Structured Programming Using THINK™ Pascal on the Macintosh

J. Winston Crawley
Shippensburg University

William G. McArthur
Shippensburg University

Norman M. Jacobson
University of California, Irvine

PRENTICE HALL, *Englewood Cliffs, New Jersey 07632*

```
Library of Congress Cataloging-in-Publication Data

Crawley, J. Winston.
   Structured programming using Think Pascal on the Macintosh / J.
Winston Crawley, William G. McArthur, Norman M. Jacobson.
     p.   cm.
   Includes index.
   ISBN 0-13-853037-8
   1. Macintosh (Computer)--Programming.  2. THINK Pascal (Computer
program language)  3. Structured programming.  I. McArthur, William
G.           II. Jacobson, Norman M.  III. Title.
QA76.8.M3C74  1992
005.265--dc20                                              91-19485
                                                              CIP
```

Acquisitions Editor/Editor-in-Chief: Marcia Horton
Production Editor: Bayani Mendoza de Leon
Cover Designer: Lundgren Graphics, Ltd.
Prepress Buyer: Linda Behrens
Manufacturing Buyer: Dave Dickey
Supplements Editor: Alice Dworkin
Copy Editor: Peter Zurita
Editorial Assistant: Diana Penha

The author and publisher of this book have used their best efforts in preparing this book. These efforts include the development, research, and testing of the theories and programs to determine their effectiveness. The author and publisher make no warranty of any kind, expressed or implied, with regard to these programs or the documentation contained in this book. The author and publisher shall not be liable in any event for incidental or consequential damages in connection with, or arising out of, the furnishing, performance, or use of these programs.

© 1992 by Prentice-Hall, Inc.
A Simon & Schuster Company
Englewood Cliffs, New Jersey 07632

All rights reserved. No part of this book may be reproduced, in any form or by any means, without permission in writing from the publisher.

Printed in the United States of America
10 9 8 7 6 5 4 3 2 1

ISBN 0-13-853037-8

Prentice-Hall International (UK) Limited, *London*
Prentice-Hall of Australia Pty. Limited, *Sydney*
Prentice-Hall Canada Inc., *Toronto*
Prentice-Hall Hispanoamericana, S.A., *Mexico*
Prentice-Hall of India Private Limited, *New Delhi*
Prentice-Hall of Japan, Inc., *Tokyo*
Simon & Schuster Asia Pte. Ltd., *Singapore*
Editora Prentice-Hall do Brasil, Ltda., *Rio de Janeiro*

TRADEMARK INFORMATION

Apple is a registered trademark of Apple Computer Inc.

Apple-DOS is a registered trademark of Apple Computer Inc.

dBase IV is a registered trademark of Ashton-Tate.

IBM is a registered trademark of International Business Machines Corporation.

Laserwriter is a trademark of Hewlett-Packard.

MS-DOS is a trademark of Microsoft Corporation.

MVS is a registered trademark of International Business Machines Corporation.

PC-DOS is a trademark of International Business Machines Corporation.

PostScript is a registered trademark of Adobe Software.

THINK Pascal is a trademark of Borland International Inc.

UCSD is a trademark of the Regents of the University of California.

Unix is a registered trademark of AT&T Bell Laboratories.

VMS is a registered trademark of Digital Equipment Corporation.

Contents

PREFACE TO THE INSTRUCTOR xv

PREFACE TO THE STUDENT xix

1   GETTING STARTED 1

    Objectives   1

    Introduction   1

  1-1   Computers and Programs   2

    Computers, 2
    Programs and Programming Languages, 2
    The Programming Environment, 3
    Pascal, 4
    Writing and Running a THINK Pascal Program, 5
    Integrated Development Environments, 6
    About this Book, 6
    Review, 7
    Exercises, 7

  1-2   Elements of the Pascal Language   8

    Basic Elements, 8
    Declarations, 10
    Action Statements, 12
    Putting the Pieces Together, 13
    DPT (Defensive Programming Tips), 14

Review, 15
Exercises, 17

1-3 Planning and Writing Looping Programs (Part 1)   17

Algorithms, Data, and Refinement, 17
Planning the Looping Program, 19
Writing the Looping Program, 20
DPT, 23
Review, 24
Exercises, 25

1-4 Planning and Writing Looping Programs (Part 2)   25

Running the Program, 26
What Can Go Wrong, 27
Program Testing, 28
Case Study No. 1, 30
DPT, 33
Review, 35
Exercises, 36

2   FUNDAMENTALS OF PASCAL PROGRAM DESIGN   37

Objectives   37

2-1 The Assignment Statement   37

Numeric Assignment Statements, 38
DPT, 43
Character Assignment Statements, 45
String Assignment Statements, 45
Examples, 47
Review, 47
Exercises, 51

2-2 Introduction to Procedures   54

An Example Procedure, 54
Some Characteristics of Procedures, 55
Standard Procedures, 57
Some Advantages of Using Procedures, 59
Some Rewards of Focusing on a Single Task, 59
A Review of Program Design, 63
DPT, 64
Review, 65
Exercises, 66

2-3 Decision Structures   66

If-Then, 67
Conditions in Pascal, 69

If-Then-Else, 70
DPT, 73
Adding to Case Study No. 1, 76
Testing, 77
Review, 80
Exercises, 80

2-4   Additional Pascal Topics   82

Formatting Output, 82
Output to the Printer, 86
Square Roots and Absolute Value, 88
Functions, 90
Integer Operations: mod and div, 91
Introducing Predefined Identifiers: maxint, 92
Real-to-Integer Conversions, 93
Integer-to-Real Conversions, 95
Real-to-Real Conversions, 96
Other Standard Numeric Library Functions, 99
DPT, 100
Review, 101
Exercises, 102

2-5   More on Decision Structures   105

Boolean Expressions, 105
Multiple-Way Branches: General, 108
The Case Structure, 112
Nested Decisions, 114
Testing, 117
DPT, 118
Review, 119
Exercises, 121

2-6   Yet More on Decision Structures   124

The "Dangling Else" Pitfall, 124
Boolean Variables, 125
Enhancements of the Case Statement, 127
Case Study No. 2, 129
Review, 134
Exercises, 135

2-7   User-Defined Functions   139

An Example, 139
The Form of a Pascal Function, 142
Parameters, 143
How to Write a Function, 144
DPT, 146
Review, 147
Exercises, 148

2-8 Modular Design and Testing   150

   Testing, 150
   Case Study No. 3, 151
   Review, 161
   Exercises, 161

3 USING LOOPS   163

   Objectives   163

   3-1 Common Applications of Loops   163

   Loop Planning, 163
   Counting, 164
   Accumulation, 167
   Largest and Smallest, 171
   Case Study No. 3 (Continued), 176
   Testing, 178
   DPT, 182
   Review, 182
   Exercises, 183

   3-2 Pascal Looping Structures   185

   Repeat-Until Loops, 185
   While-Do Loops, 186
   Repeat Versus While, 188
   For-Do Loops, 188
   Random Numbers, 190
   More Examples Using Loops, 191
   DPT: Loops, 197
   A First Look at Arrays, 200
   DPT: Arrays, 206
   Review, 207
   Exercises, 209

   3-3 Planning Loops   213

   The Loop-Planning Process, 214
   Loop Control: While-Do Versus Repeat-Until, 217
   Examples, 220
   DPT, 227
   Review, 227
   Exercises, 228

   3-4 Nested Loops and Complex Loop Termination   234

   Nested Loops, 234
   More Than One Termination Condition, 237
   Use of Multiple-Termination Conditions: Searching, 244
   Validating Input, 244
   DPT, 248

        Review, 250
        Exercises, 251

  3-5 Antibugging, Debugging, And Testing 258

        Antibugging and Debugging, 258
        Testing, 261
        Summary, 267
        Review, 267

4 MORE ON SUBPROGRAMS   269

    Objectives 269

  4-1 Parameters and Variables 269

        Review and Terminology, 269
        Reasons for Subprograms, 270
        Value and Var Parameters, 271
        Parameters: Type Matching, 273
        Choosing Parameters, 276
        Global and Local Variables; Scope, 277
        DPT, 280
        Review, 281
        Exercises, 283

  4-2 Procedures and Functions 287

        Nested Subprogram Invocation, 287
        Procedures Versus Functions, 289
        Writing a Subprogram, 291
        Examples, 292
        Recursion, 302
        DPT, 305
        Review, 307
        Exercises, 308

  4-3 Case Studies 313

        Case Study No. 4, 313
        Case Study No. 5, 324
        Case Study No. 6, 326
        Exercises, 340

5 ELEMENTARY DATA STRUCTURING   347

    Objectives 347

  5-1 Text Files 347

        Basic Text-File Operations, 348
        File-Processing Activities, 350
        Displaying and Printing Text Files, 350

Summary of File-Handling Syntax, 354
Adding Lines to a Text File, 354
Interactive File Processing, 356
Searching and Modifying Text Files, 358
Text Files as Standard I/O, 363
DPT, 364
Testing, 365
Review, 366
Exercises, 368

5-2 Records and Sets 372

Records, 372
Operations with Records, 376
Sets, 379
Set Operations, 380
An Example, 383
DPT, 383
Review, 388
Exercises 391

5-3 User-Defined Data Types 393

Scalar Types, 393
User-Defined Ordinal Types, 396
Subrange Types, 399
Type and Range Checking, 400
Error Trapping, 402
More on Records, 404
DPT, 410
Review, 410
Exercises, 411

5-4 Case Studies: Rational Arithmetic 413

Case Study No. 7 (A Rational Number Package), 413
Case Study No. 8 (An Application of the Rational-Number Package), 419
Exercises, 428

6 ONE-DIMENSIONAL ARRAYS 432

Objectives 432

6-1 Defining and Using Arrays 432

The Need for Arrays, 432
Array Declaration, 434
Array Reference, 435
Array Algorithms: Count-Controlled, 436
Array Algorithms: Condition-Controlled, 441
Initialization, Copying, and Shifting, 443
Processing Single Elements, 445

Testing, 447
DPT, 448
Review, 450
Exercises, 451

6-2 Arrays and Data Structures 456

Arrays in Pascal, 456
Data Structures, 457
Parallel Arrays and Arrays of Records, 458
Records Containing Arrays, 462
Other Combinations, 463
Testing, 467
DPT, 471
Review, 471
Exercises, 472

6-3 Searching and Sorting 478

Linear Search, 478
Binary Search, 481
Selection Sort, 484
Quicksort, 487
Comparing Efficiency Ratings, 492
DPT and Testing, 493
Review, 494
Exercises, 496

6-4 Case Studies 499

Case Study No. 9, 499
Case Study No. 10, 514
Exercises, 525

7 MORE ON ARRAYS 531

Objectives 531

7-1 More on Arrays 531

Arrays of Arrays, 531
Interactive Input and Output of Two-Dimensional Arrays, 534
Text File Input and Output of Two-Dimensional Arrays, 536
Processing Two-Dimensional Arrays, 537
Matrices, 538
Matrix Multiplication, 540
Matrix Utilities, 541
Using Part of an Array, 541
More than Two Dimensions, 544
DPT, 544
Review, 546
Exercises, 547

8 STRING MANIPULATION 551

Objectives 551

8-1 String Data and Operations 551

String Data Types, 551
Basic String Operations, 552
Built-In String Functions, 553
Built-In String Procedures, 559
String-to-Numeric Conversions, 561
DPT, 566
Testing, 569
Review, 569
Exercises, 571

8-2 String Processing 575

Some Additional String Tools, 575
Character-Conversion Techniques, 580
Longer-Length Strings, 583
Review, 588
Exercises, 588

9 POINTERS 594

Objectives 594

9-1 Pointer Variables 594

Pointers, 594
Declaring and Using Pointers, 595
Obtaining Data for Pointer Variables, 597
Managing Dynamic Memory Resources, 599
Advantages of Pointers, 605
Disadvantages of Pointers, 606
Using Pointers to Advantage, 606
DPT, 607
Review, 608
Exercises, 609

9-2 Using Pointer Variables 612

Linked Lists, 612
Saving Both Space and Time with Pointers, 616
Exercises, 625

10 RECURSION 628

Objectives 628

10-1 Thinking Recursively 628

Problem-Solving Tools, 628

The Templates of Recursion, 629
Reversing a String, 631
Subsequences and Substrings of a String, 633
Some Counting Problems, 635
A Power Set of a Set, 638
Mutual Recursion, 640
Review, 643
Exercises, 643

10-2 Recursive Programming 646

Factorial, 647
Reversing a String, 648
Recursive Sorting, 648
Subsequences and Substrings of a String, 649
Strings of Length N Using M Letters, 649
Number of Divisors of an Integer, 652
Obtaining a Number as a Sum, 653
The Power Set of a Set, 654
Mutual Recursion, 660
DPT, 660
Testing, 660
Review, 664
Exercises, 664

10-3 Recursion, Iteration, or . . . ? 666

Program Measurements, 666
Measuring Time and Space, 667
A First Comparison, 670
The Fibonacci Numbers, 671
Combinatorial Coefficients, 674
Reversing a String, 676
Sorting , 677
Prefix Expressions, 679
Some Final Thoughts on Recursion, 680
Review, 680
Exercises, 680

11 FILE I/O 683

Objectives 683

11-1 Introduction 683

File Terminology, 684
Pascal Files, 685
Review, 688
Exercises, 688

11-2 Sequential Files: Control Breaks 690

An Example, 690
Control Breaks: General, 693

Using Subprograms with Control Breaks, 696
Review, 697
Exercises, 701

11-3   Sequential Files - Merge and Update   705

The Merge Algorithm, 705
Sequential-File Update, 708
Review, 709
Exercises, 710

11-4   Random-Access-File Techniques   712

Random-Access-File Commands, 713
Random-Access-File Algorithms, 716
Inactive Records, 717
Review, 718
Exercises, 718

A ADDITIONAL THINK PASCAL FEATURES   722

A-1   Transfer Statements (Labels, Goto, Exit)   722

A-2   Variant Records   725

A-3   Nested Procedures   727

A-4   Units   732

Introduction, 732
Defining a Unit, 733
An Example, 733
Compiling and Using a Unit, 736

B SYNTAX DIAGRAMS   738

B-1   Basic Program Layout   739

B-2   Program Structures   743

B-3   Unit Structure   748

B-4   Data Structures   749

B-5   Expressions   753

C FILE UTILITIES   756

C-1   Exists   756

C-2   OpenRead   756

C-3   OpenWrite   757

C-4	FileBuild	758
C-5	FileList	759

D   THE ASCII CHARACTERS   **761**

REFERENCES   **771**

INDEX   **773**

Preface to the Instructor

This book is intended as an introduction to computer problem solving using structured programming methodologies; the THINK Pascal language is used as the vehicle for discussing and providing examples of the presented material. Throughout the book, emphasis is placed on approaching problems systematically and approaching solutions using well-known techniques of proven effectiveness. The text contains numerous example programs, written in a consistent style.

The pedagogical philosophy of the book is the *spiral approach*: topics are first gently presented in a simple context, and then presented again in a richer context when the students' experience allows them to understand a complete exploration of the topic. Decision structures, looping structures, subprograms, and arrays, as well as other topics, are treated in this fashion. In each case, by the time the student reaches the complete discussion of the topic, he or she will have worked with simple instances of the concept for some time.

The authors take the role of partners in the learning process. The use of the word "we" is intentionally ambiguous so that it can refer to the authors, to the teacher and students, or to all concerned in various places throughout the book. The authors have drawn upon their many years of teaching university-level computer science courses as well as their extensive experience as consultants to the computer industry. Many of the ideas expressed in the book have been used in actual applications in various businesses and industries.

The first six chapters of the book form an appropriate outline for a first course in computer programming. The enrichment material in the second part of the book can be used as additional topics for the first course or as a supplement for subsequent courses. The second part of the text touches on most of the topics normally found in a second course in the computer science curriculum.

The book can be used in a traditional teacher–student classroom setting or it can be used by an individual for self-study. In either case, there are many features of the book that will help the student to master the subject matter.

Getting Started

"Getting Started" is the title of the first chapter of the text, and its purpose is just that: to cover enough material quickly to enable the student to write simple looping programs. This chapter sets the stage for the spiral approach; topics introduced here are expanded at the beginning of Chapter 2.

Examples

The text is extremely rich in examples. In addition to 10 major case studies, there are a large number of complete program examples. These are supplemented by numerous examples consisting of either a single module or a segment of code. The authors have tested all program examples, using THINK Pascal version 4.0.

Thorough Explanations

The student is not left to figure out the material just by studying the examples. All concepts are carefully explained; most are carefully explained more than once, as part of the spiral approach.

Emphasis on Program Design

The major emphasis of the text is the entire program-design process. Special attention is paid to commonly encountered algorithm types, such as counting and searching. Guidelines are given on choosing appropriate designs and appropriate language tools to implement those designs.

Exercise Sets

Whether the text is used in a classroom or for self-study, proper study of the book must include solving many of the exercises that appear at the end of each section. We have included an exceptionally large number of exercises to choose from. Some of the exercises are for drill and practice, and some are intended as programming projects, with varying degrees of effort required. Solutions for a representative selection of the exercises appear in the Instructor's Guide.

Review Sections

Most sections contain a review that can be used for various purposes. The student can use the review portion before reading the section as a preview of the material to come. The student can also use the review sections in order to diagnose the degree of understanding of the presented concepts or as study guides for examinations. The instructor can use the review sections as a convenient outline for the preparation of lectures and examinations.

Finally, the review portions can be used by either student or instructor to gain a quick understanding of the topics and order of presentation of the book.

Defensive Programming Tips (DPT)

Most sections contain Defensive Programming Tips (DPT) in which the major sources of problems are discussed and suggestions are made for avoiding difficulty in programming. These ideas are unified and expanded upon in a special Antibugging, Debugging, and Testing section.

Testing Guidelines

The text contains numerous testing sections which present many ideas in this frequently overlooked area of programming. Topics include strategies for selection of test cases and the use of stubs and drivers to perform incremental testing. These discussions, like the rest of the text, follow the spiral approach. The topic is introduced in the very first chapter; as new programming ideas are presented, new ideas for testing the programs are discussed in parallel. There is also the special unifying Antibugging, Debugging, and Testing section mentioned earlier.

Language Reference

In Appendix B, we present a concise summary of the THINK Pascal programming language via the use of syntax diagrams with semantic explanations. This material will be useful for reference not only in the first course, but in subsequent courses using THINK Pascal. In addition, an experienced programmer who wants an efficient introduction to THINK Pascal can use this appendix as a study guide, with excursions into the textbook presentations when needed.

Documentation

Use of consistent and meaningful comments is emphasized throughout the text, in part by setting an example in all the program examples. In addition, the Instructor's Guide discusses documentation at some length. This may be useful if you wish to introduce your students to some of the ideas involved in external documentation of programs.

Software Engineering

The authors are advocates of the principles of software engineering. This fact has had a great influence on the flavor of the textbook: its emphasis on program design, with the particular language and dialect used as tools for implementation of design; its emphasis on modularity beginning early in the text; its emphasis on arrays and records as tools for meaningfully structuring data; its emphasis on testing throughout the text; and its emphasis on documentation as part of the design process. The student who uses this text will receive, along with an introduction to programming, an introduction to the software-engineering approach to programming.

Acknowledgments

We are grateful to Henry Etlinger, Rochester Institute of Technology, and Chris Kay, DeVry Institute of Technology (Chicago), and other anonymous reviewers of the text, who provided many useful suggestions for improvements. Special thanks to Professor Thomas A. Standish and student Manny Powers, University of California at Irvine, for their meticulous reviews of a draft of this text. The ICS21 classes at UCI used the predecessor to this text; their efforts to find mistakes and their suggestions for improving it were most appreciated.

When possible, we have incorporated suggestions made by our reviewers, students, and colleagues. Strong points of the text can be attributed to the reviewers as well as the authors; any remaining inadequacies are the sole responsibilities of the authors.

J. Winston Crawley

William G. McArthur

Norman M. Jacobson

Preface to the Student

The purpose of this book is to help you learn how to program a computer. Writing a program involves two major subtasks: designing the program and translating the design into the actual program. In this textbook, we translate the designs into the particular programming language known as THINK Pascal. It is, therefore, easy to come to the conclusion that the book is a book about THINK Pascal. However, of the two skills you will develop, the program-design skill is by far the more important. This skill can be transferred to writing programs in any of a large number of other languages that are in common use.

In this preface, we would like to point out a few features of the book that can help you use it effectively.

First of all, there are many examples in the text. You should study the examples, relate them to the material being discussed, and adapt their ideas to your own programs.

The exercise sets contain many "drill-and-practice" type problems, as well as problems calling for programming projects. After reading a section, you might wish to work through all or most of these exercises and check your answers. This would give an indication of your comprehension of the material in the section.

There are review portions at the end of each section. These can be used in several effective ways. For example, you could use them as an outline prior to reading the section. After you read the section, you could use the review portion to gauge your understanding of the material. They should prove especially helpful when reviewing for tests.

Most sections contain a portion on "Defensive Programming Tips." In these, we attempt to give you the benefit of our programming and teaching experience. We identify common problem areas with the hope that you will be able to avoid these areas if you are forewarned. You may also find these portions helpful in figuring out what is going wrong if your program is not working properly.

Throughout the text, there are pointers on how you can do a good job of testing your program. This involves running the program with data specifically designed to find any errors that may be there. It is, of course, much better to find the errors yourself than to have the instructor point them out to you after you have turned in the program!

Appendix B contains a language reference. After you have achieved some fluency in writing Pascal programs, you may find this appendix a useful tool. You may look there to answer questions about how specific Pascal statements are written or how they work. You will find this especially useful if you retain this text as a reference for later courses.

J. Winston Crawley

William G. McArthur

Norman M. Jacobson

1 *Getting Started*

OBJECTIVES

This chapter gets you started by presenting just enough information to allow you to design and run simple yet meaningful programs. After completing this chapter, you will be able to:

- use basic terminology relating to computers and programming
- recognize the basic structure of THINK Pascal programs and use a few of THINK's statements
- begin to design and write programs
- run a program and, in general terms, verify that it works correctly

INTRODUCTION

There is more to writing good computer programs than simply sitting down at a computer and typing away. In developing software, a programmer first spends time thinking about the task the program is to undertake and designing the approach the program will take to accomplish that task. Then the programmer enters the program into the computer, following rules to exhibit its structure, have its approach apparent, minimize the number of errors that might occur, and make it easy to read, understand, test, and (as the need arises) modify and enhance.

The goal of this book is to help you learn how to design and implement good programs. By imitating the examples we present in this chapter, you will be able to write simple THINK Pascal programs. Beginning in Chapter 2, and continuing throughout the book, you will add to your knowledge of program design, the THINK Pascal language, and the process of testing a program to see that it meets its specifications.

1-1 COMPUTERS AND PROGRAMS

Computers

The digital computer has become an increasingly common device in our society. It appears in a variety of sizes, shapes, and functional capabilities. Computers are sometimes classified as **mainframe computers**, **minicomputers**, or **microcomputers**. A microcomputer can be easily moved from an office to a car in just a few trips. A minicomputer would probably require a hand cart to move its components, and one would load it into a van or pickup truck instead of a car. A mainframe computer would require professional movers with the proper equipment to move it, and one would probably load it into a large truck. The boundaries between these and other classifications for computers are not really well-defined, but the previous categories are widely used in discussions concerning computers. Other less-used categories are **supercomputers** (very high-speed computers used for complex problems) and **laptop computers** (so called because they are small enough to fit on one's lap). Whatever the size, all computers possess the following components:

Input Devices: Enable the computer to receive data from the outside world; for example, keyboards, mice, light pens.

Output Devices: Enable the computer to send data to the outside world; for example, cathode-ray-tube (CRT) displays, printers, loudspeakers.

Processing Unit: Provides for computation and transformation of data.

Storage: Saves data for later use.

Computers are most often identified with the manner in which the user interacts with the input and output devices. This interaction, known as the **user interface**, is accomplished by a combination of the input and output devices and the computer **programs** that control those devices.

Programs and Programming Languages

A computer **program** is a collection of instructions that guides the computer through its operations. The program can be in a form directly understandable by the computer, **machine language**, or it can be written in a **high-level language**, a form that requires some translation by other programs before the computer can use it. A program is usually thought of as an unambiguous sequence of instructions, directed at the computer, to accomplish a specific task. There are many computer languages, including Assembler Language, COBOL, FORTRAN, BASIC, Algol, and Pascal, to name a few. Figure 1-1 contains an example of a computer program written in the THINK Pascal dialect of the Pascal programming language. You are not expected to understand the details of the program at this point, but see if you can read it and get a general idea of what it does.

The steps in the logical flow of a computer program are collectively called an **algorithm**, which can be communicated to other humans in a specialized algorithmic language such as flowcharting or pseudocode. Some programming languages, including Pascal, are rich and flexible enough to be used as their own algorithmic languages. A computer program and its associated algorithm are used for written communication with the computer and

```
program NetBill;
{Written by: XXXXXXXXXX on XX/XX/XX}
{Purpose:    To add sales tax to price}

   const
     rate = 0.06;

   var
     Bill: real;          {bill including tax}
     Price: real;         {retail price}
     Tax: real;           {sales tax}

   begin
     Write('Enter the Price: ');           {price prompt}
     Readln(Price);                         {read the price}
     Tax := Rate * Price;                   {compute sales tax}
     Bill := Price + Tax;                   {compute bill including tax}
     Writeln('The bill is:   $ ', Bill);    {print bill}
   end.
```

Figure 1-1 First program.

other people. For this reason, there is an intimate relationship between computer programming and expository writing. We can find direct analogies in programming for the writing activities of outlining, preparing a rough draft, peer reviewing, etc. As is the case for writing, programming is a discipline that requires much practice and hard work to obtain proficiency. Programming also includes some expository writing in the preparation of written descriptions and explanations, called **documentation**, for a computer program.

The Programming Environment

Operating systems. The "master" program of the computer, which is responsible for accepting commands to the computer and handling the input and output of data for the computer, among other tasks, is known as the **operating system.** It is responsible for the computer's "personality": change a computer's operating system, and the way the computer communicates with input, output, and storage devices—and the user—changes, perhaps dramatically. Operating systems are usually known by name, for example, Unix, MVS, MS-DOS, and Apple-DOS.

Editors. A program can be created by pure thought or by laborious manual effort with pencil and paper; but in either case, the program must be put into a form that is acceptable to the computer if it is to actually perform its function. The activity of entering the program into the storage area of the computer is accomplished by use of a computer program called an **editor**. The editor allows for entering the text of the program, storing the program for later use, and changing the program by adding, correcting, and deleting portions of it. The editor can be supplied as a utility that is purchased with the computer (e.g., EDLIN on the IBM PC); it can be a separate, more general, word processing program; or it can be an intimate part of the particular Pascal implementation (e.g., THINK Pascal).

Translators. The reason for writing a computer program is to use it eventually to accomplish some task. Before the program can be executed—**run**—it must be stored on the computer via an editor, and then submitted to a **translator** to be converted into a form the computer can execute. There are two kinds of translators: **interpreters**, which execute each action of the program as it is translated, and **compilers**, which first translate the entire program into a machine-readable **object file** and then (after linking) execute it. THINK Pascal uses the compiler approach to translation.

Compilers and interpreters are designed specifically for a particular language (THINK Pascal), a particular kind of computer (a Macintosh), and a particular operating system (the one the Macintosh employs).

Libraries. Even though programs vary widely, they often contain many of the same activities, such as calculating certain mathematical results or communicating with a screen or keyboard. Rather than requiring each programmer to invent (and reinvent) the sequences of instructions to accomplish these commonplace activities, standard **libraries** containing these instructions are usually associated with a particular computer and a specific computer language.

Linkers. For compiled languages, a **linker** is used to link a program's object file with any needed library procedures. The resulting file is called an **executable file**, and is the one from which the computer actually runs the program. (Interpreters do not use linkers, since they execute a program immediately as each line is translated.)

Utilities. A programmer's duties often include writing, testing, documenting and modifying programs. These tasks can require the programmer to perform such mundane (but necessary) activities as renaming programs, deleting obsolete programs, making copies of reusable parts of programs, and printing the text of programs or the data on which they operate. These and related activities are usually made possible by a collection of computer programs called system **utilities.** In the case of a microcomputer, the programmer is also usually responsible for obtaining diskettes for program storage, for preparing the diskettes for use, and for making backup copies of diskettes and hard disks; utilities also help with these chores.

The Environment. All of the previous items are facets of the computer programming **environment**. Pertinent information concerning the programming environment can be obtained from the several manuals that accompany any computer system. Consult with the local computer center or the course instructor to determine which manuals should be read or referenced for the computer you are using.

Pascal

The Pascal programming language was named for the French mathematician and philosopher **Blaise Pascal** (1623–1662), who is perhaps best known for his early work in the mathematical theory of probability, his invention of a mechanical calculator, and his book *Pensées*. In the late 1960s, **Niklaus Wirth** of Switzerland invented the Pascal language, which he announced in 1971 in the paper "The Programming Language Pascal," published in the journal *Acta Informatica*. In his 1971 report, Wirth explained he developed Pascal to be used as a convenient language to teach computer programming and as an efficient tool for writing large programs.

Pascal has been implemented in various forms on various computers, but a few common variations have been identified as "standards" for Pascal. These Pascal implementations include ANSI (American National Standards Institute) standard Pascal, ISO (International Standards Organization) Pascal, and UCSD (University of California at San Diego) Pascal. In this textbook, a particular Pascal that runs on a particular class of computers has been chosen for use in examples. The authors have chosen THINK Pascal, as implemented for the line of Macintosh computers, as the basis for all examples (and language-specific discussions) in the book. Each of the complete program examples has been tested for this particular Pascal implementation. THINK Pascal is one of several language dialects that are descended from UCSD Pascal. Other UCSD Pascal implementations will be consistent with nearly all of the material in this book. Pascal implementations that follow other Pascal standards will have some variance with the discussion of the book, but, in their essential features, all versions of Pascal are the same.

The major features of the Pascal language are that it is a structured language that encourages and enforces good programming habits; it has a rich assortment of data structures for wide-ranging applications; and it is implemented on nearly all computer systems, both large and small.

The computer community has embraced the Pascal language and has employed it successfully for applications in most categories of programming: accounting systems, educational courseware, scientific data processing, and operating systems. The nearly universal acceptance and applicability of the language make Pascal a good choice for a first programming language and an important part of the education of any computer scientist.

Writing and Running a THINK Pascal Program

You must master an editor before you can progress very far in writing and running THINK Pascal programs. The editor integral to the THINK Pascal language is sufficient for entering and modifying your programs, but you may wish to learn to use more powerful editors for writing documentation.

Once you enter your program (via the editor) and believe it to be correct, you invoke the THINK compiler (usually by issuing the Go command). The compiler attempts to verify that the program has correct form and informs you of any deviations from that correct form. It is natural to resent any agent that points out errors, but in this case, the compiler is being helpful; by noting the errors and stopping program compilation, it prevents the computer from executing an erroneous (and potentially embarrassing or catastrophic) program.

Each compiler has its own manner for detecting and reporting program errors, but the underlying principles are the same. Common errors are pointed out as "pitfalls" at appropriate places throughout the textbook. These pitfalls form a part of various sections throughout the text entitled Defensive Programming Tips (DPT). These sections contain general information on defensive programming, the art of programming in such a way as to avoid errors.

Once the compiler has approved the program and translated it (placing that translation into an object file), the program is linked and executed. In THINK Pascal, the linking and execution are done automatically when you tell THINK to "Go." (In other environments, linking and execution are separately invoked steps.)

Since the compiler does not attempt to understand intention, it cannot certify that the compiled program will behave in the manner you intended. You must, therefore, test and (if needed) correct the program before it can be considered acceptable.

Integrated Development Environments

Some Pascal implementations (such as THINK Pascal) offer program editing, compiling, debugging, and execution as parts of an integrated program-development environment. This offers advantages because the compiler can cooperate with the editor and aid in the correction of compiler-detected errors. Upon detecting an error, the compiler typically causes the editor to be loaded and to indicate the point in the program where the error occurred. This kind of environment makes it easy to find and repair typographical errors, significantly reducing the time it takes to make the program acceptable to the computer. An inherent danger in this type of environment is for one to assume that, since a program can be so easily corrected, it does not have to be well planned. Proper planning is essential to all programming and cannot be replaced by ease of revision.

About this Book

The most important topic of this text is using the computer to solve problems through the design of well-written programs. This involves the entire design process, some of whose components include:

1. Understanding what the program should do
2. Planning for the data that the program will utilize
3. Planning for the steps required to accomplish the desired task
4. Converting the plan into a form acceptable to the computer (THINK Pascal, in this text)
5. Including appropriate documentation to explain the program to those who will use it or to those who must understand how it works
6. Running the program and verifying that it does what it is supposed to do

As you can see, this involves much more than simply learning Pascal. Your programming work in the future may or may not utilize Pascal. For example, you might use COBOL or C, or some yet-to-be-invented language. What you learn about good program design will, however, be applicable in any of these environments.

On the other hand, talking about program design is not sufficient; to learn programming principles and practice programming techniques, you need to write and run actual programs. To write programs, you must learn some computer language; we think Pascal is good one to learn, since it is designed to foster good programming techniques. Therefore, a major component of this text involves details of the Pascal language.

The particular dialect we discuss in the text and use in the examples is THINK Pascal as implemented on the Macintosh. Choosing a specific Pascal implementation allows us to present examples in the text that have actually been run and allows you to learn a popular and useful programming language.

We discuss enough of the THINK Pascal environment to allow you to edit, compile, print, and run your Pascal programs, but we do not address all its capabilities (by far); those topics can fill a small book in their own right. There are several places where you can find detailed information about the THINK environment. One good reference is Chapters 3 to 9 of *THINK Pascal User Manual* (the main reference manual that accompanies the THINK Pascal language); a few others are listed in the References.

Note. We use the term THINK Pascal when we discuss that Pascal dialect in particular. We use the term "Pascal" when we discuss features common to several Pascal dialects.

REVIEW

Terms and Concepts

algorithm
compiler
documentation
editor
environment
executable file
high-level language
input devices
interpreter
laptop computers
libraries
linker
mainframe computers
machine language
microcomputers

minicomputers
object file
operating system
output devices
Pascal, Blaise
processing unit
programs
run
storage
supercomputers
translator
user interface
utilities
Wirth, Niklaus

EXERCISES

1. Invoke THINK Pascal and create a new project called NetBill.π. Then create a new program and, using THINK Pascal's editor, enter the example program in Figure 1-1 exactly as it is. Then, use the editor to change the "written by" line to your name and the correct date. Use THINK's features to store the program on disk, add it to the project, and to obtain a printed listing of it.
2. Run the example program of Figure 1-1 as changed by Exercise 1.
3. Change the line appearing as "Rate = 0.06" to the form "Rate := 0.06". Compile this (erroneous) version of the program to notice how THINK Pascal displays error messages.
4. Make several arbitrary changes to the example program of Figure 1-1 (for example, eliminate one of the ";" characters). Study the error messages the compiler produces. After several iterations of arbitrary changing and compiling, do you think that a correct program can be effectively constructed in a random manner?

1-2 ELEMENTS OF THE PASCAL LANGUAGE

In this section, we discuss the basic form of a Pascal program and some of the elements that comprise it. In Figure 1-2, we have added line numbers to the program of Figure 1-1. The line numbers are not part of the program and would not normally be present. They have been added so that we can easily refer to the lines.

The program begins with a statement giving the name of the program (line 1). This is followed by **declarations** specifying the names of the **constants** (line 7) and **variables** used (lines 10 to 12). Finally, there are **statements** specifying the actions to be performed (lines 15 to 19). The statements in lines 15 to 19 are separated by semicolons (;). A statement can occupy more than one line, if needed, or more than one statement can be placed on a given line. However, it is preferable to place one statement per line, as in Figure 1-2.

Basic Elements

In the following discussion, this example is used as a basis for a more thorough introduction to Pascal programs. Let's begin with the individual pieces that make up the program.

Pascal programs are made up of words (similar to words in ordinary text), numbers or other constants, punctuation characters, and operators. Some of the words have predefined meanings to the Pascal compiler (for example, *program*, *Write*, *Readln*, *begin*, *end*, and a number of others). These words must be used in certain restricted ways. Other words can be defined by the programmer.

Programmer-defined words (such as Rate, Tax, Price, and Bill) are called **identifiers.** Identifiers start with a letter (a–z, A–Z) and can contain letters or digits (0–9). In Pascal, uppercase and lowercase letters are equivalent when used in identifiers and in predefined words. (Although THINK Pascal allows the use of an underscore (_) in an identifier, we usually do not do so in this text.) The maximum number of characters in an identifier is 255.

In addition to following the rules for identifiers, you should make identifiers meaningful and easy to read. This approach makes it easier for others to understand your programs. In this text, we use lowercase letters, but with uppercase for the first letter of each major word that makes up the identifier. For example, an identifier made up of the two English words "pay" and "rate" is written as "PayRate". The following shows a few legal and illegal identifiers.

TaxAmount	(legal)
Tax-Amount	(illegal; dash not allowed)
XY3Z	(legal, but not good!)
Sum1	(legal)
1Sum	(illegal, begins with digit)
largevalue	(legal, but does not follow our convention)

Numbers are basically of two types, either **integer** or **real.** Integer numbers are written as a string of digits, without a decimal point, whereas reals are written with a decimal point. Reals can also contain an exponent part written with an "e" or "E," possibly a sign, and a short integer number. (If the exponent part is used, the decimal point is not required.) The following are examples of valid integer (left-hand column) and real (right-hand column) constants.

```
1)     program NetBill;
2)
3)     {Written by: XXXXXXXXXX on XX/XX/XX}
4)     {Purpose:    To add sales tax to price}
5)
6)     const
7)       rate = 0.06;
8)
9)     var
10)      Bill: real;    {bill including tax}
11)      Price: real;   {retail price}
12)      Tax: real;     {sales tax}
13)
14)    begin
15)      Write('Enter the Price: ')         {price prompt}
16)      Readln(Price);                     {read the price}
17)      Tax := Rate * Price;               {compute sales tax}
18)      Bill := Price + Tax;               {compute bill including tax}
19)      Writeln('The bill is:   $ ', Bill) {print bill}
20)    end.
```

Figure 1-2   First program with line numbers.

15	0.2
−23	0.0025
475	−25.6738
−10000	2.4E3
0	2.4e+3
−5	0.25E−2
−0	2e5
−9999	−5.0

The exponent part is interpreted as a power of 10 multiplying the rest of the number. The 2.4E3 and 2.4e+3 are equal and mean 2.4 times 10 to the third power, or 2400. The 0.25E−2 means 0.0025 and the 2e5 means 200,000. This representation is sometimes called **scientific notation**. In Pascal, we do not use commas within numbers, either real or integer. The numbers 0 and 0.0, although they have the same "value," are different in Pascal. The first is an integer and the second is real. (There are instances, to be covered later, where we must be careful to use either an integer value or a real value, so the distinction can become an important one.)

There are some restrictions to observe in writing numbers in Pascal:

1. Commas are not used.

2. No blanks are allowed between the minus sign and the number.

3. If an exponent is used, it must be an integer.

4. For real numbers (with a decimal point), there must be at least one digit on each side of the decimal point.

1-2 ELEMENTS OF THE PASCAL LANGUAGE

In addition to numbers, we can use **characters** and **character strings** in Pascal programs. These values are written using single quotes (apostrophes) before and after the value. A character value consists of exactly one character enclosed in single quotes, as, for example,

```
'A'
'a'
' '     (a single character, a blank)
```

A character string (or just **string**) can contain more than one character, as in these examples:

```
'The value of the money is '
'Strings are lists of characters'
```

If you wish to represent an apostrophe within a character or string constant, it is written using two apostrophes, as shown here:

```
'Why don''t you come along?'     (a string containing an apostrophe)
```

Finally, the following is a valid string:

```
''     (no character at all, a null string)
```

Operators are sometimes denoted by special symbols such as "–", "+", etc. Sometimes more than one special symbol is used for an operator, such as ":=" or "<=". Sometimes the name of the operator is spelled out, as in "and" and "or". Commas, semicolons, colons, and other special symbols are used as punctuation in different statements.

Blanks are used in Pascal to separate words. They can be used either before or after any punctuation symbol or operator represented by a special symbol. They must be used between any words or alphabetic operators. For example, the word "program" and the program's name in the program header (line 1 of the example) must be separated by at least one space. Blanks may not be used within an identifier nor within any of the special words that Pascal uses. Similarly, identifiers and words may not be broken from the end of a line to the beginning of the next.

Wherever we would use a blank in Pascal, except for blanks within strings, we may use a **comment**. A comment is simply text describing the program to a human reader and is ignored by the Pascal compiler. We write comments by enclosing them in braces, "{" and "}". The compiler ignores information starting with a left brace, "{", until it finds a right brace, "}". After the right brace, the compiler begins to process the information again. Comments should be used to describe your program, what it does, how it works, and who wrote it. (Lines 3, 4, 10 to 12, and 15 to 19 of the sample program contain comments.)

We can also use blank lines any place a single blank could appear. We frequently use blank lines to separate the program into parts, each of which carries out a single, basic action. These blank lines, although they are not comments, are, like comments, ignored by the compiler.

Declarations

All identifiers that we are going to use in a program must be preceded by a declaration. (Actually, there are a few exceptions, which are discussed later.) At present, our identifiers are one of three items: the program name, the name of a constant, or the name of a variable.

The program name is declared in the program header and is not used elsewhere within the program. In our sample program, the program header is line 1; the name of the program is NetBill. All program header lines are identical to that in the sample, except "NetBill" is replaced with the name of the particular program.

Next, all of the constant declarations are gathered together in a section beginning with the word "const". They are of the form:

```
name = value;
```

An example of such a section is

```
const
   TaxRate = 0.06;
   MonthinYear = 12;
```

Another example appears in lines 6 and 7 of the sample program. The const section appears before the section declaring variables and is used to define constants that we regard as particularly important. Constants can also be declared with character or character string values, as in these examples:

```
const
   Comma = ',';
   Company = 'XYZ Corp.';
```

Variables, in contrast with constants, have values that can be changed as the program is executed. Their names follow the rules for identifiers. Each variable has a type associated with it that tells what kind of value can be placed in it. Some of the common types are real, integer, and **char** (for character). Real variables are those that store numbers that have an explicit fractional part (such as 3.5, –2.353, and 10.0), whereas integer variables store numbers that do not have a fractional part (such as 3, –2, and 10). In each case, there are limits on the size of the numbers. These limits will vary from machine to machine, but in THINK Pascal on the Macintosh, standard integers can range from –32768 to +32767, long integers—type **longint**—can range from about –2 billion to +2 billion, and real variables can range from about -3.4×10^{38} to $+3.4 \times 10^{38}$. Real variables also have a limit on their precision, which also varies from machine to machine; in THINK Pascal, type real variables have at most eight decimal digits of accuracy, and occasionally only 6 or 7 digits of accuracy. (The reason is that reals are represented internally by numbers in base 2. The principal effect of this is that some simple decimal values, such as 0.1, are not represented exactly.) So, computations with reals can have slight inaccuracies.

Char variables hold a single character. Any character that the Macintosh can represent (there are 255 of them) can be placed in a char variable.

THINK Pascal also allows string variables, which may contain a string of zero characters (called the null string), one character, or more than one character, up to a maximum of 255 characters. To declare a string variable in THINK Pascal, we give the variable the type *string*. If no size is specified, it implies the variable can contain from 0 to 255 characters. If we wish the maximum allowed size of the string to be less than 255 characters, we indicate the maximum size by placing it in square brackets after the *string*. For example, if we declare

```
Name: string[20];
```

we are saying that the variable Name can contain anywhere from 0 to 20 characters. The number in the brackets (following the word *string* in the declaration) must lie in the range from 1 to 255 inclusive.

The variable declarations are collected together in a *var* section, such as the following:

```
var
    i, j, k: integer;
    Cost: real;
    Price: real;
    Letter: char;
    Line: string[133];
```

Note here that the colon (:) is used to separate the variable names from the type, and that commas (,) are used to separate variable names. Each declaration ends in a semicolon. The order of declarations doesn't matter; we could declare Line before Cost, for example.

In the sample program, all of the variables are real, and the variable declarations are contained in lines 10 through 12.

Notes

1. For variables, we declare the type explicitly. For constants, on the other hand, the value defines the type. The constant 0.06, for example, is real.
2. In THINK Pascal, a string of 1 character is considered to be equivalent to a character. So 'A' is both a string constant with a length of 1 and a *char* constant. It can be used in a context where a string would be appropriate or in a context where a character would be appropriate.
3. One of Pascal's major strengths is to allow the programmer to build up new types out of existing ones. These types are declared in the *type* section, a section similar to the *const* and *var* sections. How to define your own types is discussed later.

Action Statements

The statements describing the actions to be performed are written between the words *begin* and *end*. These statements are separated by semicolons. Notice, in the example, that lines 14, 19, and 20 do not have semicolons. This is because the *begin* and *end* are not regarded as statements in Pascal but rather as symbols that group statements. Line 19 does not need a semicolon because it is not followed by another statement. (Actually, a semicolon could have been placed at the end of line 19 because Pascal permits a so-called empty or null statement.) The final "end" is followed by a period.

The statement in line 15 is a **Write statement**, which displays whatever is within the parentheses on the computer display screen. In this case, the string within single quotes is displayed. (The quotes will not be displayed because they serve merely to delimit—mark the beginning and end of—the string.) The message this Write statement prints out is called a **prompt.** It explains to the user (of the program) what the program expects to be entered. Line 19 is similar, but after displaying the string within the single quotes and the value of the variable Bill, the **Writeln** statement advances the output display to a new line.

The Write and Writeln statements can write any number of expressions, variables, or constants. They are displayed one after the other, starting with the leftmost item within the parentheses. In all cases, the *value* of the expression, variable, or constant is written. The output from a Write or Writeln that follows another Write statement appears on the same line as the output from the first Write statement (if there is room). The output from a Write or Writeln that follows a Writeln statement always begins on a new line. For example, the sequence of statements

```
Writeln(A, B);
Writeln(C, D)
```

prints the current values of A and B on one line, and the current values of C and D on the next. Contrast this with

```
Write(A, B);
Writeln(C, D)
```

which prints all four values on the same line.

The form of the Writeln statement is

```
Writeln(list of things to be displayed)
```

where the list contains the expressions, variables, and constants separated by commas. It is also possible to use a Writeln statement without any list of items, as in

```
Writeln
```

This causes a blank line to be displayed. Later, we will see how to control the form in which the values are printed.

The statement in line 16 reads the value entered by the user of the program and places that value in the variable Price. The **Readln** is of the form

```
Readln(list of variable names)
```

It reads through the end of the input line. Like the Writeln, the names in the list are separated by commas. The statement reads a value for every variable in the list. If the user types more values than there are variables, the extra values are ignored.

The Write, Writeln, and Readln statements described here are commonly called **input/output**, or **I/O, statements** because they cause the transfer of data into or out of the computer's central processing unit. Pascal has other I/O statements that are considered later.

Lines 17 and 18 are examples of assignment statements. The expression on the right of the := operator is evaluated, and the result is assigned to the variable appearing on the left of the := operator. Expressions in Pascal are similar to normal algebraic expressions, except that variable names can contain several characters. This means that one cannot imply multiplication by writing two variable names next to each other as in ordinary algebra. Therefore, the * is used to indicate multiplication. The operators +, −, and / are used to indicate addition, subtraction, and division, respectively. The assignment statement is discussed in more detail in Section 2-1.

Putting the Pieces Together

The general form of a Pascal program, for our first simple programs, follows. The italicized portions are those the programmer supplies; the rest is a part of every Pascal program.

```
program name;
  const constant declarations
  var variable declarations

begin
  program steps
end.
```

It is possible to omit some of these parts. For example, if there are no constants to be declared, the const section can be omitted. However, if a section is needed, then it must appear in the place indicated in the previous outline. To write a program, we must know what steps we wish the program to perform, and how to express those steps in Pascal. We must know exactly what variables we need and decide on the names to give those variables. Finally, we must write our program in the general form indicated here. The next two sections present more information on this process.

DPT (Defensive Programming Tips)

This is the first of a series of sections that occur throughout the text. We abbreviate the section names as DPT. The purposes of the sections are to help you avoid errors in writing your programs and to quickly decipher those errors that do occur. (Even if the compiler detects the error for us, it cannot always determine exactly what we really did wrong.)

The name of the section indicates our general approach. We program "defensively," trying to protect against errors. This can involve any number of related ideas. One of the ways we can avoid errors is to be aware of what types of errors are frequently made, or of what types of misconceptions can occur. In this first DPT section, we can identify the following:

1. All variables must be declared. If we forget, the compiler generates an error message.

2. THINK's font when it is first "started up" is Geneva. Geneva has a lowercase l (letter l) that looks very much like 1 (the digit 1); it has a 0 (zero) and O (uppercase letter O) that are indistinguishable when viewed on the screen. So, we recommend you avoid variable names of "l" or "O", and be on the lookout for one symbol (1 or 0) masquerading as the other (l or O). If the THINK compiler is finding fault with what appears to be a perfectly valid statement (such as Value := 0), check for similar-looking characters. (To help distinguish these symbols, you can change the font the THINK editor uses to one that makes clear the differences between these characters; Helvetica works well. To change the font, select the Source Options choice from the Edit menu, click on "Geneva" and select the font you wish from the menu that appears.)

3. Misspelling an identifier, especially one with a special meaning to the compiler, can cause problems. If we misspell a variable name, we will probably be warned that we forgot to declare that variable. Misspelling a word such as "end" can so thoroughly confuse the compiler that its error messages are totally unrelated to the actual problem.

4. All declaration lines (const or var sections) end with a semicolon.

5. Action statements are separated by semicolons, and special words such as *begin* and *end* are not statements, but delimiters.

6. There is sometimes confusion between "=" and ":=" in Pascal. This is partially caused because algebra uses an "=", whereas Pascal uses a ":=". For example, the algebraic formula

$$d = rt$$

can be written as the assignment statement

$$\text{Distance} := \text{Rate} * \text{Time}$$

in Pascal. Constant declarations use "=" and assignment statements use ":=" as the operator.

7. The assignment symbol ":=" is a double symbol. The colon and the equal sign must be adjacent. Do not put a blank between them.

8. We must use * to signify multiplication. If, in the example just given we wrote

$$\text{Distance} := \text{RateTime}$$

the compiler would interpret "RateTime" as a variable and would tell us we forgot to declare it. What we really forgot was the multiplication symbol.

9. There is sometimes confusion over strings that contain digits. The string '156', for example, is not the same as the integer 156. The latter can be used in arithmetic computations, the former cannot.

REVIEW

Terms and Concepts

assignment statement
character string
char
characters
comment
constants
declarations
identifiers
input/output (I/O) statements
integer
longint
null string

prompt
Readln
real
scientific notation
statements
string
variables
Write statement
Writeln statement

Pascal Syntax

Basic Elements

1. Identifiers: First character is a letter; others are either a letter or a digit; maximum length 255 (THINK); lowercase and uppercase are equivalent.

2. Numbers: Integer—no decimal point (3, –7, etc.); real—decimal point (3.5, –2.1, etc.); or exponential form (2.3E5, 5e–2, etc.).

3. Character values: Single character enclosed in single quotes (the apostrophe character); two apostrophes to represent one ('''').

4. String values: Enclosed in single quotes; two apostrophes to represent one ('don''t', etc.).

5. Operators: +, –, *, and / are to do arithmetic (assignment) statements.

6. Comments: Form: {*any string as a comment*} — can be placed anywhere a blank could go.

7. Constant declarations: Form: *name = value*;

8. Variable declarations: Form: *variable list*: *type*; type can be real, integer, char, string, or string[maximum length], where the "maximum length" specified is in the range 1 to 255.

First Program Form

```
program name;
 const
   constant declarations
 var
   variable declarations
begin
  program steps
end.
```

Statements

```
Readln(list of variable names)
Write(list of expressions, variables, or constants)
Writeln(list of expressions, etc.)
variable := expression
```

DPT

1. Declare all variables.
2. Do not type letters O, 1, l for digits 0, 1, etc.
3. Watch for misspelling a keyword or an identifier.
4. End all declarations with a semicolon.
5. Separate statements with a semicolon.
6. Do not use = in an assignment statement or := in a const declaration.
7. Do not add space in the := operator.
8. Use an * to indicate multiplication.
9. '156' is not the same as 156.

EXERCISES

1. Decide whether the following are valid THINK Pascal identifiers. For those that are not valid, explain why not.
   (a) Beta
   (b) T10056t
   (c) 1Time
   (d) Tax Rate
   (e) X
   (f) First.Time
   (g) FirstTime
   (h) firsttime

2. Decide whether the following are valid Pascal constants. For those that are not valid, explain why not, and for those that are valid, give the type of the constant.
   (a) 123
   (b) 1.23
   (c) 1,234.00
   (d) '123'
   (e) 'Now is the hour'
   (f) 'X''t'
   (g) 'John's'
   (h) 123.05E+25

3. For each of the following, decide on appropriate variable names for the quantities involved, and give the required declarations.
   (a) social security number, age, hourly pay, number of hours worked
   (b) student name, three test grades, average test grade
   (c) section number, number of students, number who passed the course, number who failed, average grade of the class
   (d) number of bears in a sample, total height in centimeters of all the bears, average height in centimeters
   (e) state name, population, number of cities over 250,000 population, square miles, population density (population per square mile), percentage of population with high school education or above

1-3 PLANNING AND WRITING LOOPING PROGRAMS (PART 1)

The first two sections introduced some basic concepts. In the first, we had an overview about computers and about the Pascal programming language. The second section went into more detail about THINK Pascal and discussed a simple but complete program. In this section, we go through the steps one takes to develop a complete program.

Algorithms, Data, and Refinement

Before we write the program, however, we would like to discuss the program-development process. This discussion will be brief at this point, but it will be built upon throughout the text. As we will see, writing a program requires thought. The first step is a careful statement of the problem to be solved, known as the **specification**. This defines what needs to be done, presents the available information about the task, and usually describes how the program is to function from the user's point of view.

Using the specification as a starting point, we must analyze what is required and develop a plan for achieving the desired results. The plan we develop is usually called a **design**. A design is a careful, perhaps detailed, statement of what the program will accomplish and how it will accomplish it. In many ways, it is similar to a program. In fact, the completed program can be viewed as a very detailed design. However, an effective design may not require the amount of detail that the program will have. And it certainly does not have to satisfy the rigid **syntax rules** (for example, concerning the placement of semicolons) of a programming language such as Pascal.

Programs (and, therefore, designs) deal with data. Many of the programs we will write, especially early in the text, follow this general pattern: read some data, calculate some values based on that data, print the answers. This pattern can be repeated for a number of sets of data. For example, the program we will develop shortly will calculate the areas of a number of rectangles, given the length and width of each rectangle.

Part of planning a program involves planning for the data needed, and the variables to hold that data. It is frequently useful to first determine what input data the program must read (for example, length and width). In connection with this, we can determine the expected output data (for example, area of the rectangle). As we will see as our examples get more complex, we frequently need some extra data to aid in our calculations. Thus, we may categorize the variables we use as "input," "output," and "other."

For a reasonably complex problem, the first design (plan) we devise may not be detailed enough to enable us to write the program. We may have to go back and fill in details for some of the steps. This process can be repeated indefinitely, until we finally reach a point that we can successfully write a program based on the plan. The process of filling in details in the design is called **refinement**. Refinement is an expected part of the program design process. Sometimes students expect that the first algorithm they write will be sufficiently detailed. This just is not so, in general. In fact, purposefully taking several refinement steps can lead to better programming.

As our final comment on program planning, we note that there are four basic **program structures** that we use to build our algorithms, and thus our programs. The word structure, as used here, simply refers to ways of putting together the pieces of the program. These four fundamental program structures are as follows:

1. **Sequence**. This structure consists of a number of steps that are to be performed in order (in "sequence"). The program steps are simply listed in the proper order. The example in the previous section used this type of structure.

2. **Loops**. Loops are program structures that allow repetition. If we have a step (or a sequence of steps) that should be repeated a number of times, we place the steps in a loop.

3. **Decision**. Sometimes the steps to be performed depend upon some condition. For example, in many companies, the rule used to calculate an employee's pay depends upon whether the employee worked more than 40 hours that week. A decision structure in a program allows the program to perform different sets of steps based upon various conditions.

4. Subprograms. There are several other terms related to this program structure. Among these are **modules, submodules, functions**, and **procedures**. Briefly, a subprogram is a piece of a program designed to perform a certain task or calculation. This program structure is useful in breaking down a complicated task into a number of less complicated subtasks. Its use frequently goes hand in hand with the refinement process described earlier.

The example that follows utilizes the first two of these program structures, as well as a limited form of the third. More details concerning all these structures are given as we proceed through the text.

Planning the Looping Program

Let us develop the example referred to earlier. We wish to write a program that calculates the areas of rectangles. Early in the planning process, we analyze the data required for the program and begin a list of necessary variables. For this program, the output (the value the program calculates) is the area. The input (the values on which the output depends) consists of length and width. The program description does not specify whether these should be integer or real; we choose to make them real so the program can handle lengths and widths which have fractional parts (such as 3.25). We can write this preliminary variable list:

Input:	Length	Real	Length of rectangle
	Width	Real	Width of rectangle
Output:	Area	Real	Area of rectangle

Along with planning the data, we begin our plan for the program. If we were calculating the area of a single rectangle, we might list this sequence of steps:

    ask the user to enter a length and a width
    read values for Length and Width variables
    calculate the value for the Area variable (Length times Width)
    print the value of the Area variable

Because we are to write a program that handles many rectangles, we realize we will need a loop structure. The program must repeat the four steps listed a number of times.

As with all the loops we will write, we must decide on how to terminate the loop. Although there are a number of possible ways to achieve this **loop control**, we concentrate on one specific technique for the early part of this text. This technique consists of asking the user to supply some special value as input, to signal that there are no more rectangles to be processed. For example, we might use a value of 0 for the Length variable as a signal that the repetition should cease. This special value is referred to by many names, including **sentinel, terminal value, dummy value, trailer value**, and **terminating value**. We generally describe the value as a terminating value.

Unless the user is told that a length of 0 will terminate the process, the user will not know what to do to stop the program. We, therefore, print some instructions to notify the user of this fact. This step occurs once, at the very beginning of the program.

This discussion leads to the following refined variable list and design.

Note. We have added a constant named EndOfData to our list. This constant is used as part of the loop control.

Strictly speaking, we now have a constant and variable list. However, we use the simple term "variable list" throughout the text.

Constant:	EndOfData		Value 0, used to terminate loop
Input:	Length	Real	Length of rectangle
	Width	Real	Width of rectangle
Output:	Area	Real	Area of rectangle

print instructions
repeat these steps until the user enters 0 for the Length:
    ask the user to enter a length and a width
    read Length, Width values
    calculate Area value (Length times Width)
    print Area value

As we see in the next section, this algorithm, together with the variable list and some knowledge of Pascal looping mechanisms, is detailed enough to allow us to write the program.

Writing the Looping Program

The program whose plan we have just developed is typical of many programs. We may indicate the pattern as follows:

print instructions
repeat these steps until the user enters the terminating value:
    "prompt" the user to supply input
    read the input values
    perform calculations
    print answers

In this section, we continue our example by writing the desired Pascal program. The methods we use apply to any program that follows this pattern.

There are other ways that this same general plan could be realized as a Pascal program. In Chapter 3, we analyze all the possible looping structures in some detail. For now, however, we concentrate on learning one possible way to write the program.

The complete program is given in Figure 1-3. As before, the line numbers to the left are for reference; they are not part of the program.

To write a program such as this, we need to know the following about Pascal:

1. The general program layout
2. How to declare constants and variables
3. How to print (messages, values of variables)
4. How to read values for variables

5. How to perform calculations

6. How to write loops, including loop control

The first five in the list were introduced in the last section. We provide a quick review based on the program in Figure 1-3.

Lines 1, 14, and 31 form the basic program layout. Line 1 names the program. Between lines 1 and 14 are the declarations (and some comments), and between lines 14 and 31 are the statements to be performed by the program.

Lines 6 and 7 define the constant EndOfData, with a value of 0. Lines 9 to 12 declare (and comment on) the variables the program uses.

Lines 15 to 18 use Writeln to print a series of lines as instructions to the user. Lines 21 and 22 issue the prompt, requesting input. Line 21 prints a blank line, thus separating the prompt from the previous answer. Line 22 prints the actual prompt, staying on the same line to wait for user input.

Line 23 reads the values the user entered. The area is calculated in line 26 and printed by line 27. Line 27 is worth examining a little closer. As we described in the last section, Writeln can be used to print any constants, expressions, or variables. The message enclosed in apostrophes is printed verbatim, and the current value of the Area variable is printed. Another possibility would have been to write

```
Writeln (Area, ' is the area of the rectangle.')
```

printing first the value and then the message of explanation.

Note. We generally include a blank space within a message to separate it from any variable value being printed. For example, consider the blank just before the word "is" in the example just given and the one just after the word "is" in line 27 of the sample program. Another example appears in line 22, where the blank space provides a separation between the colon and the data the user will enter.

Lines 20, 24, 25, 28, and 29, which are in italics, provide the looping and the loop control. Lines 20 and 29 form the skeleton of a **repeat-until loop**. The form is

```
repeat
   list of steps to be repeated
until condition
```

In our example, we want to repeat lines 21 to 28 until the user inputs a length of 0 (that is, EndOfData).

There is a slight subtlety here, however. When we wrote the plan, we surely did not intend the program to calculate and print the area after the user indicated he was done (by entering a length of 0). Although we did not say so explicitly, it was clear that those two steps should only be done when the user inputs an actual rectangle's length and width. In a program, however, we must explicitly make sure that this is what happens. This is what lines 24 to 28 accomplish. They say, in essence,

> "If the user entered an actual length and width value, then calculate and print the area of that rectangle."

```
1)    program Rectangles;
2)
3)    {Written by: XXXXXXXXX XX/XX/XX}
4)    {Purpose:    To calculate the areas of rectangles}
5)
6)      const
7)        EndOfData = 0;   {used to terminate loop}
8)
9)      var
10)       Length: real;    {length of rectangle, input}
11)       Width: real;     {width of rectangle, input}
12)       Area: real;      {area of rectangle, calculated}
13)
14)   begin
15)     Writeln(' This program calculates areas of rectangles. You');
16)     Writeln('supply the length and width when asked, separated by');
17)     Writeln('a space. To stop the process, enter a length of 0,');
18)     Writeln('along with any value for the width.');
19)
20)     repeat
21)       Writeln;
22)       Write('Enter length and width: ');
23)       Readln(Length, Width);
24)       if Length <> EndOfData then
25)         begin
26)           Area := Length * Width;
27)           Writeln('The area is ', Area)
28)         end
29)     until Length = EndOfData
30)
31)   end.
```

Figure 1-3   A looping program.

More precisely, they say,

> "If the Length variable's value is not equal to 0 (EndOfData), then do these two steps: calculate the area, print the area."

The *if* statement's form is

```
if condition then
  begin
    steps to be done if condition is true
  end
```

Notice (line 24) that "<>" means "not equal to" in a condition. As with ":=", this is a double symbol, so no blank is allowed between the "<" and the ">".

This completes our description of the sample program. In the next section, we discuss what happens when the program is run. Before we quit, however, we want to discuss two topics briefly: indentation and semicolons.

Pascal programs are free-form. Any division into individual lines, and any indentation or spacing patterns, are optional. However, a judicious use of blank space and indentation can improve a program's readability. THINK Pascal automatically employs several formatting features, some that are fixed, and some that you can change. For those formatting options which can be changed, we stick with the **defaults**, that is, the settings you have when you first invoke THINK Pascal. Among other conventions used to improve program readability, THINK:

- displays key words in bold (lines 1, 6, 9, 14, 20, 24, 25, 28, 29 and 31)
- indents the lines between the *begin* and *end* that bracket the body of the program (lines 15 to 31)
- indent the steps that are repeated in a loop (lines 21 to 28)
- indents the steps inside an *if* statement (lines 24 to 28)
- uses blank spaces to improve readability (around the "<>" in line 24, the ":=" and "*" in line 26, and the "=" in line 29)

We also do some formatting ourselves. In particular, we usually place blank lines before and after loops (lines 19 and 30), and arrange comments so they are easy to find and read (lines 3, 4, 7, 10, 11, and 12).

One thing that frequently bothers beginning Pascal programmers is the placement of semicolons. Within the declarations, the rules are fairly rigid and not too difficult. Within the body of the program, they can cause more difficulty. We have more to say about this later. For now, notice that semicolons are used *between* steps. For example, consider the *if* statement form:

```
if condition then
    begin
        steps to be done if the condition is true
    end
```

Semicolons are used between the steps to be done if the condition is true. If there are 10 steps, there will be 9 semicolons; if 2 steps, then 1 semicolon. In the sample program, a semicolon separates the two steps on lines 26 and 27 within the *if* statement.

Likewise, in the sample program, the steps within the *repeat-until* loop are separated by semicolons. There are five steps—the two Writelns, two Readlns, and the *if*. (The entire *if* is considered to be one step of the loop body.) Thus there are four semicolons, at the ends of lines 21, 22, 23, and 26.

Similarly, the entire body of the program contains five steps—four Writelns and the *repeat-until* loop. There are, therefore, four semicolons (lines 15, 16, 17, and 18).

Keep in mind that semicolons go between statements and that such words as *repeat*, *if*, *begin*, and *end* are not (by themselves) statements.

DPT

The sample program suggests two possible pitfalls. The first relates to the use of the *if* statement in the program. As indicated in the previous discussion, we do not want to do the calculations and print the answer for the user's terminating entry. The purpose of the dummy entry is to say, "I'm finished." In the type of program illustrated by the example, we always have an *if* statement whose meaning is, "If the user did not enter the dummy value, then perform the calculations and print the answers."

What happens if we forget this? The program calculates and prints a meaningless answer for the terminating value. Although this is not as serious as some errors, we should try to write our programs to do exactly what they are supposed to do.

The second possible pitfall relates to the use of semicolons. This issue is explored in much more detail later. For now, we simply advise you to be careful. In writing programs that use the sample program as a guide, use the placement of semicolons in the example to guide you.

REVIEW

Terms and Concepts

decision
default
design
dummy value
functions
loop control
loops
modules
procedures
program structure
refinement

repeat-until structure
sentinel
sequence
specification
submodules
subprograms
syntax rules
terminal value
terminating value
trailer value

Four Program Structures

sequence

loop

decision

subprogram (module, submodule, function, procedure)

Pascal Statements

```
repeat
   steps to be repeated
until condition

if condition then
   begin
      steps to be done if condition is true
   end
```

General Plan for Sample Program (and Similar Programs)

print instructions
    repeat these steps until the user enters a terminating value:
        prompt the user to supply input
        read the input values
        perform calculations
        print answers

General Program Form for Sample Program (and Similar Programs).
Italicized portions are those that depend on the specific program.

```
program name;
    declarations

begin
   Writeln(instructions);
   Writeln(more instructions);

   repeat
      Writeln;
      Writeln(prompt);
      Readln(input variables);
      if not the terminating value then
         begin
            calculate;
            Writeln(answers)
         end
   until terminating value

end.
```

EXERCISES

1. By following the example given in this section, and by using the typical algorithm and program form just given in the Review, write programs for the following. You should make a variable list, decide on an appropriate terminating value to terminate the loop, write an algorithm, and finally write the program.

   (a) The area of a square can be found by multiplying the length of a side by itself (side × side). Write a program to find the areas of squares.
   (b) The perimeter of a square is four times the length of the side. Write a program to find the perimeters of squares.
   (c) Write a program that repeatedly reads two real numbers. For each pair of real numbers it reads, it should calculate and print their sum.

2. What changes would you make to the program in Exercise 1(c) in order to find the difference rather than the sum?

3. What changes would you make to the program in Exercise 1(c) if the numbers were integers rather than real numbers?

1-4 PLANNING AND WRITING LOOPING PROGRAMS (PART 2)

We now discuss the execution of the program shown in Figure 1-3. In Figure 1-4, we show the results of running the program. The printout in the figure begins with the output the program produces.

Note. Before running the program, select the text window (by selecting Text in the Window menu) and make it about as large as the screen. This will make it easier to see the program's output. There is a way to have your program automatically size and show the text window. Since it relies on Pascal features we explore in Chapter 2, we discuss it there.

Running the Program

In Figure 1-4, the underlined portions indicate what the user typed when the program ran. All other portions the program itself generated. Throughout the text, when we illustrate a sample run of a program, we will do the same thing; underlining will indicate user input.

```
This program calculates areas of rectangles. You
supply the length and width when asked, separated by
a space. To stop the process, enter a length of 0,
along with any value for the width.

Enter length and width: 4.0 5.0
The area is  2.0e+1

Enter length and width: 2.5 2.0
The area is  5.0e+0

Enter length and width: 0.05 0.05
The area is  2.5e-3

Enter length and width: 0.001 0.001
The area is  1.0e-6

Enter length and width: 175.72 39.045
The area is  6.9e+3

Enter length and width: 1000.0 1000.0
The area is  1.0e+6

Enter length and width: -5.0 -4.0
The area is  2.0e+1

Enter length and width: 10   15
The area is  1.5e+2

Enter length and width: 4
5
The area is  2.0e+1

Enter length and width: 7 8
The area is  5.6e+1

Enter length and width: 0 0
```

Figure 1-4   Sample input and output.

The four Writeln statements in the program caused four lines of instructions to be printed. This was followed by the prompt (a blank line, then the message "Enter length and width:"). The computer then waited for the desired input to be supplied on the same line by the person running the program. When the user hit the "Return" key to indicate the end of the line of input, the two numbers 4.0 and 5.0 were read into the variables Length and Width, respectively.

The computer next checked the Length variable. Since its value was not 0, the Area value was calculated and printed. Notice that the answer is printed in the exponential notation 2.0e+1. As was explained in Section 1-2, this means 2.0 times 10 to the power 1, or 20.0.

Note. In Section 2-4, we discuss how to exercise some control over the exact form in which the answers appear. This allows us to display output in a more familiar form, rather than the exponential form shown in Figure 1-4.

The prompt, input, calculate, and print cycle was repeated a number of times, as illustrated in the figure. The last five input lines are of particular interest. They illustrate the following points:

1. The program was not designed to detect erroneous input, so the data line "–5.0 –4.0" was accepted. In future sections, we learn how to write more sophisticated programs that do not allow erroneous data to be processed.
2. We may supply whole-number values when the program is reading real variables.
3. We may put more than one blank space between the numbers.
4. If we only enter one number on a line when the program is reading two variables, it continues to wait for further input.
5. The last data line contains the terminating value of 0. Because the program is reading two variables, we had to supply a value for both the Length and Width. Because the Length is 0, the calculation and print of the Area did not occur, the loop terminated, and the program was finished.

What Can Go Wrong

Unfortunately, any human endeavor is subject to errors. In computer programs, these errors are frequently called **bugs**, and removing them from your program is called **debugging**. The programming process includes a number of techniques whose goal is to eliminate errors. The DPT (Defensive Programming Tips) sections throughout the text provide guidelines for avoiding common bugs and for removing those that do occur.

The compiler itself can be a useful tool in uncovering certain types of bugs. It is especially valuable for the type of error that is caused by a typing mistake or by a lack of familiarity with the programming language. For example, the following list shows some possible errors in the rectangles program. For each, it shows the error message THINK Pascal generated.

omit semicolon line 16	Semicolon (;) or END expected after the previous statement
omit right parenthesis, end of line 27	This doesn't make sense.
write Area = Length * Width, line 26	This doesn't make sense as a statement.
misspell "until" on line 30	This doesn't make sense.
omit left parenthesis in line 27	This doesn't make sense.
< > rather than <> on line 24	This doesn't make sense.
spell "Area" on line 26 as "Ara"	"Ara" is not declared.

As you can see, sometimes the error message tells exactly what the error is, but sometimes it does not. To fix the error, we might see if the error message does correctly describe the problem. If not, we may need to review the Pascal rules to see what we did wrong. Sometimes, the error will have occurred earlier in the program. For example, misspelling "Area" in line 12 might cause an error message in line 26.

These errors are often called **compile-time errors, compilation errors**, or just **compile errors** (or sometimes "compiler errors," even though the problem is with the program, not the compiler). Another class of errors is known as **run-time errors.** They are not caused by violations of the language's syntax rules, but by some problem occurring when the program is running.

For example, here are some errors that could occur as the rectangles program is running:

The user entering a number that is too large

The user entering an invalid character when a number is being read

The product of the two numbers entered is too large

THINK Pascal will, when an error occurs, locate the portion of the program that was running at the time. As with the compile-time errors, it may take some investigating to find the error's exact cause.

Writing programs fully protected from errors in user input requires a sophistication generally beyond the scope of a first course. However, we can (and will) write programs that avoid other common run-time errors, such as division by zero.

A third type of error is sometimes called a **logic error**. The computer does not indicate that anything went wrong, but the program is nonetheless incorrect. As a simple example, replacing the "*" in line 26 with a "+" could not be detected by the compiler. We would detect it when we observed the incorrect answers.

Program Testing

Testing a program begins, at least informally, as soon as planning is begun. As we design the algorithm, we are probably thinking about how the algorithm will perform with some sample input. For complex programs, we may write down some input data to help guide our plans.

In addition, there are several types of more formal testing we may perform as we develop the program. First, we may **hand-trace** either the design or the program, using some sample data. This involves "playing computer," tracing the actions the computer will perform, step by step. For example, we might step through the algorithm or program for the rectangles example using input data lines of "2.5 4.0" and "0.0 0.0". This hand-tracing process can be done before running the program to detect errors in our planning process.

A second type of testing uses the compiler as a tool. This involves running the program and fixing the compile-time errors that may be present.

Eventually, we get all the syntax errors fixed and get a "clean compilation." If we are very careful typists, we might even get a clean compilation the first time we run the program. In addition, we may not have any obvious run-time errors. At this point, we must avoid the tendency to think that we are done. We still need to test the program for any remaining bugs.

There are two general types of bugs that we hope to detect by doing this testing. The first involves an error in thinking about the algorithm, and the second involves erroneous coding of the algorithm into Pascal. In an attempt to uncover these errors, we run the program with a variety of input data, and we examine the answers carefully to see if they are correct.

The only way to test a program thoroughly would be to run it with every possible combination of input. However, this is impossible in practice. We must be satisfied with a compromise—a carefully chosen sample of input data.

It is difficult to say what constitutes adequate testing, especially for a complex program, where bugs are sometimes discovered months or years after a program has been pronounced correct. However, we can give some general guidelines.

In testing the sample program, we used data that illustrate a few of the principles involved. First, we included some input for which the answers could easily be verified by doing the calculations in our head. If the program contained an error, such as adding the length and width rather than multiplying them, these input lines would have allowed us to detect the error quickly. However, not all the data were of this form. Some of the input included some more realistic values, such as 175.72 and 39.045. We did, however, use a calculator to make sure that the answers for these input lines were also correct.

A second principle illustrated by the sample test data concerns **boundary conditions**. The length and width could be any number from just slightly greater than zero on up. We included data very close to the lower limit, or boundary, for the input. In fact, we included both 0.05 and 0.001 as test data. Although there was no stated upper limit for the length and width, we did also check with some relatively large numbers (1000.0 for each). Experience has shown that errors are more likely to occur for data near boundaries, so these tests may be among the most important that we do. (However, not all our tests should be boundary tests. We should also include some data that are between the boundaries. In our sample test run, we had a number of values between the very small and the very large.)

A third principle concerns "bad" data, that is, data we do not expect the program to process correctly, but still might encounter. In this example, we entered negative numbers for the length and width. Since the program was not designed to detect negative values, we got a wrong answer. In later programs, where the program is supposed to detect such errors and print warning messages about them, this type of testing becomes very important.

There are a number of other important testing principles that we introduce later in the text when we write programs for which the principles become pertinent. For now, we can summarize the three ideas we have presented:

1. Check all answers. Include some data that are easy to check.
2. Test near boundaries; also test a random sampling away from the boundaries.
3. Include some erroneous input, especially if the program is designed to detect and warn about such errors.

The THINK Pascal environment contains a number of tools and options to help you detect compile-time and run-time errors. Most of these features are found in the Debug menu. We list a few of the more immediately useful features here for your reference; detailed information about these features and information about more advanced THINK Pascal debugging aids can be found in the THINK Pascal User Manual.

- By selecting the Observe option, you can see the Observe window, in which are printed the values that variables and expressions take on as your program executes. You can call up the Observe window any time the program stops—including when it stops because of a run-time error. Looking at variables' values when a program aborts is often very helpful in finding and fixing bugs.
- The Step Into and Step Over options allow you to execute your program one statement at a time, stopping after each statement. You can watch the Observe window as you step through the program to see how variables' values change—this approach can often let you see exactly where your program went wrong.
- The Stop Signs option lets you place a pause in your program, so you can execute all the statements to a given point and then stop. You can look at the Observe window, perhaps do other forms of checking, and then continue the program with the Go or Run command.
- You can also enter expressions into the right half of the Observe window, and THINK Pascal will evaluate them (if they are valid at this point in the program) or print a short error message (if they are not). This feature allows you to manipulate variables to help you determine the condition that caused a program to abort or to produce incorrect output.
- The Instant window, which you can access by selecting the Instant selection, allows you to enter THINK Pascal statements and execute them immediately (by clicking on the Do It button). You can execute virtually any statement which would be legal at the point the program was stopped, even if the program was stopped because of a run-time error. You can use the Instant window to try out bug fixes to be sure they do actually fix the bug before making the code a part of your program.

Case Study No. 1

To conclude this section, we develop another example similar to the one developed in the previous section. We expand this case study in later sections.

Statement of Problem. A class instructor needs a program to calculate the total of the scores on three tests for each of his students. The student's name should be printed along with the score.

Preliminary Analysis. In order to output the student's name, the program has to obtain the name from the instructor (the user) as the program is run. The other input consists of the three test scores. Output contains the student's name and the total of the three scores. (Note: Having the name with the total on the output is especially useful if the program produces a printed copy of the output.)

Algorithm and Variables List. Based on the preliminary analysis, we can develop this list of variables (and one constant):

Constant:		EndOfData	Value '', indicates end of input
Input:	Name	String[20]	Student name, also printed
	Score1	Integer	Test scores
	Score2	Integer	
	Score3	Integer	
Output:	Total	Integer	Total of 3 scores

Recall that the string[20] variable type signifies a string of characters of maximum length 20. The EndOfData constant '' can be matched by the user by just pressing the Return key when prompted for a name.

The algorithm involves a loop of the same general form as that in the previous example: obtain input, calculate answers, and print answers. We choose to ask for the student's name first, then for the three test grades.

Note. In general, we avoid entering character or string values on the same input line as numerical data. In the conversational programs we are writing, obtaining a few data at a time is a good idea. In addition, there are subtleties involved in mixing numeric and nonnumeric data on the same line. We choose not to get bogged down in these subtleties now.

To terminate the looping process, the user is asked to enter an empty name. In some of our previous programs, we told the user to press Return to terminate the program, so it did not return to THINK Pascal before the user had a chance to read the output. Here, though, the name prompt serves the same purpose: the output remains on the screen until an empty name is provided. So, for this program, we don't need a special termination message.

This planning leads to the following algorithm. (Steps marked (*) are not done if the user enters an empty name.)

    print instructions
    repeat the following until the user inputs an empty name:
        prompt for the name
        read Name
        prompt for the three scores (*)
        read Score1, Score2, Score3 (*)
        calculate Total (*)
        print Name and Total with a message (*)

Compare this algorithm to the algorithm for the areas of rectangles. You see that it is almost identical in form. The only difference is that the reading of the name is separated from the reading of the scores. This general form of algorithm is frequently appropriate for the types of programs written in the early chapters of the text.

Test Plan. At this point, we might pause to plan our testing strategy. Recalling the discussion earlier in this section, we might include the following types of tests for the three scores (we are assuming that valid test scores are in the range from 0 to 100). It may be a good idea to jot down the expected result for each test, as shown here.

Easy to check:	70, 70, 70	: 210	
	50, 100, 50	: 200	
More realistic:	87, 94, 78	: 259	
	68, 92, 75	: 235	
Boundaries:	0, 0, 0	: 0	
	100, 100, 100	: 300	(program does not
	−1, −5, −10	: −16	check for bad data)
	101, 101, 101	: 303	

As we gain more sophistication in our testing, we will discover some other tests that might be important here. Notice that we have, for instance, included some bad data (101 and −1) right on the boundary between data values that produce correct and incorrect results.

In addition to these specific tests, we would include some randomly chosen input lines.

Write Program. We now write the program, which is shown in finished form in Figure 1-5. Again, we have numbered the program lines for reference.

The following paragraphs contain brief notes on how we translated our plan into THINK Pascal.

1. Lines 3 to 5 form the header comments for the program, explaining what the program does and listing information about the authorship.

2. Lines 17, 31 to 32, and 47 also contain comments. This is the first instance of a program that uses this type of comment; they are sometimes called **section comments**, because they appear at the beginning of important sections of the program. They lead the reader to a quick understanding of the section's purpose and actions.

In this program, there are three major portions: the loop body, the steps performed before the loop, and the steps performed after the loop. We have, therefore, inserted brief comments before each of these three portions. The comments not only help someone reading our program to understand it, but help us understand it when we come back to it after a period of time. Section comments, in addition to the header comments, provide a valuable piece of documentation for any program.

In order to make them stand out, we always surround section comments by blank lines. In general, judicious use of **white space** (blank lines) makes the program easier to read.

In this text, we consistently utilize section comments. Early in the text, they are directed partially to the reader of the book, sometimes explaining some Pascal or programming features. Later, they are directed primarily to the reader of the program and may be briefer.

3. Lines 1, 15, and 49 form the basic structure of the program. They are similar to the previous program.

4. Lines 7 to 13 contain the constant and variable declarations, based directly on the variable list. For each, we have provided a brief comment.

5. The algorithm step, "print instructions," generates lines 19 to 29. Notice that, in line 20, in order to print the word "student's," which includes an apostrophe, we must add a second apostrophe.

6. The *repeat* step in the algorithm leads to several things in the program. First, lines 34 and 45 form a Pascal *repeat-until* loop, used to accomplish the repetition. In addition, we must remember that we do not want to do the steps following reading the name if the user has entered an empty name. Thus, we also include the *if* statement beginning in line 38. This *if* statement automatically includes the *begin* in line 39 and the *end* in line 44.

In THINK Pascal, a blank name would not be considered the same as an empty name; the user must hit return without typing any characters to terminate the loop.

7. The prompt asking for the name results in lines 35 and 36. We include a Writeln to print a blank line before the prompt.

8. The step "Read Name" results in line 37.

9. The prompt asking for three scores is in line 40. Line 41 reads the three scores, and line 42 calculates the Total. The next section has more details on the Pascal assignment statement.

10. "Print Name and Total with a message" generates line 43. Notice that we print a message, then the Total variable, then another brief message, and then the Name variable. The resulting printed line reads like a sentence. Notice also the extra spaces around the word "for" to separate it from the total and from the name.

Run Program. The results of a short sample run are given in Figure 1-6. Only a portion of the actual run is shown. The total run tested all the planned test items (from step 4 before), along with some other randomly chosen input. Notice that the word "student's" is printed by the program with just the one apostrophe.

DPT

1. The entire section on Program Testing can be viewed as a defensive programming tip. In particular, hand tracing an algorithm or program can uncover a logic error in a fraction of the amount of time it takes to find it after running the program.

2. Comments aid in making a program understandable. They do, however, introduce a pitfall. If we forget the closing bracket ("}") to end the comment, the compiler ignores parts of the program. This can cause error messages seemingly unrelated to the actual mistake.

3. The *begin* in line 39 and the *end* in line 44 of the Case Study program (Figure 1-5) are mandatory.

```
1)    program TestScores;
2)
3)    {Written by: XXXXXXXXX XX/XX/XX}
4)    {Purpose:    To calculate the total on three tests, and}
5)    {            print that total with the student's name}
6)
7)      const
8)        EndOfData = '';    {empty string to terminate input}
9)
10)     var
11)       Name: string[20];              {student name, input}
12)       Score1, Score2, Score3: integer; {three test scores, input}
13)       Total: integer;                {total of test scores, calculated}
14)
15)   begin {TestScores}
16)
17)   {*** Before the loop, print instructions}
18)
19)      Writeln('This program totals test scores. For each');
20)      Writeln('student you will be asked to enter the student''s');
21)      Writeln('name. You may use up to 20 characters for the');
22)      Writeln('name when you type it in. After that, you will');
23)      Writeln('be asked to type in the three test scores, in the');
24)      Writeln('range from 0 to 100. Enter these all on one line,');
25)      Writeln('separated by blank spaces.');
26)      Writeln('  The program will then print the name and the');
27)      Writeln('total score, and repeat the whole process. When');
28)      Writeln('you wish to terminate the program, just tap the');
29)      Writeln('return key when asked for the name.');
30)
31)   {*** In the loop, read name, scores; calculate and print total;}
32)   {    quit when user enters empty name}
33)
34)     repeat
35)       Writeln;
36)       Write('Enter the name (just tap return to quit): ');
37)       Readln(Name);
38)       if Name <> EndOfData then
39)         begin
40)            Write('Now enter the three scores: ');
41)            Readln(Score1, Score2, Score3);
42)            Total := Score1 + Score2 + Score3;
43)            Writeln('The total is ', Total, ' for ', Name)
44)         end
45)     until Name = EndOfData;
46)
47)   {*** After the loop, stop the program}
48)
49)   end.
```

Figure 1-5 A looping program with instructions.

```
    This program totals test scores. For each
student you will be asked to enter the student's
name. You may use up to 20 characters for the
name when you type it in. After that, you will
be asked to type in the three test scores, in the
range from 0 to 100. Enter these all on one line,
separated by blank spaces.
    The program will then print the name and the
total score, and repeat the whole process. When
you wish to terminate the program, just tap the
return key when asked for the name.

Enter the name (just tap return to quit): John Jones
Now enter the three scores: 70 70 70
The total is      210 for John Jones

Enter the name (just tap return to quit): Sue Smith
Now enter the three scores: 50 100 50
The total is      200 for Sue Smith

Enter the name (just tap return to quit): A. B. Simpson
Now enter the three scores: 70 100 89
The total is      259 for A. B. Simpson

Enter the name (just tap return to quit):
```

Figure 1-6   Sample input and output.

REVIEW

Terms and concepts

boundary conditions
bugs
compile-time errors
debugging
hand-trace

logic error
run-time errors
section comments
white space

Program testing

THREE PHASES

1. Hand-tracing the algorithm
2. Removing syntax errors
3. Running the program with test data

TEST DATA

1. Some easy to check (but all should be checked, perhaps using a calculator)
2. Test near boundaries and away from boundaries
3. Test bad data

EXERCISES

1. Enter and run the first sample program (Figure 1-3).
2. Using the program from Exercise 1, experiment with compile-time and run-time errors; some suggestions:
    (a) Make changes, such as misspellings, and notice the error messages generated. Include omitting the "}" at the close of some comments.
    (b) Change the "*" to a "/" and enter a width of 0 to obtain a "division by 0" run-time error.
    (c) Enter inappropriate data (such as words) for the length or width.
    (d) Enter extremely large numbers for length and width.
3. Enter and run the second sample program (Figure 1-5).
4. Enter and run the programs for Exercise 1 of Section 1-3.
5. Determine an appropriate set of test data for each of the programs from Exercise 1 of Section 1-3. Be sure to include some that are easy to check, some that are near any boundaries, some not near the boundaries, and some bad data (if applicable).
6. By following the method used in Case Study No. 1, write programs to perform the following tasks:
    (a) The perimeter of a triangle is the sum of its three sides. Write a program to find the perimeters of triangles.
    (b) The distance traveled in miles is the product of the speed in miles per hour and the number of miles traveled. Write a program that reads in appropriate input, and calculates the distance traveled, for a number of different inputs.
    (c) Given a number that represents inches, we can compute the equivalent number of centimeters by multiplying the number by (about) 2.54. Write a program that accepts from the user inputs in inches and outputs the same measures in centimeters.
    (d) Write a program that, for each employee in a company, accepts as input the employee's name, hours worked this week, and hourly wage, and prints that employee's name and weekly pay. The weekly pay is the product of the number of hours the employee worked and that employee's hourly wage.
    (e) Write a program that determines the amount of money each customer of a company owes, based on this rule: the new amount owed is 1.015 times the old amount owed. The program accepts as input each customer's name and old amount and prints out that information, along with the customer's new amount owed.
7. Tell how to modify the first example (Figure 1-3) so that, just before it stops, it prints "Enjoy the day!" preceded by a blank line.
8. Tell how to modify the first example (Figure 1-3) to read the user's name at the beginning of the run, then print the message "Enjoy the day," and followed by the user's name. (For instance, if the user is Dana, print "Enjoy the day, Dana".)
9. Tell how to modify the second example (Figure 1-5) to read the date as a string of characters and print it out prior to obtaining the lists of names and grades. (Just print out the data exactly as the user enters them.)

2 Fundamentals of Pascal Program Design

OBJECTIVES

Chapter 1 introduced sufficient information about writing programs and the THINK Pascal programming language to enable you to write some short programs (which, hopefully, you have done by now). In this chapter, we build on this foundation by discussing program design and Pascal in more detail. After completing this chapter, you will be able to:

- add to your knowledge of the four building blocks of program structure: sequencing, looping, decisions, and subprograms
- use more complex assignment statements
- use complex arithmetic and conditional expressions
- understand why using procedures and functions is recommended in programming
- use several of Pascal's predefined procedures and functions in your programs
- define your own procedures and functions
- improve the format of your program output, both to the screen and to the printer
- employ more complex decision structures in your programs
- perform more in-depth testing of your programs

2-1 THE ASSIGNMENT STATEMENT

We begin our study by providing a more complete description of the assignment statement than that of the previous chapter.

Recall that the assignment statement assigns values to variables. The form of the statement is

```
variable := expression
```

where "variable" represents any Pascal variable name, and "expression" represents some combination of variables, constants, and operations. The ":=" is called the **assignment operator**. (Although made up of two symbols, ":" and "=", it is treated as if it were a single symbol.)

The purpose of an assignment statement is to give a new value to a variable. Each variable has a particular place in the computer memory where its value is stored, so the effect of an assignment statement is to store a new value in that memory location. We say that the new value is "assigned to the variable."

When the assignment statement is executed, there are two major events that occur, in this order:

1. The expression on the right side of the assignment operator is evaluated. Because the expression can be complicated, the evaluation process can involve several variables and subexpressions. The current value of all variables is used in calculating the value the expression represents.
2. The value obtained by evaluating the expression on the right side of the assignment operator is assigned to (placed into) the variable on the left side of the assignment operator.

In the remainder of this section, we first look at numeric assignment statements and then at a few simple character and string assignments.

Numeric Assignment Statements

A **numeric assignment statement** is one for which the value on the right side of the assignment operator is a number and the variable on the left side of the assignment operator is a numeric type. For example, the following are numeric assignment statements (all variables are real):

```
TaxRate := 0.06
Balance := Balance + 345.68
X := Y
Price := 1.5 * Cost
```

The first example gives the variable "TaxRate" a value of 0.06. The second changes the variable "Balance" by adding 345.68 to the previous value of "Balance". The third copies the value of the variable "Y" to the variable "X", and the fourth gives the variable "Price" the product of the variable "Cost" multiplied by 1.5. The variable "Y" in the third example and the variable "Cost" in the fourth example are not changed by the execution of the assignment statements. Only the variables on the left side have their values changed.

Note. The assignment operator ":= " is suggestive of a left-facing arrow, which reminds us that values flow from right to left. There is no space between the colon and the equals sign.

Precedence. As you may have noticed, the assignment statement appears somewhat similar to an algebraic formula. For example, the formula

$$d = rt$$

tells us how to calculate the distance *d* for a given value of *r* (rate) and *t* (time). In a formula such as this, just as in an assignment statement, the quantity on the left is the quantity that we wish to calculate, using the formula or expression on the right. Our Pascal rendering of this formula might be

```
D := R * T
```

or, more clearly,

```
Distance := Rate * Time
```

Formulas typically involve combinations of variables and constants using such operators as addition, subtraction, multiplication, and division. For example, the familiar formula

$$F = (9/5)C + 32$$

(for determining the Fahrenheit temperature corresponding to a given Celsius reading) involves division (9 divided by 5), multiplication, and addition. The inverse formula

$$C = (5/9)(F - 32)$$

involves division, subtraction, and multiplication. The formulas also introduce parentheses to control the order in which the operations are to be performed. (In the last case, they ensure that the quantity "F – 32" is evaluated before being multiplied by "5/9".)

The following rules are commonly used as conventions in determining the order of operations in algebraic formulas.

1. A unary minus (as in "–5 + 6") is evaluated by acting upon the constant, variable, or parenthetical group that immediately follows to the right of the minus sign.
2. Multiplication and division are performed before addition and subtraction, unless parentheses force another sequence of evaluation. When multiplications or divisions occur in a row, they are evaluated from left to right.
3. Addition and subtraction are then performed, again from left to right.
4. Within a parenthetical expression, the evaluation occurs according to these rules (including this one).

The following is a set of examples that illustrates these rules:

$$3 + 4 \cdot 7 \text{ is } 31$$
(Multiplication takes precedence over addition.)

$$(3 + 4)7 \text{ is } 49$$
(Parentheses force evaluation of addition first.)

$$-5 + 9 \text{ is } 4$$
(The unary minus acts first.)

$$8/4 \cdot 2 \text{ is } 4$$
(Division and multiplication go from left to right.)

$$8/(4 \cdot 2) \text{ is } 1$$
(Parentheses force evaluation of multiplication first.)

$$7 - 4 - 2 \text{ is } 1$$
(Subtractions go from left to right.)

$$7 - (4 - 2) \text{ is } 5$$
(Parentheses force evaluation of right subtraction first.)

$$6 \cdot (5 - (2 + 1)) \text{ is } 12$$
(Innermost parentheses are evaluated first.)

The Pascal symbols for the arithmetic operators are:

+	addition
–	subtraction (and unary minus)
*	multiplication
/	division

Note (for the curious). There is no standard Pascal operator for exponentiation. We discuss an alternative in Section 2-4.

In algebra, you may recall, a dot indicates multiplication, as in the formula

$$y = a \cdot b$$

Later, you were allowed to drop the dot, writing

$$y = ab$$

Consider, however, the corresponding Pascal assignment statement

```
Y := AB
```

Because Pascal variable names can be (and are encouraged to be) more than one letter long, we cannot be sure whether the right side refers to a single variable "AB" or to the variable "A" multiplied by the variable "B". To clarify the situation, we must always include a symbol for multiplication. For historical reasons, the asterisk symbol was chosen to represent the multiplication operator in Pascal.

In algebra, we are accustomed to seeing fractions that have expressions for both numerator and denominator; for example,

$$\frac{a + 2b}{c - 3d}$$

In Pascal, we use the slash (/) symbol for the division operator. Note that a naive translation of the last formula into the Pascal assignment statement

```
Z := A + 2 * B / C - 3 * D
```

yields an erroneous result. The correct translation to Pascal is

```
Z := (A + 2 * B) / (C - 3 * D)
```

Note. The reason the first statement is incorrect is that, without the parentheses, the subexpression 2 * B / C is calculated before the addition and subtraction. For example, suppose the variables A, B, C, and D contain the values 4, 6, 8, and 2, respectively. The correct value for z is

$$(4 + 2 * 6) / (8 - 3 * 2) =$$
$$(4 + 12) / (8 - 6) =$$
$$16 / 2 =$$
$$8$$

The incorrect assignment statement yields

$$4 + 2 * 6 / 8 - 3 * 2 =$$
$$4 + 12 / 8 - 6 =$$
$$4 + 1.5 - 6 =$$
$$5.5 - 6 =$$
$$-0.5$$

The precedence rules for the arithmetic operators of Pascal coincide with the algebraic rules:

1. Unary minus (–) first
2. * and / next, left to right
3. + and – next, left to right
4. Parentheses can be used to group operations

Because the precedence rules in Pascal are the same as those for algebraic formulas, most algebraic formulas can be rewritten as Pascal assignment statements with little difficulty. We must, however, remember to use the asterisk (*) for multiplication and the slash (/) for division, and to group numerator and denominator expressions with parentheses.

The following illustrates the correspondence between algebraic formulas and Pascal assignment statements:

ALGEBRAIC FORMULA	PASCAL ASSIGNMENT STATEMENT
$y = x + t$	Y := X + T
$x = 2y$	X := 2 * Y
$x = y/z + r$	X := Y / Z + R
$y = ax + b$	Y := A * X + B
$a = x(t + w)$	A := X * (T + W)

2-1 THE ASSIGNMENT STATEMENT

Note. It is permissible to add extra parentheses to an expression in order to emphasize the meaning of subexpressions. For example, we can write

```
Y := (B * A) / C
```

instead of the equivalent

```
Y := B * A / C
```

if we wish to emphasize that the multiplication comes before the division. Similarly, we can write

```
Y := (40 * R) + (1.5 * R * T)
```

if we wish, although no parentheses are required to obtain the desired precedence.

Real and Integer Expressions. In the examples just given, we have usually been assuming that all variables are real. As mentioned earlier, Pascal does make a distinction between integer and real quantities. Some implications of this are discussed in detail in Section 2-4. However, a brief discussion is in order here.

Fortunately, Pascal's way of handling expressions is what we would normally expect. For example:

$$2.5 + 7 \text{ is } 9.5$$

(Adding a real to an integer is allowed.)

$$5 * 6.43 \text{ is } 32.15$$

(Multiplication (and division or subtraction) is also allowed.)

$$5 / 2 \text{ is } 2.5$$

(Dividing two integers gives just what we expect here.)

$$4 / 2 \text{ is } 2.0$$

(The answer from the division operator "/" is always real.)

Only the last example may be somewhat unexpected.

In general, then, we can write our assignment statements in a completely natural way. For example, if the Price of an item is a real and the Quantity purchased is an integer, an assignment

```
TotalCost := Price * Quantity
```

is acceptable (TotalCost is real).

There is one important restriction to note. We cannot assign a real expression to an integer variable. For example, suppose we know that a real number R is evenly divisible by 10. If N is an integer, an assignment such as

```
N := R / 10
```

would still generate a `type mismatch` compile-time error because "/" always returns a real result. Section 2-4 addresses this issue further.

DPT

For the most part, assignment statements in Pascal are straightforward. If we know what formula or expression is needed to calculate a new value for a variable, we place the expression to the right side of the assignment operator and the variable to the left. There are, however, seven points that deserve special emphasis.

    1. The main point to remember is that the assignment operator is written as ":=". A common mistake made by those new to Pascal is to use the "=" alone as the assignment operator. Another common mistake is to put space between the colon and the equals sign. Fortunately, the Pascal compiler detects and reports any such erroneous symbol usage.

    2. Multiplication cannot be implicit in an expression; it must always be made explicit by use of the symbol "*". The compiler generally detects this error, but it might give a misleading error message. For example, if we write

```
Y := AB
```

instead of

```
Y := A * B
```

the error message says that the identifier AB is unknown (because it is undeclared).

    3. Extra parentheses may be needed to group numerators and denominators when using the division symbol "/". The compiler does not detect a failure to do so and the program yields incorrect results.

    4. Using "/" to divide always yields a real value, and a real value cannot be assigned to an integer variable.

    5. Although the assignment statement is similar to an algebraic formula, it is not at all similar to an algebraic equation. For example, an assignment statement similar to

```
K := K + 1
```

is commonly used in Pascal programs. The meaning of the statement is

    (a) Evaluate the right side by taking the current value of the variable K and adding 1 to it.

    (b) Change the value of the variable K to the value obtained on the right side. If we translate the assignment statement into the algebraic equation

$$k = k + 1$$

we obtain an unsolvable equation and a surprising equality if we attempt to solve it ($0 = 1$).

    6. A variable should never appear on the right side of an assignment statement until it has been given a value. For example, if the variable K has not yet been given a value in a Pascal program, then the statement

```
K := K + 1
```

2-1 THE ASSIGNMENT STATEMENT

will have an unpredictable result. The resulting value of K will not be under the control of the programmer or the program. When you are reading through your Pascal code to check it for correctness, ask for each instance of a variable that appears on the right side of an assignment statement: "How did this variable receive its value?" In particular, look to see that the variable has received a value via an earlier Readln statement, or by being on the left side of an earlier assignment statement.

   7. Be careful to avoid assignments that result in numeric overflow, that is, never let the value to be assigned into the left-hand variable be larger in magnitude than the type of the variable permits. This problem can occur with any numeric type, but is most common with integers.

   The integers in THINK range between –32768 to +32767. Suppose we had this series of assignment statements (where I is an integer):

```
I := 100
I := I * I
I := I * 5
```

After the first assignment, I will contain 100; after the second, 10,000; and after the third, I does *not* contain 50,000. Because the last assignment results in a number that is too large to be stored as an integer, integer overflow occurs. I contains the value –15,536! Notice that no run-time error is generated; THINK cheerfully takes the value it finds in I after the overflow occurred and uses it as if nothing unusual had happened.

   Fortunately, you can tell THINK Pascal to check your program for overflow during arithmetic operations that involve integers; to do so, you must turn on the "overflow" option. One way to do this is to click on the V next to your program's name in the project window. (Of course, you must add your program to the project for its name to appear in the project window.) A box will appear around the V, indicating overflow checking is on for that program. To turn overflow checking off, just click on the V again; the box will disappear. Enabling overflow checking instructs the THINK compiler to place additional code into your program so that, when an overflow occurs, the program stops with a run-time error. This extra code does cause the program's execution to slow down, so most programmers turn overflow checking on while the program is being debugged, and turn it off when the program is ready to use.

   "Boxing" the V turns overflow checking on for the entire program, which is what we usually want. Sometimes, though, we want to check just part of a program. If our program only does integer arithmetic in one section, we might want to check for overflow only in that section.

   A way to check for overflow in part of a program is by placing the **compiler directive** {$V+} in the program at the point overflow checking is to begin and the directive {$V–} at the point it is to end. (You can turn verification on again later in the program by issuing another {$V+} directive.) Compiler directives are specific strings placed within curly brackets that give instructions to THINK as it compiles the program. THINK knows these specific strings are not comments because of the '$' symbol that begins them. Each should be placed on its own line of the program. (You can do overflow checking for the entire program by issuing {$V+} at the start of the program and {$V–} at its end. This use of $V directives is equivalent to "boxing" the program's V option on the project window.)

We strongly recommend that you turn on the check for integer overflow in any program that includes integer arithmetic. We will assume that the V option has been turned on in any example programs we give that contain integer arithmetic.

Character Assignment Statements

A variable of type *char* can have as its value any single character. Some of these characters correspond to the characters that can be generated on the keyboard and printed on a printer. The two most common ways to assign values to a char variable are by the use of a char **literal** or by use of the built-in function **Chr**. If X and Y are char variables, we can also assign the value of Y to X by use of the statement

```
X := Y
```

A char literal consists of exactly one character enclosed between apostrophes. For example, the statement

```
Letter := 'C'
```

assigns to the variable "Letter" the value of uppercase "C". In similar fashion, but less obviously, the statement

```
Blank := ' '
```

assigns to the variable Blank a single blank space. Note that the statement

```
Blank := ''
```

does not have the desired effect because there is no blank space between apostrophes. In fact, this generates a compile-time error.

If you want to represent the apostrophe as a char variable, type it twice in succession as in the statement

```
Apostrophe := '''';
```

The standard Pascal function "Chr" generates a char value from any of the numbers from 0 to 255. The character set used on the computer determines the meaning of any particular instance of this function; the Macintosh uses the **ASCII** (American Standard Code for Information Interchange) character set (as do most microcomputers, and many other kinds of computers). For instance, the value of Chr(67) is the uppercase letter "C" because "C" has the ASCII code of 67. The assignment statement

```
Letter := Chr(67)
```

assigns the character 'C' to the variable Letter. (Appendix D contains a list of ASCII values for characters.)

String Assignment Statements

In THINK Pascal, a variable of the type *string* has associated with it a maximum length that is either (a) declared with it in the *var* section of the program or (b) assumed to be 255 characters, if no size is provided with its declaration. The most common ways to assign values to a string variable are by using string literals or the concatenation operator. Other string operations are discussed in Chapter 8.

A string literal consists of 0 or more characters enclosed between apostrophes. The **null string** is denoted by '' (two apostrophes next to each other) and means a string of no characters. This particular string is also referred to as the **empty string.** Note that the string literal consisting of one blank space, ' ', is not the same as the null string. Also note that a string literal consisting of a single character is indistinguishable from a char literal. For example, the expression

```
'c'
```

could represent either a string literal or a char literal. Another point to remember is that the following two strings are different:

```
'The lazy fox'
'The lazy fox '
```

The latter string contains one more character (a blank space) than does the former string.

Suppose that the string variable ShortWord has a maximum size set to 4 (is declared as string[4]) and that the following statement is executed:

```
ShortWord := 'longest'
```

In THINK, a run-time error occurs because 'longest' is 7 characters and ShortWord can accommodate only 4. Suppose that for the same variable ShortWord, the following statement is executed:

```
ShortWord := 'is'
```

This does not have the same effect as does the statement

```
ShortWord := 'is  '
```

because the lengths of the two string literals in question are different. A string variable with a maximum length 4 can contain a string of length 0, 1, 2, 3, or 4.

As in the case of char variables, if you want to include the apostrophe within the string literal, use two consecutive apostrophes. For example, to assign the value "Wanda's" to the string variable Whose, we would use the statement

```
Whose := 'Wanda''s'
```

Concatenation is done in THINK Pascal by using the predefined *concat* function. We can think of concatenation as the pasting together of two strings. For example, if First, Second, and Third are strings of declared sizes 8, 6, and 7, respectively, then the execution of the statements

```
First  := 'apple';
Second := 's';
Third  := concat(First, Second)
```

would result in Third having the value 'apples'. First must be declared to be at least of size 5, and Second of at least size 1; Third can be of any size (up to 255). If the string 'apples' is too large to fit into the space reserved for Third, it is **truncated** to fit—the rightmost characters of apples are lost. For example, if Third were declared as *string[3]*, it would contain 'app' after the concatenation was done. Some other possible methods of placing the value 'apples' in the variable Third are as follows:

METHOD ONE

```
First := 'apple';
Third := concat(First, 's')
```

METHOD TWO

```
First  := 'apple';
Second := Chr(115);
Third  := concat(First, Second)
```

METHOD THREE

```
Third := concat('apple', 's')
```

METHOD FOUR

```
Third := 'apples'
```

If concatenation yields a string value with a length greater than 255, then THINK Pascal truncates the string to 255 characters.

Note. The relationship between variables of type *char* and *string* with respect to the assignment statement is simply that variables of type char and strings of length 1 behave similarly. Thus, we can assign a string to a char variable provided the length of the string is exactly 1.

Examples

In Figures 2-1 and 2-2, we present complete Pascal programs that utilize numeric and string assignment statements. In each case, the program reads lines of input until the value chosen to denote end-of-data is read.

Note. In entering the strings in Figure 2-2, the user placed a blank prior to "MORNING!" and "now". If she had not done so, the output would have appeared as "GOODMORNING!" and "Goodbye fornow".

REVIEW

Terms and Concepts

ASCII
assignment operator (:=)
Chr
compiler directive
concatenation (+)
empty string
literal
null string

numeric assignment statement
precedence
truncation
+
−
*
/

```pascal
program Volume;

{Written by: XXXXXXXXX XX/XX/XX}
{Purpose:    To compute the volume of cones}

  const
    EndOfData = 0;          {Terminating value for Radius}
    Pi = 3.1415927;

  var
    Radius: real;           {Radius of Base of the cone}
    Height: real;           {Height of the cone}
    Volume: real;           {Volume of the cone}

begin {Volume}

{*** In loop, read Radius and Height, compute and print Volume}

  repeat
   Writeln;
   Write('Enter the Radius: ');
   Readln(Radius);
   if Radius <> EndOfData then
    begin
      Write('Enter the Height: ');
      Readln(Height);
      Volume := Pi * (Radius * Radius) * Height / 3;
      Writeln('The volume of the cone is: ', Volume)
    end
  until Radius = EndOfData

end.
```

SAMPLE INPUT AND OUTPUT

```
Enter the Radius: 3.7
Enter the Height: 10.85
The volume of the cone is:   1.6e+2

Enter the Radius: 34.6
Enter the Height: 2.3
The volume of the cone is:   2.9e+3

Enter the Radius: 0
```

Figure 2-1   Numeric assignment.

```
program Join;

{Written by: XXXXXXXXX XX/XX/XX}
{Purpose:    To concatenate two strings}

  const
    EndOfData = '';          {Terminating value for Prefix}

  var
    Prefix: string[20];      {First string}
    Suffix: string[20];      {Second string}
    Joined: string[40];      {Joined strings}

  begin {Join}

  {*** In loop, read Prefix and Suffix}

    repeat
      Writeln;
      Write('Enter the first string: ');
      Readln(Prefix);
      if Prefix <> EndOfData then
        begin
          Write('Enter the second string: ');
          Readln(Suffix);
          Joined := concat(Prefix, Suffix);
          Writeln('The joined string is: ', Joined)
        end
    until Prefix = EndOfData

  end.
```

SAMPLE INPUT AND OUTPUT

```
Enter the first string: GOOD
Enter the second string:  MORNING!
The joined string is: GOOD MORNING!

Enter the first string: Goodbye for
Enter the second string:  now.
The joined string is: Goodbye for now.

Enter the first string:
```

Figure 2-2   String assignment.

Pascal Syntax

```
variable := expression
```

(One or more variables or constants are contained in "expression".)

POSSIBLE OPERATORS

1. For numbers: +, –, *, /
2. For strings: concat (concatenation)

ACTION

1. Evaluates expression using current values of variables
2. Assigns result to variable

PRECEDENCE

1. Unary minus
2. * and /, left to right
3. + and –, left to right
4. Parentheses can group

TRUNCATION

1. The results of string operations are truncated to fit the maximum length of the string variable. An assignment of a string literal to a string variable too small to contain it results in a compile-time error.

DPT

1. Use := for assignment.
2. Use * for multiplication.
3. May need parentheses to group numerators and denominators.
4. Using a / (slash) yields a real answer; real values cannot be assigned to integer variables.
5. Assignment is not an algebraic equation; it is more like an algebraic formula.
6. Make sure that a variable has been given a value before it is used on the right side of an assignment statement.
7. Avoid assignments that result in numeric overflow; integers are especially susceptible to this condition.

EXERCISES

1. Give the value of the following Pascal expressions:

    (a) 3 * 2 + 7
    (b) 4 / 3
    (c) 6 + 5 / 2
    (d) 3 / 2 + 1
    (e) 3 * (2 + 5)
    (f) 3 - 7 + 2
    (g) 3 - (7 + 2)
    (h) concat('A', 'B')
    (i) 4 * 3 / 2
    (j) 4 * (3 / 2)
    (k) 8 / 2 * 4
    (l) concat('4 * 6', '5')

2. Assume that A, B, and C are real and X, Y, and Z are integer. Also assume that at the time the assignment statement is executed, the variables have the values:

    A 3.2   B 6.0   C 1.5
    X 4   Y 63   Z 17

    What value is given to the variable on the left side of each assignment statement?

    (a) A := 0.5 * A
    (b) X := X + 1
    (c) B := A / 2
    (d) A := 12.3
    (e) Y := X * Z
    (f) C := C - A - B

3. Convert the following algebraic formulas to Pascal assignment statements. Assume that all variables are real.

    (a) $y = ax + b$
    (b) $t = \frac{1}{2}a + r$
    (c) $w = \frac{x+y}{2}$
    (d) $j = k + 5$
    (e) $s = 5t$
    (f) $r = \frac{x}{y+3}$
    (g) $w = \frac{x+3y}{r+a-3}$
    (h) $j = (k+3)j$

4. For the following assignment statements, determine what value is assigned to the variable on the left. Assume all variables are of type *string* and the declared size of Str3 is 3, Str5 is 5, and Str7 is 7. Further, suppose the string variable Bees has the value 'bbb' and that Sees has the value 'cccc'.
   (a) `Str3 := Bees`
   (b) `Str5 := Bees`
   (c) `Str3 := Sees`
   (d) `Str3 := concat('b', Bees, Sees)`
   (e) `Str7 := concat('b', Sees)`
   (f) `Str7 := concat('b', Bees, Sees)`
   (g) `Str3 := 'cbc'`
   (h) `Str3 := 'Str3'`
   (i) `Str7 := concat('''b''', 'c')`
   (j) `Str5 := concat('', Bees)`

5. Write Pascal assignment statements to perform each of the following calculations. Use meaningful variable names and give declarations for your variables.
   (a) Calculate the area of a rectangle given its length and width.
   (b) Convert inches to centimeters (1 inch = 2.54 centimeters).
   (c) Find the average of three real numbers.
   (d) Find a person's age in months given his age in years and months (for example, 3 years, 4 months yields an answer of 40 months).
   (e) Find the local tax given the income. The rule is: 5 percent of the portion of the income in excess of $1,000. (Assume that the income is at least $1,000.)
   (f) Prefix a last name with "Professor".
   (g) Calculate the batting average given the times at bat and the number of hits.
   (h) Find the percentage of mutated ants in an ant colony given the number of mutated ants and the total number of ants in the colony.
   (i) Convert a speed in kilometers per hour to meters per second.
   (j) Convert a swimmer's time (seconds) for the 50-meter freestyle to an estimate of the time for the 50-yard freestyle by multiplying the time by 0.9.

6. Using the assignment statements you wrote in Exercise 5, plan and write complete programs that calculate the indicated values for a number of input lines.

7. Write a complete Pascal program to read a person's name and print the message:

   `Hi, <name read in>, how's it going?`

   For example, if the user enters the name "Stacy", then the program will output

   `Hi, Stacy, how's it going?`

8. Write a program to allow experimentation with the Chr function. For each numeric value input by the user (in the range 0 to 255), it should print the corresponding character. Use the program to experiment. Is Chr(0) a character you can see on the screen? (Is it "printable?") What is Chr(68)? What happens if you enter a value not in the prescribed range?

9. Using three separate Readln statements, write a program to read a person's last name, then the first name, and finally the middle initial. Use string variables for the first and last names and a char variable for the initial. The program should create a variable AddressLine that has the

contents "To the parents of <first name> <middle initial>. <last name>" (such as "To the parents of Smedley Z. Oglethorpe"), and print AddressLine on the screen.

10. Write a complete Pascal program to calculate how long it would take someone who wishes to lose weight to reach a specific goal weight. Prompt the user (with meaningful messages) for these inputs:

Current weight
Goal weight
Gender (female or male)
Rate of weight loss (slow, moderate, fast)
Activity level (sedentary, moderately active, very active)
    (Sedentary means never exercises; moderately active means exercises three times a week for at least 30 minutes; very active means exercises virtually every day for at least 60 minutes.)

And print these outputs:

Current number of calories person is taking in
Number of calories to cut out of the person's diet
Calories to take in to reach goal weight
Number of days to reach goal weight
Other informational messages (see below)

Use the following information:

If female and sedentary, factor is 10
If male and sedentary, factor is 13
If female and moderately active, factor is 13
If male and moderately active, factor is 15
If female and very active, factor is 15
If male and very active, factor is 20

Current calorie intake = factor × Current weight
Goal calorie intake = factor × Goal weight

Goal calorie intake must not drop below 1100. (If it did, the person may not be getting enough calories to maintain her or his health.) If the above formula would result in an intake of less than 1100 calories, set the goal intake to 1100 calories, and tell the user you have done so and the reasons behind the decision.

If rate is slow, Daily calorie reduction = 500 calories
If rate is fast, Daily calorie reduction = 1500 calories
If rate is moderate, Daily calorie reduction =
Current calorie intake – Goal calorie intake, but is at minimum 500 and at maximum 1500 calories. If the formula generates an amount less then 500, set the amount to 500; if it generates an amount greater than 1500, set the amount to 1500, and explain to the user that a larger calorie reduction may be unhealthy.

EXERCISES

Daily calorie reduction of 500 calories a day results in 1 pound lost in 1 week (7 days); higher reductions cause proportionally larger weight losses (for example, a 1000-calorie-a-day reduction results in 2 pounds lost in 1 week).

Number of days = (500 calories minimum * 7 days) /
    Daily calorie reduction * Number of pounds to lose

Run the program on several test cases. Does it work well for all cases of weight loss (goal weight less than current weight)? Does it work correctly if someone wants to gain weight (goal weight greater than current weight)? What happens when the goal and current weights are equal? What does the program suggest if a sedentary female currently weighs 105 pounds and wishes to weigh 97? Does this advice make sense?

Note: This is a programming exercise, not a proven diet plan. Although this approach to weight reduction is based on formulas developed by health care professionals, it should not be used as an actual guide to weight loss. Should you wish to lose weight, consult with a health care professional to obtain a diet and exercise plan that is suited to your particular situation.

2-2 INTRODUCTION TO PROCEDURES

Previously (in Section 1-3), we discussed the four building blocks used for developing programs:

1. Sequencing
2. Looping
3. Decisions
4. Subprograms

The examples discussed so far have used the first three techniques. Sequencing appears in any program where we have a series of steps to perform, one after the other. We should expect to continue to find segments of all of our programs that fall into the sequencing category. Looping has been used in many of our examples to provide the structure in which we could repeatedly read values, make calculations, and print the results. Thus far, the loops have been terminated by the user entering a terminal (dummy) value. Decisions have been used to ensure that the dummy value is not processed inside of our read, calculate, and print loops. Subprograms are introduced in this section in one specific context. The variety of subprogram that we discuss is known in Pascal as a **procedure**.

An Example Procedure

The algorithm used to develop the program for the example (Case Study No. 1) from Section 1-4 is reproduced here as Figure 2-3 and its corresponding program as Figure 2-4. As we study the algorithm and then go on to read the program, we are struck by the fact that the printing of instructions has seemed to attain relatively more importance in the Pascal program than it had in the algorithm. In the algorithm, the task of printing the instructions occupies one line out of a total of nine algorithm lines. However, in the program, the printing of instructions occupies 11 out of a total of the 25 lines of Pascal (ignoring blank

```
          print instructions
          repeat the following until the user inputs an empty name
              prompt asking for name
              read Name
              prompt asking for three scores
              read Score1, Score2, Score3
              calculate Total
              print Name and Total with a message
          print the termination message
```

Figure 2-3   Looping algorithm.

and comment lines) that lie between the *begin* and *end* for the program. It seems that the proportion of lines dedicated to instructions in the algorithm is appropriate and that the program is harder to understand because of its inordinate emphasis on printing instructions.

The process of refining the algorithm line "print instructions" into the details of the instructions themselves has hindered readability of the resulting program. It would be nice if one could just say "print instructions" in the Pascal program and obtain the desired results when the program is executed. In fact, as we will see, we can attain that goal by the use of procedures.

The form of a Pascal procedure is similar to that of a Pascal program. This similarity lends itself well to the concept of subtasks of a task, which is what we will be using procedures to implement. When we remove the lines of the Pascal program of Figure 2-4 and place them within the confines of a Pascal procedure (named Instructions), we obtain the result shown as Figure 2-5.

Note there are two essential details that differentiate the procedure from a program:

1. The keyword *procedure* appears instead of *program*.

2. The final *end* is followed by a semicolon (;), not a period.

A more significant difference is that a Pascal procedure cannot be run by itself, but must be **called** (invoked) by another program unit to execute. In order to call our example procedure, the Pascal program just has to invoke its name with the command:

```
Instructions
```

When it does so, the statements in the Instructions procedure are executed. The program then continues with the statement following the invocation of the procedure.

For the Pascal program to invoke a procedure, it must have access to it. To achieve this, we simply include the procedure definition in the region of the program's code that immediately follows the *var* section and immediately precedes the *begin* of the program.

The program with procedure Instructions included appears as Figure 2-6. We have indicated, in italics, the differences between this and the program in Figure 2-4.

Some Characteristics of Procedures

We note here some of the properties of Pascal procedures illustrated in the example procedure, Instructions.

```pascal
program TestScores;

{Written by: XXXXXXXXX XX/XX/XX}
{Purpose:    To calculate the total on three tests, and print that total}
{            with the student's name.}

  const
    EndOfData = '';                    {empty string to terminate input}

  var
    Name: string[20];                  {student name, input}
    Score1, Score2, Score3: integer;   {three test scores, input}
    Total: integer;                    {total of scores, calculated}

begin {TestScores}

{*** Before the loop print instructions}

  Writeln(' This program totals test scores. For each');
  Writeln('student you will be asked to enter the student''s');
  Writeln('name. You may use up to 20 characters for the');
  Writeln('name when you type it in. After that, you will');
  Writeln('be asked to type in the three test scores, in the');
  Writeln('range from 0 to 100. Enter these all on one line,');
  Writeln('separated by blank spaces.');
  Writeln(' The program will then print the name and the');
  Writeln('total score, and repeat the whole process. When');
  Writeln('you wish to terminate the program, just tap the');
  Writeln('return key when asked for the name.');

{*** In the loop, read name and scores; calculate and print total;}
{    quit when user enters empty name}

  repeat
    Write('Enter the name (just tap return to quit): ');
    Readln(Name);
    if Name <> EndOfData then
      begin
        Write('Now enter the three scores: ');
        Readln(Score1, Score2, Score3);
        Total := Score1 + Score2 + Score3;
        Writeln('The total is ', Total, ' for ', Name)
      end
  until Name = EndOfData;

{*** Stop the program}

end.
```

Figure 2-4   Instructions in program.

```
procedure Instructions;
{Written by: XXXXXXXXX XX/XX/XX}
{Purpose:    To print instructions}

begin {Instructions}
  Writeln(' This program totals test scores. For each');
  Writeln('student you will be asked to enter the student''s');
  Writeln('name. You may use up to 20 characters for the');
  Writeln('name when you type it in. After that, you will');
  Writeln('be asked to type in the three test scores, in the');
  Writeln('range from 0 to 100. Enter these all on one line,');
  Writeln('separated by blank spaces.');
  Writeln(' The program will then print the name and the');
  Writeln('total score, and repeat the whole process. When');
  Writeln('you wish to terminate the program, just tap the');
  Writeln('return key when asked for the name.')
end; {Instructions}
```

Figure 2-5 Instructions procedure.

Name: A Pascal procedure has a name that is formed according to the rules for Pascal identifiers. The name of a procedure should not conflict with any of the program variables or constants (there are more specific details on this issue later).

Body: A Pascal procedure must have its lines of code contained between the *begin* and *end;* pair (note the mandatory semicolon after *end*).

Use: A program calls a procedure by specifying its name as an entire statement (including the semicolon, if needed).

Place: A Pascal procedure must be completely contained (from *procedure* to *end;*) in the area of the program that follows the *var* section and that precedes the *begin* of the program.

Note. We are discussing the simplest form of a Pascal procedure in this section. In subsequent sections, we treat other types of subprograms.

Standard Procedures

From the beginning, we have been dealing with procedures that are supplied with the Pascal language. In particular, we have used two procedures: Readln and Writeln. When we used the statement

```
Writeln
```

in our examples, we were using the procedure in the same manner that we have used the procedure "Instructions" in this section. We used Writeln to print a blank line in order to format our program's output in a more readable fashion. In our other uses of Writeln and Readln, we supplied some information for the procedures by enclosing that information within parentheses following the procedure name. For example, in the statement

```pascal
program TestScores;

{Written by: XXXXXXXXX XX/XX/XX}
{Purpose:    To calculate the total on three tests, and print that total}
{            with the student's name}

  const
    EndOfData = '';                      {empty string to terminate input}

  var
    Name: string[20];                    {student name, input}
    Score1, Score2, Score3: integer;     {three test scores, input}
    Total: integer;                      {total of scores, calculated}

  procedure Instructions;

    {Written by: XXXXXXXXX XX/XX/XX}
    {Purpose:    To print instructions on entering test scores}

  begin
    Writeln(' This program totals test scores. For each');
    Writeln('student you will be asked to enter the student''s');
    Writeln('name. You may use up to 20 characters for the');
    Writeln('name when you type it in. After that, you will');
    Writeln('be asked to type in the three test scores, in the');
    Writeln('range from 0 to 100. Enter these all on one line,');
    Writeln('separated by blank spaces.');
    Writeln(' The program will then print the name and the');
    Writeln('total score, and repeat the whole process. When');
    Writeln('you wish to terminate the program, just tap the');
    Writeln('return key when asked for the name.')
  end;

begin {TestScores}
{*** Before the loop print instructions}

  Instructions;

{*** In the loop, read name and scores; calculate and print total;}
{    quit when user enters empty name}

  repeat
    Write('Enter the name (just tap return to quit): ');
    Readln(Name);
    if Name <> EndOfData then
      begin
        Write('Now enter the three scores: ');
        Readln(Score1, Score2, Score3);
        Total := Score1 + Score2 + Score3;
        Writeln('The total is ', Total, ' for ', Name)
      end
  until Name = EndOfData;

{***  Stop the program}

end.
```

Figure 2-6   Procedure placement and use.

```
Readln(Score1, Score2, Score3)
```

we communicated to the procedure Readln that we wished to receive keyboard input for the three specified variables. Later, we encounter other **standard Pascal procedures** and we also learn how we can communicate with our own procedures.

Some Advantages of Using Procedures

Simplification: By using the procedure Instructions, we were able to simplify the code of the **main program** so as to make it more understandable. Both the main program and the procedure are sometimes referred to as **modules** of the program.

Focus: By using the Instructions procedure, we are able to take a closer look at the function of supplying directions without being distracted by the other details of the program. Some people call this kind of focus "divide and conquer." The activity of dividing a program into modules is called **modularization**.

Reuse: Some other program might have a similar set of directions. We are able to reuse the idea of giving instructions, and, with the THINK Pascal editor, we can "cut and paste" the code of the procedure and make some minor textual changes. Some call this kind of reuse "not reinventing the wheel."

We can assure you there are many more advantages to using procedures, but we will discuss them when we have presented the ideas with later examples.

Some Rewards of Focusing on a Single Task

When we isolate the task of supplying instructions for a program, we may realize that there are at least two categories of users: novices and experts. A novice user is grateful for detailed explanation and, in fact, can hardly be satisfied in his quest for clarification. On the other hand, an expert user is put off by the condescending tone of directions and may be angered by the inconvenience and loss of valuable time resulting from having to view unnecessary and unwanted details. Although these ideas about users are obvious, the implications might not be considered during program design; "print instructions" is just one of many tasks that the program has to perform. However, when the only task under scrutiny is that of giving the user directions, we might more naturally consider the user's needs.

A simple solution to the novice-versus-expert-user dilemma is to ask the user if directions are desired. Thus, we may wish to refine the algorithm step

    print instructions

into the rough steps

    ask the user if directions are desired
    if the answer is yes then
        print instructions

These steps can be refined into a smooth algorithm for the Instructions procedure as follows:

```
print 'Do you want instructions (Y or N)?'
read Answer
if Answer = 'Y' then
    print detailed instructions
```

In this algorithm, we have introduced another use of the *if-then* decision structure. We translate this use of the decision into Pascal in a manner similar to what we used to decide whether to execute the body of a *repeat-until* loop in our previous examples.

We have introduced a more subtle idea in the use of the variable "Answer". The main program does not use this variable and so it need not be known (declared) in the main program. Such a variable is said to be a **local variable** for the procedure in which it appears. As we see, the variable is declared and used exclusively within the procedure Instructions. Since the variable Answer is intended to hold a single character, we use the type *char* in its declaration.

The program TestScores, including the modified procedure Instructions, appears as Figure 2-7. Changes have been shown in italics for emphasis.

Note that the modified procedure Instructions now contains a *var* section just as does the main program. It is the procedure's *var* section in which all of its local variables are declared. Remember that these are the variables, such as Answer, used within the procedure itself and not in the main program.

Note. We now know enough about procedures to write one which will automatically size the text window and place it in front of all the other THINK windows. Here is its definition:

```pascal
procedure MakeTextVisible;

    const
        LeftEdge = 5;
        TopEdge = 40;
        RightEdge = 510;
        BottomEdge = 340;

    var
        TextWindowSize: Rect;

    begin
        SetRect(TextWindowSize, LeftEdge, TopEdge, RightEdge, BottomEdge);
        SetTextRect(TextWindowSize);
        Showtext
    end;
```

SetRect is a predefined procedure that defines the shape of a rectangle (a kind of data called a Rect); we call the rectangle TextWindowSize. SetTextRect then sets the text window to be the shape of the TextWindowSize rectangle. Showtext displays the text window at its set size.

The constants LeftEdge, TopEdge, RightEdge, and BottomEdge tell where the left, top, right, and bottom edges of the text window are to be placed, according to the

```pascal
program TestScores;

{Written by: XXXXXXXXX XX/XX/XX}
{Purpose:    To calculate the total on three tests, and print that total}
{            with the student's name}

  const
    EndOfData = '';                     {empty string to terminate input}

  var
    Name: string[20];                   {student name, input}
    Score1, Score2, Score3: integer;    {three test scores, input}
    Total: integer;                     {total of scores, calculated}

  procedure Instructions;

    {Written by: XXXXXXXXX XX/XX/XX}
    {Purpose:    To print instructions on entering test scores}

    var
      Answer: char;   {user response to question, input}

  begin {Instructions}
    Writeln;
    Writeln('Do you want directions (Y or N)?');
    Readln(Answer);
    if Answer = 'Y' then
      begin
        Writeln(' This program totals test scores. For each');
        Writeln('student you will be asked to enter the student''s');
        Writeln('name. You may use up to 20 characters for the');
        Writeln('name when you type it in. After that, you will');
        Writeln('be asked to type in the three test scores, in the');
        Writeln('range from 0 to 100. Enter these all on one line,');
        Writeln('separated by blank spaces.');
        Writeln(' The program will then print the name and the');
        Writeln('total score, and repeat the whole process. When');
        Writeln('you wish to terminate the program, just tap the');
        Writeln('return key when asked for the name.')
      end
  end; {Instructions}

begin {TestScores}

{*** Before the loop print instructions}

  Instructions;
```

Figure 2-7 Local variable (continues next page).

```
{*** In the loop, read name and scores; calculate and print total;}
{    quit when user enters empty name }

 repeat
  Writeln;
  Write('Enter the name (just tap return to quit): ');
  Readln(Name);
  if Name <> EndOfData then
    begin
      Write('Now enter the three scores: ');
      Readln(Score1, Score2, Score3);
      Total := Score1 + Score2 + Score3;
      Writeln('The total is ', Total, ' for ', Name)
    end
 until Name = EndOfData;

{*** Stop the program}

end.
```

SAMPLE INPUT AND OUTPUT (RUN NO. 1)

```
Do you want directions (Y or N)?
Y

      This program totals test scores. For each
student you will be asked to enter the student's
name. You may use up to 20 characters for the
name when you type it in. After that, you will
be asked to type in the three test scores, in the
range from 0 to 100. Enter these all on one line,
separated by blank spaces.
      The program will then print the name and the
total score, and repeat the whole process. When
you wish to terminate the program, just tap the
return key when asked for the name.

Enter the name (just tap return to quit): Delores Hayes
Now enter the three scores: 67 87 97
The total is      251 for Delores Hayes

Enter the name (just tap return to quit): Tim Rae
Now enter the three scores: 45 65 23
The total is      133 for Tim Rae

Enter the name (just tap return to quit):
```

Figure 2-7   (continues next page).

SAMPLE INPUT AND OUTPUT (RUN NO. 2)

```
Do you want directions (Y or N)?
N

Enter the name (just tap return to quit): Jim Smith
Now enter the three scores: 67 87 97
The total is       251 for Jim Smith

Enter the name (just tap return to quit): Sally Tie
Now enter the three scores: 34 67 100
The total is       201 for Sally Tie

Enter the name (just tap return to quit):
```

Figure 2-7   Local variable.

Macintosh's built-in screen coordinate system. The settings given in MakeTextVisible shape the text window so it just about fills a small-sized Macintosh screen without covering up THINK's menu bar at the top of the screen. You might want to experiment with the edge settings to best position the window for the size of screen you are using.

To use MakeTextVisible in your program, place its definition into your program before the *begin* of the main program. Then call it with the statement

```
MakeTextVisible
```

in your main program before you do any input or output.

A Review of Program Design

We show in what follows the variable lists and designs for the main program and the procedure "Instructions" that led to the Pascal program of Figure 2-7.

FOR THE TESTSCORES MAIN PROGRAM

Constant:	EndOfData	Value "	Null string for dummy name
Input:	Name	String[20]	Student name, also printed
	Score1	Integer	Test scores
	Score2	Integer	
	Score3	Integer	
Output:	Total	Integer	Total of 3 scores

print instructions (using procedure Instructions)
repeat the following until the user inputs an empty name:
   prompt asking for name
   read Name

　　　　prompt asking for three scores
　　　　read Score1, Score2, Score3
　　　　calculate Total
　　　　print Name and Total with a message
　　　print the termination message

FOR THE INSTRUCTIONS PROCEDURE

　　Input:　　　　　Answer　　　　char　　　　　User response 'Y' or 'N'

　　print 'Do you want directions (Y or N)'
　　read Answer
　　if Answer = 'Y' then
　　　　print detailed instructions

In this example, we have explicit use of the four building blocks that are used to erect the program structure: sequencing, looping, decisions, and subprograms.

Sequencing. We can find several instances of sequencing in our example. Recall that sequencing refers to program steps that are performed one after another in the same order that we read them from top to bottom. One instance of sequencing is seen in these steps of the main program:

　　prompt asking for three scores
　　read Score1, Score2, Score3
　　calculate Total
　　print Name and Total with a message

Looping. We have a single loop in the main program of our example that has the form that we have been using throughout the previous portions of the book. This loop is of the form *repeat . . . until*. In subsequent sections of the book, we encounter other forms of looping that can be represented in Pascal. An important feature of the kind of loop that we are currently using is that the user stops the loop when she inputs a terminating value (for Name, in this case).

Decisions. We have seen two instances of decisions in our example. Both the decision structures are of the form *if . . . then*. Our roster of decision structures will grow as we proceed through the book.

Subprograms. We have encountered two different kinds of procedures in our example. We have been using the standard Pascal procedures Readln and Writeln in previous sections, and we have introduced our first use of a defined procedure (Instructions). Once again, Pascal has many variations on the subprogram theme, which we study later.

DPT

The following are the most common pitfalls that threaten the Pascal programmer who is using procedures.

1. If the programmer does not declare the variable Answer as a local variable of the procedure Instructions, then the compiler produces an error message indicating that a variable has been used without a prior declaration.

2. The final *end* of the procedure body must be followed by a semicolon. If omitted, the compiler usually detects its absence (although the error message you receive may point to a part of the program well beyond the end of the procedure's definition, and may not be very illuminating).

3. The final *end* of the procedure body must not be followed by a period. The compiler reports the inappropriate presence of a period (with the message "';' expected").

4. The name of a procedure must not be used as the name of a variable used by the main program, or as the name of another procedure declared within the main program. If this error is made, the compiler generally detects and reports this redundancy.

5. The programmer must be aware of the execution sequence of the program. A procedure executes only when called (invoked). Execution of a program always starts with the first statement after the *begin* of the main program. When a procedure is called, execution continues with the first statement after the *begin* of the procedure body. When execution reaches the final *end* of the procedure, then it continues with the next statement after the procedure call.

REVIEW

Terms and Concepts

call	modules, modularization
local variable	procedure
main program	standard Pascal procedures

Procedures

1. Heading line containing the name of the procedure.
2. Declarations similar to a main program.
3. The initial *begin*.
4. The body of the procedure.
5. The final *end*, followed by a semicolon.

Properties

Name:	identifier for the procedure
Body:	code between the *begin* and *end;*
Use:	just mention the name to activate
Place:	define after *var* section

> **DPT**
>
> 1. Declare local variables.
> 2. Place ";" after *end* of procedure body.
> 3. Do not place "." after *end* of procedure body.
> 4. Do not also use the name of the procedure as a variable or constant.
> 5. Remember to invoke the procedure in the main program.

EXERCISES

1. Rewrite the program of Figure 1-3 (Section 1-3) to utilize an instruction printing procedure.
2. Run the revised program from Exercise 1. Is there any difference in what appears on the screen as the program is running? Could a user tell whether the program uses a procedure?
3. Choose one of the parts (a to e) of Exercise 6 in Section 1-4. Rewrite and run the program using an Instructions procedure that asks the user if the instructions are to be shown.
4. Consider the enhanced version of the Instructions procedure (Figure 2-7). What will happen if the user accidentally enters 'y' instead of 'Y' when asked if the instructions are to be shown? Suggest possible solutions. (Note: At this point, you have not covered enough Pascal to code some of the possible solutions; however, you should be able to describe in words what you might do.)
5. Suppose there are 37 lines of instructions to print. (Many Macintosh displays allow the THINK text window to be large enough to print out 26 lines before lines start scrolling off the top of the window.) Enhance the Instructions procedure so it prints the first 25 lines, then pauses until the user hits return, and then prints the remaining 12 lines. (Hint: To implement the pause, try a Readln with no variables listed with it.)
6. (Challenge) What do you think would happen if the main program in our example of Figure 2-7 contained its own variable named "Answer"? Under those circumstances, what if we forgot to declare "Answer" in the Instructions procedure?

2-3 DECISION STRUCTURES

In this section, we begin our formal study of decision structures. Recall that decisions are one of the four program structures described in Chapter 1. (The other three are sequences, loops, and subprograms.) We can classify decisions in three general categories:

1. There are some steps to be done if some specific condition is true. (We have already seen examples of this type.)
2. There is one set of steps to be done if some condition is true and a different set of steps if the condition is not true.
3. There are a number of conditions, one of which could be true, and a set of steps corresponding to each condition.

We examine **multiple-way branches**, this third category of decisions, in some detail in Section 2-5. In this section, we limit our attention to the first two categories.

In order to successfully use decision structures in a program, there are three steps to be followed. First, we recognize that we need a decision structure; that is, that the choice of steps to be performed depends upon some condition or conditions. Words such as "if", "depends upon", "whether or not", and so on, used in describing the task to be done, can indicate the need for a decision structure. Second, we should classify the structure as one of the three types previously listed, identifying the conditions and the corresponding steps. Third, we must accurately reflect the decision structure using the appropriate Pascal code.

If-Then

The **if-then structure** is the first category of the decision structure previously described. It is used when we have a set of steps to be performed when a condition is true, and nothing is to be done when the condition is false. We have already seen two uses of this structure. First, we have used it several times to perform calculations and print the answers, provided the user did not enter the terminating input value. Second, the instruction printing procedure in Section 2-2 used it to print instructions, provided the user specified he wished to see the instructions.

To code this structure in Pascal, we use the *if* statement. We have used the *if* statement in this form:

```
if condition then
   begin
      list of steps to be performed if condition is true
   end
```

The individual steps in the list of steps are separated by semicolons. There is a second form of the *if* statement that is frequently convenient. If there is exactly one statement to be performed when the condition is true, we can use the form

```
if condition then
   one statement to be performed if condition is true
```

Notes

1. To be precise, this is the only form of the *if* statement. However, the "one statement" can be a **compound statement**, which consists of a list of statements enclosed in a *begin* and *end*. This is the form we have seen before.

2. There are many ways to present the form of statements in a language. One choice, which we are using throughout, is a semiformal description with italics to indicate items that will be filled in based on the situation. Our descriptions of the *if-then* are of this form. In this form, the language descriptions look somewhat like a sample of the item they explain.

Two other popular ways to present the language are (a) by a more formal notation called the **Backus-Naur** or **Backus Normal form (BNF)**, and (b) by means of **syntax diagrams.** For those who prefer this more diagrammatic presentation, Appendix B presents the language elements by means of syntax diagrams.

Note. Although it is not a requirement of the language, we do indent the *if* statement as illustrated here and in the examples that follow. It is difficult to give a single rule that explains the particular indentation style we use. One might say the indented statements in some sense "belong to" the statements they are indented from. For example, the statements within a *repeat-until* loop are indented from the *repeat* and the *until*. The statements within a compound statement are indented from the *begin* and the *end*. The statement to be performed if the condition is true is indented from the *if*. Our advice is to follow the examples when you write your own programs. A good, consistent use of indentation helps anyone reading the program to understand the program's structure and, therefore, what it does and how.

As an example of the *if* statement, suppose we wish to write Pascal code to print a person's name if his blood is type O. We may use a decision structure in either of these forms:

```
if BloodType = 'O' then         if BloodType = 'O' then
   begin                           Writeln(Name)
      Writeln(Name)
   end
```

Notes

1. This is only a segment, or piece, of a program. The complete program would include declarations, among them those for BloodType and Name:

   ```
   BloodType: char;
   Name: string[20];
   ```

   It would also, more than likely, include various looping, input, output, and assignment statements. It might even include other decision structures. In order to concentrate our attention on the details of Pascal decisions, many of the examples in this section present only segments of a program.

2. If the *if* statement given in this example were followed by another statement in the complete program, there would be a semicolon between the *if* statement and that next statement.

For our second example, let us write a Pascal segment that adds 1 to a variable named HighCount and adds the income to a variable named HighTotal, provided the income is greater than $25,000. Assuming that among the declarations we have

```
HighCount: integer;
HighTotal: real;
Income: real;
```

the solution can be given as

```
if Income > 25000.00 then
    begin
        HighCount := HighCount + 1;
        HighTotal := HighTotal + Income
    end
```

In this case, there are two statements, so we must use the *begin* and *end* to group them. Notice the semicolon separating the two statements. Notice also how we "add 1" to a variable. The assignment statement assigns a new value to HighCount. The new value is the old value of HighCount plus 1.

Conditions in Pascal

These two examples illustrate the use of the *if-then*. To complete our discussion, we need to know the rules for writing a conditional expression. Actually, the rules are fairly complex, so we do not tackle them all at this point.

Simple conditions can be written to compare any two expressions. The expressions must be "compatible." For example, we cannot compare integers to character strings. There are six possible relationships in the comparison:

PASCAL NOTATION	MEANING
=	is equal to
>	is greater than
<	is less than
>=	is greater than or equal to
<=	is less than or equal to
<>	is not equal to

In performing the comparisons, the two expressions can be as simple or as complex as we require. For example, each of the following is a valid condition:

```
Sum = 15
R - C <= 0
0.05 * Nickels < 0.25 * Quarters
State = 'Virginia'
Name > 'Brown'
```

The last two examples involve string variables (State and Name). In THINK Pascal, two strings are equal if their values and lengths are identical.

When we compare two strings in THINK Pascal to see if one is greater than the other, we get an ordering where a blank space precedes any digit, which precedes any uppercase letter, which precedes any lowercase letter and the letters and digits are in the expected order. Thus,

```
' ' < '0' < '1' < ...'9' < 'A' < 'B'... < 'Z' < 'a' < 'b' < ... < 'z'
```

In our example, Name > 'Brown', the condition is true for any value beginning with C, D, and so on, or any lowercase letter. It is also true for any value beginning with 'Brown' but longer than five characters. If we compare two strings in THINK Pascal, the longer is considered greater if they match up through the last character of the shorter.

This set of rules is fairly complex, but it does ensure that, in most situations, a string comparison has the results we would expect in everyday usage (except for lowercase, which is handled differently from a dictionary).

Some other verbal conditions, such as "is not greater than," can be seen to be equivalent to one of those listed earlier. In fact, we can give a list of **negations** for each of the six relationships, as shown in the table that follows. (The negation of a condition is the result of using the word *not* with the condition.) For example, the negation of "greater than" (>) is "not greater than," which is equivalent to "less than or equal to" (<=).

CONDITION	NEGATION
=	<>
>	<=
<	>=
>=	<
<=	>
<>	=

The use of comparisons in conditions is illustrated by our earlier examples and is further illustrated in the following subsection.

If-Then-Else

The second general category of a decision structure is commonly referred to as an **if-then-else structure**. It recognizes that sometimes there are two sets of steps to be performed: one if the condition is true and the other if it is not. Pascal has a statement that is specifically designed to handle this situation. Its form is summarized as follows:

```
if condition then
        statement to be performed if condition is true
else
        statement to be performed if condition is false
```

As for the *if-then*, the "statement to be performed" can be a compound statement (a list enclosed between a *begin* and an *end*). Thus, for example, if both branches are compound statements, we will have

```
if condition then
   begin
      list of steps to be performed if condition is true
   end
else
   begin
      list of steps to be performed if condition is false
   end
```

> **Note.** In each "list of steps," the steps are separated by semicolons. However, there must be no semicolons before or after the *else*. Again, the indentation pattern shown is optional, but useful in conveying the statement's structure to a reader.

In the English language, situations that require this type of decision structure frequently are described using the word "otherwise." Other possible indications that two branches are involved might include phrases such as "if not, ..."

As an example, let us give a code segment for the following situation: We wish to double the value of an integer variable J if its current value is less than 5, otherwise triple the value. In addition, we will print a message telling which occurred.

Notice that this does fall in the general category of decision we are discussing. There are two possible branches: J is less than 5 or it is not. The *if-then-else* is therefore appropriate, and we write

```
if J < 5 then
   begin
      J := 2 * J;
      Writeln('J was doubled to ' ,J)
   end
else
   begin
      J := 3 * J;
      Writeln ('J was tripled to ', J)
   end
```

Notice that each branch includes two steps, so each branch uses a *begin* and *end*.

For our next example, we will find the smaller of two test scores, Score1 and Score2, placing the answer in the variable SmallScore. Assuming these declarations,

```
Score1, Score2: integer;
SmallScore: integer;
```

we can write:

```
if Score1 < Score2 then
   SmallScore := Score1
else
   SmallScore := Score2
```

"But," you might ask, "What if the scores are equal?" The answer is that, for example, if the two scores are both 90, the answer should be 90. This program segment takes the else branch because the condition 90 < 90 is false. It sets SmallScore to Score2, which is 90. Thus, when they are equal, the segment does yield the correct answer.

For our final example in this subsection, we develop a short program that uses a decision structure. This common example occurs in companies that pay for overtime. In its simplest form, the rule might be that any hours in excess of 40 earn "time and a half." This means that the pay for those hours is 1.5 times the pay for the usual hours. We will write a program to calculate pay, given the hours worked and the hourly pay rate.

2-3 DECISION STRUCTURES

We begin, just as we did for the programs in Chapter 1, with a tentative variable list and a preliminary algorithm.

Constant:	EndOfData	Value 0	Used to terminate loop
Input:	Hours	Real	Hours worked
	HourlyRate	Real	Pay per hour
Output:	Pay	Real	Pay (before taxes, etc)

print instructions
repeat these steps until the user enters 0 for hourly rate
    prompt for hours and hourly rate
    read Hours, HourlyRate
    if HourlyRate is not 0 do these steps:
        calculate Pay
        print Pay

We have chosen an HourlyRate value of 0 for the terminating entry.

Since the pay is not calculated by a single formula, we need to refine this step. The rule described previously indicates that the method to use depends on how many hours were worked. This leads us to an if-then-else decision structure, with the condition "Hours > 40" determining what steps to perform. If the condition is *true*, we pay overtime; if *false*, we do not. We obtain the following incomplete Pascal segment. (The italicized portion needs more refinement.)

```
if Hours > 40 then
   calculate Pay using overtime rule
else
   Pay := Hours * HourlyRate
```

To refine the first branch, we might do the calculations in three steps:

1. Calculate the regular pay for the first 40 hours.

2. Calculate the overtime pay for the remaining hours. This is the number of overtime hours (Hours – 40) times the overtime rate (HourlyRate * 1.5).

3. Add the two to get Pay.

If so, we would write

```
if Hours > 40 then
   begin
      RegularPay  := 40 * HourlyRate;
      OvertimePay := (Hours - 40) * HourlyRate * 1.5;
      Pay := RegularPay + OvertimePay
   end
else
   Pay := Hours * HourlyRate
```

Notice that this adds two variables, RegularPay and OvertimePay, that were not in the plan for our original variables list. In addition, we must write the three steps enclosed in a *begin* and *end*. The complete program appears in Figure 2-8. The decision structure for calculating the pay is in italics. Observe that it is placed precisely where the pay calculation would have gone if pay were calculated by a single assignment statement.

One other point to observe is the form of the output in the sample run. The default for printing a real number is exponential notation. In the next section, we learn some techniques for obtaining a more readable output for real numbers.

DPT

There are a number of points to be observed in connection with decision structures in Pascal:

1. The negation of "greater than" is "less than or equal to." It is not "less than." Similar comments apply to other comparisons.

2. There is sometimes confusion concerning the use of ":=" and "=" in Pascal. Pascal uses "=" to mean "is equal to" and uses it in comparing two quantities or in identifying a named constant with its value. Therefore, it can be used in connection with an *if* statement, a *repeat-until* loop, and some other situations we have not yet seen. The ":=" symbol, on the other hand, assigns a new value to a variable.

3. Due to the imprecision with which real values are stored in the computer, comparing two real quantities for equality can be misleading. For example, if we obtain a value for a variable X by adding 10 0.1's, the resulting value might not be exactly 1.0. Section 2-4 discusses this issue further.

4. The issue of where to place semicolons and where not to can be confusing. The compiler can catch some incorrect placements, but not others.

In general, semicolons separate statements in a list of statements. (Observe that the lists of statements are either set off by a *begin* and an *end*, or by a *repeat* and an *until*.) Based on what we have studied so far, we can formulate some guidelines.

Use a semicolon when the next step begins with:

a Readln or Writeln

a procedure name (e.g., Instructions)

a variable for an assignment statement

an *if* (there are exceptions to this)

Do not use a semicolon right before these words:

end   (marking the end of the list of steps)
until   (also marking the end of the list of steps)
begin   (exception—at the start of the procedure or the main program)
else

```pascal
program Payroll;
{Written by: XXXXXXXX XX/XX/XX}
{Purpose:    To calculate pay based on hours worked and hourly pay rate,}
{            where the rule used depends on whether overtime was earned}
{Procedures used: Instructions, to print instructions for user}

  const
    EndOfData = 0;        {used to terminate loop}

  var
    Hours: real;          {hours worked, input}
    HourlyRate: real;     {hourly pay rate, input}
    Pay: real;            {pay before taxes, output}
    RegularPay: real;     {pay for first 40 hours}
    OvertimePay: real;    {pay for overtime hours}

  procedure Instructions;
  begin
    {The details of this procedure are left as an exercise}
  end; {Instructions}

begin {Payroll}

{*** Before the loop, print instructions for the user}

  Instructions;

{*** Read hours and hourly rate; use if-then-else structure to}
{    calculate pay; print answers. Quit when rate of 0 is entered.}

  repeat
    Writeln;
    Write('Enter hours and hourly rate (rate 0 to quit): ');
    Readln(Hours, HourlyRate);
    if HourlyRate <> EndOfData then
       begin
         if Hours > 40 then
            begin
              RegularPay := 40 * HourlyRate;
              OvertimePay := (Hours - 40) * HourlyRate * 1.5;
              Pay := RegularPay + OvertimePay
            end
         else
            Pay := Hours * HourlyRate;
            Writeln('The pay earned was ', Pay)
       end
  until HourlyRate = EndOfData

{*** After loop, terminate program}

end.
```

Figure 2-8   If . . . then . . . else (continues next page).

SAMPLE INPUT AND OUTPUT

```
Enter hours and hourly rate (rate 0 to quit): 40 5.50
The pay earned was    2.2e+2

Enter hours and hourly rate (rate 0 to quit): 34 23.45
The pay earned was    8.0e+2

Enter hours and hourly rate (rate 0 to quit): 0 0
```

Figure 2-8   (continued).

Do not use a semicolon right after these words:

begin
if
then
else
repeat

For the short term, you can refer to these concrete guidelines. For the long term, you will want to remember the general rule:

Use semicolons to separate statements in a list of statements.

5. As described earlier, the rule for the *if-then* and *if-then-else* statements requires a *begin* and *end* only when there is more than one statement in the branch. The fact that the compiler follows this rule can lead to some strange interpretations if we forget the *begin* or *end*. For example, consider

```
WRITTEN              INTENDED
if X > Y then        if X > Y then
   T := 1;              begin
   S := 3;                T := 1;
                          S := 3
                       end;
```

The compiler assumes that only the T := 1 goes with the *if*. The S := 3 assignment is executed whether or not X is greater than Y.

Similarly, consider

```
WRITTEN              INTENDED
if X > Y then        if X > Y then
   S := 0;              begin
   T := 0;                S := 0;
else                      T := 0;
   S := 1;             end
   T := 2;          else
                       begin
                         S := 1;
                         T := 2
                       end;
```

2-3 DECISION STRUCTURES

The compiler, when it sees the *else*, thinks that the *if* terminated with the assignment S := 0. It, therefore, indicates an error on this line. However, it would not detect the error in the *else* branch.

Even experienced Pascal programmers can fall into the trap of forgetting the *begin* and *end*. Leaving it off for the special case allowed by the compiler (one statement in the branch) increases the likelihood of making this mistake.

One way to avoid this trap is to always use a *begin* and *end*, even if the branch contains only one statement. There are some trade-offs involved in this. In addition to avoiding the pitfall, it makes the program easier to modify in the future. On the other hand, the extra, unneeded begins and ends can hinder program readability.

6. Finally, programmers sometimes view an *if-then-else* as equivalent to two *if-then* statements. In fact, this is frequently true. For example, these two segments of code have identical meanings:

```
if Score1 < Score2 then           if Score1 < Score2 then
   SmallScore := Score1              SmallScore := Score1;
else                              if Score1 >= Score2 then
   SmallScore := Score2              SmallScore := Score2
```

However, these do not:

```
if J < 5 then                     if J < 5 then
   J := 2 * J                        J := 2 * J;
else                              if J >= 5 then
   J := 3 * J                        J := 3 * J
```

For example, suppose that J has a value of 4 when the segment is executed. In the left-hand segment, since J < 5 is *true*, the first branch is executed, causing J to become 8. The *else* branch is not executed. In the right-hand segment, since J < 5 is *true*, the first *if* statement changes J to 8. Now the condition J >= 5 in the second *if* statement is examined. Since it is true (8 >= 5 is *true*), the second *if* statement changes J to 24.

To avoid this type of pitfall, we should *not* code *if-then-else* structures with two consecutive *if* statements.

Adding to Case Study No. 1

In this section, we consider further modifications to Case Study No. 1, begun in Section 1-4. The program is one that, for each student, calculates the total score on three tests. In Section 2-2, we added a procedure to handle the printing of instructions for the user. (The latest version of the program appears in Figure 2-7.)

We now consider two possible enhancements. First, we could modify the algorithm to also print an indication of whether the student is passing or failing. If we assume that a total score of 210 is a passing grade, then we might reason as follows:

If the Total is 210 or higher, then the student's result is "passing," otherwise it is "failing."

We may add a string variable to our list of variables, which we call Result. This variable is assigned either the word "passing" or the word "failing" based on the total score. Thus, we have this segment of Pascal to add to our main program:

```
if Total >= 210 then
   Result := 'passing'
else
   Result := 'failing'
```

We place this immediately after the step that calculates the Total variable, on which it is based, and modify the Writeln statement to include this variable in its list of items to print.

Our second modification, in addition, prints a message identifying those students who are exempt from the final exam (total score above 290). We would like the output to look something like this for such a student:

```
The total is 298 for John Smith - passing
********* EXEMPT FROM FINAL *********
```

Since the message appears after the line with the total, name, and result, we place the steps to do this after the Writeln statement that prints these values.

Notice that this is an *if-then* situation; no message is desired for those who are not exempt. Thus, we write

```
if Total > 290 then
   Writeln('********* EXEMPT FROM FINAL*********')
```

Figure 2-9 contains the modified program, with the changes in italics. Notice that these changes do not directly affect the Instructions procedure, although we should probably modify it to reflect the changes. This modification is left as an exercise. (The sample input and output were generated by running the program exactly as it appears, without inserting the body of the Instructions procedure in the program.)

Testing

In Section 1-4, we introduced some of the concepts involved in program testing. At this point, we are concerned with testing after we have obtained a clean compilation. By this we mean that the compiler has not listed any syntax errors. The program runs, and we want to see whether it is generating correct answers. In that section, we listed three principles:

1. Check all answers. Include some data that are easy to check.
2. Test near boundaries; also test a random sampling away from the boundaries.
3. Include some erroneous input, especially if the program is designed to detect and warn about such errors.

In this subsection, we look at the second of these principles in more detail.

When a program includes branching, boundary testing becomes especially important. By a "boundary" we mean a point at which the rule for determining the answer changes. Experience has shown that programs are more likely to contain errors at or near boundary points than at other points. As a result, we want to include special tests to make sure that the program works at and near boundaries.

For example, consider our case study program. There are now a number of different boundary points. Of course, there are still the boundaries of 0 and 100 for each individual score, which we included in our original test plan in Section 1-4. In addition, we now have two more boundaries, based on the total score: scores 210 and 290. At 210, the rule for

```pascal
program TestScores;

{Written by: XXXXXXXXX XX/XX/XX}
{Purpose:   To calculate the total on three tests, and print that}
{           total with the student's name}

  const
    EndOfData = '';         {empty string to terminate input}

  var
    Name: string;                        {student name, input}
    Score1, Score2, Score3: integer;     {three test scores, input}
    Total: integer;                      {total of test scores, calculated}
    Result: string;                      {'passing' or 'failing' result}

  procedure Instructions;
  begin
    {The Instructions procedure is placed here, exactly as it appears in}
    {Figure 2-7.}
  end; {Instructions}

begin {TestScores}

{*** Before the loop print instructions}

  Instructions;

{*** In the loop, read name and scores; calculate and print total; }
{    determine whether passing or failing, and whether exempt from final;}
{    quit when user enters empty name}

  repeat
    Writeln;
    Write('Enter the name (just tap return to quit): ');
    Readln(Name);
    if Name <> EndOfData then
      begin
        Write('Now enter the three scores: ');
        Readln(Score1, Score2, Score3);
        Total := Score1 + Score2 + Score3;
        if Total >= 210 then
          Result := 'passing'
        else
          Result := 'failing';
        Writeln('The total is ', Total, ' for ', Name, ' - ', Result);

        if Total > 290 then
          Writeln('********* EXEMPT FROM FINAL *********')
      end
  until Name = EndOfData;

{*** Stop the program}

end.
```

Figure 2-9   If . . . then (continues next page).

SAMPLE INPUT AND OUTPUT

```
Enter the name (just tap return to quit): Joan Smith
Now enter the three scores: 78 67 87
The total is      232 for Joan Smith - passing

Enter the name (just tap return to quit): Tim Rae
Now enter the three scores: 34 99 71
The total is      204 for Tim Rae - failing

Enter the name (just tap return to quit): Sally Tie
Now enter the three scores: 60 61 59
The total is      180 for Sally Tie - failing

Enter the name (just tap return to quit): Alex Wilkins
Now enter the three scores: 100 95 96
The total is      291 for Alex Wilkins - passing
* * * * * * * * EXEMPT FROM FINAL *********

Enter the name (just tap return to quit):
```

Figure 2-9   (continued)

determining pass or fail changes, and at 290, the rule for telling whether the student is exempt from the final exam changes. It is a good idea to include test cases that result in values exactly on the boundary, just below the boundary, and just above the boundary. Hence, in our test plan, we might write

BOUNDARY ON PASSING

70, 69, 70	total 209, fail
65, 76, 69	total 210, pass
100, 50, 61	total 211, pass

BOUNDARY ON EXEMPTING FINAL

100, 90, 99	total 289, not exempt
95, 97, 98	total 290, not exempt
99, 96, 96	total 291, exempt

In addition to these boundary values, we would also include other passing and failing grades chosen randomly and other exempting and non-exempting grades chosen randomly.

Note.   Of the three tests listed for the boundary on passing, the first two are the most vital: 209 is the highest failing grade and 210 is the lowest passing grade. For the second list, the second and third tests are the most vital.

In general, in testing a program involving branching, we choose some test cases that exercise the boundary points, as well as others chosen more randomly within the different branches.

REVIEW

Terms and Concepts

Backus-Naur form (BNF)
compound statement
if-then structure
if-then-else structure
multiple-way branches
negations
syntax diagrams

Pascal Syntax

Conditions

```
expression relationship expression
```

The relationship is one of =, >, <, >=, <=, and <>.
The expressions must be "compatible" (e.g., cannot compare integers to strings).

String Comparisons

```
' '<'0'<...<'9'<'A'<...<'Z'<'a'<...<'z'
```

To be equal, the strings must have the same length. For example,

```
' John ' < ' Johnson '
'Joe' > 'Bill'
'An' < 'an'
'Sue    ' <> 'Sue'
```

are all *true*.

Decisions

if-then:

```
if condition then
    statement
```

The statement can be a compound statement, yielding:

```
if condition then
   begin
       list of statements separated by semicolons
   end
```

if-then-else:

```
if condition then
    statement (can be compound statement)
else
    statement (can be compound statement)
```

EXERCISES

1. Run the payroll program exactly as it appears in Figure 2-8. Then add appropriate steps for the instructions procedure and run it again.

2. Give an appropriate decision structure (*if-then-else* or *if-then*) for each of these situations. Use appropriate variables, and give both the necessary declarations and the segment of Pascal for the decision.

   (a)

INCOME	TAX RATE (%)
Less than $8000.00	2.0
$8000.00 or higher	4.5

   (b) If the sex code is "M", add 1 to the variable Males, otherwise add 1 to the variable Females.

   (c) The commission rate is 3 percent if the sales amount is less than $150. If the sales amount is $150 or more, the commission rate should be 5 percent.

   (d) Sales tax is 6 percent on any purchase of $500 or less, but only 3.5 percent on a purchase over $500.

   (e) If the tax is greater than $550, a penalty of 6 percent should be added to the tax.

   (f) If T is currently 0, do nothing; otherwise add 1 to the value of T.

   (g) Calculate the bonus based on the current value of Years and Sales. If Years is 5 or less, then the bonus is nothing; otherwise it is 0.1 percent of the sales.

   (h) If the average of the three test scores is greater than 59.5, print "passes".

   (i) If the ratio of two integers I and J is above 4.7, then calculate K as the sum of I and J; if not, K is the difference.

   (j) If Sex is 'female', then daily caloric need is 16 times body weight in pounds. If Sex is 'male', then daily caloric need is 18 times body weight in pounds. (Assume that Sex has one of the two listed values.)

3. For each program segment of Exercise 2, determine all boundary values and come up with a minimum set of test cases for each branch at and near each boundary value.

4. Add appropriate input, output, and looping steps to create an entire program built around the situations described in Exercises 2(a), (c), (d), and (g). Where it makes sense, add names to the list of data input by the user.

5. Modify the case study example (Figure 2-9) to print "IMPROVING" for those students whose third grade is better than the average of the first two grades. What additions would be needed in the test plan?

For each of Exercises 6 to 10, (a) determine the input and output and give a variables list; (b) write and refine an algorithm; (c) create a test plan; (d) write the program in Pascal; and (e) run the program, utilizing your test plan to help locate errors.

6. Each line of data has three integers, A, B, and C. These form a "Pythagorean triple" if $A*A + B*B = C*C$. Write an algorithm to read each input line; print the values of A, B, and C; and print a message: either "is a Pythagorean triple" or "is not a Pythagorean triple".

7. The amount of sales is quantity times price. The discount is 1 percent of the sales amount if the quantity is over 100, otherwise 0. The net price is the sales amount minus the discount. The commission is 3 percent of the net price if the net price is less than $250, 5 percent for $250 or more. The program should input quantity and price, then calculate and print the sales amount, discount, net price, commission rate, and commission.

8. The first input line contains the beginning balance of a savings account for a year. This is followed by a series of inputs, each representing one transaction for the account. Each consists

EXERCISES

of a transaction code ('W' = withdrawal, 'D' = deposit) and an amount. Write a program to determine the final balance at the end of the year by adding and subtracting from the running balance based on each transaction. (You can assume that the code is either a 'W' or a 'D'.)

Revise the program to print a running account of the transactions for the account, including the beginning and ending balances for each transaction.

9. Each data set has an employee name, an incentive factor (in the range 0.01 to 0.15), a weekly base salary, and the number of units produced during the week. Write a program to calculate the payroll for the company. A person's actual salary is computed from the base salary as follows: If the number of units produced is less than 500, then 10 cents is deducted from the pay for each unit by which the quota of 500 was missed. If the units produced is 500 or more, then the base salary is increased by an amount consisting of the incentive factor times the number of units produced above the quota.

Modify the program to also print a message "at or above quota" or "below quota" for each employee.

10. The data are the same as in Exercise 9. However, this time the salary is computed as follows: If the number of units produced is less than 750, the salary is merely the base salary. If 750 or more units are produced, the incentive factor is treated as a percentage; this percentage of the base salary is added to the base salary to obtain the actual salary.

11. Write a complete Pascal program to input sex, current weight in pounds, goal weight, and daily caloric intake. Use the calculation of Exercise 2(j) to calculate and print the projected number of days that are required to attain the weight loss. Use the relationship

$$3500 \text{ calories} = 1 \text{ pound}$$

and calculate the daily caloric need based on the average of the current weight and the goal weight.

2-4 ADDITIONAL PASCAL TOPICS

In this section, we explain how to control the appearance of output from a THINK Pascal program and introduce the use of the printer. We also investigate some of THINK's built-in features that aid us in writing our programs. We discuss integer and real numbers in more detail and show how we can convert numbers from real to integer and from integer to real.

Formatting Output

You probably were not overjoyed by the form of the output of our example program's real numbers. Instead of seeing an old friend such as "23," you observed scientific notation such as "2.3e+1". The two forms for the number are mathematically equivalent, but they are quite different from the point of view of simplicity and understandability. Admittedly, there are certainly cases in which one would prefer scientific notation to the explicit presence of all the decimal positions; for example, we probably would prefer the scientific form "3.5e-12" to the explicit form "0.0000000000035". The best approach is for the programmer to decide on the form of the output as part of the program design process. We now describe the **formatting** tools Pascal provides for programmer control of the way numbers should look when a program prints them.

Output Position. Whether we output to a display screen or to a printer, we write the first character of the output to a particular location. This location has both vertical (row) and horizontal (column) attributes with respect to the top and left margins of the screen or sheet of paper. We refer to this location as the **output position.**

THINK Pascal treats the top line of the text window or a sheet of paper as line 1 and the leftmost character position as column 1, often referred to as position (1,1).

If we cause the output position to become (1,1), then we refer to this action as "going to **top-of-form.**" In the case of output to a screen, top-of-form is usually accompanied by erasing all the information that may have been on the screen.

THINK Pascal also provides the standard procedure Page; calling Page places the text window's cursor at top-of-form and also erases (clears) the entire screen. To move to the top-of-form and clear the screen just say

```
Page
```

in your program. (See what follows for how to advance the printer to the top-of-form.)

For the rest of this discussion, we assume that we are in some given print position, and that we wish to control the output of the next item, including the print position at which it will appear.

Output of Integers. Suppose that we wish to output the integer variable Area, starting at the current print position and within the next three output columns. In this case, we can use one of the two Pascal statements:

```
Writeln(Area:3)
```

or

```
Write(Area:3)
```

The effect of "Writeln(Area:3)" is to output the value of Area right-justified within the next three columns and to set the print position to column 1 of the next line. The effect of "Write(Area:3)" is to output the value of Area right justified within the next three columns and to set the print position to the next column of the same line (i.e., three columns from the original print position).

Note. "Right-justified" means that the number is printed in the columns allotted as far to the right as possible. For example, if we print a two-digit number right justified in five columns, it will be preceded by three blanks.

We illustrate the results for an Area that has a value of 12. The # stands for blank spaces, | for the left margin, and ^ for where the cursor stops after printing is complete.

```
Writeln(Area:3)

              |    #12
              |^

Write(Area:3)

              |    #12^
              |
```

2-4 ADDITIONAL PASCAL TOPICS

If you send output to the text window, as much of each line will appear as there is room in the window to display it. (You can change the window's size before or after you run your program, or while it is stopped, but not while it is running. The wider you make the window, the more of an output line you can see.) It is possible to print out more on a line than you can expand the text window to see. If that occurs, consider reformatting your output.

If the value to be output is larger than the number of columns specified, then the output will begin in the current print position and extend to the right for as many columns as are necessary to represent the number. We should also note that the "-" sign for a negative number occupies an output column.

We can use any reasonable number of columns in place of the "3" used in the previous example. If "Writeln(Area)" or "Write(Area)" is used without specifying the number of columns, the resulting form of the output will be as if "Writeln(Area:0)" or "Write(Area:0)" were used.

To provide maximum flexibility for the programmer, the number of columns can be expressed as an integer variable or expression. For example, if "Width" is an integer variable or constant, we can use the statement

```
Writeln(Area:Width+3)
```

Output of Reals. In order to specify the format for a real number output, we can specify not only the number of columns to be used (the **field width**), but also the number of decimal places (the **precision**). Suppose that "Number" has the value 34.567. We now show various possibilities for printing out "Number". In all cases, we assume that the current print position is in column 1. (The | symbol signifies the left margin of the output.)

STATEMENT	OUTPUT	COMMENT
Writeln(Number:6:3)	|34.567	Perfect fit!
Writeln(Number:6:2)	| 34.57	Blank on left, rounded
Writeln(Number:7:2)	| 34.57	Right-justified
Writeln(Number:7:0)	| 35	No decimal point!
Writeln(Number:2:2)	|34.57	Takes all it needs
Writeln(Number:7)	| 3.5e+1	If number of decimal
Writeln(Number:8)	| 3.5e+1	places is not given,
Writeln(Number:9)	| 3.5e+1	THINK uses a minimum
Writeln(Number:10)	| 3.5e+1	width of 10!
Writeln(Number:11)	| 3.46e+1	Aha! How far will it go?
Writeln(Number:12)	| 3.457e+1	
Writeln(Number:13)	| 3.4567e+1	
Writeln(Number:14)	| 3.45670e+1	Now just trailing zeros
Writeln(Number:15)	| 3.456700e+1	
Writeln(Number:16)	| 3.4567001e+1	Where did the one come from?
Writeln(Number:17)	| 3.45670013e+1	It's a precision problem
Writeln(Number:18)	| 3.456700134e+1	
Writeln(Number:19)	| 3.4567000134e+1	
Writeln(Number:18:10)	| 34.5670013428	More digits than accuracy!
Writeln(Number)	| 3.5e+1	THINK's default
Writeln(Number:0)	| 3.5e+1	Minimum configuration
Writeln(Number:0:10)	|34.5670013428	Precision 10

As we can see from the listing, the possibilities are many. One principle that we note is that the desired precision is always printed, even if the field width must be violated in order to do it. (The example with field width = 0 and precision = 10 provides an extreme situation.) The next priority after precision is field width. In THINK Pascal, whenever the number of decimal places is not provided, the width is always a minimum of 10—if you give a width less than 10, THINK makes it 10. (Depending upon the number, THINK may not use all 10 spaces when printing it, but 10 spaces are reserved nonetheless.)

Another principle to remember is that representation of real numbers in a computer is usually not exact; that is why the number 3.4567 does not print out exactly if we print too many decimal places.

Again, to provide maximum flexibility for the programmer, the field width and precision can be expressed as integer variables or expressions. For example, if "Width" and "Places" are integer variables or constants, we can use the statement

```
Writeln(Number:Width+3:Places-1)
```

Character and String Output. A field width value can also be used with a char variable or a string variable. The treatment of the two is identical, so we combine them in our discussion.

Suppose that Name is a string variable whose current value is 'Joe'. The following listing indicates the output for various field widths. Observe that the current length of the string, not its maximum length, determines what is printed.

STATEMENT	OUTPUT	COMMENT
`Writeln(Name)`	`│ Joe`	
`Writeln(Name:4)`	`│ Joe`	Preceded by one blank
`Writeln(Name:7)`	`│    Joe`	Four blanks
`Writeln(Name:2)`	`│Jo`	Will print only the first two characters

The output is right-justified if the width is the length of the string or larger. If the width is shorter than the string's length, then the string is truncated (on the right) when it is printed.

A technique that can be useful is illustrated by the following example:

```
Writeln(Test1:5, ' ':7, Test2:5, ' ':7, Total:5)
```

This prints Test1, Test2, and Total. In between, the ' ':7 prints a blank space, right-justified in a field of width 7. This has the effect of printing seven blank spaces. For example, for values 95, 68, and 100 for the three tests, this would print the following. (The ƀ symbols on the line represent blank spaces.)

```
ƀƀƀ95ƀƀƀƀƀƀƀ68ƀƀƀƀƀƀƀ100
```

This technique can be useful in creating tables of output.

To complete this discussion of formatting output, we show two ways to produce the output line

```
The Weight of Player 85 is 211.6 pounds.
```

For this example, we suppose that the integer variable "Number" contains the value 85 and that the real variable "Weight" contains the value 211.6.

FIRST METHOD

```
Writeln('     The Weight of Player ', Number:1,' is ', Weight:1:1,
         ' pounds.')
```

SECOND METHOD

```
Write('     The Weight of Player ');
Write(Number:1);
Write(' is ');
Write(Weight:1:1);
Write(' pounds.');
Writeln
```

The running of these two segments of code should produce identical results. In the first, the entire line is written with one Writeln. In the second, the Write is used to print each part of the line. The final Writeln moves the print position to the following line.

Which is preferable? It is a matter of choice. There are several exercises at the end of the section that will help to clarify this subject.

Output to the Printer

For many programs, it is more appropriate to print some or all of the output on the printer than in the text window. In THINK Pascal, there are two basic ways to send output to a printer.

One approach is to redirect all output that would have gone to the text window to go to the printer. This is done by checking the "Echo to the printer" box on the Run Time Environment Settings screen. (You get to that screen by selecting Run Options from the Run menu.) This tack allows you to send output to the printer quickly, without changing your Pascal program, but it is inflexibile, since *all* text output now goes to the printer.

The more flexible approach is to include a directive to send output to the printer in those Write and Writeln statements whose output is intended to be on paper rather than in the text window.

The first step in doing this is to come up with a name to refer to the printer. Say we choose the name Report. In the *var* section, we declare Report to be a *text* variable:

```
Report: text;
```

Next, we tell THINK Pascal that this name is the one we wish to use to stand for the printer by placing the statement

```
rewrite(Report, 'Printer:')
```

in the body of the program, before we send any output to the printer:

We now use the name Report in those Write and Writeln statements whose output we wish to go the printer:

```
Writeln(Report, 'This will go to the printer.')
```

Notes

1. We cannot use the term "Printer:" directly in Write or Writeln statements. The printer is considered to be a *device* (akin to keyboards, screens, and disk drives) and THINK Pascal requires that we send output that does not go to the screen to a *file*. So we use the steps mentioned previously to "connect" the printer to a text file (that we called Report) to work around this limitation. Files we will discussed in detail in Chapter 5.

2. Output to certain printers, particularly some kinds of laser printers, may not actually print out until the Pascal statement

   ```
   close(Name assigned to Printer:)
   ```

   is issued. Include the close statement once, right before the end of the program. If you forget to include a close statement, the program could abort, go into an infinite loop, or fail to send the output to the pointer.

Moving the Printer to Top-of-Form. Not all printers behave the same way when it comes to controlling the position of the print head. However, on most printers, moving the printer to position (1,1)—the top of the next page—can be accomplished in THINK Pascal with the statement

```
Page(Name assigned to the printer)
```

For example, if the printer had been connected to the name Report,

```
Page(Report)
```

would cause the printer to go to the top of the next page.

The Appearance of Output Sent to the Printer. The appearance of output on a printed page is often quite different from the way it appears on a screen. A printed page is sometimes organized into a table consisting of columns of information, whereas the screen usually shows lines of interactive dialogue. The program shown in Figure 2-10 illustrates both of these points. The purpose of the program is to produce a small table of square roots. Note the way that the page and column headings are handled using the formatting techniques discussed earlier in this section.(The expression "Sqrt(Number)" in the Writeln calculates the square root of the number. It will be more fully explained in the next section.)

Note. As illustrated by this example, a program can send output to both the printer and the screen. Sometimes we display the answers on the screen and we also print the answers on paper to obtain a permanent record. For example, we might modify the example to read

```
if Number <> EndOfData then
  begin
    Writeln('The square root is ', Sqrt(Number):1:4);
    Writeln(Report, ' ':29, Number:4, ' ':7, Sqrt(Number):10:4)
  end
```

Observe that the form of the output for the printer can differ from that for the screen.

```pascal
program RootTable;

{Written by:  XXXXXXXXXX XX/XX/XX}
{Purpose:    To create a small table of square roots on the printer}

  const
    EndOfData = -1;         {terminating value}

  var
    Number: integer;        {user input}
    Report: text;           {name for printer}

begin  {RootTable}

{*** Assign the printer the name report, and prepare it to receive output}

  reset(Report, 'Printer:');

{*** Print headings}

  Writeln(Report, ' ' : 30, 'TABLE OF SQUARE ROOTS');
  Writeln(Report, ' ' : 28, '---------------------------');
  Writeln(Report, ' ' : 28, 'Number    Square Root');
  Writeln(Report, ' ' : 28, '------    -----------');
  Writeln(Report);

{*** Read numbers in a loop, calculate square roots and print}

  repeat
    Write('Enter a number (-1 to terminate): ');
    Readln(Number);
    if Number <> EndOfData then
      Writeln(Report, ' ' : 29, Number : 4, ' ' : 7, Sqrt(Number) : 10 : 4)
  until Number = EndOfData

{*** Terminate program}

    {Close(Report)}
    {Include if necessary}

end.
```

Figure 2-10 Output to a Printer (continues next page).

Square Roots and Absolute Value

There are several built-in THINK Pascal library functions that can help the programmer with numerical calculations. Among the most common and useful are those that take the **square root** (Sqrt) of a number or the **absolute value** (Abs) of a number.

In order to calculate a square root, the programmer uses the form

    Sqrt(*exp*)

where "exp" is any real or integer variable or expression. The value of the square root function is always a real number and only makes sense when "exp" has a nonnegative value. Some example values of the square root function are listed.

SAMPLE INPUT AND OUTPUT

Screen display:

```
Enter a number (-1 to terminate): 2
Enter a number (-1 to terminate): 4
Enter a number (-1 to terminate): 6
Enter a number (-1 to terminate): 8
Enter a number (-1 to terminate): 10
Enter a number (-1 to terminate): 12
Enter a number (-1 to terminate): 14
Enter a number (-1 to terminate): 16
Enter a number (-1 to terminate): 18
Enter a number (-1 to terminate): 20
Enter a number (-1 to terminate): 22
Enter a number (-1 to terminate): 24
Enter a number (-1 to terminate): -1
```

Printer:

```
       TABLE OF SQUARE ROOTS
       -------------------------
       Number        Square Root
       --------      -----------
          2            1.4142
          4            2.0000
          6            2.4495
          8            2.8284
         10            3.1623
         12            3.4641
         14            3.7417
         16            4.0000
         18            4.2426
         20            4.4721
         22            4.6904
         24            4.8990
```

Figure 2-10 (continued)

NUMBER	SQRT(NUMBER) TO TWO PLACES
25	5.00
0.3	0.55
0	0.00
-1	* * * error, Number must be positive or zero
1	1.00
0.5	0.71

Some example Pascal statements that use the square root are

```
Deviation := Sqrt(Variance);
Range := 3 * Sqrt(Number + 5);
Writeln(Sqrt(Number):6:2);
Root := (-B + Sqrt(B * B - 4 * A * C)) / (2 * A)
```

2-4 ADDITIONAL PASCAL TOPICS

In order to calculate an absolute value, the programmer can use the form

```
Abs(exp)
```

where "exp" is any real or integer variable or expression. The value of the absolute value function is an integer if "exp" is an integer and is real if "exp" is real. Some example values of the absolute value function are

NUMBER	Abs(Number)
25	25
-10.3	10.3
0	0
-0.0	0.0

Some example Pascal statements that use the absolute value are

```
Magnitude := Abs(Measurement);
Writeln(Abs(Number):5);
Distance := Abs(X - Y);
GeoMean := Sqrt(Abs(N*M));
if Abs(X - 1) < 0.00001 then
    Writeln('The number is close to 0')
```

Note that the square-root and absolute-value functions can be combined as in the expression "Sqrt(Abs(N*M))". (This expression means to take the square root of the absolute value of N*M. That is, first N*M is calculated, then its absolute value is determined, and finally the square root of that absolute value is obtained.)

In earlier sections, we observed that real arithmetic is not always precise. The reason for this has to do with the way real numbers are stored in the computer. For example, if we add 0.1 ten times, placing the answer in Sum, the *if* statement

```
if Sum = 1.0 then
   Writeln('Precisely 1.0')
```

might not print the message.

One approach to dealing with this difficulty uses the absolute value function. We would expect that Sum would be very close to 1.0. We might write

```
if Abs(Sum - 1.0) < 0.000001 then
   Writeln('Sum is "close to" 1.0')
```

(The expression "Abs(Sum - 1.0)" calculates the difference between Sum and 1.0.) If absolute precision is required, then real variables are not appropriate.

Functions

Sqrt and Abs are just two examples of standard THINK Pascal functions. Others are discussed later in this section. One (Chr) was introduced very briefly in Section 2-1. The examples given earlier illustrate a number of important ideas associated with functions in general.

1. The **call** (or **invocation** or **use**) of the function takes the form

   ```
   function-name(argument)
   ```

   The **argument** (or **parameter**) is the value the function uses in doing its calculation. For example, in the expression

   ```
   Sqrt(Variance)
   ```

   the variable Variance is the argument. It represents the number whose square root is to be calculated. (As we will see later, some functions have two or more arguments and some have none.)

2. The use of the function can take place almost anywhere that a variable or expression can be used. For example, it can appear on the right side of an assignment statement, in the condition for an *if* statement, or in the list of values to be written by a Writeln statement. It may not appear in a call to Readln or on the left side of an assignment statement.

3. The precedence rules are expanded when a function appears in an expression. Function values are calculated first, prior to unary minus. This involves calculating the value of the argument with the usual precedence rules. For example, consider the following expressions. The operations are done in the indicated order.

Sqrt(3*2+30)/5	First, evaluate the argument:
Sqrt(6+30)/5	* first
Sqrt(36)/5	+ to finish the argument
6.0/5	Then, use the function
1.2	Finally, do the division

Integer Operations: mod and div

In Section 2-1, on the assignment statement, we included a discussion of the "/" operator for division. This operator is sometimes called the "real division" operator because the result is always real. This is true even if the numbers being divided are integers. Some examples follow:

N	M	N / M
15	0.3	50.0
6.3	21	0.3
−32	5	6.4
100	5	20.0
45	0.0	error; division by 0 is undefined

Pascal also allows for the concept of integer division, which is similar to the long division that is practiced by students in elementary school. In long division, we speak of a **quotient** and a **remainder** when we divide one integer into another.

Similarly, in Pascal, we have two operations available: **div** to compute the quotient of two integers, and **mod** to compute the remainder. The div and mod operations are used in the same way that the more familiar operations +, -, *, and / are used. Some examples of the operations of div and mod follow:

N	M	N div M	N mod M
5	2	2	1
−5	2	−2	−1
5	−2	−2	1
−5	−2	2	−1
23	23	1	0
−38	7	−5	−3
12	19	0	12
9	0	error; division by 0 is not allowed	
5	2.0	error; both numbers must be integers	

For two integers N and M, the following relationship holds:

$$N = M * (N \text{ div } M) + (N \text{ mod } M)$$

as long as M is not equal to zero. This statement is known as the **division relation** and is the basis for many other numerical algorithms.

The operators div and mod have the same precedence as * and /. Thus, we can summarize the precedence rules so far as:

1. Function evaluation. This involves evaluating the arguments (using these rules), then invoking the function.
2. Unary minus.
3. *, /, div, and mod (left to right).
4. + and − (left to right).
5. Can use parentheses to group.

Introducing Predefined Identifiers: maxint

The THINK Pascal programming language supplies some assistance to the programmer in the form of **predefined identifiers**. As the term suggests, these identifiers can be used without the programmer declaring them, and, in addition, they have values that have already been established.

One of the most useful of these identifiers is **maxint**, which establishes the largest valid integer value that can be used for a specific implementation of Pascal. For THINK Pascal, maxint is 32767. This means that any positive integer values must range from 0 to 32767, inclusive. Depending upon how a particular computer represents integers, negative integers can range from -maxint to −1 or -(maxint + 1) to −1. (For THINK Pascal, the latter range applies.)

REAL NUMBERS AND INTEGER NUMBERS

Accuracy: Integer arithmetic is accurate. Real arithmetic can be inaccurate.

Limits.   Integer numbers are limited to the range of –maxint – 1 to maxint inclusive. Real numbers also have limits of magnitude but the range is immensely greater (–3.4e38 to 3.4e38 in THINK), so the practical limit is more one of precision than magnitude.

Operators: Integer numbers can use the *div* and *mod* operators. Real numbers cannot use these operators.

Figure 2-12 Real versus integer.

Note. Since maxint is a predefined constant, it is not declared in the program. In fact, if "maxint" were declared as a constant or variable, it would no longer function as intended. For the curious, some experiments are suggested in the exercises.

There are a number of standard predefined identifiers that will be introduced later. Implementations of Pascal often have their own special (nonstandard) predefined identifiers. (THINK Pascal has several.) Using these has the advantage of simplifying and speeding up program implementation, but also has the disadvantage of hindering **program portability**—moving the program to non-Macintosh computers. If a program written on the Macintosh is also intended to be run on other computers, the use of nonstandard identifiers should be minimized. This practice reduces the amount of rewriting of program code that will be necessary to allow the program to run on the other machines.

Real-to-Integer Conversions

One of the most difficult aspects of numerical programming is the distinction between integers and real numbers. We are accustomed in algebra to deal with integers as merely special cases of real numbers and not as an entirely different set of entities with their own rules and operators. However, as we have already seen, there are differences between the "worlds" of real numbers and integers in Pascal. Some of the differences are summarized in Figure 2-12.

One way to manage the differences between the two types of numbers might be to avoid mixing them; however, it is not always possible (or desirable) in practice. For example, if we were attempting to calculate the average amount of rainfall per day for the month of June in a particular area, we would probably calculate the total amount of rain for the month (to tenths of an inch) and divide by 30. We see here that the total amount of rain is "naturally" a real number and the number 30 is "naturally" an integer (the number of days in the month). Therefore, our calculation of the average would involve a **mixed-mode** computation (a mix of a real and an integer).

Suppose the total rainfall is contained in the variable TotalRain and the number of days is contained in the variable Days. If the variable Average is to contain the answer, we have already seen that the statement

```
Average := TotalRain div Days
```

is illegal because TotalRain is a real variable. The alternative choice

```
Average := TotalRain / Days
```

is not only legal, but it accomplishes the purpose. The way that we know which division to select is our realization that the result Average is to be a real quantity. The rule that we need to remember about the operator "/" is

N / M is always real, regardless of the types of N and M.

There are other cases of mixing modes that are not so easily handled. For example, suppose that we have an amount of money in the real variable Allowance and we wish to calculate the number of video games that we can play at a quarter per game. The number of games should be expressed as an integer (it is not usually possible to purchase one-half of a video game) and might be represented in the integer variable Games. We are naively led to the following mixed mode Pascal statement

```
Games := Allowance / 0.25
```

Unfortunately, as we indicated in Section 2-1, this is illegal and leads to a run-time error. For this type of situation, Pascal provides the built-in function **Trunc**, which converts a real number to an integer number by merely dropping the fractional part (that which follows the decimal point) of the real number. Thus, the THINK Pascal statement that we should use is

```
Games = Trunc(Allowance / 0.25)
```

Some examples of the results of this conversion are

ALLOWANCE	ALLOWANCE/0.25	GAMES
10.34	41.36	41
5.20	20.8	20
1.99	7.96	7

As another example, suppose that a teacher grades on the basis of a final average according to

90 – 100 = A
80 – 89 = B
70 – 79 = C
60 – 69 = D
under 60 = F

Suppose further that the final average is based on three 100-point examinations according to the computation

```
FinalAverage := (Exam1 + Exam2 + Exam3) / 3
```

where FinalAverage is a real variable, and Exam1, Exam2, and Exam3 are integer variables. Consider the hypothetical student who has earned:

$$Exam1 = 90$$
$$Exam2 = 89$$
$$Exam3 = 90$$
$$FinalAverage = 89.67$$

Should the student be awarded a grade of B for the course? Many teachers would handle this situation by treating FinalAverage as an integer variable instead of real. In this case, the value of FinalAverage would be 89 if we computed

```
FinalAverage := (Exam1 + Exam2 + Exam3) div 3
```

or if we computed

```
FinalAverage := Trunc((Exam1 + Exam2 + Exam3) / 3)
```

Pascal provides us with another possibility via the built-in function **Round**. If we computed the final average for the student in question with the formula

```
FinalAverage := Round((Exam1 + Exam2 + Exam3) / 3)
```

then the value of FinalAverage would be 90 and the student would receive a grade of A for the course. The following illustrates results of the Round function:

Exam1	Exam2	Exam3	(Exam1 + Exam2 + Exam3)/3	FinalAverage
90	89	90	89.67	90
89	90	89	89.33	89

The following further illustrates the effect of the Round and Trunc functions. (Suppose Number is a real variable.)

NUMBER	Round(Number)	Trunc(Number)
12.1	12	12
11.99	12	11
−1.3	−1	−1
2.5	3	2
2.49	2	2
−2.5	−3	−2
−2.49	−2	−2
−0.5	−1	0

Integer-to-Real Conversions

Sometimes it is desirable to treat an integer number as a real number. For example, suppose that the integer variable Count represents the number of old dollar bills that Jack has torn in trying to smooth them out. If we wanted to output the value of the torn money, we might try the statement

```
Writeln('The value destroyed is $', Count:7:2)
```

However, this statement is not allowed because "Count" is an integer variable. One remedy would be to use the statement

```
Writeln('The value destroyed is $', Count/1:7:2)
```

Although this statement has the desired result, its form does not reflect what we are trying to accomplish, and so is poor programming style. Here's a better solution: Suppose that Value is a real variable. Then, the job can be accomplished by the following statements

```
Value := Count;
Writeln('The value destroyed is $', Value:7:2)
```

The statement "Value := Count" is an **implicit conversion** from an integer value to a real value.

Real-to-Real Conversions

Often, when we are dealing with a real number, we want to know what number comes before the decimal point (the **integer part**) and what number comes after the decimal point (the **fractional part**). For example, if we are studying the distribution of our allowance into bills and change then

> The integer part of the amount is the number of dollar bills that we could receive.
> The fractional part of the amount represents change that we could receive.

THINK Pascal does not provide built-in functions to obtain the integer and fractional parts of a real number, but they are easily computed. To obtain the integer part of real number Number (and to keep that part type *real*), we use the expression:

```
Trunc(Number) * 1.0
```

(Although this is not the best programming style, it is the best we can manage and accomplish the task.)
To obtain the factional part, we just subtract the integer part from Number:

```
Number - (Trunc(Number) * 1.0)
```

To complete the discussion of the distribution of our allowance, suppose that the real variable Amount represents the money that we are to receive. The Pascal program of Figure 2-13 asks the user to input the amount of allowance to be received and distributes the allowance into $20, $10, $5, and $1 bills, and quarters, dimes, nickels, and pennies for the change.

```pascal
program Allowance;
{Written by: XXXXXXXXXXXX XX/XX/XX}
{Purpose:    To distribute an allowance into $20 , $10 , $5 and $1}
{            bills and quarters, dimes, nickels, and pennies}

   const
      EndOfData = 0;          {Used to terminate loop}

   var
      Amount: real;           {Value of allowance, input}
      Dollars: integer;       {Number of dollars to distribute}
      Twenties: integer;      {Number of twenty dollar bills}
      Tens: integer;          {Number of ten dollar bills}
      Fives: integer;         {Number of five dollar bills}
      Ones: integer;          {Number of one dollar bills}
      Cents: integer;         {Number of cents to distribute}
      Quarters: integer;      {Number of quarters}
      Dimes: integer;         {Number of dimes}
      Nickels: integer;       {Number of nickels}
      Pennies: integer;       {Number of pennies}

begin {Allowance}

{*** Print heading}

   Writeln;
   Writeln('              A L L 0 W A N C E S');
   Writeln('              -------------------');
   Writeln;

{*** Read amount, calculate and print distribution}

   repeat
      Writeln;
      Write('Enter the amount of the allowance (0 to quit): ');
      Readln(Amount);
      Writeln;
      if Amount <> EndOfData then
         begin
            Writeln('        DISTRIBUTION');
            Writeln;
            Dollars := Trunc(Amount);
            Cents := Round(100 * (Amount - Dollars));

{*** Distribute the bills}

            Twenties := Dollars div 20;
            Dollars := Dollars mod 20;
```

Figure 2-13 Mod and div (continues next page).

```
                    if Twenties > 0 then
                       Writeln('$20 bills: ', Twenties : 0);
                    Tens := Dollars div 10;
                    Dollars := Dollars mod 10;
                    if Tens > 0 then
                       Writeln('$10 bills: ', Tens : 0);
                    Fives := Dollars div 5;
                    Dollars := Dollars mod 5;
                    if Fives > 0 then
                       Writeln('$5 bills: ', Fives : 0);
                    Ones := Dollars;
                    if Ones > 0 then
                       Writeln('$1 bills: ', Ones : 0);

   {*** Distribute the change}

                    Quarters := Cents div 25;
                    Cents := Cents mod 25;
                    if Quarters > 0 then
                       Writeln('Quarters: ', Quarters : 0);
                    Dimes := Cents div 10;
                    Cents := Cents mod 10;
                    if Dimes > 0 then
                       Writeln('Dimes: ', Dimes : 0);
                    Nickels := Cents div 5;
                    Cents := Cents mod 5;
                    if Nickels > 0 then
                       Writeln('Nickels: ', Nickels : 0);
                    Pennies := Cents;
                    if Pennies > 0 then
                       Writeln('Pennies: ', Pennies : 0);
                    Writeln
                 end
         until Amount = EndOfData;

   {*** Stop the program}

   end.
```

Figure 2-13 (continues next page)

Notes

1. Consider the step

```
Cents := Round(100 * (Amount - Dollars);
```

near the top of the loop. If the amount is 17.23, we would expect 100 * (Amount − Dollars) to be 23.0. However, due to the imprecision of real numbers, it might be just below or just above 23.0. To be on the safe side, we use Round rather than Trunc to convert to an integer.

SAMPLE INPUT AND OUTPUT

```
            A L L O W A N C E S

Enter the amount of the allowance (0 to quit): 234.56

       DISTRIBUTION

$20 bills: 11
$10 bills: 1
$1 bills: 4
Quarters: 2
Nickels: 1
Pennies: 1
Enter the amount of the allowance (0 to quit): 123

       DISTRIBUTION

$20 bills: 6
$1 bills: 3

Enter the amount of the allowance (0 to quit): 10.34

       DISTRIBUTION

$10 bills: 1
Quarters: 1
Nickels: 1
Pennies: 4
Enter the amount of the allowance (0 to quit): 0
```

Figure 2-13 (continued)

2. Consider the two steps

```
Twenties := Dollars div 20;
Dollars := Dollars mod 20;
```

Suppose that Dollars has the value 114. The first step sees how many twenty dollar bills this represents. The second sees how much is left to be distributed as smaller bills (114 mod 20 is 14). The Dollars variable is changed to this value and the program continues.

Other Standard Numeric Library Functions

There are several other standard functions available in THINK Pascal for numeric computation. Each of these is supplied with an argument and returns a value. In the following table, we list the functions we have discussed, along with the other commonly used standard numeric functions.

Note. Functions that are standard in one version of Pascal are often not standard in another version. Standard functions are those available in an implementation of Pascal without the programmer needing to take special action.

Standard Numeric Functions			
Function	Argument	Value	Comment
Abs	Either	Same	Absolute value
ArcTan	Either	Real	Arctangent in radians
Cos	Either	Real	Cosine of angle given in radians
Exp	Real	Real	Exponential function (e^x)
Ln	Real > 0	Real	Natural logarithm
Round	Real	Integer	Rounds off
Sin	Real	Real	Sine of angle given in radians
Sqr	Either	Same	Square
Sqrt	Real >= 0	Real	Square root
Trunc	Real	Integer	Truncates fractional part

DPT

Defensive programming tips for the topics covered in this section consist primarily of remembering several key points.

1. Division by 0 is illegal. A good program will check the value of the divisor before attempting the division, as in this example:

```
if NumberOfTests = 0 then
   Writeln('No tests taken')
else
   begin
      Average := TestTotal / NumberOfTests;
      Writeln('The average is ', Average : 6 : 2)
   end
```

2. Both *mod* and *div* require integer operands and yield integer results.
3. *Sqrt* provides a real answer; *Abs* provides an answer of the same type as its argument.
4. The division operator (/) always yields a real result.
5. The trigonometric functions (*Sin*, *Cos*) require arguments in radians. (Recall that we can convert degrees to radians by multiplying by $\pi/180$.)
6. An assignment of the form

   integer variable := real expression

   is illegal. We must explicitly choose whether to round or truncate. (The existence of this rule in Pascal is itself an aid to defensive programming—it forces us to face the issue head on.)

REVIEW

Terms and Concepts

absolute value (Abs)
ArcTan
argument
call, invocation
close statement
Cos
div
division relation
Exp
field width
float
formatting
fractional part
implicit conversion
integer part
Ln
mod

output position
maxint
mixed mode
parameter
precision
predefined identifiers
Printer
program portability
quotient
remainder
Round
Sin
Sqr
square root (Sqrt)
top-of-form
Trunc
wrap

Output in Pascal Programs

Formatting

1. For integer, character, or string variables and expressions, we can use

```
Writeln(exp : fw) or Write(exp : fw)
```

where "exp" represents an integer, character, or string variable or expression to be output, and "fw" represents an integer variable or expression for the field width to be used. We can omit the field width.

2. For real variables and expressions, we can use

```
Writeln(exp : fw : prec) or Write(exp : fw : prec)
```

where "exp" represents a real variable or expression to be output, "fw" represents an integer variable or expression for the field width to be used, and "prec" represents an integer variable or expression for the precision (number of decimal places) to be used. We can omit the precision or both the field width and the precision.

Output to a Printer. To direct output to a printer, declare a variable of type *text*

```
printer name: text;
```

connect the name to the printer device:

```
reset(Printer name, 'Printer:')
```

and add the Printer name to your Write and Writeln statements as in:

```
Writeln(Printer name, X, Y, Z)
```

Paging

1. Can accomplish a new page on the screen by calling procedure

   ```
   Page
   ```

2. Can accomplish (for many printers) a new page on the printer output by the statement

   ```
   Page(Printer Name)
   ```

Library Functions

1. See the previous table, "Standard Numeric Functions," for a list.
2. Form to use (call or invoke) a function:

   ```
   function-name(argument)
   ```

3. Can use:
   - (a) on the right side of an assignment statement
   - (b) in the condition of an *if* statement
   - (c) in a Writeln
   - (d) **not** on the left side of an assignment statement
   - (e) **not** in a Readln

DPT

1. Avoid division by 0.
2. *Mod* and *div* require integers and yield integer results.
3. *Sqrt* yields a real. *Abs* yields the same type as its argument.
4. Division (/) yields a real.
5. *Sin* and *Cos* require radian arguments.
6. Must use *Trunc* or *Round* for real-to-integer conversion.

EXERCISES

1. Write a Pascal program to read an integer into the variable Number and write it using several variations of the statements "Writeln(Number:3)", "Writeln(Number:4)" ... Discover the number of columns that you have available for output on your terminal or printer.

2. What is the result of the following lines of Pascal code?

   ```
   Writeln;
   Write(3);
   Write(4);
   Write(5)
   ```

3. Write a Pascal program to read a real number into the variable Number and write it using several variations of the statements "Writeln (Number:7:2)", "Writeln(Number:7)",

"Writeln(Number)", and so on (changing the "7" and "2" to other choices). Discover the number of columns and the precision used by "Writeln(Number)".

4. Suppose that player numbers range from 0 to 99 and that player weights range from 145.0 to 312.9 pounds. Write a Pascal program to read the numbers and weights of players and produce printed output similar to the following:

```
       THE PLAYERS' BEEF
   -----------------------------

   Player Number        Weight
   -----------------------------
          12             185.3
          89             298.8
          55             216.2
```

5. Give Pascal expressions corresponding to the following algebraic expressions:
   (a) $1 + \sqrt{x}$
   (b) $\sqrt{1 + x}$
   (c) $|x - y|$
   (d) $|3 - 2x| + y$
   (e) x^3
   (f) $\left|\dfrac{x+2}{y+3}\right|$
   (g) $\sqrt{b^2 - 4ac}$
   (h) $\sqrt{(|r + 5| - 5/(5 - y))}$
   (i) $\sqrt{(x - y)/|z|}$

6. A variable Money contains a real number that is to represent a money figure. Give Pascal steps to round the value in Money to the nearest cent (e.g., if Money is 100.5372, the answer would be 100.54).

7. Give the value of the following expressions (if an expression is illegal, give the reason):
   (a) `5 mod 2`
   (b) `2 mod 5`
   (c) `103 mod 7`
   (d) `1900 mod 4`
   (e) `Abs(16-11)`
   (f) `Abs(15-23*2)`
   (g) `Trunc(23/4)`
   (h) `23 div 4`
   (i) `200 div 11 mod 4`
   (j) `200 div (11 mod 4)`
   (k) `5 * Sqrt(96/4 + 1)`
   (l) `Sqrt(4) div 2`
   (m) `Abs(-16) div 5`
   (n) `100 div 4 div 5`
   (o) `100 div (4 div 5)`
   (p) `100 div (4 / 5)`
   (q) `100 / (4 / 5)`
   (r) `5123 div 100 mod 10`

EXERCISES

8. Write a Pascal program that in a loop reads a real number, calculates the square root and absolute value of the number, and prints the results. If the number input is negative, then print an appropriate message in place of the square root (which does not exist). After each number is processed, ask the user whether to continue.

9. Write a Pascal program that in a loop reads two integer numbers N and M; calculates the expressions N div M, N mod M, and N / M: and prints the results. If M is equal to 0, then print an appropriate message in place of the three expressions. After each number is processed, ask the user whether to continue.

10. Write a Pascal program that in a loop reads two integer numbers N and M; calculates the expressions N div M, N mod M, and M * (N div M) + (N mod M): and prints the results. Is the division relation N = M*(N div M) + (N mod M) true in all cases for which M does not have the value 0?

11. (For the curious) Try the following experiments with the predefined identifier "maxint":
    (a) Violate the range of valid integers established by maxint by input, output, and calculation. What happens?
    (b) Change the program of Figure 2-11 by declaring maxint as a variable of the *integer* type.
    (c) Write a program in which you declare maxint as a constant whose value is different from that used in your implementation. Does the range of valid integers change?

12. Suppose that you output the real variable Number with the statement "Writeln(Number:7:0)". Is the output statement equivalent to "Writeln(Trunc(Number):7)" or "Writeln(Round(Number):7)"? Write a Pascal program to discover which it is.

13. Does "Writeln(Trunc(100 * (23.46 – Trunc(23.46))))" output the value 46? Think of a safer alternative and then test both this statement and your alternative.

14. (a) Write a segment of Pascal code that, for a given four-digit positive integer, will calculate the second digit. (If the number is 3613, the answer is 6.) Hint: See Exercise 7(r).
    (b) Do the same for the third digit.
    (c) Do the same for the first digit. The fourth digit.

15. Using Exercise 14, write a program that reads a series of four-digit positive integers and calculates their value "reversed." (For input 3612, the answer is 2163.)

16. Hand-trace the program of Figure 2-13, that is, trace its calculations for several different values for the Amount variable. Record the values for the different variables. Try these input values: 37.62, 2.99, and 0.41. This process should help you understand how the program works.

17. A barrel holds 11 monkeys, a crate holds 7 monkeys, and a coconut holds 1 monkey. Write a Pascal program that asks the user for a quantity of monkeys and distributes the monkeys to minimize the number of containers used.

18. A runner reports the number of minutes run daily in a diary with a running (no pun intended) total for the year. Write a Pascal program to ask the user for the total amount of minutes run for the year, and output the equivalent amount of time in months, weeks, days, hours, and minutes.

19. An electrical supplier sells wire in rolls of 500, 300, and 75 feet. Write a program to ask the user for the total number of feet of wire required, and output the number of 500-, 300-, and 75-foot rolls, and the number of feet left over. (For 1695, the answers would be three 500-foot rolls, and three 75-foot rolls, for a total of 1725 feet; the buyer is required to buy an extra 30 feet. The program's output would be 3, 0, 3, and 30.)

20. A familiar trigonometric identity translated into Pascal states that

```
Sqr(Sin(X)) + Sqr(Cos(X)) = 1
```

Write a Pascal program to read values for X and print the left side of the identity rounded to two decimal places.

21. Another trigonometric identity translated into Pascal states that

```
ArcTan(Sin(X) / Cos(X)) = X
```

unless Cos(X) = 0. Write a Pascal program to read values of X and print the two sides of this identity, both rounded to two decimal places.

22. Pascal does not come with a standard operator for raising one integer to another integer power. For two integers N and M, the value of "N raised to the Mth power" is expressible as

```
Round (Exp(M * Ln(N)))
```

Write a Pascal program that asks the user for two positive integer values and outputs the first raised to the power of the second by means of the previous formula.

23. (Challenge) Write a Pascal program for computing "N raised to the Mth power" for positive integers N and M using a loop and only multiplication and the "Sqr" function. Try to write an efficient algorithm. Hint: To compute 2 to the 6th power, here are some possibilities:

Five multiplications:

$$2*2 = 4$$
$$2*4 = 8$$
$$2*8 = 16$$
$$2*16 = 32$$
$$2*32 = 64$$

Three multiplications:

$$2*2 = 4$$
$$4*4 = 16$$
$$4*16 = 24$$

2-5 MORE ON DECISION STRUCTURES

This section continues the discussion of Section 2-3. In that section, we examined decision structures with two important limitations:

1. The condition involved consisted of comparing two expressions.
2. There were only two branches (*if-then-else*), and one branch might be empty (*if-then*).

In this section, we learn about some more complex forms the condition can take and about how to develop multiple-way branches. In addition, we examine **nested decisions** (decisions within decisions).

Boolean Expressions

The technical term for the condition in the *if* statement is a **Boolean expression**. A Boolean expression in Pascal is one whose value is either *true* or *false*. (Such an expression is also called a **logical expression**, although that is not the official Pascal terminology.)

One simple way to obtain a Boolean expression, as we have seen, is to compare two quantities using one of the six **relational operators** (=, <>, >, <, <=, and >=). In addition, comparisons such as this can be combined, as illustrated in the following examples:

```
(X > 0) or (Y > 0)
(Sex = 'F') and (Age > 21)
(Grade = 'A') or (Grade = 'B') or (Grade = 'C')
(State <> 'PA') and (State <> 'VA')
```

As you can see, we can combine one or more comparisons using an *and* or an *or*. When we combine using *and*, the resulting condition is *true* provided all of the individual conditions are *true*. When we use *or*, the resulting condition is *true* if one (or more) of the individual conditions is *true*.

We can, therefore, paraphrase the meaning of these four examples as

either X or Y (or both) is positive
female over age 21
Grade is either an A, B, or C
State is not Pennsylvania, and it is also not Virginia

Note. The parentheses in these examples are mandatory. In general, when we combine individual comparisons, those comparisons must be placed in parentheses. This is true because the relational operators (<, =, etc.) have lower precedence than *and* and *or*.

The *and* and *or* used to combine the comparisons are called **Boolean operators** (or **logical operators**). They operate on Boolean expressions (the individual comparisons) to create new Boolean expressions.

There is a third Boolean operator in Pascal: *not*. This operator forms the **negation** (the logical opposite) of a Boolean expression. For example,

```
not (X = 0)
```

means the same as

```
X <> 0
```

These operators, just as the arithmetic operators, have precedence rules. The order of precedence is

not: highest
and: next
or: lowest

This means that we sometimes have to include parentheses to obtain the desired order of operations. We illustrate these ideas by a series of examples; each example is a Pascal Boolean expression corresponding to a particular English language condition. (We make up variable names for quantities in the examples. In a complete program, of course, these variables must be declared.)

1. Not a female over age 21. We need the negation of the condition "female over age 21", which was one of our earlier examples. The easiest way to negate a condition is simply to place the entire condition in parentheses and precede it by the *not* operator:

```
not ((Sex = 'F') and (Age > 21))
```

Another way to negate the condition is to negate each individual comparison, and change the *and* to *or*. To see why this works, we may reason as follows: If a person is not a female over age 21, there are two possibilities: The person either is not female or is not over 21 (or both). We write

```
(Sex <> 'F') or (Age <= 21)
```

2. Operation code is one of '+', '−', '*', or '/'. There are two possible approaches: The first uses *or* to link the possibilities:

```
(Operation = '+') or (Operation = '-') or
(Operation = '*') or (Operation = '/')
```

Pascal also provides an easier way to state this condition:

```
Operation in ['+', '-', '*', '/']
```

This condition says that Operation has one of the values listed between the square brackets. This list is called a **set**. We study the general concept of sets in Pascal at a later time. For now, we simply note that it is useful in conditions of this type:

```
variable in [list of values separated by commas]
```

The variable and the list of values must be of the same **ordinal** type. Of the types we have studied so far, they can be *integer* or *char* because these are ordinal types. They cannot be *real* or *string*, which are not ordinal types.

3. Operation code is not one of '+', '− ','*', or '/'. We can negate either solution from number 2:

```
not((Operation = '+') or (Operation = '-') or
    (Operation = '*') or (Operation = '/'))

not(Operation in ['+', '-', '*', '/'])
```

Alternatively, we can negate each comparison and change each *or* to *and*. We reason that the operation code is not a '+', it is also not a '−', and so on. This yields

```
(Operation <> '+') and (Operation <> '-') and
(Operation <> '*') and (Operation <> '/')
```

4. The sum is between 25 and 35, inclusive. To be between, the sum must satisfy two conditions: It must be at least 25, and it must be no more than 35. Since it must satisfy both, we use *and*:

```
(Sum >= 25) and (Sum <= 35)
```

The word "inclusive" causes us to use >= and <= rather than > and <.

5. The answer is neither 'Y' nor 'N'. When we use neither/nor in English, we mean that both conditions are false. Therefore, we use *and* to join the conditions:

```
(Answer <> 'Y') and (Answer <> 'N')
```

Alternatively, we can reason that the answer is not in the set consisting of 'Y' and 'N', and write

```
not(Answer in ['Y', 'N'])
```

6. Data are good, meaning that the code is 'T' and the numerical value is either below 10 or above 500. We write

```
(Code = 'T') and ((Value < 10) or (Value > 500))
```

The extra parentheses grouping the two conditions joined by *or* are necessary. Because *or* has lower precedence than *and*, we need the parentheses to force the *or* to be performed first.

7. Data is bad (see number 6). We must negate the condition in number 6:

```
not ((Code = 'T') and ((Value < 10) or (Value > 500)))
```

Although there are other ways to negate an expression involving both *and*'s and *or*'s, we suggest using the *not* operator.

Note. In some of these examples, we have used **DeMorgan's laws** for negating compound conditions. The negation of a compound condition consisting of individual conditions joined by *and* may be formed by:

1. negating each individual condition; and
2. changing each *and* to *or*.

Likewise, to negate a compound condition consisting of several conditions joined by *or*, we:

1. negate each individual condition, and
2. change each *or* to *and*.

If both *and* and *or* appear in a compound condition, properly applying DeMorgan's laws requires a great deal of care, hence our suggestion to simply use the *not* operator.

Multiple-Way Branches: General

Now we will learn how to write multiple-way branches in Pascal. These are a direct extension of the *if-then* and *if-then-else* decision structures.

Multiple-way branches occur when the steps to be performed depend on certain conditions in three or more different categories. As a simple example, suppose we have variables BobHeight and JimHeight, containing the heights of Bob and Jim (in inches). We wish to print a message telling which is taller or stating that they are the same height. We identify three possibilities:

1. BobHeight > JimHeight
2. BobHeight = JimHeight
3. BobHeight < JimHeight

We write, in Pascal,

```
if BobHeight > JimHeight then
  Writeln('Bob is taller')
else if BobHeight = JimHeight then
  Writeln('They are the same height')
else
  Writeln('Jim is taller')
```

In general, the form for this structure (which we informally call an *if-elseif* structure) is the following:

```
if condition 1 then
  statement to be done if condition 1 is true
else if condition 2 then
  statement to be done if condition 2 is true
else if condition 3 then
  statement to be done if condition 3 is true
  .
  .
  .
else
  statement to be done if none of the listed conditions is true
```

As usual, any of the statements can be compound statements (lists of statements grouped using *begin* and *end*). For example, if each statement were a compound statement, we would have this form:

```
if condition 1 then
  begin
     steps to be done if condition 1 is true (separated by semicolons)
  end
else if condition 2 then
  begin
     steps to be done if condition 2 is true (separated by semicolons)
  end
else if condition 3 then
  begin
     steps to be done if condition 3 is true (separated by semicolons)
  end
else
  begin
     steps to be done if none of the previous conditions are true
     (separated by semicolons)
  end
```

We simply deal with the branches one at a time by specifying

1. a condition that identifies the branch
2. the steps for the branch to be performed if the condition is *true*

A word about the **semantics** (i.e., the meaning) of this structure may be in order. Because we have "else if condition 2 then", condition 2 is not be examined if condition 1 is *true*. Likewise, condition 3 is not examined if either of the first two conditions is *true*, and so on. The basic meaning of the structure is

> Examine the conditions in the order listed. For the first one (and only the first one) that is *true*, perform the indicated steps. If none is *true*, perform the steps in the final *else* branch.

Notes

1. The final *else* is optional, just as it is in the *if-then* structure. If there are no steps to be done when none of the listed conditions is *true*, we simply omit the last branch.
2. As in Section 2-3 on the *if-then* and *if-then-else*, *begin* and *end* indicate to the compiler that there is more than one step in the branch.
3. In the example just given, the three conditions are **exhaustive conditions**; they exhaust all the possibilities. In the third branch, we were able to omit the condition, writing

```
else
   Writeln ('Jim is taller')
```

We could, however, make the condition explicit if we wished:

```
else if JimHeight > BobHeight then
   Writeln( 'Jim is taller' )
```

To further illustrate these ideas, we develop three more program segment examples.

In the first example, we utilize the following simple tax table, similar to the one used by the federal government:

INCOME	TAX
Below $10,000	0
$10,000 or more but less than $15,000	7% of income over $10,000
$15,000 or more	$350 plus 10% of income over $15,000

We immediately identify three conditions, with the corresponding formulas for the tax:

1. Condition: Income < 10000

    Formula: `0`

2. Condition: 10000 <= Income < 15000

    Formula: `0.07 * (Income - 10000)`

3. Condition: Income >= 15000

    Formula: `350 + 0.10 * (Income - 15000)`

Before we begin coding in THINK Pascal, it will be helpful to think about the conditions more carefully. Because of the semantics (meaning) of the *if-elseif* structure, we can simplify the second condition. We do not need to verify that Income >= 10000. If it were not, the first condition would already have been *true*. Similarly, by the time the third branch is reached, we know the Income must be at least 15000. The three conditions are exhaustive, so we can omit the third condition. This discussion leads us to write

```
if Income < 10000 then
   Tax := 0
else if Income < 15000 then
   Tax := 0.07 * (Income - 10000)
else
   Tax := 350 + 0.10 * (Income - 15000)
```

In the second example, let us assume that a company has had a sales contest, with the eastern branch (code 'EA') winning and the northwestern branch (code 'NW') coming in second. Each employee in the winning branch is to have a bonus of $1000 added to her next check, with a $500 bonus for the second-place employees. We could write

```
if Branch = 'EA' then
   Pay := Pay + 1000
else if Branch = 'NW' then
   Pay := Pay + 500
```

In this example, we definitely need the condition in our second branch. This is not an *if-then-else* structure. There is an implicit third branch ("none of the above") with no steps.

Note. We could make the third branch explicit, adding

```
else
   Pay := Pay
```

to the previous code. However, assigning a variable's value to itself does not change the value, so these extra two lines are pointless.

For our final example, assume we are given a variable Letter known to contain a valid letter grade (A, B, C, D, or F). We are to print an appropriate message ("excellent" for A, etc.) and also add 1 to an appropriate variable (ACount for A, etc.). We can write

```
if Letter = 'A' then
   begin
      Writeln('excellent');
      ACount := ACount + 1
   end
else if Letter = 'B' then
   begin
      Writeln('good');
      BCount := BCount + 1
   end
else if Letter = 'C' then
```

2-5 MORE ON DECISION STRUCTURES

```
    begin
        Writeln('average');
        CCount := CCount + 1
    end
else if Letter = 'D' then
    begin
        Writeln('below average');
        DCount := DCount + 1
    end
else
    begin
        Writeln('failing');
        FCount := FCount + 1
    end
```

The Case Structure

Pascal offers an alternative approach to coding certain decision structures. This approach applies when the conditions on which the branches are based consist of seeing whether a variable has a certain value, such as the last decision-structure example of the previous subsection. We introduce this new **case structure** by rewriting that example:

```
case Letter of
'A':
    begin
        Writeln('excellent');
        ACount := ACount + 1
    end;
'B':
    begin
        Writeln('good');
        BCount := BCount + 1
    end;
'C':
    begin
        Writeln('average');
        CCount := CCount + 1
    end;
'D':
    begin
        Writeln('below average');
        DCount := DCount + 1
    end;
'F':
    begin
        Writeln('failing');
        FCount := FCount + 1
    end
end
```

The semantics for this example are simple: Based on the value of Letter, the list of statements given for that value is executed.

In its simplest form, the *case* statement has the structure that follows. Later, we learn about some possible extensions.

```
case variable of
  value 1:
    statement for first value;
  value 2:
    statement for second value;
  .
  .
  .
  value n:
    statement for last value
end
```

Note that each branch except the last ends with a mandatory semicolon. The last branch need not have a semicolon. Also, there is an extra *end* with no matching *begin* to mark the completion of the *case* structure.

As usual, any of the statements can be a compound statement, as in our example. Notice that there are two *ends* at completion: one for the final branch and the other for the entire *case* structure.

Consider the following example:

```
case NumberOfChildren of
  0:
    Writeln('Childless');
  1:
    Writeln('Have only one child');
  2:
    Writeln ('About Average')
end
```

What happens if the value of the variable NumberOfChildren is not one of those listed? The answer is: nothing. We could modify the example:

```
case NumberOfChildren of
  0:
    Writeln('Childless');
  1:
    Writeln('Have only one child');
  2:
    Writeln ('About Average')
  otherwise
    Writeln ('Larger than the average family')
end
```

The structure illustrated is the following. If we wish, we can place semicolons after the "value n" statement and the *otherwise* statement. There must be semicolons after the "value 1" statement, etc.

2-5 MORE ON DECISION STRUCTURES

```
case variable of
   value 1:
      statement 1;
   value 2:
      statement 2;
      .
      .
      .
   value n:
      statement for last value
   otherwise
      statement for any value not listed
end
```

Note. Just as for the set condition "*variable* in [*list*]", the variable and the list of values in the *case* structure must be of the same type. Moreover, that type cannot be *real* or *string*. Among the types we have studied, only *integer* and *char* types can be used in the case structure.

Nested Decisions

When we write any type of decision structure (*if-then*, *if-then-else*, *if-elseif*, or *case*), each branch of the structure can be either a single statement or a compound statement of this form:

```
begin
   list of steps for the branch, separated by semicolons
end
```

One or more of the steps can itself involve a decision structure. (In fact, we have been using this type of structure without calling attention to it; see, for example, Figure 2-9 in Section 2-3.)

We describe this situation by saying that we have **nested decisions**. One decision is contained totally within (nested within) a branch of another decision structure. Generally speaking, the need for this type of structure arises quite naturally as we refine our algorithm. For example, consider the following.

We wish to calculate a bonus based on the years an employee has worked with the company and the number of sales made. The bonus for people with 10 years or more of service is based on the number of sales for the year: less than 500 earns a bonus of $100, 500 to 1000 earns $150, and over 1000 earns $250. For those with less than 10 years, the rules are: 0 to 4 years, $20; 5 to 7 years, $50; 8 to 9 years, $70 plus $1 for each unit sold in excess of 1000.

This is a fairly complex problem made more so by the fact that the information has been presented in a somewhat disorganized fashion. Our first task is to organize the rules just given. As we attempt to organize the information, we may come up with four branches based on the number of years:

CONDITION (YEARS)	BONUS
0–4	$20
5–7	$50
8–9	Based on sales (rule 1)
10 or more	Based on sales (rule 2)

We begin to write:

```
if Years <= 4 then
  Bonus := 20
else if Years <= 7 then
  Bonus := 50
else if Years <= 9 then
  here we must place the code for rule 1
else
  here we must place the code for rule 2
```

To refine the algorithm (and the Pascal), we must determine the structure for rules 1 and 2. These are fairly simple:

RULE 1

```
if NumberOfSales <= 1000 then
  Bonus := 70
else
  Bonus := 70 + (NumberOfSales - 1000)
```

RULE 2

```
if NumberOfSales < 500 then
  Bonus := 100
else if NumberOfSales <= 1000 then
  Bonus := 150
else
  Bonus := 250
```

The entire decision structure simply consists of our original code with the appropriate code for rules 1 and 2 inserted:

```
if Years <= 4 then
  Bonus := 20
else if Years <= 7 then
  Bonus := 50
else if Years <= 9 then
  begin
    if NumberOfSales <= 1000 then
      Bonus := 70
    else
      Bonus := 70 + (NumberOfSales - 1000)
  end
else
```

```
begin
   if NumberOfSales < 500 then
      Bonus := 100
   else if NumberOfSales <= 1000 then
      Bonus := 150
   else
      Bonus := 250
end
```

Notice that we have written each of the inserted statements as a compound statement. Strictly speaking, this was not necessary because each *if-then-else* is a simple statement. However, we will generally follow this practice in writing nested decisions. One advantage is that it avoids the so-called "dangling else" pitfall, discussed in the next section.

Note. Consider these two code segments, where we have exaggerated the indentation to emphasize the differences:

```
if BobHeight > JimHeight then
   Writeln('Bob is taller')
else if BobHeight = JimHeight then
   Writeln('They are the same height')
else
   Writeln('Jim is taller')

if BobHeight > JimHeight then
   Writeln('Bob is taller')
else
      if BobHeight = JimHeight then
         Writeln('They are the same height')
      else
         Writeln('Jim is taller')
```

To the compiler, they are identical. The compiler does not concern itself with indentation patterns or new lines. To the reader, however, they suggest two ways of viewing the problem:

1. As a "three-way branch." Bob's height is either greater than, equal to, or less than Jim's.
2. As a nested decision. Either Bob is taller or he isn't. If he isn't, there are two possibilities: either he is the same height or he isn't.

Which is correct? Both are. Which is better? It depends on the specific problem. In this example, we like the first segment better because we view the situation as a three-way branch (>, =, <). Sometimes the choice is not so clear. For example, a program used by a bank might contain a decision structure with three branches:

1. Deposits
2. Checks that are good (sufficient funds)
3. Checks that bounce (insufficient funds)

Another, equally valid way to structure this would be as two branches:

1. Deposits
2. Checks

with a decision structure in the second branch with two subbranches

2. (a) Good checks
2. (b) Checks that bounce

Testing

Two important testing strategies, introduced in Section 2-3, apply equally well here:

1. Test the boundaries for each branch.
2. Include other tests for each branch not at the boundary points.

For example, for the previous program segment that calculates a bonus, we might devise the following test plan:

BRANCHES AND BOUNDARIES FOR YEARS

Boundaries:	Years = 0	Others:	Years = 3
	Years = 4		Years = 6
	Years = 5		Years = 12
	Years = 7		
	Years = 8		
	Years = 9		
	Years = 10		

BRANCHES AND BOUNDARIES FOR NUMBEROFSALES (FOR YEARS IN 7–9 RANGE)

Boundaries:	NumberOfSales = 0	Others:	NumberOfSales = 529
	NumberOfSales = 1000		NumberOfSales = 1325
	NumberOfSales = 1001		

BRANCHES AND BOUNDARIES FOR NUMBEROFSALES (FOR YEARS 10 OR OVER)

Boundaries:	NumberOfSales = 0	Others:	NumberOfSales = 217
	NumberOfSales = 499		NumberOfSales = 632
	NumberOfSales = 500		NumberOfSales = 1107
	NumberOfSales = 1000		
	NumberOfSales = 1001		

A third strategy is a new one for this section:

3. When complex conditions are involved (with *and* or *or*), we should test all possible combinations of the individual parts. As an example, for the condition female over age 21 we should include test cases covering these four possibilities

FEMALE	OVER AGE 21	SAMPLE TEST CASE	EXPECTED RESULT
True	True	'F', 30	True
True	False	'F', 20	False
False	True	'M', 27	False
False	False	'M', 17	False

As another example, for the condition "valid data," where to be valid the code must be 'T' and the numerical value either below 10 or above 500, we would have

CODE = 'T'	VALUE < 10	VALUE > 500	SAMPLE TEST CASE	EXPECTED RESULT
True	True	True	Impossible	
True	True	False	'T', 5	True
True	False	True	'T', 519	True
True	False	False	'T', 17	False
False	True	True	Impossible	
False	True	False	'R', 9	False
False	False	True	'M', 1000	False
False	False	False	Q, 490	False

DPT

The first two tips are generally similar to some of those discussed in Section 2-3. The others are new.

  1. We must take care in the placement of the semicolon. In the *if-elseif* type of structure, the only semicolons are those occurring between the statements of the branches, within a *begin/end* series of steps. However, the case structure introduces special semicolons at the end of each branch but the last.

  2. The *begin* and *end* delimiters on a branch are required when the branch contains more than one statement. They should be used, as a defensive programming measure, if the branch consists of another decision structure.

  3. When we use *and*, *or*, or *not* with comparisons, the comparisons must be enclosed in parentheses.

  4. The precedence order (in the absence of parentheses) is *not*, then *and*, then *or*. Parentheses may be required to obtain the desired meaning when two or more of these occur in the same condition. In particular, one way (frequently, the easiest and best way) to negate a condition is to place the entire condition in parentheses preceded by *not*.

  5. In mathematics and in everyday language, we take certain shortcuts in describing conditions. For example, we can write

$$5 < x < 10$$

to mean x is between 5 and 10, and we can say

$$x \text{ is less than } y \text{ and } z$$

to mean that x is less than both.

In Pascal, there are no such shortcuts. We must write the conditions explicitly:

```
(5 < X) and (X < 10)
(X < Y) and (X < Z)
```

6. Suppose we wish to write

```
if Y/X > 5 then . . .
```

To be safe, we ought to make sure that X is not 0. We might be tempted to combine the check that X is not 0 with the original condition, as shown here:

```
if (X <> 0) and (Y/X > 5) then . . .
```

However, this does not work. The difficulty occurs because both conditions are checked when the *if* statement is executed. If the first condition (X <> 0) is false, then the second condition (Y / X > 5) causes a run-time error, due to division by 0. (Run-time errors are often called "bombs"; the term is often used as a verb in sentences such as "Drat! My program just bombed!")

Note. There are languages in which the computer would not bother checking the second condition if the first were *false*. In fact, some versions of Pascal might behave this way. However, THINK Pascal always checks all parts of a compound condition. To avoid this pitfall, we must write something like

```
if X > 0 then
   begin
      if Y / X > 5 then . . .
```

We see some more common instances of this type of pitfall later.

---

7. The case statement has its own *end*, which is in addition to any use within the individual branches. The compiler usually detects the error of omitting this *end*.

REVIEW

Terms and Concepts

Boolean expressions
Boolean operators
case structure
DeMorgan's laws
exhaustive conditions
logical expressions
logical operators

multiple-way branches
negation
nested decisions
ordinal
relational operators
semantics
set

Pascal Conditions

1. Can combine comparisons using relational operators *not*, *and*, and *or*.
2. The precedence is

   not: highest
   and: next
   or: lowest

3. Can use this form (for integer or char variables and values):

   `variable in [list of values separated by commas]`

4. Can negate any condition by:

   `not (condition to be negated)`

If-elseif structure.   (Any branch can be a compound statement.)

1. Form

```
if condition 1 then
   statement to be done if condition 1 is true
else if condition 2 then
   statement to be done if condition 2 is true
  else if condition 3 then
   statement to be done if condition 3 is true
  else
   statement to be done if none of the previous
      conditions is true
```

2. Meaning: Examine the conditions in the order listed. For the first one (and only the first one) that is true, perform the indicated statement. If none is true, perform the statement in the final *else* branch, if present.

Note: The final else branch is optional.

Case structure.   (Any branch can be a compound statement.)

1. Form:

```
case variable of
  value1:
      statement 1;
  value2:
      statement 2;
  .
  .
  .
  last value:
      statement for last value
  otherwise
      statement for any value not listed
end
```

Note the following:

(a) Semicolons after each branch but the last.

(b) Final *end* means "end of the case structure."

(c) If no branch applies and no *otherwise* clause is present, the *case* statement performs no action.

Testing

1. Test all boundaries of branches.
2. Test all branches away from boundaries.
3. Test all combinations of parts of complex conditions.

DPT

1. Semicolon placement must be watched, especially with a case statement.
2. *Begin/end* must be used for branches with more than one statement.
3. Comparisons are to be enclosed in parentheses in complex conditions.
4. Precedence (*not*, *and*, *or*) must be followed; use extra parentheses as necessary.
5. Final *end* is required for a *case* statement.
6. All the parts of a compound condition are evaluated. Hence, for example,

   ```
   if (X <> 0) and (Y / X > S) then . . .
   ```

   will bomb if X is 0.

EXERCISES

1. For each of the following, choose variable names and write Pascal Boolean expressions for the given condition:
   (a) Married male
   (b) Not a married male
   (c) Neither married nor male
   (d) Either a freshman ('FR') or a sophomore ('SO')
   (e) Neither a freshman nor a sophomore
   (f) Either a freshman with a GPA of 4.0, a sophomore with a GPA of 3.7 or higher, or a junior or senior with GPA of 3.5 or higher
   (g) I divides evenly into both J and K
   (h) One of I, J, or K is even
   (i) All of I, J, and K are multiples of 10
   (j) J is between 0 and 100, inclusive
   (k) J is not between 0 and 100, inclusive
   (l) Made a passing grade (A, B, C, or D)
   (m) x and y are both positive

(n) x and y are not both positive
(o) Exactly one of x and y is positive
(p) Neither x nor y is positive
(q) The pair (x,y) lies in the unit box in the plane; that is, both lie between 0 and 1, inclusive.
(r) Either z is negative or both x and y are greater than 5.
(s) y is greater than 5, and either z is negative or x is greater than 5.

2. Integer variables I, J, K, and L have values 4, 7, 12, and 19, respectively. What is the value of each of these logical expressions?
   (a) (I > J) and (K > L)
   (b) (J < 10) or (K = 7) and (L > 10)
   (c) ((J < 10) or (K = 7)) and (L > 10)
   (d) not(I < J) or (I <> K) and (K <> L)
   (e) not((I < J) or (I <> K)) and (K <> L)
   (f) (not(I < J) or (I <> K)) and (K <> L)
   (g) I in [3, 4, 5]
   (h) not(K in [10, 11, 15])

3. Negate the following logical expressions:
   (a) X = 45
   (b) I < J
   (c) Class <> 'SR'
   (d) (Y < Z) or (Y >= Z + 4.0)
   (e) (Class = 'FR') and (Sex = 'M') and (GPA < 3.2)
   (f) (I mod J = 0) or (I mod K = 0)
   (g) (Percent > 0.49) and (Years < 4) and (Bonus > 5.53)
   (h) (Class = 'FR') or (Class = 'SO') and (Hours < 35)
   (i) ((Class = 'FR') or (Class = 'SO')) and (Hours < 35)
   (j) I in [3,4,5]
   (k) (I in [6,7]) or (J in [6,7])
   (l) not(I in [3,4,5])

4. Choose variable names and write a Pascal segment for each of the following situations:
   (a) Football players are marked on their performance in the preceding game. A grade above 93 percent is considered excellent, below 75 percent poor. Your segment should, given a name and grade, print the name, grade, and appropriate message ("excellent" or "poor").
   (b) Given three test grades, print "improving" if the third test score is greater than the average of the first two tests; print "declining" if it is 5 or more points less than the average.
   (c) For a quadratic equation $ax^2 + bx + c$, the value $b^2 - 4ac$ is called the "discriminant." This value determines how many real roots the equation has (none if it is less than 0, one if it is 0, and two if it is greater than 0). Write a segment that, given a, b, and c, prints a message telling the number of roots the equation has.
   (d) Given a value representing a roll of the dice, print one of these messages based on the roll value:

   'You win' (7, 11)
   'You lose' (2, 12)
   'Roll again' (anything else)

(e) (Simplified roulette) The following variables have assigned values, and you are to write a segment based on them: (1) a number indicating the result on a roulette wheel (0 to 32); (2) the amount of a bet; (3) a char variable telling the type of bet made (value 'E'—even, 'O'—odd, or 'N'—number); and (4) the number bet on if the char variable is 'N' (1 to 32). Your segment should calculate the winnings based on these rules: If the number on the wheel was 0, you lose. If you bet on a number and you matched it, you win 30 times the bet. If you bet 'E' (even) or 'O' (odd) and were correct, you win twice your bet.

(f) Given three numbers representing a date, the segment should print the date. The input numbers 11, 7, 85, for example, would cause the date "November 7, 1985" to be printed.

(g) Revise part (f) to assign the date value to a string variable rather than printing the date.

5. Follow the instructions of Exercise 4.

(a) Wage tax rate is based on city codes, as given in the listing

CITY CODE	TAX RATE
'MUR'	0.005
'MORR'	0.01
'JCY'	0.03
'BSTA'	0.005
Others	0.0

Compute the taxes for a given annual wage and city code.

(b) Write a segment to calculate charges for a checking account. For "regular" accounts, the charge is $5.00, unless the lowest monthly balance is $500.00 or more, in which case there is no charge. For "special" accounts, the charge is 20 cents per check; for "VIP" accounts, there is no charge. Hint: Use a variable AccountType with value 'R', 'S', or 'V' to determine the type of account.

(c) Taxes in a certain state are based on taxable income and are calculated differently depending on whether the person is single or married. The taxable income is either 0 or the weekly income minus $13 for each dependent, whichever is more. The taxes are given by the listings:

TAXABLE INCOME	TAX (MARRIED)
Less than $145.00	1% of income
$145.00–$293.00	2% of income
Over $293.00	$50.00, plus 3% of amount over $293.00

TAXABLE INCOME	TAX (SINGLE)
Less than $130.00	1% of income
$130.00–$250.00	2% of income
$250.01–$350.00	$60.00, plus 3% of amount over $250.00
Over $350.00	$100.00

Write a Pascal segment to calculate taxable income and tax for a taxpayer given the needed information.

(d) A certain small company manufactures five items. The prices are listed. Write a Pascal segment that, given a valid item number, calculates the price.

ITEM NUMBER	PRICE
4927	100.50
2178	3000.00
2111	100.50
1137	143.50
1342	25505.00

(e) Revise part (d) to print an error message if the item number is invalid.

6. Indicate some tests that should be in a test plan for each of the following exercises.
   (a) Exercise 4(a)
   (b) Exercise 4(b)
   (c) Exercise 4(c)
   (d) Exercise 4(d)
   (e) Exercise 5(b)
   (f) Exercise 5(c)
   (g) Exercise 5(e)

7. (a–s) For each of Exercises 1(a) through 1(s), create a test plan relating to the condition. Use a table format similar to that used in the testing section.

2-6 YET MORE ON DECISION STRUCTURES

In this section, we complete our formal study of decision structures. We introduce a few more ideas relating to decisions and conclude with a case study.

The "Dangling Else" Pitfall

Consider these two segments of Pascal code, where we have exaggerated the indentation to emphasize the difference:

```
if X > 5 then            if X > 5 then
    if Y > 0 then           if Y > 0 then
        Z := 1                  Z := 1
else                     else
    Z := 2                  Z := 2
```

Under exactly what conditions will the step "Z := 2" be performed? The indentation patterns suggest what the author had in mind: for the left-hand code, when X > 5 and Y <= 0; for the right-hand code, when X <= 5. However, the compiler pays no attention to indentation. To the compiler, these two segments are the same. Moreover, the interpretation the compiler takes is the one implied by the left-hand indentation pattern:

Each *else* is matched with the most recent unmatched *if* (within the same *begin* . . . *end* grouping).

(THINK helps us remember this rule by automatically indenting this code using the left-hand pattern.)

To obtain the meaning desired by the right-hand example, we would use *begin* and *end* as illustrated in what follows. In fact, in the interest of defensive programming, we should use a *begin* and *end* for both program segments. This would make sure that we obtained the desired results. Here are the two examples rewritten in this fashion:

```
if X > 5 then              if X > 5 then
    begin                      begin
        if Y > 0 then              if Y > 0 then
            Z := 1                     Z := 1
        else                       end
            Z := 2             else
    end                        Z := 2
```

The problem illustrated by this example arises when the *then* branch of an *if-then-else* consists of another decision structure. It, therefore, pays to be especially careful when writing nested decisions. Our defensive programming tip is as follows:

> When the *then* branch of a decision structure involves another decision structure, use a *begin . . . end* to surround the nested decision structure.

(In fact, when we nest decisions, we frequently include all the nested decision structures within *begin . . . end* groupings.)

Some of the exercises give other examples illustrating this point.

Boolean Variables

In the preceding section, we discussed the Boolean expression. It is an expression whose value is either *true* or *false*. It should not surprise you to learn that Pascal has variables capable of holding such values. Just as integer variables store integer values and char variables store one-character values, Boolean variables store Boolean values.

These variables are declared as are other variables and used analogously to the ways in which real and integer variables are used. Remember that the only values they can contain are *true* and *false*. For example, we can declare

```
var
    X, Y: integer;
    XBigger: boolean;
    YZero: boolean;
    BothPositive: boolean;
```

and include steps such as these in our program:

```
XBigger := X > Y;
YZero := Y = 0;
BothPositive := (X > 0) and (Y > 0);
Writeln('Is X bigger? ', XBigger, ' Are both positive? ', BothPositive);
if XBigger and BothPositive then
    Writeln('Both are positive but X is larger');
```

2-6 YET MORE ON DECISION STRUCTURES

This example illustrates several points about Boolean variables. These and other points are described in the following list:

1. The Boolean expressions that we assign to Boolean variables are of exactly the same form as those used in an *if* statement.

2. The assignment "YZero := Y = 0" assigns *true* to YZero if the condition "Y = 0" is true, *false* if not. To understand this step, you must realize that "Y = 0" is a comparison (Boolean expression) whose value is either *true* or *false*. This value is assigned to the boolean variable YZero.

Another way to accomplish the same thing would be

```
if Y = 0 then
   YZero := true
else
   YZero := false
```

3. The Boolean operators *and*, *or*, and *not* act with and yield Boolean values. Thus,

```
XBigger and BothPositive
```

is *true* if both XBigger and BothPositive are true, *false* otherwise. An equivalent way to write this is

```
(XBigger = true) and (BothPositive = true)
```

The "= true" is redundant, but it is allowed. When you first start working with Boolean variables, this second approach may seem clearer. However, you will soon become used to the first approach, especially because it reads "more like English."

4. Similarly, these two *if* statements are equivalent:

```
if not YZero then                if YZero = false then
   Writeln('Y is not 0');           Writeln('Y is not 0');
```

5. We can print Boolean values. The resulting output is either the word TRUE or the word FALSE.

6. We cannot read values for Boolean variables using the Readln procedure. (We can, if we wish, read a char variable and use it to assign a value to a Boolean variable, as in this code segment.)

```
Readln(Ch);
if Ch in ['T','t'] then
   BVar := true
else
   BVar := false
```

7. Boolean variables can be used in case statements and in the "*variable* in [*list of values*]" type of condition. For example, the following three segments are equivalent, although the first is most readable:

```
if X > Y then          XGreater := X > Y;         XGreater := X > Y;
   T := 0              if XGreater in [true] then case XGreater of
else                      T := 0                     true:
   T := 5;             else                             T := 0;
                          T := 5                     false:
                                                        T := 5
                                                  end;
```

8. Boolean variables are useful whenever we have a "yes or no" situation. They can make a program more readable. For example, the line

```
if UpperClassman and HighAverage then
```

is easier to follow than the line

```
if ((Class = 'JR') or (Class = 'SR')) and (GPA > 3.75) then
```

Of course, this is only true if we choose meaningful variable names. To be appropriate, a Boolean variable's name should be suggestive of what its *true* value denotes.

9. You may have noticed that we have used "boolean" and "Boolean" in our descriptions. The capital letter usage is based on the fact that the name "Boolean variable" is named after logician George Boole. The lowercase usage is consistent with our treatment of other standard types (integer, real, char, and string). The compiler, of course, does not care about uppercase or lowercase.

10. We can even use boolean constants that are declared using a declaration such as

```
const
   TestPhase = true;
```

The program might have steps such as these:

```
Readln(Number1, Number2);
if TestPhase then
   Writeln('Values entered: ', Number1, Number2);
```

This idea is frequently used to allow extra information to be printed during program development. When the program is turned over to the user, the declaration would be changed to

```
const
   TestPhase = false;
```

and the extra information would no longer be printed. (Later, if modifications were to be made, the extra prints could be reinserted simply by changing the constant's value back to *true*.)

Enhancements of the Case Statement

Here we present some minor enhancements to the *case* statement. To illustrate the first enhancement, consider this example:

```
case Letter of
  'A':
    Writeln('Above average');
  'B':
    Writeln('Above average');
  'C':
    Writeln('Average');
  'D':
    Writeln('Below average');
  'F':
    Writeln('Below average')
end
```

This has the same meaning as the following, slightly shorter, version:

```
case Letter of
  'A', 'B':
    Writeln('Above average');
  'C':
    Writeln('Average');
  'D', 'F':
    Writeln('Below average')
end
```

Instead of placing just a single value before the colon for each branch, we can place a list of values separated by commas.

In fact, THINK Pascal extends this idea a little further by allowing a range of values to be entered. For example, consider this fragment that calculates a letter grade based on an integer average:

```
case Average of
  90..100:
      LetterGrade := 'A';
  80..89:
      LetterGrade := 'B';
  70..79:
      LetterGrade := 'C';
  60..69:
      LetterGrade := 'D';
  0..59:
      LetterGrade := 'F'
end
```

The first branch of the example is equivalent to either a branch written as

```
90, 91, 92, 93, 94, 95, 96, 97, 98, 99, 100:
 LetterGrade := 'A'
```

or to a list of 11 separate branches for all possible grades.

The general form of one branch of the *case* statement would also allow a list of single values and ranges as in

```
10..14, 17, 19..21, 25:
   statement for these values
```

The listed statement would be executed for any of the values 10, 11, 12, 13, 14, 17, 19, 20, 21, or 25. (The values and ranges in the *case* statement as a whole may not overlap.)

This feature is useful when applicable, but some care should be taken in using it. Values should be grouped only if they really belong together, not if they just happen to have the same statement to be executed. As a simple example, consider the code segment

```
case ItemNumber of
      10, 931:
         Price := 0.94;
end
```

When the price for item number 931 changes, there is a danger that we will also change the price for item number 10. Even if we remember to avoid this, the program will be more difficult to modify than if we had separate branches for these two item numbers.

Case Study No. 2

This case study explores some decision structures, including the use of a Boolean variable. It also introduces some rudimentary error-checking concepts.

Statement of Problem. We want a program that inputs two 1- to 4-digit positive integer numbers and an operation code. The operation code is a "+", "−", "*", or "/". The program should print output similar to

```
1103 + 1407 = 2510
317 - 419 = -102
3 * 15 = 45
```

where the result of the operation is the number following the equals sign.

Preliminary Analysis. As we learned in Section 2-4, there are two possible interpretations of division for integers. We write the program to print both answers when division is the requested operation.

We need to design the exact form of the input. As described earlier, we separate the numeric and character input to avoid some subtleties of input. The program first asks for the two numbers (using a line with both numbers zero to terminate the loop). It then requests the operation to be performed. We use a Boolean variable, as discussed earlier in this section, to control the loop. Its value is *true* when the user enters the terminating values, *false* otherwise.

Algorithm and Variable List. Based on the preliminary analysis, we may write this variable list:

Constant:	EndOfData	Value 0	Used to terminate loop
Input:	Number1	Integer	First number
	Number2	Integer	Second number
	Operation	Char	Operation code (+, −, *, or /)

2-6 YET MORE ON DECISION STRUCTURES

Output:	Result	Integer	Result of operation
	Result2	Real	Second answer
Other:	UserIsDone	Boolean	True when user enters terminating values

Our algorithm follows a structure similar to earlier ones. In particular, we use a procedure to print instructions. (Steps followed by an (*) are not performed when the terminating values have been entered.)

> print instruction (using procedure Instructions)
> repeat these steps until user enters both numbers as 0:
>   prompt for two numbers
>   read Number1 and Number2
>   prompt for operation (*)
>   read Operation (*)
>   depending on Operation value, choose a branch: (*)
>   '+' : Result is sum, print Result
>   '–' : Result is difference, print Result
>   '*' : Result is product, print Result
>   '/' : Result is integer quotient, Result2 is real quotient; print both
> print a closing message and stop

(Of course, there are other possible approaches we could have taken.)

This algorithm, like previous ones in the text, does not deal with errors. In this case study, we consider two possible error situations. Others are suggested in the exercises.

First, it is possible that the operation code entered might not be valid. We might add a fifth branch based on the Operation value:

> anything else: print an error message

Second, division by 0 is an error. We might modify the "divide" branch to read:

> '/': check Number2
>   if it is not 0 do these steps:
>   calculate Result as the integer quotient
>   calculate Result2 as the real quotient
>   print both answers
>   otherwise do this:
>   print an error message

We will code this refined algorithm.

Test Plan. The test plan is fairly simple. We want to exercise all possible paths for the decision structure, especially including the possibility of a faulty operation code or division by 0. In fact, we might include several different faulty codes.

If we reread the statement of the problem, we see that the input is to consist of one- to four-digit integers. This implies a range of 0 to 9999. We want to include test data that exercise both boundaries (0 and 9999) for each number. In addition, we should include some numbers in between.

These considerations raise an important question. What happens if the numbers are not in the correct range? Ideally, the program should perform error checking here; this is the subject of one of the exercises. As the program stands, there are several possibilities:

1. The answer could be entirely correct. For example:

```
15101 - 14323 = 678
```

2. We could get strange but correct output such as

```
-5 + -4000 = -4005
```

3. The numbers could be so large that the answer (or even the numbers themselves) is too large for the computer to store in the kind of variable we have declared the answer to be, resulting in **numeric overflow**. In some Pascal implementations, overflow causes a run-time error; in THINK Pascal the program does produce output, but it is (often radically) incorrect. For example, if we were to execute the program segment

```
N := 30000;
N := N * 2;
Writeln(N)
```

where N is an integer, THINK's output would be −5536! The overflow occurs because N takes on the value 60,000, but the largest integer THINK can properly store is 32,767.

In our test plan, we might include some input in all these categories. In any case, the test plan does point out the need for further work on the algorithm, as indicated in the exercises.

One final test might involve entering a zero for exactly one of the two numbers. This test table contains the cases necessary to check that the looping process does not terminate unless both are zero.

NUMBER 1 ZERO	NUMBER 2 ZERO	TEST CASE	EXPECTED RESULT
True	True	0, 0	Terminate loop
True	False	0, 5	Continue loop
False	True	7, 0	Continue loop
False	False	17, 2	Continue loop

Write Program. Figure 2-14 contains the program that is based on the algorithm, as modified by our error-handling discussion. Various exercises deal with alternate coding approaches, enhancements, and modifications. In particular, we have chosen to use the *if-elseif* approach to handle the various operation codes. Exercise 6 asks you to rewrite this using the case statement approach.

Observe the use of the Boolean variable UserIsDone. This avoids the pitfall of improper negation of the condition for terminating the loop.

Revise/Enhance Program. Although we do not do so at this point, this program could benefit from some revisions. The main module (not including the const or var declarations or the Instructions procedure) occupies about a page. More importantly, it has loop and decision structures nested to four levels:

```pascal
program OperationCodes;

{Written by: XXXXXXXX XX/XX/XX}
{Purpose:    To perform addition, subtraction, multiplication, or division}
{            (both integer and real) for two integers.}
{            The program also illustrates some error-handling ideas.}
{Procedures used: Instructions, to print instructions for user}

  const
    EndOfData = 0;          {terminating data indicator}

  var
    Number1: integer;       {first number, input}
    Number2: integer;       {second number, input}
    Operation: char;        {operation code, input}
    Result: integer;        {result of operations, output}
    Result2: real;          {second answer for division, output}
    UserIsDone: Boolean;    {true if terminating value entered}

  procedure Instructions;
  begin
     {Left to the reader}
  end; {Instructions}

begin {OperationCodes}

{*** Before the loop, print instructions}

  Instructions;

{* * * In loop, obtain two numbers and operation; perform operation;}
{      print answer (two answers for division).}
{      Check for two errors: bad operation and division by zero.}
{      Stop when both numbers are terminating values.}

  repeat
    Writeln;
    Write('Enter two integer numbers (both 0 to stop): ');
    Readln(Number1, Number2);
    UserIsDone := (Number1 = EndOfData) and (Number2 = EndOfData);
    if not UserIsDone then
      begin
        Write('Now enter the operation: ');
        Readln(Operation);
        if Operation = '+' then
          begin
            Result := Number1 + Number2;
            Writeln(Number1 : 0, ' + ', Number2 : 0, ' = ', Result : 0)
          end
        else if Operation = '-' then
          begin
            Result := Number1 - Number2;
            Writeln(Number1 : 0, ' - ', Number2 : 0, ' = ', Result : 0)
          end
```

Figure 2-14 Case Study No. 2 (continues next page).

```
        else if Operation = '*' then
         begin
           Result := Number1 * Number2;
           Writeln(Number1 : 0, ' * ', Number2 : 0, ' = ', Result : 0)
         end
        else if Operation = '/' then
         begin
           if Number2 <> 0 then
             begin
               Result := Number1 div Number2;
               Result2 := Number1 / Number2;
               Writeln(Number1 : 0, ' / ', Number2 : 0, ' = ', Result : 0,
                       ' (integer)');
               Writeln(Number1 : 0, ' / ', Number2 : 0, ' = ', Result2 : 1 : 2,
                       ' (real)')
             end
           else
             Writeln('*** Division by 0 is not allowed! ***')
         end
        else
          Writeln('*** Error made in operation. You entered: ', Operation)
        end

   until UserIsDone;

{*** Stop}

end.
```

SAMPLE INPUT AND OUTPUT

```
    Enter two integer numbers (both 0 to stop): 45 67
    Now enter the operation: *
    45 * 67 = 3015

    Enter two integer numbers (both 0 to stop): 2 0
    Now enter the operation: +
    2 + 0 = 2

    Enter two integer numbers (both 0 to stop): 23 4
    Now enter the operation: /
    23 / 4 = 5 (integer)
    23 / 4 = 5.75 (real)

    Enter two integer numbers (both 0 to stop): 3 19
    Now enter the operation: -
    3 - 19 = -16

    Enter two integer numbers (both 0 to stop): 0 0
```

Figure 2-14 (continued)

1. a *repeat* loop
2. an *if* to avoid processing the terminating data
3. an *if-elseif* based on the operation code
4. an *if-then-else* to handle division by zero

Both the length of the module and the level of nesting are close to the limits of easy comprehension. The program should probably be modularized, even as it now stands. If any more sophisticated error checking were incorporated, it would certainly be desirable to modularize further. However, in order to do a good job with the modularization, we need to develop more tools, which are presented in the next chapter.

REVIEW

Terms and Concepts

numeric overflow

Pascal Syntax

Case Statement. A branch can have a form as indicated by the example:

```
10, 11..14, 16..18, 25:
 statement
```

Boolean Variables and Constants

1. Constant declaration:

```
const
   constant-name = true;
   constant-name = false;
```

2. Variable declaration:

```
var
   variable name: boolean;
```

3. Assignment:

```
variable := any boolean expression
```

4. Use in *if*. Examples:

```
if XGreater then . . .
if Valid and (Sex = 'M') then . . .
if Valid and Male then . . .
```

(XGreater, Valid, and Male are boolean variables that have an assigned value.) Note:

```
if XGreater then . . .
```

means

```
if XGreater = true then . . .

if not Male then . . .
```

means

```
if Male = false then . . .
```

5. Output: Use Write or Writeln: prints TRUE or FALSE.
6. Can use in case statement or in "*variable* in [*list*]" condition.

DPT

1. Cannot read Boolean variables.
2. Always use *begin . . . end* for a *then* branch if the branch consists of another decision structure.

EXERCISES

1. For a certain honor fraternity, freshmen and sophomores must have a 3.8 grade point average (GPA) to be eligible. Others must have a 3.5 grade point average.
   (a) Here is a segment of Pascal code that is supposed to print a message if the person is eligible. Does it correctly accomplish its task? If not, revise it so it does.

   ```
   if (Class = 'FR') or (Class = 'SO') then
     if GPA >= 3.8 then Writeln('eligible')
   else
     if GPA >= 3.5 then Writeln('eligible')
   ```

   (b) Modify the segment to print the message 'not eligible' if the person is not eligible.
   (c) Modify the segment of part (b) to assign a value (*true* or *false*) to a Boolean variable Eligible rather than printing a message.

2. (a) Consider this segment of Pascal code, which calculates a letter grade based on a numerical average. Some people are taking the course for a "pass-fail," others for a letter grade.

   ```
   if Code = 'P' then
     if Average >= 70 then
       Letter := 'S'
     else
       Letter := 'U'
   else
     if Average >= 90 then
       Letter := 'A'
     else if Average >= 80 then
       Letter := 'B'
   ```

```
      else if Average >= 70 then
         Letter := 'C'
      else if Average >= 60 then
         Letter := 'D'
      else
         Letter := 'F'
```

The part in italics is a decision structure within the *then* branch of the main decision. It violates our defensive programming tip by not being included in a *begin . . . end* grouping. Does the code segment do what it should?

(b) These two segments have the same meaning:

```
if Average >= 70 then          if Average >= 70 then
   Letter := 'S'                  Letter := 'S'
else                           else if Average < 70 then
   Letter := 'U'                  Letter := 'U'
```

Does substituting the right-hand version for the italic part of the program segment in part (a) change the meaning of that program segment?

(c) Comment on the relationship of this example to our defensive programming tip concerning the "dangling else."

3. For each condition listed, choose the appropriate variable names, including a Boolean variable. Give the variable declarations needed (the var section), and give an assignment statement to assign an appropriate value to the Boolean variable.
   (a) A given number is even.
   (b) The data are valid (either an 'M' or 'S' for the code, and the number of dependents between 0 and 12).
   (c) Eligible for an honor fraternity (freshman with 4.0 GPA, sophomore with 3.8 or better, or junior or senior with 3.5 or better).
   (d) All three values are odd.
   (e) A given number is a multiple of both M and N.
   (f) A given number is either positive or negative.
   (g) Improving (third test better than the first two).
   (h) vowel (one of 'A', 'E', 'I', 'O', or 'U').

4. Write the following decision structures using case statements. Assume Grade is an integer that can range from 0 to 100.
   (a)
   ```
   if Grade >= 60 then
         Writeln('Passing')
   ```
   (b)
   ```
   if Grade >= 60 then
         Writeln('Passing')
      else
         Writeln('Failing')
   ```

5. (a) Rewrite the solutions to Exercises 4(d) and 5(d) of Section 2-5 using the enhancements to the case statement. Which is better for those problems: your original solution or the new one? Why?
   (b) Write a decision structure to assign a value of +1, 0, or –1 to a quiz. The quiz is worth 15 points, and scores from 11 to 15 earn a +1, scores below 7 earn –1, and all others earn 0.

6. Write segments of Pascal code to assign a value for a Boolean variable as indicated by the following descriptions or questions:
   (a) Is the average of the four test scores at least 70?
   (b) Is the test average "close to" the homework average? They are close if they differ by no more than one letter grade. (Use 90 percent = A, etc.)
   (c) Repeat part (b) so that scores below 50 are not considered close to a 'D' score.
   (d) Are three given values Value1, Value2, and Value3 in increasing order?
   (e) Is Y within 10 units of X?
   (f) Is a four-digit number a "palindrome," that is, the same backward or forward? For example, 5115 is; so is 220, because as a four-digit number, it would be 0220.
   (g) Are three given points (x,y), (z,w), and (t,u) on the same straight line? Assume all values are integers.
   (h) Is a person qualified for a rent rebate program? The answer is yes (true) for income of $10,000 or less. It is also yes for income between $10,000 and $13,000 inclusive, provided the number of dependents is at least two. For all others, the answer is no (false).

Exercises 7 to 11 refer to Case Study No. 2.

7. Write the necessary Instructions procedure.
8. Rewrite the *if-elseif* structure, which handles the operation code, using the case statement.
9. One possible approach for handling input data error is to check the data, print an error message if it is faulty, then "fix" it. Although there are more sophisticated approaches, this approach is better than simply ignoring errors.
   (a) Modify the check for the operation code in Case Study No. 2. As soon as Operation is read, check its validity. If it is not valid, print a message like

   ```
   Invalid code 'T', changed to '+'
   ```

   Then change it to '+' and continue.

   (b) Do a similar check for Number1 and Number2. If they are not in the proper 0 to 9999 range, change them to 1.

10. Revise Case Study No. 2 to handle the operations listed below. Include any necessary changes to the test plan.
    (a) +, −, *
    (b) / = real division
    (c) I = integer division
    (d) M = mod
    (e) D = isolate digit. (Number2 must be in the range 1 to 4, or an error message should be printed.) For example,

    ```
    6279 D 3 = 7
    6279 D 1 = 6
     279 D 1 = 0
    ```

11. Rewrite the program so that numeric overflow is less likely. Some approaches to consider:
    (a) Change the declarations of Number1, Number2, Result, or Result2.
    (b) Check the entered numbers to be sure they are not too large.
    (c) Place the result into a real number, checking that it is within the allowed range of the Result (or Result2) variable, and then place the result into Result (or Result2).

EXERCISES

The remaining exercises deal with programs you will develop yourself.

12. Write complete Pascal programs for the following, using a planning process similar to that used in the various case studies.
    (a) Given a year in the range from 1920 to 1990, the program should print a message telling whether or not the year is a leap year. (A leap year is one divisible by 4.)
    (b) Revise part (a) to work for any year less than 4000. For years in this range, the rule is more complicated. For example, 1900 was not a leap year, but 2000 will be. In general, a year divisible by 100 is not a leap year unless it is also divisible by 400.
    (c) Revise part (b) to print the message 'I can't handle years 4000 or above' if the input year is not less than 4000.
    (d) Write a program to read a four-digit number representing "military" time. Assume the input is valid. It should add one minute to the time, and print the original time and the new time. Sample output might be:

    ```
    1912 plus one minute is  1913
     759 plus one minute is   800
    ```

    Hint: Use *mod* and *div* to split the given time into hours and minutes.

    (e) Repeat part (d), but input three values: hours, minutes, and either "a.m." or "p.m." Assume valid input. Sample output:

    ```
    11:59 a.m. plus one minute is 12:00 p.m.
    ```

    Hint: Can you think of a way to have 0 print as "00"?

13. Follow the instructions of Exercise 11.
    (a) The input consists of these items: a name, the person's gross income, and a code for the county (P = Pembroke, R = Richland, T = Tioga). The three counties have different tax rates: Pembroke County, 2 percent; Richland County, 1.5 percent; and Tioga County, 3 percent. Write a program to print a listing of name, county code, gross income, tax rate, and tax. Print an error message for any input containing an invalid county code.
    (b) A salesperson's commission is based on two factors: the sales amount and the number of years with the company. The basic commission rate is found by using this table:

SALES AMOUNT	RATE (%)
Less than $500.00	5
$500.00–$1000.00	7
$1000.01–$1499.99	8
$1500.00 on up	10

    In addition, the commission is doubled if the salesperson has worked over 7 years with the company. If the salesperson has worked over 15 years, it is doubled and $5 is added for each year over 15. Write a program to calculate commission rate and commission for each employee.
    (c) Calculate a customer's bill for an order of some quantity of a single item. We assume there are only four items available, as shown:

ITEM NUMBER	UNIT PRICE
100	24.03
247	105.00
16	10.35
240	16.00

A discount is allowed for a large order: If the total bill is $1000.00 or over, a 2 percent discount is given; from $800 to $999.99 earns a 1 percent discount.

(d) The first input contains a number indicating a beginning inventory (the number of items presently in stock). Each subsequent input consists of a code (P = purchase or S = sale) and a quantity. For a sale, the quantity should be subtracted from the current inventory; for a purchase, added to the inventory. Write a complete program to maintain the running status of the inventory.

If there is insufficient inventory to cover a sale, print a message and reject the sale. If the resulting inventory is below 750 after a sale, issue a "time-to-reorder" message; if it is below 250, issue a message of the sort "URGENT— time-to-reorder".

14. Indicate some tests that should be in a test plan for each of the following exercises.
    (a) Exercise 11(a)
    (b) Exercise 11(b)
    (c) Exercise 11(d)
    (d) Exercise 12(b)
    (e) Exercise 12(c)
    (f) Exercise 12(d)

2-7 USER-DEFINED FUNCTIONS

For some time, we have been routinely utilizing Instruction procedures in our examples and exercise solutions. The use of a separate module to perform the instruction printing subtask has a number of benefits. Perhaps the major benefit is that the details of instruction printing do not interfere with developing or displaying the major logic of the program.

In this section, we develop this theme a little further. We study **user-defined functions**, which we can write to perform a subtask consisting of calculating a single value. As we will see, using a function we write ourselves is similar to using a standard function such as Sqrt.

An Example

Suppose we wish to write a program to calculate the area of a triangle given the three sides. Following the general method used in earlier programs, we might devise this plan. (Steps with an asterisk are not executed for the terminating value.)

    print instructions (using the Instructions procedure)
    repeat these steps until the user enters 0 for A
        issue prompt
        read values A, B, C (the three sides)
        calculate the area based on A, B, C (*)
        print the area (*)

We choose to write a function whose name will be AreaFn to perform the details of calculating the area. By drawing on our knowledge of user-written procedures and standard functions, we can complete the Pascal code for the main program. In particular:

1. A user-written function must be defined before it is used. We place its definition after the variable declarations and before the *begin* of the main program. This is the same as for a user-written procedure.
2. To use a user-written function in an assignment statement, we must place the necessary arguments (parameters) in parentheses after the function name. These parameters are the values the answer is based on. This is the same as for a standard function, such as Sqrt.
3. In the module that uses the function, we cannot have another variable with the same name as the function. We might choose another variable (perhaps Area) to store the answer from the function. This is the same as for a standard function.

Figure 2-15 contains the resulting program, with the parts related to the issues just discussed in italics.

To continue with this example, we must learn how to write a function. The key to the process is that, as for a procedure, we simply write the steps necessary to perform the subtask, along with one statement declaring that these steps form a function. As with the procedure, the function can, if desired, declare local variables for its own use.

There are some major differences, however, between a function and the type of procedure we have studied to this point. Before we discuss these issues in detail, let us examine them as they relate to the AreaFn function. The Pascal function is given in Figure 2-16, with lines numbered for easy reference. It uses a mathematical formula for the area based on the sides.

Note. In order to complete the program in Figure 2-15, we would merely insert this code in place of the comment that shows where it goes.

From this example, we can learn a great deal about writing functions.

1. Line 1 declares that AreaFn is a function. The final *real* following the colon says that the value the function calculates is real.
2. Line 1 also describes the function parameters for the function. There are three, and all three represent real values. The function uses the names A, B, and C to represent them. In the example, we have chosen names that happen to match those used in the main program. This was not necessary, but it is allowed.
3. Lines 2 to 7 represent the type of header comments we use for functions. We include a brief description of the parameters (lines 5 and 6).
4. A function, like a procedure, can declare local variables. Lines 8 to 9 declare the local variable S, the semiperimeter of the triangle. This variable is used only within the function. It is not available to the main program.
5. A function can, in turn, use another function or procedure. In line 13, the AreaFn function uses the standard square root function (Sqrt).

```
program Triangles;

{Written by: XXXXXXXX XX/XX/XX}
{Purpose:    To calculate areas of triangles}
{Procedures used: Instructions, to print instructions}
{Functions used:  AreaFn, to calculate the area}

  const
    EndOfData = 0;

  var
    A, B, C: real;  {sides of triangle, input}
    Area: real;     {area of triangle, output}

  procedure Instructions;
  begin
    {stub}
  end;

{We will place the area function at this point in the program when it has}
{been developed. Its name will be AreaFn. (See Figure 2-16)}

begin {Triangles}

{*** Before the loop, print instructions}

  Instructions;

{* * * In loop, read the 3 sides of the triangle, use the area function}
{       to find the area, and print the result. Quit on entry of A = 0.}

  repeat
    Writeln;
    Write('Enter three sides of triangle (first 0 to stop): ');
    Readln(A, B, C);
    if A <> EndOfData then
       begin
         Area := AreaFn(A, B, C);
         Writeln('The area is ', Area)
       end
  until A = EndOfData;

{*** After the loop, terminate the program.}

end.
```

Figure 2-15 Use of a user-defined function.

6. The function sends its answer to the program using it by placing the answer into the function name. Line 13 performs this step.
7. The body of the function is bracketed by *begin* (line 11) and *end* (line 14). The final *end* is followed by a semicolon. We add a comment on each of these lines, identifying that these are the beginning and end of the module AreaFn.

2-7 USER-DEFINED FUNCTIONS

```
1)  function AreaFN (A, B, C: real): real;
2)
3)  {Written by: XXXXXXXX XX/XX/XX}
4)  {Purpose:    To calculate the areas of a traiangle based on its sides}
5)  {Parameters: A, B, and C are the three sides. This function assumes they}
6)  {            do form the sides of a triangle.}
7)
8)        var
9)              s: real;   {semiperimeter (half the perimeter)}
10)
11)     begin {AreaFn}
12)           S := (A + B + C) / 2;
13)           AreaFn := Sqrt(S * (S - A) * (S - B) * (S - C))
14)     end; {AreaFn}
```

Figure 2-16   Code for AreaFn.

The Form of a Pascal Function

This example illustrates the general form of a Pascal function:

1. A header line identifying the function and its parameters.

2. Declaration of local constants and variables, if any.

3. A list of statements forming the "body" of the function (bracketed by *begin* and *end;* and separated by semicolons).

The body must contain at least one statement that gives a value to the function name. It can contain more than one such statement. The entire function (from header line through the final *end;*) is placed after the variable declarations and before the *begin* of the main program.

The header line has this form:

```
function function-name (list of parameters) : result type;
```

The "result type" can be *real, integer, char, string* (without an explicit size—*string*[7] is not allowed), or *boolean*. It represents the type of value the function calculates and returns.

The "function-name" follows the usual rules for Pascal identifiers. The "list of parameters" can be simple, as in the example, or it can be quite complex. There are alternative ways to express the same list. For example, these two lists are equivalent:

```
A, B, C: real
A: real; B: real; C: real
```

The first says, "There are three parameters: A, B, and C. All three are real." The second says, "There are three parameters. The first is A, which is real. The second is B, which is real. The third is C, which is real." In general, we can describe the "list of parameters" as containing one or more repetitions of this basic pattern:

```
variable list: type
```

Within each list, the variables are separated by commas. If there are several occurrences of the pattern, they are separated by semicolons.

The following sample header lines should help clarify these points:

```
function Lowest(Score1, Score2, Score3: integer): integer;
function Lowest(Score1: integer; Score2: integer; Score3: integer): integer;
function LetterGrade(Average: real): char;
function Average(A, B, C, D, E: integer): real;
function Raise(Salary: real; Tenured: boolean): real;
function F(X, Y: real; T, U, V: integer; A, B: Char): real;
```

Notes.

The result type does not have to match the type of the parameters.

Strings can be passed as parameters, but only without an explicit size. Strings with an explicit size can be passed as parameters, but doing so requires the concept of a "named data type," which we have yet to cover. So, this is legal:

```
function Bonus(category: string): real;
```

but this is not:

```
function Bonus(category: string[10]): real;
```

Parameters

A complete discussion of parameters is given in Chapter 4. However, a few comments are in order at this point.

The parameters for a function are called **value parameters**. This means that a value (such as 7, 3.0, or 'Hello there') comes into the function through the parameter. When the main program uses the function, the values of the function's arguments are calculated and placed into the parameter variables listed in the function's definition.

For the AreaFn function we just wrote, any of the following would be legal uses, assuming that all the variables are real and have assigned values.

```
Area := AreaFn(A, B, C)
Area := AreaFn(X, Y, Z)
Area := AreaFn(Side1, Side2, Side3)
Area := AreaFn(3.0, 4.0, 5.0)
Area := AreaFn(X + 3.5, Y / 17.2, (Z + W) / 3.2)
```

In each case, the first parameter is evaluated and the value is placed into the variable A within the function, the second evaluated and placed into B, and the third evaluated and placed into C.

We can summarize the use of parameters by a function as follows:

1. The program invoking the function must supply the correct number of parameters (three, in our example).

2. The values supplied must be of the proper type (*real*, in our example).

3. The values must have the proper meaning (the three sides of a triangle, in our example).
4. The parameter correspondence occurs by position, not by name. The names used can match those in the function (as in our first use given before), but they don't have to (as in all the other sample uses given).

How to Write a Function

There are five general steps involved in writing a function.

1. Decide That a Function is Appropriate. This step occurs as part of the design of the module that will use the function. A function is appropriate whenever there is a subtask that involves calculating one value. If the steps involved in the calculation are complex, then certainly a function is in order. Even if the steps are simple, however, using a function can make the main program easier to follow.

For example, the standard function Round is not necessary; rounding can be accomplished in a single step without using it. However, an assignment such as

```
NumberPerDay := Round(Total / NumberofDays)
```

is far easier to understand with the function than without it.

2. Determine Function Name and Result Type. We name our function with an identifier descriptive of what it calculates. The only restriction is that the name must be different from any other variable name, procedure name, or function name declared in the main program.

The result type is the type of the value the function calculates and returns. It can be *real*, *integer*, *char*, (unsized) *string*, or *boolean*.

3. Identify the Parameters. A function calculates a value as an answer. If we ask, "What is the answer based on?" we will be identifying the parameters. We choose a variable name for each of these parameters.

In choosing the variable names, we can use the same names that the main program uses for these quantities. This is allowed, but it is not necessary.

4. Write an Algorithm and Identify Local Variables. This is, in a sense, a segment of an algorithm. It contains only those steps needed to calculate the answer, based on the parameters. The algorithm should place the final answer into the identifier that is the function name.

To obtain the answer, additional variables may be required. These should be declared as local variables within the function.

5. Code the Algorithm. Steps 2 and 3 have identified all the information required for the header line. We declare any local variables identified during step 4, and write the body of the function implementing the algorithm of step 4.

Note. If an exercise reads, "Write a function to . . . ," then you should begin at step 2. The authors will already have accomplished step 1.

An Example. As an example of the function design process, we carry out steps 2 to 5 for the following problem. (This problem is essentially Exercise 12(c) of Section 2-6.)

Write a function to calculate a customer's bill for an order of some quantity of a single item. We assume there are only four items available, as shown:

ITEM NUMBER	UNIT PRICE
100	24.03
247	105.00
16	10.35
240	16.00

A discount is allowed for large orders: if the total bill is $1000.00 or over, a 2 percent discount is given; from $800 to $999.99, a 1 percent discount is given.

Step 2. Determine the function name and the result type. Because the bill is in dollars and cents, we use a real function, named BillFn.

Step 3. Identify the parameters. For a function, the parameters are the variables on which the answer depends. In this case, the bill depends on what the item is and on how many of the items are being purchased. We begin our variable list:

Value parameters:	ItemNumber	Integer	Item number purchased
	Quantity	Integer	Quantity purchased

Step 4. Write an algorithm and identify local variables. The algorithm contains three major steps: (1) calculate the price; (2) calculate the total cost before discount; and (3) deduct the discount, if applicable. A more refined algorithm follows, along with local variables to be added to the variable list. (We are assuming that ItemNumber and Quantity are valid. Perhaps they have been checked in the main program.)

Local variables:	Price	Real	Unit price of item
	TotalCost	Real	Total cost before discount

Algorithm:

1. Calculate Price, based on ItemNumber, as indicated in this table (use a *case* structure)

ITEM NUMBER	UNIT PRICE
100	24.03
247	105.00
16	10.35
240	16.00

2. Calculate TotalCost as Price times Quantity

3. Calculate BillFn by subtracting a discount based on TotalCost, as indicated in this table (use an *if-elseif* structure)

2-7 USER-DEFINED FUNCTIONS

```
function BillFn (ItemNumber, Quantity: integer): real;

{Written by: XXXXXXXX XX/XX/XX}
{Purpose:    To calculate the total bill based on item ordered and quantity.}
{Parameters: The first is the item number purchased,}
{            the second the quantity of that item which was purchased.}
{            Both are assumed to be correct.}

   var
     Price: real;              {price of item, from the table}
     TotalCost: real;          {total cost, before discount}

begin {BillFn}

   case ItemNumber of
     100:
       Price := 24.03;
     247:
       Price := 105.00;
     16:
       Price := 10.35;
     240:
       Price := 16.00
   end;

   TotalCost := Price * Quantity;
   if TotalCost >= 1000 then
      BillFn := TotalCost - 0.02 * TotalCost
   else if TotalCost >= 800 then
      BillFn := TotalCost - 0.01 * TotalCost
   else
      BillFn := TotalCost

end; {BillFn}
```

Figure 2-17 Another function.

TotalCost: 1000.00 or more	Subtract: 2% of TotalCost
800–999.99	1% of TotalCost
below 800	nothing

Step 5. Code the algorithm. We must write the header line, declare the local variables, and write the necessary steps for the body of the function. We have used blank lines to highlight the three major steps of the function. The solution appears as Figure 2-17.

DPT

In writing or using functions, beware of a few common misconceptions and language subtleties.

1. Functions are written to perform calculations. As a general rule, they contain no I/O statements. They obtain the values they use from the parameters, not from reading input. They do not print the answer, but rather send it back to the calling module.
2. Any variables used in the function should be one of these: a parameter, the function name, or a local variable. Local variables are declared and used strictly within the function. They have no effect outside the function.
3. Each module should declare only the variables it uses. For example, the main module should not declare the function's local variables.
4. For the answer to reach the **calling program** (the program that invokes the function), it must be placed into the function name variable.
5. The parameters as supplied by the calling program must match those in the function by type, number, and purpose. The names may or may not match. In fact, the supplied values can be constants or even complicated expressions.
6. The result type is the type of the calculated answer. It does not have to match the types of the parameters. (In fact, the parameters can be of several different types.)
7. Within the function, we should not use the function name in a condition or on the right side of an assignment statement. For example, consider the BillFn function written in this section. We wrote these lines:

```
TotalCost := Price * Quantity;
if TotalCost >= 1000 then
   BillFn := TotalCost - 0.02 * TotalCost
```

These similar lines are **incorrect**:

```
BillFn := Price * Quantity;
if BillFn >= 1000 then
   BillFn := BillFn - 0.02 * BillFn
```

The use of BillFn in the *if* statement and both uses on the right side of the assignment statement are treated as invocations of the BillFn function. This is not what we intended at all. Although the function name looks like any other variable name, it cannot be truly used as a variable. For now, only use the function name inside a function on the left side of the assignment statement. (In Chapter 4, we learn some other uses.)

If we make the error just described, the compiler will detect it; a call to BillFn is supposed to supply two parameters, and these do not.

REVIEW

Terms and Concepts
calling program
user-defined functions
value parameters

Parameters. Parameters (arguments) in the calling program must match those in the function as to number, type, and purpose. They may or may not match in name. Any expression of the proper type can be supplied as a parameter by the calling module.

Pascal Syntax

1. Function is declared after variable declarations and before the *begin* for the main program.
2. Header statement:

   `function` *function-name (parameter list): result type;*

3. Parameter list: one or more occurrences of the following separated by semicolons:

   list of variables separated by commas: type

Considerations for Using Functions

Writing a Function

1. Decide if a function is appropriate (for a subtask to calculate a value).
2. Choose a function name and determine the result type.
3. Identify and name the parameters.
4. Write an algorithm. (Might introduce local variables.)
5. Code as a Pascal function. Write the header line using the function name, parameter information, and result type. Declare local variables. Code the algorithm.

Invoking a Function

1. Include a function call, along with required parameters, in an expression. (This is usually in an assignment statement, but it can be in a condition or a call to Writeln.)
2. Supply expressions representing the supplied values for the parameters, using variables or constants of the calling module.

EXERCISES

1. Find the errors, if any, in the following function header lines.
   (a) `function` Max(A);
   (b) `function` Cube(A; B; C: integer): integer;
   (c) `function` Cube(A: integer): real;
   (d) `function` Maxtwo(A, B: real): integer;
   (e) `function` 2Times(A; integer, B: real): char
   (f) `function` XTimesY(X real, Y real);
   (g) `function` Salary(Years: integer; Department: string[8]): real;

2. Write function header lines for the following:
   (a) A real function XDivY with two real parameters X and Y.
   (b) An integer function Largest with three integer parameters A, B, and C.
   (c) A char function LetterGrade with an integer parameter Grade.
   (d) A real function Salary with parameters: Department(integer), Years(integer), Bonus(real), Rank(char), and NumberSupervised(integer).

3. Write a function to find the smaller of two real numbers.
4. Write a function to find the largest of three integer numbers.

5. Write a function to find the smallest of three integer numbers.
6. Write a function to calculate the total surface area of a cone. The formula is
$$A = \pi r \sqrt{r^2 + h^2} + \pi r^2$$
7. Write a function to determine the letter grade for a given numerical average. Use the 90–80–70–60 scale.
8. Write a function to calculate the final average based on the homework average, test average, and final exam percentage. If the homework average is 0.70 or higher, the final average is the higher of the test average and the final exam percentage. Otherwise the final average is the sum of 0.3 times the homework average, 0.4 times the test average, and 0.3 times the final exam.
9. (a) The vacation days per year are based on the employee type and years of experience as defined by the following rules: All type 'A' employees get 7 days and all type 'E' employees get 21 days. Type 'S' employees earn 10 days if they have 6 or fewer years of experience, otherwise 15 days. All other types get 0 days. Design a function to calculate the vacation days up to the point of Pascal coding.
   (b) Code the function.
10. (a) Write a function to find the larger of two integer numbers.
    (b) Use the function you wrote in part (a) in an assignment statement to accomplish this task: The variable Try should be given an initial value that is the larger of M and N.
    (c) Use the function you wrote in part (a) in an assignment statement to accomplish this task: The final grade for the course is to be the final exam grade or the average of the two midterm test grades, whichever is larger.
11. (a) Write a function Round2 with two parameters: a real number to be rounded and an integer telling the number of places. For example:
```
Round2(3.1416, 3) is 3.142
Round2(17.1498, 1) is 17.1
Round2(16.5, 0) is 17.0
```
    (b) Use the function you wrote in part (a) to calculate BasketsPerDay as Baskets divided by Days rounded to the nearest hundredth.
    (c) Repeat part (b), but round to the nearest whole number. What is the difference between this answer and the one supplied by the standard Round function?
    (d) Use the function of part (a) to find the average on three tests rounded to the nearest tenth.
12. Write functions for the situations described by each of the following exercises from Section 2-5. Note: If the situation calls for printing the answer, instead calculate that answer as the function value.
    (a) Exercise 4(c)
    (b) Exercise 4(e)
    (c) Exercise 5(a)
    (d) Exercise 5(c) (tax only)
    (e) Exercise 5(d)
13. In Section 2-6, you wrote some assignment statements and segments of code to assign values to Boolean variables. By choosing appropriate parameters, rewrite the following exercises from Section 2-6 as Boolean functions:
    (a) Exercise 3(a)
    (b) Exercise 3(b)

(c) Exercise 3(c)
(d) Exercise 3(h)
(e) Exercise 6(c)
(f) Exercise 6(d)
(g) Exercise 6(f)
(h) Exercise 6(g)
(i) Exercise 6(h)

14. For each of these exercises from Section 2-6, determine a portion of the program that might reasonably constitute a function. Then write a function to perform the identified calculation subtask.
    (a) Exercise 10(b)
    (b) Exercise 10(d)
    (c) Exercise 11(a)
    (d) Exercise 11(b)
    (e) Exercise 11(c)

15. The library functions Sin and Cos require the parameter values to be supplied in radians. Write functions called DegreeSin and DegreeCos that calculate their values for an angle given in degrees. (Degrees can be converted to radians by multiplying by $\pi/180$.)

16. Write a function Tan that calculates the tangent of an angle supplied in radians. (Watch for an error condition.)

2-8 MODULAR DESIGN AND TESTING

Testing

A program that contains subprograms raises some issues about the way in which we test the program. For example, with a main program and one procedure, there are four possibilities:

1. We could write the entire program, then start testing the whole program as a single unit.

2. We could make sure the main program works, separately make sure the procedure works, then put them together, and see if they work together.

3. We could make sure the main program works, then add the untested procedure, and make sure the package works.

4. We could make sure the procedure works, then add it to the untested main program, and make sure the package works.

Of course, with two subprograms the possibilities increase.

The third and fourth alternatives are examples of **incremental testing**. For programs containing large numbers of subprograms, incremental testing has been found to work better than the other two methods. The first method has the disadvantage that, when an error occurs, it can be difficult to determine which subprogram caused the error. The second method is an improvement, but it has been found that pieces that work perfectly well separately sometimes do not work well when combined. If we combine them all at once, it can be difficult to see which particular combinations are causing the problems.

Method 3 from the previous list is an example of **top–down testing**. The top level (main) module is tested first, then the lower level modules are added, one at a time, and the program is tested again. In this form of testing, so-called **stubs** are needed for the subprograms that have not yet been written and tested. We would test the main program with the stub versions of the subprograms. When we get this running properly, we would replace one of the stubs by the actual subprogram and perform more testing of the resulting program. This would be followed by replacing another stub by the actual subprogram and the program as a whole is tested again. This continues until the entire program has been tested.

Method 4 is an example of **bottom–up testing**. The lowest level modules are tested; when they are running correctly, the module that calls them is added and the combination is tested. This form of testing requires a **driver** main program, a substitute for the actual main program that is used to "drive" the subprograms that are being tested.

We will have more to say about incremental testing in general, and about top–down and bottom–up testing, in other testing sections later in the text. In the case study that follows, we illustrate simple instances of both top–down testing with stubs and bottom–up testing with drivers.

Case Study No. 3

This case study develops a complete program that uses a number of subprograms. It is a simplified payroll program. Part of the case study describes some strategies for testing a program that includes subprograms.

Statement of Problem. Write a program that calculates weekly pay and the amount of state tax to be withheld from the paycheck. The pay is the hourly rate times the number of hours, except that hours over 40 earn time and a half. The state tax is based on the following rules:

> First, $12 is deducted from the income for each dependent. Then the tax is determined by the following table:

RESULTING INCOME	TAX
Less than 0	0
$0–$300	2% of resulting income
Over $300	$15.00 plus 2.5% of the amount over $300

Preliminary Analysis. The problem is not well described because it does not specify the necessary input. We will have to discover what input will be required by analyzing the problem. It is clear that we need at least the hourly rate and the number of hours in order to calculate the weekly pay. The tax is based on the pay, which we calculate, and the number of dependents, another part of the input. Finally, we assume that the input will contain an integer clock number.

For output, we will print the clock number, weekly pay, and state tax withholding.

We will not do complete error checking on the input: that will be left to the exercises. However, we do check one possible error: hours less than 0. One final note: "Time and a half" means that if a person works over 40 hours, then the first 40 are paid at the normal rate and all other hours are paid at 1.5 times the normal rate.

Algorithm and Variable List

1. *Main Program.* For the main program, we have the following input and output variables, based on our analysis:

Constant:	EndOfData	Value 0	Used to terminate loop
Input:	ClockNumber	Integer	Employee clock number (also printed)
	HoursWorked	Real	Hours worked by employee
	HourlyRate	Real	Rate of pay per hour
	Dependents	Integer	Number of dependents
Output:	Pay	Real	Pay for week
	StateTax	Real	State tax withheld for week

The algorithm is quite similar to ones we have written before. (As we have been doing, we mark steps with an (*) to indicate they are not done for the terminating data.)

```
print instructions (use procedure Instructions)
repeat these steps until a clock number of 0 is entered:
    issue prompt for clock number
    read ClockNumber
    issue prompt for hours, rate, # dependents (*)
    read HoursWorked, HourlyRate, Dependents (*)
    if HoursWorked < 0 then (*)
       print an error message (including HoursWorked)
       set HoursWorked to 0
    calculate Pay (*)
    calculate StateTax (*)
    print ClockNumber, Pay, and StateTax (*)
```

We chose to use a procedure named Instructions for the subtask "print instructions." In addition, we write functions called PayFn and TaxFn for the "calculate Pay" and "calculate StateTax" subtasks. We refine those two steps as follows:

calculate Pay: `Pay := PayFn(HoursWorked, HourlyRate)`
calculate StateTax: `StateTax := TaxFn(Pay, Dependents)`

In doing so, we have supplied as parameters the values on which the calculations are based.

Note. Given in Figure 2-18 is a **hierarchy chart** for the program. This is a visual description of the fact that it contains four modules and that the main module calls the other three. Along with the diagram, we give a short description of what task each module performs.

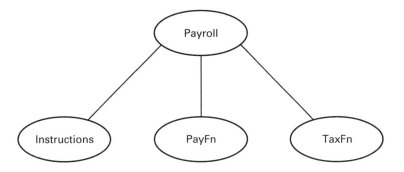

Main program (Payroll):	Reads data (some minor checking), calls functions, and prints answers in a loop
Instructions:	Procedure that prints instructions
PayFn:	Function that calculates weekly pay
TaxFn:	Function that calculates state tax withholding

Figure 2-18 Hierarchy chart.

---

2. *PayFn Function.* This completes the design for the main program. Next we design the PayFn function. We have already decided that it should be a real function with two parameters (hours and rate).

The basic algorithm was developed as a part of an earlier example, in Section 2-3 (page 72). That algorithm used the variables Hours and HourlyRate for the hours and rate, respectively. We will make use of the earlier work, so we choose to use these variable names for our parameters.

Note. One of these variable names happens to match the name used in the main program and the other does not. This is perfectly acceptable. One of the reasons for this flexibility in naming parameters is to make it easy to use previous work on the same or similar problems.

That algorithm also contained two other variables, which will become local variables for the function. We obtain this variable list and algorithm:

Value parameters:	Hours	Real	Hours worked
	HourlyRate	Real	Hourly pay rate
Local variables:	RegularPay	Real	Pay for first 40 hours
	OvertimePay	Real	Pay for overtime hours

Algorithm:

    if Hours > 40 then do these steps:
       calculate RegularPay (formula 40 * HourlyRate)
       calculate OvertimePay (formula (Hours − 40) * HourlyRate * 1.5)

2-8 MODULAR DESIGN AND TESTING

```
    calculate PayFn as RegularPay + OvertimePay
otherwise do this step:
    calculate PayFn as Hours * HourlyRate
```

3. *TaxFn Function.* We now design the TaxFn function. It is a real function with parameters representing the pay (a real quantity) and the number of dependents (an integer quantity). We choose names that match those in the main program. In addition to the parameters, we need a local variable for the taxable income.

Value parameters:	Pay	Real	Week's pay
	Dependents	Integer	Number of Dependents
Local variables:	TaxableIncome	Real	Taxable income

The algorithm, based on the verbal description, is

```
    calculate TaxableIncome
    calculate TaxFn based on TaxableIncome, using this table (use an if-elseif structure)
```

RESULTING INCOME	TAX
Less than 0	0
$0–$300	2% of resulting income
Over $300	$15.00 plus 2.5% of the amount over $300

Note. You might wonder about the use of the local variable TaxableIncome. Could we not just modify the parameter Pay, then use that in our TaxFn calculation? The answer is yes. However, this relies on the fact that for value parameters, Pascal is designed so that the Pay variable in the main program is not modified. Value parameters behave much like local variables. There are languages that do not provide this protection. In such languages, the use of the local variable would be mandatory. It is good defensive programming not to change a value parameter.

However, in this situation, we should use the local variable in any case. In general, it is a good design practice to use different variables where different quantities are being handled. "Pay" is the weekly pay and "TaxableIncome" is the portion that is taxable. These are not the same concepts, so we should use two different variables.

---

4. *Instructions Procedure.* We leave the plan for the Instructions procedure to the reader.

Note. In working with subprograms, what we just did was typical. We developed and presented each module's plan as a separate piece, starting with the main program and working our way to the subprograms. This is part of what is meant by **top–down design**.

Test Plan. We now develop the test plan. This consists of two parts: a planned order to write and test the modules and a set of test data for each module. We choose this order: PayFn, TaxFn, main program, and Instructions. Notice that this is "bottom–up" in the sense that PayFn and TaxFn are developed before the main program that uses them. On the other hand, it is "top–down" in the sense that the main program is developed before its procedure Instructions. Quite frequently in large projects, a mixture of the two methods is used.

When we write a test plan for each separate module, this is sometimes referred to as **unit testing.** We will outline a plan for each module.

Note (On Testing Philosophy). In this case study, we present an "idealized" approach to the joint process of testing and program development. This means that, under ideal circumstances, we should follow guidelines similar to those presented here. But what if circumstances are not ideal? If we do not "have time" to do the thorough testing required, shall we just forget about testing altogether? The answer is no. In testing programs (as in most human endeavors), the choice is not really all or nothing. Even if our test plan is not perfect, any test plan is better than none at all.

There are, of course, risks in taking shortcuts. If at all possible, we should do a thorough testing. If we must skimp, we should try to do the most critical tests in any case. (In general, boundary tests are probably the most critical.)

With the preceding discussion in mind, we now develop our unit test plans.

Main: Branches and borderlines on bad vs. good hours:

hours = –0.1   hours = –5
hours = 0   hours = 30
hours = 0.1

Note. There are other possible "bad data" situations, which will be explored in the exercises. (In testing the main program, we will repeat some of the branch tests that we have done for the pay and tax functions.)

PayFn: Branches and borderlines on hours:

hours = 39.9   hours = 25
hours = 40.0   hours = 50
hours = 40.1

TaxFn: Branches and borderlines on number of dependents:

dependents = 0   # dependents = 5
dependents = 1

2-8 MODULAR DESIGN AND TESTING

Branches and borderlines on taxable income: For each test, we show the desired taxable income. Because the taxable income depends on the pay and the number of dependents, we also indicate how we plan to achieve the desired taxable income. Notice that we use a variety of values for the number of dependents.

tax. inc. = −1	(pay 23 #dep 2)
tax. inc. = 0	(pay 12 #dep 1)
tax. inc. = 1	(pay 1 #dep 0)
tax. inc. = 299	(pay 299 #dep 0)
tax. inc. = 300	(pay 360 #dep 5)
tax. inc. = 301	(pay 337 #dep 3)
tax. inc. = −50	(pay 10 #dep 5)
tax. inc. = 100	(pay 148 #dep 4)
tax. inc. = 400	(pay 400 #dep 0)

Note. We have chosen to test our borderlines 1 dollar below and above rather than 1 cent below and above. At a 2 percent tax rate, a 1 cent difference in income would lead to only a very small change in the tax.

In doing the actual testing, we found that a taxable income of 301 yielded an answer of 15.02 when printed with two decimal places. It was not clear that the 2.5 percent rate was being used correctly, so we immediately tried a taxable income of 302, which yielded the correct answer of 15.05.

Instructions: Since the design of the Instructions procedure has been left to the exercises, we also leave the details of the test plan to the exercises. It should include tests of branches based on whether instructions are wanted.

Write Program. We write the program in the order indicated in our test plan. We begin with the PayFn function. In order to test the function, we need a driver main program. This is a temporary main program written for the sole purpose of testing the function. Because it is temporary, we do not include many comments or complicated instructions, and we use shorter-than-usual variable names.

Note. For large projects, or for programs that are expected to be in service for a long period, drivers and stubs are often kept as part of the program's documentation. They serve as a record of what testing was done, and are used to retest the program's modules if changes need to be made to them. In these situations, the drivers and stubs are written with complete comments, instructions, and mnemonic variable names.

The function, along with a possible driver, is given in Figure 2-19.

```
program DriverforPayFn;

  const
    EndOfData = -1;

  var
    Hours: real;
    Rate: real;
    Pay: real;

  function PayFn (Hours, HourlyRate: real): real;

    {Written by: XXXXXXXX, XX/XX/XX}
    {Purpose:    To calculate the pay for one person}
    {Parameters: The first is the number of hours the person worked.}
    {            The second is the hourly rate of pay. Both are assumed}
    {            valid.}

    var
      RegularPay: real;        {pay for first 40 hours}
      OvertimePay: real;       {pay for hours over 40}

  begin {PayFn}
    if Hours > 40 then
        begin
           RegularPay := 40 * HourlyRate;
           OvertimePay := (Hours - 40) * HourlyRate * 1.5;
           PayFn := RegularPay + OvertimePay
        end
    else
        PayFn := Hours * HourlyRate
  end; {PayFn}

begin {Driver}
 repeat
   Writeln;
   Write('Enter hours and rate (-1 to quit) : ');
   Readln(Hours, Rate);
   if Hours <> EndOfData then
       begin
         Pay := PayFn(Hours, Rate);
         Writeln('Hours = ', Hours : 2 : 2, ' Rate = ', Rate : 2 : 2,
'Pay = ', Pay : [2 : 2]);
       end
   until Hours = EndOfData
end.
```

Figure 2-19 Driver program for a function (continues next page).

2-8 MODULAR DESIGN AND TESTING

SAMPLE INPUT AND OUTPUT

```
Enter hours and rate (-1 to quit) : 34 5.67
Hours = 34.00 Rate = 5.67 Pay = 192.78

Enter hours and rate (-1 to quit) : 45 6.04
Hours = 45.00 Rate = 6.04 Pay = 286.90

Enter hours and rate (-1 to quit) -1 0
```

Figure 2-19   (continued)

We test the PayFn function by running the Driver program. If there are any errors in the function, we correct them, and test PayFn again. We continue in this way until PayFn seems correct, then proceed to the next step.

In the next step, we do exactly the same thing for the TaxFn function. The details are left as an exercise.

We are now ready to write the main program. We do so, inserting the already tested functions in the proper spot. (We should not retype the functions; rather, we should use our system's editor to load them into the proper place in the program. This approach is faster than retyping the functions and avoids typing errors that could cause bugs.)

We test the main program together with the two functions we have already written and tested. However, notice that the main program also calls for a procedure that has not been written. In order to test the main program, we write a stub for the Instructions procedure. This stub can be very simple; for example,

```
procedure Instructions;
begin
   Writeln('Instructions procedure successfully called')
end;
```

When we run the main program, this message will be printed prior to entering the loop. The actual procedure is added later. Figure 2-20 contains the program we tested at this point with the actual functions and the stub procedure.

The final steps are to replace the stub by the actual Instructions procedure and run our tests for this procedure. At this point, we have a complete program. We would probably do some more testing, similar to some that we did for the individual pieces, to try to make sure that the program as a whole is working as it should.

Modifications.   One of the advantages of modularity is that it makes modifications easier. For example, we develop some additions to the program in the next chapter that do not affect any of the subprograms, so they do not have to be retested. As another example, if we modified the pay function, only this function and the program as a whole would have to be retested.

The exercises suggest some modifications to the case study.

```
program Payroll;

{Written by: XXXXXXXX XX/XX/XX}
{Purpose: To calculate pay and state tax for a number of employees.}
{         The input consists of a clock number, the number of hours worked,}
{         the hourly rate, and the number of dependents}

{Procedures used : Instructions, to print instructions for user}

{Functions used:  PayFn, to calculate the pay based on hours and rate}
{                 TaxFn, to calculate the tax based on the pay and the}
{                        number of dependents}

  const
    EndOfData = 0;                 {terminating data indicator}

  var
    ClockNumber: integer;    {employee clock number, input}
    HoursWorked: real;       {hours worked, input}
    HourlyRate: real;        {rate of pay, input}
    Dependents: integer;     {number of dependents, input}
    Pay: real;               {pay for week, output}
    StateTax: real;          {state tax, output}

  procedure Instructions;

  begin {Instructions (stub version)}
    Writeln('Instructions procedure successfully called')
  end; {Instructions}

{Function PayFn as shown in Figure 2-19 is inserted here}

  function TaxFn (Pay: real; Dependents: integer): real;

    {Written by: XXXXXXXX, XX/XX/XX}
    {Purpose:    To calculate the tax for one person.}
    {Parameters: The first is the person's pay for the week.}
    {            The second is the number of dependents. Both are}
    {            assumed to be valid.}

    var
      TaxablePay: real;    {portion of pay used for taxing}

  begin {TaxFn}
    TaxablePay := Pay - 12 * Dependents;
    if TaxablePay < 0 then
      TaxFn := 0
    else if TaxablePay < 300 then
      TaxFn := 0.02 * TaxablePay
    else
      TaxFn := 15 + 0.025 * (TaxablePay - 300)
  end; {TaxFn}
```

Figure 2-20 Payroll program (continues next page).

```
begin {Payroll}

{*** Before the loop, print instructions}

  Instructions;

{* * * In loop, obtain clock number, hours, rate, and number of dependents.}
{      Check for dummy value. Check for invalid hours. Calculate and print}
{      pay and tax.}

  repeat
    Writeln;
    Write('Enter clock number for next employee: ');
    Readln(ClockNumber);
    if ClockNumber > EndOfData then
      begin
        Write('Now enter the hours, rate, and number of dependents: ');
        Readln(HoursWorked, HourlyRate, Dependents);
        if HoursWorked < 0 then
          begin
            Writeln(HoursWorked, ' is invalid; changed to 0.');
            HoursWorked := 0
          end;
        Pay := PayFn(HoursWorked, HourlyRate);
        StateTax := TaxFn(Pay, Dependents);
        Writeln(ClockNumber, ' earned ', Pay : 2 : 2, ' and was taxed ',
                StateTax : 2 : 2)
      end
    until ClockNumber <= EndOfData;

{*** Stop}

end.
```

SAMPLE INPUT AND OUTPUT

```
Instructions procedure successfully called

Enter clock number for next employee: 345
Now enter the hours, rate, and number of dependents: 34 5.67 8
345 earned 192.78 and was taxed 1.94

Enter clock number for next employee: 101
Now enter the hours, rate, and number of dependents: 44 6.78 3
101 earned 311.88 and was taxed 5.52

Enter clock number for next employee: 0
```

Figure 2-20 (continued)

REVIEW

Terms and Concepts

bottom–up testing
driver
hierarchy chart
incremental testing
stubs
top–down design
top–down testing
unit testing

Testing

1. Use an incremental approach (top–down, bottom–up, or a mixture).
2. Develop a unit test plan for each module.
3. Use drivers and stubs where needed.

EXERCISES

1. Rewrite the following programs from Section 2-6, using a function for an appropriate calculation subtask. (You will have to identify an appropriate subtask to be placed into a function.)
   (a) Exercise 10(d)
   (b) Exercise 11(a)
   (c) Exercise 11(b)
   (d) Exercise 11(c)

2. Write unit test plans for the functions you identified in Exercise 1.

3. Describe a unit test plan for these exercises in Section 2-7.
   (a) Exercise 3
   (b) Exercise 4
   (c) Exercise 5
   (d) Exercise 7
   (e) Exercise 9
   (f) Exercise 11

4. Write a driver program and test each function referred to in Exercise 3 using your test plan devised in that exercise.

5. Modify Case Study No. 1 (Section 1-4) to calculate and print the letter grade for each student. Use a function that you write and test prior to inserting it into the case study program. Test the revised program.

6. Write a complete program, modeled after Case Study No. 2, to accomplish the following. It should read a real number, a one-digit integer number, and a code for the operation to be performed. (The real number is of the form xxx.yyy.) It should use functions where appropriate. The valid operations

P (part):	123.456	P	1	is	123
	123.456	P	2	is	456
D (digit):	617.354	D	2	is	1
	617.354	D	6	is	4

R (rotate):	123.456	R	1	is	612345
	123.456	R	−1	is	234561
	123.456	R	0	is	123456
S (split and add):	123.456	S	1	is	1 + 2 + 3 + 4 + 5 + 6 = 21
	123.456	S	2	is	12 + 34 + 56
	123.456	S	3	is	123 + 456

The integer number is in these ranges: 1 to 2 for 'P', 1 to 6 for 'D', −1 to 1 for 'R', and 1 to 3 for 'S'. In each case, the answer is 0 if the integer number is not in the proper range.

7. Write a complete program to calculate wages and state taxes for a number of employees. Input consists of name, clock number, marital status, number of dependents, and job code. Wages are based on department and job code. If we let Department be the first digit of the four-digit clock number, the wages are as indicated in the following table (any entry not appearing indicates an error):

| Department = 1 | | Department = 2 | | Department = 3 | | Department = 4 | |
Job	Wages	Job	Wages	Job	Wages	Job	Wages
A	157.00	A	345.00	A	264.00	A	130.00
B	171.00	B	415.00	B	289.00	B	175.00
C	306.00	Any	653.00	C	315.00	C	210.00
D	339.00	Other		D	347.00	Any	239.00
				E	389.00	Other	

State taxes are based on the description given in Exercise 5(c) of Section 2-5.

Exercises 8 to 14 refer to Case Study No. 3.

8. Write an algorithm and a test plan for the Instructions procedure. The person should be able to get instructions by either entering a lowercase or a capital Y.
9. Write a driver program for the TaxFn function. Run the driver program with the function to test the function.
10. Modify the PayFn function to allow "double time" for all hours in excess of 50. Write a revised test plan.
11. Modify the TaxFn function to deduct 10 percent of the original income from the taxable income prior to calculating the tax. Write a revised test plan.
12. Think of some other possible input errors, and modify the main program to check for them. Note: Some errors violate "reasonableness" standards. For example, an hourly wage of $1,000 would be unreasonable.
13. Modify both functions to use named constants (*const* declarations). What are the advantages of this? Are there any disadvantages?
14. Add code to create a printed report. Before the loop, print some column headings. Then, for each employee, print (in columns) the clock number, hours worked, hourly rate, dependents, pay, and state tax.

3 Using Loops

OBJECTIVES

The primary topic of this chapter is loops. It also provides more detail in areas of program design and testing, espceially as they apply to loops. After completing this chapter, you will be able to:

- use loops to accomplish common programming tasks
- employ the *while-do* and *for-do* loops effectively
- generate pseudorandom numbers
- become familiar with the elementary aspects of arrays
- control loop termination using more complex conditions
- add to your knowledge of antibugging, debugging and testing techniques

3-1 COMMON APPLICATIONS OF LOOPS

Loop Planning

We discuss loop planning in detail throughout this chapter. However, before we begin this section's major topic (some common loop applications), let us give a brief overview of the loop-planning process.

We may view a loop as consisting of two components. First, we have the actual steps that we wish to perform repeatedly. This is frequently referred to as the **body** of the loop. For example, the bodies of the loops we have written up to this point have generally contained three major steps:

1. read data values
2. calculate an answer, and
3. write a line of output.

The second component of a loop is the **loop control.** Whenever we write a loop in a program, we must incorporate some way to **terminate** (or exit from) the loop. The loop control consists of the portion that causes the steps of the loop to be performed the proper number of times. In our sample programs so far, the loop control has been of a type we might call "direct user control." The steps in the loop were repeated until the user indicated, by entering a terminal data value, that there were no more data to be read. There are many other possible types of loop control, which we study in later sections of this chapter. For now, we continue to use the "terminal data value" loop control used in earlier examples.

In addition to the body and the loop control, there can be other steps closely related to the loop. These steps occur either before or after the loop. For example, many applications of loops require steps, called **initialization** steps, to be performed before the loop begins. For example, programs that accumulate totals generally must initialize the variable containing the total to zero before the loop. Many other problems require variables to be initialized. Similarly, after the loop, we may need steps that use the information gathered or calculated in the loop. For example, many times we print totals after a loop has finished summing up a set of values.

In this section, we present three common applications of program loops. These are **counting** how many times some condition occurs as the loop executes; **accumulating** the total of some set of values; and **finding** either the **largest** (maximum) or **smallest** (minimum) of some set of values. In each case, we concentrate on three major issues:

1. The initialization steps required
2. The steps that should be part of the loop body
3. The steps to be performed following the loop body

Note. Counting, accumulating, and finding largest or smallest are tasks that can appear in a wide variety of programs. In order to concentrate our attention on these three tasks, we present them in a context where the program consists of reading some values, calculating some answers, and then printing them. We examine the steps that must be added to these examples in order to count, to accumulate, or to find the largest or smallest.

Counting

Consider the following problem. A program is to read a series of nonzero integers. The end of the input is indicated by a terminal value of 0. For each number, except the 0, the program is to print a message telling whether the number is even or odd. Pascal provides a Boolean function "Odd(n)" that is *true* if n is odd and *false* if n is even. The following fragment shows the main loop of the program (EndOfData is the constant 0):

```
repeat
   write('Enter number (0 to quit): ');
   Readln(Number);
```

```
        if Number <> EndOfData then
            if Odd(Number) then
                Writeln(Number:5, ' is odd.')
            else
                Writeln(Number:5, ' is even.')
    until Number = EndOfData
```

We would like to modify this example so that our program prints the number of even values at the end of the loop. Generally, we need to keep four points in mind when writing a program involving counting:

1. A **counter**, a variable to contain the count value, is needed. It should normally be an integer variable.
2. This variable must be initialized to 0 before starting the count.
3. Whenever the condition to be counted is reached, one must be added to the counter variable.
4. After leaving the loop (or the part where the counting occurs), the counter is used in some way, perhaps by printing it.

For our specific example, we use an integer variable, EvenCounter, as our counter variable. The modified program fragment is shown in Figure 3-1. The changes are in italics. Notice that the changes correspond to the considerations listed previously. (Notice, also, that the "even" branch of the *if-then* now contains two steps. We therefore use a *begin* and *end* to group these into one compound statement .)

Note. In the following example, we use the term **record**, which, as used here, is related to files. In an employee file, for example, the information about one employee is called a record. It would contain the name, social security number, and other information for that employee. We use record here to signify the collection of data about one entity, usually one person. The user can supply this data through a single Readln or through several Readlns. This use of the term "record" occurs throughout this section and later in the text.

```
    EvenCounter := 0;
    repeat
      Write('Enter number (0 to quit): ');
      Readln(Number);
      if Number <> EndOfData then
          if Odd(Number) then
              Writeln(Number:5, ' is odd.')
          else
            begin
                Writeln(Number:5, ' is even.');
                EvenCounter := EvenCounter + 1
            end
    until Number = EndOfData;

    Writeln('There were ', EvenCounter, ' even numbers.')
```

Figure 3-1 Counting.

3-1 COMMON APPLICATIONS OF LOOPS

```
  OldCounter := 0;
  TotalCounter := 0;
  repeat
    Write('Enter I.D. and age (age 0 to quit): ');
    Readln(IDNumber, Age);
    if Age <> EndOfData then
       begin
          TotalCounter := TotalCounter + 1;
         if Age >= 30 then
             OldCounter := OldCounter + 1
       end
  until Age = EndOfData;
  Percent := (OldCounter / TotalCounter) * 100;
  Writeln;
  Writeln(Percent:1:2, '% age 30 or over.')
```

Figure 3-2   Two counters.

It is possible, of course, to have a program that does no processing other than the counting, as illustrated in the next example:

Each record contains an identification number and an age. Write a program to determine what percentage of the people represented are age 30 or older.

Here we need two counters because, to calculate the percentage, we must determine how many are 30 or older and also how many there are all together.

Here is the resulting variable list.

Input:	IDNumber	Integer	Identification number
	Age	Integer	Age
Other:	OldCounter	Integer	Number age 30 or older (a counter)
	TotalCounter	Integer	Number all together (a counter)
	Percent	Real	Percent 30 or older

Once again, we must initialize both counters at 0 before entering the loop that reads data and does the counting. Each time through the loop, add 1 to the OldCounter variable if the Age is 30 or above. This is similar to the previous example. Also add 1 to TotalCounter for every employee entered, regardless of age. After the loop, use the counters to calculate Percent, then print the answer. The program segment appears in Figure 3-2 with the counting steps in italics.

Notice the step that calculates the percentage:

```
  Percent := (OldCounter / TotalCounter) * 100
```

Notice that real division (/) is used. Integer division (div) would not work because we would always obtain a result of zero. Also notice the program assumes that TotalCounter is not 0. Probably for this problem that is a reasonable assumption; however, there are instances where a count of 0 is quite possible, and in those instances, we would want to guard against the possibility of dividing by 0.

Accumulation

Now consider the accumulation process, which finds the total of all the values in a list. For example, we may have a file with employee number and net pay and want to write a program to determine the total payroll for a pay period. Or we may have a list of names and test scores and wish to determine the average score on a test. (To find the average, we would add all the scores and divide by the number of students.)

The procedures used in accumulation are similar to those used in counting. First, we need a variable, called an **accumulator**, to keep track of the running total. The required steps before, during, and after the loop are as follows:

1. Before the loop, initialize the accumulator to 0.
2. In the loop, add the appropriate value to the accumulator. (As in the case of counting, this step can be conditional.)
3. After the loop, use the total. Either print the total obtained or use it in further calculations (such as in obtaining an average).

These steps are analogous to what happens in a cash register at a grocery store checkout. In the cash register, the accumulator is usually a piece of hardware within the machine. With each new grocery item, its price is added to the total. In this way, the accumulator maintains a running total. At any point in the process, it contains the total up to that point (the subtotal). When all the items have been processed, it contains the final total.

Now let us write a program to print a list of salespeople and to determine the total sales during the week. Assume that each set of inputs contains a salesperson number, a department number, a basic commission rate, and a sales amount for the week.

This is a typical accumulation problem. We wish to accumulate, or add, the week's sales amount for all employees. Because we are accumulating real quantities, the accumulator is real. The program initializes the accumulator to 0 prior to entering the loop, adds each sales amount to it in the body of the loop, and prints the answer after the loop. In addition to the accumulator, we need variables for the quantities represented in the input.

Input:	IDNumber	Integer	Salesperson number
	Department	Integer	Department number
	Rate	Real	Commission rate
	Sales	Real	Sales for week
Other:	TotalSales	Real	Total sales for week (printed at end)

The program segment merely incorporates what we have already decided should be done before, in, and after the loop. The loop is controlled by the user entering a terminal data value. See Figure 3-3, where the accumulation steps are in italics.

Notes

1. This program fragment uses the THINK feature Writeln(Report, . . .), introduced in Chapter 2, to print on the printer.

2. The Header procedure invoked at the beginning contains a series of Writeln(Report, ...) statements to print column headings at the top of the page.

Suppose that we now consider a slightly more complicated problem. In addition to the accumulation, we perform other processing in the loop, and not every record is included in the total. For the same set of input used in the previous example, this time we want to write a program to print a report of commissions earned and to find the average commission earned by department 100.

In this problem, we again need an accumulator, this time used to calculate the total commission department 100 earned. We also need a counter to count the people in department 100. As before, we initialize both the counter and the accumulator to 0 before the loop. After the loop, we use these values to calculate the average. In doing the counting and accumulating, we include only those in department 100. However, we do calculate the commission for each person, regardless of department number.

Let us use a function CommFn to calculate the commission, and assume that the commission is based on the commission rate and the sales amount. Then the step to calculate the commission can be refined as

```
Commission := CommFn(Rate, Sales)
```

Figure 3-4 shows a main program that contains stubs for its three subprograms (two procedures and a function). This version can be used to perform preliminary testing of the main program. The submodules can be added one at a time.

```
Header;
TotalSales := 0;
repeat
   Write('Enter salesperson number (0 to quit): ');
   Readln(IDNumber);
   if IDNumber <> EndOfData then
      begin
         Write('Now enter department, rate, sales: ');
         Readln(Department, Rate, Sales);
         Writeln(Report, IDNumber : 10, ' ' : 7, Department : 5, ' ' : 7,
               Rate : 5 : 3, ' ' : 7, Sales : 9 : 2);
         TotalSales := TotalSales + Sales
      end
until IDNumber = EndOfData;

Writeln;
Writeln('Total Sales is ', TotalSales : 3 : 2);
Writeln(Report);
Writeln(Report, 'Total sales is ', TotalSales : 3 : 2)
```

Figure 3-3 Accumulation

```
program Commissions;

{Written by: XXXXXXXX XX/XX/XX}
{Purpose:     To calculate and print a commission report;}
{             included is a summary for department 100 personnel}
{Procedures used: Header, to print headings}
{                 PrintLine, to print a detail line}
{Functions used:  CommFn, to calculate commission}

  const
    EndOfData = 0;                  {used to terminate loop}

  var
    IDNumber: integer;              {salesperson number, input}
    Department: integer;            {department number, input}
    Rate: real;                     {commission rate, input}
    Sales: real;                    {sales for week, input}
    Commission: real;               {commission for week}
    TotalComm: real;                {total for dept 100}
    CountDept100: integer;          {count of dept 100}
    Average: real;                  {average for dept 100}
    Report: text;                   {name for the printer}

  procedure Header;

  begin {Header, stub version}
    Writeln(Report, 'Header routine output')
  end; {Header}

  procedure PrintLine (ID, Dept: integer; Rate, Sales, Comm: real);

  begin {PrintLine, stub version}
    Writeln(Report, ID : 5, Dept : 5, Rate : 10 : 2, Sales : 10 : 2,
            Comm : 10 : 2)
  end; {PrintLine}

  function CommFn (Rate, Sales: real): real;
  begin {CommFn, stub version}
    Writeln('CommFn entered with rate = ', Rate : 5 : 2, ' sales = ',
            Sales : 1 : 2);
    CommFn := 150
  end; {CommFn}

begin {Commissions}
{*** Set up printer file, Print headings, and initialize count and total}
  rewrite(Report, 'Printer:');
  Header;
  TotalComm := 0;
  CountDept100 := 0;
```

Figure 3-4 Accumulation with a function (continues next page).

```
{*** Read data, calculate commission, adjust count and total}
  repeat
    Write('Enter salesperson number (0 to quit): ');
    Readln(IDNumber);
    if IDNumber <> EndOfData then
      begin
        Write('Now enter department, rate, sales: ');
        Readln(Department, Rate, Sales);
        Commission := CommFn(Rate, Sales);
        PrintLine(IDNumber, Department, Rate, Sales, Commission);
        if Department = 100 then
          begin
            TotalComm := TotalComm + Commission;
            CountDept100 := CountDept100 + 1
          end
      end
  until IDNumber = EndOfData;
{*** Calculate and print average commission}
  if CountDept100 = 0 then
    Writeln(Report, 'No one in department 100')
  else
    begin
      Average := TotalComm / CountDept100;
      Writeln;
      Writeln(Report, 'Average commission for department 100 is ',
              Average : 1 : 2)
    end;
end. {Commissions}
```

SAMPLE INPUT AND OUTPUT

On the terminal:

```
Enter salesperson number (0 to quit): 56
Now enter department, rate, sales: 100 .05 250
CommFn entered with rate = 0.05 sales = 250.00
Enter salesperson number (0 to quit): 34
Now enter department, rate, sales: 99 0.125 1000.10
CommFn entered with rate = 0.13 sales = 1000.10
Enter salesperson number (0 to quit): 0
```

On the printer:

```
Header routine output
56    100    0.05    250.00    150.00
39     99    0.13   1000.10    150.00
Average commission for department 100 is 150.00
```

Figure 3-4   (continued)

Now let us plan the function CommFn. We have already named it and established that its parameters are the commission rate and the sales amount. We have this variable list:

Value parameters:	Rate	Real	Commission rate
	Sales	Real	Sales amount

Suppose the commission is simply rate times sales if sales is less than $250, otherwise it is 1.2 times rate times sales. Then the function is easy to write:

```
function CommFn(Rate, Sales: real): real;

{Written by: XXXXXXXXXXXX XX/XX/XX}
{Purpose:    To calculate one person's commission}
{Parameters: Rate  - the commission rate, real}
{            Sales - the amount of the sales, real}

begin {CommFn}
  if Sales < 250 then
     CommFn := Rate * Sales
  else
     CommFn := 1.2 * Rate * Sales
end; {CommFn}
```

This would go in place of the stub version. The other modules are left to the reader.

To summarize, with a problem involving accumulation, a special accumulator variable is needed. Before the loop, initialize the accumulator to 0; in the loop, add to the accumulator, if appropriate; after the loop, either print the total or use the result.

Largest and Smallest

We now discuss using a loop to determine the largest of a set of values. As a simple example, not directly related to the computer, consider the following problem.

You (as a person) are given a large stack of cards, each containing a number. You are asked to determine the largest number on any of the cards. You are told that the numbers could be positive, negative, or zero. How would you solve this problem?

Before reading on, stop a moment and consider exactly how you would find the largest number if someone handed you such a deck of cards and you had to sequence through the deck one card at a time. Try to be as detailed as you can in describing your solution.

There are a number of possible solutions to this problem. Perhaps your solution was similar to the following: "Pick up the first card in my left hand. Then repeatedly pick up one card in my right hand until I run out of cards; anytime that the card in my right hand is larger than the one in my left hand, I will replace the card in my left hand. At the end, the card in my left hand will be the one with the largest number on it."

If your algorithm was similar to this one, you have described a method for using a loop to determine the largest item in a list. We know a loop is involved because you will repeat the steps of picking up a card and perhaps replacing the card in your left hand. You are using your left hand as a storage location for the largest value encountered so far and your right hand as a storage location for each of the other cards in succession. Before the loop, when you pick up the first card in your left hand, you are giving an initial (default) value to the largest value; if no other cards have a larger value, then at the end, this one is the largest.

It might be helpful to write this algorithm in the slightly more formal style we have been using for our other algorithms.

> Large is assigned the first value
> repeat the following until there are no more values
>   Next is assigned the next value
>   if Next > Large then
>   change Large to the value of Next
> print Large

This is a form of algorithm that we can use whenever we wish to find the largest using a loop.

As an example, consider a set of inputs that contains a name and a yearly salary. The program in Figure 3-5 determines the largest yearly salary. It is based on a specific instance of the general algorithm used before to describe how to find the largest number by hand. Observe how similar the process of finding the largest is to that of counting or accumulating. All three processes involve these properties:

1. A special variable is used to obtain the summary information (count, or total, or largest value).
2. This variable is initialized prior to the loop.
3. In the loop, this variable is modified based on the values read, perhaps involving comparisons of various types.
4. After the loop, the summary value is either printed or used to determine other values of interest (for example, an average).

In finding the largest of a set of values, there are two distinct approaches to initializing the variable that will store the largest value. The first is illustrated by the example in Figure 3-5. LargeSalary's initial value is the first person's salary.

Another possible approach is to give this variable a small initial value. Consider this simplified fragment.

```
Large := 0;
repeat
  Readln(Number);
  if Number > 0 then
     begin
        if Number > Large then
           Large := Number
     end
until Number <= 0;
Writeln(Large)
```

We are reading a collection of positive values. Hence, in finding the largest, an initial value of 0 is appropriate. The first number is larger and replaces Large.

```
program FindLargest;

{Written by: XXXXXXXX XX/XX/XX}
{Purpose:    To demonstrate the process of finding the largest.}
{            The program reads a series of names and salaries, and finds}
{            the largest salary.}
{Procedures used: Instructions, to print instructions for use}
  const
    EndOfData = '';   {null string terminates program}
  var
    Name: string;           {employee name, input}
    Salary: real;           {salary, input}
    LargeSalary: real;      {largest salary, calculated}
  procedure Instructions;
  begin
    {stub}
  end;
begin {FindLargest}
{*** Print instructions and initialize using first data}
  Instructions;
  Writeln;
  Write('Enter first person''s name: ');
  Readln(Name);
  Write('Enter first salary: ');
  Readln(Salary);

  LargeSalary := Salary;

{*** Repeatedly obtain name and salary. Check each salary against the}
{    largest so far, changing LargeSalary when appropriate}
  repeat
    Writeln;
    Write('Enter next name (tap RETURN to quit): ');
    Readln(Name);
    if Name <> EndOfData then
      begin
        Write('Enter next salary: ');
        Readln(Salary);
        if Salary > LargeSalary then
          LargeSalary := Salary
      end
  until Name = EndOfData;
{*** Print largest salary}
  Writeln;
  Writeln('The largest salary found was ', LargeSalary : 1 : 2)
end.
```

Figure 3-5 Finding the largest value (continues next page).

SAMPLE INPUT AND OUTPUT

```
Enter first person's name: Joe Robertson
Enter first salary: 13000

Enter next name (tap RETURN to quit): Sue Johnson
Enter next salary: 12903

Enter next name (tap RETURN to quit): Sara Michaels
Enter next salary: 17045

Enter next name (tap RETURN to quit):
The largest salary found was 17045.00
```

Figure 3-5   Finding the largest value.

Note.   Giving Large an initial value of 0 works only because the first number read is larger than 0. When working with negative numbers, use a different initial value.

The general rule for determining an appropriate initial value will be based on the possible range of values in the list of numbers involved. The initial value should be chosen to be smaller than the smallest number in this possible range. In this way, the first value in the list is larger than the initial value, and Large is changed to this first number.

In the preceding examples, the quantity whose largest value we wished to find happened to be one of the fields in our input. Of course, this need not be the case. For example, our input might contain the hourly rate and number of hours and we might wish to find the largest gross pay. To do so, we would have to calculate the pay for each person and compare this pay with the largest we had found so far.

Another point that may have struck you as you examined Figure 3-5 is that you might want to know, in addition to the value of the largest salary, the name of that employee who has the largest salary. To do so, we simply need another variable to keep track of the desired information. Add the declaration

```
LargeName: string;   {name of person with largest salary}
```

Because this variable is associated with LargeSalary, it is given a value whenever LargeSalary is given a value. Before the loop, LargeSalary is assigned the value of the first person's salary, and we should follow this by

```
LargeName := Name;
```

If it turns out that this first salary is the largest, then LargeName has the first person's name stored.

Within the loop, we replace the step

```
if Salary > LargeSalary then
   LargeSalary := Salary
```

by the step

```
if Salary > LargeSalary then
   begin
      LargeSalary := Salary;
      LargeName := Name
   end
```

Because we have found a new largest salary, we need to record both that salary and the associated name. (Notice that we need a *begin* and *end* to form a compound statement within the *if*.)

Finally, after the loop, we can print both the largest salary and the associated name:

```
Writeln ('The largest salary, ', LargeSalary : 1 : 2,
         ' was earned by ', LargeName)
```

There are two further topics to be discussed concerning the preceding example. The first is the matter of ties. Suppose there are two people in the company with the same largest salary. Our program identifies only the first person. (Why?) Although this problem can be fixed, it is relatively difficult to do, especially prior to studying arrays in depth (Chapter 6). So, for the present, we assume our data sets consist of unique values.

The second topic relates to the alternate method for initializing LargeSalary. Because the salaries are nonnegative, we could use a value of –1 as the initial value. If we did so, then only these two steps would be required before the loop:

```
Instructions;
LargeSalary := -1
```

When the first data value is read, Salary is compared to LargeSalary. It is bigger, so LargeSalary and LargeName are given the values from this first employee.

Note. When the possible range of values is known, using a default value is easier. On the other hand, initializing with the first data value is more general, since it does not depend on knowing the range of values.

Consider, however, the problem of finding the largest salary earned by a female. In this instance, we could not initialize using the first data value. We would have to use the first data value for a female. This would complicate our program substantially, so we would be inclined instead to use a default of –1, as in the previous example.

In short, it is important for you to know both methods of initialization.

Until now, all the examples have had to do with finding the largest value in a list. Finding the smallest is similar; there are only two differences:

1. When initializing the variable (perhaps called Small), start either with the first value or with a number larger than the possible range of values.

2. In the loop, change Small when a smaller value than the current smallest is found.

For example, the program given in Figure 3-6 reads name, age, and sex code and finds the name, age, and sex of the youngest person. Key portions are italicized.

Keep in mind that for a problem in which we are to find the largest of some value, and perhaps other information concerning the record possessing that largest value, special variables are needed for the largest (say, Large) and for all the other information concerning the record with the largest value. Before the loop, either initialize Large to a suitable small value or initialize Large and all the other variables based on the first data record. In the loop, change Large and all the associated special variables whenever a record is found with a larger value than that currently stored in Large. After the loop, either print the answers or use them in further calculations. Finding the smallest value is similar.

Case Study No. 3 (Continued)

As a comprehensive illustration of the topics discussed in this section, we modify the program written in Section 2-8 as Case Study No. 3. The main program for that case study appears in Figure 2-20.

Statement of Problem. Case Study No. 3 calculated wages and state tax withholding for a number of employees. We wish to modify that program to report how many employees had tax withholding of $10 or less, who had the largest amount of tax and what that amount was, and what the average pay was.

Preliminary Analysis. One of the advantages of modularity is that modifications can be restricted to specific portions of the program. For example, these modifications do not change the methods for calculating the wages or the tax withholding, so those two functions remain entirely unchanged. The only changes involve the main program. (You might want to consider minor changes to the Instructions procedure, but those are not presented here.)

Algorithm and Variable List. In a problem of this type, we need to plan for the additional variables needed. All the variables originally used in the main program are still used. Here is a list of the additional variables:

Variable	Type	Description
LowCount	Integer	Number with tax < 10 (Counter)
Large	Real	Largest tax
LClock	Integer	Clock number for person with largest tax
TotalPay	Real	Total pay (Accumulator)
EmpCount	Integer	Number of employees (Counter)
Average	Real	Average pay

The rest of the planning involves inserting the proper steps before the loop, in the loop, and after the loop, using standard methods for these types of problems.

Test Plan. When a program is modified, it should be run again using the test plan that was used when it was developed. This ensures that code that originally worked still does work. (This is sometimes called **regression testing**.) In addition, additional tests should be devised relating to the steps added. Details of the types of tests needed are covered in the next section.

Write Program. The complete modified main program is shown in Figure 3-7. We have run the program for the same input as in the original case study. Again, note that the functions would not be modified.

```pascal
program FindSmallest;

{Written by: XXXXXXXX XX/XX/XX}
{Purpose:    To demonstrate finding the smallest and associated information.}
{            The program finds the name, age, and sex of the youngest person.}
{Procedures used: Instructions, to print instructions for user}

  const
    EndOfData = '';    {null string terminates program}

  var
    Name: string;      {employee name, input}
    Age: integer;      {age, input}
    Sex: char;         {sex code, input}

    SmallAge: integer;    {smallest age}
    SmName: string;       {name of youngest}
    SmSex: char;          {sex of youngest}

  procedure Instructions;
    begin
    {stub}
    end;
begin {FindSmallest}

{*** Print instructions and initialize}

  Instructions;
  SmallAge := 100;   {high default value}

{*** Repeatedly obtain input data. Check each age against youngest so far,}
{    changing SmallAge and all associated variables when a younger person}
{    is found.}

  repeat
     Writeln;
     Write('Enter name (hit return to quit): ');
     Readln(Name);
     if Name <> EndOfData then
       begin
          Write('Age: ');
          Readln(Age);
          Write('Sex code: ');
          Readln(Sex);
          if Age < SmallAge then
              begin
                 SmallAge := Age;
                 SmName := Name;
                 SmSex := Sex
              end
       end
   until Name = EndOfData;
```

Figure 3-6 Finding the smallest value (continues next page).

```
{*** Print answers}

  Writeln;
  Writeln('The youngest person was ', SmName);
  if SmSex in ['M', 'm'] then
     Write('He ')
  else
     Write('She ');
     Writeln('is ', SmallAge : 1, ' years old.')
end.
```

SAMPLE INPUT AND OUTPUT

First run:

```
        Enter name (hit return to quit): Sally Frisling
        Age: 9
        Sex code: F
        Enter name (hit return to quit): Joe Salzburg
        Age: 21
        Sex code: M

        Enter name (hit return to quit): Mike Sawyer
        Age: 15
        Sex code: m

        Enter name (hit return to quit):

        The youngest person was Sally Frisling
        She is 9 years old.
```

Second run:

```
        Enter name (hit return to quit): Barry Purnell
        Age: 45
        Sex code: m

        Enter name (hit return to quit):

        The youngest person was Barry Purnell
        He is 45 years old.
```

Figure 3-6 (continued)

Testing

It may require several runs of the program to test adequately a program involving counting, accumulation, or finding the largest/smallest. Among the most important types of tests are these:

```
program Payroll;

{Written by: XXXXXXXX XX/XX/XX}
{Purpose:    To calculate pay and state tax for a number of employees.}
{            The input consists of a clock number, the number of hours}
{            worked, the hourly rate, and the number of dependents.}

{Modified:   XXXXXXXX XX/XX/XX - to report how many employees had tax}
{            withholding of $10 or less, who had the largest amount of tax}
{            and what that amount was, and what the average pay was.}
{            These changes affect only the main program.}

{Procedures used: Instructions, to print instructions for user}
{Functions used:  PayFn, to calculate the pay based on hours and rate}
{                 TaxFn, to calculate the tax based on the pay and the}
{                        number of dependents}

  const
    EndOfData = 0;            {terminating data indicator}

  var
    ClockNumber: integer;     {employee clock number, input}
    HoursWorked: real;        {hours worked, input}
    HourlyRate: real;         {rate of pay, input}

    Dependents: integer;      {number of dependents, input}
    Pay: real;                {pay for week, output}
    StateTax: real;           {state tax, output}

    LowCount: integer;        {# with tax < $10}
    LargeTax: real;           {largest state tax}
    LClock: integer;          {clock # of person with most tax}
    TotalPay: real;           {total pay for week}
    EmpCount: integer;        {counter of employees}
    Average: real;            {average pay for week}

  procedure Instructions;
  begin
    {stub}
  end;

{function PayFn, as shown in Figure 2-19, is inserted here}
{function TaxFn, as shown in Figure 2-20, is inserted here}

begin {Payroll}

{*** Before the loop, print instructions and initialize}
```

Figure 3-7   Case Study No. 3 (payroll) (continues next page).

```
    Instructions;
    LowCount := 0;
    LargeTax := 0;
    TotalPay := 0;
    EmpCount := 0;

{*** In loop, obtain clock number, hours, rate, and number of dependents. }
{    Check for dummy value . Check for invalid hours. Calculate and print}
{    pay and tax. Also modify summary information (counters , etc .)}

    repeat
      Writeln;
      Write('Enter clock number for next employee: ');
      Readln(ClockNumber);
      if ClockNumber > EndOfData then
        begin
          Write('Enter the hours, rate, and number of dependents: ');
          Readln(HoursWorked, HourlyRate, Dependents);
          EmpCount := EmpCount + 1;
          if HoursWorked < 0 then
            begin
              Writeln(HoursWorked, ' is invalid; changed to 0.');
              HoursWorked := 0
            end;
          Pay := PayFn(HoursWorked, HourlyRate);
          TotalPay := TotalPay + Pay;
          StateTax := TaxFn(Pay, Dependents);
          Writeln(ClockNumber, ' earned ', Pay, ' and was taxed ', StateTax : 2);
          if StateTax < 10 then
            LowCount := LowCount + 1;
          if StateTax > LargeTax then
            begin
              LargeTax := StateTax;
              LClock := ClockNumber
            end {if}
        end {if}
    until ClockNumber <= EndOfData;

{*** Print summary information and stop}
```

Figure 3-7   (continues next page)

FINDING THE LARGEST

1. Largest first (no ties)
2. Largest last (no ties)
3. Largest in middle (no ties)
4. All the same value

```
      Writeln;
   if EmpCount = 0 then
         Writeln('No employees entered')
   else
         begin
           Average := TotalPay / EmpCount;
           Writeln(LowCount, ' employees had less than $10 withheld');
           Writeln('Clock #', LClock : 1, ' paid the most tax -- $',
                   LargeTax : 1 : 2);
           Writeln('The average pay was $', Average : 1 : 2)
         end;

end.
```

SAMPLE INPUT AND OUTPUT

```
      Enter clock number for next employee: 345
      Enter the hours, rate, and number of dependents: 34 5.67 8
      345 earned 192.78 and was taxed 1.94

      Enter clock number for next employee: 101
      Enter the hours, rate, and number of dependents: 44 6.78 3
      101 earned 311.88 and was taxed 5.52

      Enter clock number for next employee: 0

      2 employees had less than $10 withheld
      Clock #101 paid the most tax -- $5.52
      The average pay was $252.33
```

Figure 3-7 (continued)

COUNTING

1. No data input at all
2. Data input, but count is still 0 for what is being counted
3. Everything in the input list is in the category being counted

ACCUMULATION

1. This is similar to counting.

It may help to understand these tests if they are viewed as the boundary values for the answers to questions such as:

1. Where in the list is the largest found?
2. How many ties are there?
3. How many items in the list of data?
4. How many items in the category being counted or accumulated?

3-1 COMMON APPLICATIONS OF LOOPS

As we mentioned earlier, boundary situations are those that are most likely to yield errors in our programs. Hence, these types of tests are the most fruitful because they are the most likely to uncover the errors that the program contains.

DPT

The most frequently encountered pitfalls in writing programs using the methods of this section may be briefly described as follows:

1. Forgetting to initialize counters and accumulators.

2. Improper initialization of "Large" or "Small" variables.

There are two choices. One is to give the variable a value based on the first input data. In this case, we also initialize any associated variables (for example, LargeName) being used to maintain additional information concerning the record with the highest value.

On the other hand, we can initialize based on the known range of values. In this case, initialize Large (or Small) in such a way that the first record is certain to contain a larger (or smaller) value. If we choose this approach, the associated variables such as LargeName need not be initialized.

Notice that both approaches require that there be at least one set of valid data. If it is conceivable that there will be no input, we should handle this possibility, perhaps by displaying a "no valid data" message.

3. Improper assignment statements. A typical error of this type is

```
if Salary > LargeSalary then
   begin
      Salary := LargeSalary;
      Name := LargeName
   end
```

The two assignment statements are both reversed. Remember that the variable to be changed should be on the left-hand side. LargeSalary and LargeName are to be changed; write

```
if Salary > LargeSalary then
   begin
      LargeSalary := Salary;
      LargeName := Name
   end
```

REVIEW

Terms and Concepts

accumulation
accumulator
body
counter
counting
finding largest/smallest

initialization
loop control
record
regression testing
terminate

Algorithm Techniques

Counting

Before loop: initialize to 0
In loop: add 1 to counter, if appropriate
After loop: print or use answer

Accumulation

Before loop: initialize to 0
In loop: add to accumulator, if appropriate
After loop: print or use answer

Finding the Largest

Before loop: initialize to a "small" value, or value from first record
In loop: change Large and associated variables when new value is larger
After loop: print or use answer

Finding the Smallest

Before loop: initialize to a "large" value or a value from the first record
In loop: change Small and associated variables when new value is smaller
After loop: print or use answer

EXERCISES

1. For each of the following, determine appropriate initial values for Large for an algorithm to find the largest of the quantity indicated. Then determine appropriate initial values for Small for an algorithm to find the smallest.
   (a) age
   (b) age of elementary school children
   (c) IQ
   (d) salary of managers in a small company
   (e) number of children in a family
   (f) numbers ranging from –23,000 to +1700
   (g) balances in checking accounts that just had an overdraft
   (h) balances in checking accounts

2. Each record (i.e., set of input data) has a name and a letter grade (A, B, C, D, or F). Write a program to count the number that passed and the number that failed. (All grades except F are passing.)

3. Each record has a name and a numerical average. Write a program that, for each record, calculates the variable Result as follows: If the numerical average is 60.0 or higher, the variable should be given the value "pass", otherwise the value "fail". The program should print the name, numerical average, and Result for each person, and tell how many passed.

4. (a) In a certain company, a bonus is based on the number of years worked and a skill code (a one-character code). For skill level 'E', the bonus is $15 for each year worked. Write a program to read a set of records, each with name, years worked, and skill code, and print a list of the bonuses for persons with skill level 'E'.

(b) Modify your program to print the following summary information: percentage of employees with skill level 'E' and total bonus for skill level 'E' employees.
(c) Modify your program to show which skill level 'E' employee had the largest bonus.

5. Each record has an ID number, sex code, age, and number of children.
   (a) Write a program to count the number of females under age 21.
   (b) Write a program to find the average number of children for persons under age 25.
   (c) Write a program to find the age and ID number of the oldest person with no children. (Assume that there is such a person.)
   (d) Revise part (c) to find the age and ID number of the youngest person who has children.

6. Each record contains, for a single course, the number of credits and a letter grade (A, B, C, D, or F). There is one record for each course taken by John Smith during his college career. Write a program to calculate his grade point average. The quality point average is the total of the quality points divided by the total number of credits. (A, 4 quality points per credit; B, 3 per credit; C, 2 per credit; and D, 1 per credit.)

7. Modify the latest version of Case Study No. 1 (Figure 2-9, Section 2-3) to count how many passed, how many failed, and the percentage of those who were exempted from the final.

8. Modify Case Study No. 2 (Section 2-7) to count how many of each possible operation were performed.

9. Devise test plans for the following:
   (a) Exercise 2
   (b) Exercise 4(b)
   (c) Exercise 4(c)
   (d) Exercise 5(b)
   (e) Exercise 5(c)

10. Write a program to handle all the transactions on a single checking account during a month. Input starts with a record indicating an account number, account type, and a beginning balance. This is followed by a number of transaction records, each containing a code (C: check, D: deposit) and an amount.
    Output should be a table with each transaction and the resulting balance, as illustrated:

```
ACCOUNT # 12345      BEGINNING BALANCE = 123.14 TYPE = R
-------------------------------------------------------------
        CODE             AMOUNT           BALANCE
        ----             ------           -------
         C               150.00            -26.86
***OVERDRAFT - - $5.00 CHARGE ***          -31.86
         D                30.00             -1.86
         C                 1.00             -2.86
***OVERDRAFT - - $5.00 CHARGE ***           -7.86
         D               100.00             92.14
         C                10.05             82.09

                  CLOSING BALANCE = 82.09
```

The following summary information should be given: minimum balance, number of bad checks, and total of the checks not including the bad checks.

3-2 PASCAL LOOPING STRUCTURES

Pascal has three looping structures. We have seen the **repeat-until loop**, which we have used in all our programs to this point. In those programs, the condition that terminated the loop was that the user entered a terminal data value. In this section, we study the *repeat-until* looping structure in more detail. In addition, we will learn about the other two looping statements available in Pascal, the **while-do loop** and the **for-do loop** (usually just called the **while** and **for** loops).

In writing programs, there are two related tasks. We must design the algorithm, that is, determine what the program should do and how it should do it. And we must write the program in some suitable programming language. In connection with loops, this implies that there are two topics to study: how to design loops and how to write loops in THINK Pascal. In this section, the basic form of the three loops is studied and a few examples are presented. The next section begins a thorough study of the techniques of loop design that will enable us to make good use of these three looping structures.

This section also introduces two concepts not directly related to loops. They are random numbers and arrays. We will use these concepts in some of our examples in this and later sections. With random numbers, we can develop some interesting examples of loops that involve simulation of random events such as coin tossing. Arrays are the subject of a complete chapter (Chapter 6), but it is helpful to gain familiarity with the concept now.

Repeat-Until Loops

We begin with *repeat-until* loops. Recall that the general form of the loop is

```
repeat
  statement(s)
until condition
```

It is not necessary to use a *begin* and *end* to delimit the body of the loop because the two key words *repeat* and *until* already delimit it. Recall also that the loop executes the statements forming its body repeatedly until the condition is *true*. The body of the loop executes one or more times. The precise semantics (meaning) of the *repeat-until* are as follows:

1. Perform the loop body.

2. If the condition is *true*, terminate the loop, otherwise go back to step 1.

We can summarize this by saying that

The test for terminating a *repeat-until* loop occurs at the bottom of the loop

The condition used after the keyword *until* can be a Boolean constant, a Boolean variable, or a more complex Boolean expression. Any condition that could be used in an *if* statement can also be used in a *repeat-until* loop.

As an extreme example of a *repeat-until* loop, one that keeps the computer busy for a long time, we could (but, of course, we wouldn't) use the construct:

```
repeat
until false;
```

This example is extreme for two reasons. First of all, it uses the Boolean constant *false* for its condition. Second, the body of the loop is empty. This is an infinite loop; it will run forever. Another extreme example that we are not likely to use in a program is

```
repeat
until true;
```

which will act as though no statement is there at all.

To gain further understanding of the *repeat-until* loop, consider this program segment:

```
I := 5;
repeat
   Writeln(I);
   I := I + 5
until I > N
```

The table gives a list of the numbers printed for various values of the variable N. It also indicates what value the variable I has following termination of the loop.

N	NUMBERS PRINTED	VALUE OF I AFTER LOOP
17	5, 10, 15	20
20	5, 10, 15, 20	25
5	5	10
4	5	10

Because the loop termination condition is not checked until the bottom of the loop, the loop always executes at least once. Note especially the last line of the table (N = 4). Even though I is already greater than 4 when the loop begins, the body executes once, printing 5 and changing I to 10.

While-Do Loops

The *while-do* loop (which we will call the *while* loop), like the *repeat-until* loop, is a condition-based loop. That is, there is a condition whose truth or falsity determines how long the repetition continues. The general form of this looping construct is

```
while condition do
   statement that forms body of loop
```

In most circumstances, the statement that forms the body of the loop is a compound one, so that our general form usually has the appearance:

```
while condition do
   begin
      body of loop
   end
```

The condition, like that in the *repeat-until* loop, can be any Boolean constant, Boolean variable, or more complex Boolean expression.

The meaning of the *while* loop is to continue to execute and reexecute the body of the loop as long as the condition remains true. Two extreme examples, analogous to those for the *repeat-until* loop, are

```
while true do;
```

which executes an empty loop body forever; and

```
while false do;
```

which is an empty loop that executes 0 times. Although a silly example, the second loop does illustrate the important point that a *while* loop executes 0 or more times.

To contrast the *repeat-until* loop with the *while* loop, consider these two program segments:

```
I := 5;                 I := 5;
repeat                  while I <= N do
  Writeln(I);             begin
  I := I + 5                Writeln(I);
until I > N                 I := I + 5
                        end
```

First, note that the loop bodies are identical (a Writeln and an assignment). However, the *while* loop requires a *begin* and an *end* to group the two statements of the loop body into one compound statement.

An important point to observe relates to the conditions controlling the two loops. In the *repeat-until*, we have "I > N", and in the *while*, we have "I <= N". These are negations of each other. In the *while* loop, the condition expresses "how long the program stays in the loop" (as long as I <= N). In the *repeat-until* loop, on the other hand, the condition expresses "when the program terminates the loop" (when I > N). In general, the conditions for similar *repeat-until* and *while* loops are negations of each other.

On the surface, then, these two loops are similar in meaning. However, the table illustrates a fundamental difference between the two looping structures.

VALUE OF N	PRINTED BY REPEAT-UNTIL	PRINTED BY WHILE-DO
5	5	5
4	5	None

The semantics of the *while* loop are as follows:

1. If the condition is *true*, go to step 2, otherwise the loop terminates.

2. Perform the loop body, then go back to step 1 to check the condition.

Thus, if N is 5, the loop body is executed, printing I (5) and changing I to 10. Because the condition is now *false*, the loop terminates. On the other hand, if N is 4, the loop terminates immediately without ever performing the loop body.

We can summarize these semantics of the *while* loop by saying that

The test for terminating a *while* loop occurs at the top of the loop.

Repeat Versus While

To summarize, the key differences between these two condition-based looping structures are as follows:

1. (a) *Repeat-until* tests after each execution of the body
1. (b) *While* tests before each execution of the body

2. (a) *Repeat-until* condition is *true* to exit the loop
2. (b) *While* condition is *false* to exit the loop

3. (a) *Repeat-until* body is always performed at least once
3. (b) *While* body might not be performed.

For-Do Loops

In this subsection, we consider the *for-do* (or just *for*) loop. This loop counts the number of times the computer executes the body of a loop and terminates the loop after a certain number of executions. The general form is

```
for control variable := start to end do
   statement that forms body of loop
```

As with the *while* loop, the statement that forms the body of the loop is most frequently a compound one, so that our general form usually has the appearance:

```
for control variable := start to end do
   begin
      body of loop
   end
```

The control variable successively takes on the values from the indicated starting value to the indicated ending value. An alternative form, discussed in what follows, uses the key word *downto* in place of the key word *to* in the *for* statement.

Perhaps the easiest way to understand the meaning of the *for* loop is by example. The table shows the output of the following program fragment for various values of the variables Start and End.

```
for I := Start to End do
   Writeln(I)
```

START	END	NUMBERS PRINTED
1	4	1, 2, 3, 4
13	19	13, 14, 15, 16, 17, 18, 19
2	2	2
3	2	None

The *for* loop can also count "down" from the starting value to the ending value as in

```
for I := Start downto End do
   Writeln(I)
```

Again, we can summarize the semantics of this loop:

START	END	NUMBERS PRINTED
4	1	4, 3, 2, 1
17	12	17, 16, 15, 14, 13, 12
5	5	5
5	6	None

We can summarize the *for* loop as follows:

1. The control variable successively takes on the values from the indicated starting value to the indicated ending value. For each value assumed by the control variable, the loop body is executed once.
2. The starting and ending values can be given by constants, variables, or more complex expressions. For now, the control variable and these expressions should all be integers.
3. If the *for* statement uses *to* and the final value is less than the initial value, then the body is not executed. Likewise, if the *for* statement uses *downto* and the final value is greater than the initial value, the body is not executed.
4. After the loop terminates, the control variable is "undefined." This means that the program cannot depend upon its having some specific value.
5. The control variable can be used within the loop body, but do not modify it.
6. If any variables are involved in the starting and ending values, they should not be modified within the loop. Doing so will not modify the behavior of the loop, but it will be confusing to the reader of the program.
7. A *for* loop, in contrast to a *while* or *repeat* loop, cannot be infinite (as long as you do not change the control variable's value inside the loop). It terminates after a predetermined number of passes.

Notes

1. This loop is sometimes referred to as a **count-controlled loop**, which means that it is possible to know exactly how many times the loop body will be executed. The control variable can be thought of as "counting" the passes through the loop.
2. The logic of the loop "for I := I to N" is essentially equivalent to the following *while* loop form:

```
while I <= N do
   begin
      {loop body}
      I := I + 1
   end
```

3-2 PASCAL LOOPING STRUCTURES

Random Numbers

We pause momentarily in our study of Pascal loops to introduce the notion of **random numbers**. Using random numbers in conjunction with loops allows us to write programs that simulate chance (such as rolling a die).

Many computer languages include functions that generate "random" numbers. What this means is that every time the function is used, a value results in what looks like a random pattern. (These numbers are sometimes (and more precisely) called "pseudorandom numbers," and the functions that generate them are sometimes called "pseudorandom number generators." This refers to the fact that the generated numbers look random, but that they are actually generated by a (complicated) formula.) In many languages, using the random number generator is a simple matter of calling a procedure. Unfortunately, in THINK Pascal for the Macintosh, there are several steps we must take to ensure the random-number generator behaves as we would like. We discuss each of those steps in turn in the next few sections.

The Random Function. Many languages provide a random-number function that returns a random number greater than or equal to zero and less than 1. THINK Pascal's random-number function, called Random, returns integers in the range of –32768 to 32767. For example, the following fragment would print out eight values within that range:

```
for I := 1 to 8 do
  begin
     Value := Random;
     Writeln(Value)
  end
```

Changing the Range of Random Numbers. Most of the time, we desire random numbers within a range smaller than –32768 to 32767. To change the range, the easiest way is to use the *abs* function, along with the *mod* and addition (or subtraction) operations. For instance, to simulate the roll of one 6-sided die, we would want a random number between 1 and 6. We can obtain this range with the statement:

```
RandomValue := abs(Random mod 6) + 1
```

The *mod* operation produces an integer in the range of –5 to 5 (the remainder of dividing the random number by 6); the absolute-value function makes the result of the *mod* operation positive (producing an integer from 0 to 5); adding 1 gives us the desired range of 1 to 6.

Seeding the Random-Number Generator. Random produces the same sequence of random numbers each time the program is run. To make the sequence of random numbers different each run of the program, RandSeed (a predefined variable) must be assigned a new value each time the program is run. This assignment, done once in the program prior to the first use of the Random function, is known as **seeding** the random-number generator.

One approach to seeding the random-number generator is to ask the user to enter an arbitrarily chosen integer. This is a poor choice, since the user should not be bothered with the particulars of THINK's random-number generator. A much better approach is to have the program itself provide the seed.

The Macintosh has an internal clock that keeps track of the date and time. It does so by counting the number of seconds since midnight of January 1, 1904, and then converting that count into the current date and time. The predefined procedure GetDateTime, when called, places into its parameter the number of seconds since New Year, 1904. This parameter makes an excellent random number seed; it changes every second, and the same number never appears twice.

To seed Random, use the statement:

```
GetDateTime(RandSeed)
```

An Example. Random functions such as this can be used to perform a variety of **simulations** of randomly occurring events in the real world. Figure 3-8 is a complete THINK Pascal program that contains all the statements needed to set up and use the random-number generator, including a function that simulates rolling a pair of dice. Each "abs(Random mod 6) + 1" gives a value from 1 to 6 and represents one of the dice. The total on the two dice is placed into the function name RollOf Dice. Notice that this function has no parameters. The answer is obtained using Random, not from parameter values.

For the simulation to be valid, each outcome must be equally likely. This is the reason for simulating each die by a separate call to the Random function.

More Examples Using Loops

In this section, we present a number of examples of the use of count-controlled and condition-based loops. In each case, we show only a program segment so that we can concentrate our attention on the looping process itself. In Section 3-3, we develop some complete programs from scratch.

Suppose we wish to estimate the number of rabbits that would be present in an area after 10 years if the number of rabbits doubles each year and there are two rabbits to start. We could count the rabbits using a variable Rabbits and the years using a variable Years. Both Years and Rabbits would be integers. At the start, Rabbits would be 2. After the first year, Rabbits would be 4 and Years would be 1. After the second year Rabbits would be 8 and Years 2. Figure 3-9 contains two solutions.

Notice how much simpler the second code fragment is than the first one. We do not have to write the initialization statement, the modification statement, nor the test for leaving the loop. They are all included in the *for* statement.

Once you are familiar with the *for* statement, it is much clearer to read a fragment like the second one. It takes a few seconds of study to determine from the *while* loop just what the initial and final values are and, in fact, that the *while* was being used for a count-controlled loop.

You should also notice that, in this case, there is only one statement in the body of the *for* loop, and, thus, we could omit the *begin* and *end* to get:

```
Rabbits := 2;
for Years := 1 to 10 do
  Rabbits := Rabbits * 2;
Writeln('After 10 years there are ', Rabbits : 1, ' rabbits')
```

```
program RollSomeDice;

{Written by: XXXXXXXXXX XX/XX/XX}
{Purpose:   To illustrate the use of the random number generator}

  var
    i: integer;

  function RollOfDice: integer;

    {Purpose: To simulate the roll of a pair of dice}

    var
      Roll1: integer;      {first die}
      Roll2: integer;      {second die}

    begin {RollOfDice}
      Roll1 := abs(Random mod 6) + 1;
      Roll2 := abs(Random mod 6) + 1;
      RollOfDice := Roll1 + Roll2
    end; {RollOfDice}

begin {Main program}

  GetDateTime(RandSeed);    {Seed the random number generator}

  for i := 1 to 10 do
    Writeln('This roll of the dice was ', RollOfDice : 2);

end. {Main program}
```

Figure 3-8   Simulating rolling dice.

Note.   The comments "{for}" and "{while}" are included following the *end;* of the loops at the programmer's option. As in other such situations, we make a judgment on whether the program is more easily understood by the inclusion of a comment. As programmers, we should keep in mind that comments can be illuminating, neutral, or annoying; we should strive for the first kind, ignore the second, and avoid the third.

On the other hand, it is true that programmers tend to underestimate the illuminating value of comments within their own work.

For another example, the fragment in Figure 3-10 simulates an experiment in which we roll a pair of dice 1200 times, counting the number of 7's that occur.

Our next example (shown in Figure 3-11) is a procedure that prints a row of asterisks. In addition to the looping structure, it illustrates an important aspect of procedures:

Procedures can have value parameters, just like those for functions.

Solution #1

```
    Rabbits := 2;

    Years := 1;
    while Years <= 10 do
      begin
        Rabbits : = Rabbits * 2;
        Years := Years + 1
      end; {while}

    Writeln('After 10 years there are ', Rabbits : 1, ' rabbits')
```

Solution #2

```
    Rabbits := 2;
    for Years := 1 to 10 do
      begin
         Rabbits := Rabbits * 2
      end; {for}

    Writeln('After 10 years there are ', Rabbits : 1, ' rabbits')
```

Figure 3-9   While and for loops.

```
    Count7 := 0;
    for I := 1 to 1200 do
      begin
         Dice := RollOfDice;
         if Dice = 7 then
            Count7 := Count7 + 1
      end; {for}
    Writeln(Count7 : 1, ' 7''s occurred in 1200 rolls')
```

Figure 3-10   Counting sevens.

This procedure has one parameter, called Number, which tells how many asterisks to print. We assume that Number lies between 0 and 70, so that the asterisks will easily fit on a single line.

We use a count-controlled (*for*) loop. We could use either a *repeat-until* or a *while* loop, but a *for* loop is easiest to write and understand for this example.

Two points should be observed, in addition to the looping structure and the parameter. First, we use Write rather than Writeln in the loop, so that all the asterisks stay on one line. The Writeln after the loop terminates the line. Second, we declare I, the loop's control variable, as a local variable within the procedure.

So far our examples have been count-controlled (*for*) loops. We now consider some condition-based loops (*while* and *repeat-until* loops).

3-2 PASCAL LOOPING STRUCTURES

```
procedure Asterisks(Number: integer);

{Written by: XXXXXXXXXX XX/XX/XX}
{Purpose:    To print a line containing 1 to 70 asterisks.}
{Parameters: Number - how many asterisks to print (assumed to be}
                     in the range 1 to 70)}

var
   I: integer;       {for loop control variable}

begin {Asterisks}
   for I := 1 to Number do
      begin
         Write('*')
      end; {for}

   Writeln
end; {Asterisks}
```

Figure 3-11   Printing N asterisks.

Figure 3-12 contains a program segment that accepts an unknown number of exam scores as input, terminated by the value −1. It calculates the average of the scores, and prints the number of scores read and the resulting average to one decimal place. Along with the program segment, we show some sample runs. (For the sample runs, the program segment was expanded into a complete program.)

In this example, the program reads the first test score prior to the loop, and then the remaining test scores in a loop. As long as the score entered is not −1, the looping continues. The loop body counts and accumulates the scores using the techniques covered in Section 3-1. After the loop, the average score is printed.

Figure 3-13 contains our first example of the *repeat-until* loop. In the example, we make use of random numbers and the dice rolling function (RollOfDice), which was introduced previously. The purpose of the program is to roll the pair of dice the first time to obtain a value, called the "point," which we will subsequently attempt to match. Then we roll the dice over and over until we match the point with a roll. We count the number of rolls that it takes to match the point and, when we finally do match it, we print the number of rolls that it took.

For our second *repeat-until* example, we return to Case Study No. 1, developed in Chapter 1. That case study calculated the total on three exam scores for a number of students, terminated by a null student name. For this example, we change the specification of the problem to state that there is no terminating value for the student name, but after the processing of the test scores total for a student, the user will be asked if the processing is to continue. See Figure 3-14.

The type of loop presented in this example can be used for many interactive programs that are to perform repeatedly an activity until the user decides to terminate the progression by stating that the activity is not to continue.

PROGRAM SEGMENT

```
{*** Read and total scores}

Total := 0;
Number := 0;
Write('Enter score (-1 to quit): ');
Readln(Score);

while Score <> -1 do
  begin
     Total := Total + Score;
     Number := Number + 1;
     Write('Enter score (-1 to quit): ');
     Readln(Score)
  end; {while}  {*** Calculate and print average.}
Writeln;
if Number > 0 then
  begin
     Average := Total / Number;
     Writeln(Number : 1, ' exam scores were processed.');
     Writeln('The average is: ', Average : 1 : 1)
  end
else
  Writeln('*** No scores were input ***')
```

SAMPLE INPUT AND OUTPUT

Run 1:

```
Enter score (-1 to quit): 89
Enter score (-1 to quit): 56
Enter score (-1 to quit): 77
Enter score (-1 to quit): 83
Enter score (-1 to quit): 92
Enter score (-1 to quit): -1
5 exam scores were processed.
The average is: 79.4
```

Run 2:

```
Enter score (-1 to quit): -1
*** No scores were input ***
```

Figure 3-12 Average value.

Notice the use of the condition "Answer in ['N', 'n']" to terminate the loop. This causes the loop to terminate if the user tries to say no with a lowercase n. Even though the program asked for uppercase input, it seems reasonable to interpret a lowercase n as desiring termination of the input process.

3-2 PASCAL LOOPING STRUCTURES

PROGRAM SEGMENT

```
GetDateTime(RandSeed);

{*** Roll the point}

Point := RollOfDice;
Writeln('The point is: ', Point : 1);
Writeln;

{*** Roll until a match occurs; count the tries}

Count := 0;
repeat
  Roll := RollOfDice;
  Writeln('This try: ', Roll : 1);
  Count := Count + 1
until Roll = Point;

Writeln;
if Count = 1 then
  Writeln('It took 1 try to match the point: ', Point : 1);
else
  Writeln('It took ', Count : 1, ' tries to match the point: ', Point : 1);
```

SAMPLE INPUT AND OUTPUT

Run 1

```
The point is: 1
This try: 9
This try: 9
This try: 7
This try: 5
This try: 10
This try: 10
This try: 8
This try. 11
This try: 4
This try: 1
It took 10 tries to match the point: 1
```

Run 3 (Note: Run 2 took 49 tries to match the point 10)

```
The point is: 7
This try: 7
It took 1 try to match the point: 7
```

Figure 3-13 Repeat-until loop.

PROGRAM SEGMENT

```
{*** Process name and scores until the user decides to quit}
repeat
  Writeln;
  Write('Enter the name: ');
  Readln(Name);
  Write('Now enter the three scores: ');
  Readln(Score1, Score2, Score3);
  Total := Score1 + Score2 + Score3;
  Writeln('The total is ', Total : 1, ' for ', Name);
  Writeln;
  Write('Do you wish to continue (Y,N)? ');
  Readln(Answer)
until Answer in ['N', 'n']  {allow both uppercase and lowercase 'no'}
```

SAMPLE INPUT AND OUTPUT

```
Enter the name: John Smith
Now enter the three scores: 75 81 99
The total is 255 for John Smith
Do you wish to continue (Y,N)? Y
Enter the name: Joe Jones
Now enter the three scores: 23 25 88
The total is 226 for Joe Jones
Do you wish to continue (Y,N)? n
```

Figure 3-14 Case Study No. 1 revisited (grades).

DPT: Loops

1. The *repeat-until* loop body is always executed at least once. The *while* loop body can be executed 0 times. In either case, the computer does not continuously monitor the condition. It is checked only at the bottom of the loop (for a *repeat-until*) or at the top (for a *while* loop). Notice this is the reason we have consistently had checks in our loops such as "if Name <> EndOfData then . . .".

2. Two particularly insidious pitfalls exist when using *for* loops. These relate to semicolons and to using *begin* and *end*.

To illustrate the problem, consider the program fragment of Figure 3-10, which is reproduced here but with two commonly made errors.

```
Count7 := 0;                        Count7 := 0;
for I := 1 to 1200 do;              for I := 1 to 1200 do
  begin                               Dice := RollOfDice;
    Dice := RollOfDice;               if Dice = 7 then
    if Dice = 7 then                    Count7 := Count7 + 1;
      Count7 := Count7 + 1    Writeln(Count7 : 1, ' 7''s out of 1200')
  end {for}
Writeln(Count7 : 1, ' 7''s out of 1200')
```

3-2 PASCAL LOOPING STRUCTURES

In the left-hand example, a semicolon is placed after the key word *do*. This causes the loop to have a single null statement as its body. The computer executes this null statement 1200 times, and then executes the compound statement once. The answer printed is either 0 or 1. The result of the second error, in which the *begin* and *end* is missing, is similar. This time the loop body consists of the single statement "Dice := RollOfDice". After this is executed 1200 times, the *if* and Writeln are executed, with an answer of 0 or 1.

Because the compiler does not detect these errors, we must take extra care to avoid them. Defensive programming suggests that we double check each *for* loop for the presence of an unwanted semicolon after the *do*. The second pitfall can be avoided by consistently using a *begin* and *end* even for single-statement loops.

3. The same possibilities for errors exist with the *while* loop. The consequences are, if anything, more disastrous than with the *for* loop. Consider, for example, these two modifications of the example of Figure 3-12.

```
while Score <> -1 do;
  begin
     Total := Total + Score;
     Number := Number + 1;
     Write('Enter the score (-1 to quit): ');
     Readln(Score)
  end; {while}

while Score <> -1 do
  Total := Total + Score;
  Number := Number + 1;
  Write('Enter next score (-1 to terminate): ');
  Readln(Score);
```

THINK accepts each of these as legal and meaningful Pascal. However, the meaning is not what we intended. In the first segment, we have an empty loop

```
while Score <> -1 do;
```

followed by a compound statement. In the second, we have the loop

```
while Score <> -1 do Total := Total + Score
```

followed by three statements not in the loop body.

What happens when we execute the program? If the score entered is not −1, the program loops forever. This is the most likely occurrence. If the user enters a −1 to abort the program, it instead asks for one more score and prints a meaningless answer.

Note. THINK's automatic formatting of programs will help us avoid these errors, since it displays the previous *while* statements quite differently. The statement group

```
while Score <> -1 do;
  begin
     Total := Total + Score;
     Number := Number + 1;
```

```
            Write('Enter the score (-1 to quit): ');
            Readln(Score)
        end; {while}
```

would be formatted (using THINK's default format settings) as

```
        while Score <> -1 do
            ;
        begin
            Total := Total + Score;
            Number := Number + 1;
            Write('Enter the score (-1 to quit): ');
            Readln(Score)
        end; {while}
```

and this block of code

```
        while Score <> -1 do
            Total := Total + Score;
            Number := Number + 1;
            Write('Enter next score (-1 to terminate): ');
            Readln(Score);
```

would appear as

```
        while Score <> -1 do
            Total := Total + Score;
        Number := Number + 1;
        Write('Enter next score (-1 to terminate): ');
        Readln(Score);
```

But we should not rely solely on THINK's formatting to point out our errors for us. THINK formats our program only when we hit certain keys, so we can go for quite some time before THINK formats our (incorrect) code. And we could easily write erroneous code that would be formatted in the same way as correctly written code.

---

4. Another potential problem exists with the *while* loop or the *repeat-until* loop. This problem could be caused by the omission, or by the erroneous coding of, the line that changes the value of the condition. In the example considered previously, if the line

```
        Readln(Score)
```

is either missing or in error, the loop can continue forever or terminate at the wrong time. The most common mistake in this example might be the omission of the statement, but another possibility would be reading another variable (perhaps Number) rather than Score. This kind of error can be avoided by the consistent use of meaningful variable names. It would be far more likely that a mistake could occur if the variables "A" and "B" were used rather than Number and Score. We should make it a regular practice to ensure the condition used for loop control can change its value to terminate the loop, and that the change will occur in exactly the correct manner.

3-2 PASCAL LOOPING STRUCTURES

A First Look at Arrays

In this section, we see a brief, simple introduction to arrays in Pascal. As we will see, an **array** is a type of variable that allows us to work with lists of related values. Although simplified, this first look is sufficient for us to understand some meaningful examples in the sections to come. In Chapter 6, we study arrays in more detail.

We all know about the value of being able to have lists of things. As an example in a program context, recall Case Study No. 1, developed in Chapter 1. In that case study, we made use of three variables for test scores: Score1, Score2, and Score3. Suppose that we had 10 scores. Would we want to use 10 variable names? What about 100 scores? Let us use the concept of a list to help out. We could think of the 3 (10, or 100) scores as a list with a single name Scores. To illustrate, in our previous way of thinking about this problem, we might write

Score1: 89
Score2: 78
Score3: 91

for a particular set of scores.

Thinking of the scores as a list, we might write:

Scores: 89, 78, 91

for the same set of scores. We can now locate the first score by its position on the list, rather than by a separate variable name.

So it is with Pascal arrays. If we declared Scores as an array (we see how in what follows), then we can refer to the first score as Scores[1], the second as Scores[2], and so on.

You are probably thinking that we haven't really gained anything. In fact, what we have said so far can be summarized as follows:

OLD WAY OF THINKING	NEW WAY OF THINKING
Score1: 89	Scores[1]: 89
Score2: 78	Scores[2]: 78
Score3: 91	Scores[3]: 91

But, here is a big advantage: Suppose that I is a variable that contains one of the numbers 1, 2, or 3. How can we refer to the Ith score? Compare:

OLD WAY OF THINKING	NEW WAY OF THINKING
??????????	Scores[I]

Note. A frequent error made by beginning programmers is assuming that ScoreI would work for the "old way of thinking." It would not. However, it is the right idea. What we need is an array, so that we can use the similar form Scores[I].

Suppose that we wanted to calculate the total of the three scores. Compare:

OLD WAY OF THINKING

```
Total := Score1 + Score2 + Score3
```

NEW WAY OF THINKING

```
Total := 0;
for I := 1 to 3 do
  begin
     Total := Total + Scores[I]
  end {for}
```

Notes. Study the "new way of thinking" carefully. Here's how it works:

1. Total starts at 0.

2. The first pass through the *for* loop, I has the value 1. The reference to Scores[I] therefore refers to Scores[1]. This is added to Total, so Total is now equal to the first score.

3. The second pass through the loop, I is 2, so Scores[I] refers to Scores[2]. After this is added to Total, Total is equal to the sum of the first two scores.

4. On the third (and final) pass, I is 3, so Scores[I] refers to Scores[3]. Total becomes equal to the sum of the three scores.

This use of a *for* loop to gain access to each array value is typical of a large number of algorithms using arrays.

Another big advantage of this new list (array) way of thinking comes when the lists are longer. For example, suppose that we wanted to calculate the total of 20 scores. Compare:

OLD WAY OF THINKING

```
Total := Score1 + Score2 + Score3 + Score4  + Score5  +
         Score6 + Score7 + Score8 + Score9  + Score10 +
         Score11 + Score12 + Score13 + Score14 + Score15 +
         Score16 + Score17 + Score18 + Score19 + Score20
```

NEW WAY OF THINKING

```
Total := 0;
for I := 1 to 20 do
  begin
     Total := Total + Scores[I]
  end {for}
```

Suppose that we wanted to calculate the total of 100 scores. Compare:

OLD WAY OF THINKING

Exercise for the unconvinced reader

NEW WAY OF THINKING

```
Total := 0;
for I := 1 to 100 do
  begin
     Total := Total + Scores[I]
  end {for}
```

For the discussion that follows, assume that we have an array called Scores that contains five scores:

Scores: 76, 87, 80, 85, 88

In the array notation, this means that

Scores[1] is 76
Scores[2] is 87
Scores[3] is 80
Scores[4] is 85
Scores[5] is 88

If we wish to refer to the third score, then we say that its **value** is 80.

With this terminology in mind, consider the following table, for which we suppose that the variable I has the value 3, the variable J has the value 5, and the variable K has the value 7:

REFERENCE	VALUE	COMMENT
Scores[1]	76	
Scores[3]	80	
Scores[I]	80	Scores[3] since I is 3
Scores[I + 1]	85	Scores[4] since I + 1 is 4
Scores[I] + 1	81	One more than Scores[3]
Scores[J]	88	Scores[5]
Scores[K]	Illegal	Scores[7] does not exist
Scores[K – 3]	85	Scores[4] since K – 3 is 4

There are three points to note well:

1. It is okay to use I + 1 as an indicator of which score we want, but be sure to do the arithmetic in the proper place. That is, the two legal expressions:

```
Scores[I] + 1
Scores[I + 1]
```

almost always have different values. The first means "one more than the Ith score." The second means "the $(I + 1)^{st}$ score."

2. Reference to a score (e.g., Scores[7]) that is not on the list is illegal.

3. We refer to the expression that appears inside of the square brackets ([]) as an **index** (sometimes called a **subscript**) of the array. We can extend the previous table to include this concept as follows:

INDEX	REFERENCE	VALUE
1	Scores[I]	76
3	Scores[3]	80
I	Scores[I]	80
I + 1	Scores[I + 1]	85
I	Scores[I] + 1	81
J	Scores[J]	88
K	Scores[K]	Illegal
K − 3	Scores[K − 3]	85

Now suppose that we are going to have 20 scores for each student of a course, but that it is the middle of the term and we only have values for 10 of each student's scores. We have here two variations of the concept of size of the array Scores. Because there will be 20 scores, we have the **potential size** or maximum allowable size of 20 for the array. Because there are now 10 scores, we have the **actual size** of 10 for the items in the array that are in use.

The price that we have to pay for this more powerful way of referring to data is that we must declare each array within the Pascal module that uses it. In the declaration of an array, we include both type and size information. The size information is for the potential size of the array.

Declaring Arrays. For now, we will use a simplified scheme for declaring our arrays. First, assume the arrays are lists of integer numbers. Second, assume that if a program has to use two or more arrays, then they have the same size. Remember that size refers to the potential (maximum allowable) number of items in the array and not the number of items in the array actually in use. Further, assume that the potential size of 1000 suffices for all of our early work with arrays.

The way that we declare our arrays is to include the following among our declarations in the main module:

```
const
    MaxIndex = 1000;  {size of arrays}
```

This *const* statement sets the mnemonic constant MaxIndex equal to 1000. Using a named constant not only helps us remember what the quantity 1000 means in this context (that it is the potential size of the arrays we will use), but also allows us to change the size of the arrays easily.

```
type
    IntegerArray = array[1..MaxIndex] of integer;
```

The type statement, among other things, allows a programmer to define **data structures** that hold more than one value. The array is one such data structure; there are others. The type statement is very powerful and useful, but also quite complex. As we talk about data structures in later chapters, we will discuss the type statement in detail.

This type statement indicates that we want to define our own data structure, IntegerArray. It will be an array, indexed from 1 to MaxIndex, and contain integer values.

For each particular array (Scores, for example), we will include among our declarations:

```
var
    Scores: IntegerArray;          {Test scores}
```

This statement declares a variable Scores and defines it to be of type IntegerArray, which was itself defined to be an array of MaxIndex (1000) integers. So Scores is an array of 1000 integers.

Out-of-Bounds Conditions. Be careful not to refer to an array item that is past the potential size of the array. In general, Pascal will not pick up this **out-of-bounds condition**. The program assigns a meaningless value to the non-existent array position. It may also on occasion exhibit strange behavior or produce unexpected and unusual run-time errors.

You can have THINK Pascal check your program for out-of-bounds conditions by turning on **range checking**, (Out-of-bounds checking is one aspect of range checking.) We can turn on range checking by using a project window option or a compiler directive.

Clicking on the R option next to your program's name in the project window will cause a box to appear around the R, indicating range checking is on for that program. To turn range checking off, just click on the R again; the box will disappear. Range checking causes additional instructions to be placed into your program to do the checking, so execution is usually slower than when range checking is off. So, most programmers turn range checking on while the program is being debugged, and turn it off when the program is ready to use.

We can turn on range checking for part of a program by placing the compiler directive {$R+} in the program at the point range checking is to begin and the directive {$R-} at the point it is to end. (You can turn range checking on again later in the program by issuing another {$R+} directive.)

We strongly recommend that you turn on range checking in any program that uses arrays. In all our program examples from now on, we will assume the R option is turned on (boxed) for any program that uses arrays.

An Example. We illustrate declaring an array with the program in Figure 3-15, which is Case Study No. 1 rewritten using an array. In this case, the actual number of elements of the array that are being used is 3. Note that we have changed the way that the data are input from all on one line to the use of a separate line for each data item. Also, the example has been simplified so that it deals with only one student. Array usage is indicated by italics.

Note. This program can be and was written earlier without arrays. However, the use of arrays gives some additional flexibility. If the values of the individual scores were needed after computing the total, then it would be difficult to write the program without arrays if the number of scores were increased. For example, suppose we needed to compute

```
program TestScores;

{Written by: XXXXXXXXX XX/XX/XX}
{Purpose:    To calculate the total on three tests, and}
{            print that total for one student}

  const
    MaxIndex = 1000;          {size of arrays}

  type
    IntegerArray = array[1..MaxIndex] of integer;

  var
    Name: string;             {student name, input}
    Scores: IntegerArray;     {test scores, input}
    Total: integer;           {total of test scores, calculated}
    I: integer;               {loop index}

begin {TestScores}

{*** Read name and scores; calculate and print total}

  Writeln;
  Write('Enter the name: ');
  Readln(Name);
  Writeln('Now enter the scores');

  Total := 0;

  for I := 1 to 3 do
    begin
      Write('Enter score ', I : 1, ' : ');
      Readln(Scores[I]);
      Total := Total + Scores[I]
    end;

  Writeln('The total is ', Total : 1, ' for ', Name);

end.
```

SAMPLE INPUT AND OUTPUT

```
Enter the name: John Smith
Now enter the scores
Enter score 1 : 78
Enter score 2 : 85
Enter score 3 : 91
The total is 254 for John Smith
```

Figure 3-15

the number of grades that were within 10 percent of the average grade, and furthermore the number of grades was to be a variable N. We can compute the average using code like this:

```
Total := 0;
for I := 1 to N do
    begin
       Readln(Scores[I]);
       Total := Total + Scores[I]
    end; {for}

Average := Total / N;
```

Once we have the average, we can count the number of scores within 10 percent of the average by

```
Count := 0;
for I := 1 to N do
    begin
       if (Scores[I] <= 1.1 * Average) and
          (Scores[I] >= 0.9 * Average) then
         Count := Count + 1
    end; {for}
```

DPT: Arrays

1. Remember that arrays must be declared. The actual size of an array can never exceed the potential size of an array. To avoid problems, use our suggested declaration scheme for your early work with arrays.

2. Don't write the expression Scores[I] + 1 when you mean the expression Scores[I + 1]. Think about what the two expressions mean.

3. Make sure range-checking is on for any program that uses arrays, especially during program development.

4. Do not refer to an array item that is past the potential size of the array. Range checking ensures THINK catches the error, but it's still an error!

5. Use square brackets "[]" for your array references and do not use parentheses "()". If you use parentheses instead of square brackets, THINK usually provides an error message, but one that may not be too helpful in identifying and fixing the problem. For instance, if I is an integer, and ABC is an array of the type we defined before, then

```
ABC(3) := 5
```

produces the error message

```
This doesn't make sense.
```

and the statement

```
I := ABC(3)
```

results in the message

```
Assignment type incompatibility.
```

Depending upon how the array is used, any one of several not-too-helpful error messages might appear. Avoid the problem; use square brackets.

6. Be sure to initialize all array locations you plan to use in your program. This is most often done with a Readln into the array item, such as

```
Readln(Scores[1])
```

or with an assignment statement, such as

```
Scores[1] := 15
```

If you use an array item that has not been initialized, there will be an unpredictable (and meaningless) value in it, but THINK will use it. No run time error results.

REVIEW

Terms and Concepts

actual size
array
count-controlled loop
data structures
for-do
index
out-of-bounds condition
potential size

random numbers
repeat-until
seeding
simulations
subscript
while-do
value

Pascal Syntax

Procedures

1. Procedures can have value parameters.

Loops

1. General form of *repeat-until* loop:

```
repeat
  statement(s)
until condition
```

2. General form of *while-do* loop:

```
while condition do
  statement that forms body of loop
```

3. Usual form of *while-do* loop:

```
while condition do
  begin
      body of loop
  end
```

4. General form of *for-do* loop (can use *downto* for *to*)

```
for control variable := start to end do
    statement that forms body of loop
```

5. Usual form of *for-do* loop (can use *downto* for *to*)

```
for control variable := start to end do
   begin
      body of loop
   end
```

Arrays

1. For now, declare arrays using the following among the declarations:

```
const
   MaxIndex = 1000;           {size of arrays}
type
   IntegerArray = array [1..MaxIndex] of integer;
var
   Array name: IntegerArray;
```

2. Refer to the Ith element of the array Scores by the expression:

```
Scores[I]
```

DPT

Loops

1. A *while* loop executes 0 or more times.
2. A *repeat-until* loop executes 1 or more times.
3. You usually need a *begin* and *end* to enclose the body of a *for* loop or a *while* loop.
4. Be careful that you do not place a semicolon directly after the *do* of the *for* loop or the *while* loop.
5. Make sure that the condition part of a *while* loop can become false sometime during the execution of the loop.
6. Make sure that the condition part of a *repeat-until* loop can become true sometime during the execution of the loop.

Arrays

1. Declare arrays.
2. Scores[I + 1] and Scores[I] +1 are different.
3. Do not violate array bounds.
4. Use "[]" and not "()" to bracket array indices.
5. Initialize all array items to be used in your program.

EXERCISES

Exercises 1 to 14 can be solved without arrays.

1. Trace the following segments by determining what values are printed and the value of I following loop termination.

   (a) `I := 1;`   (Trace for N = 6, 7, 15)
   ```
   while I < N do
      begin
         Writeln(I);
         if Odd(I) then
            I := I + 3
         else
            I := I + 5
      end
   ```

   (b) `I := 6;`   (Trace for N = 6, 7, 15)
   ```
   repeat
      Writeln(I);
      if Odd(I) then
      I := I + 3
      else
      I := I + 5
   until I >= N
   ```

   (c) `I := 1`   (Trace for N = 10, 1, 0)
   ```
   while I <= N do
    I := I + 1;
   Writeln(I)
   ```

   (d) `I := 1;`   (Trace for N = 10, 1, 0)
   ```
   repeat
      I := I + 1;
      Writeln(I)
   until I > N
   ```

2. Show the output from the program fragment:
   ```
   N := 2;
   while N < 100 do
     begin
        N := Sqr(N);
        Writeln(N)
     end
   ```

3. Show the output from the program fragment:
   ```
   S := 0;
   for I := 1 to 10 do
     begin
        Writeln(I);
        S := S + I
     end;
   Writeln(S)
   ```

4. Hand-trace this program segment for the indicated input values of the variables I and J. What values does the Writeln print?

```
Readln(I,J);
repeat
   I := 2 * I;
   if I <= J then
      I := I + 1
until I > J;
Writeln(I)
```

(a) 2, 4
(b) 3, 14
(c) 0, 12
(d) –1, 0

5. Each segment is supposed to print a table of the powers of 2 that are less than or equal to N, where N is known to be at least 2. By hand-tracing with different values of N, determine whether they are correct.

(a)
```
Readln(N);
I := 0;
P := 1;
repeat
   Writeln(I,P);
   if P <= N then
      begin
         I := I + 1;
         P := P * 2
      end
until P > N
```

(b)
```
Readln(N);
I := 0;
P := 1;
while P <= N do
   begin
      Writeln(I,P);
      I := I + 1;
      P := P * 2
   end
```

(c)
```
Readln(N);
I := 0;
P := 1;
Writeln(I,P);
while I <= N do
   begin
      I := 1 + 1
      P := P * 2;
      Writeln(I,P)
   end
```

(d) ```
    Readln(N);
    I := 0;
    P := 1;
    S := 0;
    while P <= N do
       begin
          Writeln(I,P);
          I := I + 1;
          S := S + P;
          P := S + 1
       end
```

6. Write program segments to print tables of feet and inches for the following:
   (a) feet from 1 to 30
   (b) feet from 30 back to 1
   (c) feet from 1 to N
   (d) feet from N back to 1

7. (a) Write a program segment to compute the sum $1 + 2 + \ldots + 75$. Hint: See Exercise 3.
   (b) Write a function to find the sum of the integers between (and including) two given integers. Assume that the first is less than or equal to the second.
   (c) Using the function written in part (b), write an assignment statement to find the sum of the N integers beginning at First. For example, if First is 7 and N is 3, the answer is 24 (7 + 8 + 9).

8. (a) How could Random be used to simulate a situation with equally likely outcomes ranging from 5 to 15?
   (b) How could Random be used to simulate a roulette wheel with numbers from 1 to 30, and 0 and 00?
   (c) How could Random be used to simulate a situation with equally likely outcomes 3, 6, 9, 12, 15, and 18?

9. Write a program fragment to throw a pair of dice and print the value thrown until it is 7 (also print the value 7).

10. Write a program fragment to throw a pair of dice and print the value thrown as long as it is not a 7 (do not print the value 7).

11. (a) Write a program to simulate generating 1000 random numbers in the range 1 to 10,000, and print the largest number generated.
    (b) Write a program to simulate generating 1000 random numbers in the range 1 to 1000, and count how many times the number generated matches the control variable's value.

12. (a) Write a program fragment to print all multiples of 19 that are less than 642 (19, 38, 57, and so on).
    (b) Extend part (a) to write a procedure that prints all multiples of M that are less than N.

13. (a) Modify the rabbits example so that, instead of doubling each year, it either stays the same, doubles, or triples, with each equally likely.
    (b) Modify part (a) to print the population at the end of each year for 10 years rather than after the entire 10 years.
    (c) Modify part (b) to print the population at the end of each year up to and including the year the population exceeds 10,000.

EXERCISES
```

14. A sum of $200 is deposited and compounded at 5 percent annually. Write program fragments to do the following. Note: This is similar to the rabbits example, but instead of doubling each year, the amount is multiplied by 1.05.
    (a) Print the amount in the account at the end of each year for 9 years.
    (b) Print the amount in the account at the end of each year until the amount exceeds $475.

Exercises 15 to 20 refer to arrays.

15. Suppose the array Ages contains the values:

    Ages: 12, 23, 45, 2

    Suppose that the variable Oldest has the value 3 and the variable Terrible has the value 4.

    (a) What is the value of the expression Ages[2]?
    (b) What is the value of Ages[Oldest]?
    (c) What is the value of Ages[Terrible]?
    (d) Show how to refer to the value 12.
    (e) Show how to declare the array in a program.

16. Suppose the array Days contains the values:

    Days: 31, 28, 31, 30, 31, 30, 31, 31, 30, 31, 30, 31

    (a) What is the value of the expression Days[2]?
    (b) What is the value of the expression Days[2] + 1 (which you might use in a leap year)?
    (c) Write a fragment of Pascal to print all of the values of the array Days.
    (d) What Pascal statement could you use to change the value of Days[2] to 29?

17. Determine the values printed by the following program segments, where A is an integer array as described in this section:

    (a)
    ```
    for I : = 1 to 7 do
       begin
          A[I] := I
       end; {for}

    for I := 7 downto 1 do
       begin
          Writeln(A[I])
       end; {for}
    ```

    (b)
    ```
    for I : = 1 to 5 do
       begin
          A[I] := 2 * I - 5
       end; {for}
    J := 3;
    A[J + 2] := A[J] + 2;
    A[J] := A[J] - J;

    for I : = 1 to 5 do
       begin
          Writeln(A[I])
       end; {for}
    ```

(c) ```
for I := 1 to 15 do
  begin
    if I mod 3 = 0 then
      A[I] := I + 5
    else
      A[I] := I
  end; {for}

while A[I] <= 12 do
  begin
    if A[I] >= 5 then
      Writeln(I, A[I]);
    I := I + 1
  end; {while}
```

18. Change the Pascal program of Figure 3-15 so that it uses six scores instead of three.
19. Modify your answer to Exercise 18 to change the declaration of the constant MaxIndex to 4 instead of 1000. That is, use the lines

```
const
  MaxIndex = 4;          {size of arrays}
```

Compile your program and run it. What happens? Try this both with and without range checking turned on.

20. Modify the answer to Exercise 18 so that, after printing the value of Total, it prints the value of Scores[10]. Compile the program and run it. What happens? What is the interpretation of the value printed for Scores[10] within the context of the program?

21. In the discussion of the old way of thinking and the new way, we did not have a correct alternative to offer for the "new way" statement `Writeln(Scores[I])`. There is a possible alternative given by the following case statement:

```
case I of
  1:
    Writeln(Score1);
  2:
    Writeln(Score2);
  3:
    Writeln(Score3)
end {case}
```

What do you think of this alternative? Which approach, the new or the old, would you prefer if there were 20 scores? If there were 100?

3-3 PLANNING LOOPS

In the first two sections of the chapter, we have covered several applications of loops. These include counting, accumulating totals, and finding largest or smallest values in a list of input. In addition, we have learned about two new looping constructions: the *for* loop and the *while* loop. By imitating the sample program segments of the last two sections, you have (we hope) written some looping structures similar to the examples. However, you may not
```

yet feel confident to design loops for applications that are not exactly like those examples. It is impossible to make a small set of rules that cover all possible programs that involve looping. However, some general planning strategy is quite useful in loop design. In this section, we present one approach to loop planning and illustrate it with a number of examples.

The Loop-Planning Process

The general approach to loop design can be outlined in four steps:

1. Recognize the need for a loop.
2. Plan the loop control.
3. Design the loop body and any necessary initialization and finalization steps.
4. Double check the loop control.

As we will see, in actual practice the steps interact. For example, the loop control can affect the initialization steps.

Let us begin with a brief description of the four steps.

1. Recognize the Need for a Loop. The purpose of a loop is to provide repetition. A program that must repeat one or more steps usually includes a loop for this purpose.

Part of recognizing the need for a loop involves identifying, in a general way, what is to be repeated. It may be helpful to think in terms of what one **pass** through the loop (i.e., one repetition of the loop body) accomplishes. For example, for a specific program, this might be:

Completely process one set of user input, or
Print one element of the array, or
Simulate one roll of a pair of dice, or
Double the number of rabbits

In the third step, where we plan the body of the loop, this general statement of the purpose of the loop is refined.

2. Plan the Loop Control. Planning **loop control** involves identifying the conditions under which the loop will terminate. For example, the four loops described before might terminate:

When the user enters a special terminal data value, or
When all the array elements have been printed, or
When the roll is a 7, or
When the number of rabbits exceeds 10,000

Note. Identifying a termination condition for a loop is equivalent to identifying under what conditions the loop will continue. For example, we can say that "the loop will terminate when the user enters a length of 0" or that "the loop will continue as long as the user does not enter a length of 0." Similarly, we can say that "the loop will terminate when the number of rabbits exceeds 10,000" or that "the loop will continue as long as the number of rabbits is 10,000 or less."

In general, the conditions for termination and for continuation of the repetition are negations of each other. The types of loop control can be categorized as follows:

1. *Count Control.* Most frequently, this involves a specific number of repetitions of the loop body. A *for* loop is the most appropriate structure.

2. *Direct User Control.* We have seen two types of direct user control. In the first, the user enters a special terminal value to indicate the end of a set of data. In the second, the program specifically asks the user if the process is to be repeated, and reads a yes or no answer. We can develop "standard" ways to handle these types of loops, consistent with our personal programming style. Up to this point in the text, we have used *repeat-until* loops for these types of problems.

3. *File Control.* When we learn about files in Chapter 5, we will see that loops are sometimes controlled by terminating upon reaching the end of the file. At that time, we will learn some standard ways to write this type of program.

4. *General Condition.* This is a catch-all category for any loop that does not fit one of the previous categories. For this type of loop, we choose an appropriate *repeat-until* or *while-do* looping structure. Sometimes the choice of which to use is obvious and sometimes it is not. There can be trade-offs to consider. This subject is dealt with in more detail in the next section, which discusses choosing between the *repeat* and the *while* loops.

3. Design the Loop Body, Initialization, and Finalization. The loop body consists of the steps to be repeated. As we learned in Section 3-1, certain types of looping tasks include specific types of **initialization** and **finalization** steps. For example, in a program to find the average age of a group of individuals, we would initialize a counter and accumulator to 0 prior to the loop. After the loop, we would calculate the average by dividing the accumulator by the counter and print the result.

The exact nature of the initialization steps may relate to our choice of looping structure. For example, for a *while* loop, we may have to include some preliminary steps to make sure that the condition for the loop "makes sense" the first time we execute the loop body. Thus, designing the initialization portion and the choice of loop control in step 2 may interact with each other.

By the end of this step, our algorithm should be ready (or almost ready) to write in Pascal.

4. Double Check the Loop Control. The major reasons for double checking can be summarized by these phrases:

Don't be "off by 1."
Don't be "off by 1/2."
Don't write infinite loops.

These relate to three common errors involving loop control. The first phrase warns against writing loops that execute one too many times or one too few times. For example, consider this fragment:

```
Write('Enter a number: ');
Readln(Limit);
Writeln('The multiples of 17 that are less than ', Limit : 1);
Multiple := 17;
repeat
   Writeln(Multiple);
   Multiple := Multiple + 17
until Multiple >= Limit;
```

For any Limit that is less than 17, the fragment is incorrect; we should have used a *while* loop.

The second phrase (Don't be "off by 1/2.") warns that frequently there are some steps in the loop body that should not be executed during the last pass through the loop. For example, we have written many *repeat-until* loops that skip the calculations and printing for the terminal data value entered by the user.

The third phrase (Don't write infinite loops.) indicates that we should always make sure that the termination condition can eventually become true. As we discussed in the DPT portions of the previous section, this can be caused by Pascal errors such as erroneous semicolons or forgetting *begin-end* pairs. It can also be caused by errors in reasoning. For example, the following loop, although it is correct Pascal, is faulty:

```
I := 1;
Sum := 0;
Readln(N);

repeat
    Sum := Sum + I;
    I := I + 2
until I = N;
```

For example, if N is even, the loop will not terminate. To remedy this, we would change the termination condition to "until I >= N".

One way to double check the loop control is to **hand-trace** the loop with specific values. If the loop control involves a value that would cause many passes through the loop, we may mentally replace this value with a smaller one. For example, if the loop is to terminate when an account balance exceeds $5,000.00, we might trace an equivalent loop that terminates when the balance exceeds $500.00. This process does not prove the program correct, but it can help us locate faulty reasoning. For example, consider this fragment to find the sum of the numbers from 1 to 100:

```
Sum := 0;

repeat
   Sum := Sum + I;
   I := I + 1
until I >= 100;
```

If we hand-trace this using 3 instead of 100, we observe the following:

First pass through the loop:	Sum is set to 0 + 1 = 1
	I is set to 2
Second pass through the loop:	Sum is set to 1 + 2 = 3
	I is set to 3

Since the condition "I >= 3" is now true, the loop terminates. But it did not find the sum of the numbers from 1 to 3, only from 1 to 2. Our loop control is off by 1. (Notice that we should really have used a count-controlled *for* loop, which would avoid this problem for this example.)

To illustrate the loop-planning process we have outlined, let us design a program to find the squares of numbers input by the user. The numbers are to be in the range from 1 to 100, terminated by a value of 0. The program also will indicate what percentage of the input was greater than 50.

1. Recognize the need for a loop. A loop is needed because several numbers supplied by the user are to be handled. Each pass through the loop will process one input.
2. Plan the loop control. This loop is under direct user control: an entry of 0 terminates the process. We can, therefore, use our standard techniques for this type of problem. The loop will be a *repeat-until*, terminating when the number entered is 0.
3. Design the loop body and any necessary "initialization" and "finalization" steps. The body of the loop consists of these steps to be repeated:

   issue a prompt
   read a number
   calculate and print the square
   increment the count of numbers entered
   see if the number was over 50; if so,
       increment the count of numbers over 50

   Before the loop, we initialize both counts to 0; after the loop, we calculate and print the percentage.
4. Double check the loop control. If we code the algorithm as it stands, we will be "off by 1/2." That is, we will execute some steps for the terminal value 0. All the steps beginning with the calculation should be omitted for this last pass. (We have frequently placed an asterisk in our algorithms beside these types of steps.)

Loop Control: While-Do Versus Repeat-Until

Figure 3-16 shows one possible fragment of Pascal code for the loop designed in this example. It uses our usual techniques for writing this type of loop. However, consider the program fragment in Figure 3-17, which accomplishes the same thing in a different way. This fragment **primes the loop** by reading the first value. (This terminology is intended to suggest the act of priming a pump by adding water.) As long as the Number obtained is not 0 (EndOfData), the program calculates and prints the square and does the counting. When the Number is 0, it terminates.

```
    Entered := 0;
    Over50 := 0;

    repeat
      Write('Enter number (0 to quit): ');
      Readln(Number);
      if Number <> EndOfData then
          begin
            Square := Sqr(Number);
            Writeln(Number : 1, ' squared is ', Square);
            Entered := Entered + 1;
            if Number > 50 then
                Over50 := Over50 + 1
          end
    until Number = EndOfData;
    if Entered <> 0 then
      begin
          Percent := Over50 / Entered * 100;
          Writeln(Percent : 1 : 2, '% were over 50')
      end
```

Figure 3-16 Percentage calculation-repeat loop.

```
    Entered := 0;
    Write('Enter number (0 to quit): ');
    Readln(Number);

    while Number <> EndOfData do
      begin
          Square := Sqr(Number);
          Writeln(Number : 1, ' squared is ', Square);
          Entered : = Entered + 1;
          if Number > 50 then
            Over50 : = Over50 + 1;
          Write('Enter number (0 to quit): ');
          Readln(Number)
      end;

    if Entered <> 0 then
      begin
          Percent := Over50 / Entered * 100;
          Writeln(Percent : 1 : 2, '% were over 50')
      end
```

Figure 3-17 Percentage calculation-while loop.

If you examine the two segments, you will see that there are trade-offs:

1. The *repeat-until* form includes an extra level of nesting. This can make the program harder to understand. In addition, there is the danger that we will forget to skip the processing for the terminal data value.

2. The *repeat-until* loop body contains its steps in the "natural" order: read, calculate, print. The *while* loop body has steps in this order: calculate for the value already read, print, read another value to get ready for the next pass. This can be troublesome for beginners, although we can get used to it. In addition, there is the danger that we will forget the priming read.

3. The *while* loop duplicates the read step: it appears before the loop and at the bottom of the loop. This can lead to problems if this step is modified. (Placing the step in a procedure would help avoid this problem.)

In short, the decision of which approach to use for this type of problem is not obvious. The authors chose the first approach as a starting point for the textbook examples. Many Pascal programmers (including authors of other texts) choose the second approach.

Sometimes, as in this example, there are trade-offs, and the choice is at least partially a matter of personal style. However, there are times when one or the other loop structure seems more appropriate. We offer a few general guidelines. They are not meant to cover all possible situations, but they do indicate some of the possibilities.

1. A *while* loop executes its body 0 or more times. If it is possible that the loop should terminate immediately without executing the loop body at all, a *while* loop should be used. For example, a loop to print all the multiples of 17 that are less than some user supplied number should be a *while* loop.

2. A *while* loop is ideal for activities that involve performing a first action, and then repeating a similar action if necessary. For example, in checking the validity of input data, we can write code such as:

```
Write('Enter a number in the range 0 to 100');
Readln(Number);

while (Number < 0) or (Number > 100) do
   begin
      Writeln('Invalid entry of ', Number);
      Write('Please reenter (in the range 0 to 100)');
      Readln(Number)
   end;
```

The first read and the one in the loop are similar but not quite the same. In particular, the prompt is different.

3. A *repeat-until* loop may be better for some types of problems where the loop body must be executed in order for the termination condition to make sense. For example, in a loop to count the number of dice rolls until a 7 is reached, we might write:

```
RollCount := 0;
repeat
   Roll := RollofDice;
   RollCount := RollCount + 1
until Roll = 7;
```

An equivalent *while* loop would have to perform the roll (and count it) prior to the loop. Loop priming that duplicates the entire loop body is generally not an ideal structure.

This last statement can supply some further insight into which loop type to use. First, identify the condition that is to control the loop and also the steps that form the initialization and the body of the loop. If the condition makes sense before the loop executes for the first time, then a *while* loop is indicated. If the entire body of the loop must be executed once before the condition should be tested, then a *repeat-until* loop is the best choice. If, as frequently happens, the condition first makes sense after part but not all of the loop is executed, we must make an intelligent choice. If we use a *repeat-until* loop, part of the loop body may have to be skipped on the last pass through the loop. If we use a *while-do* loop, we may have to move the first part of the loop body before the loop to prime the loop, and duplicate those steps at the bottom of the loop to prepare for the next pass through it.

Examples

For our first example, let us write a function called SmallDivisor, which finds the smallest divisor (other than 1) of a given number. (A divisor of an integer I is an integer that yields no remainder when it is divided into I.)

    SmallDivisor(15)   should be 3
    SmallDivisor(14)   should be 2
    SmallDivisor(29)   should be 29
    SmallDivisor(175)   should be 5

The function has one parameter, Number, an integer assumed to be greater than 1. Since this is our first example, we discuss it explicitly in terms of the planning steps described earlier. In our later examples, the use of those steps is implicit, even if we do not make an issue of it.

    1. *Recognize the Need for a Loop.*   How would you go about finding the smallest divisor of some large number such as 19,327? You would perhaps start trying numbers in a definite pattern: first try 2, then 3, then 4, then 5, and so on. If we imitate this manual solution, we will be repeating a process: try a potential divisor to see if it works. Thus, a loop is appropriate.

At this point, we can see the need for these two variables:

Input parameter:	Number	Integer	Number to find divisor of; the number is assumed to be greater than 1
Local variable:	Potential	Integer	A potential divisor; takes on the values 2, 3, etc.

    2. *Plan the Loop Control.*   The appropriate loop control is the "general condition" type. We cannot use count control because we do not want to try all the potential divisors from 2 to the given number. We want to stop when we find a divisor, that is, when Number mod Potential is 0.

In the verbal description of how we would solve the problem, we indicated that our first attempt would be with Potential equal to 2. Because the given number could be even, this initial value could already be the desired answer. This implies that we should use a *while* loop rather than a *repeat* loop.

3. Design the Loop Body, Initialization, and Finalization. As part of planning the loop control, we have already identified an initialization:

```
Potential := 2
```

(This is typical—the planning steps tend to interact.) In the loop body, we must add 1 to Potential; after the loop, we assign the answer to the function name.

4. Double Check the Loop Control. In rough form, our algorithm is

set Potential to 2
see if it is a divisor; as long as it isn't do this:
   add 1 to Potential

We might hand-trace this for several possible inputs: perhaps 14, 5, and 45.

For 14: Potential: 2
   loop terminates, answer is 2

For 5: Potential: 2
   not a divisor, so Potential := 3
   not a divisor, so Potential := 4
   not a divisor, so Potential := 5
   loop terminates, answer is 5

For 45: Potential: 2
   not a divisor, so Potential := 3
   loop terminates, answer is 3

Note. These inputs were chosen by observing that a number's smallest divisor lies between 2 and the number itself. The first two inputs exercise the boundaries of this possible range. In hand-tracing, as in testing, boundaries are extremely important considerations.

Based on this tracing, we appear to have avoided the three common pitfalls (off by 1, off by 1/2, infinite loop).

See Figure 3-18 for the function. There are several things to observe about that function. First, Potential is declared as a local variable within the function. Second, the mod operator checks for divisibility. Third, the *while* loop is written using a *begin* and *end* even though there is only one step in the loop; this is a matter of personal style (and defensive programming).

There is one other, fairly subtle, point. You might wonder, since in the last step of the program, we simply assign Potential to SmallDivisor, why we couldn't just use SmallDivisor itself in the loop. To be precise, would this work?

```
SmallDivisor := 2;
while Number mod SmallDivisor <> 0 do
    begin
            SmallDivisor := SmallDivisor + 1
    end; {while}
```

```
function SmallDivisor(Number: integer): integer;

{Written by: XXXXXXXXXX XX/XX/XX}
{Purpose:    To find the smallest divisor of a given number.}
{Parameters: Number - the number whose divisor is to be found}
{            (assumed to be bigger than 1)}
   var
     Potential: integer;         {a potential divisor of Number}

begin {SmallDivisor}
   Potential := 2;

   while Number mod Potential <> 0 do
      begin
         Potential := Potential + 1
      end; {while}

   SmallDivisor := Potential
end; {SmallDivisor}
```

Figure 3-18 Smallest divisor of a number.

The answer is no. Recall our previous defensive programming tip that, in writing a function, we should not use the function name anywhere except on the left side of an assignment statement. If we use it in a condition or on the right side of the assignment statement, the compiler treats it as an invocation of the function and expects parameters. Although we learn (in Chapter 4) how to make good use of this ability of a function to invoke itself, for now we should follow the rule just described.

As a second example, let us write a function to find the number of different divisors of a given number. We are not counting 1 nor the number itself as divisors. NumDivisors(15) should be 2, because 3 and 5 are divisors. NumDivisors(7) should be 0, because there are no divisors other than 1 and 7. NumDivisors(36) should be 7, because 2, 3, 4, 6, 9, 12, and 18 are divisors.

This problem is so similar to the previous one that we might be tempted to just use the same loop control. However, there is an important difference that changes the loop control: the previous example found a particular divisor, and the loop could terminate when that divisor was found. This example determines a count; we must examine every integer between 1 and the number (excluding 1 and the number). We do not want to terminate the loop when we find a divisor. A count-control loop can be used.

We need an input parameter Number, a local variable Potential as a trial divisor, and a local variable Counter to count the number of divisors found. The Pascal code for Num-Divisors is shown in Figure 3-19.

As another example, let us use the RollOfDice function (written in Section 3-2) to write a procedure that simulates a game of chance. In this game, a pair of dice is rolled once to establish a "goal." The dice are then rolled repeatedly until the goal is matched on a future roll. The player pays $10 to play the game and wins $1 for each successful roll that does not match the goal. We wish to simulate one play of the game and print an appropriate message showing the results.

We use these variables: Goal, to record the first roll; Roll, for the subsequent rolls; and Money, to keep track of the player's money. Each pass through the loop simulates one

```
function NumDivisors(Number: integer): integer;

{Written by: XXXXXXXX XX/XX/XX
{Purpose:    To find the number of divisors of a given number}
{Parameters: Number - the number whose divisors are to be}
{                    counted (assumed to be bigger than 1)}
   var
      Potential: integer;         {a potential divisor}
      Counter: integer;           {number of divisors found}

begin {NumDivisors}

   Counter := 0;

   for Potential := 2 to Number - 1 do
      begin
         if Number mod Potential = 0 then
            Counter := Counter + 1
      end; {for}

   NumDivisors := Counter

end; {NumDivisors}
```

Figure 3-19 Count of divisors of a number.

attempt to match the goal. The loop terminates when there is a match, that is, when Roll = Goal. We have the following initialization, loop body, and finalization steps:

INITIALIZATION

obtain the Goal value
set the Money to −10 (you pay $10 to play)

LOOP BODY

obtain the Roll value
print the Roll value
add 1 to the Money

FINALIZATION

print a message (depending on whether Money is positive, negative, or zero)

We now consider whether to use a *while* loop or a *repeat* loop. The termination condition (Roll = Goal) does not make sense until we have rolled the dice. We therefore choose a repeat loop. We must be cautious, however, not to be "off by 1/2." The final step of the loop body should not be executed if the roll matched the goal. For example, if the Goal is matched on the 13th roll, as illustrated in the second sample run of the program, the player would win only $2 ($12 minus the $10 to play).

The planning just described leads us to the procedure presented in Figure 3-20.

3-3 PLANNING LOOPS

```
procedure MatchRoll;

{Written by: XXXXXXXXXX XX/XX/XX}
{Purpose:    To simulate one play of a game of chance}
{Parameters: None}
{Functions used: RollOfDice, to simulate rolling a pair of dice}

   var
      Goal: integer;      {result of first roll, the "goal"}
      Roll: integer;      {subsequent rolls of the dice}
      Money: integer;     {player's money}

begin {MatchRoll}

{*** Obtain goal and initialize player's money}

  Goal := RollOfDice;
  Writeln('The goal is ', Goal : 1);
  Money := -10;

{*** Roll until goal is matched, winning $1 for each successful roll}

   repeat
      Roll := RollOfDice;
      Writeln ('This roll: ', Roll : 1);
      if Roll <> Goal then
         Money := Money + 1
   until Roll = Goal;

{*** Print the results}

   if Money > 0 then
      Writeln ('You won $', Money : 1)
   else if Money = 0 then
      Writeln('You broke even')
   else
      Writeln('You lost $', Abs(Money) : 1)
end; {MatchRoll}
```

Figure 3-20 Game of chance (continued next page).

Sometimes a problem is "almost" a count-control problem. For example, to find the sum $1 + 2 + \cdots + 400$, we could use

```
Sum := 0;
for I := 1 to 400 do
  begin
     Sum := Sum + I
  end; {for}
```

What might we do to find the sum $2 + 4 + \ldots + 266$?

SAMPLE INPUT AND OUTPUT

First run:

```
The goal is 8
This roll: 8
You lost $10
```

Second run:

```
The goal is 7
This roll: 11
This roll: 4
This roll: 4
This roll: 11
This roll: 4
This roll: 5
This roll: 9
This roll: 8
This roll: 6
This roll: 8
This roll: 8
This roll: 12
This roll: 7
You won $2
```

Figure 3-20 (continued)

One approach is to imitate the logic of the *for* loop with a *while* loop, as described in the previous section. We would like to go from 2 to 266, but by 2's. We can write:

```
Sum := 0;
I := 2;
while I <= 266 do
  begin
    Sum := Sum + I;
    I := I + 2
  end; {while}
```

Note. Some programming languages, such as FORTRAN, COBOL, and BASIC, expand the notion of the count-control loop to include a "step size," so one could use a *for* loop to, say, sum the even numbers from 2 to 266. The Pascal *for* loop does not include a step size, so we typically use a *while* or *repeat* loop in these situations.

For the final example, we consider a problem involving an integer array. For this problem, we recall the definitions of potential size and actual size for an array. The potential size is the declared size (MaxIndex in the declaration scheme we suggested). The actual size is the number of meaningful values presently stored in the array.

Note. We are suggesting using a large potential size (MaxIndex = 1000). This means that the actual size is usually considerably smaller. This avoids some subtle pitfalls that we discuss in detail in Chapter 6.

There are two frequently used ways to indicate the actual size of an array. The first uses a separate variable to keep track of this value. The second places a **delimiter** in the array following the last meaningful value. The delimiter plays the same role that a terminating input value does. It can be any chosen value that could not possibly be mistaken for a meaningful value.

Assuming that this second method is used with a delimiter of -maxint, let us write code to find the sum of an array called A. We need a loop because there are several values to be summed. In our preliminary planning, we observe that each pass through the loop adds one of the array values to the sum. We accomplish this by causing a variable I to take on the values 1, 2, ... Then we can use A[I] to refer successively to A[1], A[2], ...

Because we do not know how many values there are, we use the general condition form of loop control, terminating the loop when we reach the delimiter. To deal with the question of whether to use a *while* loop or a *repeat-until* loop, we ask: Could it be possible that the loop body might be executed 0 times? The answer is yes; if A[I] contains the delimiter, then there are no numbers to sum.

Further planning leads to the following:

INITIALIZATION

set the sum to 0
start the subscript at 1

LOOP BODY

add the array element to the sum
add 1 to the subscript

FINALIZATION: ??

The finalization step might be to print the sum. However, we choose to write a function for this task, so the finalization step assigns the answer to the function name.

The function, based on this planning process, appears as Figure 3-21. Several points are worth noting:

1. An array can be passed as a parameter to a function. We declare the parameter using the identifier IntegerArray defined in the main program. (More details on arrays as parameters are given in Chapter 4.)
2. The termination condition is "A[I] contains the delimiter." As usual in a *while* loop, the controlling condition tells how long the loop should continue and is the negation of the condition for terminating.
3. If we forget the loop's *begin* and *end*, or the step "I := I + 1", the program may execute forever.
4. Sum and I are variables local to the function. (Recall that this means they are declared and used within the function, not in the main program.)

```
function ArraySum(A: IntegerArray): integer;

{Written by: XXXXXXXXXX XX/XX/XX}
{Purpose:    To find the sum of an array which uses a delimiter of -maxint}
{Parameter:  A, the array to be summed}

   var
      Sum: integer;              {array sum}
      I: integer;                {subscript}
begin {ArraySum}
   Sum := 0;
   I := 1;
   while A[I] <> -maxint do
      begin
         Sum := Sum + A[I];
         I := I + 1
      end; {while}
   ArraySum := Sum
end; {ArraySum}
```

Figure 3-21 Summing an array with a delimiter.

DPT

1. In writing a *while* loop, the condition for the loop must make sense when the loop is first executed. This may require some "priming" steps prior to the loop. Some or all of these steps may have to be duplicated at the bottom of the body of the loop.
2. We should double check our loops to make sure that we are not "off by 1." One way to accomplish this is by hand-tracing the execution of the loop. If the loop executes a large number of times, we can make an appropriate modification of the loop for the purpose of this tracing.
3. We should also avoid being "off by 1/2." We should check to see if there are any of the steps in the loop that should not be executed on the final pass through the loop.
4. Check for initialization steps. Many times the correct initial value for some variable is a value other than zero.

REVIEW

Terms and Concepts

delimiter
finalization
hand-tracing
initialization

loop control
pass (through a loop)
priming a loop

Loop Planning

Steps in Loop Design

1. Recognize the need for a loop.
2. Plan the loop control.
3. Design the loop body and any necessary "initialization" and "finalization" steps.
4. Double check the loop control.

Types of Loop Control

1. Count control
2. Direct user control
3. File control
4. General condition

Choosing While or Repeat

1. Sometimes there is no obvious choice; there are trade-offs.
2. Use a *while* loop if the body can be executed 0 times.
3. Use a *while* loop to execute an action, and then perform a similar action 0 or more times.
4. Use a *repeat-until* if the body must be executed once before the termination condition "makes sense."

DPT

1. May need priming steps for the *while* loop to cause a condition to "make sense" on the first pass.
2. Don't be "off by 1."
3. Don't be "off by 1/2."
4. Double check the initialization steps.

EXERCISES

1. By modifying the initialization of Potential, rewrite the SmallDivisor function (Figure 3-18) to use a *repeat* loop instead of a *while* loop. Which design seems better? Why?
2. Modify the MatchRoll procedure (Figure 3-20) to use a *while* loop. Is the revised approach better or worse? Why?
3. Each record has an ID number, yearly income, number of years worked for the company, and a four-letter department code.
   (a) Write a program to find the ID number and yearly income of the person who earned the most during the year.

(b) Modify this program to print how many years this person has worked for the company and her department code (this requires two more special variables).
(c) Write a program to find the average number of years worked by persons in department 'TRNG'.
(d) Write a program to find the ID number and income of the person who earned the least during the year.

4. Each record contains a name, four test scores, the final exam score, and a quiz grade. Give a program to print the final average and resulting letter grade for each student. Also, find who had the highest and lowest scores on the final exam, which of the four tests had the highest class average, and how many received an A for the course. (Grades are based on 90 percent for an A, 80 percent for a B, and so on.)

5. The loop that follows repeatedly divides a positive integer number by 10 until the result is 0. For example, for the number 1372, the results would be 137, then 13, then 1, then 0.

```
Readln(Number);
repeat
   Number := Number div 10
until Number = 0
```

Modify the segment to obtain a count of the digits in the Number that was read. Would the program work for Number = 0? For Number < 0?

6. Write a function to find the sum of the digits of a given positive integer. Hint: Use Exercise 5 and the fact that, for a positive number N, the expression N mod 10 "picks off" its rightmost digit.

7. Write a function to find the largest digit of a given positive integer. For 1632, the answer would be 6. For 989, the answer would be 9. Hint: See Exercise 6.

8. Write a function HighPower(Number) that, for a given positive number, finds the highest power of 2 that divides into the number. For example, HighPower(6) is 1 (2 is the highest power that divides into 6). Likewise, HighPower(24) is 3 (2^3 is the highest), and HighPower(175) is 0 (2^0 is the highest). Hint: Repeatedly divide the number by 2 until an odd number is obtained.

9. In this section, we wrote a function that found the smallest divisor (other than 1) of a number. Using a similar idea, write a function that finds the largest divisor (other than N itself) of a number N. Hint: Start high and work your way down; the first divisor found is the largest.

10. Using an idea similar to that in the SmallDivisor function of this section (Figure 3-18), write a function GCD(M,N). The input parameters are positive integers. The answer is the "greatest common divisor" of M and N, that is, it is the largest number that divides evenly into both M and N. Hint: Start at the smaller of M and N and work your way down.

11. See Exercise 10. Write a function LCM(M,N) that finds the "least common multiple" of M and N. This is the smallest number into which both M and N divide evenly.

12. The algorithms suggested in Exercises 10 and 11, respectively, for the greatest common divisor and least common multiple of M and N, run very slowly for large values of M and N. There are a number of better algorithms.

Probably the most popular and fastest algorithm for calculating the GCD of two positive integers is an algorithm credited to Euclid. One form of Euclid's algorithm is

set Big, Small to the larger and smaller of M, N
repeat these steps
   set R to Big mod Small
   Big := Small
   Small := R

```
until R = 0
set GCD to Big
```

    (a) Hand-trace this algorithm for the following pairs of numbers:
- (i) 45, 10
- (ii) 10, 45
- (iii) 100, 48
- (iv) 105, 32
- (v) 10,000; 4994
- (vi) 500, 735

    (b) Code the algorithm as a function.
    (c) Temporarily modify each of the functions in Exercises 10 and 12(b) to count and print the number of assignment statements executed. Write a main program that inputs a series of pairs of numbers and calls each function. Compare the speed of the two functions in terms of the number of assignment statements.
    (d) Modify the LCM function to take advantage of this relationship:

$$GCD(M,N) * LCM(M,N) = M * N$$

13. In this section, we wrote a function that calculated the number of divisors of a given integer.
    (a) Write a procedure that for a given N prints a table listing its divisors.
    (b) Write a main program that reads a series of records, each containing an integer. For each such integer, it should use the procedure from part (a) to print a table of divisors of the integer.

14. Write a segment of Pascal code for the following:
    (a) Print a table of feet and inches for feet = 1, 2, ..., 20.
    (b) Repeat part (a) for feet = 5, 10, ..., 150.
    (c) Repeat part (a) for feet = 0.00, 0.25, 0.50, ..., 4.75, 5.00.

15. (a) How could Random be used to simulate the toss of a coin?
    (b) Simulate tossing a coin 1000 times, counting the number of heads.
    (c) Simulate tossing a coin 1000 times, counting the number of times the toss does not match the previous toss.
    (d) Simulate tossing a coin 1000 times, determining the longest streak of consecutive heads.

16. Write a program fragment that generates a series of random numbers in the range 1 to 10, counting how many numbers must be generated until two consecutive numbers are the same.

17. We can estimate the probability of a particular outcome occurring in a random experiment by performing the experiment a large number of times and finding for what percentage the outcome occurs. For example, if we roll a pair of dice 12,000 times and there are Count7 7's, then the probability of getting a 7 is approximated by Count7/12,000. Using this idea, write program segments for the following. (Note: These can also be solved mathematically.)

    (a) What is the probability that the roll of a pair of dice is between 4 and 8?
    (b) If two people each roll a pair of dice, what is the probability that their rolls are identical?
    (c) If you toss three coins simultaneously, what is the probability that only one is a head?
    (d) If you draw a card at random from a set of 10 cards numbered 1 to 10, what is the probability that it has an even number?

(e) If you draw two cards from the set of 10 cards in part (d), replacing the first before drawing the second, what is the probability that both have even numbers?

(f) For the situation in part (e), what is the probability that the sum of the numbers on the cards is at least 15?

18. Write a program to simulate 200 rolls of a single die, counting how many 1's, 2's, 3's, 4's, 5's, and 6's occur. In addition to printing the counts, use the Asterisks procedure of the previous section (Figure 3-11) to print a graph of the answer. For each outcome, the graph contains a row of asterisks, with one asterisk for each occurrence. Sample output:

```
1 : ********************************
2 : **********************************
3 : *********************************
4 : *******************************
5 : **********************************
6 : **********************************
```

19. (a) Write a function with two parameters N and Total. The function should count how many random numbers in the range 1 to N must be generated to obtain a sum of the numbers generated that is greater than Total.

(b) By placing the call to the function in part (a) in a loop that is executed 15,000 times, calculate the average number of random numbers that must be generated in the range 1 to 100 to obtain a sum greater than 500.

20. In this exercise, we describe a technique sometimes known as the "Monte Carlo" method.

(a) Consider the following diagram containing a quarter of a circle with a radius 1 and a square with a side 1.

If we randomly dropped a large number of darts onto the figure, we would expect that the following ratio would be approximately true:

$$\frac{\text{Number in quarter circle}}{\text{Total number dropped}} = \frac{\text{area of quarter circle}}{\text{area of square}}$$

Since the area of the quarter circle is $\pi/4$ and the area of the square is 1, we get an estimate for π given by

$$\pi = 4 \left(\frac{\text{number in quarter circle}}{\text{total number dropped}} \right)$$

We can simulate this situation by generating a large number of pairs of number (x,y) in the range from 0 to 1. If $x^2 + y^2 \leq 1$, then the point is inside the quarter circle. Write a program to estimate π using this technique.

(b) The idea in part (a) can be extended to other functions. Consider the following diagram.

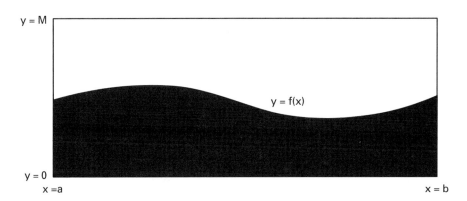

If we generate a large number of random points (x,y) with $a \leq x \leq b$ and $0 \leq y \leq M$, we would expect that the following ratio be true:

$$\frac{\text{Number of points with } y \leq f(x)}{\text{Total number of points}} = \frac{\text{area of highlighted portion}}{\text{area of rectangle}}$$

Use this method to approximate the area under the curve $y = x^2$ between 0 and 1. (The exact answer is 1/3.)

(c) Repeat part (b), using $y = 3x^3 - x$ between 1 and 2. (The exact answer is 9.75.)

21. Write a function to calculate n! for given n. (n! is n * (n – 1) * (n – 2) * · · · * 2 * 1.) Hint: Finding the product of the first n integers is similar to finding their sum.
22. Write a function that, given an integer N and a real number X, computes X raised to the Nth power by multiplying X by itself the proper number of times. (It should handle the case that N is 0 or a positive number.)
23. The expression e^x for a given real number X is given by the infinite series

$$1 + X + \frac{X^2}{2} + \frac{X^3}{2 \cdot 3} + \frac{X^4}{2 \cdot 3 \cdot 4} + \cdots +$$

Write a function Exp(X,N) that calculates the sum of the first N terms of this series. Hint: In a "for I := 1 to N do" loop, each term can be calculated from the previous term by multiplying the previous term by X / I.

24. Write a function Exp(X) that calculates the sum of the terms of the series in Exercise 23 up to and including the first term whose value is less than the current value of the sum times 0.00001.
25. The derivative of a function $y = f(x)$ at a point a is given by

$$\lim_{h \to 0} \frac{f(a+h) - f(a)}{h}$$

To demonstrate the limit process, some calculus textbooks print tables showing the value of the expression

$$\frac{f(a+h)-f(a)}{h}$$

for values of h getting closer and closer to 0. Write a program to generate such a table for $h = 1/2^n$, $n = 1, \ldots, 14$ and for $h = -1/2^n$, $n = 1, \ldots, 14$. Use these functions and points.

(a) $y = x^2$, $a = 2$ (the limit is 4)
(b) $y = \sqrt{x}$, $a = 16$ (the limit is 8)
(c) $y = 1/x$, $a = 3$ (the limit is $-1/9$)

26. The area under a positive curve can be approximated by finding the areas of a collection of rectangles. Refer to the diagram.

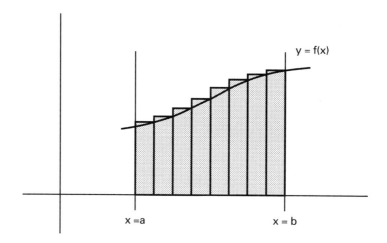

If we divide the region from a to b into n subintervals, then the area of the first rectangle is $hf(a + h)$, where $h = (b - a)/n$. The area of the second rectangle is $hf(a + 2h)$, the area of the third is $hf(a + 3h)$, and so on.

Use this idea to write a program that approximates the area under the curve $y = x^2 - 5$ between $x = 3$ and $x = 10$. Divide the interval into n = 28 regions. Repeat the process with $n = 56$, and with $n = 224$. (The actual area is 2893.)

27. Give test plans for the following exercises:
   (a) Exercise 3(a)
   (b) Exercise 3(c)
   (c) Exercise 5
   (d) Exercise 7
   (e) Exercise 8
   (f) Exercise 9
   (g) Exercise 10
   (h) Exercise 21
   (i) Exercise 22
   (j) Exercise 23

EXERCISES

Exercises 28 to 32 deal with integer arrays as described in the previous section.

28. Modify the function ArraySum (Figure 3-21) to use a separate variable to keep track of the actual size. That is, there are two parameters: the array and the actual size, N. Use a count-control loop.

29. For an array that uses a −maxint delimiter to indicate the actual size, write a segment of code to calculate the actual size as the variable N. For the array

    ```
    12, 4, -6, -maxint, . . .
    ```

    the answer is 3.

30. For an array without a delimiter and the size as a variable N, write code to place a −maxint delimiter in the array.

31. For each of the following, solve the problem twice by using the delimiter approach and the approach with a separate "size" variable.
    (a) Find the largest value in an array.
    (b) Count the even numbers in an array.
    (c) Read an array with input terminated by a dummy entry of −maxint.
    (d) Print an array, printing one number per line.

32. Give test plans for the following:
    (a) Exercise 29
    (b) Exercise 30
    (c) Exercise 31(a)
    (d) Exercise 31(b)
    (e) Exercise 31(c)
    (f) Exercise 31(d)

3-4 NESTED LOOPS AND COMPLEX LOOP TERMINATION

Many problems require combinations of the techniques discussed in Sections 3-1 to 3-3. Frequently, loops must be contained within other loops, leading to **nested loops**. In addition, the terminating conditions for loops frequently involve more than one condition. This is especially true for loops that perform **searches.** These topics are discussed in this section, along with the important topic of validating user input.

Nested Loops

Just as decisions can be nested, so also loops can be nested. As an example, consider the following program segment:

```
for Row : = 1 to 5 do
   begin
      for Seat := 1 to 8 do
         begin
            Writeln('Row #', Row : 1, ' Seat #', Seat : 1)
         end {for Seat loop}
   end {for Row loop}
```

The variable Row successively takes on the values 1, 2, 3, 4, and 5. For each value of Row, the inner *for* loop is executed, causing Seat to take on the values 1, 2, 3, 4, 5, 6, 7, and 8. Thus, the output for this segment begins with these lines:

```
Row #1 Seat #1
Row #1 Seat #2
Row #1 Seat #3
Row #1 Seat #4
Row #1 Seat #5
Row #1 Seat #6
Row #1 Seat #7
Row #1 Seat #8
Row #2 Seat #1
```

As a second example, consider this segment that, five times in a row, counts the number of rolls of the dice it takes to obtain a 7.

```
for I := 1 to 5 do
  begin
    Count := 0;
    repeat
      Roll := RollOfDice;
      Count := Count + 1
    until Roll = 7;
    Writeln('A 7 was rolled on roll #', Count : 1)
  end; {for}
```

This illustrates that a *repeat-until* loop can be one of the steps within a *for* loop. Conversely, consider this example:

```
repeat
  for I := 1 to 100 do
    begin
      Roll := RollOfDice;
      if Roll = 2 then
        Count := Count + 1
    end; {for}
  Writeln('There were ', Count : 1, ' two''s rolled')
until Count >= 3
```

This segment, which contains a *for* loop nested in a *repeat* loop, counts how many of 100 rolls of the dice are 2's. It continues to do so until a count of at least 3 occurs.

Notes

1. We follow our (and THINK's) usual indentation pattern for loops by indenting the body of each loop.
2. The terms **inner loop** and **outer loop** are frequently used in describing nested loops. In the previous example, the *for* loop is the inner loop and the *repeat* loop is the outer loop.

3. Loops can be nested to any depth. However, we should limit the levels of nesting (of both loops and decisions) to a number that does not hinder our ability to understand the program. Subprograms can be useful in this regard.
4. Loops can be nested; they may not overlap. The inner loop must be completely contained within the outer loop.

Nested loops occur quite naturally during the program design process. It is not necessary when beginning the design of a program to know at the outset that nested loops will be involved. For example, suppose we wish to print all the divisors of a series of input numbers. We might begin with an algorithm something like this:

print instructions
repeat these steps until the user enters a terminal value (≤ 0)
issue a prompt
read N
print the divisors of N (not done if N is the terminal value)

Now, to print all the divisors of N involves a count-controlled loop that, for each number I ranging from 1 to N, checks to see if I is a divisor of N. We therefore have a *for* loop nested within a *repeat* loop.

Note. Alternatively, we could use a procedure to print the divisors. The loop for printing would be in the procedure rather than nested within the main program's loop.

There is one situation, however, where we can immediately realize that nested loops can be appropriate. This situation is illustrated by the following example. Suppose that the user wishes to obtain a listing of the total sales for a number of employees. To do so, the user inputs the employee name, followed by a list of sales amounts terminated by a 0. Thus, the input will follow this pattern:

```
employee name
sales amount
. . .
terminal amount of 0
next employee name
sales amount
. . .
terminal amount of 0
. . .
```

The data itself consist of repetitions of repetitions. The set of data for an employee is repeated, and the sales figures are repeated within each set of employee data. As a general rule, we can state:

>Nested repetitions of data imply nested loops in the program.

The program in Figure 3-22 reads the data and prints a report on the printer as well as at the terminal. It includes a count of the employees processed. Notice the placement of initialization and print steps for the employee counter and for the sales amount accumulator. The counter is initialized once, before the outermost loop (the *repeat* loop), and is printed after this same loop. The accumulator, on the other hand, is initialized within the *repeat* loop, but prior to the *while* loop, and is printed following the *while* loop. This is appropriate because this total should be reinitialized to 0 for each new employee, and it should be printed for each employee.

Note. As you can see from the printer output, some adjustment in the spacing is needed to achieve better alignment. After this adjustment, the Header procedure would no longer be a stub.

The design process for a program involving nested loops is similar to that described in the previous section for single loops. As we have indicated, we may or may not immediately realize that nested loops are needed. However, once we do realize this, we should plan each loop using our usual loop-design methods.

In considering the placement of initialization and finalization steps, it may be helpful to do two things: (1) identify the primary "purpose" of each loop, and (2) visualize the loops as dividing the program into segments. For example, for the program of Figure 3-22, we would have

<pre>
                      1
    outer loop beginning (one pass = 1 employee)
                      2
    inner loop beginning (one pass = 1 sale)
                      3
                inner loop end
                      4
                outer loop end
                      5
</pre>

We can then summarize as shown:

REGION NUMBER	SUMMARY
1	Steps done once prior to handling all the employees
2	Steps done once for each employee, prior to handling the employee's sales
3	Steps done once for each sale
4	Steps done once for each employee after the employee's sales
5	Steps done once after all employees are processed

More Than One Termination Condition

For some loops, there is more than one possible condition for terminating the repetition. These loops are designed in much the same way as the simpler loops with a single termination condition. We simply use the Boolean operators *and* and *or* to write a compound-condition for loop continuation (for a *while* loop) or termination (for a *repeat-until* loop). For example, the segment of code that follows simulates a game of chance with these rules:

```
program ReadSales;

{Written by: XXXXXXXXX XX/XX/XX}
{Purpose:   To read and total a number of sales for a number of}
{           employees. The program illustrates the maxim nested}
{           repetitions of data imply nested loops.}
{Procedures used: Instructions, to print instructions}
{                 Header, to print headings}

  const
    EndOfData = 0;   {loop control}

  var
    Name: string;           {employee name, input}
    Sales: real;            {sales amount, input}
    Total: real;            {total sales, calculated}
    Answer: char;           {continue?}
    Count: integer;         {number of employees}
    Report: text;           {name for the printer}

  procedure Instructions;
  begin
   {stub}
  end;

  procedure Header;
  begin {Header - stub version}
     Writeln(Report, ' ' : 10, 'Name', ' ' : 12, 'Total sales');
     Writeln(Report, ' ' : 10, '----', ' ' : 12, '----- -----');
  end; {Header}

begin {ReadSales}

{*** Initialize and print instructions and headings}

  Rewrite(Report, 'Printer:');
  Count := 0;
  Instructions;
  Header;

{*** Read name}

  repeat
    Write('Enter name: ');
    Readln(Name);
    Count := Count + 1;
```

Figure 3-22 Counting and accumulation with nested loops (continues next page).

```
{*** Read and total sales figures}
    Total := 0;
    Write('Sales: ');
    Readln(Sales);
    while Sales <> 0 do
      begin
        Total := Total + Sales;
        Write('Sales: ');
        Readln(Sales)
      end; {while}
{*** Print total, ask user if done}
    Writeln('The total is ', Total : 1 : 2);
    Writeln(Report, Name : 20, Total : 10 : 2);
    Writeln;
    Write('Any more? ');
    Readln(Answer)
  until not (Answer in ['Y', 'y']);
{*** Print summary for entire set of data and quit}
  Writeln;
  Writeln('There were ', Count : 1, ' employees.');
  Writeln(Report);
  Writeln(Report, 'There were ', Count : 1, ' employees.');
end.
```

SAMPLE INPUT AND OUTPUT

Terminal

```
Enter name: Bob Ransome
Sales: 100
Sales: 53.40
Sales: 125.07
Sales: 0
The total is 278.47

Any more? y
Enter name: Joe Hocking
Sales: 0
The total is 0.00

Any more? Y
Enter name: Mary Wilkinson
Sales: 450
Sales: 0
The total is 450.00

Any more? n
There were 3 employees.
```

Figure 3-22 (continues next page)

3-4 NESTED LOOPS AND COMPLEX LOOP TERMINATION

Printer

```
    Name            Total sales
    ----            ----- -----
  Bob Ransome        278.47
  Joe Hocking          0.00
Mary Wilkinson       450.00
There were 3 employees.
```

Figure 3-22   (continued)

Generate a random integer from 1 to 25. If the number is 1, 2, 3, or 4, you win $5, otherwise you lose $1. Starting with $20, we play the game until we either go broke or double our money.

```
Money := 20;
repeat
   Number := abs(Random mod 25) + 1; {random number, 1 - 25}
     if Number < 5 then
         Money := Money + 5
     else
         Money := Money - 1
until (Money = 0) or (Money >= 40);
if Money = 0 then
   Writeln ('You went broke')
else
   Writeln('You doubled your money to ', Money : 1)
```

Note.   It may be useful in working with loops using multiple-termination conditions to use an **assertion** (a Boolean expression known to be true) to verbalize the situation on leaving the loop. In our example, we might insert the comment:

```
{Either Money is $0 or it is at least $40}
```

right after the loop. This assertion can help us decide what should be done next (frequently a decision structure).

To illustrate this comment, consider the following slightly modified segment, which limits play to 30 rolls:

```
NRolls := 0;
Money  := 20;
repeat
   Number := abs(Random mod 25) + 1;
   NRolls := NRolls + 1;
   if Number < 5 then
      Money := Money + 5
   else
      Money := Money - 1
until (Money = 0) or (Money >= 40) or (NRolls = 30);
```

```
{Either Money = $0, or Money >= $40, or NRolls = 30}

if Money = 0 then
   Writeln('You went broke')
else if Money >= 40 then
   Writeln( 'You doubled your money to ', Money : 1)
else
   Writeln('You neither went broke nor doubled your money. ',
        'You have ', Money : 1)
```

In an *or* condition, it is possible that more than one of the individual conditions is true. This leads to a defensive programming tip:

> Be careful in writing decision structures after loops with compound termination conditions. More than one part of the condition can be *true*.

In our example, if we wrote

```
if NRolls = 30 then
   Writeln('You neither went broke nor doubled your money. ',
        'You have ', Money : 1)
else if Money = 0 then
   Writeln('You went broke')
else
   Writeln('You doubled your money to ', Money : 1)
```

we would be incorrect. (Why?)

In addition, we must take special care to avoid some pitfalls described earlier. We must make sure, in particular, that:

1. The condition used for loop control makes sense on the first pass through the loop,

2. The condition makes sense on the last pass (i.e., when the loop terminates),

3. We are not "off by 1/2."

We illustrate these ideas with two examples.

For the first, let us simulate a game of chance in which we roll a pair of dice. The object of this game is to roll 10 consecutive numbers greater than 3. If we succeed we win, and if we fail we lose.

At first glance, this looks like it might be a count-controlled loop; however, the game should terminate immediately if a 2 or a 3 is rolled. Since the Pascal *for* loop is designed to execute precisely the number of times indicated, it is not appropriate. We, therefore, write code to explicitly count the rolls using a variable RollCount. We initialize this to 1, which is consistent with the semantics of the *for* loop "for RollCount := 1 to 10 do. . . ." The loop should terminate when RollCount indicates that we have rolled 10 rolls or when a 2 or 3 is rolled, whichever occurs first.

Because we must roll the dice to check for a 2 or 3, we use a *repeat-until* loop. A Pascal segment is given in the first half of Figure 3-23. However, it has some problems. Before you read on, and without looking at the second half of the figure, try to locate the bugs.

3-4 NESTED LOOPS AND COMPLEX LOOP TERMINATION   **241**

FAULTY PASCAL CODE

```
RollCount := 1;
repeat
  Roll := RollOfDice;
  RollCount := RollCount + 1
until (Roll <= 3) or (RollCount = 10);

if Roll <= 3 then
  Writeln('You lost with a ', Roll : 1, ' on try #', RollCount : 1)
else
  Writeln('Congratulations, you win.')
```

CORRECTED CODE

```
RollCount := 0;
repeat
  Roll := RollOfDice;
  RollCount := RollCount + 1
until (Roll <= 3) or (RollCount > 10);

if Roll <= 3 then
  Writeln('You lost with a ', Roll : 1, ' on try #', RollCount : 1)
else
  Writeln('Congratulations, you win.')
```

Figure 3-23 Wrong and right way to exit a loop.

As the first half of the figure stands, the loop is off by 1 and also off by 1/2. If we never roll a 2 or 3, the loop executes only nine times. If we do roll a 2 or a 3, the RollCount reported is one greater than the roll on which it actually occurred. With the loop the way we have written it, RollCount keeps track of which pass of the loop is occurring, and the step that adds 1 is getting ready for the next pass. The second half of the figure illustrates one correct solution. Other possible approaches, and other issues related to this example, are explored in the exercises.

For the second example, we write Pascal code that works with an array of integers named Nums. As in our previous array example, we assume that values have been read into the array. Moreover, we assume that the actual size is indicated by a variable rather than by using the delimiter method. Thus, we assume that a variable Count contains the number of values read in. For example, Nums might contain the integers 3, 15, –101, 214, –66, 14 with Count having the value 6.

We can use the following program segment to print the values in the array:

```
for I : = 1 to Count do
  begin
      Writeln(Nums[I])
  end {for}
```

This works even if Count has the value 0 because a *for* loop whose ending value is greater than its starting value executes 0 times. In our example, we do not assume that Count is positive.

```
      MoreToPrint := true;
      while (I <= Count) and MoreToPrint do
        begin
          if Nums[I] < 0 then
            MoreToPrint := false
          else
            begin
              Writeln(Nums[I]);
              I := I + 1;
            end {if}
        end {while}
```

Figure 3-24 Avoiding a pitfall with arrays.

What we wish to do in this example is to modify the program segment to print only up to the first negative value in the array. For the array values given before, only the 3 and the 15 would be printed. Because the loop should terminate (possibly) prior to printing all the values, the *for* loop is no longer appropriate. However, perhaps we can modify the following equivalent representation of the *for* loop logic:

```
      I := 1;
      while I <= Count do
        begin
          Writeln(Nums[I]);
          I := I + 1
        end {while}
```

Our planning might go something like this: The loop should continue as long as I is less than or equal to Count and Nums[I] is positive. We are tempted to make a simple modification to the *while* loop, writing

```
      while (I <= Count) and (Nums[I] > 0) do . . .
```

To consider whether this is correct, we must look in particular at whether the condition makes sense on the last pass when the loop terminates. For the condition to make sense, both halves must make sense:

```
      I <= Count
      Nums[I] > 0
```

Now if the loop terminates because it has found a negative value in the array, both parts are fine. However, suppose the loop terminates because it has printed all the array values. In this case, the variable I has a value one greater than Count, and the reference to Nums[I] makes no sense.

For example, if Count is 3, the array contains values Nums[1], Nums[2], and Nums[3]. The reference to Nums[4] in this condition refers to something that does not exist. (This is especially bad if Count is equal to the declared size of the array. Then Nums[I] would refer to a location beyond the end of the array (and only range checking being on would prevent the program from producing erroneous output).

3-4 NESTED LOOPS AND COMPLEX LOOP TERMINATION

One way to resolve this problem is illustrated in Figure 3-24. This is a well-known pitfall in dealing with arrays; you should study carefully the solution given in the figure. (In Chapter 6 on arrays, we have more to say about this pitfall.)

Use of Multiple-Termination Conditions: Searching

The examples just given are typical of many problems in which loops have more than one termination condition. In each example, we could view the loop as performing a process that would either succeed or fail. For example:

SUCCESS	FAILURE
Doubling money	Going broke
Rolling 10 times	Getting a 2 or 3 before 10 rolls
Printing the entire array	Reaching a negative value

The broad class of **searching algorithms** has this same "succeed or fail" characteristic. We study this class in some detail in Chapter 5 (in connection with files) and in Chapter 6 (in connection with arrays). In a searching algorithm, we have this general form:

repeat the steps of a loop:
    if we find for what we are searching, terminate the loop
    if we reach the end of the data without finding it,
        terminate the loop

Observe that we may not examine all the data. As soon as we find the desired item, we want to terminate. One common approach is to use a **flag** (a Boolean variable) to cause this termination to occur, as we did in the array printing example of Figure 3-24.

Another typical feature of this type of program is that the loop is followed by a decision structure. This decision structure is used to choose an action based on which individual condition caused the loop to terminate.

Validating Input

Perhaps you have heard the phrase "garbage in, garbage out." This is a rather cynical reaction to shortcomings that are sometimes found in programs. The phrase indicates that if you supply the program with invalid data, you may very well get answers that are not to be trusted.

Unfortunately, that is an accurate observation for some programs in current use. There are some programs in which no effort is made to see if the data being supplied make sense. Certainly there is some excuse for this with beginning programmers, and it is not always possible to anticipate every possible error in input. However, we should make an effort to avoid writing programs that process nonsensical data as if it were reasonable.

Already in this text, we have indicated some techniques involved in **editing input** (or **validating input**), that is, making sure that it has an appropriate value. For example, recall Case Study No. 2, which read two numbers and an operation symbol, and applied that operation to the two numbers. In that case study, the program checked user input for two errors: attempting to divide by 0 and entering an invalid operation symbol. In this section,

```
{*** Read and total scores}

Total   := 0;
Number  := 0;
Write('Enter the score (-1 to quit): ');
Readln(Score);
while Score <> -1 do
  begin
     Total := Total + Score;
     Number : = Number + 1;
     Write('Enter the score (-1 to quit): ');
     Readln (Score)
  end; {while}

{*** Calculate and print average}

Writeln;
if Number > 0 then
  begin
     Average := Total / Number;
     Writeln(Number : 1, ' exam scores were processed. ');
     Writeln('The average is: ', Average)
  end
else
   Writeln(' *** No scores were input *** ')
```

Figure 3-25 Reading without data validation.

we examine some commonly used methods for examining the input as soon as it is read and not proceeding any further unless it is valid. This is not always possible to do: the validity of the data may depend on some calculation not yet performed. However, it is frequently possible.

Consider, for example, the program segment of Figure 3-25, which obtains user input for the variable Score.

An algorithm for this program segment might contain a step:

read value for Score

Suppose we replace this algorithm step by

read a valid value for Score

We can view the task of obtaining Score and making sure that it is valid as a subtask. We might choose to write a Pascal procedure to perform the task.

A procedure to read a value for Score might begin by issuing a prompt and reading Score. Then the procedure would check the value read to make sure it was valid. If it was not valid, the procedure would print an error message and read a new value for Score. Notice, moreover, that this new value might also be invalid. Thus, the procedure should continue printing an error message and reading a new value "as long as" the Score is not valid. We have described this rough algorithm:

3-4 NESTED LOOPS AND COMPLEX LOOP TERMINATION

```
procedure GetScore(var Score: integer);

{Written by:  XXXXXXXXX XX/XX/XX}
{Purpose:     To accept a valid score (-1 or higher).}
{Parameter:   Score, the score read (passed back to the calling program}

begin {GetScore}
  Write('Enter the score (-1 to quit): ');
  Readln(Score);
  while Score < -1 do
    begin
      Writeln('You entered an invalid score: ', Score : 1);
      Writeln('The score must be positive (or -1 to quit)');
      Write('Re-enter the score: ');
      Readln(Score)
    end {while}
end; {Get Score}
```

Figure 3-26 Data-validation procedure.

issue a prompt
read Score
as long as the Score is not valid, do these steps:
    print an error message
    read a new value for Score

A Pascal procedure to accomplish this task is contained in Figure 3-26. It accepts any score greater than or equal to –1 as valid. (A score of –1 is valid because that is the terminating value for the loop.)

This procedure, like some of the procedures developed earlier in this chapter, has a parameter. However, the way it uses its parameter is new. This is our first example of a **var parameter**.

All our previous parameters have been **value parameters**, which means that the calling program passes a value into the submodule (function or procedure). A var (short for "variable") parameter, on the other hand, is used when the submodule is passing information back to the calling program via the parameter. A submodule can modify a var parameter's value. As a result, the calling program must supply a matching variable for the parameter. This matching variable in the calling program is modified whenever the parameter is modified within the submodule.

If the data are invalid, the GetScore procedure prints the value that the user entered prior to printing an error message. Although this was not required by the problem description (or even the algorithm), it is a good idea.

Note. If a procedure has a var parameter, then the statement that invokes that procedure must supply a *variable* to match the parameter. *Constants and expressions cannot match var parameters.* This is one of the important distinctions between value and var parameters.

```
{*** Read and total scores}

Total := 0;
Number := 0;

GetScore(Score);

while Score <> -1 do
  begin
      Total := Total + Score;
      Number := Number + 1;
      GetScore(Score)
  end; {while}

{*** Calculate and print average}

Writeln;
if Number > 0 then
  begin
      Average := Total / Number;
      Writeln(Number : 1, ' exam scores were processed.');
      Writeln('The average is: ', Average : 1 : 1)
  end
else
  Writeln('*** No scores were input ***')
```

Figure 3-27 Reading using the data validation procedure.

We now consider what changes would be made to the original program segment as a result of writing this procedure to edit (validate) the input. Figure 3-27 is the revised program segment that now uses the GetScore procedure. The changes are in italics. As far as the calling program segment is concerned, the process of prompting the user, accepting input, checking the input, and persisting until the input is valid is all contained in the one statement GetScore(Score).

Note. As is frequently the case, the calling module and the submodule use the same name (Score) for the parameter. We remind you, however, that this is not a requirement of the Pascal language. If the person writing the submodule had chosen a different variable name, the program segment would still have worked the same. The parameter correspondence is by position in the list of parameters, not by name.

Note that the keyword *var* in the parameter list is that which determines that the value of the parameter can be changed and passed back to the caller. If the *var* keyword were omitted from the header line of procedure GetScore, then the program would still compile correctly. However, the value of Score in the main program could not be changed by the procedure GetScore, so that Score would have some "random" value that would depend on factors outside of the user's control. A way to avoid this problem is to test each module

3-4 NESTED LOOPS AND COMPLEX LOOP TERMINATION **247**

separately. An independent test of the GetScore procedure would quickly show the effects of the absence of the *var* keyword.

We show a sample driver program for the procedure GetScore as Figure 3-28. In this case, we wish to test the procedure to be sure that it handles negative, zero, and positive integers correctly.

When we use the driver program to test the GetScore procedure, we precede each call of GetScore with the message "GetScore called." If the program should hang up or abort, we can tell that it happened in that procedure. We also print a message when GetScore returns, and we include the value returned to produce a record of the testing. In the driver, we have called GetScore three times in order to try three different test cases:

CASE 1

−5 (bad input)
−2 (bad input)
−1 (good input)

CASE 2

−2 (bad input)
−2 (bad input)
23 (good input)

CASE 3

15 (good input)

Although this is not an exhaustive test plan, it does have sufficient cases (including the boundary between good and bad input) for us to have a large degree of confidence that the procedure works correctly.

DPT

The DPT subsections of Sections 3-1 to 3-3 should be reviewed. In addition, there are some specific tips relating to the material of this section.

1. Check for initialization and finalization steps. For nested loops, make sure the steps are associated with the correct loop. It can be helpful to verbalize what each pass through the loop accomplishes. For example, in the program of Figure 3-22, each pass through the outer loop processes one employee, and each pass through the inner loop processes one sales amount for the employee. The step to initialize the counter of employees should occur prior to the loop that processes the employees. The step to initialize the sales accumulator should occur for each employee, so it is placed within the outer loop, but before the inner loop.

2. Examine loops with compound (multiple) conditions for continuation or termination especially carefully. The entire condition should make sense on the first pass and on the

```
program Driver;

{Written by: XXXXXXXXX XX/XX/XX}
{Purpose:    To test the GetScore procedure}
{Procedures used: GetScore, to get a score of -1 or higher}

    var
       Score: integer;     {Valid score from GetScore}
       I: integer;         {Loop index}

{procedure GetScore as shown in Figure 3-26 is inserted here}

begin {Driver}

 {*** Call GetScore 3 times}

   for I := 1 to 3 do
      begin
         Writeln;
         Writeln('GetScore called.');
         GetScore(Score);
         Writeln('Value returned from GetScore: ', Score : 1)
      end;
end.
```

SAMPLE INPUT AND OUTPUT

```
GetScore called.
Enter the score (-1 to quit): -5
You entered an invalid score: -5
The score must be positive (or -1 to quit)
Re-enter the score: -2
You entered an invalid score: -2
The score must be positive (or -1 to quit)
Re-enter the score: -1
Value returned from GetScore: -1

GetScore called.
Enter the score (-1 to quit): -2
You entered an invalid score: -2
The score must be positive (or -1 to quit)
Re-enter the score: -2
You entered an invalid score: -2
The score must be positive (or -1 to quit)
Re-enter the score: 23
Value returned from GetScore: 23

GetScore called
Enter the score (-1 to quit): 15
Value returned from GetScore: 15
```

Figure 3-28 A driver for testing.

last pass. The possibility of being "off by 1/2" is greater for this type of loop than for those where the condition is a simple condition.

3. Take care in writing decision structures after loops with multiple-termination conditions. Sometimes more than one of the individual conditions can occur during the same pass through the loop. In this case, the order in which the individual conditions are examined can be important.

4. Use a var parameter if a value is to be passed from the procedure to the calling program using that parameter. Using a var parameter when one is not required can lead to inadvertently modifying a value in the calling program that should not have been modified.

5. On the other hand, use a var parameter when appropriate. Failure to do so will prevent the value that is obtained in the subprogram from being passed to the calling program.

6. When a procedure does use a var parameter, the statement that invokes the procedure must use a variable that matches that parameter.

REVIEW

Terms and Concepts

assertion
editing input
flag
inner loop
nested loops
outer loop

searches
searching algorithms
validating input
value parameter
var parameter

Pascal Syntax

Var parameter form:
　var *list of parameters*

Var parameter use:
　To allow a subprogram to send a value back to the calling program

Program Design

1. Nested loops: Each loop is designed in the usual way; each loop is coded in the usual way.
2. Nested data repetitions can imply nested loops are needed.
3. More than one termination condition: Use a compound condition in the *while* or *repeat* loop control.
4. Loops with compound-termination conditions are frequently followed by a decision structure.

5. General form of algorithm to edit input:

prompt
read data
as long as the data is not valid do the following:
    error message
    prompt for reentering data
    read data

6. General form of search loop:

set flag to indicate not yet found
initialize so first pass examines first item
as long as not yet found and more to examine do
      examine an item;
      if it is the one sought, set flag to indicate found;
      if not, move on to the next item

DPT

1. Check the initialization and finalization steps. For nested loops, associate them with the correct loop.

2. For loops with compound-termination conditions:

    (a) Condition must make sense on the first and last passes.
    (b) Do not be off by 1/2.
    (c) Take care in writing a following decision structure.

3. Use a var parameter when, and only when, that parameter is being used to pass back a value to the calling program.

4. Only variables can match var parameters.

5. Test each module separately.

EXERCISES

1. For each program segment, find the output that would be produced.

(a)
```
for I := 1 to 3 do
    begin
        Sum := 0;
        for J := 1 to 4 do
            Sum := Sum + J;
        Writeln(Sum)
    end
```

(b)
```
Sum := 0;
for I := 1 to 3 do
    begin
        for J := 1 to 4 do
```

```
            Sum := Sum + J;
          Writeln(Sum)
      end

(c) J := 1;
    repeat I := 1;
      while I <= J - 2 do
        begin
          Writeln(I);
          I := I + 3
        end;
      J := J + 1
    until J >= 15
```

2. Using the program of Figure 3-22, what changes would you make for each of the following?
   (a) As it stands, the program's printer output is not done well. Change the output to align the columns better and to right-justify the name within its allotted 20 columns.
   (b) How many individual sales did each person have?
   (c) What was the total sales amount for the entire company?
   (d) Who had the highest total sales?
   (e) What was the largest individual sales amount for the entire company? Who had it?
   (f) How many individuals had no sales?
   (g) Among those employees who had at least five individual sales, who had the lowest total?

3. Consider the program segment of Figure 3-23.
   (a) Write a correct segment that uses a *while* loop with RollCount initialized to 1.
   (b) Following the lead of a typical *for* loop, we initialized RollCount to 1. Another possibility is to initialize to 0. Write a correct segment that does so by using either a *while* or a *repeat* loop.
   (c) What other corrections can fix the problems of the faulty code?

4. Write a complete Pascal program to produce the output:

```
Row 1     Seat 1    _____
          Seat 2    _____
                       . . .
          Seat 7    _____
Row 2     Seat 1    _____
          Seat 2    _____
                       . . .
          Seat 7    _____
                       . . .
Row 5     Seat 1    _____
          Seat 2    _____
                       . . .
          Seat 7    _____
```

5. Simulate an election in which candidate A is expected to receive 60 percent of the vote and candidate B 40 percent. There are 30,000 votes, and your loop should simulate each vote. Hint: Generate a random number from 1 to 10, with 1 to 6 indicating a vote for A and 7 to 10 a vote for B.

Your program should answer three questions: How many times in the counting was the vote tied? What was the last time the vote was tied? What was the largest lead candidate A ever had? The output might be similar to this:

```
The vote was tied 100 times.
The last tie occurred when counting the 9177th ballot.
At ballot 23417, A was ahead by 7913 votes, the largest lead.
```

6. (a) Write a program that reads a beginning balance, an interest rate, and an ending balance. It should print the amount in a savings account at the end of each year until the current balance exceeds the read-in ending balance. The interest for each year is calculated by multiplying the interest rate by the current balance.
   (b) Modify part (a) to allow a deposit to be made at the end of each year.
   (c) Modify part (a) to place an asterisk in the left margin for the first year (if any) in which the current balance exceeds twice the original balance.
   (d) Modify part (a) to print, for each year, the beginning balance and the ending balance for that year on a single line.

7. (a) Write a program segment that simulates rolling a pair of dice until a 5, 6, or 7 is rolled. If it took an even number of rolls and a 5 or 7 occurred, it should print the message "you win", otherwise it should print the message "you lose".
   (b) Write a program segment that repeats the action for part (a) a total of 100 times. Instead of printing "you win" and "you lose", it should count and print the number of wins and losses.

8. A deposit of $10,000 is compounded annually at 8 percent. At the end of each year, after the interest has been added, $1,000 is to be withdrawn from the account.

   (a) Write a program that prints the balance in the account every year up to, but not including, the year in which $1000 can no longer be withdrawn.
   (b) Modify the program to show how many $1,000 withdrawals were made and the amount that remains the final year.

9. Write procedures to input each of the following lists of variables with the indicated restrictions. For this exercise, the error message handling can simply print a single error message "invalid data".
   (a) Name and sex code, where the sex code must be either "M" or "F".
   (b) Four test scores, each of which must be in the range 0 to 100, inclusive.
   (c) A single integer that must be larger than 2 and no more than 10,000.
   (d) Two integers that must both be positive and even.
   (e) A color code (three characters) that must be either "RED", "GRE", "BLU", "BLA", "WHI", or "ORA".

10. Modify the procedures in Exercises 9(b) and 9(d) to have the error message tell exactly what is wrong with the input data.

11. (a) Write a program that generates a random number in the range 1 to 1000 and then asks the user to guess the number. The program should terminate with a message telling how many tries it took the user to guess the number. For incorrect guesses, it should print the messages "too high" or "too low".
    (b) Modify the program to allow no more than seven guesses.

12. By thinking about your guessing strategy for Exercise 11, write a program in which the computer tries to guess the number the user is thinking of. Hint: The program might want to keep track of a range in which it knows the answer lies.

13. For each number from 1 to 200, print a list of its divisors in a form similar to this:

```
Divisors of 1: 1
Divisors of 2: 1
               2

Divisors of 3: 1
               3

Divisors of 4: 1
               2
               4
 . . .
```

14. Suppose we generate random numbers in the range from 1 to 10. On the average, how many numbers would have to be generated until two consecutive numbers are the same? To answer the question, write a program to perform the experiment 1000 times.

15. A person offers you a game of chance that involves rolling a pair of dice until either 2, 7, or 11 comes up. If 2 or 11 comes up, you win $5, if a 7 comes up, you lose $2. Should you play the game (assuming you are a betting person in the first place)? To answer the question, write a program to play the game 1000 times.

16. Some state lotteries operate on the following principle: You bet $1, choose a number in the range 0 to 999, and win $500 if your number is drawn in the lottery. A person described a sure-fire system to win: Bet on the same number every day, eventually it is bound to turn up. This exercise explores the wisdom of that system.

(a) Assume that the person has $1,500 with which to play the lottery 300 times a year for 5 years (50 weeks a year, 6 days a week). Write a program to allow the user to choose a number, then simulate 5 years of play. At the end of the simulated 5 years, tell the person how much of the original $1,500 is left.

(b) Suppose 1000 people all tried this system. What would be the average amount left after the 5 years? To answer the question, write a program to simulate the 5 years of play 1000 times using a single chosen number.

(c) Modify part (b) to simulate each of the 1000 people choosing a different number to play for the 5 years.

17. Suppose that 5000 people all decide to play the daily number lottery game until they either go broke or win once. Each person starts with $1,000. Based on a simulation of the situation, answer these questions: What percentage will go broke? What percentage will quit with more than $1,000? What percentage will quit with between $0 and $1,000? (See Exercise 16 for a description of the lottery game.)

18. Modify the procedure MatchRoll of Figure 3-20 so that if a roll of the dice (after the first roll) comes up with either a match of the goal or the value of 7, then the loop terminates. The program should print the message "you win" if the goal was matched or "you lose" if a 7 was rolled. (If the first roll of the dice comes up with a 7, then roll for another point.) (Hint: Use another *repeat-until* loop for the rolling of the point and change the condition of the original *repeat-until* loop.)

19. Write a program to simulate a simplified game of craps. The simplified rules of the game are as follows:

   (a) Roll the dice for a first time. If the roll is a 7 or 11, then you win; if the roll is a 2 or 12, then you lose; otherwise, the point is equal to the roll.
   (b) If you have a point, then roll the dice repeatedly until you match the point (which makes you a winner) or you roll a 7 (which makes you a loser).

20. Use the program from Exercise 19 to write another program that simulates the running of 100 games of craps. Instead of printing whether you are a winner or loser, use variables Wins and Losses to count the number of times that you win and lose. Ask someone who knows some probability theory (or a gambler) what the odds of winning at craps are. Compare the results from the program with the theoretical odds.

21. A given real function Approx(X) computes an approximation to the answer to some problem, starting with an initial approximation X. For example, if we write

    ```
    XNew := Approx(XOld)
    ```

    then XNew is a new approximation that is, we hope, better than the previous approximation XOld.

    Write a loop to compute a series of approximations starting with an initial value XOld equal to 1.0. The loop should compute XNew := Approx(XOld) and then replace XOld by XNew before redoing the calculation. The loop should terminate when either

    $$\left| \frac{\text{XNew} - \text{Xold}}{\text{XNew}} \right| < 1.0 \times 10^{-4}$$

    or when 50 iterations of the loop have been completed. Print a message showing which occurred and the latest value of XNew.

22. Write a program for each of the following situations:

   (a) Each record has a beginning balance and an interest rate. The interest is compounded annually: the balance after 1 year is the original balance plus the interest for that year; the interest for the second year is based on this new balance, and so on. Write a program that, for each record, shows how many years it takes for the balance in the account to be more than twice the starting balance.
   (b) The setup is the same as for part (a). However, for each record, the algorithm should print out a table showing the year number, the beginning balance for that year, the interest for the year, and the ending balance for the year up through and including the year in which the balance exceeds twice the starting balance. Print one new page per record.
   (c) Modify part (b) so that it does not print a line of information for the final year when the balance goes over twice the starting balance.
   (d) Repeat part (a), but with no data records. Instead, use a beginning balance of $1,000.00 and interest rates of 4 to 20 percent in steps of 0.25 percent, that is, 4 percent, 4.25 percent, 4.5 percent, etc.

23. Find and print the smallest divisor of each odd number from 3 to 201.

24. The input data consist of repetitions of this pattern:

    account record for a checking account
    0 or more transaction records for this account
    terminal transaction record (code "L")

EXERCISES

For each account, generate output similar to that illustrated in Exercise 10 of Section 3.1.

Then modify the program to do the following for each account:

(a) Count the checks and deposits.
(b) Determine the lowest and highest balance.
(c) Calculate the average check amount.
(d) Calculate the service charge for the month. The first record of each group will contain an account type (R, S, or V). For regular (R) accounts, the service charge is $3.00 unless the minimum balance is at or above $750, in which case it is 0. For special (S) accounts, the charge is $0.20 per check. For VIP (V) accounts, the charge is based on the average of the minimum and maximum balances. If this is less than $500, there is a $7.00 charge; $500 to $1,000, a $5.00 charge; over $1,000, free.

25. Using the Random function to simulate the throw of a pair of dice, write programs for the following:

(a) Simulate an experiment in which we roll the dice once, and then attempt to match that number on future rolls. If we succeed in five or fewer rolls, print how many rolls it took; otherwise print a message reporting failure.

(b) Write a program to repeat the experiment of part (a) 10,000 times, reporting the percentage of successes and the average number of rolls for the successes. For example, the output might be

```
Succeeded 75% of the time, with 3.72 average rolls for each successful
experiment.
```

(c) Simulate a game in which two players roll dice. Player A starts with $15 and player B with $23. When they roll, the player with the higher number wins $1. They agree to go until one or the other is broke or 100 rolls, whichever occurs first. Print an appropriate message at the end.

(d) Place the game in part (c) in a loop to simulate it a number of times in order to answer the question: Is the game fair?

26. To see if a number N ($\geq$ 2) is prime, it suffices to check for divisors in the range from 2 to $\sqrt{N}$. If no divisors are found, then N is prime. Using this fact, write a Boolean function that tells if a number is prime or composite (not prime).

27. For a function $y = f(x)$, finding a root for the function means finding a value x that yields $y = 0$. For many functions (the continuous functions), the following is true: if $f(a)$ and $f(b)$ have different signs, then there must be at least one root between a and b.

One way to approximate that root is by the bisection method, described as follows: Let m be the midpoint of the interval from a to b. If $f(m) = 0$, then you have found a root, so quit. If $f(a)$ and $f(m)$ have opposite signs, there must be a root between a and m; if not, there must be a root between m and b. In either case, you can repeat this process with one or the other of the subintervals. Since the subintervals get smaller as you proceed, you will be getting closer and closer to the root. Quit after some predetermined number of passes.

Write a program that uses this method to approximate the root of $y = x^3 + 4.5x^2 - 0.19x - 0.14$ that lies between 0 and 1. Stop after 30 iterations and use m as the approximation, unless a root is found before 30 iterations have occurred.

28. Suppose Otto the Automaton is a robot whose tasks require it to walk metal ramps, high above the factory floor, that connect assembly lines. Its builders are concerned that its direction-sensing circuitry could be damaged in unpredictable ways (such as by an electric charge running

through a ramp on which it is moving), so they have asked you to run some simulations of what might happen if Otto loses its directional sense.

Each ramp is as pictured in the figure. Label the squares on the ramp as illustrated by the example labeling in the figure.

```
                           Factory Floor

              (1,5)                               (7,5)

                           (3,4)                  (7,4)

Assembly                                          (7,3)   Assembly
line                                                      line
        Start
        here                                      (7,2)
        (1,3)
              (1,1)                (5,1)          (7,1)

                           Factory Floor
```

(a) For one simulation, assume the circuitry completely fails; with each step, Otto is equally likely to stagger left, right, forward, or backward. Print an indication of the location after each stagger, and a message at the end: "fell off the ramp", backed off the ramp", or "made it across".

(b) Put part (a) in a loop that executes 1000 times. Replace the prints by counting steps. Tell how many times each of the three possible outcomes occurred.

(c) Repeat parts (a) and (b) with Otto's circuitry only partially damaged, resulting in a 0.4 probability of staggering forward, a 0.25 probability of staggering left or right, and a 0.1 chance of staggering backward. Hint: Generate a random number from 1 to 20, with 1 to 8 representing forward, 9 to 13 left, 14 to 18 right, and 19 to 20 back.

29. Give test plans for the following:
  (a) Exercise 2(c)
  (b) Exercise 6(a)
  (c) Exercise 6(c)
  (d) Exercise 9(b)
  (e) Exercise 9(c)
  (f) Exercise 12
  (g) Exercise 24, without modifcations
  (h) Exercise 24, with parts (a) to (d)

Exercises 30 to 34 refer to integer arrays as discussed in Section 3-2.

30. Write a program to read an array of 10 integers and to print the first integer that is greater than or equal to the average of the 10 numbers. Hint: After you calculate the average of the numbers, use a *repeat-until* loop to search the array.

31. Repeat Exercise 30 using a *while* loop.

EXERCISES

32. Should you repeat Exercise 30 using a count-control (*for*) loop?
33. Write a program to read an array of an unknown number of positive integers (terminated by a 0) and to print the position and the value of the first integer that is greater than or equal to the average of the numbers that are input.
34. Put the steps of Exercise 30 in a loop, and terminate by asking the user if the steps are to be run through again.

3-5 ANTIBUGGING, DEBUGGING, AND TESTING

Many sections of a textbook represent material to be mastered, perhaps through memorization, preferably through concentrated practice and understanding. Many sections of this book fall in that category. For example, you should come to understand counting applications thoroughly; if you are asked to do any problem that involves counting, the techniques involved should be fairly automatic.

This section has a somewhat different flavor. In it, we attempt to gather together some ideas that will aid you in writing correct programs and in feeling confident that they are correct. The section does not cover any new algorithmic techniques. It does contain some techniques and ideas that can form a part of your program-development style no matter what the specific program is designed to accomplish.

In some of your early programs, the program logic was relatively simple. On the other hand, all the rules about how to write the Pascal statements were new and perhaps confusing. As a result, your programs may have generated many compile-time errors. These errors include, for example, forgetting the final parenthesis in a Writeln statement, leaving out a semicolon, or misspelling the word "integer" in a declaration. It is possible that once you got past the list of errors generated by the compiler and any misunderstandings about the THINK Pascal language, your programs ran correctly.

At this point in your study of programming, your programs are becoming more complex, but you are getting used to the Pascal language. It is possible that you are able to resolve compiler-generated errors with little difficulty. However, you may be discovering that, even with no compiler-detected errors, the program is just not doing what it should. In the first section, we discuss antibugging and debugging, two related techniques that seek to avoid this situation or to allow you to correct this situation as easily as possible.

The second section is on program testing. We have included sections on this topic from time to time in the text, and we will continue to do so. Here we attempt to pull together some of the ideas into a single summary discussion of program testing.

Antibugging and Debugging

We begin with two related concepts: antibugging and debugging. Both terms come from the common use of the word **bug** to describe an error in a computer program. They tend to relate to the types of errors that occur after you have obtained a clean compilation. Errors that the compiler detects are not the primary subject of this section. Those errors can generally be fixed by careful examination of the subject line of code, comparing it to the required syntax (form) for that type of statement. The errors we discuss here are more subtle, frequently requiring more work to uncover.

The purpose of **antibugging** is to avoid bugs, and the purpose of **debugging** is to help you uncover and remove those bugs that do occur. The two concepts are closely related. Of course, if the antibugging is done sufficiently well, then no debugging is necessary. In a way, debugging can be thought of as adding more antibugging to the system to flush out those bugs that the original antibugging was not sufficient to prevent.

We cover these concepts by presenting a list of ideas that can be useful either in antibugging or in debugging. Where it is appropriate, we indicate differences between using the ideas for antibugging and using them for debugging. Following the list, we discuss a few issues that arise when using these ideas.

1. Awareness of Pitfalls. This is emphasized throughout the text, especially in the DPT sections. By being aware of what some common errors are, we can avoid making those errors. This is a form of antibugging. On the other hand, if errors do occur, we can review the known pitfalls to see if we have made any of the common errors and to see if the particular pitfall accounts for the observed behavior of the program. This is a form of debugging.

2. Hand-Tracing. This refers to "playing computer" and executing the algorithm or program by hand. Deciding on the data to hand-trace is in some ways similar to deciding on test data. We want to use that data that is most likely to uncover any errors, just as we do in testing.

It is sometimes useful to hand-trace a slightly modified form of an algorithm. For example, if an output table is to contain 40 lines per page, it could take a long time to hand-trace sufficiently to make sure that exactly 40 lines are printed prior to moving to a new page. We might want to write and hand-trace the same program modified to print three lines per page. If the modified program works correctly, we can have some assurance that the original program also works.

3. Echo Printing of Input. Sometimes a program appears to be performing calculations incorrectly when actually it is the input data that are at fault. As a simple example, we might have this:

```
Write('Enter pay rate and hours worked: ');
Readln(Hours, Rate)
```

The user who, in response to the prompt, types a line containing 5.50 and 40 will not realize that the program interprets this as 5.5 hours at $40 an hour.

To avoid this type of problem, we could always echo print all input to the program. This would be antibugging. Alternatively, we could insert the echo prints when errors do occur. This would be debugging.

4. Edit (Validate) Input. This topic was discussed in Section 3-4. If we check all input for correctness and reasonableness, we can avoid many problems. For example, the error described in the previous paragraph would be uncovered by an input procedure that made sure that the pay rate was in the expected range.

5. Diagnostic Prints (Trace Prints). This idea expands upon the idea of echo printing the input. **Trace prints** are print statements that trace the execution of the program. A few examples:

(a) If the program does many complex calculations, it might be desirable to print the partial answers as they are calculated. For example, in a function that calculates the total taxes for an individual, each specific tax could be printed as soon as it is calculated. The print statement could use a variable name, as in

```
Writeln('SocSec = ', SocSec : 1 : 2)
```

or a more meaningful message as in

```
Writeln('Social security withheld = ', SocSec : 1 : 2)
```

Which you use is up to you; the output from these print statements is not seen by the program's user.

(b) Trace prints can be useful in examining the progress of a loop. For example, in Figure 3-19, we wrote a function to calculate the number of divisors of a given integer. At the bottom of the loop in that function, we might print Number, Potential, Number mod Potential, and Counter to verify that the count is occurring properly. Similarly, a program to locate a particular name in a file might print each name that it reads within the search loop.

(c) Trace prints are frequently used in programs that involve a number of subprograms. They might consist of a print statement at the beginning of each subprogram and one at the end of each. The one at the beginning might print the message "Entering subprogram xxxxx", where xxxxx is the subprogram name. This print might also print the value of the parameters. (This is similar to echoing all user input.) The print statement at the end could print the message "Leaving subprogram xxxxx" and again print the parameters.

For trace prints to aid our error detection, we would compare the output to that we expect to see. This implies that we are hand-tracing the program or algorithm to determine what to expect. By seeing exactly where the output begins to differ from what we expect, we can focus our efforts on the portion of the program that is causing the error.

The term **diagnostic prints**, which is frequently used to describe trace prints, conveys the idea of using these prints as a debugging tool to "diagnose" errors. Many programmers, however, do not wait until errors occur; they routinely include trace prints in all their programs.

Note. Programs that involve random numbers may need trace prints even to know if the answer is correct. For example, if the program is supposed to count the number of 7's rolled in a dice simulation, we should print each dice roll to check the answer. (Of course, we might temporarily modify the program to perform the simulation only 10 to 20 times rather than 12,000 times.)

The various prints (echo prints of input and trace prints) raise an important issue. There can very well be differences between the program during development and the program as delivered. The extra prints are useful in uncovering and fixing bugs, but the person who is running the finished program certainly does not want to see them. This person is interested only in the final answer, not in all the details of how the program reached that answer. Thus, the final version must not print the trace messages.

There are several ways to remove the extra print statements. The simplest is to delete them. However, this has the disadvantage that if they are needed later (for example, when modifications are made to the program), they must be done over. Another alternative frequently used is to "comment them out." This means to place them in braces, as illustrated here:

    {Writeln('Length = ', Length : 1 : 2);}

If the prints are needed again, the comment braces can be removed. A variation of this might involve something like this:

    {Debug: Writeln('Length = ', Length : 1 : 2);}

This makes them stand out more, and thus they are easier to locate when they need to be reactivated. In addition, they look different from ordinary comments. Other possibilities exist for handling this problem; some are discussed in later sections.

Testing

In this section, we summarize a number of **testing** concepts, most of which have been presented in more detail earlier in the text. Because whole textbooks have been written on the subject, our treatment here will be obviously at an elementary level. Becoming an expert tester (or expert programmer) requires several courses and significant experience. Our goal in this section (and this text) is to make you aware of the need for testing and have you develop the ability to come up with a reasonable test plan for the types of programs you are writing.

We should emphasize that the purpose of testing is to find bugs. For some (perhaps most) people, testing is psychologically difficult: They do not really want to find bugs in the program they have just spent so much time developing. For that reason, many companies that develop computer software have groups whose primary job is to test the programs others have written. In the context of a programming course, however, you will generally be doing your own testing. It may help to adopt the attitude, when a test case indicates a problem, that the bug was there and would probably have been noticed by the person grading the program. The fact that your test uncovered the bug is, therefore, a benefit, not something to get upset about.

We begin with some general testing concepts. This is followed by a few specific pointers for testing programs that use some of the algorithm concepts we have studied, such as counting and searching. Finally, we discuss top-down and bottom-up testing. Further explanations of all these topics can be found in the various testing sections throughout the text.

1. Check Your Answers. Some of the test cases should contain data for which the correct answer is easily determined, preferably without using a calculator. This allows you to see at a glance whether there are obvious bugs in the program. However, this does not imply that you should ignore the other test cases. After you have verified that the program is working correctly for those that are easy to check, check all the answers. Never stop work on a program for which there are known errors; correct all bugs you find. Some of the techniques described in the previous section can be helpful in tracking down and removing the bugs.

2. Class Testing. **Class testing** is sometimes referred to as **branch testing** because it frequently relates to branching in the program. For example, when a program contains a decision structure

```
if Value < 1000 then
   Rate := 0.04
else if Value < 5000 then
   Rate := 0.07
else
   Rate := 0.10
```

we can identify three branches or classes for the variable Value: under 1000, 1000 or greater but less than 5000, and 5000 or greater.

However, we generally should base our analysis of what classes there are on the problem description in addition to, or instead of, the actual algorithm or program. Even if the programmer found some way to calculate the Rate without using a decision structure, the testing should treat the calculation of Rate as one involving three classes for Value. As a simple example, in rounding a real number to the nearest integer, we can identify two classes of input: input with fractions less than 0.5 and input with fractions 0.5 or greater. The rounding process treats these two classes of input differently, so we want to test both classes. The fact that the built-in Round function is used rather than a decision structure does not change the need for that testing.

Class testing frequently involves ranges of values, as in the previous example. It sometimes involves specific values rather than ranges. For example, if the price of a window depends upon its color, we might identify these classes for the color: white, brown, cream, etc.

In class testing, we want to include test cases that exercise each identifiable class. In fact, if the class consists of a range of values, we should generally include a number of realistic, randomly chosen values within that class.

3. Bad Data. In the previous example, which calculated the variable Rate, we actually missed at least one important class: Value less than 0. This represents an error class for which the program should ideally generate some sort of error message. In addition, the problem statement or analysis can indicate that values larger than 100,000 are considered unreasonable and probably indicate a data-entry error. If so, then another class of bad data (larger than 100,000) exists and should be tested.

Just as we generate test cases for each class of good data, we generate test cases for each error class. It is important to note here that each error should be tested separately. For example, if the sex code must be "M" or "F", and the grade must lie between 0 and 100, we identify three classes of bad data:

Sex code incorrect

Grade less than 0

Grade greater than 100

Each should be tested by itself. A single record with an incorrect sex code and a grade less than 0 is not adequate.

4. Boundary Values. Experience has shown that errors are more likely to occur for boundary values than for any other values. Thus, test cases that exercise the boundaries are likely to be more valuable in uncovering bugs.

Boundary values are frequently related to class testing. If a class consists of a range of values, then there are boundaries at each end of the range. For example, in the calculation of Rate based on Value (described previously), we can identify these boundaries:

0	(between good data and bad data)
1000	
5000	
100,000	(between good data and bad data)

Since 1000 is the lowest number in the class for which the Rate is to be 0.07, we include a test case with Value equal to 1000. We also want to test the upper boundary of the class where the Rate is 0.04, so we include a value just below 1000, perhaps 999, or 999.99, or even both. A similar approach holds for the other boundaries.

A couple of comments may help here. First, we might wish to test both just below and just above the boundary. In the previous example, we would add test cases 1000.01, or 1001, or both. Second, the actions for the two classes are sometimes not distinguishable for numbers very close to the boundary. For example, consider this decision structure:

```
if Amount <= 500 then
   Tax := 50
else
   Tax := 50 + 0.10 * (Amount - 500)
```

If Amount is 500.01, then Tax would be 50.001, which would appear as 50.00 if printed as a dollars and cents figure (using Amount:l:2, perhaps). Because this cannot be distinguished from the answer for 500.00, we might include a test case a little further from the boundary (e.g., 500.10).

Finally, we should note that some boundaries are related to output rather than input. For example, if we are supposed to print exactly 45 lines per page, we should include a test where the output ends on the 45th line of a page and a test where it ends on the first line of the following page.

5. Special Cases. This is closely related to boundary testing, and, in fact, you may wish to view special cases and boundary as the same thing. An example of a special case test might involve a program finding the average check amount for a month in a checking account. We would want to include a test where there were no checks at all.

For many, if not all, special case tests, we can view the test as a boundary test in connection with a "how many?" or a "where?" question. For example, if we ask, "How many of the transactions for the month were checks?" the answer would be, "Anywhere from no checks to all checks." Our special case where there were no checks is one of the two boundaries for the possible range of answers to the question. Similarly, in looking for the largest of a set of numbers, we could ask, "Where in the list could the answer occur?" The answer is, "Anywhere from first to last," and we have two boundaries (first and last) for that range.

6. Compound Conditions. Consider the following description of who gets a bonus: Any employee with an attendance record of 95 percent, or who sold more than 500 units, or who recruited at least one new customer. This policy can be coded as a simple *if-then* construction. However, in testing the program, it is not really sufficient to just test both branches. We should test various combinations of the three conditions involved. As you can see in the following table, there are eight possible combinations.

ATTENDANCE > 95%	SOLD > 500	RECRUITED
No	No	No
No	No	Yes
No	Yes	No
No	Yes	Yes
Yes	No	No
Yes	No	Yes
Yes	Yes	No
Yes	Yes	Yes

We should check all combinations in a situation such as this. As usual, the "boundaries" (all no, all yes, exactly one no, exactly one yes) are the most critical tests.

A particularly important example of compound conditions occurs in validating input data. To be valid, the data typically must meet a number of criteria. This implies a number of combinations, similar to those for the example just given. Experience has shown that for each way in which the data could fail to be acceptable, there should be a test case that is correct except for that one particular item.

7. Path Testing. In a program with several different decision structures, it is desirable to test all possible paths through the program. For example, consider the segment:

```
if Category = 3 then
  Bonus := 100
else
  Bonus := 250;
if Total > 1000 then
  Bonus := Bonus * 2;
```

There are four possible paths: (1) category 3, total > 1000; (2) category 3, total ≤ 1000; (3) category not 3, total > 1000; and (4) category not 3, total ≤ 1000. We should test all possibilities.

As you can imagine, for a large program, the number of paths can grow quite rapidly. This is one strong argument for modularity. We write small modules and test them independently using drivers. Some of the tests for each module might involve thorough **path testing** of that module.

8. Loop Termination. In Section 3-4, we studied loops with more than one termination condition. For this type of loop, we should include at least one test case for each possible termination condition. As a simple example, consider a search loop that is looking for the name "John Jones" in a data file. Since he might not be in the file, we would use a loop with two conditions for termination; either we find "John Jones" or we reach the end of the file and therefore know he is not in the file. Both possibilities should be tested for in our test plan. (Notice the idea on which this approach is based is similar to that for path testing.)

9. Include Random Tests. Sometimes when we carefully plan our tests, we can fall into the trap that our tests are too orderly. For a grading program, for example, our test sequence might go: 100, 90, 89, 80, 79, etc. These are all important boundary tests for a 90–80–70–60 grading scale. However, it would be good to mix up the tests. In addition, we would want to include some random testing.

This point was driven home to one of the authors in a recent program. The user was allowed to perform a sequence of activities. It turned out that a certain activity X worked fine unless it came right after activity Y. In testing, the user never had that particular combination. However, during the demonstration of the product, the combination arose. How much better it would have been to uncover the bug during testing rather than during demonstration!

We now consider how some of the general concepts just listed apply in specific types of algorithms. We are especially interested here in special case tests. For example, for a counting problem, we might identify the following tests:

No data input

Data input, but count is 0

Everything input is in the class being counted

A similar list would apply for accumulation. For finding the largest (or smallest) value, we could list tests such as:

No data input

Exactly one data item (would be both largest and smallest)

First is largest (no ties)

Largest in middle (no ties)

Last is largest (no ties)

All values the same

In a program that searches for a particular value in a file (or a set of user input, or an array), we can list tests such as:

Not found

Found, only one in file

Found, first one in file (file containing > 1 record)

Found, last one in file (file containing > 1 record)

Found, somewhere in middle of file

3-5 ANTIBUGGING, DEBUGGING, AND TESTING

Generalizing this last situation slightly, we can come up with the following types of tests for algorithms that use either count-control or general-condition loops:

Loop terminates on first pass through loop
Loop terminates on last possible pass through loop

We now turn to a brief review of **top–down testing** and **bottom–up testing.** To illustrate the difference, consider the following hierarchy chart of modules. The main module A uses modules B and C to accomplish subtasks. B, in turn, uses subprograms D and E, whereas C uses subprogram F.

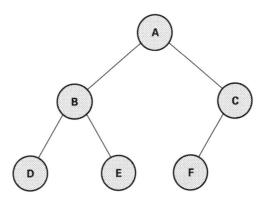

In both types of testing, we test one module at a time in the context of modules that are already tested. For example, one possible order for top–down testing is

A (stubs for B and C)
B (using the tested A, and stubs for D, E, and C)
D (using the existing A and B, and stubs for E and C)
E (using the existing A, B, and D, and a stub for C)
C (using the existing A, B, D, and E, and a stub for F)
F (using the existing A, B, D, E, and C)

Other orders are also possible, such as A, B, C, D, E, and F. In bottom–up testing, on the other hand, we would start with the lowest-level modules, perhaps in this order:

D (using a driver)
E (using a driver)
B (using a driver to call it, and the existing D and E)
F (using a driver)
C (using a driver, and the existing F)
A (using the existing B, C, D, E, and F)

Again, other orders are possible, such as F, C, D, E, B, and A.

Sometimes it is helpful to combine the two techniques. For example, suppose that the logic of main program A depends heavily on parameters it obtains from B, and that those parameter values cannot be easily imitated by a stub. We might first develop the subsystem consisting of B, D, and E. The resulting order might be B, D, E, A, C, and F.

SUMMARY

This section, in contrast with many others in the text, can be most useful as a reference to be applied to your programming projects. It, together with DPT and testing sections throughout the text, can be useful in writing programs that avoid bugs and in discovering, uncovering, and removing those that do occur.

REVIEW

Terms and Concepts

antibugging
bottoms–up testing
bug
class/branch testing
debugging

diagnostic prints
path testing
testing
top–down testing
trace prints

Antibugging and Debugging Tips

1. Beware of pitfalls.
2. Hand-trace algorithms and programs.
3. Echo print input.
4. Edit (validate) input.
5. Use trace prints.

Testing

Tips

1. Check answers.
2. Test all classes.
3. Test with bad data.
4. Use boundary values.
5. Use special cases (boundary values for "how many" or "where").
6. Test combinations for compound conditions.
7. Test all paths (use small modules to make this easier).
8. Test all possible loop-termination conditions.
9. Include random tests.

Specific Tests for Counting Problems, Etc.

1. Counting (accumulation is similar)

   No data input
   Data input, but count is 0
   Everything input is in the class being counted

2. Finding the largest (or smallest)

   No data input
   Exactly one data item (would be both largest and smallest)
   First is largest (no ties)
   Largest in middle (no ties)
   Last is largest (no ties)
   All values the same

3. Searching in file (array search similar)

   Not found
   Found, only one in file
   Found, first one in file (file containing > 1 record)
   Found, last one in file (file containing > 1 record)
   Found, somewhere in middle of file

4. Any loop with count or general-condition control

   Loop terminates on first pass through loop
   Loop terminates on last possible pass through loop

4 More on Subprograms

OBJECTIVES

By the end of this chapter, you will have an almost complete picture of the technical aspects of Pascal subprograms. After completing this chapter, you will be able to:

- employ value parameters and var parameters, and be able to determine when to use each type
- use local and global variables and to discern the differences between them
- use strings and arrays as parameters
- invoke subprograms from within other subprograms
- use elementary recursive functions
- use subprograms effectively when designing your programs

4-1 PARAMETERS AND VARIABLES

Review and Terminology

A Pascal program consists of a number of **modules**. The **main module** (or **main program**) is always present; there may or may not be **submodules** (**subprograms**). Pascal has two types of subprograms: **procedures** and **functions**. We generally use a function for a subtask whose purpose is to calculate one value and a procedure for any other subtask. The main program can **invoke** (or **call**) any subprogram. A procedure is invoked by using its name as a statement; a function is invoked by including it as part of an expression, frequently in an assignment statement.

It is possible for one subprogram to invoke a second subprogram. In this case, we can use the terms **calling program** (or **calling module**) and **called program** (or **called module**) in describing the situation. If module A invokes module B, for example, then module A is the calling module and module B the called module.

The terms **parameter** and **argument** are frequently used interchangeably. For example, in a function declared with the header

```
function AreaFn(A, B, C: real): real;
```

the variables A, B, and C are the parameters. These are sometimes called the **formal parameters**. When we use the function in an assignment statement such as

```
Area := AreaFn(Side1, Side2, Side3)
```

the variables Side1, Side2, and Side3 are supplied as parameters to match the formal parameters A, B, and C. To distinguish between these two uses of the word, we refer to Side1, Side2, and Side3 as the **actual parameters**. Some programmers reserve the word "argument" to mean "actual parameter."

Formal parameters and actual parameters correspond by position within the list of parameters. The names may or may not be the same. However, the types must match. If a function expects to receive a real value as its second parameter, then the second actual parameter must be real. Moreover, the purpose of the parameters must match. For the function with header

```
function Volume(Radius, Height: real): real;
```

the actual parameters supplied when the function is invoked should represent the radius and height in that order. Reversing the order would almost certainly cause erroneous answers.

Reasons for Subprograms

There are at least four reasons for using subprograms. We mention them briefly here. These themes, especially the fourth, are expanded upon throughout the text.

    1. *Repetition.* Sometimes a task must be executed several times within a program. If so, writing the task as a procedure or function precludes having to place the detailed steps for the task in several places in the program. In fact, by using parameters judiciously, it may be possible to unify several almost identical tasks as a single submodule.

    2. *Universal Use.* Some procedures might be needed in more than one program. Perhaps a large group of programmers all need the same procedure. By writing a subprogram and making it available to the entire group, we can avoid duplication of effort. (This saves not only the effort of copying the code, but also that of creating the code in the first place.) Further, programmers working on subsequent projects often discover that the new program needs to perform many of the same tasks as the already written program. By **reusing** procedures from the old program in the new one, much development effort, time, and money can be saved.

    3. *Teamwork.* A large portion of programming in the "real world" is done by programming teams. Rather than having the whole team work on the whole program, the program is generally divided into subprograms. Each subprogram is written by one or two team members.

4. *Modularity.* Using subprograms enables us to break up a large project into more manageable pieces. This is important not only during the initial development of a project, but also during subsequent modification. Modularization allows us to focus our attention on the specific task at hand during development. For the person who must later modify the program, it makes the program easier to understand. In addition, it allows that person to concentrate on the piece that needs to be changed.

Of these four reasons, the most important is the last. As we have seen in some of our examples involving subprograms, it is extremely useful to be able to allocate subtasks to either functions or procedures. This aids in the top–down design of our program. As we design the main program, we identify various tasks or calculations that we allocate to procedures or functions. This allows us to complete the design of the overall solution to our problem without getting bogged down in the details of the subtasks. We then come back and design the subprogram for each identified subtask. Of course, if the subtask is complex, we may in turn identify further subtasks. This would lead to one subprogram in turn invoking another subprogram. We continue in this fashion until we have designed the entire program. Because we start with the main program and work our way down to successively more and more detailed pieces, we refer to this as **top–down design** and refinement.

Note. Top–down design is similar to but different from top–down testing. In coding and testing a program that has already been designed, it can make sense to use top–down testing, or bottom–up testing, or some suitable combination. However, the design process should always be top–down.

Value and Var Parameters

Parameters are the primary means of communication between a calling program and a called program. Values used by the submodule are passed into the submodule, and answers can be passed back. As a simple example, consider this procedure that calculates the quotient and remainder of two integers.

```
procedure QuotRem(I, J: integer; var Quotient, Remainder: integer);
begin
  Quotient := I div J;
  Remainder := I mod J
end;
```

The parameters I and J are used to pass values to the procedure; the parameters Quotient and Remainder pass back the answers.

In this example, I and J are **value parameters** and Quotient and Remainder are **var parameters**. The way these parameters work is very different. Consider the following simple main program.

```
program Sample;
var
  A, B, Q, R: integer;
```

4-1 PARAMETERS AND VARIABLES

```
{procedure QuotRem goes here}

begin
  A := 34;
  B := 6;
  QuotRem(A, B, Q, R);
  Writeln(Q, ' ', R)
end.
```

When QuotRem is invoked, the actual parameters A, B, Q, and R "correspond to" the formal parameters I, J, Quotient, and Remainder, respectively. For the two value parameters A and B, the present value is calculated and sent to the procedure's variables I and J, respectively. Thus, I and J are 34 and 6, respectively.

For the var parameters, however, no values are calculated. Rather, the procedure is informed where in the computer's memory the variables Q and R are stored. It then uses those locations for any reference to its formal parameters Quotient and Remainder. Thus, the assignment

```
Quotient: = I div J
```

divides I (34) by J (6) and places the result directly into the variable Q in the calling program. At this instant, Q already contains the answer 5. The next step, likewise, places its answer (4) directly into the variable R in the main module. When the procedure terminates, the answers are there, ready for the Writeln statement to print. Figure 4-1 summarizes this discussion.

Notes

1. When the procedure is invoked, the expression "A" is evaluated and its value (34) is placed in the QuotRem variable I.
2. Likewise, the value of the second argument ("B") is placed into J.
3. The variable Quotient in the QuotRem procedure has no storage space of its own. The procedure call establishes the correspondence between it and the main program's variable Q.
4. Likewise, the procedure call establishes that Remainder in QuotRem refers to R in the main program.

This fundamental difference in how the parameters are handled helps explain various rules concerning value and var parameters. Among these are the following:

1. The actual parameter for a value parameter can be any expression of the proper type. It need not be a variable. For example,

```
QuotRem(A + B, 17, Q, R)
```

would be legal.

Reason: The value of the actual parameter is calculated and passed into the formal parameter variable in the submodule. Therefore, the actual parameter can be an expression.

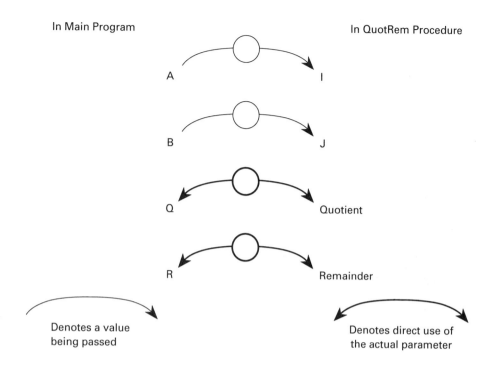

Figure 4-1 Passing parameters.

2. The actual parameter for a var parameter must be a variable (of the proper type). It cannot be a constant or other expression.

   Reason: The formal parameter variable in the submodule does not occupy its own memory space. Instead, it works directly with the memory location the corresponding actual parameter occupies.

3. Changing a value parameter in a submodule has no effect in the calling module.

   Reason: The communication using a value parameter consists solely of sending a value to the submodule when the submodule is invoked.

4. Changing a var parameter in a submodule immediately changes the corresponding actual parameter.

   Reason: The communication using a var parameter consists of the submodule working directly with the corresponding actual parameter.

Parameters: Type Matching

The communication that occurs through parameters is based on the position in the parameter list. It is not based on the name. Thus, in our previous example, we had these correspondences:

MAIN MODULE	QuotRem
A	I
B	J
Q	Quotient
R	Remainder

The names used in the calling program may or may not match.

However, the number, use, and type must match. In the example, the main module must supply four actual parameters, each of type integer. These parameters must represent the two numbers to be divided and the resulting quotient and remainder, in that order. In this section, we examine type matching for parameters in some detail.

For example, suppose we have an integer function whose header is given as

```
function Double(Number: integer): integer;
```

It should not be surprising that assignments such as

```
Twice := Double(Number)
```

and

```
Again := Double(Twice)
```

are legal (provided Twice, Number, and Again are integer). Also, because the parameter is a value parameter, we can write

```
Four := Double(2)
Final := Double((2 * I - 5) mod 3)
```

In addition, because a single element of an integer array is an integer variable, we can declare an integer array as

```
type
    IntegerArray = array[1..1000] of integer;

var
    Grades: IntegerArray;
```

and then use an assignment such as

```
Grades[I + 1] := Double(Grades[I])
```

We can summarize this by saying that

For a formal parameter of type integer, the actual parameter can be an integer variable or a single member of an integer array. If the parameter is a value parameter, it can be any integer expression whatsoever.

Note. Similar comments apply for *real*, *char*, *string*, and *boolean* parameters. That is, when we learn about arrays of reals, for example, we will see that a real array element can match a real parameter.

```
function ArraySum(List: IntegerArray; N: integer): integer;

{Written by:  XXXXXXXXXXXX XX/XX/XX}
{Purpose:     To add the numbers in an array}
{Parameters:  The array to be summed, and an indication of how many}
{             numbers are stored in the array}
var
   I: integer;          {for loop control}
   Sum: integer;        {accumulates the sum}

begin
   Sum := 0;

   for I := 1 to N do
      begin
         Sum := Sum + List[I]
      end; {for}

   ArraySum := Sum
end;
```

Figure 4-2   Array parameter.

Parameters can also be arrays. For example, consider the function in Figure 4-2. The two parameters are List, an IntegerArray, and N, the number of integers in the list. The type IntegerArray has been declared in the main module, as we have been doing for several sections now.

To use an array as a parameter, it must be given a **named type**. The following is illegal as a header:

```
function ArraySum(List: array[1..1000] of integer; N: integer): integer;
```

We must use the type name "IntegerArray" and not the definition of that type.

A similar comment applies to the use of strings as parameters. For example, the following procedure header might seem reasonable; however, it is illegal:

```
procedure PrintLine(Name: string[20]; Age: integer; Department: string[5]);
```

The parts in italics are illegal. Rather, we must, in the main module, include type declarations such as

```
type
   String20 = string[20];
   String5 = string[5];
```

Then the procedure header would be

```
procedure PrintLine(Name: String20; Age: integer; Department: String5);
```

In the calling program, the actual parameters corresponding to Name would be declared as String20 rather than as string[20].

4-1 PARAMETERS AND VARIABLES

Note. The type *string* in THINK Pascal is considered to be the (predefined) named type for *string[255]*. So it is legal (and often convenient) to use *string* as the type of string variables used as parameters.

We can summarize this discussion as follows:

When using arrays or explicitly sized strings as parameters, the formal and actual parameters must be of the same type. That type must be a named type defined in the "type" declarations of the main module.

Choosing Parameters

Understanding the preceding discussion is valuable, but the real test comes in applying it to programs. In this section, we describe some general advice on choosing parameters.

1. The parameters for a function represent values on which the function answer is based. They are called **input parameters** to emphasize the fact that the information flows into the subprogram from the calling program. They should be value parameters because the function should not modify its input.
2. For a procedure, we can have a mixture of input parameters and **output parameters**. Output parameters represent "answers" determined by the procedure. Put another way, *they represent the information passed back to the calling module*. Output parameters must be var parameters. Values passed into the procedure (input parameters), on the other hand, should be value parameters.

Note. A potential for confusion exists in this terminology. Notice that the terms input and output, when used to describe parameters, have nothing to do with reading from the keyboard or printing to the screen. An output parameter, for example, is one calculated by the procedure and returned to the calling module. That does not mean the procedure should print its value. Since we cannot invent our own terminology, we must learn to recognize the distinction between, for example, an input parameter and input from the user.

3. Sometimes a procedure has a parameter representing a value that is passed in, modified, then passed back. For example, a procedure can modify a bank balance by adding a deposit or subtracting a withdrawal. Such a parameter, called an **update parameter**, must be a var parameter.
4. There can be memory considerations that override this advice for array parameters, or, more generally, when the combined size of value parameters is very large. For example, consider the ArraySum function of Figure 4-2. Because the parameter List is a value parameter, it occupies storage space in the function. When the function is invoked, the actual parameter is automatically copied (all 1000 integers) to the formal parameter; this action takes a small amount of time as well as requiring memory. If the array were a var parameter, it would not occupy space and no copying would be needed. Instead, the function would work directly with the calling module's array, which is the actual parameter. In general, if the amount of memory needed by the

current set of value parameters exceeds what is available, the program bombs. (In THINK Pascal for the Mac, the available memory depends upon the amount installed in the particular Macintosh; in general, the more memory on the machine, the more that is available for value parameters.)

For these reasons, many programmers habitually use var parameters for all arrays. However, see the note that follows.

Note. Defensive programming argues against the practice of making all arrays var parameters. Value parameters protect the programmer from inadvertently modifying a parameter in the calling program. If we use a var parameter, we must take extra care that any modification of the parameter is intended to modify the corresponding actual parameter.

Thus, there is a design trade-off between defensive programming and efficiency. Unless the program contains an exceptional number of subprogram calls, we suggest that value parameters be used as a general rule. For most interactive applications, the extra time for copying the array to the value parameter is not noticeable, and the amount of available memory should be sufficient.

Note. The terms *input parameter*, *output parameter*, and *update parameter* are generic terms. That is, they apply to writing subprograms in a number of languages that support parameters for subprograms. They describe the desired use of the parameter as information flowing into the subprogram (input), as information flowing out of the subprogram (output), or as a combination (update). The term *value parameter* is also used as a generic term, and generally has a similar (but not necessarily identical) meaning as when it is used in a Pascal context. The term *var parameter* is strictly Pascal; the generic term for a similar way of handling parameters is **reference parameter.**

Global and Local Variables; Scope

At this point in the text, a program is of this form

> Program header line
> Constant definitions (*const*)
> Type definitions (*type*)
>
> Variable declarations for the main module
> Zero or more procedures and functions
> Main module action steps (*begin . . . end*)

Our discussion here is limited to this context. See Appendix A for a more complete discussion.

Each of the procedures and functions in the scenario described previously can, in turn, declare its own constants, types, and variables. For example, the first procedures we learned about were Instructions procedures that declared a variable "Answer." These variables are called **local variables**; they are usable "locally" within the particular procedure or function. They are not accessible in the main program or in any of the other procedures or functions.

Consider the following rather frivolous program:

```
program Demo;

   var
      I,  J: integer;

   procedure Manipulate;

   var
      I, N: integer;

   begin {Manipulate}
      I := 1;
      N := 2;
      J := I + N
   end; {Manipulate}

begin {Demo}
   I := 10;
   J := 11;
   Manipulate;
   Writeln(I, ' ', J);
end. {Demo}
```

The main module (Demo) has two variables I and J. The procedure has two variables I and N. The I variable in the Manipulate procedure is not the same as that in Demo. Examine the following diagram:

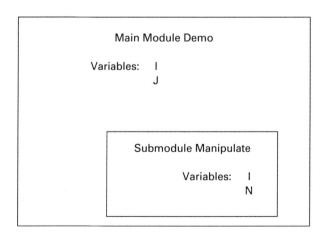

To understand how Pascal interprets these variables, imagine that the box enclosing the submodule Manipulate is a one-way mirror, with the outside surface silvered. From within Manipulate, we can see out, but it is impossible to see in.

278　　　　　　　　　　　　　　　　　　　　　　　MORE ON SUBPROGRAMS   CHAP. 4

Thus, within Manipulate, three variables are **visible**: the local variables I and N and the **global variable** J. The variable I in the main module is not visible because the compiler will assume that any reference to I means the locally defined I.

Within Manipulate, therefore, any references to I and N refer to the local variables I and N. However, Manipulate also references (and changes) J. Because J is not declared locally, it is assumed to be global. The reference to J refers to the globally defined J in the main module.

> Any variable used in a submodule, which is not declared either as a local variable or a parameter for that submodule, is assumed to be global. If the main module has a variable by that name, that main module variable is used. (If not, a syntax error—undefined variable—exists.)

In our example, the assignments I := 1 and N := 2 do not affect the main module. The assignment J := I + N changes J in the main module to 3. The Writeln prints the unchanged I (10) and the modified J (3).

Notes

1. The visibility of a variable is called its **scope**. Scope is discussed in more depth in Appendix A. For the programs that we will write:

    (a) The scope of anything defined in the main program includes the entire program. However, local declarations of the same name "hide" the global version. (The variable I in our example illustrates this hiding process.)

    (b) The scope of anything defined within a subprogram is that subprogram only.

2. The term "global" refers to the fact that the main program's declarations are visible throughout the entire program.

It is possible to contrive perfectly horrendous examples illustrating the results of this global default. For our purposes, however, we need to concentrate on three issues:

    1. *Accidental Global Variables Can Be a Disaster.* Defensive programming requires that we take extra care that all variables used in a module are declared in the module (either as parameters or as local variables). This prevents the submodule from having unwanted "side effects." The only exception is when we specifically design the module to use global variables.

    2. *Global Type Declarations Are Useful, Indeed Necessary.* For example, to pass arrays and explicitly sized strings as parameters, the type (IntegerArray, String6, etc.) should be declared in the main module.

    3. *Intentional Global Variables Should Be Used Sparingly, If At All.* The primary means of communication among modules should be parameters. Some languages, such as BASIC and COBOL, force modules to communicate via global variables. Sometimes this seems easier than parameters for introductory-level programs. However, experience has shown that using globals leads to increased program complexity. Excessive use of global variables makes it harder to get large programs working and makes it harder to modify them.

A little reflection on some of the reasons for using subprograms helps clarify these points. For example, one important reason is modularity. This term implies units that perform predictable tasks with specified input. By using parameters, we have a complete list of the input and output for the subprogram, right in the subprogram header. If globals are used, we must study the code itself to see which variables are used and which are modified. Moreover, if a variable does not have the desired value, it can be quite a task to track down which module changed it.

Two other considerations relate to the concepts of universal use and teamwork. First, to be truly universally useful, a module must not require certain declarations in the calling program. For example, the standard subprograms (Writeln, Sqrt, etc.) do not require us to declare certain variables in order to use them. All their communication occurs through the parameters.

Second, part of the advantages of allocating pieces of a project to different team members is lost if they must collaborate on all the variable names. By using local variables and parameters, it is possible to concentrate one's attention on the key issues: What data does each module need, what data does it generate, and what procedures are needed to transform the input data to the output data?

Our general rule is to use parameters rather than globals for communication.

DPT

1. The most insidious difficulties with Pascal subprograms involve inadvertent side effects. If a subprogram fails to declare a variable it uses, the compiler looks in the main program for a variable of that name. If it fails to find one that is good, it prints an error message for the undefined variable. On the other hand, if it does find a variable by that name, it assumes that the reference in the submodule meant to refer to this variable as a global variable.

Special care must be taken with *for* loop control variables. The use of variables I, J, and K for these variables is very common. Hence, the likelihood of the main module containing a variable of the same name increases.

One possible way to detect this involves unit testing each module. When we test a module, we can use a driver with "unusual" variable names. Perhaps each variable name in the driver could begin with a sequence such as "XXXX." Any variable not declared in the submodule would almost certainly fail to have the same name as a variable in the driver routine. This would allow the compiler to detect undeclared local variables for the module.

2. Attention must also be paid to the choice of value and var parameters. If a parameter is used to pass a value into the module, it should be a value parameter. Var parameters should be reserved for parameters that communicate answers to the calling module.

Two things can go wrong here. If a parameter should be declared as *var*, failing to do so prevents the calling module from getting its answer. On the other hand, suppose we use *var* for what should have been a value parameter. Then, if the submodule modifies the parameter, the corresponding variable in the calling program is modified.

Another point: If the parameter is a var parameter, we cannot supply an expression as the actual parameter. If we do, the compiler detects the error and tries to tell us what is wrong. The actual compiler message can vary. For example, if we use an expression such as I + J, it stops at the plus sign and tells us that it expected either a comma (if there is another parameter following) or a right parenthesis (if this is the last parameter). If we use a number, it tells us that the number is an illegal identifier.

3. Remember that variables defined within a subprogram are local. They cannot be used outside that subprogram.

4. When a subprogram has several parameters, we must pay close attention to the order of the parameters. When we invoke the submodule, we must supply the actual parameters in the proper order.

5. Parameters must match by type. This can be a little confusing with arrays. For example, suppose List has been declared as an integer array; consider this program segment.

```
for I := 1 to 50 do
  begin
     Root := Sqrt(List[I]);
     Writeln(List[I] : 10, Root : 10)
  end; {for}
```

The first 50 elements of the array "List" are passed, one at a time, to the standard Sqrt function. This function's parameter is a single number. Since each List[I] is one number, the invocation is correct.

On the other hand, the function ArraySum of Figure 4-2 has an integer array (type IntegerArray) as its first parameter. The step

```
Sum := ArraySum(List,50)
```

calculates the sum of the first 50 elements of the array List. Notice that in this case, we pass the entire array. There is no subscript.

REVIEW

Terms and Concepts

actual parameter	module
argument	named type
call	output parameter
called module	parameter
called program	procedure
calling module	reference parameter
calling program	reuse
formal parameter	scope
function	submodule
global variable	subprogram
input variable	top–down design
invoke	update parameter
local variable	value parameter
main module	var parameter
main program	visible

Reasons for Subprograms

1. Repetition
2. Universal use
3. Teamwork
4. Modularity

Communication Between Modules

Value versus Var Parameters

1. Value
   (a) Actual parameter can be any expression (of proper type).
   (b) Value of expression is passed to the formal parameter when the subprogram is invoked.
   (c) Nothing is passed back to the calling program.
   (d) Usually supplies input values to the subprogram.

2. Var
   (a) The actual parameter must be a variable.
   (b) No value is passed to the subprogram; instead, the subprogram works directly with the calling program's actual parameter.
   (c) Changes (within the subprogram) to the formal parameter immediately modify the calling program's actual parameter.
   (d) Usually supplies "answers" to the calling program or updates a variable of the calling program.

Type Matching for Parameters

1. Any expression of the proper type matches a value parameter.
2. An integer variable or one element of an integer array matches an integer var parameter. (Similarly for *real*, *boolean*, *char* and (unsized) *string*).
3. Arrays can be passed to match arrays of the same type. The type must be a named type declared in the "type" section of the main program.
4. Strings can be passed to match strings of the same named type.

Global versus Local Variables

1. Local: Declared within the subprogram where it is used.
2. Global: Not declared within the subprogram where it is used, but declared in the main program.
3. When interpreting the use of a variable, the compiler:
   (a) checks for a local declaration first
   (b) checks for a global declaration if there is no local one
   (c) generates an error message if there is neither a global nor a local declaration

DPT

1. Declare all local variables. Be especially careful to declare control variables of *for* loops (I, J, etc.).
2. Unit test modules.
3. Avoid using global variables.
4. Use value parameters to supply input to a subprogram. Use var parameters to supply answers to the calling program or to update a variable.
5. Do not attempt to use a subprogram's local variables (or its formal parameters) outside that subprogram.
6. Do not supply an expression for a var parameter.
7. Watch the order of the parameters.
8. Remember that parameters must be named types. (Use IntegerArray, not array[l..1000] of integer; use String20, not **string**[20]).
9. Only arrays can match array parameters.
10. Either simple variables or single-array elements can match nonarray var parameters.

EXERCISES

1. Suppose that the main program contains these declarations:

   ```
   const
     MaxIndex = 1000;

   type
     IntegerArray = array[1..MaxIndex] of integer;

   var
     L: IntegerArray;
     I, J, K, T, U, V: integer;
     B, C, X: real;
     S: string[20];
   ```

   For each of the following, you are given a procedure or function header and an invocation of that procedure or function. Decide whether each is legal; if not, explain why not.

   (a) `procedure P1(A, B: integer);`
   `P1(I, J, K);`

   (b) `function F1(A, B: real): integer;`
   `T := F1(B, C);`

   (c) `function F2(X: array[1..1000] of integer): integer;`
   `U := F2(L);`

   (d) `procedure P2(A: integer; B: real): real;`
   `X := P2(T, U);`

(e) **function** F3(I: integer): integer;
    F3(I);

(f) **procedure** P3(L: integer);
    P3(L);

(g) **procedure** P1(**var** R: integer);
    P1(L[5]);

(h) **procedure** P5(A: integer; **var** B: integer);
    P5(7, V + 12);

(i) **function** F4(Q : **string**[20]): integer;
    I := F4(S);

2. The following is a procedure to swap two integer numbers.

```
procedure Swap(var N1, N2: integer);
   var
      T: integer;      {temporary variable}

begin {Swap}
   T  := N1;           {save a copy of N1}
   N1 := N2;
   N2 := T
end; {Swap}
```

(a) What would be printed if we use this procedure in a program containing these steps?

```
I := 5;
J := 16;
Swap(I, J);
Writeln(I, J)
```

(b) Repeat part (a) assuming that the Swap procedure failed to declare its parameters as var parameters.
(c) What would happen if the Swap procedure failed to declare its local variable T?

3. Suppose that an integer array named A has been declared using our usual method and contains these as its first 10 values:

$$5 \quad 2 \quad 6 \quad 17 \quad -3 \quad 4 \quad 9 \quad -2 \quad 15 \quad -53$$

(a) Is this use of the procedure Swap from Exercise 2 legal?

```
Swap(A[1], A[5])
```

If so, what would the array look like after the procedure invocation?

(b) Repeat part (a) for this invocation:

```
Swap(A, A[10])
```

What occurs?

(c) What would be printed by this program segment?

```
for I := 1 to 5 do
  begin
      Swap(A[I], A[11-I])
  end; {for}
  for I := 1 to 10 do
      Write(A[I] : 6);
  Writeln
```

What is the purpose of the final Writeln?

(d) What would be the effect of this program segment?

```
for I := 1 to 9 do
begin
  Swap(A[I], A[I+1])
end; {for}
```

(e) What would be the effect of this program segment?

```
for I := 1 to 9 do
  begin
      if A[I] > A[I+1] then
          Swap(A[I], A[I+1])
  end; {for}
```

4. The following is a procedure that prints the digits of a positive integer in order from right to left.

```
procedure RightToLeft(N: integer);

   var
      Number: integer;       {holds "working copy" of N}

begin {RightToLeft}
  Number := N;
  repeat
      Writeln(Number mod 10);    {print right digit}
      Number := Number div 10    {then strip it off}
  until Number = 0
end; {RightToLeft}
```

(a) Hand-trace the procedure with various values of the parameter N to see how it works.
(b) Is the variable Number really needed? That is, could we just write the loop as follows?

```
repeat
   Writeln(N mod 10);
   N := N div 10
until N = 0
```

(c) What would happen in part (b) if N were inadvertently listed as a var parameter?

EXERCISES

5. Each of the following procedure and function headers is illegal. For each, indicate the type declarations that the main program needs and modify the header line to be legal.

   (a) `procedure Shift(var Scores: array [1..1000] of integer);`
   (b) `procedure Print(Name: string[20]; Initials: string[5]; Score: integer);`
   (c) `function Inorder(String1, String2: string[15]): boolean;`
   (d) `function Largest(A: array[1..75] of integer; N: integer);`

6. Type and run the following program. What happens? Why?

```
program Exercise;

   var
     I: integer;

   procedure PrintRow(RowNumber: integer);

   begin {PrintRow}
     Write('Row # ', RowNumber : 1, ':');
     for I := 1 to 10 do
        Write(RowNumber*I : 5);
     Writeln
   end; {PrintRow}

begin {Exercise}
   for I := 1 to 10 do
      PrintRow(I)
end.
```

7. For each of the following, write a header line for a function or procedure to do the indicated task. Do not write the entire submodule.

   You need to identify parameters and decide whether they should be value or var parameters. If you make any assumptions about type declarations, state those assumptions.

   (a) Calculate a person's commission based on a sales amount and commission rate.
   (b) Convert a date from Julian form to the usual form. For example, day 1 is January 1, day 33 is February 2, etc. The answer consists of a month and a day within that month. Assume that this is not a leap year.
   (c) Modify part (b) to include a parameter telling the subprogram whether or not this is a leap year.
   (d) Reverse a number viewed as a four-digit number. For example, 4172 would become 2714 and 319 would become 9130.
   (e) Sort an array containing 1000 integers.
   (f) Repeat part (e) assuming that a variable N indicates how many of the possible 1000 places in the array actually contain numbers.
   (g) Split a name into first and last names. For example, for "John Smith", the answers would be "John" and "Smith".
   (h) Add a bonus to the salary. The amount of the bonus depends on three things: the person's rank, department, and number of years in the company.

4-2 PROCEDURES AND FUNCTIONS

In this section, we study the syntax (form) and semantics (meaning) of Pascal subprograms. To a great extent, the section merely brings together material you have studied previously, but it also discusses two new major areas:

1. In previous sections, we have not used subprograms that invoked other subprograms (except for the built-in subprograms such as Readln or Sqrt). As we will see, you can write subprograms that invoke other subprograms you have written.

    This capability is extremely important in top-down design. When we break a program into subtasks, some of those subtasks can still be complicated. We want to subdivide them further, and this involves subprograms invoking other subprograms.

2. We introduce the important notion of **recursion**. This involves a subprogram invoking itself to solve a simpler version of the same problem. There are certain types of problems for which a **recursive** solution (one using recursion) is the easiest to create and to understand.

Nested Subprogram Invocation

Subprograms can in turn invoke other subprograms. For example, we can have the pattern of calls suggested by this hierarchy chart:

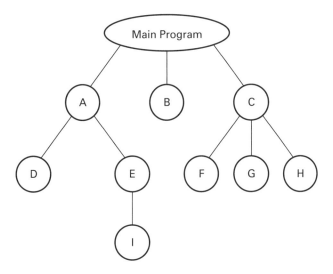

This suggests that the main module uses modules A, B, and C to perform needed subtasks. In turn, module A invokes both modules D and E, and module E invokes I. We refer to this situation as **nested invocations** (invocations within invocations). When module I completes its task, control returns to module E; when E completes, control returns to module A; and when A completes, control returns to the main module.

To write a program with the indicated hierarchy, it is only necessary to remember this rule:

In Pascal, everything must be declared before it is used.

Thus, for instance, because module A uses module E, the declaration for module E must precede that for module A. One possible program layout is this:

Program header
Constants, types, and variables for main module (globals)
Module D
Module I
Module E
Module A
Module B
Module F
Module G
Module H
Module C
Main module

Each module declares any necessary parameters and local variables.

As another example, consider the following:

```
program Nested;

    var
        Number: integer;

{This program illustrates nested invocation}

    function Double(I: integer): integer;
    begin {Double}
        Double := 2 * I
    end; {Double}

    procedure Triple (var X: integer);
    begin {Triple}
        X := Double(X) + X
    end; {Triple}

begin {Nested}
  Number := 10;
  Writeln('Before call: ', Number : 1);
  Triple(Number);
  Writeln('After call: ', Number : 1);
  Readln
end.
```

The main program uses the Triple procedure to triple the value of the variable Number. The procedure accomplishes this by invoking the function Double (which calculates twice the number), then adding the number to that. Double must be declared before Triple.

Note. In addition to nesting invocations, it is possible to nest declarations. That is, we can declare one procedure within another. In the previous example, Double is used only by the Triple procedure, not by the main program. It could, therefore, be declared within Triple.

For an advanced programmer, there are some advantages to nested definition. For very large programs with a chance of inadvertent duplicate module names, defining a module where it is used is sometimes useful.

On the other hand, nested definition increases the likelihood of accidental use of globals. Since this is a common pitfall encountered by beginners, we have chosen to defer our detailed discussion of this concept to Appendix A. (Any program we write in this text can be written quite effectively without using nested declarations.)

Procedures Versus Functions

In both form and use, there are many similarities between procedures and functions. The major difference between the two can be summarized by noting that a function returns exactly one value, and that value is returned to the calling program by the function name.

Both types of subprograms have this general form:

Header line

declarations of local constants, types, and variables

Body (a compound statement)

There are three differences between the two:

1. In the header line, one uses the word *function*, and the other the word *procedure*.
2. The header line for a function includes an indication of the type of the answer.
3. The body of a function must include at least one assignment statement giving a value to the function name. A procedure cannot give a value to the procedure name.

The header lines have this form:

`function` *function-name parameter-list*: *result-type;*

`procedure` *procedure-name parameter-list;*

The parameter-list is optional. If it is present, it consists of one or more repetitions of the following pattern, enclosed in parentheses, separated by semicolons:

`var` *list of variables separated by commas*: *type*

The keyword "var" is optional. If it is included, the parameters in that list are var parameters, otherwise they are value parameters. The type of the parameters can be any named type (*boolean*, *char*, String20, IntegerArray, etc.).

For a function, the header line contains a result type. This can be any of the following:

integer
longint
real
Boolean
char
string
a named string type

(as well as a few other types we have yet to cover).

It cannot be an array type. If we wish to return an array answer to the calling program, it must be a var parameter of a procedure. (A function returns exactly one value, and Pascal does not view an array as being a single value.)

The methods used to invoke a procedure differs from that used to invoke a function. A procedure is invoked by using its name, with necessary parameters, as a single statement. For example,

```
Triple(Number)
```

invokes the Triple procedure, passing the parameter Number. A function is invoked by using it in an expression, as in these three examples:

```
I := 1;
repeat
  I := I + 1
until Double(I) > 17

Y := Double(X) - 35 div Double(Z)

Writeln(T : 1, ' times 2 = ', Double(T) : 1)
```

In addition to the differences in form, there are differences in use. These differences arise from the view that the job of a function is to calculate its answer. It should have no other effects (known as side effects). This view is not enforced by the compiler, but it is a commonly accepted programming practice. In accordance with this view, we have the following rules.

1. All parameters for a function are value parameters. Procedures can use value or var parameters or a mix of the two.
2. Functions should not do any input or output (exception: temporary diagnostic prints, as described in Section 3-5). A procedure may or may not include I/O, depending on whether that is part of its identified subtask.
3. Functions should never use global variables. (Procedures should "almost never" use global variables.)

The following table summarizes some of the important differences between a function and a procedure.

Item	Function	Procedure
Name	Has a type (integer, etc.)	Does not have a type
	Function name is assigned a value within the function	Procedure name is never assigned a value
Use	Used to calculate a single real, boolean, char, integer or string value	Used to perform a task other than calculating a single value
	Invoked by using in an expression	Invoked by using its name as a statement
Parameters	Uses value parameters	Can use value or var parameters

Writing a Subprogram

In writing any type of subprogram, it is important to identify precisely the task to be performed. For example, many of our algorithms have been of this form:

    print instructions
    repeat these steps until user enters terminal value
        obtain input
        if not terminal input then do these steps:
            calculate answers
            print answers

We can use subprograms to refine the step "calculate answers." If so, these subprograms would probably not involve any I/O operations. They would receive input from the main program through value parameters and send back answers using var parameters (or through function names).

On the other hand, we can have subprograms whose task specifically involves input or output. For example, a procedure to obtain valid input would issue prompts, read values, and check for validity. Thus, some procedures do include I/O.

The key to proper design is defining precisely what task the subprogram is to accomplish.

We can summarize the steps for writing a subprogram as follows:

1. *Identify the Task to Be Performed.* Determine whether to use a function or a procedure. Choose a name for the subprogram, and determine the type (real, etc.) if it is to be a function.

2. *Decide on Parameters.* "Answers" passed to the calling program are var parameters. Values needed to perform the task are value parameters. Any parameter that is updated (used as input and then modified) must be a var parameter.

(All parameters for a function should be value parameters.)

3. *Devise a Plan for the Submodule.* This can involve identifying further subtasks. Both an algorithm for the required actions and a list of local variables should be generated. Remember that the algorithm for a function must include assigning a value to the function name.

4. *Write the Subprogram in Pascal.* The first and second steps just listed supply information for the header line. The third step supplies the local variable declarations and the body of the subprogram.

These four steps are always necessary. The degree to which they must be written depends on two things: the complexity of the task and your skill as a program designer and programmer. For most programmers, jotting down some notes and thoughts enhances the process.

Examples

Let us write a number of example functions and procedures. These examples are relatively simple. Their purpose is to illustrate some of the variety possible in working with Pascal subprograms. The examples here are not recursive. In the next section, we present some recursive examples. In addition, Section 4-3 contains some complete program case studies.

For the first example, we find the largest and smallest of three given integers. Since there are two answers, we write a procedure rather than a function. We name the procedure MaxMin.

The parameters include the three given integers, which we name Num1, Num2, and Num3. These are value parameters. The answers, which are var parameters, are Maximum and Minimum, also integer.

We are now ready to devise an algorithm. Several different ones are possible. However, the one that follows has certain advantages.

> Give Maximum and Minimum default values of Num1
> compare them to Num2 and adjust if necessary
> compare them to Num3 and adjust if necessary

One major advantage is that this algorithm can easily be adapted to more than three numbers. In fact, it is based on our standard method of finding the largest or smallest of a long list of input.

We can now write this in Pascal. There are no local variables. The step "compare them to Num2 and adjust if necessary" becomes

```
if Num2 > Maximum then
   Maximum := Num2;
if Num2 < Minimum then
   Minimum := Num2
```

The code for Num3 is similar.

See Figure 4-3 for the complete subprogram and a sample call.

For our next example, let us do some string processing. Suppose we are given three variables containing the city, state, and zip code of an individual. We would like to build a line suitable for an address on an envelope, similar to the following:

Jefferson City, TN 37760

Since there is one answer and no need to change any information the subprogram is supplied, a function is more appropriate than a procedure. We choose to write a function of type

SUBPROGRAM

```
procedure MaxMin(Num1, Num2, Num3 : integer; var Maximum, Minimum: integer);

{Written by: XXXXXXXXXX XX/XX/XX}
{Purpose:    To calculate the largest and smallest of three numbers}
{Parameters: Num1, Num2, Num3 - input, the three numbers}
{            Maximum - output, the largest}
{            Minimum - output, the smallest}

begin {MaxMin}

{*** Give Maximum and Minimum default values}

  Maximum := Num1;
  Minimum := Num1;

{*** Compare to second number}

  if Num2 > Maximum then
     Maximum := Num2;
  if Num2 < Minimum then
     Minimum := Num2;

{*** Compare to third number}

  if Num3 > Maximum then
     Maximum := Num3;
  if Num3 < Minimum then
     Minimum := Num3

end; {MaxMin}
```

SAMPLE CALL (I, J, K, Large, and Small are integer variables)

```
Readln(I, J, K);
MaxMin(I, J, K, Large, Small);
Writeln('The largest is ', Large : 1, ' and the smallest is ', Small : 1)
```

Figure 4-3 Procedure with two tasks.

string with parameters City, State, and ZipCode, also of type *string*. We then use concatenation to obtain the address line. See Figure 4-4.

For our next example, let us write a subprogram to check three integers to see if they are in increasing order. Because the answer is either yes or no, a Boolean function is appropriate. For parameters, we need the three numbers to be checked, which we will call First, Second, and Third. No local variables are involved. The algorithm is quite simple, but we do need to resolve one issue: Does "increasing order" allow duplicates? Are 6, 6, and 8

SUBPROGRAM

```
function AddressLine(City, State, ZIP) : string;
{Written by: XXXXXXXX, XX/XX/XX}
{Purpose:    To concatenate a city, state, and zip code into an address}
{Parameters: City  - input, the city part of the address}
{            State - input, the state part of the address}
{            Zip   - input, the zip code part of the address}
begin {AddressLine}
  AddressLine := City + ', ' + State + ' ' + ZIP
end; {AddressLine}
```

SAMPLE CALL

```
Writeln(Name);
Writeln(StreetAddress);
CityState := AddressLine(City, State, ZipCode);
Writeln(CityState)
```

Figure 4-4   String-valued function.

in increasing order? This could be answered either way, but for this example, we choose to assume the answer is no. The function appears as Figure 4-5. Study both the function and the alternate approach given for the function body.

To illustrate subprograms that deal with arrays, let us calculate the "elementwise sum" of two arrays. Here is what we mean. A and B are two variables of type IntegerArray, each containing N values. For example, if N is 5, then A and B might be

$$A: 6, 1, 3, -5, 2$$
$$B: 2, 5, -3, 1, 7$$

We wish to calculate Sum, found by adding corresponding elements of A and B. For the example, Sum would be

$$Sum : 8, 6, 0, -4, 9$$

To do so, we need a procedure. Conceptually, there is a single answer (Sum), but that answer is an array. Pascal does not allow a function to have an array type as its type, so we must use a procedure.

There are four parameters we need: the two arrays A and B, the answer array Sum, and the variable N, which shows how many values the arrays contain. Of these, only the answer (Sum) is a var parameter.

The algorithm needs to accomplish the following steps:

```
Sum[1] := A[1] + B[1];
Sum[2] := A[2] + B[2];
           .
           .
           .
Sum[N] := A[N] + B[N]
```

SUBPROGRAM

```
function InOrder(First, Second, Third : integer) : Boolean;

{Written by: XXXXXXXX, XX/XX/XX}
{Purpose:    To see if three given numbers are in strictly increasing}
{            order}
{Parameters: First, Second, Third - input, the numbers to be tested}

begin {InOrder}
  if (First < Second) and (Second < Third) then
     InOrder := true
  else
     InOrder := false
end; {InOrder}
```

ALTERNATE BODY

```
begin
  InOrder := (First < Second) and (Second < Third)
end;
```

SAMPLE CALL

```
Readln(Score1, Score2, Score3);
if InOrder(Score1, Score2, Score3) then
  Writeln('Improving')
else if InOrder(Score3, Score2, Score1) then
  Writeln('Going steadily downhill')
else
  Writeln ('Neither steadily increasing nor steadily decreasing')
```

Figure 4-5 Boolean function.

If we use a *for* loop to cause the variable I to take on the values 1 through N, then the body of that *for* loop would be

```
Sum[I] := A[I] + B[I]
```

The first time through the loop, I is 1, and Sum[1] is calculated as A[1] + B[1]. The second time through, Sum[2] is calculated as A[2] + B[2], and so on. Observe that I is a local variable for the procedure. See Figure 4-6 for the subprogram and a driver main program used to test the procedure. Study the matchup of the formal parameters (A, B, Sum, N) to the actual parameters (Arr1, Arr2, Answer, N). You may wish to adapt the driver to write drivers to test your own subprograms that have array parameters.

One approach to printing tables of output involves using procedures to print detail lines and headers. As a simple example of one possible approach, consider the program of Figure 4-7, which has lines numbered for reference purposes. That program is similar to one we wrote in Chapter 2 (Figure 2-10). It prints a table of square roots for numbers input by

```
program Driver;

{Written by: XXXXXXXX XX/XX/XX}
{Purpose:    To test the AddArrays procedure}
{Procedures used: AddArrays,  to add two arrays}

   const
     MaxIndex = 1000;            {array size}
     EndOfData = 0;              {terminal value}

   type
      IntegerArray = array[1..MaxIndex] of integer;

   var
     Arr1, Arr2: IntegerArray;   {the two arrays to add, input}
     N: integer;                 {the size of the arrays, input}
     Answer: IntegerArray;       {the sum array, output}
     I: integer;                 {loop control variable}

   procedure AddArrays (A, B: IntegerArray; var Sum: IntegerArray; N: integer);

     {Written by: XXXXXXXX XX/XX/XX}
     {Purpose:    To add two arrays elementwise}

     {Parameters: A, B - input, the arrays to be added}
     {            Sum - output, the sum}
     {            array N - input, the present size of the arrays}
     {                 (that is, the number of actual values in the arrays)}

         var
             I: integer;    {control variable - for loop}

     begin {AddArrays}
         for I := 1 to N do
             begin
                 Sum[I] := A[I] + B[I]
             end {for loop}
     end; { AddArrays }

begin {Driver}
    Write('Enter array size (0 to stop): ');
    Readln(N);

    while N <> EndOfData do
        begin

{*** Get first array}

            Writeln('Enter first array, one number per line');
            for I := 1 to N do
                begin
                    Readln(Arr1[I])
                end; {for loop}
```

Figure 4-6   Procedure to calculate an array (continues next page).

```
{*** Get second array}

            Writeln('Enter second array, one number per line');
            for I := 1 to N do
                begin
                    Readln(Arr2[I])
                end; {for loop}

{*** Use procedure to calculate sum}

            AddArrays(Arr1, Arr2, Answer, N);

{*** Print answer}

            Writeln('The sum array is: ');
            for I := 1 to N do
                begin
                    Writeln(Answer[I])
                end; {for loop}

{*** Prepare for next pass}

            Writeln;
            Write('Enter array size (0 to stop): ');
        end; {while}

{*** Stop}

end.
```

SAMPLE INPUT AND OUTPUT

```
Enter array size (0 to stop): 3
Enter first array, one number per line
4
-6
7
Enter second array, one number per line
-6
6
203
The sum array is:
      -2
       0
      210

Enter array size (0 to stop): 0
```

Figure 4-6   (continued)

the user. In Chapter 2, we simply assumed that the list would occupy no more than one page. If it did go beyond one page, headers appeared only on the first page.

The hierarchy chart illustrates the overall structure of the program:

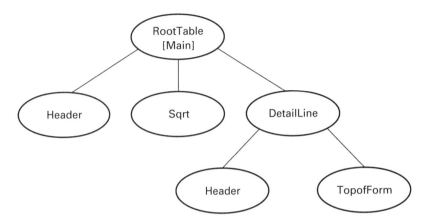

RootTable: Reads values in a loop and calculates square roots using Sqrt

Header: Procedure to print column headings on printer (it is used both by DetailLine and the main module)

Sqrt: Built-in square root function

DetailLine: Procedure to print one line of output on printer, advancing to a new page with new headings when the previous page is full

TopOfForm: Procedure to send a "form feed" to the printer, to advance to a new page

The program in Figure 4-7 contains some interesting features. First, notice that the header printing routine prints and then increments a PageNumber variable (lines 33 and 39). The main program initializes its value at 1 (line 82), and the Header procedure updates it. (PageNumber could not be local. If it were, it would never change its value.)

We chose to make PageNumber a parameter (rather than a global variable), for the reasons discussed in Section 4-1. However, the trade-off is that PageNumber must be "passed through" DetailLine in order that Header (called from within DetailLine) has access to it. Some programmers feel that passing through variables is cumbersome, especially if it must be done through several procedures; they would make PageNumber (and, perhaps, LineCount) global variables. We think the benefits of avoiding global variables usuallly outweigh the awkwardness of passing through parameters.

We use the predefined function Page as the method of going to the top of a new page (line 64). This causes the printer to advance the paper to what it thinks is the top of a new page. Provided the paper was at the top of a page when the printer was turned on, this generally works out correctly. If Page did not function correctly for a particular printer, we would need to write our own top-of-form procedure.

The DetailLine procedure not only prints the output line, but also counts how many have been printed. If 45 lines have been printed, it calls Header (line 65) to advance to a new page prior to printing the line. LineCount, which is initialized to 0 by the main program

```
1)     program RootTable;
2)
3)     {Written by: XXXXXXXXXX XX/XX/XX}
4)     {Purpose:    To create a table of square roots on the printer}
5)     {            with new headings on each new page}
6)     {Functions used: Sqrt, the built-in square root function}
7)     {               Page, the built-in paging function, to advance to a new}
8)     {                    page}
9)     {               Header (called by DetailLine as well as main module), to}
10)    {                    print headings}
11)    {               DetailLine, to print one line of the table }
12)
13)        const
14)          EndOfData = -1;                     {terminating value}
15)          MaxLines = 45;                      {maximum lines per page}
16)
17)        var
18)          Number: integer;          {user input}
19)          LineCount: integer;       {line count}
20)          PageNumber: integer;      {page number}
21)          Report: text;             {name for printer}
22)
23)
24)        procedure Header (var PageNumber: integer);
25)
26)        {Written by: XXXXXXXXXX  XX/XX/XX}
27)        {Purpose:    To print headings at the top of a page}
28)        {Parameters: None}
29)        {Globals used: Page Number, printed and incremented by 1}
30)        {              Report, the name for the printer}
31)
32)        begin {Header}
33)          Writeln(Report, ' ' : 29, 'TABLE OF SQUARE ROOTS', ' ' : 10, 46,
34)               'page ', PageNumber);
35)          Writeln(Report);
36)          Writeln(Report, ' ' : 28, 'Number        Square Root');
37)          Writeln(Report, ' ' : 28, '------    -----------');
38)          Writeln(Report);
39)          PageNumber := PageNumber + 1
40)        end; {Header}
41)
42)        procedure DetailLine (Number: integer; Root: real; var PageNumber,
43)                              LineCount: integer);
44)
45)        {Written by: XXXXXXXXXX XX/XX/XX}
46)        {Purpose:    To print a detail line (one line of a table).}
47)        {            If the page is full, it first advances to a new page}
48)        {            and prints heading.}
49)        {Parameters: Number - input, the integer number to be printed}
50)        {            Root - input, the square root, also to be printed}
```

Figure 4-7 Header and DetailLine procedures (continues next page).

```
51)     {              PageCount, passed onto Header to print page number}
52)     {              LineCount - update, used to see if it is time to start}
53)     {                       a new page;}
54)     {              set back to 0 for each new page}
55)     {Procedures used: Page, to advance to a new page}
56)     {              Header, to print headings}
57)
58)     begin {DetailLine}
59)
60)     {*** Check for full page}
61)
62)        if LineCount = MaxLines then
63)           begin
64)             Page(Report);
65)             Header(PageNumber);
66)             LineCount := 0
67)           end; {if}
68)
69)     {*** Print the line and increment the count of lines on this page}
70)
71)        Writeln(Report, ' ' : 29, Number : 4, ' ' : 7, Root : 10 : 4);
72)        LineCount := LineCount + 1
73)     end; {DetailLine}
74)
75)
76) begin {RootTable}
77)
78) {*** Initialize line counter and page number, and print headings}
79)
80)    Reset(Report, 'Printer:');
81)    LineCount := 0;
82)    PageNumber := 1;
83)    Header(PageNumber);
84)
85) {*** Read numbers in a loop, calculate square roots and print}
86)
87)    repeat
88)      Writeln;
89)      Write('Enter a number (-1 to terminate): ');
90)      Readln(Number);
91)      if Number <> EndOfData then
92)      begin
93)       Writeln('The square root is ', Sqrt(Number) : 10 : 4);
94)       DetailLine(Number, Sqrt(Number), PageNumber, LineCount)
95)      end; {if}
96)    until Number = EndOfData;
97)
98) {*** Stop program}
99)
100) end.
```

Figure 4-7   (continues next page)

SAMPLE INPUT AND OUTPUT

Terminal:

```
Enter a number (-1 to terminate :  6
The square root is       2.4495

Enter a number (-1 to terminate): 4
The square root is       2.0000

Enter a number (-1 to terminate): 10
The square root is       3.1623

Enter a number (-1 to terminate): 0
The square root is       0.0000

Enter a number (-1 to terminate): 1231
The square root is 35.0856

Enter a number (-1 to terminate): 97
The square root is       9.8489

Enter a number (-1 to terminate): 50
The square root is       7.0711

Enter a number (-1 to terminate): -1
```

Printer (with MaxLines temporarily changed to 3 rather than 45):

First page:

```
TABLE OF SQUARE ROOTS           page 1
Number       Square Root
------       -----------
    6           2.4495
    4           2.0000
   10           3.1623
```

Second page:

```
TABLE OF SQUARE ROOTS           page 2
Number       Square Root
------       -----------
    0           0.0000
 1231          35.0856
   97           9.8489
```

Third page:

```
TABLE OF SQUARE ROOTS           page 3
Number       Square Root
------       -----------
   50           7.0711
```

Figure 4-7 (continued)

4-2 PROCEDURES AND FUNCTIONS

(line 81), is incremented by DetailLine (line 72). Whenever a new page is begun, it is reset to 0 (line 66).

The global constant MaxLines (declared in line 15) indicates how many lines we want on each page. This is used by DetailLine to see if the page is "full" (line 62). This proved useful in preliminary testing of the program. We changed its value (temporarily) to 3, which allowed us to test multiple pages of output more quickly.

Note that if the user terminates the program without entering any numbers, a report consisting just of header lines is printed. If we wanted a report only when numbers were entered, then setting LineCount to MaxLines in line 81, and removing the call to Header at line 83, would accomplish this change. If −1 were entered, then DetailLine would not be called, and so no report would print. If a number were entered, then DetailLine would be called; since its first action is to check for MaxLines (line 62), a report header would be printed, followed by a detail line for the entered number.

Another approach would be to print a special version of the report when no numbers were entered, perhaps one consisting just of the report title and a message that no roots were calculated. Then the program would need a flag; it would be set to *true* if numbers were entered, and *false* if none was entered. The value of the flag can then be checked to determine which type of report is to be printed. Think about what else you would need to change in the program so it would implement this change to the reporting process.

Finally, observe that the main program passes the value "Sqrt(Number)" as the DetailLine procedure's second parameter (line 94). Because that parameter is a value parameter, this is legal.

This example can appear complicated at first. However, you should study it carefully. It contains some ideas you may wish to use (or improve upon) in programs that create tables of printed output.

Recursion

Pascal subprograms are allowed to call themselves. A subprogram that calls itself is a **recursive** subprogram, and the process of calling itself is called **recursion**.

Recursion is an extremely useful tool in certain areas of computer science. For some applications, it represents the easiest approach to understanding and solving a problem. In addition, it is frequently easier to prove a subprogram's correctness when the subprogram is written recursively.

In this section, we examine a few recursive subprograms. Our purpose is twofold. First, we wish to develop a mode of thinking that lends itself to finding recursive solutions to problems. Second, we want to understand how recursion actually works. We begin this study here; Chapter 10 provides a more in-depth examination of the topic.

For our first example, consider the problem of raising an integer number to an integer power. We wish to calculate

$$a^n$$

where both a and n are integers, and n is not negative. Suppose we decide to write a function with the header

```
function Power(A, N: integer): integer;
```

How do we go about writing the function's body?

One possibility is to observe that the following property holds:
$$a^n = a \cdot a^{n-1}$$
A naive approach might be this:

```
function Power(A, N: integer) : integer;
begin {Power}
   Power := A * Power(A, N-1)
end; {Power}
```

Although naive, this is almost correct, and it captures the spirit of recursion very nicely:

Restate the problem in terms of a "simpler" form of the same problem

In this case, a^{n-1} is "simpler" than a^n because the exponent is one less.

To see what is wrong with this function, let us trace its execution for A = 4 and N = 3. When the function is invoked, space is set aside in the computer memory for the two value parameters. We can visualize the situation as shown:

Power:
   A 4 N 3

The first step that Power takes is to invoke itself with actual parameters A and N − 1 (4 and 2, respectively). This causes additional space to be set aside for a second **instance** of the two value parameters:

Power:
   A 4 N 3
>> >> >> >> >>
   Power:
      A 4 N 2

The >> >> >> >> >> signifies that the first-level Power has invoked the second-level Power.

The second-level Power in turn invokes a third level, which invokes a fourth level, which invokes a fifth level. At this point, we have

Power:
   A 4 N 3
>> >> >> >> >>
   Power:
      A 4 N 2
   >> >> >> >> >>
      Power:
         A 4 N 1
      >> >> >> >> >>
         Power:
            A 4 N 0
         >> >> >> >> >>
            Power:
               A 4 N −1

4-2 PROCEDURES AND FUNCTIONS

```
function Power(A, N : integer): integer;

{Written by:     XXXXXXXX, XX/XX/XX}
{Purpose:        To raise an integer to an integer power. If the numbers}
{                are too large, overflow may yield an incorrect result.}
{Parameters:     A - input, the number to raise to the power}
{                N - input, the power (must be 0 or higher)}
{Functions used: Power is called recursively}

begin {Power}
   if N = 0 then
      Power := 1
   else
      Power := A * Power(A, N-1)
end; {Power}
```

Figure 4-8   Recursive function for a^n.

As you can see, the fifth level in turn calls a sixth level, and so on forever. What we need is a way to terminate this process.

This example can suggest a possibility. The fourth-level version of Power has to calculate 4 to the 0 power, which is simply 1. Suppose we rewrite the Power function as shown in Figure 4-8.

In the tracing we did before, the fourth-level Power now does not invoke a fifth level. Since its value for N is 0, it instead returns the answer 1 to the third level. The third level multiplies this answer times A (which is 4), returning the answer 4 to the second level. The second level multiplies this by A, sending 16 to the first level. Finally, the first level multiplies this by 4, returning the answer 64 to the original caller.

There are two important principles of recursion illustrated by this example. (We have stated one previously.) They are as follows:

1. For the general case, phrase the answer in terms of a simpler version of the same problem.

2. Identify one or more simple base cases for which the answer is easy to calculate without a recursive call.

We can now identify what "simpler" means: closer to the base cases. This ensures that the process does not keep on invoking new levels infinitely.

In the example, N = 0 was identified as a base case where the answer is easy. For larger values of N, the relationship

$$a^n = a \cdot a^{n-1}$$

gave the answer in terms of a simpler version of the same problem.

Note.   This function works only for positive values of N. In the exercises, you are asked to consider negative values. The function would have to be real to handle this. For example, 4 to the −1 power means 1 divided by 4 to the 1st power, which is 0.25.

Now let us consider a nonnumerical application of recursion. Given a string, we wish to "double" it. For example, the following values of the string yield the indicated answers:

STRING	ANSWER
'A'	'AA'
'Sam'	'SSaamm'
'DoubleIt'	'DDoouubblleeIItt'
''	'' (the null string doubled is still null)

To solve this problem, we use the two principles of recursion listed before.

1. Phrase an answer in terms of a simpler version of the same problem. For strings, one way to get a simpler string is to remove the first character. The resulting string is shorter and therefore simpler. (It is closer to the base case.) We call ourselves with this shorter string, using the answer obtained to build our answer for the string as a whole.
2. Identify a simple base case. If the string is null, the answer is simply the null string.

In writing recursive subprograms, it is not necessary to trace the subprogram as we did for Power. (Once we have written it, however, tracing can help us understand how it really works.) When writing the subprogram, we think as follows:

> Assuming the recursive call does calculate the correct answer for the simpler problem, how can I use that to calculate the answer for the original problem?

In our example, suppose our string is 'fine'. We call ourselves with the simpler string 'ine' and trust that the answer is correct ('iinnee'). To finish the problem, we concatenate 'f' on the front of this twice. Figure 4-9 contains the solution that is based on this observation.

Notes

1. We have used a procedure Split to split a string into two pieces: the first character and the rest of the string. One of the exercises indicates one way this procedure could be written.
2. The *string* type allows strings of up to 255 characters, THINK's maximum size. Our procedure "works" for any input string whose length is 127 or less, since doubling a larger string will result in the rightmost characters being lost. And, on some Macintoshes, we run out of memory space because each level of the recursive Double-String procedure contains its own copies of the value parameter AString and the local variables First, Rest, and RestDoubled. See the exercises for some possible enhancements.

DPT

1. Subprograms must be declared before they are used. This implies that the lower-level subprograms in the hierarchy chart come first in the program.

```
procedure DoubleString(AString: string; var Doubled: string);

   {Written by: XXXXXXXX, XX/XX/XX}
   {Purpose:    To 'double' a string by duplicating each character}
   {Parameters: AString - input, the string to be doubled, assumed no}
   {                          longer than 127 characters}
   {           Doubled - output, the doubled string}
   {Procedures used: Split, to split off the first character of the string}
   {                 DoubleString is called recursively}
      var
         First: string;                        {the first character}
         Rest: string;                         {the rest of the string}
         RestDoubled: string;                  {the rest, doubled recursively}

   begin {DoubleString}
      if AString = '' then
         Doubled := ''
      else
         begin
            Split(AString, First, Rest);
            DoubleString(Rest, RestDoubled);
            Doubled := concat(First, First, RestDoubled)
         end {if}
   end; {DoubleString}
```

Figure 4-9   Doubling a string recursively.

2. Each module declares its own local variables. These cannot be accessed outside the module.

3. Make sure you understand precisely what task each module is to perform, and write the module to perform that task. For example, many procedures are designed to calculate answers for the calling program, which use them and perhaps later print them. If the procedure's subtask does not include printing the answers, then it should not print them. (A function should never include any I/O.)

4. Use parameters as the primary means of communication. Do not use globals without giving that use careful thought.

5. Be careful in your choice of value and var parameters. Value parameters should be used to supply values to the subprogram. Var parameters are used to pass answers back to the calling program or to modify a variable in the calling program.

6. A function cannot be used to calculate an array answer. Instead, the array should be a var parameter for a procedure.

7. Always include an assignment to the function name in a function. Never assign a value to a procedure name.

8. Remember that any reference to the function name, other than on the left side of an assignment statement, represents a recursive call. If this is what was intended, great. If not, use a local variable to obtain the answer, then assign the answer to the function name.

9. When writing a recursive function or procedure, make sure you identify the base case or cases that do not involve a recursive call. Without this, the recursive process has no way to stop.

Exactly what will happen depends on the problem. One possibility is a "stack overflow" run-time error. This means that the program has run out of memory. (Each new level of the subprogram contains space for its value parameters and also any local variables.) Another possibility is that the program attempts to do some illegal activity and terminates.

REVIEW

Terms and Concepts

instance
nested invocations
recursion
recursive

Pascal Syntax

Program Layout

Program header line
Global constants, types, and variables
Procedures and functions
Main module body (compound statement)

Form of Subprogram

Header line
Local constants, types, and variables
Body of subprogram (compound statement)

Header Line Form

```
procedure procedure-name parameter-list;

function function-name parameter-list: result-type;
```

Parameter List (Optional)

One or more repetitions, in parentheses, separated by semicolons, of:

```
var variables separated by commas: type
```

"Var" is optional; default is value parameter

Function Types Allowed

Integer
Boolean
String

Real
Char
Name string type

Function versus Procedure. See table in Procedures versus Function section.

Writing a Subprogram

1. (a) Identify the subtask.
   (b) Choose a function or procedure.
   (c) Choose a name (and a type if a function is chosen).
2. Decide on parameters (value and var).
3. Write an algorithm, identifying local variables.
4. Code in Pascal.

Recursion

Two Principles

1. Write the general case using a recursive call to solve a simpler version of the same problem.
2. Identify base case(s) not involving a recursive call.

DPT

1. Declare before use.
2. Local variables are usable only in the module.
3. Identify subtasks precisely.
4. Avoid global variables.
5. Be careful in choosing between var and value parameters.
6. Remember a function answer cannot be an array.
7. Always assign an answer to the function name (in the function). Never assign a value to a procedure name.
8. Avoid unintentional recursion.
9. When using recursion, don't forget the base case(s).

EXERCISES

1. Write a subprogram to calculate the volume and surface area of a sphere of radius r.

$$V = (4/3)\pi r^3$$
$$S = 4\pi r^2$$

2. If P dollars are deposited in a savings account earning interest i compounded annually, then after n years, the amount present is given by

$$A = P(1 + i)^n$$

Write a subprogram to calculate A and also the total interest earned, given P, i, and n.

3. Write a subprogram to determine the state tax based on the following rules. First, $500 is deducted from the income for each dependent. Then a standard deduction of 10 percent of the original income is subtracted. Finally, the tax is determined according to the following table.

RESULTING INCOME	TAX
Less than $0	0
$0 – 10,000	2% of resulting income
Over $10,000	$200.00 plus 2.5% of amount over $10,000

4. (a) Write a subprogram to find the largest and smallest of two integers I and J.
   (b) Write a subprogram to find the largest and smallest of five integers.

5. Write a subprogram to calculate the letter grade, given the number grade based on the following table. (What type of variable is the answer?)

NUMBER	LETTER
90 and up	H
75 – 89.999	C
Under 75	F

6. Write a subprogram with three integer parameters. This subprogram is to find the range of the numbers, that is, the difference between the largest of the three and the smallest of the three. Use the MaxMin procedure, developed in this section, to calculate the largest and the smallest.

7. Write a Boolean function that determines whether two given real numbers are within 0.00001 of each other.

8. One way to approximate the square root of a real number X is by the method of iteration, as given by Newton. This consists of choosing a first approximation (perhaps X itself), then repeatedly getting a new (and better) approximation by using the formula:

$$a_{new} = \frac{1}{2}\left(a_{old} + \frac{X}{a_{old}}\right)$$

Thus, we have a loop involved. We continue until

$$|a_{old} - a_{new}| < 0.00001$$

(Use the function from Exercise 7.)

Write a subprogram to approximate the square root of X in this manner. Then write a main program that invokes your program and also the built-in Sqrt function. Print both answers and compare them. How good is your subprogram? How fast?

9. (a) Write a subprogram that, given an integer and a position, finds the digit in that position of the integer. For example, for the number 29867, we would have the following answers for various positions.

EXERCISES

POSITION	ANSWER
1	7
2	6
3	8
4	9
5	2
Other	0

    (b) Using this subprogram, print the digits of a number in reverse order, one per line.

10. Write Boolean functions for the following:

    (a) Given four integer test scores, see whether or not the average is at least 60.

    (b) Repeat part (a), but the parameter is an integer array containing 14 weekly quiz scores; see if the average is at least 12.0.

    (c) Given a character, determine whether it is a vowel.

    (d) Given three integers, Value, Low, and High, see whether Value lies between Low and High, inclusive.

    (e) Given a four-digit integer, determine whether it is a "palindrome" (reads the same front to back as back to front). Examples: 1001 and 3443 are; 6117 is not. Also, 110 is because 110 is 0110 as a four-digit number.

    (f) See whether a given point (x,y) lies within the "unit square" from (0,0) to (1.1)

    (g) See whether a given point (x,y) lies within a circle with center (0,0) and a given radius.

11. Use the function written in Exercise 10(d) as a tool for the following:

    (a) Write a GetScores procedure that reads three test scores and makes sure each lies between 0 and 100 inclusive.

    (b) Write a segment of code to see if at least one of the integers I and J lies between 500 and 553, inclusive.

    (c) Write a segment of code to see if an integer A is at least 1/2 of B and no more than twice B.

12. **(a)** Write a function to simulate the following game. It should generate random numbers in the range 1 to 100, continuing until a generated number is divisible by 10.

    If the sum of the numbers generated (including the last one) is 1000 or more, the result is 'W' (win); for 500 to 999, it is 'T' (tie); and for less than 500, it is 'L' (lose).

    (b) In a large number of plays, what percentage of wins, losses, and ties might you expect? Write a program to find out.

13. THINK Pascal supplies some facilities for working with strings that we have not discussed. For example, a string is treated as very similar to an array of characters. For the following descriptions, StrngVar represents any string variable. We can write

```
StrngVar[I]
```

to obtain the Ith character of the string. If Name has the value 'John Smith', for example, then Name[l] is 'J' and Name[7] is 'm'. In addition, there are some useful functions. One is Length (StrngVar), which calculates the present length of the string. Another is Copy(StrngVar, Position, Number). The answer is a substring of StrngVar, beginning at position Position and having Number characters. These examples illustrate the functions:

```
Length('Tom Jones')        is 9
Length('')                 is 0

Copy('ABCDEFG', 3, 4)      is 'CDEF'
Copy('Alphabet', 1, 1)     is 'A'
Copy('Tom', 4, 2)          is ''    (null, 4 is beyond end of string)
Copy('Tom', 2, 5)          is 'om'  (only copies what is there)
```

Using these functions, do the following:

(a) Write a procedure to print a string, one letter per line. For the string 'find', the output would be

```
f
i
n
d
```

(b) Write a function to count the blanks in a string.
(c) Write the Split procedure that was used in this section.
(d) Find the middle character (or characters) in a string. For 'hop', the answer would be 'o', and for 'Mary' it would be 'ar'.
(e) Write a SplitLast procedure that takes off the last rather than the first character.
(f) Write a procedure that removes both the first and the last characters.

14. (a) Write a subprogram to find the sum of an array. The parameters are A, an IntegerArray, and N, which indicates how many values are in the array.
(b) Modify part (a) to "drop the lowest value." For the list

$$3, 7, 2, 5$$

the sum would be 15. Hint: As you are calculating the sum, find the lowest value. Then subtract that from the sum.
(c) Modify part (a) to drop the two lowest values.

15. Write a subprogram to find the smallest and largest values in an integer array. The parameters include a variable telling how many values are in the array.

16. As part of a check printing program, it is desired to print a line such as

```
EXACTLY 55 DOLLARS AND 04 CENTS
```

Write a procedure to accomplish this, given a real number containing the amount to be printed.

17. Repeat Exercise 16, but print words instead of numbers:

```
EXACTLY FIFTY-FIVE DOLLARS AND FOUR CENTS
```

Assume the dollars are in the range 0 to 99.

18. (a) As it stands, the Power function is not very good; because maxint is 32767, numeric overflow happens quickly. Modify the function so that it will return a value of 0 when its

answer is going to be wrong. Hint: Consider how you can tell that A * Power(A, N – I) is going to be larger than maxint.

(b) Another approach to the problem mentioned in part (a) would be to make the function a real function rather than an integer function. This expands its range of usefulness. Although the resulting answers may not be completely accurate for large values, they are at least reasonably close. Make the suggested change.

(c) Modify the Power function to handle negative integer powers. Use the fact that

$$a^{-n} = 1/a^n$$

19. Write a recursive function to calculate $n!$ (n factorial). This is defined as $n! = n \cdot (n-1) \cdot \ldots \cdot 3 \cdot 2 \cdot 1$. Hint: $n! = n \cdot (n-1)!$

20. Write a recursive GCD function to find the greatest common divisor of two positive integers m and n. An algorithm due to Euclid states that if m divides evenly into n, then the answer is m. Otherwise it is the same as the greatest common divisor of (n mod m) and m.

21. Write an LCM function to find the least common multiple of two positive integers m and n. Hint: For any two positive integers m and n, it is true that

$$\text{LCM}(m,n) * \text{GCD}(m,n) = m * n$$

22. A famous sequence of numbers is the collection of Fibonacci numbers, defined as

$$F_0 = 0$$
$$F_1 = 1$$
$$F_n = F_{n-1} + F_{n-2} \text{ for } n \geq 2$$

Using these rules, we can list the first few Fibonacci numbers:

$$0, 1, 1, 2, 3, 5, 8, 13, 21, 34, 55, \ldots$$

Observe that each one is the sum of the previous two. Write a recursive function Fibonacci(N) that calculates F_N for a given N.

23. The usual definition for the binomial coefficients is expressed in terms of factorials:

$$\binom{n}{k} = \frac{n!}{k!(n-k)!} \quad 0 \leq k \leq n$$

However, it is also possible to give a recursive definition. There are two base cases: if $k = 0$, then the answer is 1; if $n = k$, then the answer is 1. The general case is given by

$$\binom{n}{k} = \binom{n-1}{k-1} + \binom{n-1}{k}$$

Use this recursive definition to write a recursive function Binomial (N,K).

24. By imitating the example in this section, write a recursive subprogram to do the following string manipulations. You can use the Split procedure.

(a) Reverse a string. For 'ABCD', the answer is 'DCBA'.
(b) See if the string contains a given character. Hint: There are two base cases: (1) the null string and (2) a string whose first character matches the given character.
(c) Count the blanks in a string.
(d) Create a string with all blanks removed. Hint: For the complex case, you either will or will not concatenate the first character with the result from the recursive call.

25. (a) If you test the DoubleIt procedure in the text, you may find that "stack overflow" occurs for long strings. This means that the program has run out of memory due to having several versions of DoubleIt, each with a value parameter and three local variables. Experiment to discover the longest string that does not cause stack overflow. You will need to write the Split procedure, Exercise 13(c), to run this experiment.
    (b) Modify the Split procedure and the DoubleIt procedure to make the first parameter type *char* rather than *string*. Does this increase the size string that can be handled? If so, suggest other similar modifications.

26. Describe a unit test plan for these exercises in this section.
    (a) Exercise 3
    (b) Exercise 4
    (c) Exercise 5
    (d) Exercise 6
    (e) Exercise 7
    (f) Exercise 9
    (g) Exercise 13(a)
    (h) Exercise 13(b)
    (i) Exercise 13(c)
    (j) Exercise 13(d)
    (k) Exercise 14(a)
    (l) Exercise 14(b)
    (m) Exercise 15
    (n) Exercise 16
    (o) Exercise 19
    (p) Exercise 20
    (q) Exercise 24(a)
    (r) Exercise 24(b)
    (s) Exercise 24(c)
    (t) Exercise 24(d)

4-3 CASE STUDIES

In this section, we present three case studies that use a number of the ideas developed to this point in the text.

Case Study No. 4

Statement of Problem. Write a program to print all the prime numbers between 1 and N, where N is a value supplied by the user.

Preliminary Analysis. A prime number is a positive integer larger than 1 that has no divisor other than itself and 1. The first few primes are

$$2, 3, 5, 7, 11, 13, 17, \ldots$$

The number 4 is not prime (it is divisible by 2) nor is 15 (it is divisible by both 3 and 5). Notice that the number 1 is not a prime as mathematicians define the concept.

We want to put limits on the values of N that are allowed. (Why?) Suppose we specify that N must lie between 2 and 1000 inclusive.

Algorithms and Variable List

1. *Main Module.* We begin with a general description of what we must do to solve the problem:

    print instructions
    read a valid value for N
    for each integer I in the range from 2 to N
        check I to see if it is prime
        if it is, then print I

There are four natural candidates for submodules:

- A procedure to print instructions
- A procedure to read a valid value for N
- A Boolean function to see if a number is prime
- A procedure to print a number

We use a procedure for printing in order to print 20 numbers on the terminal, then pause until the user is ready to continue. (If we did not do this, the numbers would be displayed too rapidly to read.)

For our variable list, we have the following:

Constant:	MaxLines	Value 20	Maximum number of lines to be printed per screen
Input: N	Integer		Indicates the desired range
Output: I	Integer		Printed if prime
Update: LineCount	Integer		Used to print MaxLines lines per screen

LineCount is initialized to 0 in the main module and updated in the printing module. We compare it to MaxLines to see if the screen is full.

The hierarchy chart at this point is

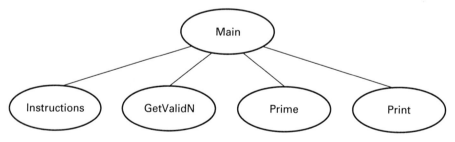

2. *GetValidN Procedure.* This is very similar to the validation procedures we have written before. The logic is

    issue prompt
    read N
    while N is not valid
     error message
     read N again

The variable N must be a var parameter.

3. *Print Procedure*. In some ways, this is similar to the procedure we used in the previous section. However, we pause just after printing the twentieth value rather than just before printing the twenty-first. Using the parameter LineCount, we write

>   print Number
>   add 1 to LineCount
>   if LineCount = MaxLines then do the following:
>   issue a message
>   wait for user to hit return
>   reset LineCount to 0

The accompanying variable list is:

Input parameter:	Number	Integer	The number to be printed
Update parameter:	LineCount	Integer	Keeps track of lines printed
Global constant:	MaxLines	Value = 20	Maximum number of lines to be printed per screen

4. *Prime Function*. A number is prime if its smallest divisor (other than 1) is the number itself. Hence, we can do the following

>   use a function Divisor to get SmallDivisor
>   if SmallDivisor = Number,
>   our answer is *true*,
>   otherwise it is *false*

The variables are

Input parameter:	Number	Integer	The number to check
Other:	SmallDivisor	Integer	The smallest divisor (other than 1)

At this point, our hierarchy chart is

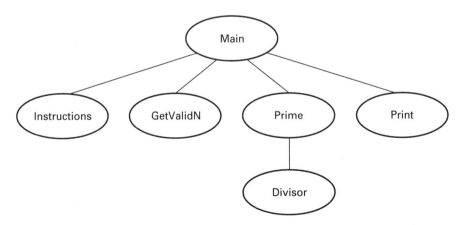

4-3 CASE STUDIES

5. Divisor Function. This function can be written by using a search loop, starting at 2 and continuing until we find a divisor for the number.

We use these variables:

Input parameter:	Number	Integer	The number for which to find a divisor (assumed to be ≥ 2)
Other:	PotentialDivisor	Integer	Takes on values 2, 3, . . . until a divisor is found

Since 2 can itself be a divisor, we need a *while* loop rather than a *repeat-until* loop.

set PotentialDivisor to 2
while we still do not have a divisor do this:
    add 1 to PotentialDivisor
assign the final value of PotentialDivisor as the function answer

Test plan. We use a top–down testing strategy augmented by a unit test for the critical module (the Divisor function). The planned tests include the following:

GetValidN: borderlines on valid:
    1, 2, 1000, 1001, others in between

Print: borderlines on total number printed:
    1, 20, 21, 40, 41, others in between

Prime:
    branches: is prime, is not
      number of factors: 1 (example, 9 = 3 · 3)
                      > 1 (example, 105 = 3 · 5 · 7)

Divisor:
    branches: smallest divisor = Num
                      smallest divisor not = Num
                      smallest divisor = 2

Except for GetValidN, all of these tests occur naturally as a part of the process of running the program.

Write in Pascal. We begin at the top level with stubs for GetValidN, Prime, and Print (Figure 4-10). Observe that we document as we go along. When we run this with a valid value of N, all the numbers from 2 to N are printed without pause.

Next we refine the procedure GetValidN and run its unit tests. This is followed by the procedure Print. Observe that because the stub version of Prime still reports that all numbers are prime, it is easy to verify that exactly 20 numbers per screen are being printed. It is also easy to force the boundary tests on the total number printed.

We now write the Prime function with a stub for Divisor. Because we want to check both branches of the Prime function, we have the stub sometimes reporting that the smallest divisor is equal to the number and sometimes not. See Figure 4-11 for the current version of the program. (Changes from Figure 4-10 are in italics.)

```
program FindPrimes;

{Written by: XXXXXXXX XX/XX/XX}
{Purpose:   To find and print the primes between 2 and a user supplied}
{           limit value ( <= 1000 ).}
{           They are printed 20 per screen, pausing after each screenful.}
{Procedures used: Instructions, to print instructions}
{                 GetValidN,  to edit the limit value}
{                 Print, to print each prime and pause after each screen}
{Functions used:  Prime, to determine if prime}
{                 Divisor, to find the smallest divisor of a number}

    const
        Maximum = 1000;          {maximum limit allowed}
        MaxLines = 20;           {maximum number of lines per screen}

    var
        N: integer;          {indicates the desired range, input}
        I: integer;          {loop control, printed if prime}
        LineCount: integer;  {used to see when screen is full}

    procedure Instructions;
    begin
       {stub}
    end;

    procedure GetValidN (var N: integer);

    {Written by: XXXXXXXX, XX/XX/XX}
    {Purpose:   To obtain a valid limit from the user.}
    {Globals used: constant Maximum, the largest value allowed for N}
    {Parameters: N - output, the valid limit (will lie between 2 and}
    {                Maximum, inclusive)}

    begin {GetValidN}
        Writeln;
        Write('Enter a number in the range 2 to ', Maximum : 1, ': ');
        Readln(N)
    end; {GetValidN}

    function Prime (Number: integer): boolean;

    {Written by:   XXXXXXXX, XX/XX/XX}
    {Purpose:    To see if a given number is prime}
    {Parameters:  Number - input, the number to be checked}
    {Functions used:  Divisor, to find smallest divisor of the number}
```

Figure 4-10   Case Study No. 4 (find primes) (continues next page).

```
      begin {Prime}
    {stub version}
        Prime := true
      end; {Prime}


      procedure Print (Number: integer; var LineCount: integer);

{Written by: XXXXXXXX XX/XX/XX}
{Purpose:    To print a number on the screen, pausing at bottom
{            of each screen}
{Globals:    constant MaxLines, indicating the max lines per screen}
{Parameters: Number - input, the number to be printed}
{            LineCount, which Main has initialized to 0 prior to the}
{                       first Print call}

      begin {Print}
          Writeln(Number : 6);
          LineCount := LineCount + 1
      end; {Print}

begin {FindPrimes}

{*** Print instructions, and initialize line counter}

      Instructions;
      LineCount := 0;

{*** Ask the user for the desired range}

      GetValidN(N);

{*** Loop to check each number in the range}

      for I := 1 to N do
          begin
              if Prime(I) then
                  Print(I, LineCount)
          end; {for loop}

{*** Terminate}

      Writeln('FindPrimes program finished');
end.
```

Figure 4-10   (continued)

```
program FindPrimes;

{Written by: XXXXXXXX XX/XX/XX}
{Purpose:   To find and print the primes between 2 and a}
{           user-supplied limit value ( <= 1000 ).}
{           They are printed 20 per screen, pausing after}
{           each screenful.}
{Procedures used: Instructions, to print instructions}
{                 GetValidN, to edit the limit value}
{                 Print, to print each prime and pause after each screen}
{Functions used: Prime, to determine if prime}
{                Divisor, to find the smallest divisor of a number}

    const
        Maximum = 1000;          {maximum limit allowed}
        MaxLines = 20;           {maximum number of lines per screen}

    var
        N: integer;              {indicates the desired range, input}
        I: integer;              {loop control, printed if prime}
        LineCount: integer;      {used to see when screen is full}

    procedure Instructions;
    begin
        {stub}
    end;

    procedure GetValidN (var N: integer);

    {Written by: XXXXXXXX, XX/XX/XX}
    {Purpose :   To obtain a valid limit from the user.}
    {Globals used: constant Maximum, the largest value allowed for N}
    {Parameters: N - output, the valid limit (will lie between 2 and}
    {                Maximum, inclusive)}

    begin {GetValidN}
        Writeln;
        Write('Enter a number in the range 2 to ', Maximum : 1, ': ');
        Readln(N);
        while (N < 2) or (N > Maximum) do
            begin
                Write('Illegal number entered.  Try again: ');
                Readln(N)
            end {while}
    end; {GetValidN}
```

Figure 4-11 Case Study No. 4 (find primes) (continues next page).

```
function Divisor (Num: integer): integer;

{Written by: XXXXXXXX, XX/XX/XX}
{Purpose: To find the smallest divisor of a number}
{Parameters: Num - input, the integer to be checked (assumed to be}
{                  at least 2)}
    begin {Divisor - Stub version}
        if Odd(Num) then
            Divisor := Num
        else
            Divisor := Num - 1
    end; {Divisor}

function Prime (Number: integer): boolean;

{Written by:   XXXXXXXX XX/XX/XX}
{Purpose:      To see if a given number is prime}
{Parameters: Number - input, the number to be checked}
{Functions used:  Divisor, to find smallest divisor of the number}

        var
            SmallDivisor: integer;
    begin {Prime}
        SmallDivisor := Divisor(Number);
        if SmallDivisor = Number then
            Prime := true
        else
            Prime := false
    end; {Prime}

procedure Print (Number: integer; var LineCount: integer);

{Written by: XXXXXXXX XX/XX/XX}
{Purpose:    To print a number on the screen, pausing at bottom}
{            of each screen}
{Globals:    constant MaxLines, indicating the max lines per}
{            screen}
{Parameters: Number - input, the number to be printed}
{            LineCount, which Main has initialized to 0 prior to}
{                    the first Print call}
    begin {Print}
        Writeln(Number : 6);
        LineCount := LineCount + 1;
        if LineCount = 20 then
          begin
            Writeln;
            Write('Tap RETURN to continue');
            Readln;
            LineCount := 0
          end {if}
    end; {Print}
```

Figure 4-11   (continues next page)

```
begin {FindPrimes}

{*** Print instructions, and initialize line counter}

    Instructions;
    LineCount := 0;

{*** Ask the user for the desired range}

    GetValidN(N);

{*** Loop to check each number in the range}

    for I := 1 to N do
        begin
            if Prime(I) then
                Print(I, LineCount)
        end; {for loop}

{*** Terminate}

    Writeln('FindPrimes program finished');
end.
```

Figure 4-11 (continued)

Notes

1. In the Prime function, we do not really need the local variable SmallDivisor. We could write the body as

```
            if Divisor(Number) = Number then
              Prime := true
            else
              Prime := false
```

2. In fact, we could write

```
            Prime := (Divisor(Number) = Number)
```

The condition "Divisor(Number) = Number" is either *true* or *false*, and the answer for Prime is the same *true* or *false* value.

Finally, we refine the Divisor function. Because this is a critical module, we give it a special unit test with a driver. (Notice that in the context of our current program, we could not tell if this function is correct. For example, if it reported that the smallest divisor of 36 is 18 and the smallest divisor of 49 is 3, our program would appear to be correct.) Figure 4-12 contains the driver with the function and a sample run. In Figure 4-13, we present a sample run of the entire program with the stub Divisor function replaced by that in Figure 4-12.

4-3 CASE STUDIES

```
program DivisorDriver;

{Written by: XXXXXXXX XX/XX/XX}
{Purpose:   To test the Divisor function}
{Functions used: Divisor, to find the smallest divisor of a number}

    const
        EndOfData = 0;              {terminating value for loop}

    var
        N: integer;                 {number to find smallest divisor of}

    function Divisor (Num: integer): integer;

    {Written by: XXXXXXXX, XX/XX/XX}
    {Purpose:   To find the smallest divisor of a number}
    {Parameters: Num - input, the number to be checked (assumed to be}
    {                  at least 2)}

        var
            PotentialDivisor: integer;          {takes on values 2, 3, ...}

      begin {Divisor}
          PotentialDivisor := 2;

          while Num mod PotentialDivisor <> 0 do
              begin
                  PotentialDivisor := PotentialDivisor + 1
              end; {while}

          Divisor := PotentialDivisor
      end; {Divisor}

  begin {DivisorDriver}
    repeat
      Writeln;
      Write('Enter an integer (2 or higher, 0 to quit): ');
      Readln(N);
      if N <> EndOfData then
          Writeln('The smallest divisor is ', Divisor(N) : 1)
    until N = EndOfData
  end. {DivisorDriver}
```

Figure 4-12 Driver for smallest divisor function (continues next page).

Enhancements. This case study has adopted a "brute-force" approach to finding primes: check each candidate by locating its smallest divisor. Moreover, the process of finding the smallest divisor has been carried out in the most straightforward manner. Many improvements are possible; the exercises suggest several that can be made.

SAMPLE INPUT AND OUTPUT

```
Enter an integer (2 or higher, 0 to quit): 2
The smallest divisor is 2

Enter an integer (2 or higher, 0 to quit): 17
The smallest divisor is 17

Enter an integer (2 or higher, 0 to quit): 77
The smallest divisor is 7

Enter an integer (2 or higher, 0 to quit): 100
The smallest divisor is 2

Enter an integer (2 or higher, 0 to quit): 0
```

Figure 4-12 (continued)

SAMPLE INPUT AND OUTPUT FOR FINAL PROGRAM

```
Enter a number in the range 2 to 1000: 100
    2
    3
    5
    7
   11
   13
   17
   19
   23
   29
   31
   37
   41
   43
   47
   53
   59
   61
   67
   71
Tap RETURN to continue:
   73
   79
   83
   89
   97
Done; tap RETURN to exit
```

Figure 4-13 Sample run for Case Study No. 4.

Case Study No. 5

Statement of Problem. Write a program that reads a series of integers from the terminal. For each number input, the program should factor the number. For example, for the series of inputs 35, 100, and 17, the output would be similar to this:

```
5    7
2    2    5    5
17
```

Preliminary Analysis. Let us restrict the input to positive numbers greater than or equal to 2. We can use a slightly modified revision of the procedure GetValidN from the previous case study. Also, we observe that the first number to be printed is the smallest divisor of the number. In the previous case study, we wrote a function Divisor that we can use to find that smallest divisor. A tentative hierarchy chart is

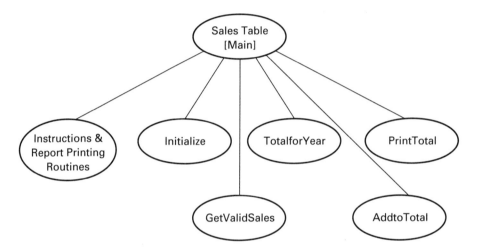

"Factor" is the procedure that does the factoring. It is always a good idea to consider whether previously written modules are either exactly or almost what we need for the current program.

Algorithms and Variable Lists

1. *Main Module.* We need only one variable and one constant.

Constant:	EndOfData	Value 1	Terminating entry
Input:	N	Integer	Number to be factored

The algorithm is

repeat these stages until the user enters the terminating value
    read a valid N (use GetValidN)
    if N is not the terminal value,
        factor the number N (use Factor)

2. *GetValidN Procedure.* This is almost identical to the procedure in Case Study No. 4. For this case study, a valid number is 1 (the terminating value) or higher.

3. *Divisor Function.* This function was written and unit tested as part of Case Study No. 4. We use editor commands to obtain an exact copy of the function to use in the present program. No further planning, writing, or unit testing is required.

4. *Factor Procedure.* This procedure is the heart of the case study. To aid in writing it, let us suppose the number to be factored is 63. If we did this by hand, we might use two steps:

$$63 = 3 \cdot 21 = 3 \cdot 3 \cdot 7$$

First, we find one factor (the smallest one), obtaining $3 \cdot 21$; then we factor 21. Similarly, for 245 and 100, we might write

$$245 = 5 \cdot 49 = 5 \cdot 7 \cdot 7$$
$$100 = 2 \cdot 50 = 2 \cdot 2 \cdot 25 = 2 \cdot 2 \cdot 5 \cdot 5$$

For a prime such as 17, we simply write

$$17 = 17$$

This discussion suggests a possible solution to our problem. We can state it in three steps:

1. Find the smallest divisor and write it.

2. Calculate the "rest of the number": divide by the smallest divisor.

3. Factor the rest of the number, if present.

For the first two steps, we need these variables:

Input parameter:	N	Integer	The number to factor
Local variables:	FirstFactor	Integer	The smallest divisor
	Quotient	Integer	N div FirstFactor

In Pascal, we write

```
FirstFactor := Divisor(N);
Writeln(FirstFactor);
Quotient := N div FirstFactor;
```

How do we factor the rest of the number (the variable Quotient)? There are several approaches; one is to simply call the Factor procedure recursively:

```
Factor(Quotient)
```

Will this work? The answer is, "Yes, almost." Remember the two important concepts of recursion:

1. Call yourself with a simpler version of the same problem.

2. Write a nonrecursive solution for the "simplest" (base) inputs.

Since Quotient is smaller than N, the first is satisfied. However, the second is not; we would have infinite recursion. To fix this, we note that when the number N is prime, we do not have anything left to factor. In this case, Quotient will have the value 1. We want to call Factor recursively only if Quotient is greater than 1:

```
if Quotient > 1 then
   Factor(Quotient)
```

Test Plan. What tests are needed for the Factor procedure? To answer this, we consider the question, "How many factors could N have?" The answer is, "One or more." This leads to two types of test input: primes and nonprimes.

A few other considerations can be included in the test plan. We should have numbers where the same factor is repeated several times, and some numbers where there is no such repetition. Some of our answers should be easy to check. We should test some large numbers whose answers we know. (We can do this by starting with the desired answer and multiplying it on a calculator.)

Based on these considerations, we devise the following list of tests with the expected answers. (Note: The program as currently designed prints one factor per line.)

17	17					
15	3	5				
64	2	2	2	2		
2261	19	7	17			
700	2	2	5	5	7	
31407	3	19	19	29		
4171	43	97				
9409	97	97				

Write Program. The program with a sample run containing some of the tests from the test plan appears in Figure 4-14.

Enhancements. One possibility, developed in the exercises, is to print the factorization on a single line rather than one number per line. We could also insert a multiplication symbol (*) between successive factors.

Case Study No. 6

In Section 4-2, we wrote a program (Figure 4-7) that created a printed list of numbers with their square roots. In this case study, we use some of the ideas from that program. In addition, we include some array-processing ideas.

Statement of Problem. For each salesperson in a company, records are kept on the amount of sales for each month of the year. A printed report is desired that, for each person, indicates three items:

Name

12 monthly sales figures

Total sales for the year

```
program PrintFactors;

{Written by: XXXXXXXX XX/XX/XX}
{Purpose:    To read a series of numbers and print a complete factoriza-}
{            tion of each}

{Procedures used: Instructions, to print instructions}
{                 GetValidN, to obtain a valid input number}
{                 Factor, a recursive procedure to perform the}
{                     factorization}
{Functions used:  Divisor, to find the smallest divisor of a}
{                     number (called by Factor)}

    const
       EndOfData = 1;                  {terminating input value}

    var
       N: integer;                     {number to be factored, input}

    procedure Instructions;
       begin {stub}
       end;

    {procedure GetValidN as shown in Figure 4-11 is inserted here}
    {with minor modifications (valid range is 1 or higher) }

    {function Divisor as shown in Figure 4-12 is inserted here}

    procedure Factor (N: integer);

    {Written by: XXXXXXXX XX/XX/XX}
    {Purpose:    To print the factors of a given number}
    {Parameters: N - input , the number to be factored}
    {Procedures used: Factor is called recursively.}
    (Functions used:  Divisor is used to find the smallest}
    {                     divisor of N}

       var
          FirstFactor: integer;  {smallest divisor of N}
          Quotient: integer;     {part left after FirstFactor is}
                                 {factored out}

    begin {Factor}

       {*** Find and print the first factor}

       FirstFactor := Divisor(N);
       Writeln(FirstFactor : 5);
```

Figure 4-14 Case Study No. 5 (recursive factoring) (continues next page).

```
     {*** If the number was not prime, factor the rest of the number}

   Quotient := N div FirstFactor;
   if Quotient > 1 then
     Factor(Quotient)
 end; {Factor}

begin {PrintFactors}
     Instructions;
     repeat
       GetValidN(N);
       if N <> EndOfData then
         begin
           Writeln;
           Writeln('The factors are: ');
           Factor(N)
         end
   until N = EndOfData;
end.
```

SAMPLE INPUT AND OUTPUT

```
     Enter a number in the range 1 or higher (1 to quit): 17

     The factors are:
        17

     Enter a number in the range 1 or higher (1 to quit): 15

     The factors are:
        3
        5

     Enter a number in the range 1 or higher (1 to quit): 64

     The factors are:
        2
        2
        2
        2
        2
        2

     Enter a number in the range 1 or higher (1 to quit): 9409
     The factors are:
        97
        97

     Enter a number in the range 1 or higher (1 to quit): 1
```

Figure 4-14 (continued)

In addition, the final page of the report should indicate the totals for the company for each month.

Preliminary Analysis. Input consists of a name and 12 sales figures. Although we could use 12 distinct variables for the sales figures, a better design would use a "real array" declared as follows:

```
const
  MaxIndex = 12;

type
  RealArray = array[1..MaxIndex] of real;

var
  SalesArr = RealArray;
```

Observe how similar this is to declaring integer arrays of size 1000, which we have done several times previously.

When we plan the output for this program, ideally we would like:

name   Jan. sales Feb. sales ... Dec. sales   Total sales

However, a typical Macintosh printer (using the standard THINK output font) prints 80 characters on a line; all this information would not fit. We therefore decide on a layout like this for each person:

name	Jan sales	Feb sales	March sales	
	Apr sales	May sales	June sales	
	July sales	Aug sales	Sept sales	
	Oct sales	Nov sales	Dec sales	Total sales

Program Design. In this case study, we do not present the detailed design for each module. Rather, we discuss the design of the program from a broader perspective.

One can view this program as containing two relatively independent components: I/O and calculations. One approach to solving the problem would be to work on one component first and then add the other. For example, we might postpone concerns about getting a "nice" output report (with headers, new pages when appropriate, etc.). Alternatively, we could tackle this aspect first. Using the program of Figure 4-7 as a starting point, we chose the latter approach. We wrote TopOfForm, Header, and DetailLine procedures, and a driver to test them. The final version of this driver program appears in Figure 4-15, along with sample input and output. (*Portions to be discussed in the Notes that follow are in italics.*)

We ran this program several times, testing:

1. Exactly one salesperson.
2. First page exactly full, no second page.
3. First page full, one entry on second page.
4. Two pages full, several entries on third page.

Notes

1. Observe the treatment of LineCount in the DetailLine procedure (italicized). Each person's print adds five lines of output. When we do not increment LineCount by 1, it is safer to use ">=" in the comparison with MaxLines.
2. The Header procedure prints the PageNumber, then increments it.
3. When we ran the test originally, the names were right-justified. Usually, lists of names are left-justified, as in

>   Bill Johnson
>
>   Timothy Axenhall
>
>   Jo Coy

   To achieve left justification, we used a local variable PrintName in the DetailLine procedure.
4. The DetailLine procedure uses

   ```
   for I := 1 to 80 do
      Write(Report, '-');
   Writeln
   ```

   to print a row of dashes.
5. The Name parameter for DetailLine must be a named type (*string*, not *string[25]*).
6. The driver routine initializes variables, assigns values to the items to be printed, and calls DetailLine the number of times indicated by the user.

With the "easy but messy" details of printing the report out of the way, we can concentrate our attention on the rest of the program.

As far as variables are concerned, we need these:

Input:	Name	String	Salesperson name
	SalesArr	RealArray	12 sales figures
Output:	YearTotal	Real	Individual's total for year
	TotalSales	RealArray	Company totals (12 totals, one per month)
Update:	PageNumber	Integer	Page number
	LineCount	Integer	Count of detail lines printed
Other:	I	Integer	*For* loop

In a loop, we want to

>   read employee name
>   read 12 sales figures
>   calculate the total for the year
>   add to the company totals
>   print the data (DetailLine)

```
program Driver;

{Written by:   XXXXXXXXXX XX/XX/XX}
{Purpose:      To test the header printing, page, and detail line routines}
{              for compatibility}
{Procedures used: Instructions, to print instructions}
{                 Header, to print headings}
{                 DetailLine, to print a set of detail lines for 1 individual}

    const
      MaxIndex = 12;           {size of arrays}
      MaxLines = 45;           {maximum lines per page}

    type
      RealArray = array[1..MaxIndex] of real;

    var
      PageNumber: integer;     {page number}
      LineCount: integer;      {line count}
      Name: string;            {name to be printed}
      SalesArr: RealArray;     {sales array to be printed}
      YearTotal: real;         {total sales to be printed}
      I: integer;              {loop control}
      NPeople: integer;        {number of salespeople to print, input}
      Report: text;            {name for printer}

    procedure Instructions;
    begin {stub}
    end;

    {procedure TopofForm, as shown in Figure 4-7, is inserted here}

    procedure Header (var PageNumber: integer);

    {Written by: XXXXXXXXXX XX/XX/XX}
    {Purpose:    To print headings at the top of a page}
    {Parameters: PageNumber - update, to keep page number current}
    {Globals used: None}

        var
          I: integer;          {loop control to print dashed line}

    begin {Header}
      Write(Report, ' ' : 27, 'LIST OF EMPLOYEE SALES');
      Writeln(Report, ' ' : 21, 'page ', PageNumber : 1);
      Writeln(Report);
      Writeln(Report, ' ' : 8, 'NAME', ' ' : 27, 'MONTHLY SALES', ' ' : 16,
              'TOTAL SALES');
```

Figure 4-15 Case Study No. 6 (sales report) (continues next page).

```
        Writeln(Report);
        Writeln(Report, ' ' : 30, 'January      February       March');
        Writeln(Report, ' ' : 30, '  April        May          June');
        Writeln(Report, ' ' : 30, '   July       August     September');
        Writeln(Report, ' ' : 30, 'October      November      December');

          for I := 1 to 80 do
            Write(Report, '-');
          Writeln(Report);
          Writeln(Report);
          PageNumber := PageNumber + 1
        end; {Header}

        procedure DetailLine (Name: string; Sales: RealArray; Total: real;
                              var PageNumber, LineCount: integer);

        {Written by: XXXXXXXXXX XX/XX/XX}
        {Purpose :   To print a detail line (one line of a table).}
        {            If page is full, it first advances to a new page and}
        {            prints headings.}
        {Parameters: Name - input, the salesman name}
        {            Sales - input, the array of 12 sales figures}
        {            Total - input, the total sales for the sale rep.}
        {            LineCount -  update, the current line; controls}
        {                         the call to Page and Header;}
        {                         following those calls it is reset to 0,}
        {                         and it is incremented for each}
        {                         person printed.}
        {Procedures used:   Header, to print headings}
        {Globals modified:  None}

        var
            I: integer;                      {loop control to print sales}
            PrintName: string[20];           {name right padded with blanks}

        begin {DetailLine}
          {stub version - adapted from Figure 4-7}

        {*** Check for full page}

            if LineCount >= MaxLines then
               begin
                  Page(Report);
                  Header(PageNumber);
                  LineCount := 0
               end; {if}

        {*** Print the lines and increment the count of lines on this page}

            PrintName := concat(Name, '          ');     {20 spaces}
            Write(Report, PrintName : 20, ' ' : 4);      {name}
```

Figure 4-15   (continues next page)

```
         for I := 1 to 3 do
            Write(Report, Sales[I] : 13 : 2);         {Jan - Feb - Mar}
         Writeln(Report);

         Write(Report, ' ' : 24);
         for I := 4 to 6 do
            Write(Report, Sales[I] : 13 : 2);         {Apr - May - Jun}
         Writeln(Report);

         Write(Report, ' ' : 24);
         for I := 7 to 9 do
            Write(Report, Sales[I] : 13 : 2);         {Jul - Aug - Sep}
         Writeln(Report);

         Write(Report, ' ' : 24);
         for I := 10 to 12 do
            Write(Report, Sales[I] : 13 : 2);         {Oct - Nov - Dec}
         Write(Report, ' ' : 3, Total : 13 : 2);      {total sales}
         Writeln(Report);
         Writeln(Report);
         LineCount := LineCount + 5

      end; {DetailLine}

begin {Driver}

{*** Initialize the page control variables}

      PageNumber := 1;
      LineCount := 0;

{*** Set up variables to be printed}

      for I := 1 to 12 do
         SalesArr[I] := 100 * I;
      Name := 'name';
      YearTotal := 7800;

{*** Perform the trial run}

      Instructions;
      Write('How many people do you want to print? ');
      Readln(NPeople);
      Header(PageNumber);

      for I := 1 to NPeople do
         begin
            DetailLine(Name, SalesArr, YearTotal, PageNumber, LineCount)
         end {for}

end.
```

Figure 4-15 (continues next page)

SAMPLE INPUT AND OUTPUT

At terminal:

How many people do you want to print? 2

On printer:

```
          LIST OF EMPLOYEE SALES                           page 1
  NAME         MONTHLY SALES             TOTAL SALES
            January      February           March
            April        May                June
            July         August             September
            October      November           December
  ---------------------------------------------------------------
  name       100.00       200.00            300.00
             400.00       500.00            600.00
             700.00       800.00            900.00
            1000.00      1100.00           1200.00          7800.00
  name       100.00       200.00            300.00
             400.00       500.00            600.00
             700.00       800.00            900.00
             000.00      1100.00           1200.00          7800.00
```

Figure 4-15 (continued)

Before the loop, we must

> initialize variables for output control (PageNumber, LineCount)
> print headings on the first page
> set the company totals to 0

After the loop, we print the company totals on a new page.

In studying the steps listed here, we chose to modularize as indicated in this hierarchy chart, which emphasizes the portion of the program we are working on now:

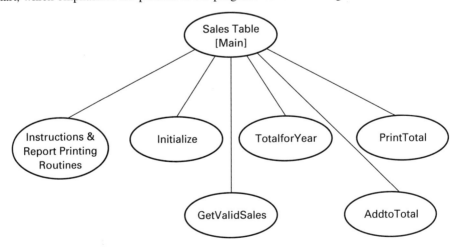

334 MORE ON SUBPROGRAMS CHAP. 4

Initialize:	Procedure to set company totals to 0.
GetValidSales:	Procedure to obtain sales amount for one month.
TotalForYear:	Function to calculate total sales for one employee.
AddToTotal:	Procedure to add one employee's sales amounts to the company totals.
PrintTotal:	Procedure to print the company summary.

The complete program appears as Figure 4-16; a small sample run appears as Figure 4-17. The program is long, but it has been modularized so that no one piece is very complicated. You should examine the main module and each procedure, using the hierarchy chart as a guide to the overall structure of the program.

```
program SalesTable;

{Written by: XXXXXXXXXX XX/XX/XX}
{Purpose:    To create a table listing the names and monthly sales}
{            figures for a number of sales employees.}
{            In addition, the total sales for each month}
{            are calculated and printed on a separate page}
{Procedures used: Instructions to print instructions}
{                 Header (called by DetailLine as well as main module),}
{                     to print headings}
{                 DetailLine, to print one line of the table}
{                 GetValidSales, to obtain a valid sales figure for}
{                     one month}
{                 Initialize, to initialize the array of sales totals}
{                 AddToTotal, to add each salesperson's sales figures}
{                     to the running total}
{                 PrintTotal, to print the total sales}
{Functions used:  CommisFn, to calculate a monthly commission}

    const
        EndOfData = '';             {terminating value for name}
        MaxIndex = 12;              {size of arrays}
        MaxLines = 45;              {maximum lines per page}
        MaximumAmount = 5000.0;     {maximum sales amount}

    type
        RealArray = array[1..MaxIndex] of real;

    var
        I: integer;                 {loop control}
        PageNumber: integer;        {page number}
        LineCount: integer;         {line count}
        Name: string;               {salesperson name, input}
        SalesArr: RealArray;        {12 sales figures for salesperson, input}
        TotalSales: RealArray;      {12 total sales figures for company}
        YearTotal: real;            {total sales to be printed}
        Report: text;               {name for printer}
```

Figure 4-16 Program to print monthly sales (continued next page).

```
procedure Instructions;
begin {stub}
end;

{procedures Header and DetailLine as shown in Figure 4-15 inserted here}

procedure GetValidSales (Month: integer; var Amount: real);

{Written by: XXXXXXXXXX XX/XX/XX}
{Purpose:    To obtain a valid sales figure (in the range from 0}
{            to MaximumAmount, a global constant}
{Parameters: Month - input, the month number to be read}
{            Amount - output, the value of the amount read}

begin {GetValidSales}
   Writeln;
   Writeln('Month # ', Month : 1);
   Write('Enter sales amount (0 - ', MaximumAmount : 1 : 2, '): ');
   Readln(Amount);

   while (Amount < 0.0) or (Amount > MaximumAmount) do
      begin
         Write('Illegal amount entered, try again: ');
         Readln(Amount)
      end {while}

end; {GetValidSales}

procedure Initialize (var Total: RealArray);

{Written by: XXXXXXXXXX XX/XX/XX}
{Purpose:    To set the total array to all zeros}
{Parameters: Total - output, the array to be initialized}

   var
      I: integer;                     {loop control}

begin {Initialize}

   for I := 1 to 12 do
      begin
         Total[I] := 0.0
      end {for loop}

end; {Initialize}

procedure AddToTotal (OnePerson: RealArray; var CompanyTotal:
                      Real Array);

{Written by: XXXXXXXXXX XX/XX/XX}
{Purpose:    To add one person's sales to the company total}
{Parameters: OnePerson - input, the array of sales for one person}
{            CompanyTotal - update, the company total array}
```

Figure 4-16   (continues next page)

```
        var
            I: integer;                          {loop control}

    begin {AddToTotal}
        for I := 1 to 12 do
            begin
                CompanyTotal[I] := CompanyTotal[I] + OnePerson[I]
            end {for loop}
    end; {AddToTotal}

    procedure PrintTotal (CompanyTotal: RealArray);

    {Written by: XXXXXXXXXX XX/XX/XX}
    {Purpose:    To print the company totals on a new page.}
    {Parameters: CompanyTotal - input, the company total array}
    {Procedures used: None}

        var
            I: integer;                          {loop control}

    begin {PrintTotal}
        Page(Report);
        Writeln(Report, ' ' : 12, 'TOTALS FOR COMPANY');
        Writeln(Report);
        Writeln(Report, '        Month Total');
        Writeln(Report, ' ---------------------------------');

        for I := 1 to 12 do
            begin
                Writeln(Report, I : 14, ' ' : 10, CompanyTotal[I] : 12 : 2)
            end {for loop}
    end; {PrintTotal}

    function TotalForYear (Sales: RealArray): real;

    {Written by: XXXXXXXXXX XX/XX/XX}
    {Purpose:    To calculate the total salesfor one person for one}
    {            year, based on the array of 12 sales figures}
    {Parameters: Sales - input, the salesperson 's set of figures}

        var
            I: integer;                          {loop control}
            Sum: real;                           {accumulates the total}

    begin {TotalForYear}
        Sum := 0.0;
        for I := 1 to 12 do
            begin
                Sum := Sum + Sales[I]
            end; {for loop}
        TotalForYear := Sum
    end; {TotalForYear}
```

Figure 4-16 (continues next page)

```
begin {SalesTable}

{*** Print instructions, initialize the page control variables, and}
{    print the first set of headings}

    Instructions;
    PageNumber := 1;
    LineCount := 0;
    Header(PageNumber);

{*** Initialize total sales array to all zeros}

    Initialize(TotalSales);

{*** Read names and sales in a loop, calculate individual yearly}
{    total, add to company totals, and print lines containing the}
{    information for one employee}

    repeat
        Writeln;
        Write('Enter name (tap RETURN to quit): ');
        Readln(Name);
        if Name <> EndOfData then
            begin
                for I := 1 to 12 do            {get sales figures}
                    begin
                        GetValidSales(I, SalesArr[I])
                    end; {for}

                YearTotal := TotalForYear(SalesArr);{calculate yearly total}
                AddToTotal(SalesArr, TotalSales);    {add person to total}
                DetailLine(Name, SalesArr, YearTotal, PageNumber, LineCount)
                                                     {print data}
            end {if}
    until Name = EndOfData;

{*** When no more input, print the total array and stop the program}

    PrintTotal(TotalSales);
    Writeln;
    Writeln('Report complete.')
end.
```

Figure 4-16 (continued)

SAMPLE INPUT AND OUTPUT (PARTIAL)

At terminal:

```
Enter name (tap RETURN to quit): Bill Frederickson

Month # 1
Enter sales amount (0 - 5000.00): 100

Month # 2
Enter sales amount (0 - 5000.00): 200
    .
    .
    .
Month # 12
Enter sales amount (0 - 5000.00): 100

Enter name (tap RETURN to quit): Sally Fielding

Month # 1
Enter sales amount (0 - 5000.00): 5001
Illegal amount entered, try again: 5000

Month # 2
Enter sales amount (0 - 5000.00): 5000.01
Illegal amount entered, try again: 5000

Month # 3
Enter sales amount (0 - 5000.00): -1
Illegal amount entered, try again: -.01
Illegal amount entered, try again: 0
    .
    .
    .
Month # 12
Enter sales amount (0 - 5000.00): 432

Enter name (tap RETURN to quit):

Report complete.
Tap RETURN to exit.
```

Figure 4-17 Sample run of Case Study No. 6 (continues next page).

On printer (first page):

```
                LIST OF EMPLOYEE SALES                          page 1
     NAME            MONTHLY SALES                    TOTAL SALES
                January      February       March
                April        May            June
                July         August         September
                October      November       December
     ------------------------------------------------------------------
     name          100.00       200.00        300.00
                   400.00       500.00        600.00
                   600.00       500.00        400.00
                   300.00       200.00        100.00      4200.00
     name         5000.00      5000.00          0.00
                   100.00       500.00        356.45
                   308.78      3800.00        405.50
                   100.00       150.00        432.00     16152.73
```

On printer (second page):

```
     TOTALS FOR COMPANY
          Month                            Total
     -----------------------------------------------------------
            1                             5100.00
            2                             5200.00
            3                              300.00
            4                              500.00
            5                             1000.00
            6                              956.45
            7                              908.78
            8                             4300.00
            9                              805.50
           10                              400.00
           11                              350.00
           12                              532.00
```

Figure 4-17 (continued)

EXERCISES

Exercises 1 to 4 refer to Case Study No. 4.

1. Write a program to read an integer N, then print the first N primes. (For example, if N = 7, then the answers are 2, 3, 5, 7, 11, 13, and 17.) Write a test plan for this program.
2. Write a program that reads a series of input integers; for each, print a message telling whether the number is prime or composite (not prime).
3. (a) It is unnecessary to check even numbers to determine if they are prime, as 2 is the only even prime number. Revise the case study to print 2 before the loop, and then check only the odd numbers (≥ 3).

(b) If we revise the main program as in part (a), then we are only checking odd numbers. Revise the Divisor function to take advantage of this fact. (That is, look for divisors that are odd numbers.)
(c) Can this revised Divisor function be used in Case Study No. 5? Explain your position.

4. If a number N is going to have a divisor other than N, then the smallest divisor is $\leq$ Sqrt(N).
   (a) Explain why this statement is true.
   (b) Revise the Divisor function to take advantage of this fact.

Exercises 5 to 7 refer to Case Study No. 5.

5. Modify Case Study No. 5 to print the factors on a single line. (Hint: Use Write rather than Writeln.) When is it appropriate to send a carriage return using Writeln?

6. Modify Exercise 5 to obtain output similar to

```
2 * 2 * 5 * 5
```

7. Modify Exercise 6 to obtain output similar to

```
100 = 2 * 2 * 5 * 5
```

Exercises 8 to 9 refer to Case Study No. 6

8. Modify Case Study No. 6 to precede the name with an asterisk (*) if the total sales are under $10,000. If any names are marked, place a footnote on the final page explaining the asterisk.

9. Add other summary statistics to the final page for Case Study No. 6:
   (a) Which months had the lowest and highest company totals?
   (b) What was the company grand total?
   (c) How many employees had at least one month with no sales?
   (d) Who had the highest total sales? What was this total?

In the remaining exercises, you will develop subprograms or complete programs. For some, ideas developed in the case studies can be useful.

10. Write the main program for the following situation. (You will want to decide which steps might be done as subprograms and what parameters would be required.)

    Each set of input data contains employee ID number, rank, number of units manufactured, basic bonus rate, and number of years experience. Your program should calculate and print basic pay and bonus pay for each employee. It should also print the ID of the person of rank 'A' with the most units produced and the average years of experience of the employees.

    The basic pay consists of $200 for code 'A', $300 for code 'B', and $355 for code 'C', plus $5 for each year of experience.

    The bonus pay is based on the number of units manufactured: 0 if under 100; basic bonus rate times basic pay if 100 to 150; 1.5 times as much if over 150.

11. (a) Write a Boolean function RelativelyPrime(A, B) that returns *true* if A and B are relatively prime, *false* otherwise. Use the GCD function developed earlier: GCD(A, B) is the greatest common divisor of A and B.
    (b) Write a driver to test the function.

12. (a) Write a Boolean function Near(Test, Homework) to do the following. Input consists of two real numbers between 0.00 and 1.00, representing a test percentage and a homework percentage. The function returns *true* if the homework percentage is no more than one letter

grade below the test percentage (using 90 percent = A, 80 percent = B, etc.); otherwise it returns *false*. For example, for a test percentage of 0.958 and a homework percentage of 0.8012, the answer is *true*. For 0.901 and 0.795, the answer is *false*.

(b) Write a main program that reads a series of data containing name, test percentage, and homework percentage. For each person, it should calculate and print the final average and the corresponding letter grade. Use subprograms where appropriate. For any subprogram you use, describe its parameters and logic. Note: The final average is

$$0.7 \times \text{test percentage} + 0.3 \times \text{homework percentage}$$

However, for a person whose homework percentage is lower than the test percentage, but "near" as defined in part (a), the final average is just the test percentage.

(c) Give a test plan for the Near function.

13. A "prime pair" is a pair of primes exactly two apart. For example, 11 and 13 form a prime pair, as do 29 and 31. Write a program to print all the prime pairs between 2 and N, where N is supplied by the user.

14. Write a program to find the roots of a quadratic equation, using the following general design. Recall that, for a quadratic equation $ax^2 + bx + c = 0$, the roots are given by

$$\frac{-b + \sqrt{b^2 - 4ac}}{2a} \quad \text{and} \quad \frac{-b - \sqrt{b^2 - 4ac}}{2a}$$

There are three distinct possibilities:

(1) $b^2 - 4ac$ is positive. Then there are two distinct real roots. For example, if $a = 1$, $b = 4$, and $c = 3$, then $b^2 - 4ac = 4$ and (plugging these values into the previous formulas) the roots are -1.0 and -3.0.

(2) $b^2 - 4ac$ is zero. Then there is a single real root. For example, if $a = 1$, $b = 2$, and $c = 1$, then $b^2 - 4ac = 0$, and the single root is -1.0.

(3) $b^2 - 4ac$ is negative. Then there are two complex number solutions, $m + ni$ and $m - ni$, where

$$m = -b/2a$$

and

$$n = \frac{\sqrt{-(b^2 - 4ac)}}{2a}$$

For example, with $a = 1$, $b = 1$, and $c = 5/4$, $b^2 - 4ac = -4$, and we have the roots of $-0.5 + 1.0i$ and $-0.5 - 1.0i$.

(Note: The quantity $b^2 - 4ac$ is known as the **discriminant**, and the letter D is used to indicate it.)

Your output should appear in a form similar to the following, with new headings on each page.

A	B	C	Type	First Root	Second Root
1.00	-2.00	-3.00	2 real	3.00	-2.00
1.00	-2.00	10.00	2 complex	1.00 + 3.00 I	1.00 - 3.00 I
1.00	-2.00	1.00	1 real	1.00	

(a) Write a DetailLine procedure to print the output line in the proper form. It should have six parameters: A, B, C, Number1, Number2, and DSign.

A, B, and C are the coefficients of the original equation. DSign is an integer that is either 1, 0, or –1, the "sign" of the discriminant (1 for positive, 0 for zero, –1 for negative). Number1 and Number2 are real; what they represent depends on the value of DSign:

(1) If DSign is 1 (D is positive), then Number1 and Number2 are the two distinct real roots.

(2) If DSign is 0 (D is 0), then Number1 is the single real root and Number2 is meaningless.

(3) If DSign is –1 (D is negative), then Number1 and Number2 are the real and imaginary parts, respectively, of the complex solutions (m and n before). You can assume that Number2 is positive. The answers are

```
Number1 + Number2 I
Number1 - Number2 I
```

(b) Write a GetData procedure that reads data records containing A, B, and C, the coefficients of a quadratic equation. We insist that A is a positive number; print an error message for faulty input.

(c) Write a procedure that calculates three values. The first is the sign of the discriminant $D = b^2 - 4ac$. The second and third are

$$-b/2a \quad \text{and} \quad \sqrt{|D|}/2a$$

(d) Using the routines developed in parts (a) to (c), write a program that reads a series of inputs, each containing A, B, and C, and prints a table of solutions to the corresponding equations.

15. Modify the program of Exercise 14 to remove the restriction that A must be positive. (Notice that if A is 0, the equation is $bx + c = 0$, which has one real solution, $x = -c/b$. However, if both A and B are 0, print an error message.)

16. Print a table of square roots for all the integers from 1 to 500, 50 per page.

17. Repeat Exercise 16, but for the real numbers 0.1, 0.2, . . . , 49.9, and 50.0.

18. An instructor gives five tests but allows each student to take either three, four, or five. (A student who takes fewer than three is treated as having taken three.) Write a program to create a printed grade report in a form similar to this:

Name	Grades					#	Total	Ave	Letter Grade
John Jones	100	-	-	95	90	3	285	95	A
Sue Smith	-	100	60	90	90	4	340	85	A
Bill Jacobs	50	40	-	-	-	3	90	30	F

Round the average to the nearest integer. Include various statistics, such as:

(a) How many took test 5?
(b) What was the average on test 5?
(c) What percentage received each letter grade?
(d) Were there any F's other than by people who apparently "gave up"?

19. Write an elementary school arithmetic tutorial package. The basic idea is to pose questions to a student and check the answers. In its simplest form, for example, the program might do the following 10 times:

pose an addition problem
read the student's answer
if the answer is right, add 1 to a count; if not, print the correct answer

At the end, it could print a count of how many were right. However, you should go beyond this simplest form. Here are some suggestions:

   (a) Include several operations: add, multiply, find least common denominator, etc. Allow the user to choose which she wants.
   (b) Allow up to three attempts to get the correct answer.
   (c) Calculate a score where getting the answer on the first try is worth more than getting it on the second try, and so on.
   (d) Allow the user to set a difficulty level, with a higher level getting harder problems (bigger numbers).

20. In this exercise, we explore some ideas related to the game of blackjack. In a simplified version of the game, an ace is worth 11 points; cards 2 to 10 are worth the face value; and jack, queen, and king are worth 10. The object is to get as high a score as possible, without going over 21, by drawing cards from a deck.

   (a) We can simulate the cards with integers 0 through 51, as shown here:

   0: ace of clubs
   1: 2 of clubs
   .
   .
   .
   9: 10 of clubs
   10: jack of clubs
   11: queen of clubs
   12: king of clubs
   13: ace of diamonds
   .
   .
   .
   25: king of diamonds
   .
   .
   .

   Write a procedure that, given an integer in the range 0 to 51, prints the card description. Hint: A case structure with 52 branches works, but is not very pleasant. Can you think of a way to use mod and div to solve this?

(b) Write a function that, given a number between 0 and 51, calculates its value. See the hint for part (a).

(c) Simulating the draw of a card is a little tricky. If we assume that the card supply consists of an infinite number of decks, then

```
Card: = abs(Random mod 52) + 1
```

works.

If we have only one deck, on the other hand, we must avoid repeating a card. One possibility is a Boolean array Dealt with index values 0 through 51, where Dealt[I] is *true* if and only if card I has already been dealt.

Write a function Card that simulates drawing a card. It should utilize the Dealt array to avoid redealing a card that was previously dealt. Note: Declaring Boolean arrays is similar to declaring integer or real arrays.

(d) Combine the ideas presented here to simulate one play of a game of blackjack. It should deal two cards, then repeatedly ask the user if it is to continue. Print a message such as "You quit with 17 points" or "You went over 21".

(e) Modify part (d) to allow several games. Shuffle the deck after each game.

(f) Modify part (d) to have the user play against the computer. Deal two cards to the user; deal two to the computer, but only print the second. Deal cards to the user until told to quit or the cards go over 21. If the cards go over 21, the computer wins. If not, print the first computer card, then deal cards to the computer with the strategy: "stay" (stop) on a total 16 or higher. If the computer goes over 21, the user wins; otherwise the user wins if her total is greater than the computer's. Shuffle the deck after each game.

21. Many enhancements to the previous exercise are possible. We suggest a few for your consideration.

    (a) Aces are worth either 1 or 11, whichever yields the higher score not over 21. (The choice can change after subsequent draws.)
    (b) Drawing five cards whose total is not over 21 is an automatic win for the user.
    (c) Betting could be allowed with a house limit and with the player staked to an initial amount.
    (d) The deck could be shuffled less frequently. (With our somewhat primitive way of telling which cards have been dealt, this could slow down the drawing of a card.)

22. It is possible to run simulations to determine probabilities for the blackjack game. These can be done with any version of the game you have written. Notice that the printing of the cards should be removed for these simulations.

    (a) How many times out of 1000 would you expect the dealer to exceed 21 using the strategy of stopping at 16 or higher?
    (b) Would a user strategy of stopping at 17 or higher likely win or lose more often? Run the game 1000 times to find out.
    (c) The user can see one but not both of the dealer's cards. Suppose the user chooses to stop at 17 if the dealer shows a 10 or higher (including an ace) and at 14 otherwise. How many out of 1000 might the user expect to win?

23. Write a program that, given a series of integers, calculates the score for a game of bowling. Each integer in the series represents the number of pins knocked down by one ball. A sample game is shown here.

EXERCISES   345

FRAME	BALLS	SCORE FOR FRAME	TOTAL	COMMENT
1	3, 6	9	9	Open frame
2	4, 6	17	26	Spare—10 plus next ball
3	7, 3	20	46	
4	10	30	76	Strike—10 plus next two balls
5	10	23	99	
6	10	15	114	
7	3, 2	5	119	
8	5, 1	6	125	
9	8, 2	20	145	
10	10	19	164	Strike in last frame gets two extra balls (spare gets one)

The following are some tips that may help you in your design.

(a) To record the score from strikes and spares, you must "look ahead" at future balls. This is a lot easier to do if you store the series of integers in an integer array.

(b) For starters, you might write a program to:

(1) Read a game into an array (terminate by an entry of –1)

(2) Print output similar to sample game shown, but with only three columns filled in (frame, balls, and comment—either "strike," "spare," or "open"). Ignore the "extra" balls for now. Assume the data are valid.

(c) Once you get part (b), finishing the problem should not be too difficult. You should, if possible, include detection of illegal situations such as this:

> Frame 1: 3, 6
> Frame 2: 4, 7—impossible

5 Elementary Data Structuring

OBJECTIVES

This chapter focuses on the file, record, and set Pascal data types. After completing this chapter, you will be able to:

- use text files in your programs
- use the record and set data types effectively
- build your own data types from records, sets, and arrays
- use records, sets, arrays, and files in combination to solve a variety of programming problems

5-1 TEXT FILES

A **text file** is organized as a number of lines, each consisting of a varying number of characters. The concept is similar to a (perhaps long) page of typewritten words.

The file can be read from or written to either line by line or character by character. We can think of reading from a text file as similar to input via a keyboard and writing to a text file as similar to output to a display screen or printer. Thus, we are already familiar with most of the details of reading and writing lines of text files. In fact, most of the programs that we have discussed thus far can be easily modified to obtain input from a text file instead of a keyboard and to produce output to a text file instead of a screen or printer. We can either read from a text file or write to it, but not both simultaneously. In order to use a text file, we must first activate it (**open the file**); then we can either read from or write to the file; when we are finished, we must deactivate it (**close the file**).

Basic Text-File Operations

Suppose we wish to work with a file that has the name "MyFriends". Text files are considered a type, just like strings or integers. Each text file used in a program is given a name for use within the program (called the **file designator** or **logical file name**), and defined to be a variable of type *text*:

```
var
   MyFile: text;
```

We are free to choose the name by which the program will refer to the file; it does *not* have to be the same name the file has on disk, which is often known as the **disk name** or **physical file name**. (This decoupling of names has certain advantages, which are discussed in what follows.)

Next, in the body of the program (sometime after the first *begin*), we open the file to make it ready for use.

If we wish to create a new file of friends' names, we can open the file with the **Rewrite** command:

```
Rewrite(MyFile, 'MyFriends')
```

Rewrite first makes the connection between the file designator (MyFile) and the corresponding disk file (MyFriends). If a file with the name MyFriends does not exist, it is created; if a file with this name already exists, it is erased and replaced by the new file (with the same disk name).

After the file has been opened, we can write to it by using the procedures Write and Writeln in conjunction with the file designator. For example, if we wish to write "Sally Jones" to the file, we could use the statement:

```
Writeln(MyFile, 'Sally Jones')
```

When we are finished with file activities, we must close the file with the **Close** command:

```
Close(MyFile)
```

The program in Figure 5-1 illustrates these ideas. This program creates a file called MyFriends and writes two friends' names into it. After you have run the program, check the contents of the file MyFriends (by using a text editor). You should see that the contents of the file are

```
            My Friends

Sally Jones
John Smith
```

If we wish to read information (input) from an existing file, we use the **Reset** command. Suppose a file of friends' names called MyFriends already existed on the disk. Then the command

```
Reset(MyFile, 'MyFriends')
```

```
program Friends;

{Written by: XXXXXXXXX XX/XX/XX}
{Purpose:   To write the names of some friends on a file}
{Procedures Used: Instructions - to print instructions}

   var
      MyFile: text;              {File designator}

   procedure Instructions;
   begin {stub}
   end;

begin {Friends}

{*** Print instructions and open the file}

   Instructions;

   Rewrite(MyFile, 'MyFriends');

{*** Write to the file}

   Writeln(MyFile, '     My Friends');
   Writeln(MyFile);
   Writeln(MyFile, 'Sally Jones');
   Writeln(MyFile, 'John Smith');

{*** Close the file}

   Close(MyFile);

{*** Print terminating message and stop program}

   Writeln;
   Writeln('Friends file created.')
end.
```

Figure 5-1   Writing to a text file.

would connect the file designator MyFile to the MyFriends disk file and open it for input. We can now use Read and Readln to input information from the file into our program; for instance:

```
Readln(MyFile, Name)
```

would read the next portion of data in the file into the variable "Name".

As with files opened for output, files opened for input must also be closed (via the Close command) when we have finished with them.

File-Processing Activities

A text file can be created by using a program similar to the one in Figure 5-1 or by using a text editor. In any case, once a file has been created, there are various activities that we can perform on the file. Among these are

> Display the file
> Print the file
> Add lines to the file
> Find a particular line in the file
> Change a particular line in the file

We now discuss each of these activities.

Displaying and Printing Text Files

Suppose that we wish to display the file on the screen. We must first declare our file designator :

```
FriendsList: text;
```

We have used a different name for the file-designator variable to emphasize that you have the choice of naming the variable as you wish. We assign the file name to the file designator with the statement:

```
Reset(FriendsList, 'MyFriends')
```

since we wish to read from the file. We read lines from the file by using the Readln procedure along with a string variable. Suppose that we have declared the string variable Line in the var section of the program. Then, we can read one line of the file with the statement:

```
Readln(FriendsList, Line)
```

The first time that we use the Readln statement, we read the first line of the file; the second time, we read the second line, and so on. Pascal provides a Boolean function **Eof** to help us in reading exactly the correct number of lines of a text file. We can test to see if we have read the entire file by the test:

```
if Eof(FriendsList) then . . .
```

If we are reading lines of the file in a loop, then we can use one of the looping constructs:

```
while not Eof(FriendsList) do . . .
repeat . . . until Eof(FriendsList)
```

Eof(file designator) is *true* exactly when there are no more data left in the file that can be read. In a program that reads using Readln, it becomes *true* immediately after the last line is read. We should use the construct

```
while not Eof(file designator) do . . .
```

for a loop where we are not sure if there are any data to be read. If we are certain that there are data that can be read, then we can use the construct

```
repeat . . .
until Eof(file designator)
```

We can display each line that is read from the file by the statement

```
Writeln(Line)
```

Finally, when we are through, we close the file with the statement

```
Close(FriendsList)
```

In Figure 5-2, we illustrate this discussion by means of a program that reads and displays the disk file MyFriends.

Note. We chose to use a *while* loop in this program. This allows the program to function correctly even if the file is empty.

After you study the program of Figure 5-2, you may note that the dependence on the particular file MyFriends is slight. In Figure 5-3, we give a general-purpose program to read and display any text file whose lines are at most 80 characters in length. The major differences between this program and the one in Figure 5-2 are italicized.

Note. In Figure 5-3, we allow the user to specify file names with lengths of up to 255 characters (the length of type *string* variables). Since the Mac allows disk file names to be at most 31 characters, you might be wondering why we need such a large-sized variable.

Up to now, we have been assuming that a file is within the same folder as the THINK Pascal compiler (or that neither is in a folder). If the file to be opened is not in the same location as THINK, its **path name** must be supplied or THINK is not able to locate the file.

On the Mac, a folder can contain files and folders; these folders in turn can contain files and folders, and so on. To specify a path to a file not in the same location as THINK, we give the disk drive name followed by all the folders in order from the first encountered to the last, followed by file's name, with each item in this listed separated by colons. For example:

```
MyDisk:Personal:Telephone Lists:MyFriends
```

would indicate the file MyFriends is in folder Telephone Lists, which in turn is in folder Personal, which resides on the disk MyDisk. (Note that blanks in disk file or folder names are legal, but not in Pascal file designators.)

By allowing a long file name, the program in Figure 5-3 becomes even more general, as files having very long path names can still be used. Were the file name variable to be a shorter string, we would be limiting ourselves to those files whose path names are no longer than the size of this short string.

```
program Display;

{Written by: XXXXXXXXX XX/XX/XX}
{Purpose:    To read and display the file MyFile}
{Procedures Used: Instructions - to print instructions}
var
   FriendsList: text;      {File designator}
   Line: string;           {For lines of the file}
procedure Instructions;
   begin {stub}
   end;

begin {Display}

{*** Print instructions and designate the file}

   Instructions;

{*** Open the file}

   Reset(FriendsList, 'MyFile');

{*** Put heading on the screen}

   Writeln;
   Writeln(' Lines of the file: ' MyFile);
   Writeln;

{*** Read and display lines of the file}

   while not Eof(FriendsList) do
      begin
         Readln(FriendsList, Line);
         Writeln(Line)
      end; {while}

{*** Close the file}

   Close(FriendsList);

{*** Print terminating message and stop program}

   Writeln;
   Writeln('All of MyFile has been displayed.');
end.
```

Figure 5-2   Reading from a text file.

You can use the program of Figure 5-3 to display the Pascal programs that you have written so far. You may find other text files that you can also display using the program.

```pascal
program FileDisplay;

{Written by: XXXXXXXXX XX/XX/XX}
{Purpose:    To read and display the contents of a text file}
{Procedures Used: Instructions - to print instructions}
   var
      AnyFile: text;          {File designator}
      FileName: string;       {Name of the file}
      Line: string[80];       {For lines of the file}

   procedure Instructions;
   begin {stub}
   end;

begin {FileDisplay}

{*** Print instructions and ask the user for the filename}

   Instructions;
   Write('Enter the filename: ');
   Readln(FileName);

{*** Open the file}

   Reset(AnyFile, FileName);

{*** Put heading on the screen}

   Writeln;
   Writeln('Lines of the file: ', FileName);
   Writeln;

{*** Read and display lines of the file}

   while not Eof(AnyFile) do
      begin
         Readln(AnyFile, Line);
         Writeln(Line)
      end; {while}

{*** Close the file}

   Close(AnyFile);

{*** Print terminating message and stop program}

   Writeln;
   Writeln('All lines of ', FileName, ' displayed.')
end.
```

Figure 5-3   User-specified file name.

Summary of File-Handling Syntax

In the examples so far, we have introduced various text file handling. Before presenting further examples of their use, let us give a brief summary. The file-handling statements are

```
var
    file designator: text;
Reset(file designator, file name)
Rewrite(file designator, file name)
Readln(file designator, . . .)
Writeln(file designator, . . .)
Eof(file designator)
Close(file designator)
```

In a typical program that uses a text file, we choose a variable name to represent the file (the file designator). We use either Reset or Rewrite to open the file (for input or output) and to assign the file designator to a particular file. We use Readln or Writeln to read or write lines of the file. If we are reading, we can use the Boolean function Eof to see if there are more data to be read. Finally, after processing is complete, we close the file using Close.

Adding Lines to a Text File

Suppose you have just made a new friend, Nancy Doe, and wish to add her to the My-Friends file. This can be done by following these steps:

> copy MyFriends to the file WorkingFile
> read the lines of WorkingFile, writing them to MyFriends
> write the new line (for Nancy Doe) to MyFriends

Copying one file to another requires that we have two files open at the same time, one for reading (Reset) and one for writing (Rewrite). We need two file designators; we must be sure to close both files when the copying is complete. After the files are open, the copying could be accomplished with this loop:

```
while not Eof(InFile) do
  begin
     Readln(InFile, Line);
     Writeln(OutFile, Line)
  end {while}
```

The copy operation is a good one to make into a procedure. We use the procedure CopyFile, which has the header line:

```
procedure CopyFile(var SourceFile, TargetFile: text);
```

Note. File parameters are required to be var parameters.

In the main program, let us assume that the file designator InFile is used for the source file and the file designator OutFile is used for the target file. When we wish to perform the copy operation, we invoke the procedure with the statement:

```
CopyFile(Infile, OutFile)
```

In Figure 5-4, we show the complete program for adding a friend to our list.

```
program AddFriend;

{Written by:   XXXXXXXXX XX/XX/XX}
{Purpose:      To add a friend's name to the file}
{Procedures Used: Instructions - to print instructions}
{                 CopyFile - to copy one text file to another}

    var
       InFile: text;           {File designator for source file}
       OutFile: text;          {File designator for target file}
       Line: string[80];       {One line of file}

    procedure Instructions;
    begin {stub}
    end;

    procedure CopyFile (var SourceFile, TargetFile: text);

    {Written by: XXXXXXXXX XX/XX/XX}
    {Purpose:    To copy one text file to another. The files}
    {            must be open.}
    {Parameters: SourceFile - file to copy from (var)}
    {            TargetFile - file to copy to (var)}

    begin {CopyFile}
       while not Eof(SourceFile) do
          begin
             Readln(Sourcefile, Line);
             Writeln(Targetfile, Line)
          end {while}
    end; {CopyFile}

begin {AddFriend}

{*** Print instructions}

    Instructions;

{*** Open the files}

    Reset(InFile, 'MyFriends');
    Rewrite(OutFile, 'WorkingFile');

{*** Copy the source file to the target file}

    CopyFile(Infile, OutFile);
```

Figure 5-4   Updating a text file (continues next page).

```
{*** Close the files}

    Close(InFile);
    Close(OutFile);

{*** Open the files to recopy lines}

    Reset(InFile, 'WorkingFile');
    Rewrite(OutFile, 'MyFriends');

{*** Copy the source file to the target file}

    CopyFile(Infile, OutFile);

{*** Write the new name to the target file}

    Writeln(OutFile, 'Nancy Doe');

{*** Close the files}

    Close(InFile);
    Close(OutFile);

{*** Print terminating message and stop program}

    Writeln;
    Writeln('New name has been added to friends file')
end.
```

Figure 5-4   (continued)

Interactive File Processing

The method of file creation that we used in Figure 5-1 is crude and inflexible. A better way of building files is for the user to respond to prompts for the information that is to be placed in the file, that is, to build the file **interactively**. For example, if we wish to build a file of friends that includes both their names and their phone numbers, we could prompt the user for the information:

file name

list of friends and phone numbers

In Figure 5-5, we show a program that creates such a file.
Note that the form of the file is

```
Friends Names and Phone Numbers

Smedley Smoke
111-2222
Lionel Train
(213)555-1234
```

```
program Build;
{Written by: XXXXXXXXX XX/XX/XX}
{Purpose:    To build a file of friends}
{Procedures Used: Instructions - to print instructions}
   const
      EndOfData = '$END';
   var
      FriendsFile: text;      {File designator}
      FileName: string;       {Name of the file}
      Name: string;           {Friend's name}
      Phone: string[13];      {Friend's phone (including room for}
                              {area code)}
   procedure Instructions;
   begin {stub}
   end;
begin {Build}
{*** Print instructions and ask the user for the filename}
   Instructions;
   Write('Enter the filename: ');
   Readln(FileName);
{*** Open the file}
   Rewrite(FriendsFile, FileName);
{*** Put heading on the file}
   Writeln(FriendsFile, '     Friends Names and Phone Numbers');
   Writeln(FriendsFile);
{*** Get names and phone numbers for file}
   repeat
      Writeln;
      Write('Enter name ($END to quit): ');
      Readln(Name);
      if Name <> EndOfData then
        begin
           Write('Enter phone number: ');
           Readln(Phone);
           Writeln(FriendsFile, Name);
           Writeln(FriendsFile, Phone)
        end {if}
   until Name = EndOfData;
{*** Close the file}
   Close(FriendsFile);
{*** Stop program}
end.
```

Figure 5-5   Interactive text-file building.

The reason why we put the names and phone numbers on separate lines of the file is a bit complicated. Suppose that we used the same line for name and phone number. A sample line of the file might be

```
Joan Smith 111-2222
```

Now suppose that we wish to read lines of the file and recover the name and phone number. How can we tell our program that the name should be "Joan Smith" rather than "Joan" and the phone number should be "111-2222" rather than "Smith 111-2222"? It would require some tricky use of formatting when building the file and subsequent care when reading the file to achieve the desired results. (We discuss some further formatting issues in Chapter 8.) We find a simple and satisfactory solution for dealing with this file in the next section; but for now, we use separate lines for separate data items to avoid difficulty.

Searching and Modifying Text Files

For our next example, we present a program that asks the user for the name of a friend and displays the friend's phone number. This program provides an example of a **search** of a file. The basic idea is to ask the user for a friend's name, to skip over the heading lines of the file, to read names and phone numbers from the file until the friend is found, and to display the phone number for the friend. Can we trust the user to ask for the name of a friend that is in the file? To answer this question, we quote from an axiom of interactive programming:

The user will make mistakes!

Our searching strategy must take into account that we may not find the friend's name in the file. We can use the Eof function to signal that we have searched the entire file and not found the friend for whom the user is looking.

Note that there are two ways for the search to terminate: successfully (finding a friend) or unsuccessfully (reaching the end-of-file). We choose to design the search in the following way:

while friend has not been found and end-of-file has not occurred:
   read name and phone number
   if friend was found, print phone number; otherwise print not found

Note that in the program, we use a compound condition in searching for the friend's name:

```
while (Friend <> Name) and (not Eof(FriendsFile)) do . . .
```

The loop can terminate in one of two ways:

1. Friend = Name (the friend has been found).
2. Eof(FriendsFile) is *true* (end-of-file has occurred).

After the loop, we wish to check to see which condition caused the search to end.
The condition that always works correctly is

```
Friend = Name
```

If we substituted the condition

```
Eof(FriendsFile)
```

in order to check how the loop has terminated, we would get the wrong result if the desired name were the last name in the file. This is a subtle point worthy of some reflection. (What is the value of Eof(FriendsFile) before the last name is read? Before the last phone number is read? After the last phone number is read?)

Note. The answers are *false*, *false*, and *true*. Thus, if the last name is the one we seek, Eof(FriendsFile) is *true* after the loop.

One other step of the program is worthy of special note. When we write a *while* loop, we must always be sure that the condition for the loop is defined when the loop begins. In our case, the condition is

```
(Friend <> Name) and (not Eof(FriendsFile))
```

Before we read the first name, the variable Name is undefined. We therefore must assign some value to it, so that "Friend <> Name" makes sense. We choose a null value because this could not inadvertently be equal to the name for which we are searching.

Figure 5-6 shows a program that searches for a friend's phone number.

```
program Search;

{Written by: XXXXXXXXX XX/XX/XX}
{Purpose:    To search for a friend and display her phone number}
{Procedures used: Instructions - to print instructions}

   var
      FriendsFile: text;      {File designator}
      FileName: string;       {Disk file name}
      Friend: string;         {Name of friend to find}
      Name: string;           {Name from file}
      Phone: string[12];      {Friend's phone number}

   procedure Instructions;
   begin {stub}
   end;

begin {Search}

{*** Print instructions and ask the user for the filename}

   Instructions;
   Write('Enter the filename: ');
   Readln(FileName);
```

Figure 5-6   Searching a text file (continues next page).

```
{*** Open the file}

   Reset(FriendsFile, FileName);

{*** Skip heading lines of the file}

   Readln(FriendsFile);        {Reads "Friends Names and Phone Numbers"}
   Readln(FriendsFile);        {Reads the blank line}

{*** Get name from the user}

   Writeln;
   Write('Enter the friend''s name: ');
   Readln(Friend);

{*** Search the file for the name}

   Name := '';                  {Required so while condition is defined}
   while (Friend <> Name) and (not (Eof(FriendsFile))) do
     begin
        Readln(FriendsFile, Name);
        Readln(FriendsFile, Phone);
     end; {while}

{*** Display the results of the search}

      if Friend = Name then
         Writeln('The phone number is: ', Phone)
      else
         Writeln('*** Friend not found.');

{*** Close the file and stop program}

      Close(FriendsFile);
   end.
```

Figure 5-6   (continued)

As our last example of text-file processing, we present a program that allows us to change the phone number of one of our friends. This program is a combination of the concepts of adding lines to a file, as illustrated in Figure 5-4, and searching a file, as illustrated in Figure 5-6. We allow the user to specify the friend's name and, if we find the friend in the file, we ask the user for the new phone number. The steps for the program are as follows:

    ask the user for the filename
      open the file
      copy the file to WorkingFile
      ask the user for the friend's name
      search WorkingFile for the friend while copying back to the file
      if found, ask the user for the new phone number and write to
        the file; otherwise, tell the user that the friend was not found
      copy the remainder of WorkingFile back to the file

We use the CopyFile procedure once again in order to perform the copying activities in the program, as shown in Figure 5-7. Two items in the figure are especially noteworthy. First, after files have been closed, they can be reassigned. Second, the Copy procedure is invoked a second time to finish the copying operation. It copies starting at the current record of Infile until end of file is reached.

```
program ChangePhoneNumber;

{Written by:   XXXXXXXXX XX/XX/XX}
{Purpose:      To change a friend's phone number}
{Procedures Used: Instructions - to print instructions}
{                 Copy - to copy one file to another}

  const
    WorkingFile = 'Search Work File';      {name of working file}

  var
    InFile: text;              {File designator for source file}
    OutFile: text;             {File designator for target file}
    FileName: string;          {Name of the file}
    Friend: string;            {Name of friend to find}
    Name: string;              {Current name from file}
    Phone: string[12];         {Friend's phone number}
    Line: string[80];          {Line of file}

  procedure Instructions;
  begin {stub}
  end;

{procedure Copy, as shown in Figure 5-4, is inserted here}

begin {Change}

{*** Print instructions and ask the user for the filename}

  Instructions;
  Write('Enter the filename: ');
  Readln(FileName);

{*** Open the files}

  Reset(InFile, FileName);
  Rewrite(OutFile, WorkingFile);

{*** Copy the source file to the target file}

  CopyFile(Infile, OutFile);

{*** Close the files.}

  Close(InFile);
  Close(OutFile);
```

Figure 5-7 Interactive text-file update (continues next page).

```
{*** Reopen the files to search for friend}

  Reset(InFile, WorkingFile);
  Rewrite(OutFile, FileName);

{*** Skip heading lines of the file}

  Readln(InFile, Line);
  Writeln(OutFile, Line);
  Readln(InFile, Line);
  Writeln(OutFile, Line);

{*** Get name from the user}

  Writeln;
  Write('Enter the friend''s name: ');
  Readln(Friend);

{*** Search for the name while copying the file}

  Name := '';
  while (Friend <> Name) and (not Eof(Infile)) do
    begin
      Readln(Infile, Name);
      Writeln(OutFile, Name);
      Readln(InFile, Phone);
      if Friend = Name then
        begin
          Writeln('The old phone number is: ', Phone);
          Write('Enter the new phone number: ');
          Readln(Phone)
        end; {if}
      Writeln(OutFile, Phone)
    end; {while}

{*** Act on the results of an unsuccessful search}

  if Friend <> Name then
    Writeln('*** Friend not found.');

{*** Finish the copying operation}

  CopyFile(Infile, OutFile);

{*** Close the files}

  Close(InFile);
  Close(OutFile);

{*** Print terminating message and stop program}

  Writeln;
  Writeln('Finished')
end.
```

Figure 5-7 (continued)

The program of Figure 5-7 assumes that the filename of the file of friends is not called WorkingFile because that is the file that is used for copying. Another assumption is that the user will enter the correct name for the file. The program will fail to work correctly if either of these assumptions is incorrect. You should experiment with this program by violating one or both of the assumptions. A program that is intended for serious use should not make any assumptions; the program should be designed to handle all contingencies. We discuss the handling of input/output errors (such as trying to read from a non-existent file) in Section 5-3.

Text Files as Standard I/O

The examples in this section have dealt with a file as the primary focus of the program. For example, we have had programs to create a file, to print its contents, to search for a value in a file, and to modify a value in a file.

As we have indicated, text-file processing has much in common with processing input from a terminal or output to either a terminal or a printer. We describe briefly several types of programs in which text files can be used as substitutes for the standard input and output devices.

When the amount of input to be supplied to a program is large, it may be more convenient for the user to build a text file using an editor, then run the program with that data. Suppose it turns out, upon examining the result of running the program, that some of the input is faulty. Then that input can be corrected (using an editor) and the program run again. This may be much simpler than rerunning an interactive program and having to redo all the input, including the correct input.

Two specific examples of this come to mind. The first is the THINK Pascal compiler. It accepts your program as a text file rather than interactively one line at a time. When there is a problem, you do not have to retype the entire program.

Second, even for a program that will be interactive, this idea can be useful during debugging and testing. Suppose your test plan includes 34 individual test cases and that the 26th uncovers a bug. After you fix the bug, you should start over with the testing. This is easy if your test cases are in a text file. When the entire run is bug-free, you can then change the input to the terminal and run through the tests one final time. (The input text file can be saved for future testing in case modifications are made to the program.)

In a similar way, we can use a file for output rather than the terminal, especially if the amount of output is extensive. As an example, suppose we are debugging and testing as described in the previous paragraph. The output from the 34 test cases might flash by so quickly on the screen that we are unable to see it. We can send the output to a file instead and examine it using a text editor after the program runs.

A similar example occurs in many production programs. Along with the interactive input and output, the program can be building a text file (called a **trace file**). The trace file contains a complete record of all output from the program and all user input. If a problem develops while the program is running, the file can be examined to isolate the difficulty. It can, if it is built carefully, even be used to rerun the program up to the point of the difficulty.

Finally, text files can be used in place of printer output. Consider this situation: You are to write a program that creates a printed report, but you do not personally own a printer (or the printer is in the shop). By redirecting all the output that would have gone to the printer to a text file, you can build a file version of the report. Later, when you have access to a printer, you can print the file (such as by opening the file within THINK and issuing the Print command) to obtain a printed report. By using this idea, you can write programs that generate two or more printed reports simultaneously.

We can achieve additional advantages using this technique. It is possible to obtain multiple copies of the report without having to run the program again, simply by printing multiple copies of the text file containing the report. And, if the printer paper jams or the printer malfunctions, the program need not be rerun to obtain the report: we simply fix the printer and print the disk file again.

DPT

1. We must open a file before we can perform input or output operations on it. Also, we must use Reset if we wish to read from the file and Rewrite if we wish to write to the file. If we fail to open the file before attempting to use it, the compiler does not detect the omission, but we encounter a run-time I/O error when we attempt to read from or write to the file. If we attempt to read from a file that has been opened with Rewrite or to write to a file that has been opened with Reset, a run-time I/O error occurs.

2. There is a danger in using Rewrite to open a file. If the file already exists, then it is deleted as soon as the Rewrite is executed. Be careful not to carelessly lose valuable files through this effect of Rewrite.

3. If we attempt to open a file using Reset and the file does not exist, a run-time I/O error occurs. We explain a mechanism for controlling this situation in Section 5-3.

4. After using a file, we should close it. If we forget to close a file that has been opened with Reset and attempt to reopen the file with either Reset or Rewrite, no error results and nothing is wrong except our programming style. If we forget to close a file that has been opened with Rewrite, we are very likely to lose some of the data that we have written to the file. If we get in the habit of always closing files, we will not encounter any difficulty.

5. Always use the file designator when performing input and output activities with a file. If we forget to include the file designator in our input and output statements, then we will find ourselves using the keyboard and screen instead of the file.

6. After searching a file in a loop with a compound exit condition, do not use the function Eof after the loop has terminated as a check on how termination occurred. Remember that as soon as the last line in a file has been read, Eof(file designator) becomes *true*.

7. Do not assume that the user of your program always does the correct thing, spells words correctly, or even types what he or she is intending to type. You already have had enough experience at using your own programs to realize that even a knowledgeable user makes mistakes. Attempt to write programs that protect the user from mistakes, instead of punishing the user for making them. We provide some special techniques for making programs "bulletproof" (immune from user errors) later in the book.

Testing

We have given several example programs that illustrate file searching. There are certain test cases that should always be tested when searching a file for a particular instance of a data item.

Empty File. Your program should not falter when it encounters a file that contains no data. You can produce an empty file to use in testing with the following Pascal program:

```
program EmptyFile;

var
  AnyFile: text;

begin {EmptyFile}
  Rewrite (AnyFile, 'EmptyFile');
  Close(AnyFile)
end.
```

Target Item Is First. Your program should be tested with a file in which the first data item is the only one that should be successfully found.

Target Item Is Last. Your program should be tested with a file in which the last data item is the only one that should be successfully found.

Target Item Is Between First and Last. Your program should be tested with a file in which some middle data item is the only one that should be successfully found.

Multiple Target Items. Your program should be tested with a file in which there are at least two data items that should be successfully found. Even more thorough testing would have several files in which the data items are in the first and last positions, two middle positions, etc.

No Target Item. Your program should be tested with a file in which there are no data items that should be successfully found, although some of the data items should be close (for example: Smith, Simth).

If we wished to test the program of Figure 5-6, searching for Joan Smith, we might use the following set of test files:

Empty File

Target Item First

   Friends Names and Phone Numbers

Joan Smith
111-2222
Bill Jones
222-1111

Target Item Last

   Friends Names and Phone Numbers

Bill Jones
222-1111
Joan Smith
111-2222

Target Item in Middle

   Friends Names and Phone Numbers

Bill Jones
222-1111
Joan Smith
111-2222
Carol Doe
333-4444

Multiple Target Items (just the phone number should be reported)

   Friends Names and Phone Numbers

Carol Doe
333-4444
Joan Smith
111-2222
Bill Jones
222-1111
Joan Smith
999-9999

No Target Item:

   Friends Names and Phone Numbers

Bill Jones
222-1111
Joan Simth
111-2222
Carol Doe
333-4444

REVIEW

Terms and Concepts

Close
close a file
disk name
Eof
file designator
interactive
logical file name
open a file

path name
physical file name
Reset
Rewrite
search
text file
trace file

Pascal Syntax. Text file manipulation: All examples use "MyFile" as the file designator.

1. To declare the file designator:

   ```
   var
     MyFile: text;
   ```

2. To open the file for output:

   ```
   Rewrite(MyFile, disk file name)
   ```

3. To open the file for input:

   ```
   Reset(MyFile, disk file name)
   ```

4. To write to the file:

   ```
   Writeln(MyFile, 'John Smith')
   ```

5. To read from the file:

   ```
   Readln(MyFile, Name)
   ```

6. To test for the end of the file:

   ```
   if Eof(MyFile) then ...
   ```

   or

   ```
   while not Eof(MyFile) do ...
   ```

   or

   ```
   repeat until Eof(MyFile) ...
   ```

7. To close the file:

   ```
   Close(MyFile)
   ```

DPT

1. Open a file with Reset before reading or Rewrite before writing.
2. Rewrite deletes an existing file.
3. Opening a non-existent file with Reset causes a run-time error.
4. Close files after using them.
5. Always use the file designator when reading or writing a file.
6. Don't test Eof outside of a loop that has used Eof as part of a compound exit condition.
7. The user will make mistakes.

REVIEW

Testing. To test a program that is searching a file for a particular object, use at least the following test cases:

1. Empty file
2. Target item first
3. Target item last
4. Target item in the middle
5. Multiple target items
6. No target item, some close

EXERCISES

1. Write a program to build a text file called ShoppingList with the following contents:

   ```
   A Shopping List
   ---------------

    2 Frozen Pizzas
   10 Bags of chips
    4 Cans of soup (assorted)
    1 Case of cola
   ```

2. Write a program to add the two lines

   ```
   3 Boxes of cough drops
   3 Bottles of aspirin
   ```

   to the file at these positions:

   (a) To the beginning of the file.
   (b) To the end of the file.
   (c) Between lines 5 and 6 of the file (after the chips).

3. Modify the programs of Exercises 1 and 2 as follows:
   (a) Obtain input from the user to be placed into the file you are creating.
   (b) Allow the user to insert new data after any line of the file. For each line of the original, do these steps:

   Read the line
   Write the line to the output file
   Ask the user if he wishes to add lines
      if so, read 0 or more lines and add them to the output file

4. Modify the program of Figure 5-3 so that after each segment of 23 lines is displayed, the user is prompted to tap a key to continue.

5. Modify the program of Figure 5-3 to output to the printer instead of displaying to the screen. Also, print a heading and page number at the top of each page except the first. Finally, print at most 58 lines of text on a page.

6. Modify the program of Figure 5-1 by omitting the Close statement. Run the program, and look at the contents of the MyFriends file. What effect does omitting the Close statement have?

7. Write a program to produce a text file with the following contents:

   ```
   program SelfMade;

     var
       N: integer;

   begin {SelfMade}
     N := 6;
     Writeln(N)
   end.
   ```

   After you have successfully created the file with your program, see if the text file can be compiled and run as a program in its own right. In a small way, you just wrote a program that wrote a program.

8. Write a program that reads a text file and prints each line, allowing the user to choose one of three options. The user can choose to delete the line, retype it, or leave it unchanged. For convenience, this last option should be chosen just by hitting return.

9. Write a program combining the ideas of Exercises 3 and 8.

10. Write a program that allows the user to build a file of student names, student numbers, and scores on an examination interactively. A sample set of lines of the file should appear as

    ```
    John Smith
    11-333-5555
    85
    ```

11. Use the program from Exercise 10 (or a text editor) to build a file that has several students with the same score on the examination. Write a program that asks the user for a score and then lists all students who have earned that score on the screen. Example input and output are as follows:

    ```
    Enter a score: 85

    Students with a Score of 85
    John Smith   11-333-5555
    Nancy Doe    22-222-6666
    *** list complete

    Enter a score: 66

    Students with a Score of 66
    *** list complete

    Enter a score: -1
    ```

12. Write a program that processes the file created in Exercise 11 by asking the user for a student number and displaying the name and score for the student. Example input and output are as follows:

    ```
    Enter a student number: 11-333-5555

    The student is:
      John Smith 85
    ```

EXERCISES

```
Enter a student number: 33-333-3333
*** Student not found.

Enter a student number: $END    {program exits}
```

13. Write a program that processes the file created in Exercise 11 by adding 5 points to Nancy Doe's score.
14. Revise Exercise 10 to allow multiple tests by making the first data item in the file N, the number of tests.
15. Write a program that uses the file created in Exercise 14 to add another test score for each student.
16. This exercise deals with a text file that, for each person, contains the following data:

    Name
    Age
    Sex
    Marital status
    Earned income for previous year
    Number of children

    You can build the file using the ideas of Exercise 10 or using a text editor.

    (a) Write a procedure to read the data for one person. This procedure will be used in part (b).
    (b) Write programs (or program segments) to answer these questions concerning the data file.

        (1) How many people are in the file?
        (2) What percentage are single (code 'S')? Female (code 'F')? Either single or female?
        (3) Who has the largest earned income? How old is that person?
        (4) What is the marital status of Mary Wikinson?
        (5) What is the average number of children for married males between the ages of 40 and 60?
        (6) Who is the first person in the file who is either widowed (code 'W') or divorced (code 'D'), has no children, and has an income over $50,000?

17. (a) Tell what changes you would make to Case Study No. 6 (Figure 4-16) if the data were in a text file rather than obtained from the user as the program runs.
    (b) Which approach do you think would be preferable to the user of the program: the original approach or the one suggested in part (a)?
    (c) Tell how you could modify Case Study No. 6 to create an output file containing name and total sales for each employee.

18. (a) Choose any program that you have written and revise it to read its input from a text file.
    (b) Choose any program that you have written and revise it to create a trace file (see page 363) containing a complete record of the program run.
    (c) Choose any program that you have written that creates a printed report and revise it to send the report to a file instead. Print the file using a text editor.

19. A text file consists of repetitions of the following data:

    Student information
    One or more groups of course information for the student
    A line containing the string XXX

The student information consists of name, total semester hours taken prior to this semester, and total grade points earned prior to this semester. Each group of course information consists of course department (e.g., CPS), course number (e.g., 121), semester hours credit for the course, and letter grade for the course. The course information groups represent courses taken during this semester.

(a) Design the exact file structure and give a small sample file for two students.
(b) Write a program to read the file. For each student, it should display the information on the screen and then use Readln to wait for the user to tap return.
(c) Modify part (b) to create a printed grade report for each student, indicating name, list of courses (department, number, grade, and grade points for course), total semester hours for the semester, total grade points for the semester, and grade point average for the semester. (Quality points for each course are found by multiplying the semester hours for the course by 4 for an A, 3 for a B, 2 for a C, 1 for a D, or 0 for an F. Quality point average is grade points divided by semester hours.)
(d) Write a program to create an output text file containing this information for each student: name, semester hours taken including this semester, and total grade points earned including this semester. The output file should follow the same general form as the input file. It can then be used as a starting point for building next semester's input file.
(e) Add a printed report to the program in part (d). Send the printed output to a file for future printing. The columns of the report are name, total semester hours, total grade points, and grade point average. See part (c) for information on grade point calculations.

21. A text file contains the following information:

A line containing the number of departments

Department information (code, number of professors) for the first department

Name and salary information for each professor in the first department

Department information (code, number of professors) for the second department

Name and salary information for each professor in the second department

And so on.

Write a program to read the text file and generate a report in this form:

```
Department          Professor         Salary
----------          ---------         ------
   XXX              XXXXXXXXXXXXXXXXX  XXXXX
                    XXXXXXXXXXXXXXXXX  XXXXX
                    XXXXXXXXXXXXXXXXX  XXXXX
   XXX              XXXXXXXXXXXXXXXXX  XXXXX
                    XXXXXXXXXXXXXXXXX  XXXXX
```

Then show what changes to make to accomplish the following:

(a) Find and print the average salary in each department.
(b) Find and print the average salary in the entire school.
(c) Count the number earning over $28,000 in the entire school.
(d) Find and print the person with the highest salary in each department.
(e) Find the number of departments that have an average salary in excess of $20,000.
(f) Find the largest average salary for a department.

For example, the answer might be:

```
BIO department has highest average salary: 25533.00
```

22. Give test plans for the following.
    (a) Exercise 3(b)
    (b) Exercise 4
    (c) Exercise 8
    (d) Exercise 11
    (e) Exercise 12
    (f) Exercise 13
    (g) Exercise 16(b)(2)
    (h) Exercise 16(b)(3)
    (i) Exercise 16(b)(4)
    (j) Exercise 16(b)(5)

5-2 RECORDS AND SETS

In this section, we introduce a powerful data structuring technique via the Pascal **record**. We continue our discussion of files that was begun in the last section and we learn some more about the Pascal **set** data structure.

Records

Record Structure. Especially when dealing with files, it is frequently the case that certain data items are associated with one another. For example, in the last section, we discussed a text file that consisted of friends' names and phone numbers. The two data items Name and Phone are associated because of their relationship with one particular individual. Recall that we stored the name and phone number in a rather awkward manner: on two separate lines of the file. Pascal provides a better way of dealing with this information via the record structure.

Note. Historically, the term "record" referred to files. However, the concept of grouping related data is an important one, whether files are involved or not. In our discussion of records, some examples involve files and others do not.

We begin by adapting the programs of the previous section, which dealt with text files, to files of records.

A record consists of data entities called **fields** that have values. The general form of the definition of a record occurs in the *type* section of a Pascal module and has the following form:

```
type
   identifier = record
         list of field declarations
   end;
```

In our example, we want to have a record called PersonalData, which has two fields: Name and Phone. We declare this data structure in the *type* area of our declarations as follows:

```
type
   PersonalData = record
      Name: string[50];
      Phone: string[12]
   end;
```

We also must declare a variable of type PersonalData, which can hold the values for one particular instance of a friend. We make this declaration in the var area of our program as follows:

```
var
   Friend: PersonalData;
```

We can refer to the individual fields of a record variable by means of the construction:

record variable name.field name

Therefore, for our example, we can refer to the fields of the variable Friend by means of the designations:

```
Friend.Name
Friend.Phone
```

If we want to use our records for a file (and we do), then we declare a file type as follows:

```
type
   PersonalFile = file of PersonalData;
```

We also declare a file designator variable in the var section:

```
var
   Friend: PersonalData;
   FriendsFile: PersonalFile;
```

Files of Records. Files of records (and, in fact, any file that is not of type *text*), are called **binary files**. The properties of binary files in THINK are somewhat different than those of text files; we discuss these properties in more detail in Chapter 11. The major differences we need to concern ourselves with now are as follows:

1. We use Read and Write rather than Readln and Writeln with binary files. We must take care not to use Readln and Writeln except with text files; otherwise, we will encounter compile-time errors. We also read and write entire records in this new setting.
2. Since a binary file does not contain text, we can no longer view our file's contents with a text editor. We would need to write a THINK Pascal program to examine its contents.

An Example. We rewrite the programs of Figures 5-5 and 5-6 using the record concept, as shown in Figures 5-8 and 5-9. Major differences are in italics.

```
program Build;
{Written by: XXXXXXXXX XX/XX/XX}
{Purpose:    To build a file of friends}
{Procedures used: Instructions - to print instructions}
  const
    EndOfData = '$END';

  type
    PersonalData = record
        Name: string;
        Phone: string[12];
      end;
    PersonalFile = file of PersonalData;

  var
    Friend: PersonalData;         {Instance of record}
    FriendsFile: PersonalFile;    {File designator}
    FileName: string;             {Disk name of file}

  procedure Instructions;
  begin {stub}
  end;

begin {Build}
{*** Print instructions and ask the user for the filename}
  Instructions;
  Write('Enter the filename: ');
  Readln(FileName);

{*** Open the file}
  Rewrite(FriendsFile, FileName);

{*** Get names and phone numbers for file}
  repeat
    Writeln;
    Write('Enter name ($END to quit): ');
    Readln(Friend.Name);
    if Friend.Name <> EndOfData then
      begin
        Write('Enter phone number: ');
        Readln(Friend.Phone);
        Write(FriendsFile, Friend);
      end {if}
  until Friend.Name = EndOfData;

{*** Close the file}
  Close(FriendsFile);

{*** Stop program}
end.
```

Figure 5-8   Writing to a file of records.

```
program Search;

{Written by: XXXXXXXXX XX/XX/XX}
{Purpose:    To search for a friend and display her phone number}
{Procedures used: Instructions - to print instructions }

  type
    PersonalData = record
      Name: string;
      Phone: string[12];
    end;
    PersonalFile = file of PersonalData;

  var
    FriendsFile: PersonalFile;      {File designator}
    FileName: string;               {Disk file name}
    Name: string;                   {Name of friend to find}
    Phone: string[12];              {Friend's phone number}
    Friend: PersonalData;           {Instance of record}

  procedure Instructions;
  begin {stub}
  end;

begin {Search}

{*** Print instructions and ask the user for the filename}

  Instructions;
  Write('Enter the filename: ');
  Readln(FileName);

{*** Open the file}

  Reset(FriendsFile, FileName);

{*** Skip heading lines of the file}

  Read(FriendsFile, Friend);   {Reads "Friends Names and Phone Numbers"}
  Read(FriendsFile, Friend);   {Reads the blank line}

{*** Get name from the user}

  Writeln;
  Write('Enter the friend''s name: ');
  Readln(Name);

{*** Search the file for the name}

  Friend.Name := '';           {Required so while condition is defined}
  while (Friend.Name <> Name) and (not (Eof(FriendsFile))) do
    begin
      Read(FriendsFile, Friend);
    end; {while}
```

Figure 5-9 Searching a file of records (continues next page).

```
{*** Display the results of the search}

    if Friend.Name = Name then
        Writeln('The phone number is: ', Friend.Phone)
    else
        Writeln('*** Friend not found.');

{*** Close the file and stop}

    Close(FriendsFile)
end.
```

Figure 5-9   (continued)

Because the file to contain the friends' names and phone numbers is no longer available for use with a text editor, we no longer use the concept of heading lines in the file.

Note.   There is one disadvantage of using files of records instead of text files. Text files can be created using an editor, and they can also be examined using an editor. This is not true for files of records. It is therefore very useful, when writing a program that works with nontext files, to first write simple programs for file creation and file display.

Appendix C contains a framework for writing file creation and display utilities. To use these frameworks, you only need to write a procedure to read one record and a procedure to display one record.

Operations with Records

Assignment.   We can assign the entire contents from one record to another record of the same type. For example, if Friend and NewFriend are both declared to be of type PersonalData, then the statement:

```
Friend := NewFriend
```

is equivalent to the two statements:

```
Friend.Name := NewFriend.Name;
Friend.Phone := NewFriend.Phone
```

This is a convenience when a record contains many fields.

Processing a Single Record.   Pascal allows a shorter way to refer to fields than the examples we have seen: NewFriend.Phone, for example. The shorter route involves the Pascal keyword **with.** The general form of the *with-do* construction is

```
with record variable name do
  begin
      list of statements
  end
```

376   ELEMENTARY DATA STRUCTURING   CHAP. 5

Between the *begin* and *end* of the *with-do* construct, we can use the names of the record's fields without using the record variable and a dot (.) as a prefix.

As an example, suppose that we wish to read the name and phone number of NewFriend from the keyboard. Our first style for doing this would be as follows:

```
Write('Enter the name: ');
Readln(NewFriend.Name);
Write('Enter the phone number: ');
Readln(NewFriend.Phone)
```

The shorter method uses the form

```
with NewFriend do
  begin
    Write('Enter the name: ');
    Readln(Name);
    Write('Enter the phone number: ');
    Readln(Phone)
  end
```

Note that because we have told Pascal that we are dealing with NewFriend, we do not have to use the record identifier as a prefix for the field names.

Records as Parameters. We can pass records as parameters to procedures or functions. For example, if we wanted to use a detail line print procedure Detail to print the friend's name and phone number, then we could declare the procedure with the heading:

```
procedure Detail(Friend: PersonalData);
```

We could then invoke the procedure from our program with the statement

```
Detail(Friend)
```

As another example, consider the following segment of code. It works with records whose fields are Name and Age. The variables Person and Large are records of this type.

```
Large.Name := '';
Large.Age := 0;
repeat
  GetRecord(Person, Quit);
  if not Quit then
    begin
      if Person.Age > Large.Age then
        Large := Person
    end {if}
until Quit;

PrintRecord(Large)
```

This segment reads a series of input consisting of Name and Age. After the loop, it prints the name and age of the oldest person (assuming no ties). We have written a number of programs similar to this, but this one is notable in several ways:

5-2 RECORDS AND SETS

1. The data items that "belong together" (name and age) are associated by putting them in a record.
2. We use variables that are records as parameters to two procedures: GetRecord, PrintRecord.
3. If a larger age is found, we assign

```
Large := Person
```

which makes a record of both the name and age of the person whose age is larger. If the record contained 10 fields, all 10 fields would be copied by the one assignment statement.

Arrays of Records. We can use the array concept with records as well as with other types of variables. For example, if we wanted to be able to deal with a list of 10 friends, we could use the declarations

```
type
   PersonalData = record
       Name: string[50];
       Phone: string[12]
     end;

   PersonArray = array[1..10] of PersonalData;

var
   Friends: PersonArray;
```

Note. We could accomplish the declaration by

```
var
     Friends: array[1 .. 10] of PersonalData;
```

However, the former method of declaring the array is more general and is recommended over this one. One advantage is that it allows passing array Friends to a subprogram.

To illustrate a few possible ways we could work with arrays of records, suppose that the PersonArray type is declared globally (i.e., in the main program's declarations). Then we can declare a procedure ReadPeople as follows:

```
procedure ReadPeople(List: PersonArray);
```

We can invoke the subprogram ReadPeople this way:

```
ReadPeople(Friends);
```

If we wish to refer to the name field of the fifth record in the array, we can use the form

```
Friends[5].Name
```

We can do extensive processing with the sixth record in the array by using the construct

378 ELEMENTARY DATA STRUCTURING CHAP. 5

```
with Friends[6] do
   begin
      .
      .
      .
   end
```

Finally, we can print the names in the Friends array by

```
for I := 1 to 10 do
   begin
      Writeln(Friends[I].Name)
   end
```

Arrays of records are dealt with in greater detail in Chapter 6.

Sets

We have used the concept of a Pascal set in some of our previous examples. In particular, when a user is asked a yes or no question, we have checked for a valid response by means of the Boolean expression

```
Ans in ['Y','y','N','n']
```

In this subsection, we discuss some additional details of Pascal sets.

A set in Pascal is similar to the mathematical notion of a collection of objects. Each object that is in the set is called a **member** or **element** of the set. Two sets are equal if they have exactly the same elements, regardless of order. All of the elements of a set must be of the same Pascal type. The legal types for elements in sets are

Integer

Boolean

Char

User-defined scalar types (discussed in the next section)

Constant sets are specified by listing the elements of the set between a pair of square brackets (for example, ['Y','y','N','n']). Some examples of set constants are

```
[1, 3, 5]
['a','b','c']
[]
```

The third example, [ ], is the **empty set,** the set with no elements. We can also specify a constant set by means of ellipses (. .). Thus, we can specify the set of all uppercase letters between A and F by

```
[A..F]
```

We declare a set type by specifying the kind of elements that may belong to sets of that type. The type of the elements of the set is called the **base type.** For example, if we wanted to work with sets of integers less than 100, we could declare the set type as

```
type
    SmallNumbersSet = set of 1..99;
```

Note. We have seen the notation value..value (as in 1..99) before: in defining array types and in listing the branches of a *case* statement. This notation indicates a subrange of the integers. Subranges are examined in more detail in Section 5-3.

If we wish to work with sets of characters, then we could declare the set type as

```
type
    CharacterSet = set of char;
```

We declare variables to have a set type in the var section of the program. For example, if we want the variables A and B to be sets of numbers less than 100, we can use the declarations

```
type
    SmallNumbersSet = set of 1..99;

var
    A, B: SmallNumbersSet;
```

Set Operations

Assignment. We can assign a set value to a set variable of the same type. Thus, if A is declared of type SmallNumbersSet as before, we can use the statement

```
A := [17,23,41]
```

to give A a value. If B is also of type SmallNumbersSet, then we can also assign a value to A with the statement

```
A := B
```

Union. If A and B are variables of the same set type, then we can form the **union** of A and B by the expression A + B. This new set is comprised of all elements that are in either A or B (or in both). For example, if A is [1,3,5] and B is [4,6], then A + B is [1,3,5,4,6]. Remember that order does not matter with sets, so we can also say that A + B is [1,3,4,6,5].

We do not allow repetition in sets. For example, if C is [1,3,5] and D is [5,7] then C + D is [1,3,5,7].

Intersection. If A and B are variables of the same set type, then we can form the **intersection** of A and B by the expression A * B. This new set A * B is comprised of all elements of A that are also members of B. For example, if A is [1,3,5] and B is [5,7], then A * B is [5]. As another example, if C is [1,3,5] and D is [1,3], then C * D is [1,3].

Difference. If A and B are variables of the same set type, then we can form the **difference** of A and B by the expression A − B. This new set is comprised of all of the elements of A that are *not* members of B. For example, if A is [1,3,5] and B is [4,6], then A − B is [1,3,5]; if C is [1,3,5] and D is [5,6], then C − D is [1,3].

Note that in general A − (A − B) is equal to A * B. Note also that D − C is [6], which is totally different from C − D. In general, A − B and B − A are not equal.

Membership Test. We have already encountered the Pascal keyword **in**. In general, if A is a variable of set type, and if X is a variable of the base type of A, then we can construct the Boolean expression "X in A", which is *true* if X is an element of A (and *false* if it is not). We must be careful not to attempt to test mismatched types with the membership test.

Set Equality. We can compare two variables of the same set type for equality by use of the "=" operator. Thus, if A and B are variables of the same set type, we can construct the Boolean expression

```
A = B
```

which is *true* if A has exactly the same elements as does B. Remember that order does not count, so that

```
[1,3,5] = [3,5,1]
```

is *true*. We can use the operator "<>" to test for inequality.

Set Inclusion. We can compare two variables of the same type to see if one is a **subset** of the other by means of the operators <, <=, >, and >= . If A and B are two variables of the same set type, then we can construct the following Boolean expressions:

A < B	*true* if every element of A is also an element of B and A is not equal to B
A <= B	*true* if every element of A is also an element of B
A > B	*true* if every element of B is also an element of A and B is not equal to A
A >= B	*true* if every element of B is also an element of A

For example, these are true conditions:

```
[1,5] < [3,1,5,6]
[6,3,2] >= [3,2]
[1,2,3] <= [1,2,3]
```

but these are not:

```
[1,5] < [2,6]
[1,2,3] > [1,2,3]
```

Input and Output. No automatic input or output of sets is allowed using the keyboard, screen, printer, or text files. We can read and write sets with files declared to be of set type in a fashion similar to that of records.

However, we can write our own code to print sets one element at a time. For example, these steps can be used to print a set A of the type SmallNumbersSet defined before. (The numbers in the set are printed one per line.)

```
for I := 1 to 99 do
  begin
```

```
       if I in A then
          Writeln(I)
   end {for}
```

Similarly, we can read a set of this type by reading the numbers one at a time and using a step such as

```
A := A + [I]
```

where I is the number read. (A would be initialized to [ ].)

Set Construction. Sets can be constructed using constants or variables of the base type. For example, if A is a set with base type *char*, and if X and Y are variables of type *char*, then we can construct a set as follows:

```
A := ['a', X, 'b', Y];
```

If X has the value 'c' and Y has the value 'd' in the last expression, then the resulting value of A is ['a', 'c', 'b', 'd']. The following is a Pascal fragment to test the validity of the example just cited:

```
var
   A: set of char;
   X, Y: char;

X := 'c';
Y := 'd';
A := ['a', X, 'b', Y];
if A = ['a', 'c', 'b', 'd'] then
   Writeln('The example is valid')
else
   Writeln('The example is invalid');
```

Parameters. Sets, with some care, can be passed as parameters. A valid scenario for passing a set as a parameter is shown in the fragment

```
type
   Kind = set of char;       {This is a named type}

var
   A : Kind;

procedure BeCareful(S: Kind);

BeCareful(A);
```

The main point is that for passing set parameters, named types must be used. The scenario that follows is invalid; the compiler will reject it:

```
var
   A: set of char;

procedure BeCareful(S: set of char);

BeCareful(A);
```

Set parameters follow the same rules that we have already seen with arrays, strings, and records.

An Example

We develop an example use of sets for obtaining valid input from a user. Quite often, a program has to ask the user for a response that consists of a single character. For example, in answering a yes-or-no question, we often consider any of Y, y, N, or n to be valid responses. If a menu has the options

> S(top the process)
> R(estart the process)
> C(ontinue the process)

then we would consider any of S, s, R, r, C, or c to be valid responses. We write a subprogram called AskUser, which as has two parameters: a prompt message to be shown to the user and a set of valid responses. It returns a valid response from the user. The steps in the subprogram are

> print the prompting message
> read response from user
> while the response is invalid do the following:
>   ask user to try again
>   read response from user
> return the valid response

Accepting single-character input from the keyboard can be a bit tricky. We take a straightforward approach and read the user's response into a variable of type *char*, using Readln. If the user enters more than one character before tapping the return key, only the first is read; the remaining characters are ignored. So as long as the user enters a string whose first character is in the set of valid responses, AskUser will return that first character. We could take the position that any input string longer than one character should be invalid, regardless of its first character; we leave it as an exercise to change AskUser to reflect that position.

In the example program shown in Figure 5-10, we exercise the AskUser function in two of the most common contexts in which it would be used. Note that in the first, we use variables in the invocation of the function, whereas in the second, we use constants. Either method is valid.

DPT

1. When we are dealing with nontext files, we use Read and Write and do not use Readln and Writeln. If we use Readln or Writeln in a program, then the compiler detects and reports the error.

2. We must be sure to use the "." when dealing with a field of a record when not within a *with-do* construct. For example, suppose that we have a record declared as

```
program Ask;

{Written by: XXXXXXXXX XX/XX/XX}
{Purpose:    To ask the user to respond}
{Procedures used: Instructions - to print instructions}
{Functions used:  AskUser - to obtain valid input}

  type
    Letters = set of char;
    Sentence = string[80];

  var
    Responses: Letters;        {Valid responses}
    Prompt: Sentence;          {Message to user}
    Answer: char;              {Answer from user}

  procedure Instructions;
  begin {stub}
  end;

  function AskUser (Message: Sentence; Valids: Letters): char;

   {Written by: XXXXXXXXX XX/XX/XX}
   {Purpose:    To ask the user to respond}
   {Parameters: Message - input, a string to be displayed}
   {            Valids - input, a set of valid responses}

   var
    Keystroke: char;            {User's response}

  begin {AskUser}
   Write(Message);
   Readln(KeyStroke);
    while not (Keystroke in Valids) do
      begin
        Write('*** Invalid response, please reenter: ');
        Readln(KeyStroke);
      end; {while}
    AskUser := Keystroke
  end; {AskUser}

begin {Ask}

{*** Print instructions}

  Instructions;

{*** Show typical "yes/no" setup}

  Responses := ['Y', 'y', 'N', 'n'];
  Prompt := 'Do you wish to continue (Y,N)? ';

  Answer := AskUser(Prompt, Responses);
  Writeln('Your answer was: ', Answer);
```

Figure 5-10 Using a set to validate input (continues next page).

```
{*** Show sample menu setup}

  Writeln('S(top the process)');
  Writeln('R(estart the process)');
  Writeln('C(ontinue the process)');

  Answer := AskUser('Selection: ', ['S', 's', 'R', 'r', 'C', 'c']);
  Writeln('Your answer was: ', Answer);

{*** Stop program}

end.
```

SAMPLE INPUT AND OUTPUT

```
Do you wish to continue (Y,N)? q
*** Invalid response, please reenter: w
*** Invalid response, please reenter: y
Your answer was: y
S(top the process)
R(estart the process)
C(ontinue the process)
Selection: y
* * * Invalid response, please reenter: n
* * * Invalid response, please reenter: s
Your answer was: s
```

Figure 5-10   (continued)

```
type
  PersonalData = record
      Name: string[50];
      Phone: string[12]
    end;
var
  Friend: PersonalData;
```

Suppose that in our program (and not in a "with Friend do" construct) we unintentionally omit the prefix and write

```
Name := 'Joan Smith';
```

One of two things happens:

  (a) If there is no string variable Name in the program, then the compiler reports that "Name " is not declared.
  (b) If there is a string variable Name in the program, then the compiler does not report any problem. This could cause the program to act erroneously without causing a compiler or run-time error. This kind of bug can be very hard to locate.

3. The preceding tip raises a very subtle point. It is legal to have a program containing these declarations:

```
type
   String20 = string[20];
   InputRecord = record
        Name: String20;
        Age: integer
      end;
var
   Person: InputRecord;
   Name: String20;
   Age: integer;
```

The identifiers Name and Age are not considered to be duplicates because the actual names of the fields within the record are

```
Person.Name
Person.Age
```

Inside a *with* statement, as indicated by tip number 1, the field name would take precedence over the variable name. Thus, the output of the fragment

```
Person.Name := 'Sam';
Name := 'Sue';
with Person do
  Name := 'Mary';
Writeln(Name, ' ', Person.Name)
```

would consist of "Sue" and "Mary".

Our defensive programming tip is to try to avoid this situation because it has the potential for confusion. Do not include a field name and a variable name that are the same.

Note. On the other hand, using identical field names within two different record structures can be appropriate. For example, this might be useful:

```
type
   String20 = string[20];
   InputRecord = record
        Name: String20;
        Score1, Score2, Score3: integer
      end;
   OutputRecord = record
        Name: String20;
        Total: integer
      end;
```

---

4. We must take care to use the file designator in all of our Read and Write statements that are intended to work with a file. If we omit the file designator, then we will read from the keyboard and we will write to the display screen.

5. We must be sure to use a subscript when dealing with a field of one element of an array of records. Suppose that we have declared the array of records

```
Friends: array[1..10] of PersonalData;
```

It would be an error to attempt to refer to one of the elements as in the following example:

```
Friends.Name := 'Joan Smith'
```

The compiler detects and reports this error.

6. We must use a named type when passing a record as a parameter to a subprogram. The compiler detects an attempt to declare a parameter as a record in the heading of a procedure or function.

7. When we specify a range of values, we must use two dots as in

```
5..99
```

A common mistake is to use three dots instead of two, as we do when using ellipses in composition. Also, some electronic spreadsheets allow the use of three dots to specify ranges of rows or columns. An example of the misuse of range specification is the following:

```
if 'C' in ['A'...'F'] then
   Writeln('You won''t see this message!')
```

The compiler detects this error.

8. When we wish to specify a range of characters, we must use single quotes around the characters at the beginning and end of the range as in the example:

```
'A'..'F'
```

Suppose that we omit the quotes, as in the example:

```
if C in [A .. F] then
   Writeln( 'Will you see this message? ' )
```

One of two things will happen:

(a) If any one of C, A, or F have not been declared as variables, then the compiler reports an undeclared variable error.

(b) If C, A, and F have been declared as variables, then the statement can be legal. For example, if all three have been declared as integer variables and if A has the value 4, C has the value 2, and F has the value 6, then the condition

```
C in [A .. F]
```

is legitimate and has the value of *false*. The main principle that will help us to avoid this kind of situation is the use of meaningful variable names in our programs. It is unlikely the variables C, A, and F would be the best choices.

9. Two sets must have the same base type in order for them to be used together in set operations. For example, we cannot construct the set union

```
[1, 2, 3] + ['A', 'B', 'C']
```

The compiler detects this type incompatibility.

10. Input and output of sets as text is not allowed. If we attempt to print a set as in the example

```
Writeln([1, 2, 3])
```

the compiler detects the error.

11. Use of the set membership condition *in* requires that the element being tested be of the base type of the set. Thus, the condition

```
1 in ['A' .. 'F']
```

is not *false*, it is illegal. The compiler usually detects this error.

12. We must remember the significance of using single quotes. We have already discussed this point in DPT number 7. But for reemphasis, remember

[X, Y, Z] is different from ['X', 'Y', 'Z']

13. We must be aware of the restrictions that apply to the use of sets. First, the base type of the set must be *integer*, *boolean*, *char*, or any of the other types that are discussed in Section 5-3. By default, THINK Pascal permits at most 256 items in a set and, when using integers in sets, we must use values between 0 and 255, inclusive. Because of this restriction, the following declaration is illegal:

```
A = set of integer;
```

THINK does give us the capability of building an integer set containing integer values outside of the range of 0 to 255. Checking the Large Sets box in the Compile Options selection of the Project menu allows us a range for integer sets from -32768 to 32767 (the full range of integers). With this option enabled, the declaration

```
A = set of integer;
```

would then be legal.

Choosing the larger integer range has the disadvantage of taking up about 8,100 more memory cells than using the 0 to 255 range, leaving less memory available for other purposes (such as for arrays). So we only use the larger range when it is truly required.

REVIEW

Terms and Concepts

base type
binary file
difference (–)
element
empty set
field
in

intersection (*)
member
record
set
subset (<, <=, >, >=)
union (+)
with

Pascal Syntax

Records

1. Define a record structure in the type section:

```
type
   identifier = record
        list of field declarations
      end;
```

2. Declare a variable to have a record type in the var section:

```
var
   variable name: record type name;
```

3. Refer to a single field of a single record:

record variable name.field name

4. Process a single record using the *with-do* construct:

```
with record variable name do
  begin
      list of statements
  end
```

5. Declare an array of records in the var section; for example:

```
Friends: array[1..10] of PersonalData;
```

6. Refer to a field of an element of an array of records, as shown in the example:

```
Friends[5].Name
```

7. Pass a record as a parameter using a named type, as shown in the example:

```
procedure Print(List: PersonalData);
```

Files of Records

1. Define a type for a file of records:

file type name = file of *record type name*;

2. Define a file designator for a file of records:

file designator: *file type name*;

3. Use Read and Write for input and output activities with a file of records:

Read(*file designator, record variable name*)

Write(*file designator, record variable name*)

Sets

1. Define a constant set using square brackets, as shown in the example:

[1, 3, 5]

2. Declare a set type in the type section, as shown in the example:

SmallNumbersSet = **set of** 1..99;

3. Refer to the empty set by

[]

REVIEW

4. If A and B are of the same set type, then the set operations are

Assignment	A := B
Union	A + B
Intersection	A * B
Difference	A – B
Equality tests	A = B
	A <> B
Subset tests	A < B
	A <= B
	A > B
	A >= B

5. If A is of set type and X has the base type of A, then we can test to see if X is a member of A with the Boolean expression

```
X in A
```

6. If X, Y, and Z are elements of the same base type, then we can construct the set containing the values of the variables

```
[X, Y, Z]
```

DPT

1. Do not use Readln and Writeln with nontext files.
2. Be sure to use the "." when dealing with a field of a record when not within a *with-do* construct.
3. Do not use duplicate names for variables and field names.
4. Make sure that you use the file designator in your Read and Write statements that are intended to work with a file.
5. Be sure to use a subscript when dealing with a field of one element of an array of records.
6. Use a named type when passing a record as a parameter to a subprogram.
7. When specifying a range of values, use two dots as in: 1..99; do not use three dots.
8. When specifying a range of characters, use single quotes around the characters at the beginning and end of the range, as in 'A'..'F'.
9. Two sets must be of the same base type in order for them to be involved in set operations.
10. Input and output of sets as text are not allowed.
11. Use of the set membership condition *in* requires that the element being tested be of the base type of the set.
12. Note that [X,Y,Z] is different from ['X','Y','Z'].
13. There can be no more than 256 elements in a set unless the range is expanded on the compiler options screen.

EXERCISES

1. Write declarations or expressions to represent each of the following:
   (a) The field Phone of the record variable Friend is assigned the value '555-1212'.
   (b) The record type Complex is to consist of the two real number fields RealPart and ImaginaryPart.
   (c) The variable Number is of type Complex.
   (d) If the field Name of the record variable Friend is equal to 'Joan Smith', then print "Found".
   (e) The set consisting of the numbers 1, 2, and 3.
   (f) The set consisting of the characters '1', '2', and '3'.
   (g) If the value of the variable N is a member of the set consisting of the numbers between 3 and 9, inclusive, then print "Yes".
   (h) The variable A is to have sets of characters as its values.

2. Write a procedure or function for each of the following:
   (a) Given a record variable of type PersonalData, print a detail line consisting of the phone number, a colon, and the name.
   (b) Given a record variable of type PersonalData, get input from the user for the name and phone number.
   (c) Given a record variable of type Complex (see Exercise 1(b)), calculate the sum of the squares of the real and imaginary parts.
   (d) Given a character set variable, ask the user for characters to be members of the set.
   (e) Given a set of characters and one character that is a member of the set, ask the user to enter a character that is a member of the set. Check for valid input and return a value of *true* if the user enters the given character and return a value of *false* otherwise. (This might be part of a program for administering a multiple-choice examination.)

3. Extend the record structure of Figure 5-9 by adding the fields:

   Address (string of size 80)
   Month of birth (integer)

4. Write a Pascal program to interactively build a file of records of the form:

   COMPANY

Name	(string)
Address	(string)
City	(string)
State	(string)
ZIP code	(string)
Number of employees	(integer)

5. Write a Pascal program to deal with the file created by Exercise 4. The program should accept the company name as input and should print the number of employees of the company.

6. (a) Write a Pascal program to list the contents of the file from Exercise 4 on the printer. You should use appropriate headings.
   (b) Modify the program of part (a) to also print the following summary information:
      (1) The number of companies.
      (2) The percentage of large companies (more than 700 employees).

(3) The company with the most employees and the number of employees.
(4) The number of the companies that are New York (state = NY) companies.
(5) The California company (state = CA) with the most employees (assume there is at least one California company).
(6) Repeat (5) without the assumption; if there is no California company, the program should say so.

7. Using the file from Exercise 4 as input, write a program to create an output file containing only the name and number of employees for those companies from North Carolina (state = NC) employing 50 or fewer employees.

8. Write a program to consist of two loops:

   First loop: Read integers between 50 and 100 and store them in a set A. The loop should terminate when the user enters a 0. Use set union to add to the set.

   Second loop: Read integers and tell the user whether or not each integer is in the set.

9. Write a program to check that THINK does not allow you to pass set parameters in a manner similar to the statement:

   procedure Check(A: **set of** char);

10. Modify AskUser so that it considers a user's input valid only if it exactly one character. [Hint: Read the user's response into a string variable and check its length before comparing it to the set of valid responses.] Write a driver program to test the modified AskUser. What happens if the user just taps Return? Enters a very long string? What other changes might you make to AskUser to make it even more particular about the input it will consider valid?

11. Write a calculator program that provides the following menu:

    ```
    O P T I O N S

    A(dd two numbers)
    S(ubtract two numbers)
    Q(uit)
    ```

    Use the AskUser function to get the user request for a menu option.
    Use a case statement for the different menu options.

12. Write a program to allow the user to complete (in any order) a list of five unrepeatable tasks:

    ```
    F(ill in a blank)
    S(olve an addition problem)
    G(uess a number)
    N(ame a famous person)
    R(ead a joke)
    ```

    Use the set difference operator to reduce the set of options, and when there are no more options left, quit. Hint: There are no options left when the set of options is equal to [ ].

13. Write a program to build a set of all prime numbers between numbers N and M input by the user. The numbers N and M must be in the range from 0 to 255, inclusive. Then, in a loop, let the user enter a number and have the program say whether the number is a prime or is a composite. Hint: Use set union to build the set incrementally.

14. Write a test plan for the following exercises:
    - **(a)** Exercise 2(c)
    - **(b)** Exercise 2(d)
    - **(c)** Exercise 5
    - **(d)** Exercise 6(a)
    - **(e)** Exercise 6(b)(3)
    - **(f)** Exercise 6(b)(4)
    - **(g)** Exercise 6(b)(6)
    - **(h)** Exercise 8
    - **(i)** Exercise 12

5-3 USER-DEFINED DATA TYPES

Pascal provides a powerful and flexible means of dealing with data in the form of user-defined data types. We have seen some examples of this facility when we dealt with arrays, records, files, and sets. In this section, we discuss some additional possibilities for structuring data through data typing.

Defining the structure of data is a significant part of the total program design effort. Choosing an appropriate structure for the data can make writing the program more straightforward than choosing an unnatural, awkward one. For example, we could deal with time in minutes and seconds by using two integer variables Minutes and Seconds, or we could use a single real variable Minutes. If we have to perform time arithmetic, we will appreciate having chosen the latter data structure. (However, due to the limitation of real accuracy, we might have to use the former structure in a program where accuracy is critical.)

In this section, we deal with scalar types, enumerated types, ordinal types, subrange types, type checking, and more information on records. We also illustrate input/output error trapping for two common situations.

Scalar Types

Pascal provides the standard **scalar types**: *integer, real, boolean,* and *char*. All of these except *real* are also referred to as **ordinal types** because it makes sense to think of them as being in order, one after another. Ordinal types are sometimes referred to as **enumerated types**. When we are looking at an element of an ordinal type, it is meaningful to talk about the previous and the next element, for all but the first and last elements. For example:

TYPE	ELEMENT	PREVIOUS	NEXT
Integer	4	3	5
Boolean	false	—	true
Char	'd'	'c'	'e'

Pascal provides three built-in functions to help in dealing with ordinal types. The function **Ord** tells us the serial order of an element within its ordinal type. If X is an element of an ordinal type, then Ord(X) is an integer value expressing its position within the type. In general, Ord begins its count at 0 rather than 1. For integers, Ord(X) is X itself. The following table gives some example values of Ord:

TYPE	ELEMENT	Ord(Element)
Integer	0	0
Integer	1	1
Integer	−4	−4
Boolean	false	0
Boolean	true	1
Char	'a'	97
Char	'A'	65
Char	3	51

For an integer, Ord acts as an identity. The values of Ord for *false* and *true* are 0 and 1, respectively. The values of Ord for char variables depend upon the particular character code set that is used for each implementation of Pascal. The values in the previous table for the char variables are those for the Macintosh, which uses a version of the popular character code set called **ASCII**, the character code set used on most microcomputers. (See Appendix D.) Figure 5-11 shows a program that allows you to print the Mac's character code set for your reference.

For elements of *char* type, the **Chr** function is the inverse of the Ord function. That is, for any char variable X:

```
Chr(Ord(X)) = X
```

Also, for any integer variable I that has a value from 0 to 255:

```
Ord(Chr(I)) = I
```

Because of the order that is associated with ordinal types, we can use the relational operators:

```
=    <>    <    >    >=    <=
```

These operators behave in the manner that the Ord function dictates. For example, if X and Y are elements of the same ordinal type, then X < Y is *true* if and only if Ord(X) < Ord(Y) is *true*. One concrete example is the ethical inequality false < true. You can test this inequality with the small program shown as Figure 5-12.

Pascal provides two additional functions that can be used with ordinal types: **Pred** and **Succ**. For any element X of an ordinal type that is not the first element of the type, Pred(X) is the element of the ordinal type that precedes X. The relationship between Pred and Ord is

```
Ord(Pred(X)) = Ord(X) - 1
```

Pred(X) is not meaningful when X is the first element of the ordinal type.

Note that if X is an element of any ordinal type except *integer*, then X is the first element of the type if and only if Ord(X) = 0. Thus, when moving "backwards" through an ordinal type using the Pred function, we should stop when Ord returns the value 0.

For any element X of an ordinal type that is not the last element of the type, Succ(X) is the element of the ordinal type that follows X. The relationship between Succ and Ord is

```
program CodeSet;

{Written by: XXXXXXXXX XX/XX/XX}
{Purpose:    To print the ASCII character set from position 27 onward}

    var
      I: integer;                      {Loop index}
      Report: text;                    {Name for printer}

begin {CodeSet}

{*** Print headings on the printer}

    Rewrite(Report, 'Printer:');
    Writeln(Report, ' ' : 30, 'ASCII Code Set');
    Writeln(Report, ' ' : 30, '--------------');
    Writeln(Report);
    Writeln(Report);
    Writeln(Report, ' ' : 28, 'Ord Value', ' ' : 6, 'Character');
    Writeln(Report);

{*** Generate the ASCII set}

    for I := 27 to 255 do
      Writeln(Report, ' ' : 31, I : 3, ' ' : 13, Chr(I));
    Close(Report)

{*** Stop program}

    Writeln;
    Writeln('ASCII list printed')
end.
```

Figure 5-11 Printing the ASCII code.

```
program Ethics;

{Written by: XXXXXXXXX XX/XX/XX}
{Purpose:    To illustrate the ethical inequality}

begin {Ethics}
  if (false < true) then
    Writeln('All is well.')
  else
    Writeln('Something is wrong.');
end.
```

Figure 5-12 An ethics lesson.

```
Ord(Succ(X)) = Ord(X) + 1
```

Succ(X) is not meaningful when X is the last element of the ordinal type.

Note that we cannot detect the last element of an ordinal type in as easy a manner as for the first element of the type. However, we can define an integer constant to be the Ord of the last item of the type we are manipulating, and match Ord(X) against it to determine if we are at the last element.

User-Defined Ordinal Types

Pascal allows for **user-defined ordinal types**, declared by naming the elements of the type in the order they are to have, from first element to last. For example, one can specify a type consisting of adventure game character classes as follows:

```
type
    Classes = (Fighter, Thief, Paladin, Monk, Cleric, MagicUser);
```

Note that the identifier Fighter, for example, represents a **constant** of the type Classes. THINK does not allow any duplication of identifiers within a program unit. So we could not use the type Classes as just specified along with any variable called Fighter within the same program unit. We can declare variables to have a user-defined ordinal type, as shown in the example:

```
var
    Class: Classes;
```

The variables and constants of a user-defined ordinal type can be used in a manner similar to other ordinal types, but with some restrictions (discussed in what follows).

As another example, we could define

```
type
    Days = (Sun, Mon, Tue, Wed, Thr, Fri, Sat);
var
    Today: Days;
```

Assignment. If Class is a variable of the type Classes, then we can use the assignment statement

```
Class := Cleric
```

If PrimaryClass and SecondaryClass are two variables of the type Classes, then we can use the assignment statement

```
SecondaryClass := PrimaryClass
```

Comparison. If Class is a variable of the type Classes, then we can use any of the comparisons

```
Class = Human;
Class <> Human;
Class < Human;
Class <= Human;
Class > Human;
Class >= Human
```

If Today and PayDay are two variables of the type Days, then we can use any of the comparisons

```
Today = PayDay;
Today <> PayDay;
Today < PayDay;
Today <= PayDay;
Today > PayDay;
Today >= PayDay
```

Use of the Functions Ord, Pred, and Succ. If Today is a variable of type Days, then we can use any of the expressions

`Ord(Today)`	
`Pred(Today)`	if the value of Today is not Sun
`Succ(Today)`	if the value of Today is not Sat

For example,

`Ord(Sun)`	is 0
`Ord(Red)`	is 4
`Pred(Sat)`	is Fri
`Succ(Wed)`	is Thr

Retyping. For the char type, the Ord function has an inverse function, Chr: Ord('A') = 65, and Chr(65) = 'A'. In THINK Pascal, the inverse function for Ord with user-defined types is the name of the type used as if it were a predefined function. It has one parameter, a legal position within that type. For example, if we define:

type
    Days = (Sun, Mon, Tue, Wed, Thr, Fri, Sat);

then Days(0) is Sun, Days(4) is Thr, and Days(6) is Sat. This THINK Pascal feature is called **retyping** and is typically not found in other versions of Pascal.

Input and Output. In standard Pascal, we cannot use any of the functions Read, Write, Readln, or Writeln with variables or constants of a user-defined ordinal type. THINK Pascal, though, does allow us to use these functions with user-defined ordinal types. For instance, if we have these declarations:

type
    Classes = (Fighter, Thief, Paladin, Monk, Cleric, MagicUser);

var
    ClassName: Classes;

the following statements are examples of legal THINK Pascal I/O statements that employ user-defined enumerated types:

```
Writeln(Fighter);
Writeln(ClassName);
Read(ClassName)
```

Notes

1. Notice that Fighter is not in quotes; 'Fighter' is a string, not a value of Classes.
2. When reading a value into ClassName, THINK looks for a value of Classes. It starts where the last Read or Readln statement left off, and then skips over any blanks or end-of-line characters. Then it starts looking at characters. If the first character encountered matches the first character of one of the type values, it reads the next input character. If these two characters match the first two characters of (at least) one of the type values, it reads the next input character, and so on, until it reads a character that doesn't match. It then takes all the characters up to *but not including* the last one read, and determines if that character sequence matches one of the type values. If so, that value is placed into ClassName; if not, a run time error occurs.

Indexes of arrays. We can employ the constants of a user-defined ordinal type as the indexes of an array. For example, to add a description when printing a name, such as "Kragthorn the Wise", we could initialize an array as follows:

```
type
    Classes = (Fighter, Thief, Paladin, Monk, Cleric, MagicUser);
    ClassesStrings = array[Classes] of string[30];

var
    PrintTitle: ClassesStrings;

begin
    PrintTitle[Fighter] := 'the Fierce';
    PrintTitle[Thief] := 'the Sneaky';
    PrintTitle[Paladin] := 'the Crusader';
    PrintTitle[Monk] := 'the Holy';
    PrintTitle[Cleric] := 'the Wise';
    PrintTitle[MagicUser] := 'Doctor of Illusionary Sciences';
```

We shall provide more details on arrays in Chapter 6.

For Loop Index. We can employ the constants of a user-defined ordinal type to control a *for* loop. For example, suppose that we have defined the ordinal type DaysOfWeek as follows:

```
type
    DaysOfWeek = (Sun, Mon, Tue, Wed, Thr, Fri, Sat);
```

and defined an array to hold strings for the days of the week spelled out (for printing purposes):

```
    NameArray = array[DaysOfWeek] of string;
```

We initialize this array to the days of the week (as strings) using this procedure:

```
procedure Initialize(var PrintName: NameArray);

{Written by: XXXXXXXXX XX/XX/XX}
{Purpose:    To initialize PrintName array}

begin {Initialize}
  PrintName[Sun] := 'Sunday';
  PrintName[Mon] := 'Monday';
  PrintName[Tue] := 'Tuesday';
  PrintName[Wed] := 'Wednesday';
  PrintName[Thr] := 'Thursday';
  PrintName[Fri] := 'Friday';
  PrintName[Sat] := 'Saturday'
end; {Initialize}
```

If we wish the user to input the amount of sales for each day of a week in order to compute a total, we could use the following code fragment (assuming that the variables DaysSales and WeekTotal have both been declared as *real* and that the variable Day has been declared to have type DaysOfWeek):

```
WeekTotal := 0.0;
for Day := Sun to Sat do
  begin
     Write('Enter the sales for ', PrintName[Day], ': $');
     Readln(DaysSales);
     WeekTotal := WeekTotal + DaysSales
  end; {for}
```

If we used "for Day := Mon to Fri do", then this fragment would ask for sales only for the days Monday through Friday.

In summary, we have seen that user-defined ordinal types allow the programmer to make clear his or her intentions within the code of the program. This clarity can make the jobs of program design, coding, debugging, and program maintenance easier and less time consuming.

Subrange Types

Pascal allows us to define ordinal types that contain part of the values of a given ordinal type lying between two values. This construction of a **subrange** type can be accomplished using built-in ordinal types or user-defined ordinal types. We specify the subrange values by means of the construction:

```
first value in the subrange..last value in the subrange
```

Some examples:

`2..5`	represents the subrange of integers 2, 3, 4, and 5
`'d'..'g'`	represents the subrange of chars 'd', 'e', 'f', and 'g'
`Thief..Cleric`	represents the subrange of the type Classes defined previously and consists of Thief, Paladin, Monk, and Cleric

We have seen subranges used in our preliminary discussions of arrays wherein we defined the type:

```
type
    IntegerArray = array[1..1000] of integer;
```

In this case, the subrange 1..1000 is used to limit the legal indexes for the arrays of the type. This use of the subrange concept is typical: to limit the values that can be used for a given situation. For example, in adventure games, characters have certain assigned qualities, such as dexterity, wisdom, and intelligence. In some such games, the values of these qualities are obtained from a roll of an 18-sided die. In addition, values under 6 are considered to be too low to be useful. So, we have a working rule that the values of these character qualities are to lie between the values 6 and 18, inclusive. This concept can be embodied in a Pascal program via a type declared as follows:

```
type
    RolledValue = 6..18;
```

We can then declare character qualities as variables of type RolledValue as follows:

```
var
    Dexterity: RolledValue;
    Wisdom: RolledValue;
    Intelligence: RolledValue;
```

We could accomplish the same result without an explicit type name by means of the lines of code:

```
var
    Dexterity: 6..18;
    Wisdom: 6..18;
    Intelligence: 6..18;
```

We consider the use of a named type to be better programming style because it allows the use of the variables Dexterity, Wisdom, and Intelligence to be passed as parameters. Use of a named type also makes it relatively easy to change the subrange (say, to 7..18).

Type and Range Checking

Pascal provides for two levels of checking for the legality of certain activities such as value assignment, input/output, array referencing, and parameter passing. At compile time, Pascal performs type checking in which each instance of the previously listed activities is checked to see if the types involved are legal for the context.

Earlier in this book, we discovered that the compiler does not allow an assignment statement that has an integer variable on the left side and a real variable on the right side. This was our first example of **type checking**. As programmers, we should be grateful that the compiler attempts to stop us from doing things that are likely to cause the program to produce erroneous results. As we have introduced different data types in this book, we have attempted to indicate what activities can be legitimately performed with each type.

In general, activities performed with objects of subrange types of the same base type pass through type checking. For example, if X is a variable of type RolledValue (defined previously as a subrange of the integers from 6 to 18) and if Y is a variable of type *integer* or any subrange of the *integer* type, then the compiler deems the assignment statement:

```
X := Y
```

legal.

In other type-checking activities, the compiler only allows variables of a named type to be passed as parameters. Also, indexes of arrays must be of the same base type as that used in the declaration of the array.

The other kind of checking occurs at both compile time and run time and is called **range checking**. The main purpose of having subrange types in Pascal is to allow for the detection of invalid values for variables that can occur as the program runs. The invalid values can result from bugs in the program or they can result from invalid user input.

In THINK Pascal, the default compiler option is for run-time range checking not to be performed; that is why we have been turning on the range-check option in all our programs that use arrays. We strongly suggest that you activate range checking for all programs under development that use arrays or subranges. If program speed is a concern, the range checking can be turned off once the program has been completely debugged. (Programs without range checking run faster than those with range checking active.)

The following are some of the common violations of range restrictions:

1. *Array Index Out of Range.* If we have declared that the array X has indexes that are integers in the range from 3 to 6, inclusive, then the array references X[7] and X[2] are invalid. These two errors are detected by the compiler whether run-time range checking is active or inactive. A slightly different set of circumstances is found in the following lines:

```
y := 7;
z := x[y]
```

This range violation is not detected at compile time, but is detected at run time if range checking has been activated.

2. *Assignment Outside of Subrange.* Suppose that the type Classes and a subrange type Elite have been declared as follows:

```
type
    Classes = (Fighter, Thief, Paladin, Monk, Cleric, MagicUser);
    Elite   = Thief..Cleric;
```

Also, suppose that the variable HiClass has been declared to be of type Elite. Then the assignment statement

```
HiClass := Fighter;
```

is a range violation that is detected at run time if run-time error checking is activated.

3. *Numeric Value Out of Range.* If real number values exceed the maximum possible value, then a run-time error occurs whether or not range checking is activated. For example, the following statement results in a run-time error:

```
X := Exp(1000)
```

In this statement, we are attempting to produce a value of order of magnitude 1 followed by 435 zeros.

4. *Illegal Value for Function.* Recall that the Chr function is defined for the ordinal values of the character set used in the implementation of Pascal, in our case, the ASCII set, which has Ord values from 0 to 255. The expression Chr(300) is illegal, yet in THINK Pascal it does not result in a run-time error, even if range checking has been turned on. (A result is returned, but its value is meaningless.) So be careful!

Examples of the same kind are the attempts to refer to the predecessor of the first element or the successor of the last element of an ordinal type. The expressions Pred(false) and Succ(true) are illegal and result in meaningless values being returned.

5. *Input of an Integer of Overlarge Magnitude.* If the user responds to a Read or Readln of an integer with a value that is above maxint or below −maxint, there are two possibilities. If checking for integer overflow has not been turned on, an incorrect value is stored in the variable; no run-time error occurs. If overflow checking is turned on, a run-time error results. This error can be trapped (i.e., noticed and dealt with within the program); we discuss error trapping in more detail in what follows.

Error Trapping

There are two circumstances that are quite aggravating when dealing with files. If you have been running the example programs of this chapter, you have probably experienced both of these situations.

The first situation occurs when you are asked for the name of an existing file. If you make a spelling mistake in entering the name of the file, the program **aborts** with a "file not found" run-time error.

The second situation can cause you to lose valuable files. It arises when you are asked for the name of a file that is to be created. If a file by the same name already exists, then it is deleted and any information that was in the file is lost. If you accidently enter the name of one of your existing program or data files, your file will be destroyed.

THINK Pascal provides a solution to both of these problems by means of **error trapping**. By default, THINK Pascal aborts the program when an input/output error is detected, but this can be changed by using the predefined procedure IOCheck. IOCheck takes one Boolean parameter. If it is set to *false*, then there is no program abort when input/output errors are detected; if the parameter is *true*, then the program does abort when input/output errors are detected.

In addition, THINK Pascal provides a built-in function IOResult that indicates the presence of an input/output error when IOCheck(false) has been issued. The values of IOResult are interpreted as follows:

IOResult = 0   means that no input/output error has occurred
IOResult <> 0   means that some input/output error has occurred

By using the compiler directives and the built-in function IOResult, we can cause our programs to behave properly. For example, Figure 5-13 contains a function Exists that will tell if a file with a given name exists on the disk. Also shown in the figure is a procedure

OpenRead that invokes the Exists function. If the file the user specified does not exist, the procedure provides the user another chance to specify the file name.

Any program that reads from a file needs to contain code similar to that in Figure 5-13. The easiest way to accomplish this is to put the code in subprograms, as illustrated in the figure. These subprograms can then be inserted in any program that needs them.

```
function Exists (FileName: string): boolean;

{Written by: XXXXXXXXX XX/XX/XX}
{Purpose:    To check a given file name for existence, using IOCheck}
{            and IOResult}
{Parameters: FileName - input, the name of thefile to be checked}

    var
       DummyFile: text;      {Used to check file name}

    begin {Exist}
       IOCheck(false);                {Turn off error messages}
       Reset(DummyFile, FileName);    {Try to open for input}
       IOCheck(true);                 {Turn on error messages}
       Exists := IOResult = 0;        {Call IOResult function to see if ok}
       if IOResult = 0 then
         Close(DummyFile)             {Don't leave open files about}
    end; {Exists}

procedure OpenRead (var InputFile: text);

{Written by: XXXXXXXXX XX/XX/XX}
{Purpose:    To obtain the name of an existing file from the user,}
{            and open it for reading.}
{Parameters: InputFile - the file to be opened}
{Functions used:  Exists, to see if the file exists}

       var
          FileName: string;      {Name of file on disk}
          ValidName: boolean;    {Name entered exists}

    begin {OpenRead}
      repeat
        Write('Enter the filename: ');
        Readln(FileName);
        ValidName := Exists(FileName);
        if not ValidName then
           Writeln(' *** File does not exist')
      until ValidName;
      Reset(InputFile, FileName);    {Open the file for output}
    end; {OpenRead}
```

Figure 5-13 Trapping I/O errors.

> **Note.** OpenRead as shown in Figure 5-13 opens a text file. For any other file type, you would simply change the parameter type to match the file to be opened.

This type of module is sometimes referred to as a "utility" module. It can be used in a large variety of programs. Another useful utility would be OpenWrite, to open a file for output. Appendix C (Utilities) contains such a module, along with the OpenRead and Exists presented here.

> **Note.** Notice that the function Exists closes the file "AnyFile" after it checks for its existence. If you use this function in your programs, do not leave out that step. (If you do leave it out, you may exceed the limit on how many files can be open at once, even in a program that only uses one or two files.)

More on Records

In this section, we look at a slightly richer record structure that combines some of the ideas that we have been developing. In our example, we use a record structure that represents some of the attributes of an adventure game character. Our record structure is defined as follows:

```
Character = record
            Name: String20;
            Class: Classes;
            Dexterity: RolledValue;
            Constitution: RolledValue;
            Wisdom: RolledValue;
            Strength: RolledValue;
            Intelligence: RolledValue;
            Charisma: RolledValue
    end;
```

The type String20, Classes, and RolledValue must have been defined prior to defining the type Character.

The name of the character is a string of up to 20 characters and would include the examples: Gandalf the Grey, Garvin, and Mirro the Ugly. The type Classes is the same as discussed previously:

```
Classes = (Fighter, Thief, Paladin, Monk, Cleric, MagicUser);
```

The type RolledValue is a subrange type that was also discussed previously:

```
RolledValue = 6..18;
```

The other fields of the record represent qualities of the character that determine the limits of the character's activities during a game. In the two programs that comprise Figures 5-14 and 5-15, we provide the means to build a file of characters and to search that file.

The Build program of Figure 5-14 makes considerable use of the random-number function Random to produce the simulated dice rolls and also to choose the character class for each character. The simulated dice rolls are supposed to be random numbers in the range from 6 to 18, inclusive. To get the random numbers in the range that we want (6 to 18), we use the expression

```
abs(Random mod HighRollLess5) + 6
```

where HighRollLess5 is 13.

In order to choose a random member of the enumerated type Classes, we begin at the first element (Fighter) and, at random, execute 0 or more instances of the Succ function to arrive at a random element in the enumerated type. Note that because the number of elements in the type is 6, we want to execute between 0 and 5 instances of Succ. This is accomplished via the lines

```
Class := Fighter;
for I := 1 to abs(Random mod ClassesSize) do
   Class := Succ(Class)
```

where ClassesSize has the value 6. Input/output error trapping is utilized via the Exists function and OpenWrite procedure to prevent the user from inadvertently deleting a file.

```
program Build;

{Written by:   XXXXXXXXX XX/XX/XX}
{Purpose:      To build a file of game characters}
{Procedures used: Instructions - to print instructions}
{Functions used:  Exists - to check for existence of a file}

   const
      EndOfData = '$END';              {Terminating value}

      ClassesSize = 6;                 {Number of classes}
      HighRollLess5 = 13;              {Highest possible roll minus 5}

   type
      String20 = string[20];
      Classes = (Fighter, Thief, Paladin, Monk, Cleric, MagicUser);
      RolledValue = 6..18;

      Character = record
         Name: String20;
         Class: Classes;
         Dexterity: RolledValue;
         Constitution: RolledValue;
         Wisdom: RolledValue;
         Strength: RolledValue;
         Intelligence: RolledValue;
         Charisma: RolledValue
      end;
```

Figure 5-14 A comprehensive example: build a file (continues next page).

```
      FileType = file of Character;

   var
      MyChar: Character;                  {Instance of record}
      AnyFile: FileType;                  {File designator}
      I: integer;                         {Loop index}

   procedure Instructions;
   begin {stub}
   end;

{function Exists, as shown in Figure 5-13, is inserted here}

{procedure OpenWrite, as shown in Appendix C, is inserted here; with}
{type text changed to type FileType}

begin {Build}

{*** Print instructions and initialize}

   Instructions;
   GetDateTime(RandSeed);    {Seed the random number generator}

{*** Ask the user for the filename and open the file}

   OpenWrite(AnyFile);

{*** Get names for file}

   with MyChar do
      begin
         repeat
            Writeln;
            Write('Enter name ($END to quit): ');
            Readln(Name);
            if Name <> EndOfData then
               begin
                  Class := Fighter;
                  for I := 1 to abs(Random mod ClassesSize) do
                     Class := Succ(Class);
                  Writeln('The class is: ', Class);
                  Dexterity := abs(Random mod HighRollLess5) + 6;
                  Writeln('The dexterity is: ', Dexterity);
                  Constitution := abs(Random mod HighRollLess5) + 6;
                  Writeln('The constitution is: ', Constitution);
                  Wisdom := abs(Random mod HighRollLess5) + 6;
                  Writeln('The wisdom is: ', Wisdom);
                  Strength := abs(Random mod HighRollLess5) + 6;
                  Writeln('The strength is: ', Strength);
```

Figure 5-14 (continues next page)

```
                Intelligence := abs(Random mod HighRollLess5) + 6;
                Writeln('The intelligence is: ', Intelligence);
                Charisma := abs(Random mod HighRollLess5) + 6;
                Writeln('The charisma is: ', Charisma);
                Write(AnyFile, MyChar)
            end {if}
        until Name = EndOfData
      end; {with}

  {*** Close the file}

    Close(AnyFile);

  {*** Stop program}

  end.
```

SAMPLE INPUT AND OUTPUT

```
    Enter the filename: CharacterFile
    File already exists. Delete(Y,N)? Y

    Enter name ($END to quit): Kragthorn
    The class is: Cleric
    The dexterity is: 6
    The constitution is: 7
    The wisdom is: 12
    The strength is: 15
    The intelligence is: 10
    The charisma is: 11

    Enter name ($END to quit): Nephron
    The class is: MagicUser
    The dexterity is: 16
    The constitution is: 18
    The wisdom is: 15
    The strength is: 14
    The intelligence is: 17
    The charisma is: 11

    Enter name ($END to quit): $END
```

Figure 5-14 (continued)

The program Search of Figure 5-15 allows the user to specify the name of a character and receive the other information associated with the character. The procedure Initialize is once again used to establish the array of print names for the character classes. Input/output error trapping is used to detect the situation where the user specifies a file that does not exist. The file-searching technique is similar to that used earlier in this chapter.

```
program Search;

{Written by: XXXXXXXXX XX/XX/XX}
{Purpose:    To search for a character and display its information}
{Procedures used: Instructions - to print instructions}
{Functions used:  Exists - to check for existence of a file}

   type
      String20 = string[20];
      Classes = (Fighter, Thief, Paladin, Monk, Cleric, MagicUser);
      RolledValue = 6..18;

      Character = record
         Name: String20;
         Class: Classes;
         Dexterity: RolledValue;
         Constitution: RolledValue;
         Wisdom: RolledValue;
         Strength: RolledValue;
         Intelligence: RolledValue;
         Charisma: RolledValue
      end;

      FileType = file of Character;

   var
      MyChar: Character;                {Instance of record}
      AnyFile: FileType;                {File designator}
      PrintName: ClassesStrings;        {For printing classes}
      I: integer;                       {Loop index}
      ToFind: string[20];               {Name to find}

{procedure Exists, as shown in Figure 5-13, is inserted here}

{procedure OpenRead, as shown in Figure 5-13, is inserted here with}
{type text changed to type FileType}

begin {Search}

{*** Print instructions and initialize}

   Instructions;

{*** Ask the user for the filename and open the file}

   OpenRead(AnyFile);

{*** Get name from the user}

   Writeln;
   Write('Enter the character''s name: ');
   Readln(ToFind);
```

Figure 5-15 A comprehensive example: search a file (continues next page).

```
{*** Search the file for the name}

  with MyChar do
    begin
        Name := '';            {Null value in case no characters in file}
        while (Name <> ToFind) and (not Eof(AnyFile)) do
          begin
             Read(AnyFile, MyChar);
          end; {while}

{*** Display the results of the search}

        if Name = ToFind then
          begin
            Writeln('The class is: ', Class);
            Writeln('The dexterity is: ', Dexterity);
            Writeln('The constitution is: ', Constitution);
            Writeln('The wisdom is:', Wisdom);
            Writeln('The strength is: ', Strength);
            Writeln('The intelligence is: ', Intelligence);
            Writeln('The charisma is: ', Charisma)
          end
        else
            Writeln('*** Character not found.')
    end; {with}

{*** Close the file}

  Close(AnyFile);

{*** Stop program}

end.
```

SAMPLE INPUT AND OUTPUT

```
Enter the filename: CharactersFile

* * * File does not exist.
Enter the filename: CharacterFile

Enter the character's name: Kragthorn
The class is: Cleric
The dexterity is: 6
The constitution is: 7
The wisdom is: 12
The strength is: 15
The intelligence is: 10
The charisma is: 11
```

Figure 5-15 (continued)

DPT

1. Perhaps the most important defensive programming tip is to make sure that range checking is in effect so the compiler can detect illegal references outside the proper range. Without this checking, almost anything can happen when we make an illegal reference. For example, if we write

```
Y := A[I]
```

and I is out of range, Y's value is totally meaningless. Even worse,

```
A[I] := Y
```

"clobbers" some memory location by placing the value of Y in it. This could, for example, give some other variable the value of Y, give some other variable a meaningless value, or even modify part of the program.

2. We must not use the functions Ord, Pred, or Succ on variables of type *real*. The compiler detects these errors.

3. Do not use Pred on the first element of an ordinal type or Succ on the last element. These may not produce an error message, but they have no reasonable meaning.

4. Do not use duplicate identifiers within a program unit. They produce a compile-time error.

One possibility for violating this rule occurs when we create user-defined ordinal types. For example, suppose we have a type declaration

```
Days = (Sun, Mon, Tue, Wed, Thr, Fri, Sat)
```

Then we cannot use Days or any of Sun, Mon, and so on as variable names. More subtly, we cannot define another type such as

```
Weekdays = (Mon, Tue, Wed, Thr, Fri)
```

The duplicate use of Mon, for example, is illegal. (However, we can define Weekday using the subrange type Mon..Fri, since subranges are portions of other ordinal types.)

5. Use input/output error-trapping techniques for friendlier programs. Remember that the programmer is responsible for the behavior of a program, even when it is being used by a less-than-attentive user.

REVIEW

Terms and Concepts

abort
ASCII
Chr
constant
enumerated type
error trapping
Ord
ordinal type

Pred
range checking
retyping
scalar type
subrange
Succ
type checking
user-defined ordinal types

Pascal Syntax

1. Functions for ordinal types:

   (a) Ord(X) shows the position of X within the type.

   (b) Succ(X) gives the successor of X.

   (c) Pred(X) gives the predecessor of X.

2. Declare user-defined ordinal type by listing the constants of the type, as in this example:

   ```
   type
        Classes = (Fighter, Thief, Paladin, Monk, Cleric, MagicUser);
   ```

3. Specify the limits of a subrange by separating the first and last elements with two dots:

   ```
   first value..last value
   ```

4. IOResult = 0 indicates no error occurred (IOCheck(false) must have been issued).

DPT

1. Use range checking during development.
2. Do not use the functions Ord, Pred, or Succ on variables of type *real*.
3. Do not use Pred on the first element of an ordinal type. Do not use Succ on the last element of an ordinal type.
4. Do not use duplicate identifiers within a program unit.
5. Use input/output error-trapping techniques.

EXERCISES

1. Evaluate the following:
   (a) Ord('b')
   (b) Succ('1')
   (c) Pred(true)
   (d) Ord(-5)
   (e) Succ(Pred('t'))
   (f) Ord(Chr(75))
   (g) Chr(Ord('d'))
   (h) Succ(Chr(68))
   (i) Pred(4)
   (j) Pred('4')
   (k) Succ(9)
   (l) Succ('9')

2. Suppose that we have defined a type as follows:

```
type
   Outcomes = (Lose,Draw,Win);
```

Evaluate the following:

(a) `Ord(Lose)` (b) `Pred(Win)`
(c) `Succ(Draw)` (d) `Lose < Draw`
(e) `Win = Lose`

3. Write an integer function Roll that returns a random integer between 6 and 18, inclusive.
4. Write an integer function Roll(Low, High: integer) that returns a random integer between Low and High, inclusive.
5. Either of the functions of Exercises 3 and 4 would prove useful for the program of Figure 5-13. Discuss pros and cons of each of the functions and choose one of them to use. Rewrite the program of Figure 5-13 using the function that you have chosen.
6. (a) Write a function of type Outcomes (see Exercise 2) as follows: Two pairs of dice are rolled. If the first pair's result is greater than the second, you win; if less, you lose; if equal, you draw.
   (b) Using the function of part (a), write a program that plays the following game. Two players start, one with $20 and one with $14. They roll the dice 100 times or until one goes broke, whichever occurs first. The winner of each roll wins $1 from the other player. The program should tell what happened.
   (c) Is the game described in part (b) fair? To answer the question, simulate the game 1000 times, calculating the average amount of money each player has left at game's end.

7. Write a function:

   function `UppercaseValue(N: integer): Uppercase;`

   which returns the uppercase letter associated with position N. (For example, for N = 0, 'A' would be returned. The type Uppercase is defined as 'A'..'Z'.

8. (Inspired by Steve's of Somerville, MA.) Define the following types:

   Fruits: Includes strawberries, raspberries, plums, and bananas
   Flavors: Includes vanilla, chocolate, tinroof, and tuttifruiti
   Toppings: Includes chocolatechips, nuts, candybars, and hardcandy
   Sundaes: A record containing a name, 3 flavors, 1 fruit, and 3 toppings

9. Write Pascal programs to build and search for sundaes as defined in Exercise 8.
10. (a) Define a procedure TimeAdd(Time1, Time2: Times; var Sum: Times). Times is a record type that includes the two integer fields Minutes and Seconds.
    (b) Define a procedure TimeSub similar to TimeAdd.
11. Define the record types:

    Point: Includes two real fields: X and Y
    Line: Includes three real fields: Ycoeff, Xcoeff, and Constant

    We want to interpret the record type Point to represent points in a coordinate plane. We want to interpret Line to represent a line in a coordinate plane via its equation:

    `(Ycoeff)*Y + (Xcoeff)*X + (Constant) = 0`

    Write the following functions:

(a) IsLine—Boolean; input parameter of type Line; returns *true* if the equation represents a line. Hint: At least one of Ycoeff or Xcoeff must be nonzero.

(b) OnLine—Boolean; determines if the input parameter of type Point lies on the input parameter of type Line.

12. Give test plans for the following:
    (a) Exercise 4
    (b) Exercise 6
    (c) Exercise 9
    (d) Exercise 10

5-4 CASE STUDIES: RATIONAL ARITHMETIC

In this section, we present two case studies. In the first, we develop portions of a package to deal with rational numbers (fractions). In order to represent the data, we use the record data structure. (As we indicated when we first discussed records, the record concept is frequently employed when files are not involved. This case study illustrates this type of use.) As the program design proceeds, we present the venerable Euclidean Algorithm for determining the greatest common divisor of two integers. It is a function that is needed for several of the activities involved with rational numbers.

The second case study illustrates the use of modules in a package by developing a working program that acts as a "calculator" for rational numbers, but which contains only two functions. In order to present the user interface, we use sets to specify valid menu options. We suggest several other functions in the exercises.

Case Study No. 7 (A Rational Number Package)

Statement of Problem. The real variables in Pascal are usually only approximately accurate representations. For example, the constant 1/3 as used in the statement

```
x := 1/3
```

does not provide the exactness that it appears to have. We might expect that following this assignment, we could use X as an accurate representation of the rational number 1/3. However, if we execute the code

```
X := 1/3;
if 3 * X = 1.0 then
  Writeln ('I''m surprised!')
else
  Writeln ('I knew it was only approximate!')
```

we see that real variables do not provide a faithful representation for rational numbers. In this case study, we develop a set of modules to provide a more faithful representation.

Preliminary Analysis. There are an infinite number of mathematical representations for a given rational number. For example, 1/2, 5/10, 25/50, –7/–14, and so on, are all representations for the same number. However, there is a unique preferred representation, namely, the one in which the numerator and denominator have no common factors and the denominator is positive.

Since the mathematical representation of a rational number contains two integer numbers, it is natural to choose a computer representation that uses two Pascal integer variables. In our case, we use a record with two integer fields to represent a single rational number:

```
RationalNumber = record
    Numerator: integer;
    Denominator: integer
end;
```

The use of this data structure allows us to deal with a rational number as a single entity when we are communicating with subprograms, and it allows us to deal with the numerator and denominator individually when necessary.

We must next decide on the operations to perform. We obviously need to provide addition, subtraction, multiplication, and division. In addition to these, it would be desirable to have operations for reading and writing rational numbers, converting a rational number to an integer or a real number, and converting an integer to a rational number. We might also provide comparison of rationals and possibly other operations.

Note that some of the operations can be expressed in terms of others. For example, subtraction involves a change of sign followed by addition. Division involves inverting one rational and multiplying. This suggests a separation of the operations into primitive and composite operations, as shown in Table 5-1.

We must next decide on the form of the operations. Most operations take several steps to perform, so it seems reasonable to use subprograms. Many operations in Table 5-1 produce a rational result. Because we cannot have Pascal functions of a record type, we use procedures for these operations. Input and output activities are normally not appropriate for functions, so we use procedures for these activities as well. It is natural to expect comparison operations to produce conditions to be used in *if-then, while-do,* and *repeat-until* con-

TABLE 5-1 OPERATIONS SEPARATED INTO PRIMITIVE AND COMPOSITE OPERATIONS

Primitive
Addition
Multiplication
Input
Output
Convert rational to integer
Convert rational to real
Convert integer to rational
Compare for equality
Compare for less than

Composite
Subtraction
Division
Compare for less than or equal

structs, so we use Boolean functions for these operations. Finally, we use an integer function and a real function for the conversion of a rational number to integer and real, respectively.

The arithmetic operations require two operands and one result. We could use another argument to indicate success or failure of the operation. However, in order to simplify the argument lists of the subprograms, we adopt the following convention: any error causes an error message and the program terminates.

Some of the operations are commutative and others are not. For example, 1/2 + 1/3 is the same as 1/3 + 1/2, but 1/2 − 1/3 is not the same as 1/3 −1/2. When we add two rational numbers to produce the sum, there are six different ways to arrange the parameters for the addition procedure. We choose our arrangement based on the principles:

1. Input parameters come before output parameters.
2. The two operands for the operation are arranged in the natural order for the equivalent operation we use in arithmetic.

Summarizing our discussion so far, we have decided to use the following procedures:

```
procedure Add(FirstNumber, SecondNumber: RationalNumber;
         var Sum: RationalNumber);
procedure Subtract(FirstNumber, SecondNumber: RationalNumber;
              var Difference: RationalNumber);
procedure Multiply(FirstNumber, SecondNumber: RationalNumber;
              var Product: RationalNumber);
procedure Divide(FirstNumber, SecondNumber: RationalNumber;
            var Quotient: RationalNumber);
```

We adopt the convention that all rational numbers that appear as parameters of the operations of Table 5-1 have the following reduced form:

1. The numerator and denominator have no common factor larger than 1.
2. The denominator is positive.

In order to produce this internal consistency of representation in the package, we use the procedure:

```
procedure Reduce(Number: RationalNumber; var ReducedNumber:
            RationalNumber);
```

Algorithms and Programs. We select a few of the operations for detailed discussion and leave the others for the exercises.

A simple method of adding the two rational numbers A/B and C/D is shown in the equation:

$$\frac{A}{B} + \frac{C}{D} = \frac{AD + BC}{BD}$$

The equation shows us that the algorithm for addition is essentially two steps:

    set the numerator to AD + BC
    set the denominator to BD

```
procedure Add (FirstNum, SecondNum: RationalNum; var Sum: RationalNum);

  {Written by: XXXXXXXXX XX/XX/XX}
  {Purpose:    To add two fractions}
  {Parameters: FirstNum - input, first fraction to add}
  {            SecondNum - input, second fraction to add}
  {            Sum - output , sum of the two fractions}
  {Procedures used: Reduce - to reduce a fraction to lowest terms }

  begin {Add}
    with Sum do
      begin
        Numerator := FirstNum.Numerator * SecondNum.Denominator +
                     SecondNum.Numerator * FirstNum.Denominator;
        Denominator := FirstNum.Denominator * SecondNum.Denominator
      end; {with}

    Reduce(Sum, Sum)
  end; {Add}
```

Figure 5-16 Adding rational numbers.

Because of our desire to maintain the reduced form for all of our results, we add a third step:

reduce the answer

This algorithm becomes the Pascal procedure of Figure 5-16. Note the use of the *with-do* construct to simplify the calculation of the numerator and denominator. Also, notice that Sum is used as the input and the output in the call to the Reduce procedure. This is very similar to the dual use of a variable in an assignment statement such as:

```
I := I + 1
```

Note. However, it can be dangerous if both parameters are var parameters. Because that is not the case here, we are safe. An alternate approach would be to use a local variable ReducedSum, and replace the line

```
Reduce(Sum, Sum)
```

by the steps

```
Reduce(Sum, ReducedSum);
Sum := ReducedSum
```

The next procedure is intended to accept the input of a rational number from the user. We call this procedure ReadOne because it reads one rational number. This procedure must not allow the user to input a denominator of 0, which would produce an invalid rational number. The steps in the algorithm for ReadOne are

prompt the user for the numerator
read the numerator
prompt the user for the denominator
read the denominator
as long as the denominator is zero do these steps:
   print a message
   read a new value for the denominator
reduce the rational number

The Pascal code for ReadOne is shown in Figure 5-17.

The next procedure, which we call WriteOne, is for output of a rational number on the terminal. We do not attempt to produce any fancy output for this discussion, but simply perform the following steps:

print a blank line
print the numerator preceded by "Numerator:"
print the denominator preceded by "Denominator:"
print a blank line

The code for the procedure WriteOne appears as Figure 5-18.

```pascal
procedure ReadOne(var Number: RationalNumber);

{Written by: XXXXXXXXX XX/XX/XX}
{Purpose:    To read a fraction}
{Parameters: Number - output, fraction to be entered by user}
{Procedures used: Reduce - to reduce a fraction to lowest terms}

begin {ReadOne}
  with Number do
    begin
      Write('     Enter numerator: ');
      Readln(Numerator);
      Write('     Enter denominator: ');
      Readln(Denominator);
      while Denominator = 0 do
        begin
          Writeln;
          Write('Denominator of 0 not allowed. Please reenter: ');
          Readln(Denominator)
        end; {while}
    end; {with}

  Reduce(Number, Number)
end; {ReadOne}
```

Figure 5-17 Reading rational numbers.

5-4 CASE STUDIES: RATIONAL ARITHMETIC

```
procedure WriteOne(var Number: RationalNumber);

{Written by: XXXXXXXXX XX/XX/XX}
{Purpose:    To print a fraction}
{Parameters: Number - input, fraction to be printed}

begin {WriteOne}
  Writeln;
  with Number do
    begin
      Writeln(' Numerator: ', Numerator);
      Writeln('Denominator: ', Denominator)
    end; {with}
  Writeln
end; {WriteOne}
```

Figure 5-18 Writing rational numbers.

The Reduce procedure has two major jobs: to eliminate any common factor bigger than 1 from the numerator and denominator and to provide for a positive denominator. The steps in the algorithm for Reduce are

determine the greatest common divisor (gcd) of the numerator and denominator
divide the numerator by the gcd
divide the denominator by the gcd
if the denominator is negative, then negate both numerator and denominator

The process of determining the greatest common divisor of two integers is a natural candidate for a subprogram. The best method for producing the gcd is an algorithm attributed to the Greek mathematician Euclid (ca. 300 B.C.). The algorithm is based on the idea that for any two positive integers N and M (not 0), we can find integers Q (quotient) and R (remainder) so that

$$N = Q * M + R$$

and such that R < M. Some examples:

N	M	EQUATION
12	10	12 = 1 * 10 + 2
34	7	34 = 4 * 7 + 6
20	3	20 = 6 * 3 + 2
43	8	43 = 5 * 8 + 3

The simplest way to find the numbers Q and R is to let Q be the integer part of N/M and let R be N – Q * M. The basis of the Euclidean Algorithm is that the gcd of N and M is the same as the gcd of M and R. Thus, the basic idea is a recursive one:
  To find the gcd of N and M:

if M is zero, N is the gcd
otherwise:
    determine Q and R
    find the gcd of M and R

The following is an example that traces the recursion for the two numbers 1101 and 24:

N	M	Q	R
1101	24	45	21
24	21	1	3
21	3	7	0
3	0		

This example calculates the gcd of 1101 and 24 as 3. Note that there is no requirement that N be larger than M because the two numbers switch places in the first step if N is smaller.

Usually, the gcd of two integers is expected to be positive even if one or both of the integers is negative. We accomplish this requirement by calculating the gcd of the absolute values of the numerator and denominator in Reduce. The code for Reduce and the recursive Gcd function appear in Figure 5-19.

The final operation we discuss is the "compare for less than." In designing the algorithm for this operation, we must consider how it is that we know that

5/8 is less than 11/16

3/5 is less than 61/99

We can tell very simply which of two fractions is smaller by using a calculator to divide the denominators into the numerators and comparing the resulting decimals. This is the strategy that we adopt for our algorithm for our operation, which we call Less:

> divide the numerator of the first number by its denominator
> divide the numerator of the second number by its denominator
> if the first quotient is less than the second, then return *true*;
>   otherwise, return *false*

The code for the operation is given in Figure 5-20. Note that the value of the function Less is produced by the assignment statement:

```
Less := (FirstQuotient < SecondQuotient)
```

Because the right side of the assignment statement provides a value of type *boolean*, the statement is valid. It is also meaningful because it clearly states that the value of the function Less is directly dependent on the sizes of the quotients for the two fractions.

Case Study No. 8 (An Application of the Rational-Number Package)

The purpose of this case study is twofold:

1. To demonstrate how the rational-number package (or, more generally, any package) might be used.
2. To illustrate a program that provides the user with a menu of choices.

Statement of Problem. Hand-held calculators typically work with decimal numbers. Write a program that acts as a calculator but works with fractions instead.

```
function Gcd(N, M: integer): integer;

{Written by:  XXXXXXXXX XX/XX/XX}
{Purpose:     To calculate the greatest common divisor of two positive}
{             integers by means of the Euclidean Algorithm}
{Parameters: N - input, first number for gcd}
{            M - input, second number for gcd}
{Functions used: calls itself recursively}

begin {Gcd}
  if M = 0 then
    Gcd := N
  else
    Gcd := Gcd(M, N mod M)
end; {Gcd}

procedure Reduce(Number: RationalNumber;
                 var ReducedNumber: RationalNumber);

{Written by:  XXXXXXXXX XX/XX/XX}
{Purpose:     To reduce a fraction to lowest terms:}
{             Numerator and denominator have no common}
{             factor bigger than 1. The denominator is positive.}
{Parameters: Number - input, fraction to be reduced}
{            ReducedNumber - output, reduced fraction}
{Functions used: Gcd - to compute the greatest common divisor}
{                abs - to calculate the absolute value}

  var
    CommonFactor: integer;                    {Greatest common factor}

  begin {Reduce}
    with Number do
      CommonFactor := Gcd(abs(Numerator), abs(Denominator));

    ReducedNumber.Numerator :=.Numerator div CommonFactor;
    ReducedNumber.Denominator := Denominator div CommonFactor;
    with ReducedNumber do
      if Denominator < 0 then
        begin
          Denominator := -Denominator;
          Numerator := -Numerator
        end {if}
end; {Reduce}
```

Figure 5-19 Greatest common divisor (reducing rational numbers).

Preliminary Analysis. We approach this problem using "menu-driven" logic. That is, we display the possible options and let the user decide which one to choose. This simulates the existence of the function keys on a typical calculator. Contrary to what most calculators do, we input first the operation and then the fraction(s) the operation should use.

```
function Less(FirstNumber, SecondNumber: RationalNumber): Boolean;

{Written by:  XXXXXXXXX XX/XX/XX}
{Purpose:     To compare two fractions to determine if the first}
{             is less than the second}
{Parameters:  FirstNumber  - input, first fraction to compare}
{             SecondNumber - input, second fraction to compare}

   var
     FirstQuotient: real;   {The first number "divided out"}
     SecondQuotient: real;  {The second number "divided out"}

begin {Less}
  with FirstNumber do
     FirstQuotient := Numerator / Denominator;
  with SecondNumber do
     SecondQuotient := Numerator / Denominator;
  Less := (FirstQuotient < SecondQuotient)
end; {Less}
```

Figure 5-20 Comparing rational numbers.

(Thus, we are using *prefix* input, whereas most calculators would use *infix* input, with the operation in the middle, or *postfix* input, with the operation entered last.)

(The Mac has facilities to produce a user interface that would look very much like a real calculator, where the mouse could be used to indicate which keys are pressed. Unfortunately, producing that kind of interface requires advanced programming concepts and techniques, so we stick with our menu-driven approach.)

Algorithms, Data, and Program. The logic of the main program is

print instructions
repeat the following until the user wants to quit:
  present the user a menu and get user choice
  depending on the choice, perform appropriate activity
print message and terminate program

The main program declares our record type for rational numbers, three variables for use as rational numbers, a variable for the user choice from the menu, and a set to be used for valid menu options. The declarations of the main program are

```
type
   Letters = set of char;
   RationalNumber = record
        Numerator: integer;
        Denominator: integer
      end;
var
   FirstNumber, SecondNumber,
   ThirdNumber: RationalNumber;   {Rational numbers input}
   Option: char;                  {User choice of menu option}
   ValidOptions: Letters;         {Valid menu options}
```

5-4 CASE STUDIES: RATIONAL ARITHMETIC

In the spirit of top-down design, the main program delegates most of its activities via calls to subprograms. To print the instructions, the procedure Instructions is used, as was shown earlier in this book. To display the menu and obtain a valid user option, the procedure Menu is used. To perform the appropriate activity, the procedure Handle is called. The only detail the main program handles is establishing the valid menu options. The code for the main program is as shown:

```
begin {Calculator}
  ValidOptions := ['R', 'r', 'A', 'a', 'Q', 'q'];

{*** Print instructions}

  Instructions;

{*** Main loop}

  repeat

{*** Display Menu and get user option}

    Menu (ValidOptions, Option);
    ClearScreen;

{*** Handle user choice}

    Handle(Option)

  until Option in ['Q', 'q'];

{ *** Stop program}

end.
```

The decision to have the main program establish the valid menu options was made because two subordinate program units depend on the valid options. The communication of the valid options to the Menu procedure is done via a parameter, but the procedure Handle has the valid options as elements of a case statement, as we will see. If an option is to be added to the list of valid options, then the following must be changed:

the set in the main program must be enlarged
another menu line must be added in Menu
another case must be added in Handle

We use the procedure Pause in several places throughout the program. Its purpose is to cause the user to tap a key on the keyboard before activity can continue. The code for the procedure is as follows:

```
procedure Pause;

{Written by: XXXXXXXXX XX/XX/XX}
{Purpose:   To wait for user keystroke}
var
     Answer: char;                   {User keystroke}
begin {Pause}
  Writeln;
  Writeln(' ' : 20, '<Tap any key followed by Return to continue.>');
  Readln(Answer)
end; {Pause}
```

The Menu procedure displays the options to the user and obtains a valid choice. The procedure is as follows:

```
procedure Menu(ValidOptions: Letters; var Option : char);

{Written by: XXXXXXXXX XX/XX/XX}
{Purpose:   To display the menu and obtain the user choice}
{Parameters: ValidOptions - input, the set of legal options}
{            Option       - output, the option selected by the user}
{Procedures used: Page    - to clear the screen}

   const
     Margin = 23;                    {Left margin for menu}
     Bel = 7;                        {ASCII Bel character}
   var
     Answer: char;                   {User response}
begin {Menu}  Page;
                                     {Clear the screen}
  Writeln(' ' : 34, 'MENU OPTIONS');
  Writeln(' ' : 34, '------------');
  Writeln;
  Writeln(' ' : Margin, 'R(educe fraction to lowest terms)');
  Writeln(' ' : Margin, 'A(dd two fractions)');
  Writeln(' ' : Margin, 'Q(uit)');
  Writeln;
  Write(' ' : Margin+5, 'Option: ');

  repeat
     Readln(Answer);
     if not (Answer in ValidOptions) then
        Write(Chr(Bel))
  until Answer in ValidOptions;

  Writeln(Answer);
  Option := Answer
end; {Menu}
```

We use the local constant Margin to determine the left "edge" of the menu display. As we add options to the calculator, the number of spaces that we want to indent each option very likely changes. Note that we do not print the invalid keystrokes on the screen, but we do cause the computer to beep (or chirp or bong or whatever, depending upon the Mac's setting) by using the Bel character. Once a valid key has been tapped, we print the valid choice on the screen.

The procedure Handle actually performs the useful work of the program. The module is organized as a *case* structure according to the options the user can select. Note that both the uppercase and lowercase alternatives for each choice are listed together, separated by a comma, to lead into the case. We use the *otherwise* for the *case* structure to detect an invalid option. This error message is useful only during debugging of the program because once the program begins to work as designed, the user cannot select invalid options. Note that in order to reduce a fraction to lowest terms, the program need only read and write the fraction because the procedure ReadOne calls Reduce before returning the user input. The code for this module is

```
procedure Handle(Option: char);

{Written by: XXXXXXXXX XX/XX/XX}
{Purpose:    To perform the appropriate activities depending}
{            on the user choice.}
{Parameters: Option - input, user choice}
{Procedures used: ReadOne  - to get a fraction from the user}
{                 WriteOne - to print a fraction}
{                 Pause    - to wait for a user keystroke}
{                 Add      - to add two fractions}

begin {Handle}
  case Option of
    'R', 'r':
      begin
        Writeln(' ':25, 'REDUCE FRACTION TO LOWEST TERMS');
        Writeln(' ':25, '-------------------------------');
        Writeln;
        ReadOne(FirstNumber);
        Writeln;
        Writeln('The reduced number is:');
        WriteOne(FirstNumber);
        Pause
      end;

    'A', 'a':
      begin
        Writeln(' ':32, 'ADD TWO FRACTIONS');
        Writeln(' ':32, '-----------------');
        Writeln;
        Writeln('Enter the first fraction: ');
        Writeln;
        ReadOne(FirstNumber);
        Writeln;
        Writeln('Enter the second fraction: ');
```

```
            Writeln;
            ReadOne(SecondNumber);
            Add(FirstNumber, SecondNumber, ThirdNumber);
            Writeln('The sum of the fractions is:');
            WriteOne(ThirdNumber);
            Pause
          end;

        'Q', 'q':
          Writeln
        otherwise
          Writeln('*** illegal option: ', Option, ' detected in procedure
                Handle')
    end {case}
  end; {Handle}
```

Now that we have discussed all of the modules of the program, it is time to put things together. To comply with the idea of defining elements before using them, it is helpful to view the hierarchy of the program. We show the program hierarchy in an alternative "paragraph" form in which indentation indicates subordination of modules:

main program
    Instructions
        Page
        Pause
    Menu
        Page
    Page
    Handle
        ReadOne
        Reduce
            Gcd
                Gcd   (denotes a possible recursive call)
        Pause
        Add
        Reduce
            Gcd
                Gcd
        WriteOne

We can see from the hierarchy that the following order of defining modules ensures that each module is defined before it is used:

Page
Pause
Instructions
Menu
Gcd
Reduce
Add
ReadOne
WriteOne
Handle

This order is by no means unique, but it does have the virtue of keeping subordinate modules close to calling modules to some extent. The assembled program appears as Figure 5-21, with a sample run given in Figure 5-22. The output could be made more attractive; we leave that as an exercise.

```
program Calculator;

{Written by: XXXXXXXXX XX/XX/XX}
{Purpose:    To provide a calculator for fractions}
{Procedures used: Instructions - to print instructions}
{                 Menu   - to display the menu and get the user option}
{                 Handle - to perform the user option}

{The declarations previously discussed are inserted here}

    procedure Instructions;
    begin {stub}
    end;

{The following modules are inserted here:}
{   Pause}
{   Menu}
{   Gcd from Figure 5-19}
{   Reduce from Figure 5-19}
{   Add from Figure 5-16}
{   ReadOne from Figure 5-17}
{   WriteOne from Figure 5-18}
{   Handle}

begin {Calculator}
  ValidOptions := ['R', 'r', 'A', 'a', 'Q', 'q'];

{*** Print instructions}

  Instructions;

{*** Main loop}

  repeat

{*** Display Menu and get user option}

      Menu(ValidOptions, Option);
      Page;

{*** Handle user choice}

      Handle(Option)

  until Option in ['Q', 'q']

{*** Stop program}

end.
```

Figure 5-21 Menu-driven calculator.

SAMPLE INPUT AND OUTPUT

```
                    MENU OPTIONS
                    ------------
                    R(educe fraction to lowest terms)
                    A(dd two fractions)
                    Q(uit)

                    Tap option: r

                    REDUCE FRACTION TO LOWEST TERMS
                    -------------------------------

         Enter numerator: 11
         Enter denominator: 33

     The reduced number is:

             Numerator: 1
           Denominator: 3
                       <Tap any key to continue.>

                    MENU OPTIONS
                    ------------
                    R(educe fraction to lowest terms)
                    A(dd two fractions)
                    Q(uit)

                    Tap option: A

                          ADD TWO FRACTIONS
                          -----------------
         Enter the first fraction:

             Enter numerator: 2
           Enter denominator: 0
   Denominator of 0 not allowed. Please reenter: 3

         Enter the second fraction:

             Enter numerator: 6
           Enter denominator: -4
     The sum of the fractions is:

             Numerator: -5
           Denominator: 6
                       <Tap any key to continue.>

                             MENU OPTIONS
                             ------------
                    R(educe fraction to lowest terms)
                    A(dd two fractions)
                    Q(uit)

                    Tap option: q
```

Figure 5-22   Sample input and output for Case Study No. 8.

5-4 CASE STUDIES: RATIONAL ARITHMETIC

Documentation. As becomes apparent when one uses a package of modules to develop a program, the documentation for such a package is different from that for a program. The fundamental reason is that the class of user is different.

If we think about the user of a program, we might picture a person sitting at a terminal running the program. Such a person needs to know enough about computers to get the computer going and initiate the program. He or she needs to know about the use of the return key, the back space key, and other similar features. However, the user need not know how to program in Pascal. (Most users are not programmers in any language.) Accordingly, the user documentation should avoid technical jargon. It should explain how to start the program, what type of input is expected, what type of output is generated, how to handle any error situations, and similar topics.

On the other hand, the user of a package of modules is definitely a programmer. She or he may not be proficient in the language in which the package was written; for example, many packages are written in assembly language. However, the user understands terms such as subprogram, input parameter, and other technical terms, and needs to know some of the technical details of the package. She or he needs to know what parameters must be supplied to the package's modules in order for them to work properly. The user needs to know what declarations must be included in the main program for use by the modules in the package. She or he wants to know precisely what output values result from given input values to modules. (The user does not, however, care about the details of how the inputs generate outputs: the algorithm and the code are not important.) The user's guide for a package of modules is, therefore, much more technical than a typical user's guide.

EXERCISES

Exercises 1 to 7 relate to the case studies of this section.

1. Write modules for one or more of the modules that were mentioned in this section but not fully discussed:
   (a) Subtract. Use procedure Add to write this one.
   (b) Multiply.
   (c) Divide. Use procedure Multiply to write this one.
   (d) Convert rational to real.
   (e) Convert rational to integer.
   (f) Compare for equality. Do not do this the same way as for Less. Take advantage of the fact that all fractions are in a standard form in order to just compare numerators and denominators.

2. In the code for Add, the product of the denominators is used as the denominator of the unreduced sum. This is not how schoolchildren do this problem; instead, the concept of least common denominator is used. This concept makes use of the mathematical idea of the least common multiple (LCM) of two integers: the smallest integer that is a multiple of each of the two integers. Because we already have a function to compute the gcd of two numbers, we can take advantage of the relationship:

   LCM of N and M = (product of N and M)/(gcd of N and M)

   (a) Write a LCM function to compute the least common multiple of two integers. In order to keep the numbers generated by the calculation as small as possible, calculate the LCM of N and M as

```
LCM := N * (M / GCD(N,M))
```

    (b) Use the LCM function to change the method used in Add to arrive at the denominator of the unreduced sum.

3. Add some more user options to the fraction calculator of Figure 5-21. Some possible options to add:

S(ubtract two fractions)
M(ultiply two fractions)
D(ivide two fractions)
I(nvert a fraction)

4. **(a)** Add an option to the fraction calculator of Figure 5-21:

C(onvert a fraction)

    Make this new option lead to a submenu:

R(eal conversion)
I(nteger conversion)
Q(uit this menu)

    (b) "Clean up" the output of user prompts and answers so it is more pleasing to the eye.

5. Use the ideas of this section to write a Pascal program for fraction drill and practice. Your program should pose random problems in the categories:

R(educe fraction to lowest terms)
A(dd two fractions)
M(ultiply two fractions)
D(ecimal equivalent of a fraction)

The program should tell the user if the answer to a problem is correct or incorrect and a running score should be kept. The user should get a "report card" when the session ends.

6. **(a)** Write a program using the rational arithmetic package to read three rational numbers A, B, and C and compute and print D1 = (A + B)/C and D2 = (A − B)/C.
    (b) Write a program using the rational arithmetic package to read rational numbers A, B, and C and an integer number X. Calculate and print P = A * X + B * X + C. The answer should be printed as an integer if possible.
    (c) Repeat part (b), but print the answer as a real number.
    (d) Repeat part (c), but first convert A, B, C, and X to real numbers. Compare the answer to that of part (c).

7. For a quadratic equation $ax^2 + bx + c = 0$, where a, b, and c are integers, the solutions may or may not be rational numbers. If the quantity $b^2 - 4ac$ (the discriminant of the equation) is a positive perfect square (1, 4, 9, 16, 25, and so on), then the solutions are rational. Write a program to read values for a, b, and c, and either print a message "no rational solutions" or else print the rational solutions. You may wish to refer to Exercise 14 of Section 4-3 for more information on quadratic equations.

Exercises 8 to 15 involve writing packages of subprograms that use Pascal's record types to represent various data.

EXERCISES

8. In Exercise 11 of Section 5-3, we defined two record types:

   Point: includes two real fields: X and Y
   Line: includes three real fields: Ycoeff, Xcoeff, and Constant

   This choice of record for a line is based on the standard form of the equation of a straight line:

   $$(Ycoeff) * Y + (Xcoeff) * X + (Constant) = 0$$

   Using these record definitions, write subprograms for the following:

   (a) Determine whether two lines are parallel.
   (b) Determine whether two lines are perpendicular.
   (c) Determine whether two lines are the same.
   (d) Given a line and an X value, find the corresponding Y value.
   (e) Given a line and a Y value, find the corresponding X value.
   (f) Given a line and a point, determine whether or not the point is on the line.
   (g) Given a line and two points, determine whether or not the points are on the same side of the line.

9. Another possible representation for a line is based on the fact that two distinct points determine a line. Thus, we define a line as a record consisting of two points. Repeat Exercise 8 for this representation.

10. A third possible representation for a line is based on the slope-intercept equation for a line:

    $$y = mx + b$$

    Provided the line is not vertical, we can represent the line as a record containing slope m and intercept b. To handle vertical lines as well, we might choose a record with three components:

    Vertical: A boolean field indicating if the line is vertical
    Slope: A real field
    Intercept: The x intercept for a vertical line $x = c$; otherwise the y intercept (b in the equation)

    Repeat Exercise 8 for this representation.

11. Write routines to convert from any of the three representations in Exercises 8 to 10 to any other representation.

12. Revise Exercise 10 to use rational numbers (as developed in this section) rather than real numbers for the slope and intercept portions of the record.

13. Using real numbers for dollars and cents operations can lead to accuracy problems. An alternate approach might be to keep each money value as a record containing two integer fields representing the dollars and the cents, respectively. For this situation:

    (a) Write a subprogram to add two such figures. Notice that there are two parts to the answer. Given 101, 50 representing $101.50, and 45, 63 representing $45.63, the answer should be 147, 13 representing $147.13. You can assume that the numbers are positive.
    (b) Write a subprogram to subtract two such figures. Assume that the first amount is larger than the second.
    (c) Write a subprogram similar to part (b) except that it does not assume that the first amount is larger than the second. Instead, it has another parameter that is used to report to the main program whether it was able to do the subtraction. If it is able, it sets this parameter to *true* and does the subtraction; if not, it sets this parameter to *false*.

(d) Write a subprogram to multiply two such figures. Assume that both are positive, and round the answer to the nearest cent. For example, 145.01 times 1.10 should be 159.51.

(e) Modify part (d) to make the second figure represent a real number with three decimal places. For example, 1, 85 to represent 1.085.

(f) Write subprograms to compare two such dollar and cents figures. One, called Equal, should tell whether or not they are equal. The second, called Larger, should tell whether or not the first is larger than the second.

(g) Extend your representation scheme to include a Boolean field that indicates if the number is positive or negative, and rewrite the various subprograms.

(h) Write a program for Exercise 14 of Section 3-2 that uses this representation for money rather than using real numbers.

(i) Write a program for Exercise 24 of Section 3-4 that uses this representation for money rather than using real numbers.

14. Maxint is 32767. This imposes a stringent limit on the size of integers than can be used. There are various ways to extend the range of values; one is suggested by analogy with what we did in Exercise 13 to represent money.

For example, to represent positive numbers with up to nine digits, we could think of the number as we typically write it by hand, as in these examples:

$$213,567,198$$
$$3,175,000$$

We might choose to use a record with three integers to represent the number of millions, thousands, and units. Using this representation, write subprograms for the following:

(a) Add two integers.
(b) Subtract two integers, assuming the first is larger.
(c) Compare two integers to see if they are equal.
(d) Compare two integers to see if the first is larger.
(e) Multiply two integers. Caution: If you multiply two 3-digit numbers, the result may be larger than maxint. Can you suggest some solutions to this problem?

15. Refer to Exercise 14. Add a field to the record indicating whether the integer is positive, zero, or negative. Write routines that use this representation scheme to find the absolute value of an integer and to compare, to add, and to subtract two integers.

EXERCISES

6 One-Dimensional Arrays

OBJECTIVES

This chapter's main objectives are to discuss in detail the array data type and its uses. We introduced the concept of an array in Chapter 3, and we have used arrays in Chapters 4 and 5. After completing this chapter, you will have:

- gained a thorough understanding of the definition and use of one-dimensional arrays
- learned how to employ the array to help structure the data our programs use
- learned how to design and implement linear search (in more detail than previously), binary search, selection sort, and quicksort
- studied two examples of array use in detail

6-1 DEFINING AND USING ARRAYS

The Need for Arrays

An **array** can be thought of as a list of values. The values must be of the same type, and they are generally related in some way. For example, we might declare an array as

```
AverageTemp: array[1..31] of real;
```

Our program can then use AverageTemp to store a list of 31 real values. Those values might represent the average temperature in Tempe, Arizona, for the 31 days of March 1988. We would refer to the first value as AverageTemp[1], the tenth as AverageTemp[10], and so on. (Notice that we would know that AverageTemp[23] refers to the average temperature on March 23; the computer would know only that it refers to the 23rd value in the array named AverageTemp.)

As a general rule, we can state that:

> An array is probably the proper choice of data type when the program needs to store a list of related values of the same type.

To illustrate this rule, we briefly describe some situations in which we might consider using an array and some in which an array is probably inappropriate. (Some of these examples are developed more fully later in the section.)

1. *Given a list of 40 test grades for a class, find how many are greater than the average.* To solve this problem, we would read the grades, add them, and divide by 40 to calculate the average. We would then have to compare each grade to the calculated average. Rather than ask the user to reenter the grades, we would want to store the grades in an array as we read them. We then could compare the values in the array to the average in order to find the desired count.

2. *Given a list of 40 test grades for a class, find the average.* This is similar to the previous problem, but we do not need an array. We can read the grades one at a time, as shown in this segment:

```
Sum := 0;
for I := 1 to 40 do
   begin
      Readln(Grade);
      Sum := Sum + Grade
   end;
Average := Sum / 40
```

As we read each grade, we do everything that is required for that grade prior to reading the next. We do not need to store all 40 grades, so we do not need an array.

3. *Data for each employee consist of name and 12 monthly pay figures. Print the name, the 12 pay figures, and the total pay for each person.* To solve this problem, it is convenient to store the 12 pay figures in an array as we read them, then print the array along with the name and total. By making clever use of Write rather than Writeln, we could avoid using an array. However, the program design is "cleaner" if we do use an array.

4. *Simulate rolling a pair of dice 12,000 times, and tell how many 2's, 3's, etc., are rolled.* For this, we will need 11 counter variables. We could use Count2, Count3, . . . , Count12 as variables. However, it is useful to think of the counters as a list of values and use a declaration such as

```
Count: array[2..12] of integer;
```

Count[7] would be the number of 7's rolled, and so on. This allows us, for example, to print the results using

```
for I := 2 to 12 do
   begin
      Writeln(I : 2, ' occurred ', Count[I] : 4, ' times.')
   end
```

(You might consider how you would print the results using variables Count2, Count3, etc.)

6-1 DEFINING AND USING ARRAYS

Notice that we would not need an array of size 12,000 to store the 12,000 simulated rolls. We would generate one at a time, adding to the appropriate counter.

5. *Given I, a number between 1 and 12 representing a month, print the month name.* This can be solved without an array, of course. For example, we could use the structure suggested here:

```
case I of
1:
   Writeln ('January');
   .
   .
   .
end {case}
```

However, if an array Month were set up by the program to contain the 12 month names, then we could simply use

```
Writeln(Month[I])
```

to accomplish the task.

Array Declaration

Arrays can be declared in Pascal using a declaration of the form

```
array[index type] of component type
```

For example, in the declaration

```
array[1..100] of integer
```

the index type is "1..100" and the component type is *integer*. This says that:

1. The **subscript** (**index**) must be an integer in the range 1 to 100.
2. Each value (component) in the array is an integer.

The example given illustrates the most common form for the index type: a subrange of the integers from 1 to some number greater than 1. However, declarations such as

```
array[2..100] of integer
array[-500..500] of real
```

are also allowed; we use them when they are appropriate for the problem to be solved.

Note. If a subscript range has a negative lower bound and a positive upper bound, then 0 is one of the valid subscripts.

The "component type" can be any of the following: integer, real, Boolean, char, a string type, or a programmer-defined scalar or subrange type.

> **Note.** In Section 6-2, we discuss a more general fashion in which the index type and component type can be defined.

There are several ways to declare a specific variable to be an array. For example, to declare an array of 50 names, we could write

```
var
   Names: array[1..50] of string[45];
```

or we could write

```
const
   MaxIndex = 50;

type
   String45 = string[45];
   NameArray = array[MaxIndex] of String45;

var
   Names: NameArray;
```

The second approach has several advantages. First, by using the constant MaxIndex, it is easier to adjust the array size in the future. Second, the array Names can be passed as a parameter to a procedure or function because it is of a named type. (Likewise, Name[3] could be passed as a parameter because it is of the named type String45.) As we will see, there are other advantages to be gained by using named types; we almost always use them when declaring arrays.

Array Reference

Suppose that we have these declarations:

```
type
   CountArray = array [2..12] of integer;
   RealArray = array[-5..25] of real;
var
   Count: CountArray
   X: RealArray,
   I, J: integer;
```

More often than not, a program step that refers to one of these arrays would be referencing a specific value of the array. To do so, it would use

   array-name[subscript]

The subscript (index) can be any integer expression in the proper **subscript range**. For example, if I and J currently have the values 5 and 3, respectively, then each of these is a valid reference:

```
Count[7]
Count[I]          refers to Count[5]
Count[2 * I]      refers to Count[10]
X[-I + J]         refers to X[-2]
```

6-1 DEFINING AND USING ARRAYS

> **Note.** If we turn range-checking on, the computer detects subscripts that are outside the range of valid subscripts.

A reference to an element of the Count array can be used anywhere an integer variable could be used. For example, we could write steps such as these:

```
Count[4] := 0
if Count[I] > Count[I+1] then . . .
Readln(Count[J])
X[I] := Sqrt(X[I+1])
```

In particular, an array element can be passed to a function or procedure (as long as it matches the type of the corresponding formal parameter). Since X[I+1] is a numeric value, it can be passed to the Sqrt function. For any function with an integer parameter, we could pass Count[12] to match that parameter.

Less frequently, a program step refers to the array name without using a subscript. Such a reference refers to the entire array. The most frequent example involves passing an entire array as a parameter to a subprogram. In such a case, the parameter in the subprogram must be of the same named type.

Another instance in which we would use the array name without a subscript involves array assignments. For example, the assignment

```
A := B
```

could be used to cause the entire array B to be copied to array A. This is possible only if the arrays are of precisely the same type. For example, it is legal with the declarations:

```
type
    IntegerArray = array[1..50] of integer;
var
    A: IntegerArray;
    B: IntegerArray;
```

It is illegal with the similar declarations:

```
var
    A: array[1..50] of integer;
    B: array[1..50] of integer;
```

Array Algorithms: Count-Controlled

The easiest program segments to write dealing with arrays are those that use a "count-controlled" logic. We can describe segments of this type generically as

```
for I := start to end do
    begin
        steps which process array element A[I]
    end; {for}
```

For example, the program in Figure 6-1 carries out the task referred to earlier in this section: read exactly 40 grades and count how many are larger than the average. Some portions are in italics for emphasis. First, we have used a named constant for the number of grades. In our preliminary testing, we changed this to a smaller value. Second, the variable I is used both to control the *for* loop and as a subscript for the array. The *for* loop causes I to take on the values 1 through 40, and, therefore, the reference "Grades[I]" refers to Grades[1] the first time through the loop, Grades[2] the second time, and so on.

```
program CountGrades;
{Written by:   XXXXXXXXXX XX/XX/XX}
{Purpose:      To read a list of grades (of a fixed length),}
{              and count how many are greater than the average}
     const
        MaxIndex = 40;          {size of grade array}
     type
        GradeArray = array[1..MaxIndex] of integer;
     var
        Grades: GradeArray;     {list of grades}
        I: integer;             {loop control, and subscript}
        Sum: integer;           {sum of grades}
        Average: real;          {average of grades}
        Count: integer;         {how many are > average}
begin
{*** Read the grades and find the sum}
     Sum := 0;
     for I := 1 to MaxIndex do
        begin
           Write('Enter grade #', I, ' ');
           Readln(Grades[I]);
           Sum := Sum + Grades[I]
        end; {for}
{*** Find and print the average}
     Average := Sum / MaxIndex;
     Writeln;
     Writeln('The average is ', Average : 1 : 2);
{*** Count how many are larger than the average, and print answer}
     Count := 0;
     for I := 1 to MaxIndex do
        begin
           if Grades[I] > Average then
              Count := Count + 1
        end; {for}
     Writeln(Count : 1, ' grades are larger than the average.');
end. {CountGrades}
```

Figure 6-1 Number of above-average grades.

Notes.   It happens that this example uses an array of integers. We can write similar examples using arrays of other "component types." For example, we can declare:

```
type
    VoicePart = (bass, tenor, alto, soprano);
    VoiceArray = array[1..50] of VoicePart;

var
    Voice: VoiceArray;
```

Assuming that some earlier steps in the program have supplied values to this array, code such as the following could be used to count the tenors in the array:

```
TenorCount := 0;
for I := 1 to 50 do
    begin
        if Voice[I] = tenor then
            TenorCount := TenorCount + 1
    end {for}
```

As another example, let us write a function that finds the largest grade in an array GradeList. To do so, we maintain a variable Large that at all times contains the largest value encountered so far. We compare each value in the array with this largest value. Our "step that processes array element A[I]" is, in this case:

```
if GradeList[I] > Large then
    Large := GradeList[I]
```

Before the loop, we must give Large an initial value; otherwise, the comparison "GradeList[I] > Large" would be meaningless the first time through the loop. We have two choices: start at a low value (0 is low enough for this example) or start with the first value. In working with an array, it is easy to start with the first value, so we do:

```
Large := GradeList[1]
```

Figure 6-2 contains the function. Observe the following:

1. We have included a parameter that indicates the number of students. This allows the function to be used more generally than if it used the array size for its loop control.
2. The *for* loop index I goes from 2 to NumberOfStudents. There is no need to compare the first grade with itself.
3. We need a local variable Large to obtain the answer. As our last step, we copy the answer to the function name. (Without this, a step "if GradeList[I] > Largest" would be considered a recursive call to the function.)

In Figure 6-3, we present a slight modification. In addition to the largest value, we wish to know the position (that is, the subscript) for which the value occurred. To do so, we add an additional variable, LargePosition. Because there are now two answers, we use a procedure rather than a function. Whenever we assign a value to Large, we also assign a value to LargePosition to keep track of where Large obtained its value. For example, if at

```
function Largest(GradeList: GradeArray; NumberOfGrades : integer): integer;

{Written by: XXXXXXXXXX XX/XX/XX}
{Purpose:    To find the largest value in an array of grades}
{Parameters: GradeList - input, the array of grades to examine}
{            NumberOfGrades - input, a count of how many students there are}
var
  Large: integer; {used to get the largest}
  I: integer;     {loop control and subscript}

begin {Largest}
  Large := GradeList[1];
  for I := 2 to NumberOfGrades do
    begin
      if GradeList[I] > Large then
        Large := GradeList[I]
    end; {for}
  Largest := Large
end; {Largest}
```

Figure 6-2   Largest value in an array.

---

the end, LargePosition has the value 3, this means that the third grade was the largest. (It is useful to notice that GradeList[LargePosition] is the largest, and, hence, we do not really need to pass back Large to the calling program.)

Notes

1. We can pass the current length of an array as a parameter to a procedure or function. The subprogram can use that parameter to make sure it uses only the portion of the array that contains meaningful data. However, the declared size of the array is fixed. It cannot be defined or redefined by the subprogram. It is set by the type declaration in the main program.

2. One of the most frequent errors made in working with arrays is confusing a subscript with the array element to which it refers. In working with arrays, we must always ask, "Do I want to refer to the subscript or to the array element indicated by the subscript?"

As another example, let us write a procedure to print an integer array. For this, we use two parameters: the array and an indication of how many values are in the array. We assume, as we have in the previous examples, that the lowest subscript is 1. We would like our procedure to print eight values per line.

We begin with steps that print one value per line, then modify the procedure to print eight per line. We might write

```
for I := 1 to NumberOfGrades do
  begin
    Writeln(Grades[I] : 7)
  end {for}
```

```
        procedure Largest (GradeList: GradeArray; NumberOfGrades: integer;
                      var Large, LargePosition: integer);
{Written by: XXXXXXXXXX XX/XX/XX}
{Purpose:    To find the largest value, and its subscript, in an}
{            array of grades}
{Parameters: GradeList - input, the array of grades to examine}
{            NumberOfGrades - input, a count of the number of students}
{            Large - output, the largest number found}
{            LargePosition - output, the position where the largest}
{                            was found (in case of a tie, it is the}
{                            first position where a largest was found)


        begin {Largest}
          Large := GradeList[1];
          LargePosition := 1;

          for I := 2 to NumberOfGrades do
            begin
              if GradeList[I] > Large then
                begin
                  Large := GradeList[I];
                  LargePosition := I
                end {if}
            end {for}

        end; {Largest}
```

Figure 6-3   Position of largest value in an array.

Each Writeln invocation prints the grade followed by a carriage return to move to the next line. What we must do to get eight grades per line is to only send a carriage return after every eight grades, so we might write

```
        for I := 1 to NumberOfGrades do
          begin
              Write(Grades[I] : 7);
              if I mod 8 = 0 then
                Writeln
          end {for}
```

Each individual grade is written (using Write not Writeln) without a carriage return. When I is 8, 16, 24, and so on, I mod 8 is 0 and the Writeln sends a carriage return.

This version almost works; however, if NumberOfGrades is not evenly divisible by 8, the last line of grades does not get a carriage return. Thus, we add

```
        if NumberOfGrades mod 8 <> 0 then
          Writeln
```

after the loop. We leave the details of writing this as a procedure to the reader.

Array Algorithms: Condition-Controlled

In the preceding subsection, we examined several types of problems where a count-controlled loop (*for* loop) is an appropriate structure. Some looping processes involving arrays, however, cannot use such a structure. An important class of problems where this is true is that involving an **array search**.

In Chapter 5, we wrote several programs that involved searching in a file. As we discovered, the loops involved in those searches used a compound condition for termination. We wanted to terminate the loop "successfully" as soon as the desired item was found or "unsuccessfully" if the entire file was traversed without finding the desired item.

A similar approach can be used in searching an array. If, for an array A, the subscripts range from 1 to N, we can cause an index variable I to assume the values 1, 2, and so on, using this basic logic:

> initialize I to 1
> as long as the search is not complete,
>   add 1 to I to move to the next array element.

When is the search complete? If A[I] is the item sought, it is complete (we have found it). If I goes beyond N (the number of items in the array), it is also complete (the item is not there). We may be tempted to write the condition "the search is complete" as

```
(I > N) or (A[I] = ValueSought)
```

However, this contains a subtle flaw: if I is greater than N, the reference to A[I] is illegal (at best, meaningless). One common solution to this problem is to use a Boolean variable Found to indicate success in the search. Our basic logic becomes

> initialize Found to *false*, I to 1
> as long as the search is not complete:
>   if A[I] is the sought value, set Found *true*;
>   otherwise, add I to 1.

The function of Figure 6-4 illustrates this approach. It searches for a given integer in an array of integers. This technique (using a Boolean variable to indicate success) can be useful in solving any problem that involves searching for the occurrence of some condition in an array.

As another example of a condition-based loop using an array, we write code that reads up to 10 nonzero integers into an integer array of size 10. We would like the procedure to stop after 10 numbers have been read or when the user enters a terminating (0) value. Moreover, the 0 should not be placed into the array, and a parameter N should indicate how many numbers were actually input.

One approach to this problem involves "simulating" the *for* loop. To read exactly 10 numbers, we could use the *for* loop on the left or the equivalent *while* loop on the right:

```
for I := 1 to 10 do        while I <= 10 do
   begin                      begin
      Readln(Number);            Readln(Number);
      A[I] := Number             A[I] := Number;
   end {for}                     I := I + 1
                              end {while}
```

```
function Search (A: IntegerArray; Key, N: integer): integer;

{Written by:   XXXXXXXXXX XX/XX/XX}
{Purpose:      To locate a given value in an array}
{              The answer is the subscript where found (0 if not found)}
{Parameters:   A - input, the array in which to search}
{              Key - input, the value for which to search}
{              N - input, the portion of the array in use}

  var
    Found: boolean;      {used to indicate success}
    I: integer;          {loop control and subscript}

begin {Search}
  Found := false;        {assume value not in array}
  I := 1;
  while (I <= N) and (not Found) do
    begin
      if A[I] = Key then
        Found := true
      else
        I := I + 1
    end; {while}

  if Found then
    Search := I
  else
    Search := 0

end; {Search}
```

Figure 6-4   Searching an array.

If we use a *for* loop, we must read exactly 10 values. With the *while* loop, we can quit when the input number is 0. One idea is to use the Boolean variable UserIsDone initialized to *false*. In the loop, because we do not want to put the 0 in the array, we write

```
if Number = 0 then
  UserIsDone := true
else
  A[I] := Number
```

The *while* loop condition is modified to

```
while (I <= 100) and (not UserIsDone) do
```

After the loop, we can calculate the size of the array as

```
N := I - 1
```

With these changes, the *while* loop solution becomes

```
I := 1;
UserIsDone := false;
while (I <= 10) and (not UserIsDone) do
  begin
      Readln (Number);
      if Number = 0 then
        UserIsDone := true
      else
        A[I] := Number;
        I := I + 1
  end; {while}

N := I - 1
```

(You should convince yourself that this is correct for the boundary values N = 0, 1, 9, and 10.)

Initialization, Copying, and Shifting

We have considered a few examples of processing an entire array. These examples have included important algorithm classes, such as finding the largest and searching, which were considered at length in earlier chapters. We now consider some array-processing methods that have no analogues in earlier chapters.

It is frequently necessary to initialize arrays to some known value. To initialize all elements of an array X with 100 elements to some value, for example, Z, we could write

```
for I := 1 to 100 do
  begin
    X[I] := Z
  end {for}
```

Of course, Z could be replaced by a constant such as 0, ' ', or other value, as might be needed.

Another common initialization is to place values equal to the index of the element into each element, as such as X[1] = 1, X[2] = 2, . . . , X[100] = 100. This can be accomplished by

```
for I := 1 to 100 do
  begin
    X[I] := I
  end {for}
```

In addition to initializing arrays, we frequently wish to copy one array, or part of one array, into another. As we have seen, if A and B are the same named type, the assignment

```
A := B
```

can be used to copy all of B to A. Suppose now that we want to copy only the first 10 elements of B to the first 10 elements of A. A simple loop such as

```
for I := 1 to 10 do
  begin
    A[I] := B[I]
  end {for}
```

suffices.

On the other hand, suppose we want to copy elements 1 to 5 and 10 to 15 of B into the first 11 positions of A. One approach is to copy B[l] through B[5] to A[l] through A[5], as in the first example, then copy B[10] through B[15] to A[6] through A[11].

There are several approaches to writing a loop to move B[10] through B[15] to A[6] through A[11]. We might make a table of subscripts, as follows:

A SUBSCRIPT	COMES FROM B SUBSCRIPT
6	10
7	11
8	12
9	13
10	14
11	15

After studying this table, we might write

```
for I := 1 to 5 do
  begin
    A[I] := B[I]
  end; {for}

for I := 1 to 6 do
  begin
    A[I+5] := B[I+9]
  end {for}
```

The second loop was written by first noting that we wished to move six elements. This led to the loop for I = 1 to 6. Now we know we want our loop body to be of the form

```
A[??] := B[??]
```

We must come up with the proper formulas for the A subscript and the B subscript. To determine the formula for the A subscript, we note that when I is 1, the subscript is 6; when I is 2, the subscript is 7; and so on. The subscript is always 5 more than I, and hence the proper formula is I + 5. Similar reasoning leads to the formula I + 9 for the B subscript.

Notes

1. The second loop could be replaced by

```
for I := 6 to 11 do
  begin
    A[I] := B[I+4]
  end {for}
```

In this case, we have chosen the index range to match the destination subscripts. By having I take on the values 6 to 11, we avoid the need to determine a formula for the A subscript. The formula for the B subscript is found by observing that it is always 4 more than the A subscript.

2. If we do not wish to devise a formula for B's subscript, we might use this alternate approach:

```
J := 10;
for I := 6 to 11 do
  begin
      A[I] := B[J];
      J := J + 1
  end {for}
```

By initializing J to 10 prior to the loop and incrementing it each time through the loop, we have J take on the values 10 to 15.

Shifting is a frequently used array operation. It is similar to copying, but involves only one array. As an example, let us write code to shift the array A to the left by one position. This means to copy A[2] to A[1], A[3] to A[2], and so on. If A contains 50 values, our last copy would copy A[50] to A[49]. We might then set A[50] to 0, or decrease a variable representing the actual length by 1. The code would be

```
for I := 2 to 50 do
  begin
      A[I-1] := A[I]
  end; {for}
A[50] := 0
```

Next consider a shift to the right. We might be inclined to write code that copies A[1] to A[2], then A[2] to A[3], and so on. However, this does not work, since A[2] is changed before we copy it to A[3]. The solution is to work from right to left: first copy A[49] to A[50], then A[48] to A[49], and so on. The code to do so is left as an exercise.

Processing Single Elements

In the examples we have considered in this section, the subscripts of the array elements have been set by the loop index or have been obtained using a formula based on that index.

The loops are of the general form

```
for I : = 1 to N do
  begin
      process A[formula involving I]
  end {for}
```

Frequently, however, we need to work with a single element of an array. We need a subscript, but because we are not in a loop, the subscript is not a loop index.

6-1 DEFINING AND USING ARRAYS

It sometimes happens that, in reading values for an array, we do not read the entire array at once. Instead, each input record can contain a subscript along with the value to be placed in the array at that position. For example, the input

```
7        150.25
```

indicates that the value 150.25 is to be placed into A[7].

It is possible to read such an input record using

```
Readln(I, A[I])
```

This practice is dangerous because it makes the program vulnerable to data-entry errors. For example, we might have an array with 10 elements in it and the data value read for I might be 25. A reference to A[25] is either recognized as an error (if we turned on range checking) or treated as a reference to some part of the computer memory outside of the array A. A much better approach is to read the array value into a temporary variable. We then check that the subscript is in the valid range before placing the value in the array. Thus, the previous Readln statement is better written as

```
Readln(I, ReadValue);
 if (I >= 1) and (I <= 10) then
  A[I] := ReadValue
else
  Writeln('Subscript value ', I : 1, ' is illegal.')
```

The following problem illustrates a second situation involving subscripts that are not loop indexes. We are to simulate rolling a pair of dice 12,000 times and to count the number of times each possible number (2 through 12) occurs.

As we discussed in the section "The Need for Arrays," it is convenient to use an array (with possible subscripts from 2 to 12) for the counters. The array can be declared as

```
type
  CountArray = array[2..12] of integer;
var
  Counter: CountArray;
```

The first step in the program involves initializing the entire array to 0:

```
for I := 2 to 12 do
  begin
    Counter[I] := 0
  end; {for}
```

The steps to do the counting can be written as

```
for I := 1 to 12000 do
  begin
    Roll := RollOfDice; {use the function we wrote earlier}
    Counter[???] := Counter [???] + 1
  end; {for}
```

Our only problem is determining the proper subscript. However, that is easily solved. If the roll is 2, we want to increment Counter[2]; if it is 3, we want to increment Counter[3]; and so on. The variable Roll gives the desired subscript. Thus, the counting step should be

```
Counter[Roll] := Counter[Roll] + 1
```

As a final indication of the use of subscripts other than the loop index itself, consider the following situation. Each child in a nursery school has been assigned to one of six different groups, numbered 1 to 6. An array Group contains the group assignments for the children. There are N children. Count how many are in each group.

We have a program segment similar to the one involving dice rolls:

```
for I := 1 to N do
  begin
      calculate subscript CountSub for Counter array;
      Counter[CountSub] := Counter[CountSub] + 1
  end {for}
```

What is the proper value for CountSub? It is the person's group number, namely, Group[I]:

```
CountSub := Group[I];
Counter[CountSub] := Counter[CountSub] + 1
```

We may combine the steps as

```
Counter[Group[I]] := Counter[Group[I]] + 1
```

(Some find the former notation a bit easier to read than the latter.)

Testing

In working with arrays, there are two natural boundaries: the first element in the array and the last element in the array. Moreover, in speaking of the last element in the array, we can mean one of two things: the last element the array is capable of holding or the last element it actually holds. For example, consider an array Names of size 50, capable of holding names for a class of 50. For a given class, it might actually contain only 33 students. The "last" element of the array could be thought of as Names[33] or as Names[50].

Likewise, in an array such as the Names array, we have boundaries on how "full" the array is. Put another way, if NStudent indicates the number of students in the class, then there are boundaries at NStudent = 0, NStudent = 1, and NStudent = 50.

Most testing involving arrays uses these considerations together with those for the specific problem. For example, in finding the largest grade in an array Grade of size 50 that currently contains NStudent grades, we can identify tests such as these:

Value of NStudent: 0, 1, 50, in between, 51 (an error)
Location of largest (assuming no ties):
   position 1, with NStudent > 1
   position NStudent, with NStudent = 1
   position NStudent, with NStudent > 1
   position NStudent, with NStudent = 50
   in between I and NStudent
Number of ties for largest:
   none
   all scores the same
   in between none and all

As another example, similar tests would apply for an array search. Among the most important tests would be these:

value not found
value found:
   in first position
   in last position in use (N), with N < declared array size
   in last position in use (N), with N = declared array size

DPT

1. Do not use subscripts in place of array elements and vice versa. In any reference to an array, we must ask, "Do we want to refer to the location (the subscript) or the value in that location of the array?"

2. Think carefully about the formula for subscripts. Because so many standard processes involve a reference A[I], we may have a tendency to assume that all subscripts are always a loop-control variable I. In this section, we have seen several examples where the proper subscript is not the loop-control variable.

3. Avoid subscripts *out of range*. An out-of-range subscript can be caused by the errors indicated in items 1 and 2. In addition, some common causes are

(a) Failing to check the input that indicates a subscript

(b) Adding values to an array without checking if the array is full

If we turn on range checking, the computer detects this error. If we do not, the out-of-range array reference is allowed. This reference refers to (and perhaps modifies) some part of the computer memory outside the array—perhaps another variable, a constant, or even the program itself. This can cause almost any type of error to occur.

4. Think carefully when using arrays as arguments for subprograms. If the subprogram expects an array as a parameter, then pass the whole array [for example, `Print(Scores)`]. If the subprogram expects a single value, pass an array element [for example, `Y := Sqrt(Total[I])`].

5. Parameters must be of a named type. For example,

    function Sum(A: IntegerArray): integer;

is legal, but

    function Sum(A: **array**[1..100] **of** integer): integer;

is illegal.

6. Be especially wary of compound conditions involving subscripts. Any condition such as the ones that follow are suspect:

(a) (I > N) or (A[I] = Value)

(b) (I <= N) and (A[I] <> Value)

(c) (I > 0) and (A[I] > Temp)

The problem is that Pascal evaluates both halves of the condition even if only the first half is needed to determine whether the condition is *true* or *false*. If the valid subscripts for the array A are 1 to N, then these three conditions are faulty because

(a) If I > N is *true*, then A[I] = Value is illegal (an out-of-range subscript).

(b) If I <= N is *false*, then A[I] <> Value is illegal.

(c) If I > 0 is *false*, then A[I] > Temp is illegal.

Notes

1. As we discussed in our array-search example, a common solution to this last problem is to introduce a Boolean variable such as Found, which represents the second half of the compound condition. This variable is initialized prior to the loop and changed within the loop body.

2. Versions of this bug can be found in the sample programs of many computer science textbooks. What this should say to you as a student is that it is an exceptionally dangerous bug: even experienced programmers can easily make this mistake. You must be especially alert to avoid the problem.

---

7. THINK Pascal reserves $2^8 - 2$ (32,766) bytes (memory units) for all *static variables*—that is, those variables whose memory needs can be determined at compilation time. Except for file variables, all of the types of variables that we have discussed to this point in the text are static variables. Since each item of an array takes at least 1 byte, arrays are a prime suspect when THINK says its memory has been exceeded: declaring one very large array (or many small ones) can cause THINK to exceed its static memory limit.

The memory needs of each array vary depending upon the array's component type. As a guide, the largest array you can declare is one that can hold 16,384 integers, 8192 reals, or only 128 strings of size 255. If the array's memory needs exceed 32,766 bytes, or the combined size of all static variables exceeds the available memory, THINK prints this error message at compile time: "Available memory for variables declared at this level has been exhausted."

A good way to resolve these errors is to make the arrays (or other data structures) smaller. You can cut down the number of items in the array, or change the component type to one that uses less memory. An often overlooked way to reduce memory usage in string arrays is to replace the component type *string*, which is 255 characters, with a named string type of a smaller size. For instance, changing

```
type
    StringArray = array[1..128] of string;
```

to

```
type
    String128 = string[128];
    StringArray = array[1..128] of String128;
```

frees up over 16,500 bytes.

6-1 DEFINING AND USING ARRAYS

REVIEW

Terms and Concepts

array
array search
index

subscript range
subscript

Pascal Syntax

Array Declaration:

`array[index type]` **of** `component type`

where the index type can be of the form low..high, and the component type can be *integer*, *real*, *string*, etc.

Array Reference:

`array-name[subscript]`

where the subscript can be any integer expression in the proper range, as is given in the declaration of the array.

Enabling range checking causes the computer to check for a subscript out of range.

Array Algorithms. Initialization, if needed:

```
for I := 1 to N do
  begin
     process involving A[I]
  end {for}
```

Searching

```
Found := false;
I := 1;
while (I <= N) and (not Found) do
  begin
     if A[I] = Value then
        Found := true
     else
        I := I + 1
  end; {while}
{at this point, take action based on whether or not found}
```

Working with a Single Element. Subscript based on some action, such as searching, formula calculation, and reading data.

Testing

1. Natural boundaries for arrays:

   First element
   Last possible element
   Last element actually present

2. Portion of array in use:

None
Completely in use
In between

DPT

1. Do not confuse a subscript and the corresponding array element.
2. Do not use a wrong subscript.
3. Avoid a subscript out of range.
4. Pass arrays to match array parameters, array elements to match real, integer, etc., parameters.
5. Parameters must be of a named type.
6. Be wary of compound conditions such as:

   `(I > N) or (A[I] = Value)`

7. Avoid very large arrays, and arrays storing long strings, so as not to exceed THINK's limit for static variables.

EXERCISES

Many of these exercises ask you to write subprograms involving arrays. To do so, you must make intelligent assumptions about the context.

For example, in Exercise 3, you must assume that the type for the array has been declared in the main program, and you must make an assumption about what that type is called. Also, you should assume that N represents the portion in use, and that the lowest subscript is 1.

(If a specific array size such as 50 or 100 is mentioned, we suggest you use a global constant such as MaxIndex in place of the specific constant.)

1. Give the appropriate constant, type, and variable declarations to declare the following arrays:
   (a) An integer array with subscripts ranging from 0 to 100.
   (b) A real array with subscripts ranging from –50 to 75.
   (c) A Boolean array with subscripts ranging from 22 to 53.
   (d) An array of days of size 100. The array values are Monday, Thursday, etc. Use an appropriate user-defined scalar type.
   (e) An array representing the positions played by a 28-member baseball team. Possible positions are P, C, 1B, 2B, SS, 3B, and OF.
   (f) An array to contain the names of up to 250 students in an introductory calculus section.
   (g) An array to contain the classes (FR, SO, JR, SR, CONTED, or GRAD) of approximately 1750 students at a small college.

2. (a) Give appropriate declarations and Pascal code to create an array containing the names of the months.

(b) Repeat part (a) for an array containing the 16 single characters "0" through "9" and "A" through "F". (The subscript for "0" should be 0, for "1" should be 1, and so on.)

3. Assume that we have an array A containing N elements. Write subprograms for the following:
    (a) Find the value of the smallest element in A.
    (b) Find the location of the first element equal to the smallest.
    (c) Find the location of the last element equal to the smallest.
    (d) Count the number of elements equal to the smallest.
    (e) Print the subscripts of all array elements equal to the smallest. Hint: This requires two loops.

4. (a) By making minor modifications to the procedure in Figure 6-3, write a function that finds the position of the largest value in an array.
    (b) Can you accomplish this task without using a variable such as Large to contain the largest value? Hint: In Figure 6-3, GradeList[LargePosition] is the same as Large.

5. (a) Given this code to read an array, terminating when the user enters a 0; N is the array size.

```
I := 0;
Readln(Number);
while Number <> 0 do
  begin
      I := I + 1;
      A[I] := Number;
      Readln(Number)
  end; {while}
  N := I
```

Modify this segment to limit the array to 10 numbers. Compare this to the segment in the section "Processing Single Elements" that accomplishes the same task.

(b) Trace your solution, and that in the section, for situations where the resulting value of N should be 0, 1, 9, and 10.

6. Previously, we gave the following solution to a problem of counting how many children in a kindergarten are assigned to each of six groups. (We assume the Counter array has been initialized to 0.)

```
for I := 1 to N do
  begin
      CountSub := Group[I];
      Counter[CountSub] := Counter[CountSub] + 1
  end {for}
```

A student has proposed the following alternative solution:

```
for I := 1 to 6 do
  begin
      for J := 1 to N do
          begin
              if Group[J] = I then
                  Counter[I] := Counter[I] + 1
          end {for J}
  end {for I}
```

Compare the two solutions to see which has fewer steps. If N is 150, how many steps are involved for each?

7. Write subprograms for the following using an integer array A. Assume the array is of size 50, but that it presently contains only N (≤ 50) values.
   (a) Find the average of the values.
   (b) Find what percentage of the values are positive.
   (c) Set a variable Location to contain the subscript of the first negative value in the array (Location is to be 0 if there are no negative values).
   (d) Set a Boolean variable to *true* if none of the array values are 0; otherwise to *false*.
   (e) Add a new value to the end of the array. The variable NewValue contains the value to be added. Assume that N < 50.
   (f) Repeat part (e), but remove the assumption that N < 50. Set a Boolean variable to indicate if the array is full.
   (g) Repeat part (f), but assume that if that value is already present in the array, it should not be added.
   (h) Repeat part (g), but assume that the numbers in the array are in increasing order and that they should still be in increasing order after the new value is inserted.

8. The standard deviation of a group of N values of A can be defined as

$$\sqrt{\frac{1}{N-1} \sum_{i=1}^{N} (A_i - \overline{A})^2}$$

(The Σ (summation) notation indicates the sum of the indicated values for i varying from 1 to N.) Write a subprogram that computes $\overline{A}$ (the average of the A values), then compute the sum of the values $(A_i - \overline{A})^2$, and finally compute the standard deviation.

9. We are given two arrays A and B of N elements each. Write a subprogram to compute

$$P = A_1 * B_1 + A_2 * B_2 + \cdots + A_N * B_N$$

10. Suppose an array of N integers is known to contain only 0's and 1's. Write code to place all the 0's at the beginning of the array and all the 1's at the end of the array.

11. Given an array representing the positions played by a 28-member baseball team, count the pitchers. (See Exercise 1(e).)

12. Given an array representing the voice parts of a 75-member choir, compute the ratio of tenors to sopranos.

13. Using the array defined in Exercise 2(a), write a subprogram to convert a date to printable form. The input is a record containing three fields (month, day, and year); the output is a string. For example, for input 11 7 90, the output would be 'November 7, 1990'.

14. Using the array defined in Exercise 2(b), write subprograms for the following:
    (a) Given an integer in the range 0 to 15, the output is the corresponding character from "0" to "9", "A" to "F".
    (b) Given a character in the range "0" to "9" or "A" to "F", the output is the corresponding integer in the range 0 to 15.

15. Write a subprogram to calculate a student's score on a 100-point true–false test. The input consists of two Boolean arrays of size 100: the answer key and the student's answers.

16. Assume that we have real arrays A and B, each containing 100 elements. Write subprograms for the following:

(a) Copy B to A.
(b) Copy the first 50 locations of B to the last 50 locations of A; that is, copy B[1-50] to A[51-100].
(c) Copy B[17-23] to A[1-7].
(d) Copy B[First] through B[Last] to the first locations of A. Assume First and Last are variables containing numbers in the range 1 to 100, with First ≤ Last.
(e) Copy the next six numbers, starting at the first nonzero number in B, into A[1–6]. You can assume that there is a nonzero number in B, located prior to or at location 95.
(f) Repeat (e), but copy six or fewer numbers. For example, if B[98] is the first nonzero number, you should copy only three numbers: B[98], B[99], and B[100]. If there are no nonzero numbers, do not copy any. Set a parameter to indicate how many were copied.
(g) Shift A one place to the right, setting A[1] to 0.
(h) Shift A two places to the left.
(i) Shift A two places to the right.
(j) Shift A in a given direction by a given amount. The parameters are A (the array), a char variable telling which direction to shift (value 'L' or 'R'), and an integer N telling how far to shift (assume N > 0).

17. A large data file contains the SAT scores for all the students in an incoming freshman class. The scores can range from 200 to 800.
(a) Write a program segment that counts how many students had each of the possible scores. What is a suitable type definition for the array of counters?
(b) Modify the code to also find which score occurred most frequently.
(c) Give two ways to find the average score.
(d) Modify part (a) to count scores in ranges of 10 points each: 200 to 209, 210 to 219, etc. Hint: Use integer division by 10.
(e) Modify part (a) to count scores in the ranges 200 to 300, 301 to 400, 401 to 500, . . . , 701 to 800.

18. (a) Write a subprogram to interchange two integers A and B. Use this subprogram to interchange the elements in positions I and J of an integer array A.
(b) Using the subprogram of part (a), write code to reverse the elements of an array A of five elements. For example, if A = (2, 4, 6, 8, 10), then the code should change A to (10, 8, 6, 4, 2). (Set this up so that elements 1 and 5 are interchanged followed by elements 2 and 4.)
(c) Repeat part (b), but allow the number of elements to be N. Does N have to be odd? Hint: First do the specific cases where N = 51 and where N = 50.

19. (a) Write code for scanning an array A and whenever A[I] > A[I+1] interchanging A[I] and A[I+1]. If the array has N elements, how many comparisons should be made? What is the value of the last element of A after the algorithm has been performed?
(b) Enclose your solution to part (a) in a loop that causes J to take on the values 1 through N − 1. Trace this algorithm using N = 5 and A = (1, 4, 5, 3, 2).

20. Write a subprogram to compare two arrays A and B of N elements each to see if the arrays are identical. In other words, the subprogram should see if the Ith element of A is the same as the Ith element of B for all I from 1 to N. If the arrays are identical, the answer is *true*; otherwise, *false*. Hint: This can be viewed as a search problem.

21. Write a subprogram to check if each element of A occurs only once in A. The answer is *true* if each does and *false* if some element occurs more than once. Hint: This can be viewed as a search problem.

22. Write a subprogram to check if each element of A occurs at least once in an array B. Hint: This, too, can be viewed as a search problem.

23. (a) A is an array of N elements, where N is larger than 7. Write code to locate the largest element in positions 7, 8, up to N, and interchange it with the element in position 7.
    (b) Redo part (a), but instead of using element 7, make that position variable, perhaps J.
    (c) Enclose your solution to part (b) in a loop that causes J to take on the values 1 through N − 1. Trace this subprogram using N = 5 and A = (1, 4, 5, 3, 2).

24. Each record in a file contains a name and 12 monthly take-home pay figures. We can use this segment of code to read and print the file:

    ```
    while not Eof(InputFile) do
      begin
         GetInput(InputFile, Name, Pay);
         DetailLine(Name, Pay)
      end {while}
    ```

    GetInput is a procedure that reads a name and 12 pay figures from the file. DetailLine is a procedure that prints the data, with headings when appropriate. We assume that these procedures have already been written. (Note: For a complete program, we would have to add steps to open and close the file, initialize line and page counts, and so on. In this exercise, we do not deal with these issues. See Exercise 25.)

    Show how to modify this segment of code to do the following:
    (a) Also print the total yearly take-home pay for each person.
    (b) Find and print the name of the person who had the highest total take-home pay.
    (c) Find the highest take-home pay for each of the 12 months. Hint: Use an array LargePay of size 12.
    (d) Find who had the highest take-home pay in each month and print (for each month) a message like

    ```
    In month 1 xxxxxxxxxxxx had the largest pay - xxxxxx.xx.
    ```

    (e) Modify part (d) to print messages like

    ```
    In January xxxxxxxxxxxx had the largest pay - xxxxxx.xx.
    ```

    Hint: Use a string array of size 12 containing the names of the months.

25. (a) Write the GetInput procedure for Exercise 24 under the assumption that the file is a text file consisting of 13 lines for each person: name, January pay, and so on.
    (b) Redo part (a) assuming that the file is of Pascal records each consisting of a name and 12 pay figures.
    (c) Using either file description from part (a) or (b), write a complete program accomplishing everything outlined in Exercise 23.

26. Give test plans for the following exercises in this section.
    (a) Exercise 4(a)
    (b) Exercise 7(a)
    (c) Exercise 7(b)
    (d) Exercise 7(c)
    (e) Exercise 7(f)
    (f) Exercise 7(g)

EXERCISES

(g) Exercise 7(h)
(h) Exercise 16(d)
(i) Exercise 18(c)
(j) Exercise 20
(k) Exercise 22

6-2 ARRAYS AND DATA STRUCTURES

In the previous section, we examined arrays in some detail, expanding the knowledge we had been gradually building over the previous three chapters. In that section, we placed a number of restrictions on the arrays under consideration: (1) the subscripts were integers; (2) the component type was integer, real, char, string, or a user-defined scalar type; and (3) we dealt (mostly) with one array at a time. In this section, we remove these restrictions and consider the important topic of **data structures** in more detail.

Arrays in Pascal

We begin with a more complete description of Pascal arrays. We can declare an array type using a declaration of the form

```
array[index-type] of component-type
```

As we have seen, a common form for index-type is a range of integers from 1 to some number greater than 1. However, there are other possibilities, including these:

1. A subrange of the integers, such as

```
2..12
-500..500
```

2. Either *boolean* or *char*.

3. A subrange of *char*, such as

```
'a'..'z'
'0'..'9'
'A ..'J'
```

4. User-defined enumerated or subrange type, such as

```
type
        Suits = (Clubs, Diamonds, Hearts, Spades);
        ValidGrade = 0..100;
        Days = (Sun, Mon, Tue, Wed, Thr, Fri, Sat);

        Distribution = array[Suits] of 0..13;
        Summary = array[ValidGrade] of integer;
        HourArray = array[Mon..Fri] of real;
```

We access an element of an array by giving the array name and the subscript, or index, in an expression of the form

```
array-name[index]
```

The "index" can be any expression of the proper type. For example, suppose we declare these arrays, using the type definitions just given:

```
var
   GradeCount: Summary;
   HandCount: Distribution;
   Hours: HourArray;
   LetterCount: array[char] of integer;
```

Then these are valid array references:

```
Hours[Mon]
GradeCount[73]
HandCount[Hearts]
LetterCount['w']
```

Moreover, if Score is an integer variable in the range 0 to 100, Today is a type Days variable in the range Mon to Fri, and ThisCharacter is a char variable, then these are legal:

```
Hours[Today]
GradeCount[Score]
LetterCount[ThisCharacter]
```

In fact, we can use any legal expression of the proper type as a subscript.

The component type in the array declaration can be any legal type. This specifically includes arrays and records. We defer the consideration of "arrays of arrays" to the next chapter. However, we consider arrays of records extensively in the remainder of this section.

Data Structures

The term **data structure** refers to "structuring data." Thus, a data structure is a way of organizing data in a meaningful way. In this text, we have already seen numerous examples of data structures, including the following:

Strings. THINK Pascal uses the string data type to organize a series of individual characters into a meaningful entity.

Records. Records are one of the most useful tools for structuring data. For example, we can organize information about a person (name, age, and so on) as a record with a field for each piece of information. A slightly different example occurred in the case study of Section 5-4, where we used a record to structure the two parts of a fraction: numerator and denominator.

Arrays. Arrays allow us to organize a large number of related items of the same type.

Files. Files provide two important services. Most people probably think first of the "long-term storage" aspect of files. However, they also provide a structuring of the data they store.

Most computer science curricula include at least one course whose primary topic is data structures; we cannot cover the entire topic in this section. However, we indicate, primarily by examples, how arrays and records can be used in various combinations to organize data in meaningful ways.

6-2 ARRAYS AND DATA STRUCTURES

Parallel Arrays and Arrays of Records

Consider the following simple example. We wish to read the names and grades for 40 individuals and print the name of each person whose grade is larger than the average grade. This is a slight extension of the program of Figure 6-1. We can solve the problem by modifying that program, as shown in Figure 6-5. The changes are in italics.

Notice especially the step that prints the name:

```
if Grades [I] > Average then
    Writeln (' ' : 3, Names[I])
```

If, for example, the third grade in the Grades array exceeds the average, then this prints the third name in the Names array. Because of the manner in which the names and grades were stored in the array, the third name corresponds to the third grade, and thus the program prints the correct name.

We say that the name and grade arrays are **parallel arrays.**

As another example, we might have parallel arrays ClockNumber, Age, Sex, and Salary, each of size 50. We can think of these arrays as the columns of a table:

ClockNumber	Age	Sex	Salary
1149	25	M	12,500
1614	20	F	14,000
2319	35	F	17,250
1003	50	M	16,750
3914	39	M	22,000

Notice that, in the table, the arrays are parallel to each other (vertically).

Pascal, with its record structure, provides an alternative way to organize the data in our example program. Rather than using two parallel arrays Name and Grade, we might use a single array of 40 records, where each record has a name component and a grade component. Figure 6-6 illustrates the differences involved with this approach.

Conceptually, parallel arrays and arrays of records are the same. We can visualize each in terms of a table, as illustrated earlier. For languages that do not provide a record structure, we are forced to use the parallel array idea; in Pascal, we have a choice.

Many of the array-processing techniques we have learned can fruitfully be used in the context of tables (either as parallel arrays or as arrays of records). For example, Figures 6-7(a) and 6-7(b) each give code to locate a student in the data structure and tell his grade. The first assumes parallel arrays and the second assumes an array of records. They both assume that the data have been read earlier in the program. The significant differences are in italics.

Note. As usual, when there are two ways to accomplish a task, there are trade-offs to be considered when choosing between parallel arrays and arrays of records. Fortunately, the thought processes involved in the two methods are similar, as illustrated by the small number of differences between Figures 6-7(a) and 6-7(b).

```
program PrintNames;

{Written by:  XXXXXXXXXX XX/XX/XX}
{Purpose:     To read a list of names and grades (of a fixed length) and }
{             print the names whose grades > the average}

    const
       MaxIndex = 40;              {size of grade array}

    type
       String50 = string[50];
       NameArray = array[1..MaxIndex] of String50;
       GradeArray = array[1..MaxIndex] of integer;

    var
       Names: NameArray;           {list of names}
       Grades: GradeArray;         {list of grades}
       I: integer;                 {loop control, and subscript}
       Sum: integer;               {sum of grades}
       Average: real;              {average of grades}
       Count: integer;             {how many are > average}

begin

{*** Read the names and grades and find the sum}

    Sum := 0;
    for I := 1 to MaxIndex do
      begin
         Write('Enter name #', I : 1, ': ');
         Readln(Names[I]);
         Write('Enter grade #', I, ' ');
         Readln(Grades[I]);
         Sum := Sum + Grades[I]
      end; {for}

{*** Find and print the average}

    Average := Sum / MaxIndex;

    Writeln;
    Writeln('The average is ', Average : 1 : 2);

{*** Prints names whose grades are larger than the average}

    Writeln;
    Writeln('Names whose grades are larger than the average:');

    for I := 1 to MaxIndex do
      begin
         if Grades[I] > Average then
            Writeln(' ' : 3, Names[I])
      end {for}

    end. {PrintNames}
```

Figure 6-5   Parallel arrays.

6-2 ARRAYS AND DATA STRUCTURES

```pascal
program PrintNames;
{Written by: XXXXXXXXXX XX/XX/XX}
{Purpose:   To read a list of names and grades (of a fixed length),}
{           and print the names whose grades are greater than the}
{           average}

  const
    MaxIndex = 40;                    {size of grade array}

  type
    String50 = string[50];
    StudentRecord = record
        Name: String50;
        Grade: integer
      end;
    StudentArray = array[1..MaxIndex] of StudentRecord;

  var
    Student: StudentArray;            {list of names and grades}
    I: integer;                       {loop control, and subscript}
    Sum: integer;                     {sum of grades}
    Average: real;                    {average of grades}
    Count: integer;                   {how many are > average}

begin
{*** Read the names and grades and find the sum}

  Sum := 0;
  for I := 1 to MaxIndex do
    begin
      Write('Enter name #', I : 1, ': ');
      Readln(Student[I].Name);
      Write('Enter grade #', I, ' ');
      Readln(Student[I].Grade);
      Sum := Sum + Student[I].Grade
    end; {for}

{*** Find and print the average}

  Average := Sum / MaxIndex;
  Writeln;
  Writeln('The average is ', Average : 1 : 2);

{*** Prints names whose grades are larger than the average}

  Writeln;
  Writeln('Names whose grades are larger than the average:');
  for I := 1 to MaxIndex do
    begin
      with Student[I] do
        if Grade > Average then
          Writeln(' ' : 3, Name)
    end {for}
end. {PrintNames}
```

Figure 6-6   Array of records.

```
{*** Read a name to search for}

Writeln;
Write('Enter a name to search for: ');
Readln(NameToFind);

{*** Locate name and print grade, or error message}

Found := false;
I := 1;
while (I <= MaxIndex) and (not Found) do
  begin
     if Names[I] = NameToFind then
        Found := true
     else
        I := I + 1
  end; {while}
if Found then
  Writeln('The grade is ', Grades[I] : 1)
else
  Writeln('Name not found.')
```

Figure 6-7a Searching parallel arrays.

```
{*** Read a name to search for}

Writeln;
Write('Enter a name to search for: ');
Readln(NameToFind);

{*** Locate name and print grade, or error message}

Found := false;
I := 1;
while (I <= MaxIndex) and (not Found) do
  begin
     if Student[I].Name = NameToFind then
        Found := true
     else
        I := I + 1
  end; {while}
if Found then
  Writeln('The grade is ', Student[I].Grade : 1)
else
  Writeln('Name not found.')
```

Figure 6-7b Searching an array of records.

Generally, the array of records more closely matches our usual notion of a table as a set of rows, each row describing one entity, a plus for this method. Using parallel arrays, it is up to the programmer to tie together the related data.

6-2 ARRAYS AND DATA STRUCTURES

On the other hand, suppose we modified the code in Figures 6-7(a) and 6-7(b) as follows: Write a procedure that finds the subscript of a given name. Using parallel arrays, we would pass the name array to the procedure. The same procedure could be used in other programs with arrays of names. Using the array of records representation, we would have to pass in the entire data structure (the array of records called Student). The procedure would not be usable (without some changes) in another program needing a procedure to locate a name in an array. (In addition, the procedure could inadvertently modify a part of the data structure totally unrelated to its purpose of looking for a name.)

Records Containing Arrays

In defining a record data type, we are allowed to use an array as one of the fields of the record. To illustrate this, we design a program that reads payroll data from a file and prints a report. For each person, the data consist of these components:

> Name
> Pay rate
> Hours worked each of 7 days (Sunday through Saturday)

The basic logic of the program involves repeating these steps for each employee:

> read the data
> calculate the total hours
> calculate the pay
> print the name and pay

An appropriate data structure involves several of the ideas developed in this section:

```
type
  String50  = string[50];
  DaysOfWeek = (Sun, Mon, Tue, Wed, Thr, Fri, Sat);
  HourArray = array[DaysOfWeek] of real;
  WorkerRecord = record
      Name: String50;
      PayRate: real;
      Hours: HourArray
    end;
  WorkerFile = file of WorkerRecord;

var
  Worker: WorkerRecord;      {individual's data}
  MasterFile: WorkerFile;    {master worker file}
```

Leaving for later the details of opening and closing files, we can write the body of the main program as

```
while not Eof(MasterFile) do
  begin
     Read(MasterFile, Worker);
     TotalHours := TotalFn(Worker.Hours);
     Pay := Worker.PayRate * TotalHours;
     DetailLine(Worker.Name, Pay)
  end; {while}
```

We have chosen to use a function to calculate the total hours, passing it the Hours array portion of the Worker record as its parameter. (Its parameter is of type HourArray.) We have also chosen to use a procedure to print the output (and to use the OpenRead procedure discussed in Chapter 5 to handle the details of opening the file). We can begin with a stub version, later adding refinements such as printing headers, etc.

The entire program is presented in Figure 6-8. Of special interest is the TotalFn function. It adds the weekday hours; any in excess of 40 are scaled by a factor of 1.5 ("time and a half"). Weekend hours are "double time", reflected in the scaling factor of 2.0. Notice the use of "for Day := Mon to Fri" to loop through the five weekdays (Monday through Friday), and of "HourList[Day]" to refer to the array elements.

Note. An array such as HourList, which uses an enumerated type for its subscripts, raises an interesting issue. With integer subscripts, we are used to expressions such as

```
A[I+1]
A[I-3]
```

To do a similar thing with enumerated types, we would have to use the functions Succ and Pred. For example, if Day has the value Wed, then HourList[Succ(Day)] would refer to the hour for Thursday, and HourList[Pred(Day)] to the hours for Tuesday.

We now consider an important data structure with an entirely different flavor. In dealing with arrays in the preceding section, we frequently maintained a count of how many values were in the array. We used a separate variable for that purpose.

Another approach that is sometimes used associates the array size more closely with the array, as indicated by these data declarations:

```
const
   EndOfData = -1;    {terminates input}
   MaxSize = 50;      {maximum size of array}
type
   IntegerList = record
       Len: integer;        {length of list}
       Values: array[1..MaxSize] of integer;
   end;
```

When we pass a parameter of type IntegerList to a subprogram, its current length (Len) automatically goes along. We do not have to remember to pass it as a separate parameter.

Note. In a subprogram that has this type of variable as a parameter, we might wish to use the Pascal *with* statement. See Figure 6-9.

Other Combinations

As we indicated earlier, our intention here is simply to suggest some data-structuring ideas. For our final example, we consider a combination of ideas from the previous two subsections. We have an array of records, where each record contains an array. Specifically, we deal with an array of student records, where each student record has these components:

```
program PayReport;

{Written by:   XXXXXXXXXX XX/XX/XX}
{Purpose:      To data from a payroll file , and print a pay report}
{Functions used: TotalFn, to find total hours, adjusted for overtime}
{               rules}
{Procedures used:  OpenRead, to open the master file}
{                  DetailLine, to print a line of the report}

   type
      String50 = string[50];
      DaysOfWeek = (Sun, Mon, Tue, Wed, Thr, Fri, Sat);
      HourArray = array[DaysOfWeek] of real;
      WorkerRecord = record
         Name: String50;
         PayRate: real;
         Hours: HourArray
        end;
      WorkerFile = file of WorkerRecord;

   var
      Worker: WorkerRecord;          {individual's data}
      MasterFile: WorkerFile;        {master worker file}
      TotalHours: real;              {total hours for week}
      Pay: real;                     {pay for week}

   function TotalFn (HourList: HourArray): real;

   {Written by: XXXXXXXXXX XX/XX/XX}
   {Purpose:    To add up all the hours, adjusting for double}
   {            time (for weekends), and time and a half (for}
   {            over 40 hours during a week)}
   {Parameters: HourList - input, array of hours for week}

      var
         Day: DaysOfWeek;     {loop control and subscript}
         Total: real;         {local variable for total}

      begin {TotalFn}

{*** Total weekday hours}

         Total := 0;
         for Day := Mon to Fri do
           begin
              Total := Total + HourList[Day]
           end; {for}
```

Figure 6-8   Record containing an array (continues next page).

```
{*** Adjust for time and a half (over 40 hours)}

    if Total > 40 then
      Total := 40 + (Total - 40) * 1.5;

{*** Add in weekend at double time}

    Total := Total + 2 * (HourList[Sun] + HourList[Sat]);

{*** Send answer back}

    TotalFn := Total
  end; {TotalFn}

{function Exists, as shown in Appendix C, is inserted here}

{procedure OpenRead, as shown in Appendix C, is inserted here, with}
{text type changed to WorkerFile}

  procedure DetailLine (Name: String50; Pay: real);

  begin {DetailLine - stub version; full version left as exercise}
    Writeln(Name, ' ', Pay : 1 : 2)
  end; {DetailLine}

begin {PayReport}

{*** Open file}

  OpenRead(MasterFile);

{*** Read records and process pay report}

  while not Eof(MasterFile) do
    begin
      Read(MasterFile, Worker);
      TotalHours := TotalFn(Worker.Hours);
      Pay := Worker.PayRate * TotalHours;
      DetailLine(Worker.Name, Pay)
    end; {while}

{*** Close file and terminate}

  Close(MasterFile);
  Writeln;
  Writeln('Report complete.');
end.
```

Figure 6-8   (continued)

```
procedure AddToEnd(var List: IntegerList; Number: integer;
                   var OK: boolean);

{Written by: XXXXXXXXXX XX/XX/XX}
{Purpose:    To add a number to the end of a list, if possible}
{Parameters: List   - update, the list to add to}
{            Number - input, the number to add}
{            OK     - output, whether or not the list was full}
{Globals used: MaxSize - global constant telling maximum size of list}

begin {AddToEnd}
  with List do
    begin
      if Len = MaxSize then
        OK := false
      else
        begin
          OK := true;
          Len := Len + 1;
          Values[Len] := Number
        end {if}
    end {with}
end; {AddToEnd}
```

Figure 6-9   Keeping the actual size with an array.

Name

4 test grades

Final exam grade

10 program grades

Final average

Letter grade

We define our data structure as

```
const
  MaxStudents = 50;

type
  String50 = string[50];
  TestArray = array[1..4] of integer;
  ProgramArray = array[1..10] of integer;
  StudentRecord = record
      Name: String50;
      TestList: TestArray;
      Exam: integer;
      ProgList: ProgramArray;
      Average: real;
      Letter: char
    end;
  StudentList = array[1..MaxStudents] of StudentRecord;
```

```
var
    Student: StudentList;      {array of student records}
```

The program in Figure 6-10 has three major steps:

1. Read the data for the class: How many students? How many tests so far? How many programs so far? And what is the student list?
2. Add the scores for a test to each student's record.
3. Rewrite the data to the same files.

Besides illustrating data structures, the program illustrates one approach to maintaining data on files over a period of time. We can read the entire set of data from the file into memory, allow the user to perform a number of steps that modify the data in various ways, then write the data back to the file. This approach works adequately well for files with a few thousand records or less; other techniques (discussed later in the text) are needed for large files (both for efficiency reasons and because of memory restrictions).

A difficulty arises in this example because we have two different types of data. First, we have the list of student records, which can be stored using a file declared as "file of StudentRecord". Second, we have the "control" information: how many students, how many tests, how many programs?

There are a number of ways to approach this problem. The program illustrates one possibility: use a **control file** to store control information about the **data file.** The data file has the data for the students in the class, and the control file has the information about the number of students, tests, and programs. (Chapter 11 discusses other file-related ideas.)

Testing

We suggest you review the comments presented in Section 6-1 on testing involving arrays. Here we discuss additional testing issues raised by this section's topics.

To begin, consider a program that reads an array of student records from a file, allows the user to make a series of changes, then writes the records back to the file. Suppose that among the possible changes to the data are these:

Delete a student
Add a student
Change a grade

In this type of program, we might want to test the relationship of various steps performed in sequence. This is sometimes called **sequence testing** or **combination testing.** For example, these are some important tests:

- delete a name, then try to delete the same name again
- delete a name, do some other steps, then add the same name
- try to add the same name twice in a row
- change a test, then later change it again for the same person
- add a name, change a test, and delete the name
- add enough names to "overflow" the array
- with the array full, try to add a name that is already there
- delete all names, then add a name

6-2 ARRAYS AND DATA STRUCTURES

```
program EnterTest;

{Written by:  XXXXXXXXXX XX/XX/XX}
{Purpose:     To allow the user to enter test scores for the class}
{Procedures used: OpenFiles, to open the files}
{                 ReadFiles, to read the files into the data structure}
{                 WriteFiles, to write the data structures back to the files}
{                 GetValidScore, to obtain a score in the range 0 - 100}

   const
      MaxStudents = 50;         {limit on array size}

   type
      String50 = string[50];
      TestArray = array[1..4] of integer;
      ProgramArray = array[1..10] of integer;

      StudentRecord = record
         Name: String50;
         TestList: TestArray;
         Exam: integer;
         ProgList: ProgramArray;
         Average: real;
         Letter: char
      end;

   ControlRecord = record
      NStudents: integer;
      NTests: integer;
      NPrograms: integer
   end;

   StudentList = array[1..MaxStudents] of StudentRecord;
   StudentFileType = file of StudentRecord;
   ControlFileType = file of ControlRecord;

   var
      Student: StudentList;              {array of students}
      Control: ControlRecord;            {control information}
      StudentFile: StudentFileType;      {master student file}
      ControlFile: ControlFileType;      {control file}
      I: integer;                        {loop control}

   procedure OpenFiles (var Master: StudentFileType; var ControlFile:
                        ControlFileType);

   begin {OpenFiles - stub version; full version left as exercise}
      Reset(Master, 'StudentInfo');
      Reset(ControlFile, 'StudentControl')
   end; {OpenFiles}
```

Figure 6-10 Array of Records Containing Arrays (continues next page).

```
procedure GetValidScore (var Score: integer);

begin {GetValidScore - stub version; full version left as exercise}
  Readln(Score)
end; {GetValidScore}

procedure ReadFiles (var StudentFile: StudentFileType;
                     var ControlFile: ControlFileType;
                     var Student: StudentList;
                     var Control: ControlRecord);

{Written by:   XXXXXXXXXX XX/XX/XX}
{Purpose:      To read the data from the control and student files}
{              into the internal data structure}
{Parameters:   StudentFile - the file designator for the student file}
{              ControlFile - the file designator for the control file}
{              Student - output, the array of student records}
{              Control - output , the control record}

var
  I: integer;    {loop control}

begin {ReadFiles}
  Read(ControlFile, Control);
  for I := 1 to Control.NStudents do
    begin
      Read(StudentFile, Student[I])
    end {for}
end; {ReadFiles}

procedure WriteFiles (var StudentFile: StudentFileType;
                      var ControlFile: ControlFileType;
                      Student: StudentList;
                      Control: ControlRecord);

{Written by:   XXXXXXXXXX XX/XX/XX}
{Purpose:      To write the data from the internal data structures back}
{              to the original files}
{Parameters:   StudentFile - the file designator for the student file}
{              ControlFile - the file designator for the control file}
{              Student - input, the array of student records}
{              Control - input, the control record}

var
  I: integer;    {loop control}

begin {WriteFiles}
  Rewrite(ControlFile, 'StudentControl');
  Rewrite(StudentFile, 'StudentInfo');
  Write(ControlFile, Control);
```

Figure 6-10 (continues next page).

```
    for I := 1 to Control.NStudents do
      begin
        Write(StudentFile, Student[I])
      end {for}

  end; {WriteFiles}

begin {EnterTest}

{*** Open files and read the data}

  OpenFiles(StudentFile, ControlFile);
  ReadFiles(StudentFile, ControlFile, Student, Control);

{*** See if another test can be entered. If so, print each student name}
{    and read the test score.}

  if Control.NTests >= 4 then
    Writeln('There have already been 4 tests.')
  else
    begin
      Control.NTests := Control.NTests + 1;
      for I := 1 to Control.NStudents do
        begin
          with Student[I] do
            begin
              Write('Score for ', Name, ': ');
              GetValidScore(TestList[Control.Ntests])
          end {with}
      end {for}
  end; {if}

{*** Write the resulting data structure back to the files}

  WriteFiles(StudentFile, ControlFile, Student, Control);

{*** Close files and stop program}

  Close(StudentFile);
  Close(ControlFile);
  Writeln;
  Writeln('Test scores updated.');
end.
```

Figure 6-10 (continued)

In this type of problem, the results of a specific step depend on what has come before. The rules for determining the important test sequences, in a context such as this, are not as precise as those for boundary or class testing. Although we can give some general guidelines, writing a good test plan is always a creative process, even more so for this type of problem than for those we have dealt with previously.

DPT

1. The most important defensive programming tip, perhaps, is an offensive programming tip: Choose your data structures wisely. Data structures that adequately reflect the "real world situation" are much easier to understand as you develop your program. Hastily chosen data structures can lead to a great amount of frustration later. Carefully chosen data structures can make the program easier to write and easier to understand.

2. Remember that subscripts are necessary to access an element of an array. For example, in the data structures used in Figure 6-10, the reference Student[5] would refer to the fifth student record. Within that record, Student[5].TestList[3] would refer to that student's third test. To access the fifth student's third test, we need both subscripts in the form indicated here.

3. The subscript must be an expression of the proper type. For example, if we declare:

```
type
   Days = (Sun, Mon, Tue, Wed, Thr, Fri, Sat);

var
   Hours = array[Days] of real;
```

then Hours[l] makes no sense, but Hours[Sun] does.

4. Don't forget to use range checking during development.

5. When we define complex data structures involving records, it is a good idea to use named data types for each component of the record. For example, use

```
type
   String50 = string[50];
   TestArray = array[1..5] of integer;
   StudentRecord = record
     Name: String50;
     Test: TestArray
   end;
```

This allows us to pass individual components, if necessary or convenient, as parameters to subprograms.

6. All other tips relating to arrays (especially in Sections 3-2 and 6-1) and to records (Sections 5-2 to 5-4) must be kept in mind when dealing with combinations of these structures.

REVIEW

Terms and Concepts

combination testing
control files
data file
data structures
parallel array
sequence testing

Pascal Syntax

1. Index type for an array declaration can be

    (a) Subrange of integers, e.g., 1..50 or –3..5

    (b) Boolean

    (c) Char

    (d) Subrange of char, e.g., 'a'..'z'

    (e) User-defined enumerated type or subrange type, e.g., Days or Mon..Fri

2. Array reference: `array-name[index]`

Data Structure Examples

1. Strings
2. Records
3. Arrays
4. Files
5. Parallel arrays
6. Arrays of records
7. Records containing arrays
8. Other combinations, e.g., arrays of records, where each record contains an array

Testing

Sequence (combination testing); for example:
    add same name twice
    delete name, then add back
    change same value twice
    etc.

DPT

1. Choose data structures carefully.
2. Use subscripts to access array elements, e.g., Student[5].Test[3].
3. Subscript must be of the proper type.
4. Use range checking.
5. Use named data types for record components.

EXERCISES

1. Define data structures for each of the following. Give the type and var declarations and show how to access each part of the data structure. (For example, Student.Grade[I].)

(a) One entry for a mailing list: name, address, expiration date, and a special 8-character code.
(b) Data for a family consisting of a husband, wife, and up to five children. Include name and age for each person.
(c) A list of rainfall figures for one year for one state. The data consist of the state name and 12 monthly rainfall figures.
(d) Repeat part (c), but store the data for all 50 states at once.
(e) Repeat part (d), but simultaneously store the data for 7 years. For each year, the data consists of the year (e.g., 1992) and the data for the 50 states.
(f) A table containing data for up to 100 employees: name, social security number, and last year's salary.
(g) A polynomial having up to 20 terms, each consisting of a real coefficient and an integer exponent.
(h) An answer key for a multiple-choice test containing up to 100 questions. Each question has possible answers a, b, c, d, or e, and has a point value assigned to it.
(i) A student's answer sheet for the test described in part (h).
(j) An array to contain the characters '0', '1', ... , '9'. The array should be set up in such a way that the element with subscript 5 contains '5' and so on. Also give the assignments to initialize the array.
(k) An array called Vowel, indexed by capital letters 'A' through 'Z', to make it easy to answer the question, "Is this capital letter a vowel?" For example, Vowel['T'] would be *false*. Also give the assignments to initialize the array.

2. The person designing the data structure for a class list has chosen to use a group of parallel arrays: Name, Testl, Test2, Test3, Test4, Test5, Test6, Exam, Average, and Letter. Name[I] contains the name of the Ith student, Testl[I] her score on the first test, and so on. Suppose that the names, test grades, and exam grade have already been read and that there are N students. Write segments of Pascal code to do the following:
   (a) Compute the values for the Average array.
   (b) Print the names of all students who received the highest average. Notice that there may be several tied for highest.
   (c) Print the highest and lowest score for each test.
   (d) Compute the average score for each test.
   (e) Assuming that the function LetterGrade calculates a letter grade, given a numeric average, write code to calculate the values for the Letter array.

3. Repeat Exercise 2, but assume that students can withdraw. When they do, the information remains in the arrays; however, their letter grade is given the value 'W'.
(a)–(d) Repeat parts (a) to (d) of Exercise 2, but ignore all students who have withdrawn.

   (e) Write code to count the number of students who have withdrawn and print the percentage of withdrawals.
   (f) Write code that, given a student name, locates that student and marks him as withdrawn. If the student has already withdrawn or if the name is not present, print an appropriate error message.

4. Repeat Exercise 2 with a different choice for the data structure. Use an array of records, each record having these fields: name, an array of six test scores, exam score, final average, and letter grade.

5. Was there any significant advantage to either of the data structures in Exercises 2 and 4? Which strategy would be more appropriate if there were 3 tests and 14 weekly quizzes? Which would be better if there were variables indicating how many scores have been entered so far?

6. In this exercise, we explore three possible data structures to represent a list of campers and the cabins to which they are assigned. There are 20 cabins, with names such as "BlackHawk," "Wigwam," and so on. For each data structure, we use an array of records, one record per camper. The record has the camper's name and a representation of the cabin. The differences are in how we represent the cabin.

Data Structure No. 1:   The cabin is given by a string variable containing the name of the cabin.

Data Structure No. 2:   The cabin is an integer code representing the cabin number.

Data Structure No. 3:   The cabin is a user-defined scalar type defined in the form CabinType = (BlackHawk, Wigwam, . . .).

For each part of the exercise, give code to solve the problem for each data structure. (You may need to define additional data, such as print name arrays; if so, describe them in words.)

(a) Print a list of campers: name and cabin name.
(b) Read a camper's name and print his or her cabin name (or an error message if the person is not in the list).
(c) For each cabin, print the cabin name and a count of the campers in the cabin.
(d) Read a name and cabin name for a camper to be added to the list. Make sure the cabin name is one of those allowed and that the camper's name is not a duplicate.

7. (a) Write a program that declares an array CountLetter indexed by the range type 'A' .. 'Z'. It should initialize the array to contain all zeros, then read a series of single-character inputs from the user. The array should be used to count how many of each letter ('A' to 'Z') are input. Output consists of a series of lines such as

```
B was entered 3 times
```

Skip any for which the count was 0.

(b) Extend part (a) to include all characters. Hint: The index type is "char" and a loop

```
for I := Chr(0) to Chr(255) do
```

can be used to move through the array.

(c) Extend part (a) to read strings rather than single characters. Hint: For a string InputString, InputString[I] is the Ith character, and Length(InputString) returns the number of characters in InputString.

8. Suppose that an array of 100 records contains data for NEmpl employees. Each record contains the employee number, name, sales, age, sex, department, and group. Give segments of code for the following. Assume that the data have been read earlier in the program.

(a) Give the appropriate declarations to declare the array.
(b) There are 10 groups. Find the total sales for each of the 10 groups putting the answers in an array of size 10. Then read an employee number and new sales amount; add this amount to that employee's sales figure and to the total for each group.
(c) Suppose that an array ValidDepartment, of size 17, contains a list of all the valid department codes. Print the employee number of all employees whose department entry is presently invalid.
(d) Add a new employee to the end of the list. Check for these errors: invalid department code, employee number already in use, and list full.
(e) Count how many are in the following age groups: under 20, 20 to 29, 30 to 39, 40 to 49, 50 to 59, and 60 or over. Use an array of counters.
(f) Count how many are in each department. Hint: The ValidDepartment array of part (c) can be used to convert a valid department name to a number from 1 to 17.

9. (a) Write a program to interactively build an array of records of the form: father's name, mother's name, number of children, and children's names (array of up to 8). At the end, print the array and write it to a file.
   (b) Write a program to read the file created in part (a) into an array, and print the array on the terminal.

10. Do the following for the example of Figure 6-8:
    (a) Write the DetailLine procedure.
    (b) Write another program to create the file this program uses. It should read data from an appropriate text file, check for errors in the data, and write it to the file of records.

11. Do the following for the example of Figure 6-10:
    (a) Write a program to create the files the program uses. At the beginning of the semester, the number of tests and programs is 0. Thus, the program should simply read a series of names and write the appropriate values to the data and control files.
    (b) Write the OpenFiles procedure. It should ask the user for a "base name" and use that to build the file names. For example, if the user enters Hist305, the file names would be Hist305Scores and Hist305Control. The procedure should print a message if the files do not exist. Hint: Use an Exists function as shown in Appendix C. You may also wish to imitate the logic of the OpenRead procedure of Appendix C.
    (c) Write the GetValidScores procedure.
    (d) Write a program to dump the data in the files. It should print the control record, and then each student record. For each student, print all 4 test scores and all 10 program scores, even if all have not yet been entered. Note: Unless the create program puts meaningful data (such as 0) in the fields of the record, the dump program may show "garbage" until later programs fill in the data.
    (e) Describe what additional programs would be needed to make the system useful to an instructor. Do you think it would be better to have a separate program for each task or to use a single menu-driven program with each task a menu option?

12. One very useful data structure is called a *stack*. A stack is a list where items are inserted and removed from only one end of the list. The term is suggestive of a stack of cafeteria trays or a stack of papers in an "in" box. A stack has the *last in, first out* property: The item removed from a stack is always the most recent one that was placed onto it.

    One way to implement a stack of integers is as a record defined by

    ```
    type
      Stack = record
          Top: integer;
          Values: array[1..MaxIndex] of integer
        end;
    ```

    "Top" contains the subscript of the top element in the stack. It is 0 for an empty stack, increases by 1 each time an item is added to the stack, and decreases by 1 each time an item is removed. Observe that this data structure is similar to the one where an array and its count are kept together by placing them in the same record.

    Write the following subprograms:

    (a) Procedure CreateEmpty(var S: Stack). It causes S to be an empty stack by setting S.Top to 0.
    (b) Function IsEmpty(S: Stack): boolean. It sees if S is empty.

EXERCISES

(c) Procedure Push(var S: Stack; Item: integer; var Overflow: boolean). It "pushes" an item on the stack, that is, adds an item to it. "Overflow" indicates whether the push succeeded. If there was no more room on the stack, it is set to *true*, otherwise to *false*.

(d) Procedure Pop(var S: Stack; var Item: integer; var Underflow: boolean). It "pops" an item from the stack, that is, removes an item from the stack and places its value into the variable Item. Underflow is set *true* if there was no item on the stack; otherwise it is *false*.

13. Using the stack operations defined in Exercise 12, write a program to reverse a series of integer inputs. (Push all input onto the stack, and then pop each item off in turn.)

14. Define subprograms to perform various operations on lists of integers. Use the data structure:

```
type
   Integerlist = record
      Length: integer;
      Values: array[1..MaxIndex] of integer
   end;
```

For example,

Length = 3
Values = 6, 7, 9

would represent a list of three integers.

(a) Read a list of integers.
(b) Print a list, eight numbers per line.
(c) Given a list and a value, place the value on the end of the list if it is positive; otherwise place it on the front of the list. Assume there is room for it.
(d) Concatenate two lists. For example, consider

    A. Length = 3   B. Length = 2
          Values = 6, 7, 9   Values = 1, 8

If C is the answer, it would be

    C. Length = 5
          Values = 6, 7, 9, 1, 8

Assume that A.Len + B.Len ≤ MaxIndex.

(e) Repeat part (d) without the assumption. The result should be truncated to the first MaxIndex values.
(f) Extract a sublist. The parameters are

    List: a list
    Posn: starting position for the sublist
    Len: the length of desired sublist
    Sublist: the resulting sublist

Assume that Posn and Len are such that the desired sublist is entirely contained within the list and that Len ≥ 0. The original list is unchanged.

(g) Repeat part (f), but without the assumptions on Posn and Len. If Posn < 1, Posn > List.Length, or if Len < 0, the resulting list should be empty. If Posn lies within the list and Len would go beyond the end, stop at the end. (For a list of length 5 with Posn = 4 and Length = 15, the resulting list would have only the fourth and fifth values of the original list.)

(h) Repeat part (f), but modify the original list by removing the extracted sublist.

(i) Insert a list into a given position "Posn" in another list. Assume that the position is between I and the length of the list into which it is being inserted.

(j) Repeat part (i), but without the assumption. If Posn < 1, place the new list at the front of the other; if Posn > the length of the list, place the new list at the end.

15. Suppose we have an array of up to 75 records for choir members. Among the fields are name, voice part, and range (e.g., 'John Smith', bass, high) would denote a "first bass," that is, a bass with a higher range than a "second bass." The voice parts are soprano, alto, tenor, and bass; the ranges are high and low. There are Number members in the choir at present. Give code for each of the following; use subprograms if appropriate. Except for part (c), assume that the data have already been read.

   (a) Give the necessary declarations for the array.

   (b) Declare and initialize "print name" arrays for the voice part and range. Using these, print a list of the choir.

   (c) Read values for the array from the terminal.

   (d) What percentage of the choir is soprano?

   (e) What percentage of the tenors are "first tenors" (high range)?

   (f) Given a name, tell his or her voice part and range.

   (g) Declare an array of four counters indexed by the voice part data type. Use this array to count the number of each voice part.

16. A file contains 50 records, each consisting of the name of a state and 12 monthly rainfall figures. Give code for the following:

   (a) Give appropriate declarations (see Exercises l(c) and l(d)).

   (b) Read the file into an array of size 50.

   (c) Rewrite the array to the file.

   (d) Given the name of a month, find the average rainfall for that month.

   (e) Given the name of a state, find which month had the largest rainfall.

   (f) Find the total rainfall for each state.

   (g) Find which state had the highest total rainfall. If there were ties, print all the states with the highest total.

17. (a) Using the random-number generator, write a function with two parameters, Range and Previous. The function should generate an integer in the range 1..Range, with the generated number not equal to Previous.

   (b) Repeat part (a), but with Range, Previousl, and Previous2. The number generated should not equal either Previousl or Previous2.

   (c) Expand on this idea by having an array Previous containing N different values. The number generated should not equal any of the values in the array. Note: In order to be assured of eventual success, assume that N < Range.

18. One of the authors was given a chance to win a prize at a movie video rental store. The game slip had nine hidden numbers. The goal was to uncover any three of the nine numbers; if the total was 15 or more, the author would win the prize.

    After failing to win, the author proceeded to uncover all nine numbers. They were 2, 9, 2, 5, 8, 9, 8, 6, and 5. What was the probability that the author would lose? To answer this, write a function of type win-or-lose that simulates one play of the game. Invoke the function 5000 times, counting how many are losses. (Hint: For the function, use an array of size 9 containing the nine values. Generate three different numbers in the range 1..9, and add those three array elements. The functions written in Exercises 17(a) and 17(b) could prove helpful.) You may wish to allow the user to enter the values for the array to make the game more general.

EXERCISES

19. (a) One way to simulate shuffling a deck of 52 cards is to generate random numbers in the range 1..52, making sure that each number is different from all those that came before. Using the function of Exercise 17(c), write a procedure to generate an array of size 52, containing the numbers 1 to 52, shuffled.
   (b) The problem with the approach in part (a) is that toward the end it may take quite some time to find a number that does not duplicate some earlier number. A better approach is this: Put the numbers 1 to 52 in the array. Then generate 52 random numbers in the range 1..52. If Num is the Ith number generated, swap A[I] with A[Num]. Write a procedure to do this form of shuffling.
   (c) Write a program to compare the times for the two methods. See the StatPack procedures in Section 10-3 for a method to time a routine. To obtain a meaningful test, you may want to invoke each procedure a number of times in a loop.

20. We can use the shuffling procedure of Exercise 19, suitably modified, to simulate the following experiment: Shuffle five cards, numbered from 1 to 5, into random order, then count how many cards are in their "correct" position. For example, if the cards are in the order 5, 2, 4, 1, and 3, then the 2 is in the correct position. For the order 1, 5, 3, 2, and 4, both the 1 and the 3 are in the correct position.
   (a) On the average, how many cards would we expect to be in the correct position? To answer this question, write a program to simulate the experiment a large number of times.
   (b) Suppose there were 10 cards, numbered 1 to 10. On the average, how many would we expect to be in the correct position?
   (c) Suppose there were 52 cards, numbered 1 to 52. On the average, how many would we expect to be in the correct position?

6-3 SEARCHING AND SORTING

Two important applications involving arrays are **searching** and **sorting**. Searching involves looking for a specific value in an array and reporting its position (subscript), or the fact that this value was not found. Sorting involves ordering the array's elements in increasing or decreasing order. For simplicity, we use integer arrays, but the techniques developed apply to any data type for which order comparisons make sense. These types include integers, reals, strings, and user-defined scalar types.

For each application, we present two solutions. The first is easier to understand; the second faster. For very small arrays, speed may not be important. For large arrays, though, it becomes quite important, so we examine solutions that are faster than the first naive solution we may devise.

Linear Search

For this and the other applications, let us assume we are dealing with an integer array A with subscripts ranging from 1 to a constant MaxIndex. We also assume the array actually contains N values, with $0 \leq N \leq MaxIndex$. In searching problems, we are also given a value to look for in the array.

The Algorithm **Linear search** is an approach to searching for what we have already seen. We simply start at the first element A[1] and proceed through the array until one of two conditions occurs:

1. We reach the end of the portion of the array containing values.
2. We find the desired value.

As we learned in Section 6-1, we have to take some care in writing the condition for the loop. Figure 6-11 shows a subprogram that accomplishes the search.

There are actually two "answers" from this subprogram. They answer the questions: (1) Is the value present? (2) If so, in what location? However, by setting the location to 0 if the value is not found, we can convey the answer to both questions in a single variable.

Note. As a general rule of program design, using "trickery" to convey two answers as if there were only one is not good programming style.

However, using a 0 to indicate "not found" is widely used and understood within the computer science community. Thus, this use is generally accepted.

```
function Search(A: IntegerArray; Key, N: integer): integer;

{Written by: XXXXXXXXXX XX/XX/XX}
{Purpose:    To locate a given value in an array. The answer is}
{            the subscript where found (0 if not found).}
{Parameters: A   - input, the array to search in}
{            Key - input, the value to search for}
{            N   - input, the portion of the array in use}

var
   Found: boolean;
   I: integer;     {loop control and subscript}

begin {search}
   Found := false;   {assume value not in array}
   I := 1;
   while (I <= N) and (not Found) do
      begin
         if A[I] = Key then
            Found := true
         else
            I := I + 1
      end; {while}

   if Found then
      Search := I
   else
      Search := 0;

end; {Search}
```

Figure 6-11 Linear search of an array.

6-3 SEARCHING AND SORTING

By making a slight modification to the linear search, we can simplify it a good deal. Its major complexity arises from not knowing whether we will find the value in the array. Suppose, before we enter the loop, we do an assignment

```
A[N + 1] := Value
```

Now, we can write our loop as

```
I := 1;
  while A [I] <> Value do
  begin
     I := I + 1
  end; {while}
```

Because we have placed the value into the array, we know it is there, so we do not need the test I <= N in the *while* condition. After the loop, we can write

```
if I = N + 1 then
   Location := 0
else
   Location := I
```

If I is N + 1, then the only occurrence of the value was the one we put in, so we set Location to 0 to show that the value was not in the original array.

Note. If N = MaxIndex, the size of the array, this does not work. The rest of our program must treat the array such that N always stays less than MaxIndex.

Some people always declare arrays to be one larger than they really need, so that techniques such as this always work. For example, the declaration

```
array[1..51] of integer
```

might be used for an array to store up to 50 (not 51) student grades.

Efficiency. When discussing the **efficiency**—the speed—of search algorithms, a very good measure is to look at the number of times we must compare a value in the array against the key value to determine if the key value is present or absent. For the linear search algorithm of Figure 6-11, asking how many comparisons occur corresponds to asking the question:

On the average, how many passes through the loop will be required?

Intuitively, we can reason as follows. We might get lucky and find the value at A[l], requiring one pass. Or it might require two, three, or four passes. At worst, it will require N passes. On average, we would expect about N/2 passes to be required (higher if many are not found).

Computer scientists describe this by saying that the linear search has average time **O(N)** (read as **order N** or **big oh of N**). Roughly speaking, this means that the time is "approximately proportional to N." So, if the array size doubles, the number of comparisons about doubles, and so the average time for the search doubles as well.

Binary Search

If the array is in order, we can use a more efficient search known as the **binary search**. The easiest way to understand this method is by looking at an example.

The Algorithm.
Suppose we have the following array:

$$15 \quad 23 \quad 36 \quad 42 \quad 79 \quad 101 \quad 125 \quad 140 \quad 142$$

The numbers are in increasing order. Because N is 9, we know that whatever value we are looking for is between position 1 and position 9, inclusive, if it is there at all. For our example, assume we are looking for the value 101.

Suppose we initialize a variable Low to 0 and a variable High to 10 (= N + 1). Then the value, if it is there, must be strictly between position Low and position High. ("Strictly between" means "between but not including.") Rather than check the positions in order, let us check the middle item of the array. We calculate

```
Middle := (Low + High) div 2
```

and examine A[Middle]. In this case, Middle is 5, so we examine A[5], which is 79. If we were looking for the value 79, we would be done—the location would be 5.

Because the number we are looking for (101) is larger than the one at position Middle (79) and because the array is in increasing order, we know it must be above the Middle position (again, if it is in the array at all). If we do

```
Low := Middle
```

then this is our situation:

1. Low is 5.
2. High is 10.
3. If the value is there, it must be strictly between position Low and position High.

We again go to the middle of the possible positions, setting Middle to (5 + 10) div 2 = 15 div 2 = 7, and examine A[7]. This time the number we are looking for is less than A[Middle], so we know it must be to the left of the Middle position. We set

```
High := Middle
```

and have

1. Low is 5.
2. High is 7.
3. If the value is there, it must be strictly between position Low and position High.

This time, we set Middle to (5 + 7) div 2 = 6, and A[6] is our desired value, so we quit with the answer 6.

Suppose, now, that we had been searching for 40. The following table summarizes what would happen:

	LOW	HIGH	MIDDLE	NEW LOW	NEW HIGH
First pass	0	10	5	0	5
Second pass	0	5	2	2	5
Third pass	2	5	3	3	5
Fourth pass	3	5	4	3	4

At the start of the fifth pass, we have

1. Low is 3.
2. High is 4.
3. If the value is there, it must be strictly between position Low and position High.

But this cannot be: nothing can be strictly between positions 3 and 4. This is how we detect that an element is not present in the array: when High – Low = 1.

The function in Figure 6-12 reflects this discussion. It uses a Boolean variable Found to indicate success, with High – Low ≤ 1 indicating failure.

Notes

1. The condition "if the value is there, it must be strictly between position Low and position High" is an example of a **loop invariant**. It is true when we start the loop, and we make sure it remains true for each successive pass through the loop.

   The concept of a loop invariant can be made very formal and used in proving that programs are correct, a process called **program verification**. For our purposes in this introductory text, we use loop invariants primarily in an informal way. We might not even use the term "invariant," but rather think in terms of what is true on each successive pass. Such reasoning can help us understand how the loop accomplishes its task, and thus can help us write correct loops.

2. Another key aspect of the correctness of the program of Figure 6-12 is that the distance between Low and High is becoming smaller on each successive pass. Thus, if the value is not in the array, the loop eventually terminates when High – Low is 1.

3. Notice that if the array is empty (N = 0), then Low starts at 0, High at 1, and we leave the loop immediately with Found still *false*.

Efficiency. To begin to assess the efficiency of the binary search, imagine an array of size 31. Each pass through the loop eliminates the middle number from consideration and also half of the remaining numbers. For example, after the first pass, we have found the number, or know that it is between positions 0 and 14, or know that it is between positions 16 and 32. In the worst possible case, this happens:

At start	31 numbers left to examine
After one pass	15 numbers left to examine
After two passes	7 numbers left to examine
After three passes	3 numbers left to examine

After four passes	1 number left to examine
After five passes	Have found the number or know it is not there

Thus, five passes is the most it could take.

Now, because $2^5 = 32$, we have $\log_2 32 = 5$. Thus, the number of passes is approximately the **log base 2** of the array size. We say that the binary search has a worst-case behavior O(log N), where the base 2 is understood. For an O(log N) algorithm, doubling the array size adds a constant amount of time to the running time. Although the average number of passes is more difficult to calculate, it is also O(log N).

Notice that for an array of size 1024, logN is 10, whereas N/2 is 512. Thus, the binary search would be significantly faster than the linear search. Yet, binary search requires the array to be sorted. If the array to be searched is not (already) sorted, then using sequential search might well be faster than first sorting the array and then using binary search.

```
function BinarySearch(A: IntegerArray; Key, N: integer): integer;
{Written by: XXXXXXXXXX XX/XX/XX}
{Purpose:    To locate a given value in an array. The answer is the}
{            subscript where found (n if not found). Because a binary}
{            search is used, the array must be in increasing order.}
{Parameters: A   - input, the array to search in}
{            Key - input, the value to search for}
{            N   - input, the portion of the array in use}
   var
      Found: boolean;   {used to indicate success}
      Low: integer;     {lower end of subarray}
      High: integer;    {higher end of subarray}
      Middle: integer;  {middle of subarray}
   begin {BinarySearch}
      Found := false;    {assume not there as default}
      Low := 0;
      High := N + 1;
      while (High - Low > 1) and (not Found) do
         begin
            Middle := (Low + High) div 2;
            if A[Middle] = Key then
               Found := true
            else
               if A[Middle] > Key then
                  High := Middle
               else
                  Low := Middle
         end; {while}
      if Found then
         BinarySearch := Middle
      else
         BinarySearch := 0
   end; {BinarySearch}
```

Figure 6-12 Binary search of an array.

6-3 SEARCHING AND SORTING

Selection Sort

We now turn to sorting algorithms. Given an array A containing *N* values, we wish to rearrange the array so that the values are in increasing order. Our first method is sometimes called **selection sort**.

The Algorithm. The underlying idea is to select the number that should be in the first position in the array and to put it there. We then select the number that should be in the second position in the array and put it there. We continue in this fashion until the proper numbers have been selected and placed into each position in the array. In order to understand the selection sort algorithm, we begin with some preliminary examples.

First, let us write a segment of Pascal to determine the subscript SmLoc of the smallest element in A. We have written algorithms of this type before. We use a *for* loop indexed by the variable J. (The reason for the use of J rather than I becomes apparent later.)

```
SmLoc := 1;
for J := 2 to N do
   begin
      if A[J] < A[SmLoc] then
         SmLoc := J
   end; {for}
```

Next we write code to exchange A[l] and A[SmLoc]. For example, if SmLoc is 7, this exchanges A[l] and A[7]. To accomplish this, we write a procedure capable of swapping any two integers. We can then invoke the procedure to swap A[l] and A[SmLoc] by a step such as

```
Swap(A[1], A[SmLoc])
```

To write the procedure, we need two var parameters, which we call X and Y. We use a temporary location to keep the value of X, moving data as indicated by this diagram, in the order indicated:

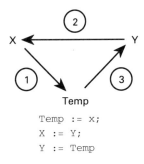

```
Temp := X;
X := Y;
Y := Temp
```

Figure 6-13 shows the Swap function.

To make use of the ideas just developed, we must generalize them slightly. Rather than starting at position 1, let us start at position I. We, therefore, write code to determine the subscript SmLoc of the smallest element in A[I] through A[N] and then exchange A[I] with A[SmLoc]. For example, if A is the following array shown and I is 4, then SmLoc is 7.

6 9 10 **25** 15 27 **13** 14 20 31

After swapping A[4] and A[7], we have A as follows:

```
procedure Swap(var X, Y: integer);

{Written by: XXXXXXXXXX XX/XX/XX}
{Purpose:    To swap two integers}
{Parameters: X, Y - update, the integers to be swapped}

   var
      Temp: integer;   {temporary variable for swapping}
begin {Swap}
   Temp := X;
   X := Y;
   Y := Temp
end; {Swap}

procedure SelectionSort(var A: IntegerArray; N: integer);

{Written by: XXXXXXXXXX XX/XX/XX}
{Purpose:    To sort an array, using the selection sort technique}
{Parameters: A - update, the array to sort}
{            N - input, the portion of the array in use}
{Procedures used: Swap, to swap two array elements}

   var
      I,J: integer;        {loop control}
      SmLoc: integer;      {location of smallest}
      Temp: integer;       {used for swapping}
begin {SelectionSort}
   for I := 1 to N - 1 do
     begin
        SmLoc := I;
        for J := I + 1 to N do
           begin
              if A[J] < A[SmLoc] then
                 SmLoc := J
           end; {for J}
        Swap(A[I], A[SmLoc])
     end {for I}
end; {SelectionSort}
```

Figure 6-13 Selection sort.

6 9 10 **13** 15 27 **25** 14 20 31

Here is the code to accomplish this swapping, with the generalizations in italics:

```
SmLoc := I;
for J := I + 1 to N do
  begin
     if A[J] < A[SmLoc] then
        SmLoc := J
     end; {for}

Swap(A[I], A[SmLoc])
```

6-3 SEARCHING AND SORTING

The selection sort method consists of applying this algorithm segment repeatedly. Starting with an array A that is not sorted, we determine the subscript SmLoc of the smallest number in A[l] through A[N], then exchange A[l] with A[SmLoc]. For example, if A is

21 17 **3** 16 12 10 19 9

then after this first swap, we have

3 17 **21** 16 12 10 19 9

We now determine the subscript SmLoc of the smallest number in A[2] through A[N], and exchange A[2] with A[SmLoc], with the results shown:

3 **9** 21 16 12 10 19 **17**

As you can see, the first exchange located and placed into A[l] the smallest number in A. The second placed the proper number (the smallest of the remaining numbers) into A[2]. A third exchange determines the subscript SmLoc (it turns out to be subscript 6) of the smallest number in A[3] through A[N], exchanging A[3] with A[SmLoc]:

3 9 **10** 16 12 **21** 19 17

After each such exchange, one more number is in its correct location. After N − 1 exchanges, N − 1 numbers are correct and the Nth is, therefore, also correct. Our algorithm is

```
for I := 1 to N-1 do
   begin
      determine the subscript SmLoc of the smallest element in
         A[I] through A[N], then  exchange A[I] with A[SmLoc]
   end {for}
```

To obtain the final procedure, we replace the body of the loop with the code we wrote earlier.

Efficiency. The selection sort is easy to analyze; we use the usual technique of counting comparisons. Because each pass through the inner loop does one comparison, counting comparisons is equivalent to counting the total passes through the inner loop. The following table should help.

WHEN I IS	J STARTS AT	AND ENDS AT	NO. OF PASSES
1	2	N	N − 1
2	3	N	N − 2
3	4	N	N − 3
.	.	.	.
.	.	.	.
.	.	.	.
N − 3	N − 2	N	3
N − 2	N − 1	N	2
N − 1	N	N	1

The total is 1 + 2 . . . + (N − 1), which is equal to

$$\frac{N(N-1)}{2} = \frac{N^2}{2} - \frac{N}{2}$$

This is roughly proportional to N^2 (for large N, the N/2 is insignificant). We therefore have an $O(N^2)$ algorithm. For such an algorithm, doubling the array size quadruples the time. Thus, selection sort is satisfactory for small arrays, but not for larger ones.

Quicksort

One of the fastest known sorting algorithms is **quicksort.** Many variations of the underlying idea have been developed. We present one of the simpler forms.

The Algorithm. Quicksort is easiest to understand as a recursive procedure, although it can be written nonrecursively. The basic idea is this:

1. Rearrange the given array so that:

    (a) Its first element has been moved to its proper spot. We call this the **pivot location** and use the variable name PivotSub for this subscript.

    (b) Everything to the left of position PivotSub is less than or equal to A[PivotSub].

    (c) Everything to the right of position PivotSub is greater than or equal to A[PivotSub].

    This is called the **partition step**.

2. Do a recursive call to sort the subarray to the left of position PivotSub.
3. Do a recursive call to sort the subarray to the right of position PivotSub.

Because when we call quicksort recursively, we are sorting subarrays of the original array, we have three parameters:

A: The array to be sorted. This is modified, so it is a var parameter.
Low: The lowest subscript of the part to be sorted.
High: The highest subscript of the part to be sorted.

If Low < High, there are at least two elements in the subarray. If not, then there is nothing to do; this (very small) subarray is already sorted. This is our base case, which we must have in any recursive algorithm.

Note. The program that originally calls the QuickSort procedure does so as shown here:

```
QuickSort(A, 1, N)
```

This says the subarray to be sorted is the entire array.

As an example, suppose the array is

$$23\ 6\ 24\ 17\ 29\ 12\ 19\ 28\ 8$$

After the partition, if it is done correctly, we have PivotSub = 6, with this situation

A[l] to A[5] contains	A[6] is 23	A[7] to A[9] contains
6, 17, 12, 8, 19		24, 29, 28
in some order		in some order

If the recursive calls work, they sort A[l] to A[5] into the order 6, 8, 12, 17, 19, and A[7] to A[9] into the order 24, 28, 29. The entire array is then sorted.

Let us use a Partition procedure for the partition step. It requires the parameters A, Low, and High and returns the value for PivotSub. Quicksort itself is fairly easy; it simply reflects everything we have just said, using the procedures Partition and QuickSort:

```
if Low < High then
   begin
      Partition(A, Low, High, PivotSub);
      QuickSort(A, Low, PivotSub - 1);
      QuickSort(A, PivotSub + 1, High)
   end {if}
```

To complete QuickSort, we must now write the Partition procedure. We present a version of the general method that is frequently described in discussing quicksort. There are a number of other possible ways to do this; some are explored in the exercises.

The method is easy to describe intuitively, although it is a bit more subtle than most algorithms in this text. For illustration, consider this small array:

$$23\ 6\ 24\ 17\ 29\ 12\ 19\ 28\ 8$$

where Low is 1 and High is 9. The idea works equally well for a piece of an array.

The idea is this. We use two pointers (variables containing subscripts) that we call I and J. We start I at the left end of the array and J at the right end. We then move them together until they meet or cross, constantly maintaining this condition (the loop invariant):

> Everything to the left of position I is less than or equal to the pivot, and
> everything to the right of J is greater than or equal to the pivot.

When I and J meet or cross (that is, I ≥ J), we can swap the pivot with the Jth element; then, everything to the right of position J is still greater than or equal to the pivot, and everything to the left of J is also to the left of I and is less than or equal to the pivot. This is the desired result. To see how this works, we step through the algorithm for the last array given.

First, starting at the left (not including the pivot number 23), locate a number that is bigger than or equal to the pivot number. Then, starting at the right, locate a number less than or equal to the pivot number. The numbers we locate are in boldface, with the variables I and J containing their subscripts:

$$23\ 6\ \mathbf{24}\ 17\ 29\ 12\ 19\ 28\ \mathbf{8}$$
$$\uparrow\qquad\qquad\qquad\uparrow$$
$$I\qquad\qquad\qquad\quad J$$

In order to maintain the loop invariant as I and J continue moving, we must swap the Ith and Jth elements:

$$23\ 6\ \mathbf{8}\ 17\ 29\ 12\ 19\ 28\ \mathbf{24}$$
$$\uparrow\uparrow$$
$$IJ$$

Continuing, we move I to the right again, then J to the left again, obtaining

$$23\ 6\ 8\ 17\ \mathbf{29}\ 12\ \mathbf{19}\ 28\ 24$$
$$\uparrow\uparrow$$
$$IJ$$

After the swap, we have

$$23\ 6\ 8\ 17\ \mathbf{19}\ 12\ \mathbf{29}\ 28\ 24$$
$$\uparrow\uparrow$$
$$IJ$$

Once more we move 1, then J, obtaining

$$23\ 6\ 8\ 17\ 19\ \mathbf{12}\ \mathbf{29}\ 28\ 24$$
$$\uparrow\ \uparrow$$
$$J\ I$$

Because I and J have crossed, we do not swap. To finish the partition, we need only place the pivot in its proper position, by swapping it with A[J], and observe that J is the PivotLocation.

Note. You may wonder why J, and not I, is the PivotLocation. To answer this, recall our invariant: Everything to the left of position I is less than or equal to the pivot, and everything to the right of J is greater than or equal to the pivot.

If I and J are equal, then either one would do. However, if they have crossed, then I is to the right of J. The invariant would say that A[I] is greater than or equal to the pivot. If we swap the pivot with A[I], we moving a large value into the left subarray, a result we do not want.

The final result of the partition process is

$$\underline{12\ 6\ 24\ 17\ 19}\ \ \ \mathbf{23}\ \ \ \underline{29\ 28\ 8}$$
$$\text{Items} \leq \text{pivot}\ \ \uparrow\ \ \text{Items} \geq \text{pivot}$$
$$\text{pivot}$$

The complete Partition and QuickSort procedures are given in Figure 6-14. The Swap procedure referred to is that of Figure 6-13.

Note. Because the recursive calls to QuickSort sort a piece of the array, there are three parameters: the array and the lower and upper bounds of the piece to be sorted.

To sort the entire array, the main program would include a call such as

```
QuickSort(GradeArray, 1, NumberOfStudents)
```

The argument "1" must be supplied as the lower bound of the array.

Efficiency. In the best case, each Partition splits the array exactly in half. To find the first pivot takes about N comparisons, as we compare the values at I and J, swapping as necessary. Making the partition itself requires no comparisons (we already know their boundaries). Looking for a pivot in one of the two partitions requires about N/2 comparisons (as each partition is half the size of the original array); there are two partitions, so the total

```
procedure Partition (var A: IntegerArray; Low, High: integer;
                     var PivotLocation: integer);

{Written by:   XXXXXXXXXX XX/XX/XX}
{Purpose:      To partition an array into three parts:}
{              1. values less or equal to the pivotal element}
{              2. the pivotal element}
{              3. values greater than or equal to the pivotal element}
{Parameters:   A - update, the array to partition}
{              Low, High - input, the portion of the array to}
{                          partition}
{              PivotLocation - output, the location for the pivot}
{                              element}
{Procedures used: Swap, to swap two elements of the array}

var
   I: integer;            {used to locate large values}
   J: integer;            {used to locate small values}
   Pivot: integer;        {the pivotal element}

begin {Partition}
   I := Low;
   J := High + 1;
   Pivot := A[Low];

   repeat

   {*** Move I to right looking for a value >= the pivot}

      repeat
         I := I + 1
      until (I = High) or (A[I] >= Pivot);

   {*** Move J to left looking for a value <= the pivot}

      repeat
         J := J - 1
      until A[J] <= Pivot;
```

Figure 6-14 Quicksort (continues next page)

number of comparisons is again about N. When each partition is itself partitioned again (creating 4 partitions), each one contains about N/4 elements; again, the total number of comparisons for each partition is about N.

If an array of N elements is partitioned in half repeatedly, (first two partitions, then four, then eight, and so on), then the number of partitions made is about log N. For each set of partitions, we have N comparisons; we have log N partition sets to examine. So the best case time for quicksort is O(N log N).

In the worst case, instead of dividing the current partition in half each time, quicksort divides it into one partition of size 1 and another of size N–1. It turns out that this kind of partitioning slows quicksort way down; in this worst case, quicksort is $O(N^2)$. This worst case occurs when the array is already in order.

```
{*** Swap if the values are out of order}

   if I < J then
      Swap(A[I], A[J])

   until I >= J;

{*** Put the pivotal element in the proper place, and return the value}
{    of its subscript to the calling module}

   Swap(A[Low], A[J]);
   PivotLocation := J

end; {Partition}

procedure QuickSort (var A: IntegerArray; Low, High: integer);

{Written by:      XXXXXXXXXX XX/XX/XX}
{Purpose:         To sort an array , using quicksort technique}
{Parameters:      A - update, the array to sort}
{                 Low, High - the portion of the array to sort}
{Procedures used: Partition, to partition the array into two pieces}
{                 QuickSort(recursively), to sort the two pieces}

   var
      PivotSub: integer;              {location of pivot element}

begin {QuickSort}
   if Low < High then
      begin
         Partition(A, Low, High, PivotSub);
         QuickSort(A, Low, PivotSub - 1);
         QuickSort(A, PivotSub + 1, High)
      end {if}
end; {QuickSort}
```

Figure 6-14   (continued)

6-3 SEARCHING AND SORTING

The calculations to compute the average case are fairly extensive; we just report that the result is O(N log N). For an algorithm that is O(N log N), doubling the array size multiplies the time by a factor just barely more than 2. This factor gets smaller as N gets larger. This is much better than an O(N^2) algorithm. Thus, for large arrays, we would definitely choose quicksort rather than selection sort.

It is important to note that the efficiency of quicksort depends partially on the efficiency of the partition process. It is possible to replace the Partition procedure with another that accomplishes the same goal but is either faster or slower than the one we described. This effects quicksort's speed. However, as long as the time to make a partition is O(N), Quicksort is O(N log N).

Some of the work that has been done in speeding up quicksort has concentrated on making the partition faster. Other work has concentrated on trying to make sure the partition splits the array as nearly in half as possible. Thus, if you examine a half dozen quicksort programs in papers or texts, you find that the major differences occur in how the partitioning works.

Comparing Efficiency Ratings

To help you get a better feel for the different efficiency ratings discussed in the section, we present a table showing the values of log N, N log N, and N^2 for various values of N. (The column labeled "Ratio" is discussed in what follows.)

N	logN	NlogN	N^2	RATIO
16	4	64	256	4.00
32	5	160	1,024	6.40
64	6	384	4,096	10.67
128	7	896	16,384	18.29
1,024	10	10,240	1,048,576	102.40
2,048	11	22,528	4,194,304	186.18
4,096	12	49,152	16,777,216	341.33
8,192	13	106,496	67,108,864	630.15

Of course, when we say an algorithm is O(expression), that means that it is approximately proportional to the expression. For example, quicksort might take approximately 0.01 N log N and selection sort approximately 0.001 N^2. If so, then the ratio of selection sort time to quicksort time would be

$$\frac{0.001 N^2}{0.01 N \log N} = 0.1 \frac{N^2}{N \log N}$$

The Ratio column is the ratio N^2/ (N log N) (which is N/log N). As you can see, with these hypothetical times, the two would be approximately equal for N = 64 (0.1 × 10.67). For N = 2048, quicksort would be almost 20 times faster.

Some of the exercises give further insight into the significance of these "efficiency ratings."

DPT and Testing

We already know about some of the pitfalls to watch for from our previous study of arrays and of the linear search. Specifically, we must take care that our array references do not include subscripts beyond the legal array limits. If we have included range-checking in the program, THINK tells us the subscripts are out of bounds; if we do not, our program may run very strangely. It may actually appear to work for several runs, then begin not to work. Remember that searching programs are especially prone to this type of error.

Avoid compound conditions that could possibly lead to errors, such as

```
while (I > 0) and (A[I] > Key) do ...
```

Remember the fairly widely used solution to this problem: a Boolean variable such as Found to indicate success.

The sorting and searching algorithms presented in this section have their own pitfalls, which seem to occur with regularity. For example, in the binary search as we have written it, our loop invariant states that the item to be found is strictly between positions Low and High. To make this true at the start, we must set Low to 0 (not 1) and High to N + 1 (not N). (See the exercises for a version of the binary search with a slightly different loop invariant.)

Another pitfall involves the partition algorithm for QuickSort. Notice that in the loop involving I, we must include the test for I = High. If we do not, the condition A[I] >= Pivot might never become true if the first element is the largest in the array. The variable I would go beyond the end of the array, leading to thoroughly unpredictable results (unless we have enabled range-checking).

Searching and sorting, then, seem to be relatively dangerous, error-prone activities, yet they are ones we cannot avoid when writing programs. What can be done to reduce our chances of making mistakes? One possibility is to make more careful use of assertions about the loops (loop invariants). A second is to make extensive use of hand-tracing with small sample arrays. Yet another is to do very careful testing.

Here is a number of tests we feel are important for any searching or sorting algorithm. First, for searching:

1. An important boundary test relates to the actual size (N) of the array. Try arrays of size 0, 1, and MaxIndex, where MaxIndex is the declared (potential) size of the array.

2. Two other important boundaries are closely related. We would want to try searching for the first and last items in the array. However, this has two possible interpretations: by the "first," we could be referring to A[1] or we could be referring to the smallest value. Both interpretations should be tested. In addition to the boundaries, we should search for items we know to be in the array, but which are not at the boundary positions.

3. We should exercise the possibility that the item sought is not present. Of special interest are values less than the smallest or greater than the largest.

4. Finally, we suggest a totally exhaustive test for a relatively small array. For example, we might set up an array such as this:

10 20 30 40 50

6-3 SEARCHING AND SORTING

and search for 5, 10, 15, 20, 25, 30, 35, 40, 45, 50, and 55 (in some random order). Notice that we have searched for each item that is there and between each pair of items, as well as below the first and above the last.

If the search does not require the array to be ordered, we might try the same test with a rearranged array, perhaps 30, 40, 10, 50, and 20.

The tests we suggest for sorting are similar:

1. Test arrays of size 0, 1, and MaxIndex.
2. Test an array that is already in order and one that is in exactly reversed order. (Also, of course, test some in random order.)
3. Test arrays with and without duplicates; perhaps include an array for which the entire array consists of the same value.
4. For some small arrays, try every possible ordering. In a graduate class, a student was assigned to present a variation on quicksort that had been published in a leading computer science journal. She was to explain the method to the class and give some analysis of the efficiency. Within a few days, she reported that the algorithm did not work. What she had tried (and the author of the article apparently had not) was testing the method on some small arrays. In particular, she tried all possible orders of the three numbers 1, 2, and 3. For more than one of these, the algorithm failed.

REVIEW

Terms and Concepts

big oh
binary search
efficiency
linear search
log base 2
loop invariant
O notation
order

parition step
pivot location
program verification
quicksort
searching
selection sort
sorting

Searching

Linear Search

Start at the beginning, keep going until found or reach the end
Order is O(N)

Binary Search

Look in the middle; keep cutting the part of the array to search in half until found or there is no part left to search
Array must be in order
Order is O(log N)

Selection Sort

Repeatedly find the smallest of those left, and swap it with the first of those left
Order is $O(N^2)$

Quicksort

Partition the array based on a pivot element, then sort the subarrays to the left and right of the pivot element recursively
Order is $O(N \log N)$

Efficiency. The approximate results on time from doubling the size of the array:

$O(\log N)$: adds a constant amount of time

$O(N)$: doubles the time

$O(N \log N)$: multiplies the time by a factor slightly above 2; the larger the array, the smaller the factor

$O(N^2)$: quadruples the time

DPT

1. Hand-trace the algorithms for some small arrays.
2. Avoid the known bugs.
3. Avoid conditions such as

   `(I > 0) or (A[I] . . . )`

Testing

Searching

1. Test arrays of size 0, 1, and MaxIndex.
2. Search for the first and the last items, and items in between.
3. Search for the smallest and the largest items, and items in between.
4. For some small arrays, try searching for each item.
5. Search for numbers less than the lowest in the array, greater than the highest, and in between but not there.

Sorting

1. Test arrays of size 0, 1, and MaxIndex.
2. Test arrays already in order and in reverse order.
3. For some small arrays, try every possible ordering.

EXERCISES

1. Under the assumption that the array is in increasing order, the linear search algorithm could be modified to give up as soon as it encounters a value larger than the one sought. Comment on this as compared to the binary search. (Which is faster for small arrays? Large ones?)

2. If a searching method is O(N) and it takes an average of 10 ms to locate a value in an array of a given size, how long would you expect it to take if the array size is doubled? Note: ms stands for milliseconds; 1 ms = $1/1000^{th}$ of a second.

3. Suppose that you are using an order $O(N^2)$ sorting algorithm, and it takes about 2 seconds to sort an array of size 60. About how long would you expect it to take for an array of size 120? 250? 500? 1000? 2000? 4000?

4. Suppose that you are using an order O(N log N) sorting algorithm, and it takes about 5 seconds to sort an array of size 60. About how long would you expect it to take for an array of size 120? 250? 500? 1000? 2000? 4000? Note: The time is scaled by a factor of approximately 2 + 2/log N.

5. Suppose that you are using an order O(N) algorithm, and it takes about 3 ms to sort an array of size 60. About how long would you expect it to take for an array of size 120? 250? 500? 1000? 2000? 4000? (See the note in Exercise 2.)

6. Suppose that you are using an order O(log N) algorithm, and it takes about 10 ms to sort an array of size 60. Assuming that each doubling adds 25 ms to the time, about how long would you expect it to take for an array of size 120? 250? 500? 1000? 2000? 4000?

7. Hand-trace the partition algorithm given in this section for these arrays:
   (a) 10, 12, 9, 14, 7, 21
   (b) 2, 22, 7, 24, 100, 5, 13, 4, 1, 23
   (c) 1, 2, 3, 4, 5
   (d) 5, 4, 3, 2, 1
   (e) 10, 10, 10, 10

8. For the following array, trace the binary search for each element of the array. For each, find the number of passes through the loop it takes to find the value.

   101 122 123 203 417 500 623

9. An alternate version of the binary search uses the loop invariant "the value, if it is there, lies at or between the positions Low and High". This method initializes Low to 1 and High to N. Write the algorithm. **Caution**: This approach contains a notorious pitfall into which many professional programmers have stumbled. Hand-trace your solution with some small arrays. Make sure you avoid an infinite loop by ensuring that the subarray remaining is smaller for each pass.

10. Write a recursive form of the binary search. Note: By rights, the array being searched should be a value parameter. However, in a recursive routine, passing an array as a value parameter uses considerable time and space because each level must maintain its own copy of the array. Make the array a var parameter.

11. What is the maximum number of passes that it could take to locate a value using the binary search of this section in an array of size 63? Of size 127? Of size 80?

12. (a) Generate a random array of size 2000, and sort it using selection sort. How long does it take? Repeat for quicksort.
    (b) Modify the two sorts of part (a) to count the number of key comparisons that occur. Run each to compare the two in terms of this count.

13. A colleague once made a bet with an unsuspecting friend. He wagered that he could locate a person in the white pages of the phone book in 20 guesses or less. For each guess, the friend

must merely indicate whether the actual name came before or after the guess in the phone book. The local phone book contains perhaps 20,000 entries. Did the colleague win the bet? If so, can you explain how? If not, why not?

14. (a) An array contains N student records, each with a last name, first name, the final average, and space for a letter grade. To aid in figuring grades, the professor desires a listing of the students in order from highest to lowest average. Write a procedure to sort the array and print the listing.

(b) For the final grade list, the names must be in alphabetical order. Write a procedure to print a listing of name and letter grade in alphabetical order by last name.

15. An array contains 50 records, each with a state name and 12 monthly rainfall figures. Write a procedure to print a listing of the states, in order from lowest to highest total yearly rainfall.

16. See Exercise 15. A naive approach might involve calculating the total rainfall for some of the records over and over again. Suggest a data structure that would allow you to calculate the total for each state only once. Note: You cannot, as the person writing the procedure, change the description of the parameters. However, you can define local variables. You may wish to write your procedure to set up the local variables, then call the procedure that actually accomplishes the sorting.

17. (a) Write a procedure that has as parameters an array, its current size (N), and a value to be inserted into the array. The array is in increasing order, and MaxIndex is the declared size of the array (N < MaxIndex). Insert the value into the array so that the array is still in order. Hint: If the value is bigger than the last, put it at the end. If not, move the last one over 1 and compare the value to the next to last. Continue until you find the proper spot.

(b) Your procedure in part (a) should be O(N). Present a reasonable argument that this is so.

(c) A student proposed accomplishing part (a) by just placing the new value at the end, then calling quicksort to reorder the array. Comment on the efficiency of this approach.

18. (a) By using the procedure of Exercise 17(a) repeatedly, write a sorting algorithm. Insert A[2] into the (sorted) subarray A[1], then insert A[3] into the (now sorted) subarray consisting of A[1] and A[2], and so on. This is known as **insertion sort**.

(b) By counting the number of array comparisons for the worst possible case, determine the efficiency of insertion sort.

19. One version of **bubble sort** has this form:

```
for I:=1 to N-1 do
   begin
      for J := 1 to N-1 do
         begin
            if A[J] > A[J+1] then
               Swap(A[J], A[J+1])
         end {for J}
   end {for I}
```

Analyze the efficiency of this algorithm by counting the number of array comparisons.

20. An easy way to accomplish the partition process for an array is to simply copy the array to another array. Then, starting with subscript 2 of the other array, return the values to the original array. If they are less than the pivot, they go to the front of the array; if not, to the end. Use two pointers, one starting at Low and increasing and the other starting at High and decreasing. Write the code for this approach. Is it easier to understand? Is it faster? On the whole, is it better?

EXERCISES

21. See Exercise 20. Another approach to the partition process can be based on a possible solution to Exercise 10 in Section 6-1. In that exercise, you were asked to arrange an array containing only 0's and 1's in such a way that all the 0's came before all the 1's. A possible solution is the following:

```
LastZero := 0;
for I := 1 to N do
  begin
     if A[I] = 0 then
        begin
           Swap(A[LastZero+1], A[I]);
           LastZero := LastZero + 1
        end {if}
  end {for}
```

The variable LastZero keeps track of where you have placed a 0; when another 0 is found, it is swapped into the next available spot and LastZero is incremented. (This approach appeared in the "Programming Pearls" column of the Communications of the ACM, April 1984, Vol. 27, No. 4. The column's author, Jon L. Bentley, says he learned the method from Nico Lomuto of Alsys, Inc.)

   (a) Trace this code for some sample arrays to make sure you understand it.
   (b) This code can be thought of as partitioning the array into two pieces: the 0's and the 1's. Using the basic idea of the code, write code for the following. You are given an array of size N. Partition the subarray from position 2 to N so that everything that is less than A[I] comes first and then comes everything that is not less than A[I].
   (c) Generalize the solution to part (b) to obtain a Partition procedure. Note: After you obtain the result of part (b), swap the first element with the last one that is smaller than it.
   (d) Trace your code from part (c) for the arrays of Exercise 5 as well as for the one traced in this section for the Partition procedure.
   (e) Explain in your own words how this method works. Is it easier to understand than the one in Figure 6-14?
   (f) Test your code by writing it as a procedure and including it in the QuickSort of Figure 6-14.

22. Quicksort performs best if the pivot element is always in the middle of the subarray being sorted. If an array is already partially sorted, this does not happen. This exercise describes two approaches to solving this problem.
   (a) Modify the partition procedure to swap A[Low] with A[RandomLoc] prior to beginning the partitioning, where RandomLoc is a randomly generated subscript in the range Low..High.
   (b) Modify the partition procedure so that, prior to beginning the search for the pivot position, it swaps A[Low] with the median of A[Low], A[High], and A[(Low + High) div 2]. The median of three numbers is the middle one. For example, the median of 5, 16, and 10 is 10; the median of 20, 12, and 20 is 20; and the median of 7, 7, and 7 is 7.

23. Write a procedure to merge two sorted arrays. Input consists of arrays A and B and the size of each. Output consists of array C and its size. Assume that the sum of the sizes of A and B is less than or equal to MaxIndex, the declared size of the three arrays.

The two input arrays are in increasing order, as should the output array. For example, if we merge the arrays A and B illustrated here, the answer is the array C, as shown:

$$A = 5\ 6\ 8\ 12\ 13$$
$$B = 4\ 6\ 7\ 9$$
$$C = 4\ 5\ 6\ 6\ 7\ 8\ 9\ 12\ 13$$

Hint: Maintain pointers for each array. Use a decision structure based on whether the A element or the B element is larger.

24. (a) Modify the procedure of Exercise 23 as follows: Input consists of an array A and three subscripts Startl, Start2, and End2. In addition, a "scratch" array is passed for the procedure to use. The arrays to be merged are both subarrays of A, namely, A[Startl] through A[Start2 − 1] and A[Start2] through A[End2]. Merge these into the scratch array, then copy the result back to A[Startl] through A[End2].
    (b) Using the procedure of part (a), write a procedure to sort an array by this method: Use a recursive call to sort the left half of the array, use a recursive call to sort the right half of the array, then use the merge procedure to merge the two halves into a single sorted array. This is called a *recursive merge sort*. Provided the procedure of part (a) is written properly, it is of order O(NlogN).
    (c) Repeat Exercise 12 for the recursive merge sort of part (b).

6-4 CASE STUDIES

In this section, we develop two case studies that indicate the broad range of possible applications of arrays. The first is a business-related application in which we use arrays to store information on prices, customer discounts, and so on. In the second, we write a package of modules that could be used in programs that need to manipulate polynomials.

Case Study No. 9

Statement of Problem. A small, locally owned store wants to computerize its point-of-sale operations. It sees a number of benefits to be derived from this automation, including automatic updating of inventory records and granting of discounts to preferred customers.

Preliminary Analysis. A system such as this involves quite a few activities. We implement only a few of them, and even then in only a simplified way. Some enhancements are suggested in the exercises.

To accomplish some of the desired point-of-sale and inventory functions, we use a file containing information about the items the store stocks. Likewise, a file contains a list of preferred customers. The following table represents sample information from the two files:

ITEM NUMBER	INVENTORY	PRICE	CUSTOMER NUMBER	DISCOUNT
101	249	3.89	4398	2%
247	1300	24.99	3898	1/2%
93	500	0.78	6756	1%
16	55	100.04	4528	1/2%
89	453	6.34		

For simplicity, let us assume that the customer file contains no more than 75 records, and the item number file no more than 500. As we did for the program of Figure 6-10, we use a control file to record the current status of the data. This file contains one record with two fields: current number of items and current number of preferred customers.

There are techniques, beyond the scope of our knowledge at this point, that would allow us to work directly with the data in the files. Instead, we read the file data into arrays, work with the arrays, and then rewrite the arrays to the files.

We use a menu-driven program similar to that in Case Study No. 8 (Section 5-4). In fact, rather than begin from scratch, we build our menu system by modifying the menu portion of the program of Figure 5-20. We choose to implement these four actions for the case study:

P—purchase:	Obtain an item number and quantities, adjust the inventory, and calculate the bill.
C—new customer:	Add a new customer to the preferred list.
S—save:	Save the data to the files.
Q—quit:	Warn the user if there is a change since the data were last saved.

Overall Data Requirements. This analysis indicates the need for these variables:

1. A control record with two fields: number of items and number of customers
2. An array of item records, each with three fields: item number, current inventory, and price
3. An array of customer records, each with two fields: customer number and base discount
4. A Boolean variable indicating whether the arrays have been changed
5. A set of valid options
6. The user option
7. File designators for the three files

In addition, the various modules were require local variables to be determined as we write the modules. In this case study, we choose to use the data listed in items 1 to 4 as global data throughout the program. The alternative would involve passing the arrays and control information as parameters to almost every subprogram.

Main Program (and Menu-Handling Procedures). The main program initializes the data just described, and then processes user requests in a loop. As mentioned, it is adapted from Figure 5-20 of Case Study No. 8. By using the code from the previous work as a starting point, we significantly reduced the time required to get started.

Figure 6-15 contains a first attempt at the program. Most of the modules are stubs. We have added an option D, which "dumps" the data. This is helpful for debugging purposes, but is removed from the version of the program delivered to the user.

```
program PointOfSale;

{Written by:   XXXXXXXXX XX/XX/XX}
{Purpose:      To handle point-of-sale procedures}
{Procedures used:  Instructions - to print instructions}
{                  Menu  - to display the menu and get the user option}
{                  Handle - to perform the user option}

  const
    MaxCust = 75;         {Customer array size}
    MaxItem = 500;        {Item array size}
    Bel = 7;              {ASCII Bel character}

  type
    Letters = set of char;
    Sentence: string[80];
    ControlRec = record
        NItem: integer;               {# of items presently}
        NCust: integer                {# of customers presently}
      end;
    ItemRec = record
        ItemNumber: integer;
        Inventory: integer;
        Price: real
      end;
    CustomerRec = record
        Number: integer;
        Discount: real
      end;

    ItemArray = array[1..MaxItem] of ItemRec;
    CustomerArray = array[1..MaxCust] of CustomerRec;

    CFile = file of ControlRec;
    CustFile = file of CustomerRec;
    ItFile = file of ItemRec;

  var
    Item: ItemArray;                  {Array of item information}
    Customer: CustomerArray;          {Array of customer information}
    Modified: boolean;                {Has data been changed?}
    ControlRecord: ControlRec;        {The control record}
    ControlFile: CFile;               {The control file}
    CustomerFile: CustFile;           {The list of customers}
    ItemFile: ItFile;                 {The list of items}
    Option: char;                     {User choice of menu option}
    ValidOptions: Letters;            {Valid menu options}
    Answer: char;                     {User answer to yes/no}
```

Figure 6-15 Case Study No. 9: first cut (continues next page).

```
{procedures Pause, Instructions, and Menu are inserted here. They are}
{minor modifications of the procedures of Figure 5-20}

  procedure Purchase;
  begin {Purchase - stub version}
    Writeln('Purchase procedure invoked');
    Pause
  end; {Purchase}

  procedure NewCustomer;
  begin {NewCustomer - stub version}
    Writeln('NewCustomer procedure invoked');
    Pause
  end; {NewCustomer}

  procedure SaveData;
  begin {SaveData - stub version}
    Writeln('SaveData procedure invoked');
    Pause
  end; {SaveData}

  procedure DumpData;

{Written by: XXXXXXXXX XX/XX/XX}
{Purpose:    To dump the data on the screen to aid in testing and}
{            debugging}
{Globals used: The following are used for the dump:}
{                  ControlRecord.NItem}
{                  ControlRecord.NCust}
{                  Item}
{                  Customer}
{                  Modified}
{Procedures used:  Pause - to wait for a user keystroke}

  var
    I: integer;                         {Loop control}

  begin {DumpData}
    if Modified then
       Writeln('Data has been modified since save')
    else
       Writeln('Data has NOT been modified since save');
    Pause;
    Page;

    Writeln('There are ', ControlRecord.NItem : 1, ' items');
    Pause;
    Page;
```

Figure 6-15   (continues next page)

```
      for I := 1 to ControlRecord.NItem do
        with Item[I] do
          begin
            Writeln('Item number: ', ItemNumber);
            Writeln('Inventory: ', Inventory : 1);
            Writeln('Price:     ', Price : 1 : 2);
            Pause;
            Page
          end; {with}

      Writeln('There are ', ControlRecord.NCust : 1, ' customers');
      Pause;
      Page;

      for I := 1 to ControlRecord.NCust do
        with Customer[I] do
          begin
            Writeln('Customer number: ', Number : 1);
            Writeln('Discount:     ', Discount : 1 : 2);
            Pause;
            Page
          end; {with}

      Writeln('End of Dump');
      Pause
    end; {DumpData}

    procedure Quit;
    begin {Quit - stub version}
      Writeln('Quit procedure invoked');
      Pause
    end; {Quit}

{procedure Handle is inserted here. It is a minor modification of the}
{procedure of Figure 5-20}

    procedure Initialize;
    begin {Initialize - stub version}
      ControlRecord.NItem := 3;
      ControlRecord.NCust := 2;

      Item[1].ItemNumber := 101;
      Item[2].Inventory := 10;
      Item[3].Price := 1.56;
      Item[2].ItemNumber := 202;
      Item[2].Inventory := 20;
      Item[2].Price := 2.56;
      Item[3].ItemNumber := 303;
      Item[3].Inventory := 30;
      Item[3].Price := 3.56;
```

Figure 6-15 (continues next page)

```
            Customer[1].Number := 1;
            Customer[1].Discount := 0.01;
            Customer[2].Number := 2;
            Customer[2].Discount := 0.02;
            Customer[3].Number := 3;
            Customer[3].Discount := 0.03;

            Modified := false
        end; {Initialize}

    begin {PointOfSale}
        ValidOptions := ['P', 'p', 'C', 'c', 'S', 's', 'Q', 'q', 'D', 'd'];

    {*** Print instructions}

        Instructions;

    {*** Load data from files}

        Initialize;

    {*** Main loop}

        repeat

    {*** Display Menu and get user option}

            Menu(ValidOptions, Option);
            ClearScreen;

    {*** Handle user choice}

            Handle(Option)
        until Option in ['Q', 'q']

    {*** Stop program}

    end.
```

Figure 6-15 (continued)

Purchase Procedure and Its Subprograms. This procedure consists of the following steps:

1. Clear the screen, input an item number, and make sure it is valid.
2. Input the quantity desired, between 0 and the available inventory.
3. Adjust the inventory (and indicate that the arrays have been modified).
4. Calculate the cost before discount.
5. Input the customer number and determine the discount.

6. Determine the net cost.

7. Display lines of information on the purchase.

We use subprograms for steps 1, 2, and 5.

We can now identify required variables and write the body of the Purchase subprogram.

Global variables:	Item	Array of item records	Used to access the price for the item
	Modified	Boolean	Have data been modified?
Local variables:	ItemSub	Integer	Subscript of item number entered
	Quantity	Integer	Number purchased
	Gross	Real	Cost before discount
	Discount	Real	Discount percentage
	Net	Real	Cost after discount

We do not directly deal with the item number or customer number. Rather, the procedures that read them report the item number subscript and the discount percentage.

In the Pascal code that follows, we have numbered the lines based on the general description of the steps given before.

1. `GetValidItem(ItemSub);`

2. `GetAmount(Quantity,ItemSub);`

3. `with Item[ItemSub] do`
     `Inventory := Inventory - Quantity;`

3. `Modified := true;`

4. `Gross := Quantity * Item[ItemSub].Price;`

5. `GetCustomer(Discount);`

6. `Net := Gross - Discount * Gross;`

7. `Writeln;`

7. `Writeln(Gross : 10 : 2, '<---Gross');`

7. `Writeln(Discount * Gross : 10 : 2,'<---Discount');`

7. `Writeln(Net : 10 : 2,'<---Net');`

7. `Pause`

   1. *GetValidItem Procedure.*   The general logic of the procedure consists of repeating these steps until a valid number is entered:

   (a) Prompt and read the item number.

   (b) Use a lookup function to calculate the subscript for the item number.

   (c) Handle three possibilities:

Not found
Found, but no inventory
Found, valid

Based on this statement of the algorithm, we can identify variables and write the required code. Notice the use of the Bel character to "beep" for an error.

Global variables:	Item	Array of item records	Used to check inventory
Parameters:	ItemSubsc	Integer	Output parameter (therefore, var)
Local variables:	ItemNum	Integer	User input
	Valid	Boolean	Is input valid?

```
repeat
  Writeln;
  Write('Enter item #:');
  Readln(ItemNum);
  ItemSubsc := ItemLookup(ItemNum);
  if ItemSubsc = 0 then
     begin
       Valid := false;
       Writeln(Chr(Bel), 'Item does not exist. Please try again')
     end
  else if Item[ItemSubsc].Inventory <= 0 then
     begin
       Valid := false;
       Writeln(Chr(Bel), 'Out of stock. Please try again')
     end
  else
     Valid := true
until Valid
```

Notes

1. At first, we wrote a *while* loop for this, but we changed to a *repeat* loop. Try writing a *while* loop yourself. Caution: Do not write a condition such as (ItemSubsc <> 0) and (condition using ItemSubsc). Why not?
2. We could not exchange the first two branches of the *if-then-else-if* decision structure. Why not?
3. ItemLookUp Function. This is a standard array lookup function. See Figure 6-16.
4. GetAmount Procedure. See Figure 6-16. Observe that this procedure needs the parameter ItemSub in order to check that the quantity entered does not exceed the inventory for that item.
5. GetCustomer Procedure (and CustomerLookup Function). These are similar to the subprograms for the item number. Notice, however, that if the customer number is not found in the customer array, this is not an error. It simply means that the discount is zero. See Figure 6-16.

2. *NewCustomer Procedure*. We perform the following steps:

(a) Obtain a customer number and a discount.

(b) Handle these possibilities:

>The customer number is already in the array.
>There is no more room in the array.
>Everything is OK; add to the array.

In step (2a), we use the CustomerLookup function described before. In step (2c), we should signal that the data have changed by setting the global Modified flag to *true*.

Based on this discussion, we can describe the variables and write the code.

Global variables:	Customer	Array of customer records	Record added to end
	Control		
	Record.NCust	Integer	Number of customer, modified
	Modified	Boolean	Has data been modified? (Set to *true*)
Global constants:	MaxCust		Maximum number of customers
Local variables:	CustomerNo	Integer	New customer number
	Disc	Real	New discount

```
Write('Enter customer number, discount:');
Read(CustomerNo, Disc);
if CustomerLookup(CustomerNo) <> 0 then
  begin
     Writeln(Chr(Bel), 'Customer already in file');
     Pause
  end
else if ControlRecord.NCust = MaxCust then
  begin
     Writeln(Chr(Bel), 'Customer list is full. ',
             'Must modify program.');
     Pause
  end
else
  begin
     with ControlRecord do
       begin
          NCust := NCust + 1;
          Customer[NCust].Number := CustomerNo;
          Customer[NCust].Discount := Disc
       end; {with}
     Modified := true;
     Writeln('Added to list');
     Pause
  end {if}
```

Figure 6-16 Case Study No. 9: refined (continues next page).

```pascal
program PointOfSale;

{*** The main program declarations and the Pause, Instructions, and}
{    Menu procedures are unchanged}

  function ItemLookup (ItemNum: integer): integer;

    {Written by:    XXXXXXXXX XX/XX/XX}
    {Purpose:       To look for an item number in the item array}
    {Parameters:    ItemNum - input, the number to look for}
    {Globals used:  Item - to check the item number}
    {               ControlRecord.NItem - to know array size}

    var
      I: integer;              {Array subscript}
      Found: boolean;          {Loop control}
  begin {ItemLookup}
    I := 1;
    Found := false;
    while (not Found) and (I <= ControlRecord.NItem) do
      begin
        if ItemNum = Item[I].ItemNumber then
          Found := true
        else
          I := I + 1
      end; {while}

    if Found then
      ItemLookup := I
    else
      ItemLookup := 0
  end; {ItemLookup}

  procedure GetValidItem (var ItemSubsc: integer);

    {Written by:     XXXXXXXXXX XX/XX/XX}
    {Parameters:     ItemSubsc - output, the subscript of the item entered}
    {Globals used:   Item - to check for out of stock}
    {Functions used: ItemLookup - to look up item number in array}

    var
      ItemNum: integer;        {Item number, user input}
      Valid: boolean;          {Is input valid?}

  begin {GetValidItem}

{*** The previously developed body of the procedure is placed here}

  end; {GetValidItem}
```

Figure 6-16   (continues next page)

```
procedure GetAmount (var Quantity: integer; ItemSub: integer);

  {Written by:    XXXXXXXXX XX/XX/XX}
  {Purpose:       To obtain a valid quantity for an item}
  {Parameters:    Quantity - output, the quantity desired}
  {               ItemSub  - input, the item's subscript}
  {Globals used:  Item - to access the inventory}

  var
     Limit: integer;              {Inventory available}

begin {GetAmount}
  Limit := Item[ItemSub].Inventory;
  Write('Quantity desired (maximum ', Limit : 1, '): ');
  Readln(Quantity);
  while (Quantity <= 0) or (Quantity > Limit) do
    begin
      Write(Chr(Bel), 'Quantity desired (maximum ', Limit : 1, '): ');
      Readln(Quantity)
    end {while}
end; {GetAmount}

function CustomerLookup (CustNum: integer): integer;

  {Written by:    XXXXXXXXX XX/XX/XX}
  {Purpose:       To look for a customer number in the customer array}
  {Parameters:    CustNum - input, the number to look for}
  {Globals used:  Customer - to check the number}
  {               ControlRecord.NCust - to know array size}

  var
    I: integer;              {Array subscript}
    Found: boolean;          {Loop control}

begin {CustomerLookup}
  I := 1;
  Found := false;
  while (not Found) and (I <= ControlRecord.NCust) do
    begin
      if CustNum = Customer[I].Number then
        Found := true
      else
        I := I + 1
    end; {while}

  if Found then
    CustomerLookup := I
  else
    CustomerLookup := 0
end; {CustomerLookup}
```

Figure 6-16 (continues next page)

```
procedure GetCustomer (var Disc: real);

   {Written by:        XXXXXXXXX XX/XX/XX}
   {Purpose:           To input customer number and determine discount}
   {Parameters:        Disc - output, the discount}
   {Globals used:      Customer - to get the discount}
   {Functions used:    CustomerLookup - to look up item number in array}

   var
      CustNum: integer;    {Customer number, user input}
      CustSub: integer;    {Customer subscript}

begin {GetCustomer}
   Writeln;
   Write('Enter customer #: ');
   Readln(CustNum);
   CustSub := CustomerLookup(CustNum);
   if CustSub = 0 then
      Disc := 0.0
   else
      Disc := Customer[CustSub].Discount
end; {GetCustomer}

procedure Purchase;

   {Written by:   XXXXXXXXX XX/XX/XX}
   {Purpose:      To handle a customer's purchase}
   {Globals used:    Item - to access the price}
   {Globals modified: Modified - changed to true}
   {Procedures used: GetValidItem - to obtain item subscript}
   {                 GetAmount - to obtain quantity desired}
   {                 GetCustomer - to get customer percentage}
   {                 Pause - to wait for a user keystroke}

   var
      ItemSub: integer;     {Subscript of item}
      Quantity: integer;    {Number purchased}
      Gross: real;          {Cost before discount}
      Discount: real;       {Discount percentage}
      Net: real;            {Cost after discount}

   begin {Purchase}

{*** The body of the previously developed procedure}

   end; {Purchase}
```

Figure 6-16 (continues next page)

```
procedure NewCustomer;
   {Written by:      XXXXXXXXX XX/XX/XX}
   {Purpose:         To add a new customer}
   {Globals used:    ControlRecord.NCust - to see if array is full}
   {                 MaxCust - to see if array is full}
   {Globals modified: Modified - changed to true}
   {                 Customer - new customer added at end}
   {Procedures used: Pause - to wait for a user keystroke}
   {Functions used:  CustomerLookup - to check for a duplicate}
   var
      CustomerNo: integer;          {New customer #}
      Disc: real;                   {New discount}
 begin {NewCustomer}
{*** The body of the previously developed procedure}
   end; {NewCustomer}
   procedure SaveData;
{Written by:      XXXXXXXXX XX/XX/XX}
{Purpose:         To save the data to the files}
{Globals used:    ControlFile - the control file handle}
{                 CustomerFile - the customer file handle}
{                 ItemFile - the item file handle}
{                 The following are written to the files:}
{                   ControlRecord}
{                   Item}
{                   Customer}
{Globals modified: Modified - set to false}
     var
        I: integer;                 {Loop control}
   begin {SaveData}
     Rewrite(ControlFile);
     Write(ControlFile, ControlRecord);
     Close(ControlFile);
     Rewrite(ItemFile);
     for I := 1 to ControlRecord.NItem do
       begin
          Write(ItemFile, Item[I])
       end {for}
     Close(ItemFile);

     Rewrite(CustomerFile);
     for I := 1 to ControlRecord.NCust do
       begin
          Write(CustomerFile, Customer[I])
       end; {for}
     Close(CustomerFile);
```

Figure 6-16 (continues next page)

```
      Modified := false;
      Writeln('Data has been saved to files');
      Pause
   end; {SaveData}

   {*** procedure DataDump, as shown in Figure 6-16}

{function AskUser, form Figure 5-10, is insered here}

procedure Quit;

{Written by:     XXXXXXXXX XX/XX/XX}
{Purpose:        To quit, first allowing a save if anything has changed}
{                since the last save}
{Globals used:   Modified - to see if a save should be offered}
{Procedures used: SaveData - to save data to the files}

   var
     Responses: Letters;      {Valid responses}
     Prompt: Sentence;        {Message to user}
     Answer: char;            {Answer from user}

   begin {Quit}
     if Modified then
       begin
         Write(Chr(Bel));
         Writeln('Data modified since last save');
         Prompt := 'Do you wish to save (Y, N): ';
         Responses := ['Y', 'y', 'N', 'n'];
         Answer := AskUser(Prompt, Responses);
         Writeln(Answer);
         Writeln;
         if Answer in ['Y', 'y'] then
           SaveData
       end {if}
   end; {Quit}

{*** Procedure Handle is unchanged}

   procedure Initialize;

     {Written by: XXXXXXXXX XX/XX/XX}
     {Purpose:    To open files and read data}
     {Globals modified: ControlFile - the control file handle}
     {                  CustomerFile - the customer file handle}
     {                  ItemFile - the item file handle}
     {                  The following are read from the files}
     {                       ControlRecord}
     {                       Item}
     {                       Customer}
     {                  Modified - set to false}
```

Figure 6-16   (continues next page)

```
  var
    I: integer;              {Loop control}

begin {Initialize}
  Reset(ControlFile, 'SalesControl');
  Read(ControlFile, ControlRecord);
  Close(ControlFile);

  Reset(ItemFile, 'SalesItem');
  for I := 1 to ControlRecord.NItem do
    begin
      Read(ItemFile, Item[I])
    end; {for}
  Close(ItemFile);

  Reset(CustomerFile, 'Customers');
  for I := 1 to ControlRecord.NCust do
    begin
      Read(CustomerFile, Customer[I])
    end; {for}
  Close(CustomerFile);

  Modified := false
end; {Initialize}

begin {PointOfSale}

{*** Main program is unchanged}

end.
```

Figure 6-16   (continued)

SaveData and Quit Procedures.   These are fairly straightforward. See Figure 6-16. We simply comment on their use of the Modified flag. The SaveData procedure sets it to *false* because now the data have not been modified since the last save. The Quit procedure allows the user to save the data if the Modified flag is *true*.

Test Plan.   We do not write a complete test plan, but rather describe a few tests to remind you of some of the testing strategies:

- Item number not in list
- Item number for item with 0 inventory
- Item number first in list; last in list; in between
- Quantity = entire remaining inventory
- Quantity one more than remaining inventory
- Quantity = 0; = 1
- Password correct, except it has trailing blanks

- New customer already in array: first, last, in between
- Customer array full
- Try to add same new customer twice
- Do several purchases of same item, driving inventory eventually to 0
- Add several customers in a row to fill the array
- New customer already in array, with array full

Case Study No. 10

In this case study, we prepare a package of subprograms rather than a single program. The modules in the package assist us when writing programs that manipulate polynomials in a single variable. Because the package of subprograms handles the details of working with polynomials, we are able to concentrate on the problem we wish to solve and not on these details.

Statement of Problem. Polynomials of degree n or less in a single unknown, say, x, can be written as

$$c_0 + c_1 x + c_2 x^2 + \cdots + c_n x^n$$

where the c's are the coefficients of the individual powers of x.

Such a polynomial can be specified completely by giving the values for the coefficients and the name of the single unknown. We want to have a collection of subprograms for performing arithmetic and other operations on polynomials of a single unknown that we call X.

Analysis. There are a number of ways to represent polynomials in the computer. Some use techniques that have not yet been covered. The one we present has a number of drawbacks. For example, there is a limit placed on the degree of the polynomials. However, it has the advantage of being one of the easiest to understand.

In the case study, then, we choose to represent the polynomials by real arrays containing their coefficients. For example, a polynomial P is represented by an array C declared as

```
type
   Polynomial = array[0..MaxDegree] of real;
var
   P: Polynomial;
```

(MaxDegree is a constant defined in the *const* section.)

Note that we are taking advantage of the fact that we can specify a lower bound other than 1 for the array subscripts. Thus, the coefficient of X^K in the polynomial is the element of the array with subscript K.

We next decide on the operations to be performed. We normally would like to provide addition, subtraction, multiplication, and division. (Division is fairly difficult and, therefore, we do not do that in this example.) Other operations that we can provide are the evaluation of a polynomial for a given value of X, and integration and differentiation by X. More computer-related operations would be reading and writing polynomials, finding the degree of a polynomial, comparing two polynomials to see if they are the same polynomial, and

TABLE 6-1 OPERATIONS TO BE PROVIDED BY POLYNOMIAL PACKAGE

(a)	Addition
(b)	Subtraction
(c)	Multiplication
(d)	Multiplication by a constant
(e)	Multiplication by X
(f)	Evaluate a polynomial
(g)	Integrate a polynomial
(h)	Differentiate a polynomial
(i)	Read a polynomial
(j)	Write a polynomial
(k)	Find the degree of a polynomial
(l)	Compare two polynomials for equality
(m)	Copy a polynomial

copying one polynomial into another. We also include some special cases of multiplication, namely, by a constant and by X. Refer to Table 6-1 for a summary of these operations.

We must next decide on the form our operations will take. Most of the operations require a number of steps to complete, and so it seems reasonable to use subprograms for the operations. Most of the operations have a polynomial for a result. In Pascal, a function cannot return an array as the function value. Since we are representing polynomials with arrays, we use procedures for these operations. Operations (f), (k), and (l) do return single values and thus could be implemented using functions.

Let us name the subprograms with names that start with "Poly" for polynomial and end with characters in some sense descriptive of the operation. Thus, we use names like PolyAdd, PolySub, PolyMult, and PolyEval. By starting with the prefix Poly, the routines are usually listed together in any automatically generated alphabetical lists of subprograms used in any program. Although this is not a consideration in using THINK Pascal, it is in many production environments.

The arithmetic operations require two operands and one result. Also, we sometimes use another argument to indicate success or failure of the operation. The operation

```
R := OP1 - OP2
```

could be represented with six different orderings of R, OP1, and OP2. However, it would be very confusing to the user of the routine to have OP1 follow OP2 or to have OP1 separated from OP2 by the result R. Therefore, the two reasonable choices for the ordering of these three seem to be R, OP1, OP2 and OP1, OP2, R. As we did in Case Study No. 7 (Section 5-4), we choose the order OP1, OP2, R.

For example, the first routine would have this header line:

```
procedure PolyAdd(P, Q: Polynomial; var Result: Polynomial);
```

Result is the array representing the result polynomial, and P and Q are the arrays representing the operand polynomials.

One remaining question is the size of the arrays to be used. We pick 50 as the maximum degree of the polynomials, writing

```
const
   MaxDegree = 50;
```

in the main program. Many of the submodules reference this global constant.

Algorithms and Programs. Most of the algorithms are very simple and short, so in many cases we omit the variable lists. Also, because we have many short programs, we show them right after the discussion of the algorithm.

Addition of two polynomials is performed by adding the coefficients of the same power of X. The sum of

$$5x^5 - 4x^2 + 6$$

and

$$6x^5 + 2x^3 + 3$$

is

$$11x^5 + 2x^3 - 4x^2 + 9$$

The first and second polynomials are represented by arrays containing

$$6\ 0\ -4\ 0\ 0\ 5$$

and

$$3\ 0\ 0\ 2\ 0\ 6$$

as their first six elements (in positions 0 through 5). The result is represented by the array

$$9\ 0\ -4\ 2\ 0\ 11$$

The algorithm uses a count-control loop to add each corresponding array element. This is easily coded, as shown in Figure 6-17. The subtraction routine is very similar to the addition routine.

```
procedure PolyAdd(P, Q: Polynomial; var Result: Polynomial);

{Written by: XXXXXXXXX XX/XX/XX}
{Purpose:    To add two polynomials}
{Globals used: MaxDegree, constant for maximum degree}
{Parameters: P, Q   - input, the polynomials to add}
{            Result - output, the resulting sum}

   var
      I: integer;          {loop control}

begin {PolyAdd}
   for I := 0 to MaxDegree do
      begin
         Result[I] := P[I] + Q[I]
      end {for}
end; {PolyAdd}
```

Figure 6-17 Adding two polynomials.

Multiplication, on the other hand, is much more complex. The product of two polynomials

$$p_0 + p_1x + p_2x^2$$

and

$$q_0 + q_1x + q_2x^2 + q_3x^3$$

is

$$p_0q_0 + (p_0q_1 + p_1q_0)x + (p_0q_2 + p_1q_1 + p_2q_0)x^2$$
$$+ (p_0q_3 + p_1q_2 + p_2q_1)x^3 + (p_1q_3 + p_2q_2)x^4 + p_2q_3x^5$$

The first polynomial has three terms and the second four terms. The product has 12 individual terms, each a product of one P term and one Q term. In other words, each P coefficient is multiplied by each Q coefficient. The power of x in the product associated with the term p_iq_j is just $i + j$. The degree of the product polynomial is the sum of the degrees of the two factors.

This is one place where it is convenient to have a routine to compute the degree of a polynomial. Let us define that routine as an integer function named PolyDegree. It has a single parameter, which is a polynomial. (We write the function later.)

In order to multiply each term of polynomial P by each term of polynomial Q, we need a nested loop structure. We use the variables IP and IQ as indices for the loops. For the degrees of P and Q, we use the variables PDegree and QDegree. Similarly, we use IR and RDegree for the index and degree, respectively, associated with the result polynomial Result.

The rough algorithm for the multiplication routine is

Compute the degree of Result and check for a legal value.
Initialize the coefficients of Result to zero.
Compute all the products of the terms of P and Q, adding them into the appropriate terms of Result.

The first step becomes

```
PDegree := PolyDegree(P);
QDegree := PolyDegree(Q);
RDegree := PDegree + QDegree;
if RDegree > MaxDegree then
   OK := false
else
   .
   .
   .
```

The output parameter OK is used to indicate to the calling program whether the multiplication was possible.

Within the else branch, we set OK to *true* and perform the second and third steps of our algorithm.

The second step becomes

```
for IR := 0 to 50 do
     R[IR] := 0.0
```

Notice that we initialize all elements of R to zero and not just the elements from 0 to RDegree. This is done so that later calculations, such as adding or finding the degree, work correctly. The main part of the algorithm are the nested loops multiplying the individual terms and adding to the proper terms in R:

```
for IP := 0 to PDegree do
  begin
    for IQ := 0 to QDegree do
      begin
        IR := IP + IQ;
        R[IR] := R[IR] + P[IP] * Q[IQ]
      end {for IQ}
  end {for IP}
```

Combining the pieces, we obtain the procedure shown in Figure 6-18.

Let us now work on the PolyDegree function used in PolyMult. The degree of a polynomial P is the highest power of X that appears in the polynomial. This corresponds to the subscript of the last nonzero coefficient for the polynomial. A simple way to find that element is to search the array from the last term back until we find a nonzero element. Note that if all the elements are zero, then the polynomial represents the constant zero and the degree is zero.

This can be written using our usual searching techniques, as outlined here:

1. Set Found to *false* and I to MaxDegree.

2. In a loop, examine P[I]. If it is nonzero, set Found to *true*; otherwise decrement 1.

3. The loop terminates when Found is *true* or I reaches 0.

4. After the loop, I is the answer. Notice this is *true* no matter which condition causes the loop termination.

Based on this discussion, we write the function given in Figure 6-19.

Now let us consider the routine for evaluating a polynomial. It requires two arguments: the array of coefficients and the value of X. The routine returns only a single value and, therefore, can be a function. Let us call the function PolyEval, with arguments P and X.

A first rough algorithm might look like

```
PDegree := PolyDegree(P);
Value := P[0];
for I := 1 to PDegree do
  add P[I] times I^th power of X to Value
```

To compute X to the Ith power, we could use

```
XToI := X;
for J := 2 to I do
  XToI := XToI * X
```

This approach would require I − 1 multiplications. To compute the value of a polynomial of degree N would require N multiplications of coefficients by powers of X plus

```
procedure PolyMult(P, Q: Polynomial; var Result: Polynomial;
                   var OK: boolean);

{Written by: XXXXXXXXX XX/XX/XX}
{Purpose:    To multiply two polynomials}
{Globals used: MaxDegree, constant for maximum degree}
{Parameters:   P, Q  - input, the polynomials to multiply}
{              Result - output, the resulting product}

  var
     IR: integer;        {index for Result}
     IP: integer;        {index for P}
     IQ: integer;        {index for Q}
     RDegree: integer;   {degree for Result}
     PDegree: integer;   {degree for P}
     QDegree: integer;   {degree for Q}

begin {PolyMult}

{*** Calculate Result degree, see if legal}

  PDegree := PolyDegree(P);
  QDegree := PolyDegree(Q);
  RDegree := PDegree + QDegree;

  if RDegree > MaxDegree then
     OK := false
  else

{*** Set OK, initialize result to 0}

     begin
        OK := true;

        for IR := 0 to MaxDegree do
           begin
              Result[IR] := 0
           end; {for}

{*** Multiply P, Q terms; add to Result terms}

        for IP := 0 to PDegree do
           begin
              for IQ := 0 to QDegree do
                 begin
                    IR := IP + IQ;
                    Result[IR] := Result[IR] + P[IP] * Q[IQ]
                 end {for IQ}
           end {for IP}
     end {if}
end;    {PolyMult}
```

Figure 6-18 Multiplying two polynomials.

```
function PolyDegree(P: Polynomial): integer;

{Written by: XXXXXXXXX XX/XX/XX}
{Purpose:    To find the degree of a polynomial}
{Globals used: MaxDegree, constant for maximum degree}
{Parameters:   P - input, the polynomial whose degree is sought}

    var
      I: integer;        {array index}
      Found: boolean;    {used to quit loop}

    begin {PolyDegree}
      Found := False;
      I := MaxDegree;

      while (I <> 0) and (not Found) do
        begin
          if P[I] <> 0 then
            Found := true
          else
            I := I - 1
        end; {while}

      PolyDegree := I
    end; {PolyDegree}
```

Figure 6-19 The degree of a polynomial.

$$(N-1) + (N-2) + (N-3) + \cdots + 2 + 1$$

additional multiplications to compute the various powers of X. The expression

$$(N-1) + \cdots + 2 + 1$$

is equal to

$$\frac{N(N-1)}{2}$$

and so the total number of multiplications needed is

$$\frac{N^2}{2} - \frac{N}{2} + N = \frac{N^2}{2} + \frac{N}{2}$$

If N were 50, this would require 1275 multiplications. This number can be reduced considerably. Notice first that the powers of X are needed in sequence. Rather than compute the Ith power of X starting from scratch, we can compute it from the $(I-1)^{st}$ power. This leads to the following code:

```
PDegree := PolyDegree(P);
XToI := 1;
Value := P[0];
```

```
    for I := 1 to PDegree do
      begin
        XToI := XToI * X;
        Value := Value + P[I] * XToI
      end; {for}
    PolyEval := Value
```

For this algorithm, the number of multiplications for a polynomial of degree N is just 2N. Note that for N = 50, this is a reduction by a factor of almost 13.

There is still a better method, commonly called **Horner's method**. A polynomial such as

$$p_0 + p_1 x + p_2 x^2 + p_3 x^3 + p_4 x^4$$

can be rewritten in a nested form as

$$p_0 + x(p_1 + x(p_2 + x(p_3 + x(p_4)))).$$

This can be evaluated in the order

$$\text{val} := p_4$$
$$\text{val} := p_3 + x * \text{val}$$
$$\text{val} := p_2 + x * \text{val}$$
$$\text{val} := p_1 + x * \text{val}$$
$$\text{val} := p_0 + x * \text{val}$$

When we are finished, val has the value of the polynomial. We have used, in this case, only four multiplications. In general, the algorithm would be that shown in the function of Figure 6-20.

Of course, here a polynomial of degree N requires N multiplications. Notice that in this situation the fastest of our three algorithms is also the shortest to write. One should not assume that this last procedure is twice as fast as the second procedure because there are other operations, such as additions, loop control, etc., involved. Still this should be faster than the others on most conventional computer systems.

The routines for integration and differentiation use similar methods. If you have not studied calculus yet, you can skip this material without affecting your understanding of the other routines in the package.

The integral of a polynomial is the sum of the integrals of each of the terms plus an arbitrary constant. The integral of the term

$$p_i x^i$$

is

$$\frac{p_i x^{i+1}}{i+1}$$

The result is a new polynomial, say, Result, with the $(i + 1)^{st}$ coefficient of Result being the ith coefficient of P divided by $i + 1$. For the degree of Result to be less than or equal to MaxDegree, the degree of P must be less than or equal to MaxDegree − 1.

```
function PolyEval(P: Polynomial; X: real): real;

{Written by: XXXXXXXXX XX/XX/XX}
{Purpose:    To evaluate a polynomial for a given x value}
{Parameters: P - input, the polynomial to evaluate}
{            X - input, the given X value}

  var
    PDegree: integer;    {degree of P}
    Value: real;         {local copy of answer}
    I: integer;          {loop control}

begin
  PDegree := PolyDegree(P);
  Value := P[PDegree];
  for I := PolyDegree - 1 downto 0 do
    begin
      Value := P[I] + X * Value
    end; {for}
  PolyEval := Value
end; {PolyEval}
```

Figure 6-20 Evaluating a polynomial (Horner's method).

Let us call our routine PolyIntegrate and use arguments P, C, Result, and OK. P is the original polynomial, C is the arbitrary constant, Result is the result polynomial, and OK indicates success. See Figure 6-21.

For our final example we write the output routine. This should be a procedure because it returns no value. It needs only the one argument, the polynomial to be printed. Let us call the routine PolyOut. Suppose we print all coefficients except the constant term as

(dddddd.ddddd) * X ^ (dd)

(where the d's stand for digits) and the constant term as

(dddddd.ddddd)

(This uses ^ to stand for exponentiation, a common notation.)

Also, let us not print any terms with a zero coefficient; however, we should be sure to print at least one term. We use a Boolean variable AnyPrinted to indicate whether any terms have been printed. The procedure is shown in Figure 6-22.

Testing. Testing a package of subprograms differs from testing a program in several ways. First, the individual subprograms cannot stand alone, and so you must write programs to call the subprograms. These programs are commonly called drivers. Second, the individual routines tend to be fairly simple, so the tests are generally fairly simple.

Probably the input and output subroutines should be tested first. In that way, you can use those routines when you test the others. A simple way to test these routines is to use a driver program that calls PolyIn (the input routine) and PolyOut in a loop. You can then check the output to see if it matches your input. The driver should also print the array corresponding to the polynomial that has been read by PolyIn to guard against errors in

```
procedure PolyIntegrate(P: Polynomial; C: real;
                       var Result: Polynomial; var OK: boolean);
{Written by: XXXXXXXXX XX/XX/XX}
{Purpose:    To integrate a polynomial}
{Parameters: P - input, the polynomial to integrate}
{            C - input, the constant of integration}
{            Result - output, the resulting integral}
{            OK - output, indicates whether or not ok}
{Globals used: MaxDegree - largest possible degree}

  var
    PDegree: integer;   {degree of P}
    I: integer;         {loop control}

  begin {PolyIntegrate}
    PDegree := PolyDegree(P);
    if PDegree > MaxDegree - 1 then
      OK := false
    else
      begin
        OK := true;
        Result[0] := C;
        for I := 2 to PDegree + 1 do
          begin
            Result[I] := P[I-1] / I
          end; {for}
        for I := PDegree + 2 to MaxDegree do
          begin
            Result[I] := 0
          end {for}
      end {if}
  end; {PolyIntegrate}
```

Figure 6-21 Integrating a polynomial.

PolyOut and PolyIn that might cancel each other. An example of such an error would be if PolyIn placed the coefficients in the wrong elements of the array and PolyOut picked up the elements in the same wrong manner. The test data for the driver should include polynomials of degree 0, 1, MaxDegree − 1, MaxDegree, and some over MaxDegree. (You may wish to reduce the size of MaxDegree for most of the tests.) Some of the polynomials should consist of just a few nonzero terms, whereas others should have all nonzero terms. The constant 0 should be one of the test values because that causes a special action in the PolyOut routine.

Once PolyIn and PolyOut are tested and appear to be correct, you can begin testing the other routines. A driver that reads two polynomials and computes their degrees, adds them, subtracts them, differentiates them, compares for equality, and multiplies by X would be a natural next step and would test a large number of the routines. These operations have been grouped because they each require one or two input polynomials but do not require any additional data. In addition, separate drivers should be used to provide each routine that has error checks with invalid data so as to check error handling.

```
procedure PolyOut(P: Polynomial);

{Written by: XXXXXXXX, XX/XX/XX}
{Purpose:     To print out a polynomial}
{Globals used: MaxDegree, constant for maximum degree}
{Parameters:   P - input, the polynomial to print}

  var
    AnyPrinted: boolean;    {to make sure at least one term is printed}
    I: integer;             {loop control}

begin {PolyOut}
  AnyPrinted := false;
  for I := MaxDegree downto 1 do
    begin
      if P[I] <> 0 then
        begin
          Writeln('(', P[I] : 12 : 5, ') * X ^ (', I:2, ')');
          AnyPrinted := true
        end {if}
    end; {for}
  if (P[0] <> 0) or (not AnyPrinted) then
    Writeln('(', P[0] : 12 : 5, ')')
end; {PolyOut}
```

Figure 6-22 Output of a polynomial.

The copy routine can be tested after the routine for comparing for equality. Finally, the last group to be tested could be the routines for evaluating a polynomial, multiplication by a constant, and integration. This group requires both a polynomial and a real value as inputs for each routine.

The detailed unit test plans for the various modules are left as an exercise. To get you started, we list a few possible tests for two of the modules.

    For PolyDegree: degree MaxDegree

                             degree 1

                             degree 0 (not zero polynomial)

                             degree 0 (zero polynomial)

    For PolyAdd: both polynomials zero

                             first polynomial zero

                             second polynomial zero

                             neither polynomial zero, result not zero

                             neither polynomial zero, result zero

Documentation. The documentation for a package of subprograms normally includes a description of what operations are provided, how the polynomials are represented, how the user has to define the data arrays that hold the polynomials, and, finally, a detailed description of each routine in the package. The detailed description should include precise descriptions of how to call each routine and precise descriptions of each argument. It is desirable to include examples of each routine's use. You can use Pascal terminology, if convenient, to describe these routines because anyone using the package has to know Pascal to write a program calling the routines. Notice that the user documentation for a package such as this differs from that for a program. For a program, Pascal terminology is not appropriate for the user's guide.

EXERCISES

Exercises 1 to 5 refer to Case Study No. 9.

1. (a) Write a program to create the data files initially used by the case study.
   (b) Modify the Initialize procedure to obtain the base part of the file name from the user, and check that files <base>Control, <base>Items, and <base>Customer exist prior to opening them. See the hint for Exercise 11(b), Section 6-2.

2. The case study uses a linear search for item number and customer number. What changes would be necessary to use a binary search? Caution: The new customer procedure would change.

3. Modify the Purchase activity as follows:
   (a) Allow the user to abort the process of obtaining a valid item number. (This avoids the possibility of being stuck forever in the Purchase procedure if the item numbers entered are all invalid.)
   (b) Obtain a list of one or more item numbers and quantities rather than just one.
   (c) Double the discount for preferred customers if the total bill is at least $500.
   (d) Add sales tax to the bill.
   (e) Add to part (b) as follows: When the user can enter several item numbers, it is possible that he or she may want to abort the whole activity. Allow this to occur at any point up to indicating that the list of input is through. This must adjust the inventory properly. Hint: One way to solve this involves building up the purchase information in an array. Assume that there are no more than 30 individual items input.

4. Modify the new customer procedure as follows:
   (a) Require the user to enter a password before a new customer can be entered.
   (b) Validate the discount entered. It must lie between 0.0 and 10.0 percent. (It can be 10.0, but not 0.0.)

5. Add the following activities. Note: To avoid a "cluttered" menu, you may want to reorganize it. For example, you might have a single menu item for the various Utility activities, such as adding an item or a customer, changing a price, etc. Choosing this item would cause a submenu to be displayed for the various utility activities.
   (a) Add an item to the list.
   (b) Remove an item from the list.
   (c) Change a price.
   (d) Change a discount percentage.
   (e) Change the password. You might wish to store the valid password in the control file.
   (f) See part (e). If the control file contains the password, it should not be in character form. Modify the program to store the password on the control file as a record containing: (1) length of the password and (2) an array of the Ord values for the characters in the password.

(g) Query: Given an item, what is the current price and inventory?
(h) Query: Given a customer number, what is the discount?
(i) Generate an order. Add a field to the item file indicating a cutoff point. When the inventory drops below that point, it is time to reorder. This activity should print a list of all items that should be reordered.

Exercises 6 to 12 refer to Case Study No. 10.

6. (a) Design and write an interactive version of the module PolyIn(P, EndOfData). You need to devise a way for the user to indicate that she or he does not wish to enter more data. In addition, you need a way to terminate the polynomial being entered. EndOfData is a Boolean parameter set to *true* if the user does not wish to enter a polynomial and set to *false* otherwise.
   (b) Design and write a file version of the module. It should read its data from a text file opened by the main program. (Prompts are not appropriate in this version.)

7. (a) Design and write the routines for multiplication of a polynomial by a constant or by X.
   (b) If you have studied calculus, design and write the routine for differentiation.
   (c) Design and write the routines for comparing for equality and for copying polynomials.

8. Think carefully about how you do polynomial division. Write a routine to divide P by Q, giving a quotient polynomial and a remainder polynomial. Hint: You may be able to write this almost entirely in terms of other routines in the package.

9. Test all of the routines written in Exercises 6 to 8.

10. The family of polynomials known as Chebyshev polynomials is used in several different areas of mathematics. These polynomials are denoted by

$$T_N(x)$$

where N is the degree of the individual polynomial. The first few of these are defined as

$$T_0(x) = 1$$
$$T_1(x) = x$$
$$T_2(x) = 2x^2 - 1$$

and

$$T_{10}(x) = 512x^{10} - 1280x^8 + 1120x^6 - 400x^4 + 50x^2 - 1$$

The polynomial of degree N can be calculated from those of degree $N - 1$ and degree $N - 2$ by the equation:

$$T_N(x) = 2xT_{N-1}(x) - T_{N-2}(x)$$

Write a program using the polynomial package to compute and print the Chebyshev polynomials for $N = 0$ through $N = 15$. How would you have to modify the package for N greater than 15? Hint: Use recursion.

11. (a) Revise each of the routines developed in the case study to use the following representation of a polynomial.

```
type
   Polynomial = record
      Degree: integer;
      Coeff: array[1..MaxDegree] of real
   end;
```

The degree is stored as part of the record, and the coefficient array contains meaningful data only for the portion indicated by the degree.

(b) Repeat part (a) for the routines developed in Exercises 6 to 8.
(c) What differences would the revised representation of a polynomial make for Exercise 10?

12. Follow the instructions for Exercise 11 for this data structure. A polynomial is represented as a list of its nonzero terms. For example, $5x^6 - 4x^3 + 7.5$ would have these values stored:

3 (there are 3 terms)
5.0, 6   a record representing $5x^6$
−4.0, 3   a record representing $-4x^3$
7.5, 0   a record representing 7.5 ($7.5x^0$)

The terms are stored in order from the highest degree to the lowest. We use the declarations:

```
const
  MaxTerms = 50; {maximum number of terms}
type
  Term = record
    Coeff: real;
    Power: integer
  end;
  Polynomial = record
    NTerms: integer;
    Terms: array[1..MaxTerms] of Term
  end;
```

Hint: The add routine can be done using the "array merge" logic, as described in Exercise 21 of Section 6-3.

Exercises 13 to 14 suggest packages of subprograms that could be developed to aid in working with certain types of problems.

13. Integers of long length can be stored in the computer as arrays, one digit per array element. For example, a 15-digit number could be represented as an integer array Number of size 15. Number[1] would contain the first digit of the number, and Number[15] the last digit.
    (a) Write a procedure to add two such numbers. It should give an indication of whether the answer fits in the array that represents the answer.
    (b) Subtract two such numbers, indicating whether it is possible to do so.
    (c) Compare two such numbers to see whether the first is greater than the second. (This might be a Boolean function.)
    (d) Multiply two such numbers.
    (e) Use this package to find the sum
    $$1 + 2 + 4 + 8 + \cdots + 2^1 + \cdots + 2^{63}$$
    (The answer is fewer than 30 digits long.)

14. Numbers in base 10 can be represented as arrays, each array element having one digit whose value is 0 to 9 (see Exercise 13). If we limit our digits to 0 to 7, we have a "base 8" number instead of a base 10 number. For example, in base 8, the array

    0 0 0 0 1 5 3

    would represent $1 * 8^2 + 5 * 8 + 3 = 107$. Write procedures or functions for the following:

EXERCISES

(a) Given an array and a base, calculate the value of the number represented by the array in that base.
(b) Given a value, convert it to an array in a given base.
(c) Print the number represented by an array, given the array and the base. For example,

ARRAY	BASE	RESULT
0, 0, 8, 0, 3	10	803
0, 1, 5, 1, 0	8	1510
0, 1, 5, 1, 0, 1, 9	16	FA19

Hint: Convert the given array to an array of characters, with leading zeros converted to blanks. Notice that for base 16, the digits are 0 to 9 and A to F, with A = 10, etc. An array containing the characters '0', '1', etc., may help.

(d)–(g) Revise parts (a) to (d) of Exercise 13 to work for arrays representing numbers in any given base.

Exercises 15 to 21 suggest other "case study" applications.

15. (a) A simple encryption ("secret code") method is to jumble the alphabet, replacing, for example, A by D, B by X, C by M, and so on. One way to implement this uses two parallel arrays. The first contains the letters in order, and the second contains the letters in the desired jumbled order (for example, D, X, M, . . .). Give the declarations and assignment statements to create these arrays.
    (b) Another approach would be to use one array indexed by the char values 'A' to 'Z'. Give the necessary declarations and assignment statements to set this up.
    (c) Write a subprogram segment to encode a single character. Assume that characters that are not letters are replaced by themselves (CAB$ might become MDX$). Use the representation of either part (a) or part (b).
    (d) Write a main program that codes or decodes lines of text. It reads a series of lines, each 65 columns long. The first character of each line should contain either a C or D to indicate whether the remaining 64 characters should be coded or decoded.
    (e) Modify your program to handle both uppercase and lowercase letters.

16. (a) Modify Exercise 15 to use the following different encryption method: A is replaced by G, B by H, C by I, and so on, each letter replaced by the sixth letter further along in the alphabet. Some care is required to handle the letters near the end properly; for example, Z is replaced by F. Use only a single array containing the letters in order.
    (b) Modify Exercise 15 to replace A by Z, B by Y, C by X, D by W, and so on. Use only a single array containing the letters in order.

17. Write subprograms for the following actions that deal with an array of records containing employee ID, sales, and rate. There are presently NEmployees employees represented in these arrays. Hint: Write a search function first.
    (a) *Inquire.* Given an ID number, print the sales amount and rate for that employee or print an error message if the given ID is faulty.
    (b) *New Sale.* Given a sales amount and ID, add the amount to the Sales figure for that ID (or print an error message). Also calculate the commission as sales amount times rate.
    (c) *Change the Rate.* Given a new rate and an ID, change the rate for that employee to the given new rate or print an error message.

(d) *Find the Largest.* Print the ID, rate, and sales amount of the salesman with the largest sales amount.

(e) *New Employee.* Given a new employee ID and rate, add that employee to the end of the list. If the ID is already in use, print an error message.

(f) *Sort.* Sort the data in order by sales (highest to lowest).

18. Repeat Exercise 17 under the assumption that the array is maintained in increasing numerical order by employee number. Notice that for part (e), the new employee goes at the proper place based on her ID, which is not necessarily at the end of the list. For part (f), create a separate sorted array. Hint: Rewrite the search function so it returns the subscript of the first table element larger than or equal to the given key. This simplifies part (e), but it also requires some changes in parts (a) to (c).

19. (a) Write a general-purpose procedure to copy a portion of the array B to the array A. Assume A and B are integer arrays, each of size 200. The routine is given A, APosn, B, BPosn, and ArrLength. APosn and BPosn represent the starting positions in the A and B arrays, respectively, and ArrLength is the number of items to be copied. You can assume that ArrLength is valid, that is, copying that many items does not run past the end of either A or B.

    (b) Rewrite part (a) to handle the possibility that ArrLength may be "too long." The routine should copy up to ArrLength items, taking care to stay within the bounds of both arrays. For example, if APosn = 199, BPosn = 3, and ArrLength = 14, only two items are copied (to A[199] and A[200]).

20. In Case Study No. 4 (Figures 4-11 to 4-13), we presented a program to find all the primes less than or equal to a number N. To do so, we checked each number I from 2 to N to see if I was prime.

    The method used to see if I is prime can be improved significantly using arrays. To see if I is prime, we checked for divisibility by all the numbers from 2 to I − 1. It would suffice to check for divisibility by all the primes from 2 to $\sqrt{I}$. If, as we located a prime, we put it into an array of primes, then this check would be easy to accomplish.

    Write a program that carries out this procedure.

21. An efficient method for determining all the primes less than some given value N is the so-called *sieve of Eratosthenes*, which consists of two major phases. The first is to write the positive integers from 2 to N. The second phase is a nested search and marking process: Starting with the first unmarked number in the list, say, K (at the start, all the numbers are unmarked), go through the list and mark off all multiples of K.

    The result of applying this process three times to the numbers from 2 to 34 is shown in the following list. The marks (X) are shown above the numbers so that we can indicate at which time the markings occurred. Notice that some numbers are marked more than once. The first mark shows all numbers divisible by 2 except for 2. The second mark shows all values divisible by 3 except for 3. The third mark shows all values divisible by 5 (4 was already marked because it is divisible by 2). Upon completion of the entire marking process, all numbers divisible by some smaller number other than 1 have been marked. Thus, the unmarked values are primes.

										X		
Third										X		
Second					X		X			X		
First			X		X		X		X		X	
	2	3	4	5	6	7	8	9	10	11	12

EXERCISES

			X					X			
Third			X			X			X		
Second		X		X		X		X		X	
First	13	14	15	16	17	18	19	20	21	22	23

		X					X				
Third	X			X			X			X	
Second	X		X		X		X		X		X
First	24	25	26	27	28	29	30	31	32	33	34

The key to the efficiency of this process is that the marking process does not require any checking of divisibility. In general, the multiples of K are in positions 2K, 2K + K, 2K + 2K, and so on. Also, notice that only values up to $K = \sqrt{N}$ need to be processed.

(a) Write Pascal code for initializing an integer array Num, with subscripts ranging from 2 to 2000, to the values 2, 3, ... , 2000.

(b) Write Pascal code that, given the array Num initialized as in part (a), carries out the marking process described for the sieve of Eratosthenes. One way of marking the numbers is to set the array element equal to zero.

(c) The values of the numbers do not actually have to be used because the positions of the numbers can indicate their values in this algorithm. Rewrite parts (a) and (b) using a Boolean array Marked, with subscripts ranging from 2 to 1000. Initialize the elements to *false*, and indicate marking by setting an element to *true*. After marking, we can determine if a value J ($2 \leq J \leq 2000$) is prime by checking to see if Marked[J] is *true* or *false*.

(d) Write a program to produce a printed table of primes up to 2000 with 10 primes printed on each line. Be sure that the last line is printed whether or not it includes 10 numbers.

22. Compare the efficiency of the programs written in Exercises 20 and 21 by timing them for various values of N.

23. Revise the program of Figure 6-10 (Section 6-2) to develop a menu-driven system that allows various activities with the files' data. You might include, for example, the ability to initialize the files, add students, delete students, change grades, calculate current averages, set values for tests and programs, and so on.

7 More on Arrays

OBJECTIVES

In Chapter 6, we described the fundamental techniques for dealing with arrays. In this chapter, we will deal with some additional array concepts that can prove useful in your programming. By the end of this chapter, you will be able to:

- use arrays of arrays with effect in your programs
- represent matrices using arrays
- accept input into and produce output from arrays

7-1 MORE ON ARRAYS

Arrays of Arrays

The form for declaring an array is

```
array [index type] of component type;
```

The index type is frequently of the form 1..N for some integer N, but it can also be, for example, a user-defined scalar type. The component type can be, among other types, *integer*, *real*, a string type, or a record type. It can also be an array type.

Thus, for example, we can declare an array to consist of three arrays, where each of those arrays consists of four real numbers. There are three ways to accomplish this. First, we could translate what we have written into Pascal more or less directly:

```
type
    ArrayofArrays = array[1..3] of array[1..4] of real;
```

Second, we could predefine the notion of an array of four real numbers and then use that in our definition of the array of arrays:

```
type
    RealArray     = array[1..4] of real;
    ArrayofArrays = array[1..3] of RealArray;
```

Finally, Pascal provides an abbreviated form of declaration as follows:

```
type
    ArrayofArrays = array[1..3, 1..4] of real;
```

In this example, we can think of the declaration as (1) showing the number of arrays (three, indexed by 1..3) and (2) describing each as consisting of four real numbers (indexed by 1..4).

The three methods simply give alternative ways to describe precisely the same type. If we declare a variable X to be of the type ArrayofArrays, then it will consist of three arrays of four real numbers each. It is useful, at times, to be able to visualize such an array of arrays. A common technique is to list the three arrays, one below the other, as illustrated here:

```
3.6    - 1.0     4.2      1.0
2.9      7.8    11.5      0.0
0.5     -0.1    -6.5     10.2
```

Because of this commonly used visualization, arrays of arrays are frequently referred to as **two-dimensional arrays.**

Within an array of arrays, we can refer to the entire array by using its name (X, in our example). We can also refer to X[1], which is the first array, consisting of the four numbers 3.6, –1.0, 4.2, and 1.0. X[2] is the second array and X[3] is the third.

It is also possible to refer to the individual numbers within the array of arrays. One way to refer to the number 4.2, for example, is to realize that it is the third number in the array X[1]. Thus, we can write

```
X[1][3]
```

Similarly, X[2][4] refers to the fourth number in X[2], whose value is 0.0 in the previous illustration.

Pascal provides an alternative way to say the same thing. Rather than writing X[1][3], we can abbreviate this as X[1, 3]. The two notations mean exactly the same thing: the third number in the array X[1]. Notice that, because of this meaning, both X[4, 2] and X[3,5] would be illegal. The first says to take the second value of X[4], and there is no X[4]. The second says to take the fifth value of X[3], and X[3] contains only four numbers.

An interpretation of X[I][J] or X[I, J], then, is as follows: the first subscript tells which array to choose, and the second which number within that array. If we are picturing the array in the table form described previously, the first subscript tells which row to choose, and the second which number within that row.

To further illustrate these ideas, in the context of a meaningful application, we work extensively with the following example. We wish to use an array to represent the monthly rainfall in inches for several cities of the United States. For each city in the list—Philadelphia, New York, Atlanta, Los Angeles, and Chicago—we have a list of 12 real numbers representing the rainfall for the 12 months. We wish to employ a data structure that allows us to specify one of the cities and one of the months of the year and obtain the average rainfall. Some alternative ways of defining the data structure are as follows:

1. *Separate Declaration*

```
type
    Months = (January, February, March, April, May, June, July,
              August, September, October, November, December);
    Amount = array[Months] of real;
    Cities = (Philadelphia, New_York, Washington_DC, Los_Angeles,
              Chicago);
var
    MonthlyRain: array[Cities] of Amount;
```

2. *Joint Declaration*

```
type
    Months = (January, February, March, April, May, June, July,
              August, September, October, November, December);
    Cities = (Philadelphia, New_York, Washington_DC, Los_Angeles,
              Chicago);
var
    MonthlyRain: array[Cities] of array[Months] of real;
```

3. *Abbreviated Joint Declaration*

```
type
    Months = (January, February, March, April, May, June, July,
              August, September, October, November, December);
    Cities = (Philadelphia, New_York, Washington_DC, Los_Angeles,
              Chicago);
var
    MonthlyRain: array[Cities, Months] of real;
```

In any of the variations for the declaration of the array, we can refer to November's rainfall in Philadelphia by either of the expressions:

```
MonthlyRain[Philadelphia][November]
MonthlyRain[Philadelphia, November]
```

Note that the second expression is an abbreviation of the first.

To put the ideas into perspective, let us look at some possible expressions and the data types that correspond to them.

EXPRESSION	DATA TYPE
MonthlyRain[Philadelphia, November]	Real
MonthlyRain[Philadelphia]	Array of real
MonthlyRain[January]	Illegal construction
MonthlyRain	Array of arrays of real

7-1 MORE ON ARRAYS

We can perform activities appropriate to the type on each kind of expression. For example, if we wished to make the rainfall figures for Chicago the same as that for Los Angeles for the entire year, then we could execute the statement

```
MonthlyRain[Chicago] := MonthlyRain[Los_Angeles]
```

If we wished to make the amount of rainfall for the month of June for New York the same as that of the month of May for Philadelphia, then we could execute the statement

```
MonthlyRain[New_York, June] := MonthlyRain[Philadelphia, May]
```

If we wish to make the monthly rainfall statistics for February the same as the rainfall statistics for January, then we could use a variable City of type Cities and the loop:

```
for City := Philadelphia to Chicago do
  MonthlyRain[City, February] := MonthlyRain[City, January]
```

Interactive Input and Output of Two-Dimensional Arrays

Suppose we wish to read in the rainfall values by having the user enter them one at a time. As your own experiences have shown, it is important to indicate clearly to the user, by using meaningful prompts, what input is required. We can expect most users to know that a prompt such as "Month2" indicates February, but we cannot expect the user to know that "City2" indicates New York. As we know, THINK allows us to print the constants of the user-defined types Cities and Months in order to prompt the user. If we wish to read in the values for the rainfall from the user by city and then by month for each city, we can use the loops:

```
for City := Philadelphia to Chicago do
  begin
    Writeln('Enter rainfall for ', City, ': ',);
    for Month := January to December do
      begin
        Write(' ' : 5, Month, ': ');
        Readln(MonthlyRain[City, Month])
      end {for}
```

If we wish the user to enter the values for the rainfalls for each city, month by month, we can use the nested loop:

```
for Month := January to December do
  begin
    Writeln('Enter rainfall for ', Month, ': ');
    for City := Philadelphia to Chicago do
      begin
        Write(' ' : 5, City, ': ');
        Readln(MonthlyRain[City, Month])
      end {for}
  end; {for}
```

Now, suppose that we have obtained the rainfall values in either of the ways shown previously and that we wish to print the values in a table that appears similar to the following:

	Philadelphia	New York	Atlanta	Los Angeles	Chicago
January	2.33	1.40	1.58	4.34	1.35
February	1.11	4.05	3.07	2.52	0.71
March	2.81	3.60	0.31	4.25	4.48
April	3.94	3.91	1.05	1.29	2.73
May	3.40	4.07	1.11	2.13	4.42
June	1.56	2.42	3.39	0.41	1.23
July	4.34	0.67	1.94	0.33	1.60
August	2.22	2.91	1.03	0.88	4.83
September	4.37	4.71	4.22	4.56	0.13
October	2.64	2.19	3.40	4.61	0.66
November	0.70	1.02	2.86	3.30	2.61
December	3.02	0.56	3.37	3.95	2.90

THINK Pascal writes out enumerated types right justified. If we want to left justify or center enumerated values when they are printed (as we do to print out the chart just shown), we first convert the enumerated values to strings, and then use string functions and Write field size designators to position the values as we desire.

To convert enumerated values to strings, we use the THINK function StringOf. The parameters to StringOf are the same kind of expressions that are legal to use in a Write statement, including field width and number-of-decimal-places designators. StringOf then returns as a string what would have been the result of writing out those values. For instance:

```
StringOf('We are writing out a string and the real value', 34.234 : 7 : 2,
         ' as a single string.')
```

will return the value:

```
We are writing out a string and the real value   34.23 as a single string.
```

as a (single) string.

In the following code fragment, we use the StringOf function to convert the enumerated values of types City and Month into strings so we can position them where we desire:

```
{*** Write out rainfall chart with cities centered over the columns and}
{    months left justified labelling each row}

Writeln;
Write(' ' : 10);
for City := Philadelphia to Chicago do
  begin
    CityName := StringOf(City);
    Left := (13 - Length(CityName)) div 2;
    Right := 13 - (Left + Length(CityName));
    Write(' ' : Left, CityName, ' ' : Right)
  end; {for}
Writeln;
```

7-1 MORE ON ARRAYS

```
for Month := January to December do
  begin
    MonthName := StringOf(Month);
    Write(MonthName, ' ' : 10 - Length(MonthName));
    for City := Philadelphia to Chicago do
      Write(MonthlyRain[City, Month] : 10 : 2, ' ' : 3);
    Writeln
  end; {for}
```

We use the string function Length to determine the number of characters each month and city name contains. We use a Write field designator to allow us to left justify the month names. We compute Left and Right, the size of the left and right halves of a city name, to allow us (using some arithmetic and Write field designators) to center that name. By using Left and Right, we avoid accumulating any "off-by-one" errors that might occur if we had used the expression

```
(13 - Length(CityName)) div 2
```

for both sides. This is another example of a small detail that makes the difference between code that accomplishes the desired result and code that surprises us with its behavior.

Text File Input and Output of Two-Dimensional Arrays

If you run a program that interactively obtains data for a large array, you may come to the conclusion that there must be a better way. It is possible to obtain data from a text file instead of from a terminal. Perhaps the most common context is where the data have been placed onto a text file by another program or the same program at an earlier time. The method also works for text files created using an editor.

The discussion given here applies only to numeric arrays. For arrays that involve strings, it is difficult to write programs that deal with text files. (With numbers, it is easy to tell where one ends and the next begins; with strings, this is much harder, and generally requires the use of special characters to mark where one string stops and the next begins. We discuss string manipulation in Chapter 8.)

Provided we take some care when we write the array, we can later read a numeric array from the text file and expect its values to be the same as they were when we wrote the array to the file.

We illustrate the methods by again referring to our rainfall array. The code given before for printing the array can be used to place the same data into a text file by simply declaring a file and placing its name in each Write and Writeln statement. This approach is appropriate if people will be examining the text file. If we want to use the file as input to a program at a later date, however, we would not want the row or column headings. The code that follows would place one month's rainfall per line of the text file RainFile:

```
for Month := January to December do
  begin
    for City := Philadelphia to Chicago do
      Write(RainFile, MonthlyRain[City, Month] : 10 : 2, ' ' : 3);
    Writeln(RainFile)
  end; {for}
```

Similar code could be used to read the data from the file:

```
for Month := January to December do
  begin
    for City := Philadelphia to Chicago do
      Read(RainFile, MonthlyRain[City, Month]);
    Readln(RainFile)
  end {for}
```

Notes

1. The spaces between the figures (written using ' ':3) are a good idea for user-read output. They provide white space between the numbers. They are mandatory if the data are to be read by another program (because they separate one number from the next).
2. The Readln(RainFile) step in the last code segment is optional. When the Read runs out of data on a line of a text file, it goes on to the next line automatically. The Readln can be useful, however, to cause the rest of the input line to be skipped. And it is useful in this example to illustrate how similar the code for reading data from a text file is to that for writing it.
3. Note that the order of the loops is important. If we write the data by month, then by city, we should read them in the same order.

Processing Two-Dimensional Arrays

We continue to refer to our rainfall example to consider some processing activities typically done with two-dimensional arrays. We consider three problems to illustrate the techniques needed for common processing situations.

Find the Average Rainfall in Philadelphia. We use real variables, TotalRain and AverageRain, whose values we can calculate with the following code fragment:

```
TotalRain := 0;
for Month := January to December do
   TotalRain := TotalRain + MonthlyRain[Philadelphia, Month];
AverageRain := TotalRain / 12
```

Note that in the loop, we use the expression

```
MonthlyRain[Philadelphia, Month]
```

in which the first subscript is a constant and the second subscript is a variable.

Find the Average Rainfall in January. We use the same two real variables as in the previous example. The following code segment can be used to calculate the values:

```
TotalRain := 0;
for City := Philadelphia to Chicago do
   TotalRain := TotalRain + MonthlyRain[City, January];
AverageRain := TotalRain / 5
```

Whereas in the first example, the constant 12 is an obvious choice to use as the number of months, the number 5 is not such an obvious choice. What if we add a city to the list? It would be better to use a constant named NumberCities that would be set to 5 in this case. When we add a city, we would change the named constant. Perhaps even better would be to simply count the cities within the loop, as shown here:

```
TotalRain := 0;
CityCount := 0;
for City := Philadelphia to Chicago do
    begin
       TotalRain := TotalRain + MonthlyRain[City, January];
       CityCount := CityCount + 1
    end; {for}
AverageRain := TotalRain / CityCount;
```

Find the Average Rainfall Overall. We use the same two real variables. In this case, we are being asked to average all the rainfall numbers in the array. It doesn't matter what order is used as long as each number is involved once and only once. We choose one of the two natural alternatives in the following code fragment:

```
TotalRain := 0;
for City := Philadelphia to Chicago do
  for Month := January to December do
     TotalRain := TotalRain + MonthlyRain[City, Month];
AverageRain := TotalRain / 60;
```

Once again, it would be better to use the expression 12 * NumberCities, or to count the number of cities, rather than using the constant 60 to calculate the average.

Matrices

A **matrix** is a mathematical structure that consists of a rectangular table in which we refer to the horizontal groupings as rows and the vertical groupings as columns.

A matrix can be written as, for example,

$$\begin{bmatrix} 3 & 2 & 1 \\ 2 & 6 & 7 \end{bmatrix}$$

We usually refer to the size of the matrix by specifying the number of rows and columns, in that order. This example is called a "2-by-3" matrix, which is frequently written as "2 × 3." A natural way to represent a matrix within a Pascal program is as a two-dimensional array. We could represent 2-by-3 matrices with integer entries by use of a declaration such as

```
var
   A: array[1..2, 1..3] of integer;
```

In a program that makes extensive use of such 2-by-3 matrices, we would want to declare a global type such as

```
type
   MatrixType = array[1..2, 1..3] of integer;
```

By using the global type, we can pass variables as parameters, which would be a common desire in any program dealing with matrices.

One operation that is often performed upon matrices of the same size is that of **matrix addition**. When we add two matrices, we get a third matrix of the same size that is obtained by adding the two elements in each of the positions of the matrices. For example,

$$\begin{bmatrix} 3 & 2 & 1 \\ 2 & 6 & 7 \end{bmatrix} + \begin{bmatrix} -5 & 4 & 0 \\ 1 & -1 & 6 \end{bmatrix} = \begin{bmatrix} -2 & 6 & 1 \\ 3 & 5 & 13 \end{bmatrix}$$

Let us design a procedure MatrixAdd to add two matrices to obtain a third. In order to create a general-purpose matrix adder, we need to have available the number of rows and columns of the matrices. Therefore, we will alter our declarations slightly to the following:

```
const
   NumberRows = 2;
   NumberCols = 3;
type
   ElementType = integer;
   MatrixType  = array[1..NumberRows, 1..NumberCols] of ElementType;
```

If A and B are two matrices that we wish to add to obtain matrix C, then the algorithm is

loop Row going from 1 to NumberRows:
   loop Col going from 1 to NumberCols:
      set C[Row, Col] to A[Row, Col] + B[Row, Col]

The two variables Row and Col must be declared as integer variables in the program. Translating the algorithm into Pascal code is quite straightforward, as we see by inspection of the code in Figure 7-1.

```
procedure MatrixAdd(A, B: MatrixType; var C: MatrixType);

{Written by: XXXXXXXXXX   XX/XX/XX}
{Purpose:    To add two matrices}
{Parameters: A, B - input, the matrices to add}
{            C    - output, the resulting sum}
{Globals used: NumberRows, NumberCols - constants for matrix size}

   var
      Row: integer;     {Loop index through the rows}
      Col: integer;     {Loop index through the columns}

   begin {MatrixAdd}
      for Row := 1 to NumberRows do
         for Col := 1 to NumberCols do
            C[Row, Col] := A[Row, Col] + B[Row, Col]
   end; {MatrixAdd}
```

Figure 7-1   Adding two matrices.

7-1 MORE ON ARRAYS

```
procedure ScalarMult(M: ElementType; A: MatrixType; var C: MatrixType);

{Written by:  XXXXXXXXX XX/XX/XX}
{Purpose:     To scalar multiply M times A}
{Parameters:  M - input, scalar to multiply by}
{             A - input, matrix to multiply}
{             C - output, resulting matrix}
{Globals used: NumberRows, NumberCols - constants for matrix size}

  var
    Row: integer; {Loop index through rows}
    Col: integer; {Loop index through columns}

begin {ScalarMult}

  for Row := 1 to NumberRows do
    for Col := 1 to NumberCols do
      C[Row, Col] := M * A[Row, Col]

end; {ScalarMult}
```

Figure 7-2   Scalar multiplication of a matrix.

Another standard activity for rectangular matrices is the operation of **scalar multiplication.** The operation consists of multiplying a specified number by each of the elements of the matrix to produce another matrix of the same size. For example, if we multiply the scalar 4 by the matrix

$$\begin{bmatrix} 3 & 2 & 1 \\ 2 & 6 & 7 \end{bmatrix}$$

we obtain the resulting matrix

$$\begin{bmatrix} 12 & 8 & 4 \\ 8 & 24 & 28 \end{bmatrix}$$

Once again, we can write a procedure, ScalarMult, to accomplish the operation. The code appears in Figure 7-2.

Matrix Multiplication

For **matrix multiplication,** the number of columns of the first matrix must be equal to the number of rows of the second matrix. The most usual circumstance for this operation is for **square matrices,** where the number of rows is equal to the number of columns. For such matrices, we still would like to maintain the operations of addition and scalar multiplication, so we would probably use a set of declarations such as

```
const
  NumberRows = 3;
  NumberCols = 3;
type
  ElementType = integer;
  MatrixType = array [1..NumberRows, 1..NumberCols] of ElementType;
```

The algorithm for multiplying two matrices is a bit complicated. If we are multiplying two matrices A and B to obtain matrix C, then we obtain the individual elements of C by the computations

```
C[Row, Col] := 0;
for Runner := 1 to NumberRows do
   C[Row, Col] := C[Row, Col] + A[Row, Runner] * B[Runner, Col];
```

Because we must calculate C[Row, Col] for each row and column combination, the code fragment for matrix multiplication is

```
for Row := 1 to NumberRows do
   for Col := 1 to NumberCols do
      begin
         C[Row, Col] := 0;
         for Runner := 1 to NumberRows do
            C[Row, Col] := C[Row, Col] + A[Row, Runner] * B[Runner,Col]
      end; {for Col}
```

As always, the variable Runner must be declared as an integer in the program (most likely, within a MatrixMult procedure, which you can write as an exercise).

Matrix Utilities

When we are dealing with operations on matrices, it is convenient to have a procedure that "pretty prints" a matrix, horizontally centered on the screen if possible. We illustrate such a routine for matrices with integer entries. We note that our procedure works for real matrices with a small number (of important) changes. The procedure, named MatrixPrint, performs many detailed computations to account for various combinations of numeric ranges, number of columns, etc. The code for MatrixPrint appears in Figure 7-3.

Another convenience for testing matrix routines is a means of quickly generating test matrices. For instance, the following fragment of code can be used to generate a random matrix, A, with values from –5 to +5 :

```
for Row := 1 to NumberRows do
   for Col := 1 to NumberCols do
      A[Row, Col] := abs(Random mod 11) - 5
```

Using Part of an Array

As we have seen when working with arrays in Chapter 6, we frequently declare an array with more room than is used. The same is true for two-dimensional arrays. For example, a program that deals with matrices might very well have many different sizes of matrices at any given time. This can be handled by declaring the type MatrixType to be the largest expected size (say, 10 by 10), then keeping track of the size of each individual matrix separately. This can be done using three variables, declared as in this example:

```
var
   A: MatrixType;
   ARows: integer;
   ACols: integer;
```

```
procedure MatrixPrint (InMatrix: MatrixType);

    {Written by:    XXXXXXXXX XX/XX/XX}
    {Purpose:       To print a matrix}
    {Parameters:    InMatrix - input, the matrix to print}
    {Globals used: NumberRows, NumberCols - constants for matrix size}

  var
    Width: integer;          {Width of an element}
    MaxWidth: integer;       {Max width of element}
    TotalWidth: integer;     {Total width of matrix}
    Row: integer;            {Index for rows}
    Col: integer;            {Index for columns}
    TestString: string;      {String for numbers}
    Entry: integer;          {Loop index for current matrix element}
    PerRow: integer;         {Number per row}
    ScreenRows: integer;     {Number of rows on screen}
    LeftMargin: integer;     {Spaces on left of row}
    ScrRow: integer;         {Loop index for row on screen}

begin {MatrixPrint}

{*** Establish the maximum width for an element}

  MaxWidth := 0;
  TestString := '';
  for Row := 1 to NumberRows do
    for Col := 1 to NumberCols do
      begin
        TestString := Concat(TestString, StringOf(InMatrix[Row, Col] : 1));
        Width := Length(TestString);
        if Width > MaxWidth then
          MaxWidth := Width
      end; {for}

{*** Decide on the number of elements per screen row}

  TotalWidth := NumberCols * (MaxWidth + 1) - 1;
  if TotalWidth <= 80 then
    begin
      PerRow := NumberCols;
      LeftMargin := (80 - TotalWidth) div 2;
      ScreenRows := 1
    end
  else
    begin
      PerRow := 80 div (MaxWidth + 1);
      LeftMargin := 0;
      ScreenRows := NumberCols div PerRow + 1
    end;
```

Figure 7-3   Output of a matrix (continues next page).

```
{*** Print the matrix}

  Writeln;
  for Row := 1 to NumberRows do
    begin
      if LeftMargin > 0 then
        Write(' ' : LeftMargin);
      Col := 1;
      for ScrRow := 1 to ScreenRows do
        begin
          for Entry := 1 to PerRow do
            if Col <= NumberCols then
              begin
                Write(InMatrix[Row, Col] : MaxWidth);
                if Entry < PerRow then
                  Write(' ');
                Col := Col + 1
              end; {if}
          Writeln
        end; {for}
      if TotalWidth mod 80 <> 0 then
        Writeln
    end; {for}
  Writeln
end; {MatrixPrint}

begin
  for i := 1 to NumberRows do
    for j := 1 to NumberCols do
      Matrix[i, j] := i + j;
  MatrixPrint(Matrix);
end.
```

Figure 7-3   (continued)

Alternatively, we could define a record type consisting of three components: the matrix, the number of rows, and the number of columns:

```
type
  MatrixType = record
      Data: array [1..10, 1..10] of ElementType;
      NumberRows: integer;
      NumberCols: integer
    end;
```

No longer are NumberRows and NumberCols global constants that apply to all matrices. Each matrix carries its own size. To illustrate, Figure 7-4 repeats the scalar multiplication example using the record data type.

7-1 MORE ON ARRAYS

```
procedure ScalarMult(M: ElementType; A: MatrixType; var C: MatrixType);
   {Written by: XXXXXXXXX XX/XX/XX}
   {Purpose:    To scalar multiply M times A}
   {Parameters: M - input, scalar to multiply by}
   {            A - input, matrix to multiply}
   {            C - output, resulting matrix}
      var
         Row:  integer;   {Loop index through rows}
         Col:  integer;   {Loop index through columns}
   begin {ScalarMult}
      C := A;
      with C do
         begin
            for Row := 1 to NumberRows do
               for Col := 1 to NumberCols do
                  Data[Row,Col] := M * Data[Row,Col]
         end {with}
   end; {ScalarMult}
```

Figure 7-4   Matrix as a record with size information.

More than Two Dimensions

You will not be surprised to learn that the notion of arrays of arrays can be generalized. For example, we can declare an array of two-dimensional arrays to obtain a three-dimensional array. One way to accomplish this is illustrated by this example:

```
var
   A: array[1..3, 1..4, 1..5] of integer;
```

This might be called a 3 × 4 × 5 array; it can be conceptualized as consisting of three separate 4-by-5 matrices. To access a single value from the array, we supply three subscripts. The first picks one of the three 4 × 5 matrices; the second chooses a row; and the third a column. Because of this view of what the array is, we might choose to print the data as three 4 × 5 arrays.

We do not pursue this subject at length. We should, however, point out that it can be useful in the type of problem typified by our rainfall example. For example, we might declare an array indexed on three subscripts, where the first chooses a year in the range 1980 to 1995, the second chooses the city, and the third chooses the month. With such a declaration,

```
MonthlyRain[1990, Philadelphia, March]
```

signifies the rainfall in Philadelphia in March 1990.

DPT

All the defensive programming techniques we learned in connection with arrays in Chapter 6 apply to two-dimensional arrays as well. In addition, there are some tips that apply specifically to two-dimensional arrays.

1. To access a single value from the array, two subscripts must be supplied. In a matrix application, the first tells the row and the second the column. More generally, the first chooses one of the arrays that make up the two-dimensional array and the second chooses one value from that array.

What happens if we use only one subscript varies with the context. For example, consider a matrix defined as

```
var
   X: array[1..2, 1..3] of integer;
```

We can visualize X as having this form:

$$\begin{bmatrix} 2 & -4 & 5 \\ -6 & 1 & 3 \end{bmatrix}$$

If we write X[l], this refers to the entire first row, an array of three integers. This may or may not be what we intended. A reference to X[3], on the other hand, is illegal. There is no way to refer to the columns of the matrix as separate entities.

Similarly, for our declaration

```
var
   MonthlyRain: array[Cities, Months] of real;
```

we need to specify both the city and the month to get a single rainfall figure. A reference such as MonthlyRain[Philadelphia] is legal and refers to the entire array of 12 rainfall figures for Philadelphia. A reference such as MonthlyRain[January], on the other hand, is illegal.

2. In addition to supplying two subscripts, we must supply them in the proper order. When the two subscript types are different, as in the rainfall example, the compiler catches this error. (This is an added advantage to choosing data types to match closely the problem being solved.) If the compiler cannot detect the error, as in the case of matrix applications, we access the wrong data item and get erroneous results.

3. Nested loops are frequently used to process the entire array in some fashion. The outer loop control is based on one of the subscripts, and the inner loop control on the other. For example, to process a matrix by rows, then by columns within each row, we would use the row subscript as the outer loop index. To process the rainfall array by months, then by city for each month, we would use the month subscript as the outer loop index. By thinking about the order in which we wish to process the data, we can properly write the loops.

4. Although we can access an entire array or a row of an array, we cannot do input or output with these structures. For example, with the declarations:

```
type
   MatrixType = array[1..5, 1..10] of integer;
var
   A, B: MatrixType;
```

the statement

```
   A[3] := B[5]
```

7-1 MORE ON ARRAYS

is legal (and assigns the values stored in the fifth row of B to the third row of A). However, the statement

```
Writeln(A[3])
```

is illegal.

REVIEW

Terms and Concepts

matrix
matrix addition
matrix multiplication
scalar multiplication
square matrix
two-dimensional arrays

Two-Dimensional Arrays

Examples of Declarations

1. type
```
ArrayofArrays = array[1..3] of array[1..4] of real;
```

2. type
```
RealArray4 = array[1..4] of real;
ArrayofArrays = array[1..3] of RealArray4;
```

3. type
```
ArrayofArrays = array[1..3, 1..4] of real;
```

Processing and I/O

1. A single row can be processed by letting the row subscript remain constant and the column subscript vary.
2. A single column can be processed by letting the column subscript remain constant and the row subscript vary.
3. An entire array can be processed by using nested loops, one controlled by varying the row subscript and the other by varying the column subscript.

DPT

1. Generally need two subscripts when working with two-dimensional arrays.
2. Don't interchange the subscripts.
3. Pay attention to which subscript is the outer loop control when writing nested loops to process arrays.
4. Only do I/O using an array's elements.

EXERCISES

1. For the two-dimensional array X shown, what is the size of the array? What is X[3][2]? What is X[2, 4]? What is X[4, 2]?

$$\begin{bmatrix} 1 & 4 & -3 & 2 \\ 10 & -5 & 5 & 7 \\ -6 & 0 & 1 & 11 \end{bmatrix}$$

2. (a) Write a Pascal program to read rainfall statistics and display a table such as that shown in this section.
   (b) Write a Pascal program to read rainfall statistics and print a table such as that shown in this section on your printer.

3. (a) Write a segment of Pascal code to print the rainfall statistics on a printer with 132 columns, one city per line.
   (b) Modify the segment to handle printers of smaller width by printing two lines for each city. Label the columns appropriately.

4. Write segments of Pascal code to allow a person to query the rainfall statistics:
   (a) Given a city name, print the total rainfall for that city.
   (b) Given a month, show which city had the most rainfall during that month.
   (c) Given a city and a month, print the rainfall.

5. Write code for the following, which deal with a 21-by-28 real matrix.
   (a) Find the largest number in the entire matrix.
   (b) Modify part (a) to also find which row and column contained the largest value. Assume there are no ties.
   (c) Modify part (b) to handle ties.
   (d) Find the largest number in each row, placing the results in an array Large.
   (e) Print the sum of each row.
   (f) For row 5, find the column number of the first positive value (0 if none are positive).
   (g) Exchange rows 14 and 19.
   (h) Exchange columns 14 and 19.
   (i) Sort the rows of the matrix so that the row with the largest sum is the first, and so on.
   (j) Repeat part (i), but sort the columns instead.

6. Write the MatrixMult procedure for multiplying two square matrices, assuming global constants for the array size.

7. Generalize the matrix addition procedure to handle matrices that are only partially used. Part of the output should be a Valid variable set to true or false depending on whether or not the operation was legal.
   (a) Use separate variables for the sizes.
   (b) Use records containing the size to represent the matrices.

8. Repeat Exercise 7 for the matrix multiplication procedure of Exercise 6. You should handle matrices that are not necessarily square.

9. Write a MatrixRead procedure that prompts the user for input as shown:

```
Enter row 1:
  element for column 1:
  element for column 2:
       .
       .
       .
```

```
        Enter row 2:
          element for column 1:

            .
            .
            .
```

10. Write a procedure similar to MatrixPrint that has another parameter specifying the number of decimal places for real numbers.

11. Write a Pascal program that acts as a matrix calculator for 3-by-3 matrices. The program should be menu-driven with the main menu:

```
            Main Menu
            ---------

    1 -- Matrix Addition
    2 -- Scalar Multiplication
    3 -- Matrix Multiplication
    4 -- Terminate Session

         Selection?
```

When the user selects an operation, the program should ask the user to input the two matrices (or the number and matrix in the case of scalar multiplication). The program should print the user input and then print the answer. Ask the user to touch a key to return to the main menu.

12. A matrix is called *sparse* if most of the entries are zeros. Suppose that we wish to work with 10-by-10 sparse matrices with entries that are either 0's or 1's. One technique for accepting input for such a matrix is to ask the user to specify the row and column pairs for each of the 1's in the matrix. Write a Pascal program to read a sparse matrix and print it using the MatrixPrint procedure.

13. Modify the program of Exercise 12 so the nonzero entries in the matrix can be any integer values.

14. Write a program to generate two random 10-by-10 matrices, multiply them, and print the answer using the MatrixPrint procedure. How many individual additions are required in the matrix multiplication operation?

15. In a square matrix, the *main diagonal* is the collection of elements that have their row equal to their column. That is, the main diagonal of the matrix A is the collection of elements A[1,1], A[2,2], etc.
    (a) Write a function to calculate the sum of the elements on the main diagonal of a square matrix.
    (b) Write a function to find the largest number on the main diagonal.
    (c) Write a function to find the average of the numbers that lie on or below the main diagonal, that is, the average of those elements A[I,J], where $I \leq J$.
    (d) Write a function to find the sum of the numbers on or below the diagonal that runs from the lower left to the upper right.

16. A square matrix A is *symmetric* if A[I, J] is equal to A[J, I] for each I and J from 1 to the number of rows of the matrix.
    (a) Write a Boolean function to determine if a given square matrix is symmetric.
    (b) Generate 1000 random 2-by-2 matrices with elements ranging from 1 to 6 and calculate the fraction of these that are symmetric. (The probability that such a square matrix is symmetric is the same as the probability of throwing doubles on a pair of dice; can you see why?)

17. Write a program to declare a 3-by-4-by-5 integer array, fill it with random integers in the range from –5 to 5, and print it as three 4-by-5 matrices.
18. Do the following for the rainfall array indexed by year, city, and month alluded to in the section "More than Two Dimensions":
    (a) Give declarations for the array.
    (b) Write a procedure that, given a year and a city, prints the rainfall figures for that year and city.
    (c) Write a procedure that prompts the user for a month *name* and a city *name*, and prints the history of rainfall for that month and city.
    (d) Write a procedure that answers the question: For a given year, which cities had a total rainfall of less than 20 inches?
    (e) Write a procedure that answers the questions: For a given year, what was the highest rainfall figure? What city had that highest figure? What month?
    (f) Write a procedure that answers the question: Within the entire structure, what year, city, and month combination had the highest rainfall figure?
19. Write programs for the following.
    (a) Read a series of birthdays represented as a month number and a day number. Keep track of how many people were born on each day. When the data have all been read, print a list of all the days on which two or more persons were born. Hint: Use a two-dimensional array of counters to count the birthdays.
    (b) Repeat part (a), but do not read the data. Instead, generate 30 random birthdays using Random.
    (c) Place the process of part (b) in a loop to execute 1000 times, and find how many of those 1000 executions resulted in at least one duplicate birthday.
20. (a) Write a function to calculate the "number of combinations of *n* items taken *k* at a time," whose value is given by

$$\frac{n!}{k!(n-k)!}$$

   (b) The $k!$ in this formula "cancels with" the last k factors of the $n!$, leaving

$$\frac{n(n-1)(n-2)\ldots(k+1)}{(n-k)!}$$

   Revise your function to take advantage of this fact.

   (c) If we have many of these to calculate in a program, we might want to set up an array Comb declared as

   `array[0..10,0..10] of integer;`

   Comb[N, K] is the number of combinations of N items taken K at a time. It is known that Comb[N, K] can be calculated by

   ```
   if K = 0 or N = K then
         Comb[N, K] := 1
   else
         Comb[N, K] := Comb[N - 1, K - 1] + Comb[N - 1, K]
   ```

   Use this fact to fill the portion of the array on and below the main diagonal.
21. Write a program to play Conway's Game of Life. On an infinite checkerboard, each square has eight neighbors:

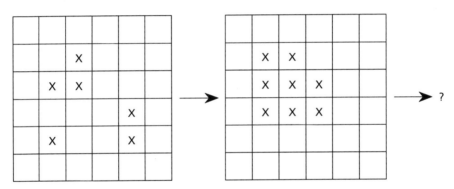

This game simulates growth and decay in a collection of interacting organisms, where cells (squares) are born, survive, or die based on how "crowded" the conditions are. The cycle occurs in "generations" by these rules (each square is either dead (empty) or alive):

Birth. If an empty (dead) square has exactly three live neighboring squares, it will be alive the next generation.

Survival. If a live square has either two or three live neighbors, it will still be alive the next generation.

Death. Any live square that does not survive dies either from overcrowding (more than three neighbors) or isolation (less than two neighbors).

For example,

Input to the program includes an initial configuration and an indication of how many generations to print. Output is one screen (or printed page) per generation (starting with the initial configuration).

Because programming an infinite array is difficult (not to mention printing it), we restrict ourselves to a 20-by-78 array if using the display or a 50-by-50 array if using the printer. Use the character "*" to denote live and " " (blank space) to denote dead. Treat the squares on the edges as infertile regions where nothing is ever born.

8 *String Manipulation*

OBJECTIVES

In this chapter, we present an in-depth discussion of string handling. Strings are the most common form of nonnumeric data that programs process. By the end of this chapter, you will be able to:

- define string variables
- process strings using the THINK Pascal string operators
- process strings using predefined and user-defined subprograms
- perform string input and output

8-1 STRING DATA AND OPERATIONS

String Data Types

We already know much about strings because we have been using them throughout the book. Strings are similar to an array of type *char* in that they consist of a sequence of characters that can be accessed by use of an index. However, strings form a distinct class of data types with their own special properties. A string can consist of from 0 to 255 characters. Note that, during the running of a program, any string that is created that is greater than 255 characters THINK truncates to 255 characters. A string variable has a maximum length that is specified when it is declared. (Variables of the type *string* have a predefined length of 255.)

For example, if we wish to work with lines of text that are less than or equal to 80 characters in length, then we might declare a variable Line as follows:

```
var
    Line: string[80];
```

Remember that the number 80 specifies the maximum number of characters that Line can contain, not necessarily the actual number of characters that Line does contain. The actual number of characters that Line contains at any time during the running of a program can vary from 0 to 80, inclusive.

When a string literal is assigned to a (string) variable, its length must not exceed that variable's size: If a string literal is assigned to a variable that is too small to contain it, THINK issues a compile-time error message. However, assigning a string variable to a string variable of smaller size results in the truncation of the value. The truncation does not cause a run-time error, but it can produce unwanted results. Yet again, reading a string into a variable that is too small to hold it does cause a run-time error. For example, suppose that we wish to have the user enter his or her name into a variable for later use. A commonly used maximum size for names is 20 characters; but there certainly are names that exceed this length. If the user enters a name longer than 20 characters and the accepting variable has a maximum length of 20, then the run-time error 'String too large' results. (By the way, we have found a string of length 50 is capable of holding most anyone's name.)

We can access the individual characters of a string by use of an index. If StringX is a string variable, then StringX[1] is the first character of the string, StringX[2] is the second character of the string, and so on. If we try to refer to a character position that is beyond the declared length of a string and if range checking is on, then a run-time error results. What happens if we try to refer to a character position that is within the declared length of the string, but that is beyond the actual length of the string (and range checking is off)? A run-time error does not occur when referring to such a position, but the reference is not meaningful. We must be careful to avoid using character positions beyond the string's actual length because of their meaningless nature. The best way to avoid trouble when dealing with strings is to view them as higher-level data constructs and to use the string operations that THINK Pascal provides.

Basic String Operations

We can use global string types in our programs so that we can more easily work with procedures and functions that deal with strings. It is tempting to simply declare all string variables within a program to be of type *string*, but we should resist the temptation because of the possible waste of memory resources. Another common type that appears in many programs using strings is String80, which can be defined by

```
type
    String80 = string[80];
```

We can compare strings with a similar set of relational operators that are used for other types of objects. **String equality** uses the symbol '=' and operates on two strings, such as

```
String1 = String2
```

The result is *true* if the actual lengths of String1 and String2 are the same and all the characters of the two strings from the first up to the actual length are the same. The result is *false* if the actual lengths of the strings are different or if any character position contains different characters. In short, the contents of the two strings must be identical. Note that the strings may be defined to be of different maximum lengths and still be compared.

If two strings are not equal, then the non-equality relation

```
String1 <> String2
```

is *true*, otherwise it is *false*.

The other **string relational operators** depend on the collating sequence of the character set that underlies the implementation of Pascal (which for THINK Pascal is the ASCII character set). The definition of "<" is as follows:

String1 < String2 is *true* if either:

(a) in some character position, the character for String1 precedes the character in the same position of String2, with all characters prior to this character position matching; or

(b) every character of String1 is equal to the character in the same position of String2 and the actual length of String1 is less than the actual length of String2.

The other relational operators (>, <=, and >=) have analogous definitions. Two important functions that we have used from time to time are Chr and Ord. Ord(character) gives the position of the character in the collating sequence. Chr is the inverse of Ord. That is, given a number n in the proper range (0 to 255), Chr(n) is the character in the nth position in the collating sequence. Thus, for example, in the ASCII collating sequence, Ord('a') is 97, and Chr(97) is 'a'.

Built-In String Functions

THINK Pascal provides standard string functions to aid in our programming with strings. The first of these functions is the integer-valued function **Length.** The function is used in the form

```
Length(string expression)
```

which returns the actual number of characters in the string expression that is provided as a parameter. Suppose that the string variable X has the value 'abc'. Then the following table of examples shows the nature of the Length function. (We use the symbol ƀ to signify a blank space to help you see the lengths more clearly.)

StringExpression	Length(StringExpression)
X	3
''	0
'a'	1
'abƀƀƀ'	5
'ƀƀaƀƀ'	5

Notice that the presence of blank spaces in a string is detected by the Length function and that blanks are counted in the same way as other characters. The Length function permits us to access only the valid character positions in a string. For example, suppose that we wish to print the contents of the string variable X vertically. The following fragment of code accomplishes the task:

8-1 STRING DATA AND OPERATIONS

```
for I := 1 to Length(X) do
  Writeln(X[I])
```

If we want to print the string "diagonally" down the screen, we could use the fragment

```
for I := 1 to Length(X) do
  Writeln(' ' : I, X[I])
```

Concat is the concatenation function; it has the form

```
Concat(list of string expressions)
```

and returns the string that results from concatenation of the parameters from left to right.

The string-valued function **Copy** is provided for extracting substrings of a string. The function is used in the form

```
Copy(string expression, start position, number of characters)
```

and returns the substring that begins in the start position and continues for the number of characters specified. Suppose that the string variable X has the value 'abc'. Then the following table of examples shows the nature of the function Copy:

Str	Start	Chars	Copy(Str, Start, Chars)
X	2	2	'bc'
Concat(X, X)	3	3	'cab'
X	1	3	'abc'
X	2	0	''
X	0	2	Run-time error
X	2	5	'bc'
X	2	−1	''
X	4	1	''
X	−1	3	Run-time error

We note that the starting position cannot be set to 0 or below or a run-time error results. On the other hand, if the starting position is set to a value beyond the length of the string (actual or declared), Copy will return the null string. If *number of characters* would cause Copy to go beyond the actual length of the string, Copy returns a substring that contains only the characters from the given starting position to the (actual) end of the string.

The integer-valued function **Pos** is provided to permit searching a string for a specified substring. The function is used in the form

```
Pos(search string, object string)
```

and returns the starting position of the leftmost occurrence of the search string within the object string. If there is no occurrence of the search string within the object string, then the value of Pos is 0. Suppose that the string variable X has the value 'abc'. Then the following table shows the nature of the Pos function:

Search	Object	Pos(Search, Object)
'b'	X	2
'cb'	X	0
'ca'	Concat (X, X)	3
'abc'	X	1
'b'	Concat (X, X)	2

When the null string is the search string, and the object string is not null, Pos always returns a 1. Yet, if both the search and object strings are null, Pos returns 0.

THINK's **Omit** function returns a given string with a selected substring removed from it. The function has the form

```
Omit(string, start position, number of characters)
```

Omit takes the passed string, removes "number of characters" characters from it, beginning at the start position, and returns the remaining characters of the string as its result. If the number of characters passed to Omit would cause the substring to be beyond the string, only the characters up to the end of the string are removed. The following table shows some results from the Omit function (where the string variable X has the value 'abc'):

Str	Start	Chars	Omit(Str, Start, Chars)
X	2	1	'ac'
X	2	2	'a'
X	2	3	'a'
X	1	3	' '
X	2	0	'abc'
X	2	5	'a'

Omit does not modify its parameters; in particular, the passed string is left unchanged.

The **Include** function adds characters to a string and returns the revised string as its result. The form of the function is:

```
Include(insertion string, original string, position)
```

Include adds the string into the original string beginning at the given position, and returns this new string as its result. (Neither the insertion string nor the original string is changed.) The following table shows Include's behavior. (Again X is a string variable with the value 'abc'.)

InsStr	Str	Pos	Include(InsStr, Str, Pos)
'a'	X	1	'aabc'
X	X	1	'abcabc'
X	X	3	'ababcc'
' '	X	4	'abc'
'12'	X	4	'abc12'
'12'	X	0	'12abc'

8-1 STRING DATA AND OPERATIONS

As an example of the use of the string functions, suppose that we are dealing with strings that may contain a substring between pairs of single quotes. Some examples of such strings are

this string contains no substrings of interest
this string also doesn't contain any
this string 'certainly' does contain one
this string also contains 'one'

For our example, we assume that the strings contain at most one substring contained between pairs of single quotes. The goal of the example is to read in a string, extract the substring between the quotes (if any), and print the substring or a message indicating that no substring was found. The substring extraction process is implemented as a procedure called Extract with three parameters:

InString:	(input) string sent in
	type = string
SubString:	(output) substring found
	type = string
NotFound:	(output) indicates whether substring is found or not
	type = Boolean

The steps of the procedure are as follows:

look for a single quote
if none found, set NotFound to true and quit; otherwise:
    set Start to the position of the single quote
    look for single quote in substring of the string which comes after Start
    if none found, set NotFound to true and quit; otherwise:
        set Finish to the position of the second single quote in the string
        set SubString to the string between Start and Finish
        set NotFound to false

We present the procedure Extract as part of the program Find in Figure 8-1. Note the correspondence of parameters in the procedure call:

```
Extract(InString, Substring, NotFound)
```

In the case of the first parameter, we have a String80 variable associated with a string variable. This is valid for value parameters. In the case of the second parameter, which is a var parameter, both variables are of type *string* because their types must match exactly.

The following lists the tests that are shown in the sample input and output for Figure 8-1. Notice that many of these are boundary tests.

1. A string with no substring to find
2. The null string
3. The null string between quotes
4. A substring at the beginning of the string

```
program Find;

{Written by:   XXXXXXXXX XX/XX/XX}
{Purpose:      To read strings and locate substrings between}
{Procedures used:  Instructions - to print instructions}
{                  Extract - to extract substrings}

  const
    EndOfData = '$END';         {terminates input loop}

  type
    String80 = string[80];

  var
    InString: String80;         {string read in}
    SubString: string;          {substring found}
    NotFound: Boolean;          {indicator for success of search}

  procedure Instructions;
  begin {stub}
  end;

  procedure Extract (InString: string; var SubString: string;
                     var NotFound: Boolean);

{Written by:   XXXXXXXXX XX/XX/XX}
{Purpose:      To find a substring between two single quotes}
{Parameters:   InString - input, the string to look in}
{              Substring - output, the substring found (if any )}
{              NotFound - output, true means no substring found}
{Functions used:  Pos - to locate the single quotes}
{                 Copy - to get substrings}

    const
      Quote = '''';              {single quote character}

    var
      Start: integer;            {location of first single quote}
      Finish: integer;           {location of second single quote}
      Rest: string;              {string after first single quote}

  begin {Extract}

{*** Find first single quote, if any}

    Start := Pos(Quote, InString);
    if Start = 0 then
      begin
        NotFound := true;
        SubString := ''
      end
    else
```

Figure 8-1 Finding quoted substrings (continues next page).

8-1 STRING DATA AND OPERATIONS

```
{*** Find second single quote, if any}

      begin
        Rest := Copy(InString, Start + 1, Length(InString) - Start);
        Finish := Pos(Quote, Rest);
        if Finish = 0 then
          begin
            NotFound := true;
            Substring := ''
          end
        else

{*** Establish substring}

          begin
            SubString := Copy(Rest, 1, Finish - 1);
            NotFound := false
          end
      end

  end; {Extract}

begin {Find}

{*** Print Instructions}

  Instructions;

{*** Read and process strings}

  repeat
    Write('Enter the string ($END to quit):');
    Readln(InString);
    if InString <> EndOfData then
      begin
        Extract(InString, SubString, NotFound);
        if NotFound then
          Writeln('*** No substring found.')
        else
          Writeln('Substring found: ->', SubString, '<-')
      end {if}
    until InString = EndOfData

{Terminate program}

  end.
```

Figure 8-1   (continues next page)

5. A substring at the end of the string
6. A substring in the middle of the string
7. A substring that covers the whole string
8. A string with only one quote

SAMPLE INPUT AND OUTPUT

```
Enter the string ($END to quit):there is none here
*** No substring found.
Enter the string ($END to quit):there is 'one' here
Substring found: ->one<-
Enter the string ($END to quit):there is 'one ' here
Substring found: ->one <-
Enter the string ($END to quit):i don't see one
*** No substring found.
Enter the string ($END to quit):'tis not here
*** No substring found.
Enter the string ($END to quit):not here'
*** No substring found.
Enter the string ($END to quit):'
*** No substring found.
Enter the string ($END to quit):''
Substring found: -><-
Enter the string ($END to quit):
*** No substring found.
Enter the string ($END to quit):'first' thing
Substring found: ->first<-
Enter the string ($END to quit):'only'
Substring found: ->only<-
Enter the string ($END to quit):and 'last'
Substring found: ->last<-
Enter the string ($END to quit):$END
Find program terminating.
```

Figure 8-1 (continued)

9. A string consisting of only one quote
10. A string that has only one quote at the beginning
11. A string that has only one quote at the end
12. A string that has only one quote in the middle

Built-In String Procedures

THINK Pascal also provides two procedures that deal with strings. The first of these procedures is **Delete,** which allows for the deletion of a substring of a specified string. The use of the procedure has the form

```
Delete(string variable, start position, number of characters)
```

This procedure has the side effect of altering the value of the string variable that is supplied as the first parameter. Suppose that the string variable X has the value 'abc'. Then the following table shows the nature of the procedure Delete:

Str	Start	Chars	Str after Delete(Stg, Start, Chars)
X	2	1	'ac'
X	2	2	'a'
X	2	3	'a'
X	1	3	' '
X	2	0	'abc'
X	2	5	'a'

Note that you can specify more characters than are remaining in the string after the start position, as is shown in the example Delete(X, 2, 5), which causes X to have the value 'a'.

The procedure **Insert** allows a substring to be inserted into a string. The procedure is used in the form

```
Insert(substring expression, string variable, start position)
```

and has the effect of changing the value of the string variable by inserting the substring beginning at the start position. Suppose that the string variable X has the value 'abc'. Then the following table shows the nature of the procedure Insert:

SubStr	Str	Start	Str after Insert(SubStr, Str, Start)
'd'	X	2	'adbc'
'd'	X	4	'abcd'
'd'	X	5	'abcd'
'de'	X	1	'deabc'

We note that you can specify a starting position that is beyond the end of the string, but no matter what number you specify, you get the substring concatenated with the string as the result.

As an example of the string procedures, we write a program that reads a string and replaces any occurrence of the word "thing" with the two words "general object." We consider a word to have on both sides a nonnumeric, nonalphabetic character. Thus, in the following strings, we find "thing" as a word:

The word "thing" is here.

The music is the thing.

We have the thing, and it has us.

The thing's attributes are right.

In the middle of the thing

thing is one of the

In the following strings, we do not find "thing" as a word:

Something is wrong.

Things go better without bugs.

To make our design simpler, we assume that there is only one occurrence of the substring "thing" within the string. We use a Boolean function Break to determine if the characters to the left and right of the substring "thing" are nonnumeric and nonalphabetic. We use the procedure ChangeThing to do the replacement of "thing" by "general object." The procedure has two parameters:

    InString: (input) string for replacement
    OutString: (output) string with replacements made

The steps for the procedure ChangeThing are as follows:

    set OutString to InString
    set Start to position of "thing" in OutString
    if Start is not zero and if characters to left and right of "thing" are both
        break characters, then:
            delete "thing"
            insert "general object" into OutString at Start

If you think about these steps, you can uncover a subtle flaw in the logic. If the word "thing" occurs at the extreme left of InString, then there is no character to its left to be a break character. A similar problem arises if the word is at the extreme right. Instead of handling these situations as special cases, we take another approach that is frequently useful: We add an extra blank at the front and rear of our string when we start, and then take them off when we are done. Now the word "thing" cannot be at either the extreme left or the extreme right. We show the code for ChangeThing in the program of Figure 8-2.

    Note.   The algorithm condition

    if Start is not zero and if characters to left and right of "thing"

is changed to

    if Start is not zero then
        if characters to left and right of "thing"

This avoids examining OutString[Start − 1] when Start is 0, which would generate a range-check error.

We make the program of Figure 8-2 more useful in the exercises.

String-to-Numeric Conversions

    SANE.   The Standard Apple Numeric Environment—SANE—contains several constant, type, and module declarations, most of which are designed to allow a programmer to perform very precise computations involving real numbers. It also contains other routines serving a variety of purposes, including ones that convert strings to numbers and numbers to strings, our concern in this section. A complete description of SANE's workings and features is beyond the scope of this text; see the references for sources that discuss SANE in detail.

    To THINK Pascal, SANE appears as a **unit**. Units (roughly speaking) are pieces of code set up for programmers to use as part of their programs. They usually contain state-

```
function Break (Character: char): Boolean;

{Written by:   XXXXXXXXX XX/XX/XX}
{Purpose:      To determine if a character is a break character or not}
{              ('0' to '9', 'a' to 'z', and 'a' to 'Z' are not break }
{              characters, all others are) }
{Parameters:   Character - input, the character to test}

begin {Break}
   Break := ((Character < '0') or (Character > '9')) and
         ((Character < 'a') or (Character > 'z')) and
         ((Character < 'A') or (Character > 'Z'))
end; {Break}

procedure ChangeThing (InString: string; var OutString: string);

{Written by: XXXXXXXXX XX/XX/XX}
{Purpose:   To replace the first occurrence of the word "thing" with}
{           the phrase "general object"}
{Parameters: InString  - input, the string to work with}
{            Outstring - output, the resulting string with the}
{                        replacements made}
{Procedures used:  Delete  - to delete "thing" }
{                  Insert  - to insert "general object"}
{Functions used:   Pos     - to locate a substring }
{                  Break   - to determine break characters}

   var
      Start: integer;                    {location of "thing"}

begin {ChangeThing}

{*** Initialize; put blanks at front and rear to avoid special cases}

   OutString := Concat(' ', InString, ' ');

{*** Replace "thing" if there}

   Start := Pos('thing', OutString);
   if (Start <> 0) then                  {if 'thing' is there}
     if (Break(OutString[Start - 1])) and (Break(OutString[Start + 5]))
        then                             {check for breaks}
        begin
           Delete(OutString, Start, 5);  {replace 'thing'}
           Insert('general object', OutString, Start)
        end; {if}

{*** Remove the extra blanks at front and rear}

   OutString := Copy(OutString, 2, Length(OutString) - 1)

end; {ChangeThing}
```

Figure 8-2   Changing substrings.

ments that perform common tasks, or statements that reference the large number of predefined variables and procedures Apple built directly into the Macintosh hardware. There are many predefined units, of which SANE is one. (We can also define units for our own or other's use. Since the topic is fairly advanced, we have placed its discussion in Appendix A.)

To incorporate one or more units into a program, we include the statement

uses
   list of unit names

immediately after the *program* statement that begins the THINK Pascal program. So to use SANE in our program, we place

uses
   SANE

after the program header.

In THINK, the project must also be set up to use SANE. To make use of the SANE unit, you must add the files SANELib.lib and SANE.p to your project. (Both of these files are supplied with THINK Pascal.) SANELib.lib should appear after the Interface.lib file in the project file list. After SANELib.lib should come SANE.p, then your program file. (For certain Macintosh computers, you may need to use SANELib881.lib instead of SANELib.lib; see the THINK Pascal User Manual for details.)

Note. You might wonder why we are going to the trouble of using SANE to do string to numeric conversions, when there is a THINK procedure (called ReadString) that can also perform them.

If we use ReadString to convert a string to a number, a run-time error will occur if the string does not "look like" a number (for example, 'X123.5'). This would cause our program to bomb whenever the user made a data entry error. It also prevents us from using a special string value to indicate that data entry is complete (as we will want to do later in this section).

SANE, though, has methods to identify strings that cannot be converted properly to numbers. Thus the programmer can catch data entry errors and use special string values without the program bombing.

Numeric-to-String Conversion. The SANE procedure **Num2Str** allows the conversion of a numeric expression into a string. The procedure is called with

   Num2Str(*format, numeric expression, string variable*)

and has the effect of converting the numeric value into its string equivalent and placing it into the string variable. The string equivalent might take on several different forms, depending upon how the format parameter is set. (For instance, the number 10 could be converted to the string "10", "10.0", "1.0e+1", and so on. All reflect the number 10, but are strings of characters rather than the numeric quantity 10.)

Some of the types of Num2Str's parameters are a bit unusual. The numeric expression can be any numeric type. The string variable must be of type *DecStr*, a SANE-defined type declared to be a string of 255 characters. The format parameter must be of type *DecForm*. DecForm is a record type:

```
DecForm = record
    Style: (FloatDecimal, FixedDecimal);
    Digits: integer
end;
```

Style has two values. FloatDecimal causes the string to look like a floating point number (a number with an exponent); FixedDecimal makes the string have the form of a fixed-point number (a number without an exponent). If Style is FixedDecimal, Digits defines the number of digits to appear after the decimal point; if Style is FloatDecimal, it is the number of significant digits.

There are many conditions that govern exactly how a given number appears, but examining the following table indicates Num2Str's nature more easily than memorizing a long series of rules.

NUMBER	STYLE	DIGITS	STRING RESULT
1	FixedDecimal	0	1
1	FixedDecimal	3	1.000
0	FixedDecimal	4	0.0000
10.25	FixedDecimal	0	10
10.25	FixedDecimal	1	10.2
10.25	FixedDecimal	2	10.25
10.25	FixedDecimal	3	10.250
–3.42	FixedDecimal	0	–3
–3.42	FixedDecimal	2	–3.42
–0.234	FixedDecimal	5	–0.23400
–8	FixedDecimal	7	–8.0000000
1	FloatDecimal	0	1e+0
1	FloatDecimal	3	1.00e+0
0	FloatDecimal	4	0.000e+0
10.25	FloatDecimal	1	1e+1
10.25	FloatDecimal	2	1.0e+1
10.25	FloatDecimal	3	1.02e+1
10.25	FloatDecimal	4	1.025e+1
–3.42	FloatDecimal	1	–3e+0
–3.42	FloatDecimal	3	–3.42e+0
–0.234	FloatDecimal	5	–2.3400e–1
–8	FloatDecimal	7	–8.000000e+0

String-to-Numeric Conversion. The SANE function **Str2Num** allows us to convert a string that represents a numeric expression into a number. The use of the function has the form

```
Str2Num(string to convert)
```

and returns the value represented by the string. The returned value is of type ***extended***, which is a real number with about 19 decimal digits of accuracy. (Type real numbers are accurate to about seven digits to the right of the decimal point.) All SANE arithmetic computations (and, in fact, many internal THINK arithmetic computations) are performed using type *extended* variables. THINK allows an extended type value to be placed into a type *real* variable (but some accuracy may be lost).

If the string does not represent a numeric expression, Str2Num returns a value called NaN(017) — Not a Number for reason 17 (an invalid conversion). NaN values cannot be printed, but can be detected using "class" functions. There are four class functions; which one is used depends upon the type of the variable being checked. Since we use real variables for our work here, we employ the ClassReal function.

ClassReal returns several values; the one of interest here is the value QNaN. If Class-Real returns QNaN, then we know the real number does not contain a legitimate numeric value. ClassReal is commonly used in a Boolean expression to see if an invalid number is present; for example:

```
Str := '23.45X7';
 .
 .
 .
Result := Str2Num(Str);
if ClassReal(Result) = QNaN then
  Writeln (Str, ' does not represent a real number')
```

The following table illustrates Str2Num's behavior:

STRING TO CONVERT	RESULTING NUMBER
' 1 '	NaN(017)
'1'	1.0
' 1a'	NaN(017)
'–'	NaN(017)
'3+4'	NaN(017)
'–3.4+'	NaN(017)
'–3.4'	–3.4
'23'	23.0
'– 23'	–23.0
'2E2'	200.0
'3e–3'	0.003
'34 '	34

In general, the strings to convert can "look like" integers or reals, with the latter in either fixed- or floating-point format. The string may contain leading blanks or tabs, but trailing blanks (or any other nonnumeric character) result in a NaN value.

An Example. As an example of using Str2Num and Num2Str, suppose that we want to have the user input real numbers representing profits and losses in a loop and that we don't wish to designate any particular real number as a terminating value. We can read the user input as a string, check to see if it is the terminating value ($END, in our example), and convert the string to a number using the Str2Num procedure, if appropriate. In our example, we are to add the numbers that are input and print the total. If the total is positive, we are to print

```
Profit: $total
```

If the total is negative, we are to print

```
Loss: ($total)
```

We could accomplish this form of output with two Writeln statements, but for the purpose of the example, we use the Num2Str procedure to build the output line and then print it. The example program is shown as Figure 8-3.

Note. Even with SANE's help, we can still input values that are not numbers, but that the previous program will treat as numbers. For example, the string "45...5" will be converted to the number 45 and 123,456 will be converted to 123. Fully "bulletproofing" input is a difficult task, one that requires us to become conversant with the Macintosh toolbox routines—which is well beyond the scope of this text. We will do what bulletproofing we can using the routines we have readily available in THINK.

DPT

1. Whenever we access a character of a string by indexing as in an array, we must be sure that the index is not out of range. This means it may not be less than 1 and it may not exceed the declared maximum length of the string. Conditions such as "(I = 0) or (Str[I] = '')" are suspect, for example. It will often not cause a run-time error if you index to a character position past the length of a string (but not past the declared maximum size of the string), but the character at that position has no meaning for your program. Use the Length function to keep your indices in the proper range.

2. Be careful of unwanted truncation when using string-assignment statements. You can anticipate truncation by use of the Length function.

3. In THINK Pascal, position 0 of a string contains the length of the string in character form. You should avoid the use of position 0: you can determine the length of a string by using the Length function, and you can change the length of a string by concatenation or substring extraction via the Copy function.

4. In one of the examples in this section, we used the statement

```
Writeln(' ' : I, X[I])
```

in order to print the Ith character of the string in X in increasing columns. You may have noted that this prints the Ith character of X in column I + 1. It may seem obvious that we can print the Ith character of X in the Ith column with the statement

```
program ProfitAndLoss;

{Written by:     XXXXXXXXX XX/XX/XX}
{Purpose:        To read profit and loss figures for a period and print}
{                the total}
{Procedures used: Instructions - to print instructions}
{                ReadString - to convert a string to a number}
{                StringOf - to convert a number to a string}

   uses
      SANE;            {use SANE for string <-> number conversions}

   const
      EndOfData = '$END';     {terminates input loop}

   type
      String80 = string[80];

   var
      InString: string;         {string read in}
      OutString: string;        {string to write}
      Total: real;              {total profit or loss}
      Amount: real;             {input profit or loss}
      StrTotal: DecStr;         {total in string form}
      Format: DecForm;          {format for numeric equivalent of string}

   procedure Instructions;
   begin {stub}
   end;

begin {ProfitAndLoss}
{*** Print Instructions and initialize}
   Instructions;
   Total := 0;
   Format.Style := FixedDecimal;     {fixed point}
   Format.Digits := 2;               {2 digits to right of decimal}

{*** Read and total profit and loss figures}
   repeat
      Write('Enter the amount ($END to quit): ');
      Readln(InString);

      if InString <> EndOfData then
         begin
            repeat
               Amount := Str2Num(InString);
               if ClassReal(Amount) = QNaN then
                  begin
                     Write('*** Invalid amount, redo ($END to quit): ');
                     Readln(InString)
                  end {if}
            until (ClassReal(Amount) <> QNaN) or (InString = EndOfData)
         end; {if}
```

Figure 8-3   Output of monetary values (continues next page).

```
        if InString <> EndOfData then
          Total := Total + Amount

    until InString = EndOfData;

  {*** Set up output}

    if Total < 0 then
      begin
        Num2Str(Format, -Total, StrTotal);
        OutString := Concat('Loss: ($ ', StrTotal, ')')
      end
    else
      begin
        Num2Str(Format, Total, StrTotal);
        OutString := Concat('Profit: $ ', StrTotal)
      end; {if}

  {*** Print the output}

    Writeln;
    Writeln(OutString)

  {*** Terminate}

  end.
```

SAMPLE INPUT AND OUTPUT

First run:

```
Enter the amount ($END to quit) :2.34
Enter the amount ($END to quit) :45.6
Enter the amount ($END to quit) :-23.4
Enter the amount ($END to quit) :$end

*** invalid amount, redo ($END to quit): $END

Profit: $ 24.54
```

Second run:

```
Enter the amount ($END to quit) :5.67
Enter the amount ($END to quit) :/34

*** invalid amount, redo ( $END to quit): -12.34
Enter the amount ($END to quit):5.6
Enter the amount ($END to quit) :-99.9
Enter the amount ($END to quit) :$END

Loss: ($ 100.97)
```

Figure 8-3   (continued)

```
Writeln(' ' : X[I] - 1)
```

However, note that the idea fails when I is equal to 1, because the statement

```
Writeln(' ' : 0)
```

prints one blank. These boundary value problems are a constant plague to programmers.

5. We cannot use anything but a string variable for the first parameter of the procedure Delete and the second parameter of the procedure Insert. We cannot use string constants or string expressions such as X + Y. The compiler detects violations of this rule.

6. Do not put quotes around the numeric expressions that you use for the Num2Str and Str2Num routines.

7. When we pass a string as a value parameter, we can mix the string types of the formal and actual parameters. We can produce more general purpose subprograms by using the *string* type for all value parameters. The situation is different for var parameters. In this case, the formal and actual parameters must have the same type. Thus, if we wish to produce more general-purpose subprograms, we must declare both formal and actual var parameters to be of type *string*.

Testing

When we are testing programs and subprograms that use string data, we should include the following in our test cases:

1. The null string should always be tested because it is a boundary value for string data.
2. Strings of maximum length should be tested because they are boundary values for the program's data.
3. When the program builds strings by concatenation or insertion of substrings, **stress testing** should be performed to attempt to force a string to be constructed of more than 255 characters.

REVIEW

Terms and Concepts

Concat
Copy
Delete
extended
Insert
Length
Num2Str

Pos
stress testing
string equality (=)
other string relational operators (<>. <, >, <=, >=)
Str2Num
Unit

Pascal Syntax

General String Manipulation

1. *Indexing.* We can refer to the Ith character of the string variable X with the char expression

X[I]

2. *Relational Operators.* For string expressions E1 and E2, we can form the Boolean expression

    ```
    E1 relational operator E2
    ```

    where the relational operators are =, <>, <, >, <=, and >=.

3. *Chr and Ord.* Chr returns a character's position in the (ASCII) collating sequence; Ord does the opposite.

4. *Length Function.* For a string expression E1, we can determine the number of characters in E1 with the integer expression

    ```
    Length(E1)
    ```

5. *Concat Function.* For string expressions E1, E2, ..., En, we can form the concatenation of the strings with the string expression

    ```
    Concat(E1, E2, . . . , En)
    ```

6. *Copy Function.* For the string expression E1, we can form the substring that begins at the Ith character of E1 and that consists of N characters with the string expression

    ```
    Copy(E1, I, N)
    ```

7. *Pos Function.* For the string expressions E1 and E2, we can find the starting position of the leftmost occurrence of E1 as a substring of E2 with the integer expression

    ```
    Pos(E1, E2)
    ```

    The value returned is 0 if there is no occurrence of E1 as a substring of E2.

8. *Omit Function.* For a string variable or literal X, we can remove N characters from the string starting at position I, and return the remaining characters of the string with the string expression

    ```
    Omit(X, I, N)
    ```

9. *Include Function.* For a string variable or literal X, we can insert a string S into X at position I, and return the modified string with the string expression

    ```
    Include(S, X, I)
    ```

10. *Delete Procedure.* For a string variable X, we can delete N characters from X, beginning with the character in position I, by use of the procedure invocation

    ```
    Delete(X, I, N)
    ```

11. *Insert Procedure.* For a string variable X, we can insert the value of the string expression E1, beginning at position I, by use of the procedure invocation

    ```
    Insert(E1, X, I)
    ```

SANE Routines

1. *Num2Str Procedure.* For an extended, real or integer numeric expression E1, we can convert E1 into the DecStr type string variable X with the format specified by F by use of the procedure invocation

    ```
    Num2Str(F, E1, X)
    ```

2. *Str2Num Function*. For a string expression E1 that is a representation of a number, we can obtain the numeric value of E1 with the type extended expression

```
Str2Num(E1)
```

DPT

1. Keep the lengths of all string expressions to within 255 characters.
2. Do not index beyond the length of a string.
3. Watch for unwanted truncation.
4. Avoid position 0 of a string.
5. Writeln(' ':0) prints one space.
6. The first parameter of Delete and the second of Insert must be a string variable.
7. Do not use quotes around numeric expressions.
8. Do not mix types for string var parameters.

Testing

1. Test the null string.
2. Test strings of maximum length.
3. Try to push against the 255-character barrier.

EXERCISES

1. Define a string variable String1 to have maximum length 10. Assign the value 'banana' to String1 and then assign the value 'grape' to String1. Print String1[6]. Experiment some more with direct changes to a string's characters. Is this a good idea?
2. Write careful, detailed definitions for the string comparisons '>', '<=', and '>='.
3. The purpose of this exercise is to illustrate the danger of altering position 0 of a string. Write a Pascal program to execute the following lines of code. Run it with range-checking on and with it off.

```
var
   X: string[80];

   X := 'This string is valid';
   Writeln(X);
   X := 'A mess it is in';
   Writeln(X);
   X[0] := Chr(20);
   Writeln(X);
```

4. Suppose X has the value 'abcde' at the beginning of each of the parts of this exercise. State the value of X after the statement of each part has been executed.
   (a) X := 'yz' + X

(b) ```
if X = 'abcde' then
    X := 'surprise'
else
    X := 'no surprise'
```
(c) `X := Concat('a', 'b', 'de')`
(d) `X := Copy(X, 2, 3)`
(e) `Delete(X, 2, 3)`
(f) `Insert('yz', X, 3)`
(g) `X := Include('a', X, 2)`
(h) `X := Omit(X, 2, 2)`
(i) `Str2Num(Pos('cd', X))`
(j) `Str2Num(X)`

5. Evaluate the following:
   (a) `Length('ab' + 'cd' + ' ')`
   (b) `Pos('de ', 'ad' + 'ef')`
   (c) `Pos('ce', 'abcde')`
   (d) `Copy('some' + 'where', 4, 3)`
   (e) `Copy('abcde', 4, 5)`

6. Suppose that X is a string variable. Is it always true that the length of Copy(X, 4, 6) is equal to 6? Explain.

7. Suppose that X is a string variable of length 4 and that Y is a string expression of length 5. Is it always true that, after execution of Insert(Y, X, 2), X has a length of 9? Explain.

8. Modify the program of Figure 8-1 to allow multiple substrings between pairs of quotes on a single line.

9. Modify the program of Figure 8-2 to allow multiple instances of the word "thing" to appear on a single line.

10. Modify the program of Figure 8-2 to accept as user inputs the word to find ("thing" in the example) and the phrase to substitute ("general object" in the example).

11. Modify the program of Figure 8-3 to allow the user to input amounts using an optional dollar sign.

12. Write a program that accepts as input the user's name and prints a continuous "snake" of the user's name on the screen. For example, for the user named Jane, we would begin with

```
J
 a
  n
   e
    J
     a
      n
       e
        J
         a
          n
           e
            .
             .
              .
```
```

13. Write procedures or functions for the following:
 (a) Given a name and an array of names, print all the names in the array that match the first five characters of the given name.
 (b) Determine whether or not an array of strings adheres to this rule: There can be no non-empty entries after the first one that is empty.
 (c) Given an array of strings, delete any duplicates by changing them to empty strings.
 (d) Given an array of strings, move all empty strings (if any) to the end of the array.
 (e) Find out how many blanks are in a given string.

14. Write procedures or functions for the following:
 (a) Given a string containing a name such as

   Johnson, Joseph Lawrence

   obtain three strings consisting of the last, first, and middle names. Assume valid input.

 (b) Create a magazine account number, given the last name, initials, city, and expiration date in the form mm/yy. The account number is in a form such as

   ```
   CRAJW-DEC89-SP
   ```

   This consists of
   (1) the first three letters of last name
   (2) the initials
   (3) a dash
   (4) the month of expiration (JAN, FEB, etc.)
   (5) the year of expiration
   (6) a dash
   (7) the first and fourth characters of city

   The "#" character is used if the last name is short (e.g., "Ho" or "Ng") or the initials are missing (e.g., no middle initial).

 (c) Given a string Str and an integer N, place N blanks into Str beginning at position N.

15. (a) Show how to use Pos to convert a given character '0', '1', etc. to its numeric value. Hint: Consider the string '0123456789'.
 (b) In base 16, the "digits" are '0' through '9' and 'A' through 'F', where 'A' represents 10, 'B' represents 11, and so on. Use Pos to convert a given base-16 "digit" to its numeric value.

16. In this exercise, you will write a program to *parse* input strings. The input to the program consists of a text file that has lines of six different types. The file should be considered as a file of commands for drawing a primitive text picture on the screen. The types of commands are identified by the first character on the line. The types are as follows:
D (Duplicate):

 a single character follows the D

 a positive integer follows the character

 examples:

 ```
 Dx20
 ```
 ```
 D#65
 ```

 meaning:
  print the specified character consecutively the specified number of times

EXERCISES

C (Center):

a string follows the C examples:

```
CA Bar Graph
CFigure3-4
```

meaning:
print the centered string on a new line, as the entire line

N (Newline):

either a positive integer or nothing follows the N

example:
```
N
```

meaning:
go to a new line

example:
```
N2
```

meaning:
go to a new line twice

P (Print):

a string follows the P

examples:
```
PLoss:
PMonth
```

meaning:
print the string without going to a new line

E (Erase):

nothing follows the E

example:
```
E
```

meaning:
clear the screen

H (Halt):

nothing follows the H

example:
```
H
```

meaning:
>halt the program

Your program should read the file one line at a time and execute the command contained on the line. For example, suppose that your program reads the following file (we use ƀ to represent a blank):

```
E
CAverage Earnings
N
P1984:ƀƀ
D$7
N
P1985:ƀƀ
D$3
N
P1986:ƀƀ
D$5
N2
CTable 3.1
H
```

The program should produce output similar to

```
    Average Earnings

1984:   $$$$$$$
1985:   $$$
1986:   $$$$$

        Table 3.1
```

8-2 STRING PROCESSING

In this section, we discuss various aspects of string processing. We begin by developing some extensions to the basic string operations that are provided as built-in features of THINK Pascal. We continue with a discussion of character-conversion techniques and provide some useful illustrations of these methods. We complete the section with a presentation of a package for dealing with arbitrarily long string data (allowing us to break the 255-character barrier).

Some Additional String Tools

The first additional tool that we discuss is the user-defined string function **Trim**, which deletes trailing blanks from a string. The function accepts a string of any type as a value parameter and returns the trimmed string as its value. Some examples of the behavior of the function Trim are shown in the following table, where we have used ƀ to signify a blank in order to clarify the action.

InString	Trim(InString)
'abcbbb'	'abc'
'bbbabc'	'bbbabc'
'bbbb'	' '
'abb'	'abb'
' '	' '

We note that Trim only deletes blanks that are on the right of the string. It does not deal with embedded blanks or blanks on the left. If the input string consists of all blanks, then the value of Trim is the null string.

The result type of the function and of its single-value parameter is *string*. The function uses the built-in Length and Copy functions to produce its value. The header for the Trim function is

```
function Trim(InString: string): string;
```

The function has a local integer variable I for use as a loop index and a local Boolean variable Found for loop control. The algorithm uses a standard searching loop, except that rather than searching forward, it searches backward. The first nonblank found represents the desired length of the result. A special check is included for the null string to avoid trying to set Trim to the first zero characters of InString.

```
if InString is null
    set Trim to null
else
[search backwards for a nonblank character]
    set I to the length of InString, Found to false
    while no nonblank character has been found and I <> 0
        decrement by 1
[return the trimmed string]
    set Trim to the first I characters of InString
```

The Trim function is shown in Figure 8-4.

The next tool that we discuss is a function that produces a string consisting of repetitions of a single character. The function **RunOf** is a string-valued function that has two value parameters: the number of repetitions and the character to be repeated. We show some examples of the behavior of the RunOf function in the following table:

Number	Character	RunOf(Number, Character)
3	'*'	'***'
1	'#'	'#'
5	' '	' '
0	'%'	' '
256	'$'	' '

We note that if the number of repetitions is specified as less than 1 or greater than 255, RunOf returns the null string.

```
function Trim (InString: string): string;

{Written by:     XXXXXXXXX XX/XX/XX}
{Purpose:        To trim trailing blanks from a string}
{Parameters:     InString - input, the string to be trimmed}
{Functions used: Length - (built-in) to get number of characters}
{                Copy   - (built-in) to extract a substring}

  const
    Blank = ' ';          {Blank space}
    Null = '';            {Null string}

  var
    I: integer;           {Loop index}
    Found: boolean;       {Has nonblank been found?}

begin {Trim}

{*** If null, return null}

  if InString = Null then
    Trim := Null
  else

{*** Search backwards for a nonblank character}

  begin
    I := Length(InString);          {Start at last position}
    Found := false;
    while (not Found) and (I >= 1) do
      begin
        if InString[I] <> Blank then
          Found := true
        else
          I := I - 1
      end; {while}

{*** Return the trimmed string}

      Trim := Copy(InString, 1, I)
    end {if}
end; {Trim}
```

Figure 8-4   The trim function.

The header for the RunOf function is

```
function RunOf(Number: integer; Character: char): string;
```

The function has a local string variable WorkString for use in creating the value to be returned. The logical steps of the algorithm for RunOf are

```
function RunOf(Number: integer; Character: char): string;

{Written by:   XXXXXXXXX XX/XX/XX}
{Purpose:      To create a string of a specified number of}
{              occurrences of a specified character}
{Parameters:   Number    - input, number of characters to generate}
{              Character - input, character to generate Procedures used}

  const
    NullString = '';        {Empty string}

  var
    WorkString: string;     {used to build up RunOf string}
    i: integer;             {loop counter}

  begin {RunOf}

{*** Return null string if invalid Number of characters}

    WorkString := NullString;
    if (Number >= 1) and (Number <= 255) then
      begin
        for i := 1 to Number do
          WorkString := Concat(WorkString, Character)
      end; {if}

{*** Return the created string}

    RunOf := WorkString

  end; {RunOf}
```

Figure 8-5   The RunOf function.

    set WorkString to the null string
    if Number is between 1 and 255 (inclusive) then
       for I = 1 to Number
          concatenate Character onto end of WorkString
    set RunOf to WorkString

The RunOf function is shown in Figure 8-5.

    Sometimes when dealing with strings, we wish they were all the same constant length. The usual character that is used to "pad" strings is the blank. We introduce the function **Pad** to pad a string to a specified length by adding spaces if necessary. Pad is a string-valued function that has two value parameters: the input string to be padded and the desired minimum length of the resulting string. Some examples that illustrate the behavior of the Pad function are shown in the following table:

InString	Margin	Pad(InString, Margin)
'ab'	5	'abbbb'
''	3	'bbb'
'abcd'	3	'abcd'
'abc'	0	'abc'
'abc'	256	'abc'

```
function Pad(InString: string; Margin: integer): string;

{Written by: XXXXXXXXX XX/XX/XX}
{Purpose:    To add blanks to the end of InString in order}
{            to extend its length to Margin}
{Parameters: InString - input, the string to pad}
{            Margin   - input, the resulting margin}
{                       (if less than current length,}
{                       or greater than 255, answer is InString)}
{Functions used: RunOf - to obtain a string of blanks}
{                Length - (built-in) to get the length of a string}

    const
        Blank = ' '; {Blank space}

begin {Pad}

{*** Pad blanks to InString if Margin is valid}

    if (Margin > 255) then
        Pad := InString                        {Do nothing if invalid}
    else
        Pad := Concat (InString, RunOf(Margin - Length(InString), Blank))

end; {Pad}
```

Figure 8-6   The Pad function.

The function uses the functions RunOf and Length to produce its value. The header for the Pad function is

```
function Pad(InString: string; Margin: integer): string;
```

The logical steps of the algorithm for Pad are

if Margin is greater than 255
   set Pad to InString
otherwise
   set Pad to the concatenation of InString with a run of
     Margin – Length(InString) blanks

The Pad function is shown in Figure 8-6.

The next tool is the procedure **Replace**, which replaces the leftmost occurrence of a substring with a replacement substring. The procedure has a var parameter consisting of the string to work on and also has two value parameters: the substring to find and the substring to replace the found string. If the substring to be found does not exist in the input string, then the procedure does not change the input string. Some examples of the behavior of the Replace procedure are shown in the following table:

Original InString	Search	Change	After Replace Called InString
'abcd'	'bc'	'efg'	'aefgd'
'abcd'	'bd'	'efg'	'abcd'
'abcd'	' '	'efg'	'efgabcd'
'abcd'	'd'	'defg'	'abcdefg'
' '	' '	'abcd'	' '
'abcd'	'bc'	' '	'ad'

The procedure uses the procedures Delete and Insert as well as the functions Pos and Length to produce its result. The header for the Replace procedure is

procedure Replace(**var** InString: **string**; Search, Change: **string**);

The procedure uses the local variable Start to indicate the beginning of the substring within the input string and a local variable Total to ensure that no attempt is made to produce a string of length greater than 255.

The logical steps of the algorithm for Replace are

[check for existence of substring]
   set Start to Pos(Search, InString)
[check the resulting length of the replaced string]
   set Total to Length(InString) − Length(Search) + Length(Change)
[do the replacement, if valid]
   if Start is not 0 and Total is not greater than 255:
     Delete(InString, Start, Length(Search))
     Insert(Change, InString, Start)

The Replace procedure is shown in Figure 8-7.

We suggest a few more string-processing tools in the exercises at the end of the section.

Character-Conversion Techniques

There are a number of instances where we want to move through a string, character by character, changing the character to some other character if appropriate. Some examples of a conversion strategy are as follows:

   Change all uppercase characters to lowercase.
   Change all lowercase characters to uppercase.
   Encode each character according to some (secret?) code.
   Decode each character according to some code.

We often wish to process an entire text file using one of these schemes. A good design methodology for these tasks is to modularize according to size of data:

   Module to change an entire text file

   Module to change an entire string

   Module to change individual characters, if appropriate

```
procedure Replace(var InString: string; Search, Change: string);

{Written by: XXXXXXXXX XX/XX/XX}
{Purpose:    To replace the leftmost occurrence of Search in}
{            InString with Change}
{Parameters: InString - update, the string to be modified}
             Search   - input, the substring to look for}
{            Change   - input, the substring to replace Search by}
{Procedures used: Delete - (built-in) to delete a substring}
{                 Insert - (built-in) to insert a substring}
{Functions used: Pos    - (built-in) to find a substring in a string}
{                Length - (built-in) to find the length of a string}
   var
      Start: integer;           {Position of Search within InString}
      Total: integer;           {Potential total length of result}

begin {Replace}

{*** Check for the existence of Search in InString}

   Start := Pos(Search, InString);

{*** Check the resulting length of the replaced string}

   Total := Length(InString) - Length(Search) + Length(Change);

{*** Do the replacement if valid}

   if (Start > 0) and (Total <= 255) then
      begin
         Delete(InString, Start, Length(Search));
         Insert(Change, InString, Start)
      end {if}

end; {Replace}
```

Figure 8-7   The Replace procedure.

The module to change an entire text file reads one line at a time into a string, calls the module that changes entire strings to make the modifications, and writes the line to the output file. The module to change an entire string loops through the string one character at a time and calls the module that changes individual characters, as appropriate.

Note that one advantage of this particular modularization is that we can use essentially the same modules for the top two levels in the hierarchy. Then, by plugging in different lowest-level modules, we can change our conversion application.

Let us begin with a discussion of changing lowercase letters to uppercase. In ASCII, lowercase letters run from positions 97 (a) to 122 (z). Uppercase letters occur at positions 65 (A) to 90 (Z). Notice that the uppercase version of a lowercase letter is exactly 32 positions prior to it in the ASCII collating sequence. So to convert a lowercase letter to its uppercase equivalent (and leave the other characters alone), we use the following THINK statement, where CntChar is the current character being checked:

```
if (CntChar >= 'a') and (CntChar <= 'z') then
    InString[I] := Chr(Ord(CntChar) - 32);
```

By placing this statement within a loop that checks each character in a string, we have the needed routine.

(Note the approach we use is dependent upon the ASCII collating sequence; moving this program to a computer that uses a different collating sequence requires changes in the program.)

We place this conversion activity in the module **LowToUp** and choose to implement it as a string-valued function. This allows us to test for a terminating value in an input loop with the statement

```
until LowToUp(String1) = '$END'
```

so that the user can enter any of the following as terminating values:

```
$END $ENd $EnD $End $eND $eNd $enD $end
```

By now you have probably typed '$end' instead of '$END' enough times to appreciate this more flexible way of handling user responses. The header for the function is

```
function LowToUp(InString: string): string;
```

We use the built-in function Length to help produce the desired value. Since InString is a value parameter, we use it as a working string inside of LowToUp with no fear of side effects. We use a local variable I as a loop index. The basic logical steps of the algorithm are

[loop through the string, converting each character]
loop I from 1 to the length of InString:
    if InString[I] is between 'a' and 'z'
        set InString[I] to uppercase version (using code above)

[return the converted string]
set LowToUp to InString

The code for the function LowToUp is shown in Figure 8-8.

The module that deals with the text file is normally the main program and is responsible for the user interface and opening and closing files. We simply list the rough steps of this module here and refer you to Figure 8-10, which is a complete example of one of the applications. The rough steps of the file-level module are as follows:

1. Print the instructions.
2. Ask the user for the filenames and open the files.
3. Convert the lines of input file into output file.
4. Close the files.
5. Print the terminating message and stop program.

We now turn to another application area, changing uppercase to lowercase. We note that it is a chore almost identical to that of converting lowercase letters to uppercase ones:

```
function LowToUp(InString: string): string;

{Written by: XXXXXXXXX XX/XX/XX}
{Purpose:    To convert lowercase to uppercase}
{Parameters: InString - the string to be converted}
{Functions used: Length - to get the length of a string}

  var
    I: integer;                {Loop index}

begin {LowToUp}

{*** Loop through the string, converting each lowercase letter}

for I := 1 to Length(InString) do
  if (InString[I] >= 'a') and (InString[I] <= 'z') then
    InString[I] := Chr(Ord(InString[I]) - 32);

{*** Return the converted string}

  LowToUp := InString
end; {LowToUp}
```

Figure 8-8 Converting a string to uppercase.

the only difference is that we add 32 to compute the new letter's ASCII value rather than subtracting 32. The code for this function (which we call **LowCase**) is shown in Figure 8-9.

Longer-Length Strings

Although it is not usually a problem, the strings of THINK Pascal are limited to a length of 255 characters. What if we wanted to deal with larger strings? In this subsection, we begin to develop a package for dealing with strings of lengths longer than 255.

Our basic data structure for dealing with **BigStrings** is a type such as the following:

```
BigString = record
    Character: array[1..MaxLength] of char;
    Length: integer
  end;
```

MaxLength is a named constant, perhaps in the 500 range. We wish to be able to perform similar activities with BigStrings as we do with the usual string types. Some of the operations we have in mind are as follows:

Inputting and outputting	Searching for substrings
Determining length	Deleting substrings
Concatenating	Inserting substrings
Extracting substrings	Replacing substrings
Comparing strings	Trimming trailing blanks
Converting a string to a BigString	Padding with blanks
Converting a BigString to a string	

```
function LowCase(InString: string): string;

{Written by: XXXXXXXXX XX/XX/XX}
{Purpose:    To convert uppercase to lowercase}
{Parameters: InString - the string to be converted}
{Functions used: Length - to get the length of a string}

  var
    I: integer;              {Loop index}

begin {LowCase}

{*** Loop through the string, converting each uppercase letter}

  for I := 1 to Length(InString) do
    if (InString[I] >= 'A') and (InString[I] <= 'Z') then
      InString[I] := Chr(Ord(InString[I]) + 32);

{*** Return the converted string}

  LowCase := InString
end; {LowCase}
```

Figure 8-9 Converting a string to lowercase

We will develop some of these activities and leave some of the others for the exercises. Before we move on to some development, let us agree to the following naming convention: If a string routine is called xxx, then we call the corresponding BigString routine by the name Bigxxx. With this in mind, the names of the routines in the package are as follows:

BigReadln	BigFromStr
BigWriteln	BigPos
BigLength	BigDelete
BigConcat	BigInsert
BigCopy	BigReplace
BigEqual	BigTrim
BigLessThan	BigPad
BigToStr	

The first routines to develop are the input and output routines because they form the interface with the user and ultimately allow the user to check on the correctness of other routines as they are developed.

The simplest routine to design is BigWriteln, so we start with it. Our version of BigWriteln accepts a single-value parameter of type BigString and prints the contents on the screen. We use a single local variable I as a loop index. The basic logic of the algorithm is

loop I from 1 to the Length of the BigString:
    Print the Ith character of the BigString
Go to a new line

The code for the BigWriteln procedure appears in Figure 8-10. The single Writeln at the end of the procedure ensures that the next data that are printed begin on the next line.

```
procedure BigWriteln(InString: BigString);

{Written by: XXXXXXXXX XX/XX/XX}
{Purpose:    To print out InString}
{Parameters: InString - input, string to print}

   var
      I: integer; {Loop index}

begin {BigWriteln}
   with InString do
      begin
         for I:= 1 to Length do
            Write(Character[I])
      end; {with}
   Writeln
end; {BigWriteln}
```

Figure 8-10   Output of a BigString.

The next routine that we wish to implement is BigReadln to allow us to input data to BigString-type variables. We read in user-entered characters one at a time until a carriage return is pressed to signal the end of input. Return is Chr(13), a fact we make use of to terminate the character-by-character input loop.

Our version of BigReadln has a single var parameter of the type BigString, which returns the string input by the user. The basic logic of the algorithm is

set Length of the BigString to 0
until we reach end of the line
   read input character
   if not a carriage return
      increment the Length of the BigString by 1
      place the character into the Character array at position Length

The code for the BigReadln procedure is shown in Figure 8-11.

The next module we develop is the integer function BigLength, which returns the length of a BigString. The function has one value parameter of the type BigString. It may surprise you that we wish to use a procedure for a "one-line" operation. The reason for this is to respect the principle of **information hiding**, which holds that the one using the program should not know the details of data structures used to represent information; instead, the program user should employ higher-level operations to gain access to the information. The code for the procedure BigLength is shown in Figure 8-12.

Next, we develop the procedure BigCopy, which extracts a substring of a BigString. Notice that the usual Copy subprogram in THINK Pascal is a function. However, BigCopy must be a procedure because functions are unable to return a record type as a result.

The procedure has one value input parameter and one var output parameter, both of the type BigString. The procedure also has two integer-value parameters: the start position of the substring and the number of characters desired. The procedure uses the local variable I as a loop index and the local variable InLen to store the length of InString. The basic logic of the steps of the program is

```
procedure BigReadln(var OutString: BigString);

{Written by: XXXXXXXXX XX/XX/XX}
{Purpose:    To read characters into OutString}
{Parameters: OutString - output, the string being read}

  var
     CntChar: char;      {Character just entered}

begin {BigReadln}
  with OutString do
     begin
        Length := 0;

{*** Take characters one at a time until end of line}

        repeat
           Read(CntChar);
           if CntChar <> Chr(13) then
             begin
                Length := Length + 1;
                Character[Length] := CntChar
             end {if}
        until CntChar = Chr(13);

     end {with}

end; {BigReadln}
```

Figure 8-11 Input of a BigString.

```
function BigLength(InString: BigString): integer;

{Written by: XXXXXXXXX XX/XX/XX}
{Purpose:    To return the length of a BigString}
{Parameters: InString - input, the string to find the length of}

begin {BigLength}
  BigLength := InString.Length
end; {BigLength}
```

Figure 8-12 Length of a BigString.

set InLen to the length of InString

[see how many to copy]
if the number of characters to copy is less than 0, then set the
    number of characters to copy to 0
if the start position is less than 1, then set the number of characters
    to copy to 0
otherwise,

if the start position plus the number of characters is greater than
InLen, then set the number of characters to the number that
will go to the end of InString

[perform the copy]
loop I from 1 to the number of characters to copy
    set the Ith character of OutString to the Start + $(I - 1)^{st}$ character
        of InString
set the length of OutString to the number of characters copied

The algorithm for BigCopy, because of our desire to remain consistent with the THINK Pascal Copy function, contains a few subtleties due to the possibilities:

Number < 0
    in this case, we wish to set Number to 0
Start < 1
    in this case, we wish to set Number to 0
Start + Number > InLen
    in this case, we wish to copy characters to the end of
    InString, so we set Number to InLen − Start + 1

The code for the procedure is shown in Figure 8-13.

The last routine that we present is the procedure BigConcat, which concatenates two elements of the type BigString. The procedure has two value input parameters, InString1 and InString2, and one var output parameter, OutString. The procedure uses the local variable I as a loop index and two local variables InLen1 and InLen2 to store the lengths of the input BigStrings. For simplicity in the presentation, we assume that the resulting length of the answer is less than or equal to MaxLength, the maximum length allowable. The basic logic of the steps of the procedure is

set InLen1 to the length of InString1
set InLen2 to the length of InString2
loop I from 1 to InLen1:
    set the Ith character of OutString to the Ith character of
    InString1
loop I from InLen1 + 1 to InLen1 + InLen2:
    set the Ith character of OutString to the $(I - InLen1)^{th}$
    character of InString2
set the length of OutString to InLen1 + InLen2

There are several special cases of concatenation to consider:

InString1 is null.

InString2 is null.

Both InString1 and InString2 are null.

Resulting OutString is as large as possible.

You should hand-trace the algorithm for BigConcat to verify that these special cases cause no difficulty for the algorithm. The code for the procedure BigConcat is shown in Figure 8-14.

8-2 STRING PROCESSING

```
procedure BigCopy(InString: BigString; Start, Number: integer;
                  var OutString: BigString);

{Written by: XXXXXXXXX XX/XX/XX}
{Purpose:    Extract a substring from a string}
{Parameters: InString - input, the string to look in}
{            Start    - input, where the substring should start}
{            Number   - input, desired length of the substring}
{            OutString - output, the substring}
{Functions used: BigLength - to find the length of a BigString}

  var
     InLen: integer;   {Length of InString}
     I: integer;       {Loop index}

begin {BigCopy}
  InLen := BigLength(InString);
  with OutString do
     begin
       if Number < 0 then
          Number := 0;
       if Start < 1 then
          Number := 0
       else if (Start + Number) > InLen then
          Number := InLen - Start + 1;
       for I := 1 to Number do
          Character[I] := InString.Character[Start + I - 1];
       Length := Number
     end {with}
end; {BigCopy}
```

Figure 8-13 Extracting a substring of a BigString.

For testing these first routines of the package, we have written a driver program. The driver main program is shown in Figure 8-15. To run the driver, the routines of the package would have to be inserted so those used by other routines are defined previously to them; one possible ordering is shown in Figure 8-15.

REVIEW

Terms and Concepts

BigStrings
information hiding
LowCase
LowToUp

Pad
Replace
RunOf
Trim

EXERCISES

1. Write Pascal procedures or functions for the following. Use THINK's built-in string type:
   (a) CountSubstr, which counts how many times a substring occurs within a given string.

```
      procedure BigConcat(InString1, InString2: BigString;
                      var OutString: BigString);

{Written by: XXXXXXXXX XX/XX/XX}
{Purpose:    To concatenate two BigStrings}
{Parameters: InString1, InString2 - input, the strings to concatenate}
{            OutString - output, the concatenated string}

   var
      InLen1: integer;                     {End of String1}
      InLen2: integer;                     {End of String2}
      I: integer;                          {Loop index}

   begin {BigConcat}
      InLen1 := BigLength(InString1);
      InLen2 := BigLength(InString2);

      with OutString do
         begin
            for I := 1 to InLen1 do
               Character[I] := InString1.Character[I];
            for I := InLen1 + 1 to InLen1 + InLen2 do
               Character[I] := InString2.Character[I - InLen1];
            Length := InLen1 + InLen2
         end {with}

   end; {BigConcat}
```

Figure 8-14 Concatenating BigStrings.

(b) IsBlank, which sees if a given string is either null or totally blank.
(c) Equal, which sees if two strings are equal when the shorter is padded with blanks to be as long as the longer. For 'Johnson' and 'Johnson ', the answer would be *true*.
(d) InsertBlanks, which inserts a given number of blanks at a given position in a given string.
(e) FindSubst, which locates a substring without respect to character case. For example, it would find 'Anne' in the string 'Dianne Wilson' in position 3.
(f) ReplaceAll, which replaces all instances of the search substring with the change substring.

2. Write the following functions:
   (a) Reverse, which reverses the order of the characters in the input string, using a loop.
   (b) Repeat part (a) using a recursive function. Run the function for a string of length 255. What happens?
   (c) Use the Reverse function of part (a) to write a function RPos that finds the rightmost occurrence of a substring in a string.
   (d) Use the Reverse function to write a function Clip that removes leading and trailing blanks from a string.

3. Think of a simple coding scheme that involves character exchange such as

   A → B
   B → C
   .
   .
   .

EXERCISES

```pascal
program Driver;

{Written by: XXXXXXXXX XX/XX/XX}
{Purpose:    To test the BigString Package}

  type
    BigString = record
      Character: array[1..500] of char;
      Length: integer
      end;

  var
    String1, String2, String3: BigString;
    Start, Number: integer;

{function BigLength inserted here}

{procedure BigConcat inserted here}

{procedure BigCopy inserted here}

{procedure BigReadln inserted here}

{procedure BigWriteln inserted here}

begin {Driver}

{*** Read two BigStrings}

  Write('Enter a string: ');
  BigReadln(String1);
  Write('Enter a second string: ');
  BigReadln(String2);

{*** Write out a BigString}

  BigConcat(String1, String2, String3);
  Writeln('The length of the string is: ', BigLength(String3));
  BigWriteln(String3);

{*** Extract a substring}

  Write('Enter start position for substring: ');
  Readln(Start);
  Write('Enter number of characters for substring: ');
  Readln(Number);
  BigCopy(String3, Start, Number, String1);
  Writeln('The length of the string is: ', BigLength(String1));
  BigWriteln(String1);

{*** Print terminating message and stop program}

  Writeln;
  Writeln('Tests completed.')
end.
```

Figure 8-15 Testing with BigStrings.

Z → A
a → b
b → c
.
.
.
z → a
0 → 1
1 → 2
9 → 0
all others stay the same

Write a function Encode to encode characters according to this scheme.

4. Write the string-level function for encoding an entire string using the result of Exercise 3.
5. Write the text-file-level program for encoding a file using the results of Exercises 3 and 4.
6. Write the character, string, and text-file-level modules for decoding files produced by the results of Exercise 5.
7. Do the following for the examples of this section:
   (a) Explain why the RunOf function has a local variable WorkString.
   (b) Modify BigConcat to simply copy the first string to the output using a record assignment, and then fill in the second string. Is this better (faster or clearer)?
   (c) Modify BigConcat to handle the situation where the sum of the lengths exceeds the maximum allowed. It should simply yield a truncated answer.
   (d) Modify the BigReadln and BigWriteln procedures to handle very long strings more smoothly. For example, BigWriteln might send a carriage return every 70 characters. BigReadln should be able to get around any terminal limitations on the length of an input line.
8. Write the following additions to the BigStrings package:
   (a) BigChar(Str, I), a char function to return the Ith character.
   (b) BigTrim(Str1, Str2), a procedure to delete trailing blanks for Str1 and return the results as Str2.
   (c) BigRunOf(Num, Chr, Str), a procedure to produce a BigString of Num consecutive characters specified by Chr.
   (d) BigPos(SubStr, Str), an integer function to locate a substring.
   (e) BigEqual(Str1, Str2), a Boolean function to determine equality.
   (f) BigLessThan(Str1, Str2), a Boolean function to determine if Str1 is less than Str2.
   (g) BigInsert(SubStr, Str, Start), a procedure to insert a substring.
   (h) BigDelete(Str, Start, Num), a procedure to delete Num characters from Str, beginning with the position specified by Start.
   (i) BigReplace(Str, Search, Change), a procedure to replace the leftmost occurrence of Search in Str by Change.
   (j) BigToStr(Bstr, Lstr), a procedure to change the BigString Bstr into the regular string Lstr. Lstr should be of the type *string*. Truncate if the length of Bstr is more than 255.
   (k) BigFromStr(Bstr, Lstr), a procedure to change the regular string Lstr into the BigString Bstr. Lstr should be of the type *string*.

9. Write a comprehensive test plan for the Replace procedure of Figure 8-7.
10. Write subprograms for the following:

(a) Given an array of strings and a new string, add the new string to the end of the list if it is not already in the list.

(b) Extract the first word from a string. Consider a word to be any sequence of nonblank characters. The given string should not be changed.

(c) Repeat part (b), but modify the original string to take the word out of it.

(d) Given a string, print a list of the words in the string, one word per line.

11. Write a program to read the lines of text and to find how many times each word that appears is used. (This is a simple form of analysis of an author's style.) Hint: See Exercise 10.

12. (a) Write a function that captures the last 10 characters of a string.

(b) Generalize part (a) to allow the number of characters to be captured to be a parameter.

13. Write a paragraph formatter. It should read a series of lines of text, interpreting lines that begin with a blank as the beginning of new paragraphs. The beginning of each paragraph should be indented five spaces. All strings of consecutive blanks should be converted to a single blank. As many words as possible should be placed on each line of output.

14. Add these enhancements to the paragraph formatter of Exercise 13:

(a) Right-justify each line except the last line of the paragraph by inserting blanks between words and keeping the words as evenly spaced as possible on the line.

(b) Do not compress blanks that immediately follow a period.

(c) Handle multiple-page printed output, leaving an appropriate margin at the top and bottom.

(d) Treat a line that begins with a period as a command, as outlined in the rest of this exercise. Any command immediately terminates a paragraph. After the command is processed, the next line is treated as the beginning of a new paragraph, but it is not indented unless it begins with a blank.

(e) The command .C means to center the remainder of the input line on an output line by itself.

(f) The command .E means to generate a top of form.

(g) The command .H signifies that the rest of the line is to be treated as a header for each page of output, centered near the top of the page. Any occurrence of the character '#' in the header line is to be replaced by the page number for each page.

(h) Within the body of the text, a '^' character is to be treated as a noncompressible space. On output, it should be replaced by a blank.

15. Develop a subprogram that creates a "printable" version of a dollar-and-cents figure given as a string of up to 10 digits. For example,

'1234567890'	yields	'$12,345,678.90'
'7891'		'$78.91'
'0000007891'		'$78.91'
'2'		'$0.02'
'135692'		'$1,356.92'

16. Write a conversion routine to change base 2 to base 8. Its input is a string representing a number in base 2. Its output is a string representing the same number in base 8. For example,

'101'	yields	'5'
'10101'		'25'
'111010110'		'726'

There is no limit, other than the built-in limits, on the length of the input string. Hint: When grouped by threes from the right, the triplets of base-2 digits yield the corresponding base-8 digit. You may have to pad the leftmost triplet with 0's on the left.

17. Write a conversion routine similar to Exercise 16 for base 8 to base 2.
18. Write a routine that converts an integer value to a string of binary digits. For example, the integer 26 would yield '11010'. Hint: If you successively divide the integer by 2, each remainder is one of the digits of the base-2 string, working from right to left. For 26:

    26 div 2 is 13   26 mod 2 is 0 → '0'
    13 div 2 is 6   13 mod 2 is 1 → '1'
    6 div 2 is 3   6 mod 2 is 0   → '0'
    3 div 2 is 1   3 mod 2 is 1   → '1'
    1 div 2 is 0   1 mod 2 is 1   → '1'

    We quit when the quotient is 0.

19. Repeat Exercise 18 for base 8. Divide and mod by 8 instead of 2. For 26:

    26 div 8 is 3   26 mod 8 is 2 → '2'
    3 div 8 is 0   3 mod 8 is 3   → '3'

    The answer is '32'.

20. Write a routine to reverse Exercise 19. That is, given a string representing a valid base-8 integer, it should calculate the integer. Assume that the integer lies between 0 and maxint.

9 Pointers

OBJECTIVES

In this chapter, we introduce the concept of pointers and their use in Pascal programs. By the end of this chapter, you will be able to:

- appreciate the value of pointers in programming
- define and use pointers in Pascal programs
- use pointers to develop your own data structures

9-1 POINTER VARIABLES

Pointers

A **pointer** is an indirect reference to a data item. We deal with pointers often in our daily lives, although we don't often call them by that name. For example, suppose you write your name on a slip of paper and put the slip in a hat for a drawing to see who gets to wash the dishes. If we think of your name as being similar to a variable with you as its contents, what is the content of the slip of paper? Your name, of course. The slip of paper is an indirect reference to you. It is indirect because it leads to you through first leading to your name. We can maintain the indirect reference to you without mentioning your name at all by writing on the slip: "the worried-looking individual sitting on the folding chair, in the corner." Also, if a stranger enters the room and sits on the red pillow, we can enter the newcomer in the competition by writing on a slip of paper: "the confused-looking individual sitting on the red pillow." The new slip of paper is a pointer to the new individual and is certainly not the name of that individual.

We use pointers to data items stored in computer memory. When data items have names (in the form of variables), we continue to use the names to refer directly to the data.

But, when new data items appear, whose names we do not know, then we use pointers to refer indirectly to the data items. We explain later in the section where to obtain these new "nameless" data items.

Declaring and Using Pointers

Declaring Pointers.
Every type of data can have a pointer type associated with it. We can declare named pointer types or we can declare variables as belonging to an unnamed pointer type. This is exactly the same case as for the other data types with which we have dealt. For example, if we wish to declare a variable Scores to be an integer array with at most 1000 cells, we can choose either of the alternatives:

```
type
   IntegerArray = array[1..1000] of integer;
var
   Scores: IntegerArray;
```

```
var
   Scores: array[1..1000] of integer;
```

The choice depends on whether it is an advantage to have the global named type available for passing as a parameter or for the declaration of other variables.

We begin with the idea of declaring pointer variables directly. Because pointers can hinder the readability of a program, it is important to select names for our pointer variables carefully. Let us suppose that we have a type called ItemType and we want to point to an item of that type. Since it's the first such pointer to ItemType, let us call the pointer variable First. In Pascal, to declare the variable First to be a pointer to ItemType, we can use the declaration

```
var
   First: ^ItemType;
```

We use the **caret** (^) to denote that First is a pointer. Note carefully where the caret is located in the declaration; it is "pointing to" the name of the type. We can visualize the situation as a box (variable) called First, whose content is a pointer — an arrow — to another variable. Since First has yet to be initialized, its arrow points to some unknown place in memory; we can illustrate this situation:

First

If we wish to name our pointer type, then we must first choose a name. We select the name ItemType_Ptr, which conveys that it represents a type that points to data of type ItemType. Using the named pointer type, we can alternatively declare the variable First as

```
type
   ItemType_Ptr = ^ItemType;  {Type for pointer to ItemType}
```

```
var
   First: ItemType_Ptr;      {Pointer variable for ItemType}
```

Note that the caret is used in exactly the same way: as a modifier of ItemType.

We can violate a principle of Pascal and declare ItemType_Ptr before we declare ItemType. It is always legal to declare the pointer first, but not always valid to declare the pointer afterwards. Therefore, we adopt the strategy of declaring the pointer first as a defensive programming measure. For example, if ItemType represents data that might appear on a shopping list, then we might have a set of declarations such as

```
type
   ItemType_Ptr = ^ItemType;
   ItemType = record
      Quantity: integer;
      Item: string[20]
   end;

var
   First: ItemType_Ptr;      {First is a pointer to ItemType}
```

Assigning Values to Pointers. We will discuss how we assign a data element to the pointer First in a bit. For now, assume First does point to some data of the type ItemType. We now concentrate on how we can use the indirect referencing of a pointer variable. The general rule is that the notation

```
First^
```

provides the indirect reference to the data and is treated as if it were a name for the data. This statement would commonly be read as "the variable First points to".

If we want the item on the shopping list to be "apples", then we make the assignment

```
First^.Item := 'apples'
```

If we want to buy six apples, then we make the assignment

```
First^.Quantity := 6
```

So now the Quantity and Item fields of the variable to which First points have been set to 6 and 'apples' (respectively):

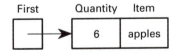

Because the data item is of a record type, we can use the *with-do* construct:

```
with First^ do
   begin
      Item := 'apples';
      Quantity := 6
   end {with}
```

If we wish to print the item, we can use the statement

```
Writeln('The item is: ', First^.Item)
```

The @ Operator.   Another way to assign a pointer a value is to assign it to the location in memory (the **address**) of an existing variable by using the "@" operator. For instance, if S is a string variable, and StrPtr is a pointer variable that points to items of type *string*, we can have StrPtr point to S as follows:

```
StrPtr := @S
```

This operation is often read "place the address of S into StrPtr", StrPtr now points to S. The @ operator is a THINK extension to standard Pascal, and is not often used. We generally stick to examples that use the more standard pointer operations.

Obtaining Data for Pointer Variables

Now that we have some idea of how to use a pointer once it is pointing to some data item, we will discuss how to obtain a data item to which it can point. Pascal provides us with the built-in procedure **New** to obtain a data item of any pointer type. If we wish to obtain a data item for the pointer variable First, then we execute the statement

```
New(First)
```

Pictorially, we have this situation before First is initialized:

and this situation after New(First) is issued:

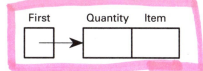

If we use the previous declarations, the following fragment of code reads and prints a shopping-list item:

```
{declarations}

New(First); {Obtains a data item to use}
with First^ do
  begin
     Write('Enter the item: ');
     Readln(Item);
     Write('Enter the quantity: ');
     Readln(Quantity);
     Writeln('You wish ', Quantity, ' ', Item)
  end; {with}
```

Suppose that we follow this fragment of code with the statement New(First). This statement assigns another data item to the pointer First and the original data item cannot be accessed because we have no way to refer to it. Besides now having "wasted" memory, we can no longer access the data stored in the first item. Pictorially, we have this situation:

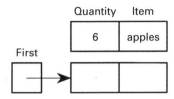

Fortunately, Pascal provides two ways for us to avoid this problem:

1. ***Keep the Old Data Item.*** If we have available another pointer variable, Before, declared to be of the type ItemType_Ptr, then we can execute the sequence

    ```
    Before := First;        {Assigns old data item to Before}
    New(First);             {Obtains new data item for First}
    ```

2. ***Discard the Old Data Item.*** Pascal provides a mechanism for recycling old data items. If we are through with the particular data item pointed to by First, then we can execute the statement

    ```
    Dispose(First)
    ```

    After the statement is executed, First no longer refers to the data item and the data item is returned to available memory for potential future use.

First still has a value, but what it points to is unpredictable, since the data item it used to point to has been "sent back to" the available memory pool. A pointer pointing to "who knows where" is called a **dangling pointer** and is often illustrated:

(You will notice the variable is in the same state as it was when first declared; we know it is a pointer, but what it points to is unknown.)

On the Macintosh (and many other computers), dangling pointers point to some random spot in memory; if the pointer is "followed" (by referring to it in a statement), very strange program behavior can result. In fact, depending upon what part of memory you happen to have entered, a Macintosh could even reboot itself!

After we dispose of what First points to, what we should do is set First to a value indicating it no longer points to anything. By assigning a pointer the predefined constant **nil**, we indicate that a pointer variable is not pointing to a valid data item. This provides a convenient test for validity of data, as we will see. Nil conforms to all pointer types and can be used for comparison purposes. Therefore, we can initialize First with the statement

```
First := nil
```

We often illustrate this situation by placing a diagonal line or a dot in the pointer variable; we use the former approach:

We can check if First refers to any valid data with the comparisons

```
if First = nil then . . .
if First <> nil then . . .
```

We can now look at a small example of the use of pointers. Suppose that we have two stores in which we shop, Ace Drugs and King Groceries. We may wish to buy an item at either or both stores. We use the two pointers AceFirst and KingFirst to refer to the items for Ace Drugs and King Groceries, respectively. The user is asked how many items are intended for each store and enters the items, if any. We restrict the user to either one item or no items for each store for now because we just want to become more comfortable with using pointers.

The code for the program appears in Figure 9-1. Note the manner in which we manage our use of the data items for the pointers:

1. We initialize both pointers to nil.
2. We call New for a data item when we are sure that we are going to use it.
3. We call Dispose to return a data item when we are through with it.
4. After we call Dispose for a pointer, we set it to nil.

(Try drawing pictures to help you get a clear understanding of how pointers are adjusted by these four steps.)

Managing Dynamic Memory Resources

The example of Figure 9-1 shows more disadvantages than advantages of using pointers. We now extend the example to achieve a more realistic and useful result.

We start with one of the most important features of the pointer type: there can be fields of the pointer type within the record structure that is pointed to. That is, we can enhance our shopping list item to include a pointer to the next item on the list. Our declarations become

```
type
   ItemType_Ptr = ^ItemType;
   ItemType = record
      Quantity: integer;     {Number to buy}
      Item: string[20];      {Item to buy}
      Next: ItemType_Ptr     {Pointer to next item}
   end;
```

We can now organize a shopping list as a structure containing many items, each of which points to the next. To summarize the organization of the list:

```
program BuyOne;

{Written by: XXXXXXXXX XX/XX/XX}
{Purpose:    To maintain two small shopping lists}
{Procedures used: New     - (built-in) gets a new data item}
                  Dispose - (built-in) returns a data item}

  type
    ItemType_Ptr = ^ItemType;
    ItemType = record
       Quantity: integer;        {Number to buy}
       Item: string[20]          {Item to buy}
       end;

  var
    AceFirst: ItemType_Ptr;      {Pointer to Ace list}
    KingFirst: ItemType_Ptr;     {Pointer to King list}
    N: integer;                  {Number of items at store}
    I: integer;                  {Loop index}
    None: Boolean;               {Indicator for empty lists}

begin {BuyOne}

{*** Initialize}

  AceFirst := nil;
  KingFirst := nil;

{*** Get and print lists in a loop}

  repeat
     Writeln;
     None := true;
     Write('How many items for Ace Drugs: ');
     Readln(N);
     if N <> 0 then
        N := 1;
     for I := 1 to N do
        begin
           New(AceFirst);
           with AceFirst^ do
              begin
                 Write('Enter the item: ');
                 Readln(Item);
                 Write('Enter the quantity: ');
                 Readln(Quantity)
              end {with}
        end; {for}
```

Figure 9-1   First use of pointers (continues next page).

```
            Write('How many items for King Groceries: ');
            Readln(N);
            if N <> 0 then
              N := 1;
            for I := 1 to N do
              begin
                New(KingFirst);
                with KingFirst^ do
                  begin
                    Write('Enter the item: ');
                    Readln(Item);
                    Write('Enter the quantity: ');
                    Readln(Quantity)
                  end {with}
              end; {for}
            Writeln;
            Writeln('Here is your shopping list: ');
            if AceFirst <> nil then
              with AceFirst^ do
                begin
                  None := false;
                  Writeln(' From Ace Drugs: ');
                  Writeln(' You want ', Quantity, ' ', Item, '.');
                  Dispose(AceFirst);
                  AceFirst := nil
                end;
            if KingFirst <> nil then
              with KingFirst^ do
                begin
                  None := false;
                  Writeln('From King Groceries: ');
                  Writeln('You want ', Quantity, ' ', Item, ' ');
                  Dispose(KingFirst);
                  KingFirst := nil
                end;
      until None;

      Writeln(' *** Shopping list is empty');

    {*** Print message and terminate program.}

      Writeln;
      Writeln('End of list')
    end.
```

Figure 9-1   (continued)

A pointer First points to the first item on the list. Within each Item, a pointer Next points to the next item on the list. For the last item on the list, Next is set to nil (to indicate it does not point to anything).

This variety of data structure is called a **linked list.** To enhance the example of Figure 9-1, we keep the logic of building the lists similar to what is already there. One addition we require is a temporary pointer variable for each list. We refer to this as Temp in our algorithm, which is as follows:

>get the number of elements, N, from the user
>loop for I going from 1 to N:
>>New(Temp)   [get a new data item]
>>set Temp^.Next to First   [link new item to first on list]
>>set First to Temp   [put new one first on list]
>>with First^ do the following:
>>>get the data for the item

Before we discuss more details, let us note some points about the **dynamic** use of memory. When we must predetermine the size of our data structures, as in the case of arrays, we are making **static** use of memory. Using pointers allows us more flexible use of memory. In our example of the two shopping lists, we can use available memory with one large list and one small list or we can have two equal-size lists. The main idea is that we do not have to decide the memory needs for each list in advance. We note a similarity with the way that Macintosh disk files use the available space on a disk; each file uses as much space as it needs within the limits of the total space available.

The previous algorithm builds a list of any length. As each new **node** (that is, data item for the list) is created, its Next pointer is set to point to what was the first item on the list. For example, suppose the user enters 3 as N for the King Groceries list and that the three items are entered in this order: 12 apples, 1 newspaper, and 5 candy bars. As the items are added, the list appears as follows.

At first, the list is empty:

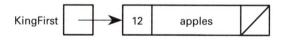

Then, the node for 12 apples is added to the front:

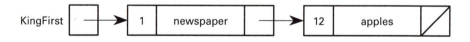

Next, the node for 1 newspaper is added to the front:

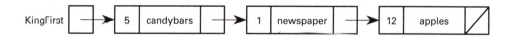

Finally, the node for 5 candy bars is added to the front:

KingFirst → 5 candybars → 1 newspaper → 12 apples

In this visual representation of the list, arrows represent pointer variables, both as named variables and as parts of records. Note the Next pointer is nil for the last item in the list.

As you can see from this example, the lists we are building have the property that the most recently added items are placed at the front of the list. If we were to also remove items from the list starting at the front, then the most recently added item would be the first to be deleted. A data structure with this approach for adding and deleting items is said to have the **last-in, first-out (LIFO)** property, and is often called a **stack**.

Using the LIFO approach, we give an algorithm for printing and disposing of each list:

while First is not equal to nil:
  print the item
  set Temp to First   [hold onto for disposal]
  set First to First^. Next   [delete the first item from list]
  Dispose(Temp)   [dispose of the unneeded item]

This algorithm works for printing and disposing of a list of any length. Note that we do not have any idea how long the list is before we print; we just print until the list is exhausted. See Figure 9-2.

```
program BuyLots;

{Written by: XXXXXXXXX XX/XX/XX}
{Purpose:    To maintain two small shopping lists}
{Procedures used: New - (built-in) gets a data item}
{                 Dispose - (built-in) returns a data item}

   type
      ItemType_Ptr = ^ItemType;
      ItemType = record
           Quantity: integer;    {Number to buy}
           Item: string[20];     {Item to buy}
           Next: ItemType_Ptr    {Pointer to list next}
         end;
   var
      AceFirst: ItemType_Ptr;    {Pointer to Ace list}
      AceTemp: ItemType_Ptr;     {Working pointer for Ace}
      KingFirst: ItemType_Ptr;   {Pointer to King list}
      KingTemp: ItemType_Ptr;    {Working pointer for King}
      N: integer;                {Number of items at store}
      I: integer;                {Loop index}
      None: Boolean;             {Indicator for empty lists}

   begin {BuyLots}

   {*** Initialize}

      AceFirst  := nil;
      KingFirst := nil;
```

Figure 9-2   Two linked lists (continues next page).

```
{*** Get and print lists in a loop}

repeat
  Writeln;
  None := true;

{*** Build the list for Ace Drugs}

  Write('How many items for Ace Drugs: ');
  Readln(N);
  if N < 0 then
    N := 0;

  for I := 1 to N do
    begin
      None := false;
      New(AceTemp);                    {get a data item to use}
      AceTemp^.Next := AceFirst;       {link the new item to list}
      AceFirst := AceTemp;             {new item is now first}
      with AceFirst^ do
        begin
          Write('Enter the item: ');
          Readln(Item);
          Write('Enter the quantity: ');
          Readln(Quantity)
        end {with}
    end; {for}

{*** Build the list for King Groceries}

  Write('How many items for King Groceries: ');
  Readln(N);
  if N < 0 then
    N := 0;

  for I := 1 to N do
    begin
      None := false;
      New(KingTemp);                   {get a data item to use}
      KingTemp^.Next := KingFirst;     {link the new item to list}
      KingFirst := KingTemp;           {new item is now first}
      with KingFirst^ do
        begin
            Write('Enter the item: ');
            Readln(Item);
          Write('Enter the quantity: ');
          Readln(Quantity)
        end {with}
    end; {for}
```

Figure 9-2 (continues next page)

```
            Writeln;

        {*** Print the shopping lists}

            Writeln('Here is your shopping list: ');

        {*** Print the list for Ace Drugs}

            Writeln('From Ace Drugs: ');
            while AceFirst <> nil do
                begin
                    with AceFirst^ do
                        begin
                            Writeln(' You want ', Quantity, ' ', Item, ' ');
                            AceTemp := AceFirst;      {save for later disposal}
                            AceFirst := Next;         {delete from list}
                            Dispose(AceTemp)          {dispose of item}
                        end; {with}
                end; {while}   {*** Print the list for King Groceries}

            Writeln('From King Groceries: ');
            while KingFirst <> nil do
                begin
                    with KingFirst^ do
                        begin
                            Writeln(' You want ', Quantity, ' ', Item, ' ');
                            KingTemp := KingFirst;    {save for later disposal}
                            KingFirst := Next;        {delete from list}
                            Dispose(KingTemp)         {dispose of item}
                        end; {with}
                end {while}

        until None;

            Writeln(' *** Shopping list is empty');

        {*** Terminate program}

    end.
```

Figure 9-2 (continued)

Advantages of Pointers

In the previous examples, we introduced the concept of pointer variables and to one frequently used application, linked lists. We trust you have a feel for how they can be useful in programs and why learning more details is worthwhile. Some of the advantages of using pointers are as follows:

Efficiency. By appropriate use of pointers, we can sometimes make our programs run faster and use less storage space. It is rare to find a technique that features both of these advantages.

Flexibility. We find that the use of pointers allows us more flexibility in planning data storage. You have already encountered some situations with arrays where you had to make some guesses for array sizes without knowing with confidence how big the arrays should be.

Higher-Level Programming. Pointers allow us to build data structures that often more closely reflect the real-world task we are tackling. Having the appropriate data structure makes the task of programming more enjoyable and makes it easier for us to write correct programs.

Disadvantages of Pointers

Pointers provide us with a powerful mechanism that can be used to make our programs better or worse. The are major advantages but disadvantages as well:

Conceptual Difficulty. Pointers are difficult to understand, and the context in which they are used is usually complex. So at times, it may be difficult to keep our algorithms and data structures under control and the program may be more difficult to understand (than a similar one that does not employ pointers).

Reduced Readability. Our programs that use pointers are difficult to read because of the notation and the indirectness of reference. We should attempt to choose names wisely and use comments to help alleviate this problem.

Lower-Level Programming. If we are not careful, we may allow pointers to lead us into lower-level rather than higher-level programming. Pointers allow us to build useful data structures, but pointers also allow us to think in terms of memory addresses instead of structures. Anyone who has programmed a computer in machine or assembler language realizes the essential harshness of a low-level programming environment.

Hidden Side Effects. If we use pointers incorrectly or unwisely, we may find hidden side effects due to complicated data dependencies in our programs. Some nasty surprises can lurk in hidden side effects.

Using Pointers to Advantage

As programmers, we cannot afford to ignore any technique that can be useful. If a technique can be misused (and most can), then we must strive to discover the circumstances in which the technique is most beneficial and let those circumstances serve as a cue as to when to use the technique. It is important to keep in mind that there are usually many alternative ways to handle a programming situation, ranging from perfectly appropriate to grossly inappropriate. The hallmark of a good programmer is the ability to select the best technique for the job. In view of the possible bad effects that pointers can have on our programming, we offer some advice on their use:

Limit the Use of Pointers. Do not overuse pointers in your programs. Make sure that you can justify every one of the pointers that you use.

Use Pointers Appropriately. The inappropriate use of pointers can confuse you and can cause your programs to behave unpredictably.

Learn About Data Structures. To really make effective use of pointers, you should know about the important types of data structures and when and how to use them. There are several different levels of textbooks (and computer science courses) dedicated to data structures.

DPT

1. We should use pointers only when they are appropriate to the problem at hand. As with any powerful concept, we have the tendency to overuse pointers in situations where standard variables would do the task as effectively.

2. Avoid low-level programming if the nature of the task indicates that you should be operating on a higher level of abstraction. There are tasks closely related to a computer's hardware that are best done with low-level techniques, but most programs should operate as closely as possible to the context in which the problem is stated rather than in terms of the machine being used to solve it.

3. The use of pointers can cause a phenomenon known as **aliasing**, a situation where a single data item has two or more different references. The danger is that any of the references can modify the data item and the others will encounter a hidden side effect. This situation can happen in the sequence

```
New(First);
{put some data into First^}
Temp := First;
Dispose(First)
```

The assignment Temp := First makes the pointers aliases; they both refer to the same data item. Therefore, when we execute the statement Dispose(First), we also lose the data item associated with Temp. One can easily forget that Temp no longer points to a valid data item; in fact, Temp has become a dangling pointer, and any use of it results in a (perhaps major) unwanted side effect.

4. Never use a pointer variable until it is assigned a value by an assignment statement or by the New procedure. An uninitialized pointer points to some chance place in memory, and its use causes unpredictable results.

5. Never use a pointer variable after use of the Dispose procedure; the pointer is now dangling.

6. Declare a pointer type before the type declaration for the "pointed-to" data items. This order of declaration is always valid, whereas the other order is illegal if the pointer type is used within the declaration of the other type.

7. Avoid reference to what a pointer points to when that pointer is nil. This is similar, in many ways, to avoiding references to arrays using subscripts that are out of range. For example, suppose we chose to use a *repeat* loop to print the list for King Groceries. We might write

```
        Writeln('From King Groceries: ');
        repeat
          with KingFirst^ do
            begin
              Writeln(' You want ', Quantity, ' ', Item, '.');
              KingTemp  := KingFirst; {save for later disposal}
              KingFirst := Next;      {delete from list}
              Dispose(KingTemp)       {dispose of item}
            end; {with}
        until KingFirst = nil
```

This works unless the list is empty. If the list is empty, the first reference to KingFirst^.Quantity (in the Writeln statement) causes a run-time error.

REVIEW

Terms and Concepts

aliasing
caret (^)
dangling pointer
dynamic
last in, first out (LIFO)
linked list
(memory) address

nil
New
node
pointers
stack
static

Pascal Syntax

1. Declare a pointer type:

```
type
    SomeType_Ptr = ^SomeType;
    SomeType = definition of the type;
```

2. Declare a pointer variable:

```
var
    pointername: SomeType_Ptr;
```

3. Assign a value to a pointer:

   (a) To indicate that it is not pointing at any data item:

   pointername := **nil**

   (b) To get a newly allocated data item:

   New(*pointername*)

   (c) To have it refer to an existing data item:

   pointername := *another pointer name*

or

```
pointername := @variable of type pointer can point to
```

4. Access the information of the data item:

```
pointername^
```

Pointername^ is used as we would use a variable name for the data item

5. Dispose of an unneeded data item:

```
Dispose(pointername)
```

DPT

1. Use pointers only when appropriate to the problem.
2. Avoid low-level programming.
3. Be wary of aliasing.
4. Don't use a pointer until it is assigned a value.
5. Don't use a pointer after it has been disposed of.
6. Declare the pointer type before the pointed-to type.
7. Avoid reference to what a pointer points to when the pointer is nil.

EXERCISES

1. Write declarations for the following:
  (a) A named type for strings of maximum length 30.
  (b) A named pointer type to the string type of part (a).
  (c) Two variables of the string type.
  (d) Two pointer variables to items of the string type of part (a).

2. Suppose that we have a data structure for students set up as follows:

```
type
  StudentType_Ptr = ^StudentType;
  StudentType = record
      Name: string[50];
      SSN: string[9];
      Roommate: StudentType_Ptr
    end;

var
  AnyOne: StudentType_Ptr;
  Student1: StudentType;
```

Assume that a program has been processing some student information.
  (a) How could you test to find if Student1 has a roommate?
  (b) How could you test to find if the student referred to by AnyOne has a roommate?

(c) Print the name of Student1.
(d) Print the name of the student referred to by AnyOne.
(e) Assign the student referred to by AnyOne as the roommate of Student1.

3. Define a data structure for members of a gourmet club that includes the following information for each member: name, favorite dessert, and spouse.

4. Suppose that we have a data structure for books defined as

   ```
   type
       BookType_Ptr = ^BookType;
       BookType = record
           Author: string[50];
           Title: string[80];
           Year: string[4];
           Comment: string[80];
           Next: BookType_Ptr
       end;

   var
       Head: BookType_Ptr; {Pointer to first book}
       Temp: BookType_Ptr; {Working pointer to book}
   ```

   Suppose that a program has built a list of books so that the first book on the list is referred to by the pointer Head, the last book on the list has its pointer Next set to nil, and each of the other books on the list has the pointer Next set to the next book on the list. (This is similar to the examples in this section.)

   (a) Write a condition to test if the list is empty.
   (b) Write a condition to test if there is exactly one book on the list.
   (c) Suppose that the pointer Temp refers to a book not on the list. Write a Pascal code fragment that puts that book at the front of the list.
   (d) Suppose that the pointer Temp does not refer to any data item. Write code to obtain a data item for Temp and put that data item at the front of the list. Record the following information for the new book:

   > author: Douglas Master
   > title: The World of Imagined Worlds
   > year: 1977
   > comment: a book about role-playing games

   (e) Write a THINK code fragment to delete the first book from the list if the list is not empty; if the list is empty, do nothing.
   (f) Assume that there are at least two books on the list. Write a Pascal fragment to delete the second book from the list.
   (g) Assume that there are at least two books on the list. Write a Pascal fragment to move the second book to the first position on the list.
   (h) Write a Pascal fragment to count the number of books on the list.
   (i) Write a Pascal fragment to print the information for the first book on the list. Assume that the list is not empty.
   (j) Write a Pascal fragment to print the information for the last book on the list. Assume that the list is not empty.
   (k) Write a Pascal fragment to delete the last book on the list. Assume that the list has at least two books.

(l) Write a Pascal fragment to delete the last book on the list. Assume that the list has at least one book.

(m) Write a Pascal fragment to delete the last book on the list, if any; handle the case where the list might be empty.

5. Modify the shopping-list data structure discussed in this section so that there are two different data types for the two different stores. Add a unit price field to the Ace Drugs record and add unit price and coupon discount fields to the King Groceries record.

   (a) Make all modifications that are necessary to the program of Figure 9-2 to reflect the new data structures.

   (b) Add code to your program of part (a) to obtain a total cost of the shopping list at each store. Assume that the coupon discount is subtracted from the price of one item only.

   (c) Modify your program for part (b) so that no item is added to the shopping list if the quantity is less than 1.

6. Use the data structure of the program of Figure 9-2 to write a program with the following body:

```
begin
  repeat
     New(AceFirst)
  until false
end.
```

Predict what happens when you run the program. Run the program and see what happens. What would happen if you added the statement "Dispose(AceFirst)" after "New(AceFirst)" in the loop?

7. (a) Use the data structure of the program of Figure 9-2 to write a program that creates an empty list, and then tries to print the first node. Predict what happens when you run the program. Run the program and see what happens.

   (b) Modify the program to create a list with one node, and then try to print two nodes.

8. Predict the behavior of the following program and then run it to see what happens:

```
program Aliases;

var
  X: ^integer;
  Y: ^integer;

begin
  Y := 2;
  X := 5;
  Writeln(X^, Y^)
end.
```

9. Run both of the following programs below and check the execution times with a stopwatch.

```
program Transfers;

  var
    X, Y: string;
    I: integer;
```

EXERCISES

```
begin
  X := '**************************************************';
  for I := 1 to 30000 do
     Y := X
end.

program Transfers;

  var
    X, Y: ^string;
    I: integer;

begin
  New(X);
  X^ := '**************************************************';
  for I := 1 to 30000 do
     Y := X
end.
```

Which is faster? Why, do you think?

9-2 USING POINTER VARIABLES

In this section, we use examples to illustrate pointer use in more detail. In the first example, we refine the sample program of the previous section that dealt with linked lists. The second example gives an application involving sorting that illustrates a somewhat different use of pointers. This serves only as an introduction to the topic; a course in data structures and algorithms typically goes into much more detail.

Linked Lists

The example of the previous section introduced some techniques for representing a list using pointers to link the individual list items. Specifically, the program in Figure 9-2 initialized two lists, read values for them, and printed them (disposing of the nodes at the same time). In this subsection, we rewrite the program with a few changes.

As you read the program in Figure 9-2, you may have said to yourself, "This program does exactly the same things for the two lists. Wouldn't it be possible to generalize the program by using subprograms?" That is exactly what we do in this section.

There are two obvious candidates for subprograms in that program:

Reading a list

Printing and deleting a list

However, we can visualize programs where printing and deleting would be totally separate activities. We, therefore, separate those activities.

In addition to these three subprograms, which apply specifically to the program at hand, we develop some "utility" modules. They are

a module to create an empty list
a module to see if a list is empty
a module to create a node with the values filled in

These modules can be used as they are, or modified slightly, for inclusion in almost any program that deals with linked lists. At first glance, they may seem to be too trivial to be worthy of submodules. (The first two are one line each.) However, they do hide information about the details of the data structure from the main program. This is part of what we mean when we talk about programming at a high level rather than a low level.

Before we write the submodules, let us see what the main program declarations and body look like using these modules. Refer to Figure 9-3. As you can see, it is much "cleaner" than the previous version. It deals with the "what" of the program, delegating the details to its submodules. Moreover, if the exact form used to represent the lists is modified in the future, we need to make only minor changes to the main module, mostly in the declarations.

Notice the use of Empty to set the variable None used for loop control.

```
program BuyLots;

{Written by: XXXXXXXXX XX/XX/XX}
{Purpose:    To maintain two small shopping lists}
{Procedures used: ReadList  - to read a linked list}
{                 PrintList - to print the values of a linked list}
{                 DeleteList - to delete a list, disposing of the nodes}
{                 NewList   - to create an empty linked list}
{                 Empty     - to see if a list is empty}

   type
      String20 = string[20];
      ItemType_Ptr = ^ItemType;
      ItemType = record
            Quantity: integer;     {Number to buy}
            Item: String20;        {Item to buy}
            Next: ItemType_Ptr     {Pointer to list next}
         end;
   var
      AceFirst: ItemType_Ptr;   {Pointer to Ace list}
      KingFirst: ItemType_Ptr;  {Pointer to King list}
      None: Boolean;            {Indicator for empty lists}

{Submodules are declared here}

begin {BuyLots}

{*** Initialize}
   NewList(AceFirst);
   NewList(KingFirst);
```

Figure 9-3   Pointers and procedures: first cut (continues next page).

9-2 USING POINTER VARIABLES

```
{*** Get and print lists in a loop}
  repeat
     Writeln;
{*** Build the lists and see if both are empty}
     ReadList('Ace Drugs', AceFirst);
     ReadList('King Groceries', KingFirst);
     None := Empty(AceFirst) and Empty(KingFirst);
{*** Print the shopping lists}
     Writeln('Here is your shopping list: ');
     PrintList('Ace Drugs', AceFirst);
     PrintList('King Groceries', KingFirst);
{*** Delete the shopping lists}
     DeleteList(AceFirst);
     DeleteList(KingFirst)
  until None;
  Writeln(' *** Shopping list is empty');
{*** Terminate program}
end.
```

Figure 9-3   (continued)

Now let us write the subprograms, beginning with the utilities. The function to see if a list is empty needs one parameter: the list to check. If we call that ListHead, then the body is simply

```
Empty := (ListHead = nil)
```

Using the same name for the parameter for the NewList procedure, we have the procedure body:

```
ListHead := nil
```

Notice that ListHead is an output parameter and is, therefore, defined as a var parameter. Finally, the Create function is of the pointer type. Given the values for the record that will be the new node, it calls New to create the node, and then fills in the values. We choose NewQuant, NewItem, and NewNext for the three parameters and write the body as

```
New(Temp);
with Temp^ do
  begin
     Quantity := NewQuant;
     Item := NewItem;
     Next := NewNext
  end; {With}
Create := Temp
```

Temp is a local pointer variable used to build up the answer; the last step assigns the answer to the function name.

The ReadList procedure is generalized from the two segments of code that were used to read the two separate lists. We use an output parameter ListHead to represent the pointer to the beginning of the list that is being read. In addition, we have an input parameter that contains the list name for use in the prompt. The body of the procedure is

```
Write('How many items for ', ListName, ': ');
Readln(N);
if N < 0 then
  N := 0;
for I := 1 to N do
  begin
     Write('Enter the item: ');
     Readln(NewItem);
     Write('Enter the quantity: ');
     Readln(NewQuant);
     Temp := Create(NewQuant, NewItem, nil);
     Temp^.Next := ListHead;    {link the new item to list}
     ListHead := Temp;          {new item is now first}
  end {for}
```

The variables N, I, and Temp are local variables that play roles analogous to similar variables in the original program. Specifically, Temp is a pointer to the new node (obtained by using the Create function). This new node is placed on the front of the list by making its Next field point to what was the list head, and then having the list head point to it. PrintList is similar; we adapted it from the printing portions of the previous program. The parameters are the list name and the pointer to the first node in the list (both are input). The body is

```
Writeln('From ', ListName, ': ');
NodeToPrint := ListHead;
while NodeToPrint <> nil do
  begin
     with NodeToPrint^ do
       Writeln(' You want ', Quantity, ' ', Item, '.');
     NodeToPrint := NodeToPrint^.Next
  end {while}
```

Notice the use of the pointer variable NodeToPrint to traverse the list. The step

```
NodeToPrint := NodeToPrint^.Next
```

represents a standard way to move on to the next node in a list. It is similar in intent to the step I := I + 1 to move on to the next item in an array. (Likewise, NodeToPrint := ListHead, which starts at the front of the list, is similar in intent to I := 1, which starts at the front of the array.)

Finally, the code to delete the list is extracted from the loops that deleted and printed in the original program:

```
while ListHead <> nil do
  begin
     NodeToDelete := ListHead;       {Save for later disposal}
     ListHead := ListHead^.Next;     {Delete from list}
     Dispose(NodeToDelete)           {Dispose of item}
  end; {while}
```

9-2 USING POINTER VARIABLES

ListHead is an update parameter that points to the first node in the list to be deleted, and NodeToDelete is a local pointer used to keep track of the node to be disposed when ListHead is advanced to the next node. Figure 9-4 contains the complete program.

Saving Both Space and Time with Pointers

In this section, we present an example that shows how the use of pointers can provide dramatic savings of both space and time. The context of the example is that we are to read a list of an unknown number of students, with the relevant information for each student including the name, section number, and grade. We wish to sort the list by name and print the list. We organize the data for an individual student in a standard manner:

```
NameType = string[50];
SectionType = integer;
GradeType = char;
StudentType = record
    Name: NameType;
    Section: SectionType;
    Grade: GradeType
  end;
```

Now, in this example, we do not know the number of students, so it is difficult to guess an accurate size for the list of students. We do not wish to use the linked-list techniques because of the requirement that we must sort the data by name, which requires fast access to the various elements of the list. An array appears to be the appropriate data structure for the student list. However, if we use an array of StudentType, then each unused array element is costing us about 24 memory locations. To play it safe, we set the array size to some large number such as 5000. We will be requiring approximately 120,000 memory locations for our student list even if we only have 25 students in the list for some particular run of the program. To save space, we use an array of pointers for the student list. We declare the list as follows:

```
const
   MaxNumber = 5000;  {Maximum size for list}

type
   NameType = string[50];
   SectionType = integer;
   GradeType = char;
   StudentType_Ptr = ^StudentType;
   StudentType = record
       Name: NameType;
       Section: SectionType;
       Grade: GradeType
     end;
   StudentArray = array [1..MaxNumber] of StudentType_Ptr;

var
   Student: StudentArray;            {Array of pointers}
```

```
program BuyLots;

{Written by:   XXXXXXXXX XX/XX/XX}
{Purpose:      To maintain two small shopping lists}
{Procedures used: ReadList   - to read a linked list}
{                 PrintList  - to print the values of a linked list}
{                 DeleteList - to delete a list, disposing of the nodes}
{                 NewList    - to create an empty linked list}
{                 Empty      - to see if a list is empty}

   type
      String20 = string[20];
      ItemType_Ptr = ^ItemType;
      ItemType = record
          Quantity: integer;            {Number to buy}
          Item: String20;               {Item to buy}
          Next: ItemType_Ptr            {Pointer to next item}
        end;

   var
      AceFirst: ItemType_Ptr;      {Pointer to Ace list}
      KingFirst: ItemType_Ptr;     {Pointer to King list}
      None: Boolean;               {Indicator for empty lists}

      function Create (NewQuant: integer; NewItem: String20; NewNext:
                       ItemType_Ptr): ItemType_Ptr;

{Written by:   XXXXXXXXX XX/XX/XX}
{Purpose:      To create a new node and fill in the values}
{Parameters:   NewQuant - input, the quantity for the new node}
{              NewItem  - input, the item name for the new node}
{              NewNext  - input, the pointer field for the new node}
{Procedures used: New - (built-in) gets a data item}

   var
      Temp: ItemType_Ptr;     {Temporary copy of answer}

begin {Create}
  New(Temp);
  with Temp^ do
    begin
      Quantity := NewQuant;
      Item := NewItem;
      Next := NewNext
    end; {With}

  Create := Temp
end; {Create}
```

Figure 9-4 Pointers and procedures: refined (continues next page).

```
function Empty (ListHead: ItemType_Ptr): boolean;

  {Written by:   XXXXXXXXX XX/XX/XX}
  {Purpose:      To see if a list is empty}
  {Parameters:   ListHead - input, the list to check (that is, a}
  {                         pointer to the list's first item)}

begin
  Empty := (ListHead = nil)
end; {Empty}

procedure NewList (var ListHead: ItemType_Ptr);

  {Written by:   XXXXXXXXX XX/XX/XX}
  {Purpose:      To create an empty list}
  {Parameters:   ListHead - output, the list created}

begin {NewList}
  ListHead := nil
end; {NewList}

procedure ReadList (ListName: string; var ListHead: ItemType_Ptr);

  {Written by:   XXXXXXXXX XX/XX/XX}
  {Purpose:      To create a list by reading from the terminal}
  {Parameters:   ListName - input, the "name" of the list}
  {              ListHead - update, the list created (assumed to be nil}
  {                         when ReadList is invoked)}
  {Functions used: Create - to create one node for the list}

  var
    N: integer;                {Number of items for list}
    I: integer;                {Loop index}
    Temp: ItemType_Ptr;        {Pointer to temporary node}
    NewItem: String20;         {Item to add to list}
    NewQuant: integer;         {Quantity to add to list}

begin {ReadList}
  Write('How many items for ', ListName, ': ');
  Readln(N);
  if N < 0 then
    N := 0;

  for I := 1 to N do
    begin
      Write('Enter the item: ');
      Readln(NewItem);
      Write('Enter the quantity: ');
      Readln(NewQuant);
      Temp := Create(NewQuant, NewItem, nil);
      Temp^.Next := ListHead;        {link the new item to list}
      ListHead := Temp;              {new item is now first}
    end {for}

end; {ReadList}
```

Figure 9-4   (continues next page).

```
procedure PrintList (ListName: string; ListHead: ItemType_Ptr);
  {Written by:  XXXXXXXXX XX/XX/XX}
  {Purpose:     To print a list}
  {Parameters:  ListName - input, the "name" of the list}
  {             ListHead - input, the list to be printed (that is, a}
  {                        pointer to the first node)}
  var
    NodeToPrint: ItemType_Ptr;     {traverses the list}
begin {PrintList}
  Writeln;
  Writeln(' From ', ListName, ': ');
  NodeToPrint := ListHead;

  while NodeToPrint <> nil do
    begin
      with NodeToPrint^ do
        Writeln(' You want ', Quantity, ' ', Item, '.');
      NodeToPrint := NodeToPrint^.Next
    end {while}

end; {PrintList}

procedure DeleteList (var ListHead: ItemType_Ptr);
  {Written by:  XXXXXXXXX XX/XX/XX}
  {Purpose:     To delete a list by disposing of all its nodes}
  {Parameters:  ListHead - update, the list to be deleted (its value}
  {             is nil when deletion is completed}
  {Procedures used:  Dispose - (built-in) to dispose of one node}
  var
    NodeToDelete: ItemType_Ptr;    {Traverses the list}
begin

  while ListHead <> nil do
    begin
      NodeToDelete := ListHead;         {save for later disposal}
      ListHead := ListHead^.Next;       {delete from list}
      Dispose(NodeToDelete)             {dispose of item}
    end {while}

  end; {DeleteList}

begin {BuyLots}
{*** Initialize}
  NewList(AceFirst);
  NewList(KingFirst);

{*** Get and print lists in a loop}
  repeat
    Writeln;
```

Figure 9-4   (continues next page).

{*** Build the lists and see if both are empty}

      ReadList('Ace Drugs', AceFirst);
      ReadList('King Groceries', KingFirst);
      None := Empty(AceFirst) and Empty(KingFirst);

{*** Print the shopping lists}

      Writeln('Here is your shopping list: ');
      PrintList('Ace Drugs', AceFirst);
      PrintList('King Groceries', KingFirst);

{*** Delete the shopping lists}

      DeleteList(AceFirst);
      DeleteList(KingFirst)

  until None;

  Writeln(' *** Shopping list is empty')

{*** Terminate program}

  end.

Figure 9-4   (continued)

If there are no students on the list, the array of pointers occupies approximately 20,000 memory locations. If we run the program with 25 students on the list, then, using pointers, we utilize approximately 20,000 memory locations as compared to 265,000 memory locations using a standard array. (And since THINK allows only 64,000 locations for all of static storage, we could not use a standard array approach with more than about 1200 students.)

Now that we have seen the space savings of the technique, we look at the time savings. We intend to sort names by using a version of the quicksort algorithm discussed in Chapter 6. Computer runs have shown that assignment statements using pointers to StudentType records are faster than assignment statements using StudentType records directly. Since quicksort uses assignment statements for swapping data items, we can expect significant time savings by using pointers.

We now discuss each of the modules of the example and indicate where the use of pointers has made a difference in the program.

The main program has the steps:

  initialize the number of students to 0
  while still students to read in
      add the student to the list using AddStudent
  while not in sorted order
      sort the student list by name using NameSort

> loop for I going from 1 to the number of students
>> print the student record for Ith student using PrintStudent

We see that the three major modules of the program are AddStudent, NameSort, and PrintStudent.

The AddStudent procedure has the single parameter Done, a Boolean type, which indicates when the user is finished. The procedure has the steps:

> set number of students to number plus 1
> get a new data item using New
> read student name from the user
> if the name is empty then:
>> set Done to true
>> return the data item using Dispose
>> set number of students to number minus 1
> otherwise:
>> set Done to false
>> read the section and grade from the user

Notice that, by using pointers, we have need of the New and Dispose procedures. In the actual procedure, we refer to the record as Student[Number]^ instead of as Student[Number]; we would use the latter if the array contained student data directly, rather than pointers to student data.

The NameSort procedure is an adaptation of the QuickSort procedure presented in Chapter 6. We have made very few changes, which are as follows:

1. We have called the sort NameSort and the partitioning procedure NamePartition.
2. We have eliminated the first parameter of both procedures.
3. We have used the global type NameType for the Pivot variable.
4. We have changed all references of the form A[expression] to the form Student[expression] ^ .Name.
5. We have declared the variable Temp to be a pointer for use in swapping.
6. We have replaced the use of the Swap procedure with the three-statement swapping logic.

These few changes allow quicksort to be used in a very different context than that of Chapter 6.

The procedure PrintStudent simply prints the information for the Ith student on one line. The only evidence of the use of pointers is in the one statement that refers to the record as Student[Number]^ instead of as Student[Number], which we would use were it not for the pointers.

The example program is presented in Figure 9-5 with the changes given before in italics.

```
program Efficiency;

{Written by:     XXXXXXXXX XX/XX/XX}
{Purpose:        To illustrate the use of arrays of pointers}
{Procedures used:  AddStudent    - adds a student to the list}
{                  NameSort      - sorts by student name}
{                  PrintStudent  - prints a student record}

   const
      MaxNumber = 5000;      {Maximum list size}

   type
      NameType = string[50];
      SectionType = integer;
      GradeType = char;
      StudentType_Ptr = ^StudentType;
      StudentType = record
          Name: NameType;
          Section: SectionType;
          Grade: GradeType
        end;
      StudentArray = array[1..MaxNumber] of StudentType_Ptr;

   var
      Student: StudentArray;        {Array of pointers}
      Number: integer;              {Actual number of students}
      I: integer;                   {Loop index}
      Done: Boolean;                {Indicator for finished}

   procedure AddStudent (var Done: Boolean);

      {Written by:     XXXXXXXXX XX/XX/XX}
      {Purpose:        To get student information and add to list}
      {Parameters:     Done - output, indicates finished when true}
      {Procedures used:  New      - (built-in) gets new data item}
      {                  Dispose - (built-in) returns data item}
      {Globals used:   Number - actual number of data items, updated}
      {                MaxNumber - maximum number for list, used}

      const
         EndOfData = '';              {Terminating value}
```

Figure 9-5   Array of pointers (continues next page).

```
      begin {AddStudent}
        if Number >= MaxNumber then
          Done := true
        else
          begin
            Number := Number + 1;
            New(Student[Number]);        {Get new data item}
            with Student[Number]^ do
              begin
                Write(' Name (Empty to quit): ');
                Readln(Name);
                if Name = EndOfData then
                  begin
                    Done := true;
                    Dispose(Student[Number]);  {Return data item}
                    Number := Number - 1
                  end
                else
                  begin
                    Done := false;
                    Write(' Section: ');
                    Readln(Section);
                    Write(' Grade (A,B,C,D,E): ');
                    Readln(Grade)
                  end
              end {with}
          end

    end; {AddStudent}

    procedure NamePartition (Low, High: integer; var PivotLocation:
                             integer);

      {Written by:   XXXXXXXXXX XX/XX/XX}
      {Purpose:      To partition an array into three parts:}
      {    1. values less or equal to the pivotal element}
      {    2. the pivotal element}
      {    3. values greater than or equal to the pivotal element}
      {Parameters:  Low, High     - the portion of the array to partition}
      {             PivotLocation - the location for the pivotal element}
      {                             (sent back to the calling module)}

      var
        I: integer;                      {used to locate large values}
        J: integer;                      {used to locate small values}
        Pivot: NameType;                 {the pivotal element}
        Temp: StudentType_Ptr;           {for swapping}
```

Figure 9-5   (continues next page).

```
      begin {Partition}
        I := Low;
        J := High + 1;
        Pivot := Student[Low]^.Name;
      repeat

   {*** Move 1 to right looking for value >= the pivot}

          repeat
            I := I + 1
          until (I = High) or (Student[I]^.Name >= Pivot);

   {*** Move J to left looking for value <= the pivot}

          repeat
            J := J - 1
          until Student[J]^.Name <= Pivot;

   {*** Swap if the values are out of order}

          if I < J then
            begin
              Temp := Student[I];
              Student[I] := Student[J];
              Student[J] := Temp
            end {if}
        until I >= J;

   {*** Put pivotal element in the proper place and return the value of }
   {    its subscript to calling module}

        Temp := Student[Low];
        Student[Low] := Student[J];
        Student[J] := Temp;

        PivotLocation := J

      end; {Partition}

      procedure NameSort (Low, High: integer);

        {Written by:   XXXXXXXXXX XX/XX/XX}
        {Purpose:      To sort students by names, using quicksort}
        {Parameters:   Low, High - the portion of the array to sort}

        var
          PivotSub: integer;   {location of pivotal element}

      begin {NameSort}
        if Low < High then
          begin
            NamePartition(Low, High, PivotSub);
            NameSort(Low, PivotSub - 1);
            NameSort(PivotSub + 1, High)
          end {if}
      end;     {NameSort}
```

Figure 9-5   (continues next page)

```
    procedure PrintStudent (I: integer);

      {Written by:  XXXXXXXXX XX/XX/XX}
      {Purpose:     To print the student record for one student}
      {Parameters:  I - input, index of student to print}

    begin {PrintStudent}
      with Student[I]^ do
        begin
          Writeln(Section : 6, ' ', Name, ' ' : 50 - Length(Name), Grade)
        end {with}
    end; {PrintStudent}

  begin {Efficiency}

  {*** Initialize}

    Number := 0;

  {*** Get students}

    repeat
      AddStudent(Done)
    until Done;

  {*** Sort the data}

    NameSort(1, Number);

  {*** Print the student records}

    Writeln;
    Writeln('            Student Records');
    Writeln('            ---------------');
    Writeln('Section       Name', ' ' : 40, ' Grade ');

    for I := 1 to Number do
      PrintStudent(I)

  {*** Terminate}

  end.
```

Figure 9-5 (continued)

EXERCISES

1. For the program of Figure 9-4, revise the ReadList procedure to read an unknown number of list items, terminated by an appropriate terminal value.
2. Modify the program of Figure 9-4 to create 10 lists. Use an array of list names and an array of pointers to the first item in each list.
3. Why does the Create function in Figure 9-4 need the Temp variable? Why not just write

   ```
   New(Create);
   with Create^ do . . .
   ```

4. In the ReadList procedure of Figure 9-4, we use Create to fill in the quantity and item portion of the new record, but we fill in the Next portion ourselves. Tell how to modify the steps so that the Create call completes the entire record.
5. The comments for the ReadList procedure in Figure 9-4 say that it assumes the list is empty when the procedure is called. By hand-tracing the procedure with a non-empty list, find what happens if the list is not empty upon entry to the procedure.
6. (a) Given is a segment of code for searching in an array. By examining the intent of each step of that code, write a segment of code for searching in a linked list. (Use the linked-list structure of the program of Figure 9-4.)

```
Found := false;
while (not Found) and (I <= N) do
  begin
    if A[I] = Key then
       Found := true
    else
       I := I + 1
  end; {while}

if Found then
  Locate := I
else
  Locate := 0;
```

(b) Write the code of part (a) as a function that returns a pointer to the node that contains the desired value or nil if there is no such node.
(c) In linked-list applications, it is often useful to obtain a pointer to the node just before the one that contains the desired value. Assuming that there is such a node and that it is not the first node, write a segment of code to accomplish this. Hint: Modify part (b).
(d) Write a procedure with the parameters that follow, using the linked list structure from the program of Figure 9-4. The procedure's purpose is to report the position of a given item in a list and establish a pointer to the list entry before the given item.

   A pointer to the first node of a list — input.
   A value to look for — input.
   An indication of the result (either NotFound, First, or NotFirst - use a user-defined type) — output.
   A pointer to the node before the one with the value (only defined if NotFirst is the result) — output.

(e) By using the procedure of part (d), write a segment of code to insert a new node containing the entry "2 toothpaste" in the list right before the entry for vegetable soup. Assume that vegetable soup is in the list.
(f) Repeat part (e), but put the new entry in the front of the list if vegetable soup is not in the list.

7. Write procedures or functions for each of the parts of Exercise 4 of Section 9-1.
8. Modify the program of Figure 9-5 by using a Create procedure in the AddStudent procedure.
9. Modify the program of Figure 9-5 by using the selection sort of Chapter 6 in place of the NameSort procedure that is shown. Use the discussion of the changes that were made to quicksort for NameSort to guide your modifications.

10. Redo the program of Figure 9-5 by using a linked list as the data structure. You will want to perform a simpler sort, such as one of the selection sorts, rather than quicksort. Compare the performance of your program with that of the program of Figure 9-5.

11. Write a function that returns a pointer to the Nth record on the student list using the data structure of Figure 9-5.

12. Write a function that returns a pointer to the Nth record of the data structure for your program of Exercise 10.

13. Modify the program of Figure 9-5 so that it prints the students in reverse order.

14. What would be needed to print the students in reverse order in your program of Exercise 10?

15. Modify the program of Figure 9-5 so it prints only the students who have received a particular user-specified grade.

16. Modify your program of Exercise 10 so that it prints only the students who have received a particular user-specified grade.

17. Modify the program of Figure 9-5 so that instead of printing all of the students, it asks the user for a student name and prints the information for that student. Use a binary search (see Chapter 6) to locate the correct student.

18. Modify the program of Figure 9-5 so that it obtains the student information from a text file with three lines per student. Offer a menu of options for the user that includes the following:

    Displaying all students

    Printing all students on the printer

    Displaying a specified student (by binary search)

    Changing a grade for a specified student (by binary search)

    Calculating the average grade for the students (using 4 for A, 3 for B, 2 for C, 1 for D, and 0 for F)

10 Recursion

OBJECTIVES

We were introduced to recursion in Chapter 4 and used it with arrays in Chapter 6. In this chapter, we take a more in-depth and focused look at the topic. By the end of the chapter, you will be able to:

- use recursion as a problem-solving strategy
- implement recursive solutions as recursive subprograms in Pascal
- analyze the running time and storage use of THINK Pascal routines
- determine when to choose recursion or some other method when alternative solutions to a problem exist

10-1 THINKING RECURSIVELY

Problem-Solving Tools

One way to view computer programming is in the broader context of problem solving. When we are presented with a problem in the "real world," it is not often obvious which line of attack leads most fruitfully to a solution. Problem solvers through the ages have developed strategies and techniques that can be helpful aids for any problem-solving effort. We have already discussed some of these tools in the text; a list of some useful tools is as follows:

- **Historical Approach.** If someone has already solved the problem, why reinvent the solution? Classical algorithms, such as the Euclidean Algorithm for the greatest common divisor and quicksort, are often well-done algorithms that can be used with few or no changes.

- **Reasoning by Analogy.** Many problems are analogous to problems that we or others have solved. With the proper changes, we can find that an old solution solves a new problem.
- **Divide and Conquer.** We have continually emphasized the advantages of simplifying a problem by cutting it into "bite-size" pieces. We have used the concept of modularity to utilize this problem-solving tool.
- **Geometric Methodology.** When appropriate, the theory and techniques of geometry can provide leverage for solving problems.
- **Algebraic Methodology.** When appropriate, the theory and techniques of algebra provide powerful tools for dealing with problems.
- **Analytic Methodology.** When appropriate, the theory and techniques of mathematical analysis, as commonly encountered in calculus courses, prove to be an effective tool for solving problems.
- **Statistical Methodology.** When appropriate, the methods of probability and statistics can provide quick, effective solutions to a wide class of problems.
- **Simulations.** Often, the best way to solve a real-world problem is to simulate it in a simpler computerized environment. Simulating the situation allows the possibility of testing the proposed solution thousands or millions of times in order to test the behavior of the solution repeatedly.
- **Recursion.** When applicable, recursion can provide a solution that is almost magical in its simplicity and effectiveness.

A good problem solver will become fluent with all of these tools. It is as important to know which tools are inappropriate as it is to know which tools are appropriate for a given problem. We should not remain ignorant of any area of problem-solving methodology; there may be times when a particular method is the only one that works. In addition, as we will see, it is better to have two solutions to a problem than just one because we can now choose the better solution for our context. Also, having two solutions to a problem means that we can use each method to test the other for correctness. There are many times when we can be confident that having two different solutions for a problem that provide the same results means that both solutions are correct. So recursion is an important problem-solving technique when it provides an alternate solution to a problem, even if the recursive solution is not the one that is finally selected as the better of the two.

The Templates of Recursion

Recursion is often seen in the context of problems that depend on one or more positive integers that in some way measure the size of the problem. A classical example is provided by the factorial function Factorial(N), which is recursively defined (and solved) by

$$\text{Factorial}(N) = N * \text{Factorial}(N-1), \text{ for } N > 0$$
$$= 1, \text{ for } N = 0$$

An algorithm for the factorial of N is

```
if N = 0 then
    Factorial := 1
else
    Factorial := N * Factorial(N - 1)
```

The simple factorial example provides evidence for the general recursive strategy:

1. Solve the previous problem in terms of smaller instances of the same problem. For the previous problem, Factorial(N) := N * Factorial(N – 1).
2. Decide what to do with the base case(s) of the problem. For the previous problem, Factorial(0) := 1.

Observe that "smaller" means "closer to the base case(s)."

This strategy also applies for problems that deal with more than one measure of size. For example, the coefficient of the mth term of the binomial raised to a power, $(a + b)^n$, is given by the **combinatorial coefficient** C(n, m), which is defined by

$$C(n, m) = 1, \text{ if } m = 0 \text{ or } m = n$$
$$= C(n - 1, m) + C(n - 1, m - 1), \text{ otherwise}$$

These numbers are often presented via a device called **Pascal's Triangle**; it is named after Blaise Pascal, the same person for which the Pascal programming language is named.

```
 1                    1  1
 2                  1  2  1
 3                1  3  3  1
 4              1  4  6  4  1
 5            1  5 10 10  5  1
 6          1  6 15 20 15  6  1
 7        1  7 21 35 35 21  7  1
 8      1  8 28 56 70 56 28  8  1
 9    1  9 36 84 126 126 84 36  9  1
10  1 10 45 120 210 252 210 120 45 10  1
```

For each line of the triangle, the value of m begins with 0 on the left and moves to 1, 2, ... Thus, the fifth row of the triangle has values of m as shown:

			m			
n	0	1	2	3	4	5
5	1	5	10	10	5	1

Thus, we can see from the table that

$$C(5, 2) = C(4, 1) + C(4, 2)$$
$$10 = 4 + 6$$

Note that our concept of a "smaller case" when we are dependent on two integers is interpreted as "either (or both) of the integers is smaller." This moves us closer to the base cases.

Reversing a String

We turn to the problem of reversing a string, making the last character first and so on. If the given string is "Joan Smith", then the reversed string is "htimS naoJ". The main point of this example is that the size of a case is not always directly available. In this case, the measure of size is the number of characters in the string. Let us denote the reversed form of a string S by Reversed(S). Then our recursive formulation is

> to calculate Reversed(S):
> let x be the first character of S
> let T be S with the first character removed
> Reversed(S) is Reversed(T) + x

Thus, if S is "plum", then x is "p", T is "lum", Reversed(T) is "mul", and Reversed(T) + x is "mulp". What is the basis case for this example? There are two choices that naturally present themselves:

> If S is null, then Reversed(S) is S.
>
> If S has exactly one character, then Reversed(S) is S.

We choose the former alternative to provide a slightly more general algorithm for reversing the string S. We use the built-in Copy function of THINK Pascal to extract substrings of a string. The substring of a string S, which consists of all of S except the first character, is thus Copy(S, 2, Length(S) – 1), where the built-in function Length provides the number of characters of S. You can refer to Chapter 8 for more details of string handling. The algorithm is

> if S is null, then
>   Reversed := S
> else
>   S := Reversed(Copy(S, 2, Length(S) – 1)) + S[1]

We saw an example of sorting numbers recursively in Chapter 6 with the quicksort algorithm. In this subsection, we consider two other sorting techniques that can be done recursively. For each example, we assume that an array X has been passed to the sorting routine Sort, along with the lower and upper limits of the array to be sorted (in that order). For example, suppose the first several members of the array X have values as shown:

subscript	1	2	3	4	5	6	7	8	9
value	33	10	50	–8	5	8	9	44	3

Then, after invoking Sort(X, 3, 7), X would appear as follows:

subscript	1	2	3	4	5	6	7	8	9
value	33	10	–8	5	8	9	50	44	3

The first example is a variation of the **selection sort** algorithm presented in Chapter 6 in which we repeatedly move the larger elements of the array to the right. The recursive idea is to move the largest element to the right and then call ourselves recursively to deal with all but the last element in the specified range. The algorithm for the selection sort version of Sort(X, First, Last) is as follows:

>if First >= Last then
>>return without doing anything
>
>else
>>interchange the largest of X[First]..X[Last] into position X[Last]
>>invoke Sort(X, First, Last-1)

The only redeeming virtue of this selection sort is that it can be so simply described. The process of exchanging the largest value to position X[Last] is accomplished via the following algorithm:

>set Large to X[First] and set Place to First
>loop for I going from First + 1 to Last
>>if X[I] > Large, then set Large to X[I] and set Place to I
>
>set X[Place] to X[Last] and set X[Last] to Large

The second example is called the **merge sort** and is slightly more complex than the selection sort. The basic idea is to divide the range of X to be sorted into roughly half, to sort each half, and to merge the two results. Suppose we want to sort the numbers

>50 −8 5 8 9

Our procedure is to divide the numbers into two parts:

>50 −8 5   and   8 9

Then, we sort the two parts into:

>−8 5 50   and   8 9

Finally, we merge the two parts into:

>−8 5 8 9 50

Of the two basic tasks to be done, sorting the parts and merging the results, the easier of the two is the sorting because we simply call ourselves recursively to do that. If we assume for the moment that the merging of the results is already defined, then our algorithm for the merge sort invocation of Sort(X, First, Last) is:

>if First >= Last then
>>return
>
>else
>>set Middle to (First + Last) div 2
>>invoke Sort(X, First, Middle)
>>invoke Sort(X, Middle + 1, Last)
>>merge the results

Actually, the merging process is not too difficult if we use an auxiliary array Temp to merge into. The algorithm for merging the sorted parts X[First], . . . , X[Middle] with X[Middle + 1], . . . , X[Last] is as follows:

>set LPlace to First
>set RPlace to Middle + 1
>set I to First

```
[work with both halves, while neither exhausted]
while LPlace <= Middle and RPlace <= Last do
    if X[LPlace] <= X[RPlace] then
        set Temp[I] to X[LPlace] and set LPlace to LPlace + 1
    else
        set Temp[I] to X[RPlace] and set RPlace to RPlace + 1
    set I to I + 1

[work with one half, when other exhausted]
if LPlace > Middle, then
    set Start to RPlace and set Finish to Last
else
    set Start to LPlace and set Finish to Middle
loop for XPlace from Start to Finish
    set Temp[I] to X[XPlace] and set I to I + 1

[copy from Temp to X]
loop for I going from First to Last
    set X[I] to Temp[I]
```

This algorithm is a bit heavy with notation, but the concept is an example of a "two-finger" algorithm: set the left finger to the first element of the first part and set the right finger to the first element of the second part; then, whichever element is smaller is moved to Temp and that finger moves; when either part is exhausted, then the other part moves to Temp one by one. We suggest that the reader try the two-finger version of the algorithm on a small example and then try to see that the more formal algorithm accomplishes the same task.

Note that in both sorting examples that we have discussed, the base case is reached when the range of the array to be sorted contains at most one element and then we do nothing but return.

Subsequences and Substrings of a String

In this section, we consider two routines that are of the general class that is sometimes called **predicates**. In each case, the routine simply reports whether a situation is true or false.

For our first case study, we are interested in whether a given string is a **subsequence** of another given string. We consider one string to be a subsequence of another if all the characters of the first string appear in the second string in the same order. It is not necessary that the characters of the first string appear consecutively in the second string. Here are some examples of subsequences of strings:

STRING	SUBSEQUENCE OF THE STRING
abcdefghijkl	bdgl
apple	pl
banana	ann
house	house
abc	(empty string)

The recursive idea in determining if one string is a subsequence of another is to locate the first character of the first string within the second, and then ask recursively if the rest of the first string is a subsequence of the rest of the second string. The base cases are as follows:

1. If the first string is null, the predicate is true.
2. If the first string is not null and the second string is null, the predicate is false.

The reason the empty string is a subsequence of any other string is that it must be true that "all of the characters of the empty string appear in the second string and in the same order." An algorithm for determining if the string InSeq is a subsequence of the string InString is:

    To calculate the predicate SubSeq(InSeq, InString):
      if InSeq is null then
        set SubSeq to true
      else if InString is null then set SubSeq to false
      else
        set Place to the leftmost location of InSeq[1] in InString
        if Place is 0 (not found), then
          set SubSeq to false
        else
          set SubSeq to SubSeq(Right(InSeq, 2), Right(InString, Place + 1))

In this algorithm, we are assuming the existence of the string-valued function Right that is given a string and a position and returns all the characters of the string that come after that position.

We turn now to a related problem of recognizing whether a string is a substring of another string. We note that the built-in THINK Pascal function Pos accomplishes this task and more because it identifies the starting location of the substring within the string. However, we discuss this problem without using the Pos function in order to explore a recursive solution.

The recursive approach is: If the first string is not the same as the leading several characters of the second string, then we check to see if the first string is a substring of the second string from its second character onward. The base cases are as follows:

1. If the first string is null, the predicate is true.
2. If the length of second string is less than the length of first string, the predicate is false.

An algorithm for determining if the string InSub is a substring of the string InString is as follows:

    To calculate SubString(InSub, InString):
      if InSub is null, then set SubString to true
      else if Length(InString) < Length (InSub), then
        set SubString to false
      else if InSub is equal to Left(InString, Length(InSub)) then
        set SubString to true
      else
        set SubString to SubString(InSub, Right(InString, 2))

In this algorithm, we assume the availability of the string function Right as discussed earlier and we also assume the existence of the string function Left, which is given a string and a position and returns all the characters of the string up to and including the specified position.

Some Counting Problems

In this section, we consider a few counting problems of varying degrees of difficulty.

For our first problem, we attempt to count the number of strings of length N that can be made by an alphabet of M letters. For example, if we use the alphabet consisting of 'a' and 'b' (M = 2) and ask for strings of length 3, then we have the following complete list:

aaa
bbb
aab
aba
baa
abb
bab
bba

The recursive idea for this problem is that we can produce all strings of length N using M letters by first producing all strings of length N – 1 using M letters and then prefixing each of them with each of the M letters. If we use the notation StringsNM(p, q) to denote the number of strings of length p using q letters, then the recursive counting formula is

$$\text{StringsNM}(n, m) = m * \text{StringsNM}(n - 1, m)$$

The basis case is that StringsNM(1, m) = m. Therefore, the algorithm for counting strings of length N using M letters is

To calculate StringsNM(n, m):
  if n is equal to 1 then
    set StringsNM to m
  else
    set StringsNM to m times StringsNM(n – 1, m)

Let us turn next to the problem of counting the number of divisors of an integer N. First, we consider some examples:

N	DIVISORS	NUMBER OF DIVISORS
1	1	1
2	1, 2	2
3	1, 3	3
4	1, 2, 4	3
5	1, 5	2
6	1, 2, 3, 6	4
7	1, 7	2

8	1, 2, 4, 8	4
9	1, 3, 9	3
10	1, 2, 5, 10	4
11	1, 11	2
12	1, 2, 3, 4, 6, 12	6

How do we approach this problem recursively? An obvious choice for measuring the size of the problem is to use the magnitude of the number itself. So, to use recursion, we must decide on a method of meaningfully reducing the size of the number. When dealing with divisors of a number, it is not a good idea to reduce the size by subtracting 1 because the divisors of a number N and the number N − 1 do not relate to one another. A better choice for reducing size is to divide the number by one of its factors. The resulting number is smaller in magnitude and shares some of the same divisors as the original number. This observation provides the crucial insight into this problem.

Our approach is to find the smallest divisor of the number and divide by it. The question is: How do we relate the divisors of the smaller number with the divisors of the larger number? If we study the previous table of divisors, we do not see an easy relationship between the divisors of 6 (12 divided by 2) and 12. However, if we look at the divisors of 3 and the divisors of 4, we see that the number of divisors of 12 is equal to the number of divisors of 3 times the number of divisors of 4. So our procedure is as follows:

To calculate the number of divisors of N:

1. Let S be the smallest divisor of N (note that S is prime).
2. Let S^K be the highest power of S that divides into N evenly.
3. The number of divisors of N is equal to (K + 1) times the number of divisors of N divided by S^K (note that K + 1 is the number of divisors of S^K because S is prime).

The basis case for this process is the number 1 because the number of divisors of the number 1 is 1. According to our procedure, we see that the number of divisors of 72 is 12 because, using the previous notation, N is 72, S is 2, and K is 3.

Our next problem is to calculate the number of ways to express a positive integer as a sum of positive integers where we don't distinguish different orderings (that is, we consider 2 + 1 and 1 + 2 to be the same). For example, the number 6 can be expressed in the following ways:

$$6$$
$$1 + 5$$
$$2 + 4$$
$$3 + 3$$
$$1 + 1 + 4$$
$$1 + 2 + 3$$
$$2 + 2 + 2$$
$$1 + 1 + 1 + 3$$
$$1 + 1 + 2 + 2$$
$$1 + 1 + 1 + 1 + 2$$
$$1 + 1 + 1 + 1 + 1 + 1$$

Note that we include 6 itself as a degenerate form of a sum. The way we choose to organize the sums in this problem is by the lowest factor that appears in the sum. This organization for the number 6 appears as follows:

Lowest factor = 1:	1 + 1 + 1 + 1 + 1 + 1
	1 + 1 + 1 + 1 + 2
	1 + 1 + 2 + 2
	1 + 2 + 3
	1 + 1 + 4
	1 + 5
Lowest factor = 2:	2 + 2 + 2
	2 + 4
Lowest factor = 3:	3 + 3
Lowest factor = 6:	6

Our procedure for counting the number of ways to express N as a sum is to count the number of ways to express N as a sum using I as the lowest factor for I = 1, 2, 3, ..., N. So far, we haven't used any recursive ideas. Let us use the notation AddendsAux(N, I) to represent the number of ways to express N as a sum using I as the lowest factor. The recursive idea is to recognize that

$$\begin{aligned} \text{AddendsAux}(N, I) = &\text{AddendsAux}(N - I, I) + \\ &\text{AddendsAux}(N - I, I + 1) + \\ &\text{AddendsAux}(N - I, I + 2) + \\ &\quad\cdot \\ &\quad\cdot \\ &\quad\cdot \\ &\text{AddendsAux}(N - I, N - I) \end{aligned}$$

The basis for our procedure has two cases:

1. If N = 1, then AddendsAux is 1.
2. Otherwise, if I > N div 2, then AddendsAux is 0.

Let us use the notation Addends(N) to denote the number of ways to express N as a sum of positive integers. Then our algorithms are as follows:

```
To calculate Addends(N):
    set Total to 0
    loop for I going from 1 to N
        set Total to Total + AddendsAux(N, I)

To calculate AddendsAux(N, I):
    if N is equal to I then
        set AddendsAux to I
    else if I is greater than N div 2 then
        set AddendsAux to 0
```

    else
        set Total to 0 loop for J going from I to N–I
        set Total to Total + AddendsAux(N–I, J)

A Power Set of a Set

A mathematical set is an unordered collection of distinct objects often presented as a list using notation such as

$$\{a, b, c\}$$
$$\{1, 0\}$$
$$\{b, a, c\}$$

Since order is not important, the two sets $\{a, b, c\}$ and $\{b, a, c\}$ are the same. A set may have no elements; in this case, it is referred to as the **empty set** and we can denote it as $\{\ \}$. A **subset** of a set is any second set, all of whose elements are members of the first set. Thus, some subsets of $\{a, b, c\}$ are

$$\{\ \}$$
$$\{a\}$$
$$\{b, c\}$$
$$\{a, b, c\}$$

A problem sometimes arises that involves the consideration of all subsets of a given set. Let us begin with the question: How many subsets does a given set have? A recursive solution to this counting problem can be formulated as follows (we use $\{a, b, c\}$ as an example):

To calculate the number of subsets of S, Subs(S):
    suppose that S is the given set   [S = $\{a, b, c\}$]
    let x be any member of S   [x = b, for example]
    let A be S with x removed   [A = $\{a, c\}$]
    note that any subset of S is either a   [$\{a\}$ is of the first kind]
        subset of A or can be derived from a   [$\{b, a\}$ is of the second kind]
        subset of A by adding x to the subset of A
Thus, Subs(S) = 2 * Subs(A)

The basic recursive idea here is illustrated by listing all of the subsets of $\{a, c\}$:

$$\{\ \}$$
$$\{a\}$$
$$\{c\}$$
$$\{a, c\}$$

If we augment each of these by adding the element b, we get the following list:

$$\{b\}$$
$$\{b, a\}$$
$$\{b, c\}$$
$$\{b, a, c\}$$

Together, these two lists of subsets contain all of the subsets of the original set $\{a, b, c\}$:

$$\{\ \}$$
$$\{a\}$$
$$\{b\}$$
$$\{c\}$$
$$\{a, b\}$$
$$\{a, c\}$$
$$\{b, c\}$$
$$\{a, b, c\}$$

What is the basis case for counting subsets? The natural choice is the empty set, which has exactly one subset (itself). Thus, an algorithm for counting subsets of a set can be presented as follows:

To calculate the number of subsets of a set of n elements, NSubs(n):

```
if n = 0 then
    NSubs := 1
else
    NSubs := 2 * NSubs(n – 1 )
```

Our discussion has provided us with the means of solving a slightly more difficult problem: that of collecting all of the subsets of a set S. The algorithm for collecting the subsets of S is

```
if S is empty then just collect { }
else
    choose any element x from S
    let A be S with x removed
    let Cl be the collection of all of the subsets of A
    let C2 be the collection of all of the subsets of A with x added to each
    our answer is the union of Cl with C2
```

An interesting exercise in recursion is to trace this algorithm to see in what order the subsets of S appear in the final collection. Suppose that the following scenario is followed in choosing x at each level of recursion:

Level 1: $S = \{a, b, c\}$, choose $x = a$
Level 2: $S = \{b, c\}$, choose $x = b$
Level 3: $S = \{c\}$, choose $x = c$
Level 4: $S = \{\ \}$, collection is $\{\{\ \}\}$
Level 3: Collection is $\{\{\ \}, \{c\}\}$
Level 2: Collection is $\{\{\ \}, \{c\}, \{b\}, \{b, c\}\}$
Level 1: Collection is $\{\{\ \}, \{c\}, \{b\}, \{b, c\}, \{a\}, \{a, c\}, \{a, b\}, \{a, b, c\}\}$

10-1 THINKING RECURSIVELY

Mutual Recursion

We now illustrate the idea of two **mutually recursive** subprograms, that is, each subprogram invokes the other. We use as the context of our discussion the concept of **prefix** arithmetic expressions.

When we symbolically represent the arithmetic expression for the sum of the numbers 2 and 3, we usually write

$$2 + 3$$

This form is known as the **infix** form of the expression. The prefix form of the expression is

$$+23$$

We keep all of our numbers as single digits for simplicity in this discussion and offer extensions in the exercises. We allow for two arithmetic operations, "+" and "*", representing addition and multiplication, respectively. One advantage of the prefix form is that parentheses are unnecessary. In the infix form, with the usual notions of precedence and associativity, we must use parentheses to denote "the product of 2 with the sum of 3 and 4," as shown:

$$2 * (3 + 4)$$

Without parentheses, the expression 2 * 3 + 4 has the value of 10, not the value of 14. However, we can represent our expression in prefix notation as

$$*2+34$$

The table shows some more examples of the prefix form:

INFIX FORM	PREFIX FORM	VALUE
2 * (3 + 4)	*2+34	14
2 * 3 + 4	+*234	10
(2 + 3) * (4 + 5)	*+23 + 45	45
2 + 3 + 4 + 5	+++2345	14
2 + (3 + (4 + 5))	+2+3+45	14
4	4	4

Our intention is to write an algorithm for the evaluation of prefix expressions. We use three main routines to accomplish the evaluation process.

The first routine, called Eval, accepts a prefix expression and returns its value. At first thought, this seems to be no more than the top-level routine, until we realize that there are often several prefix subexpressions to evaluate during the evaluation of the whole expression. Eval must be able to handle the simplest prefix expression that contains a single number with no operators. If we look at the second and third columns of the table, we see some examples of the behavior of Eval.

The second routine, called Apply, accepts an operator and an expression that can be split into the two operands for the operator. Apply returns the value attained by applying the operator to the operands. Some examples of the behavior of Apply are shown in the table:

Op	InString	Apply(Op, InString)
+	23	5
+	*234	10
*	45	20
*	2+34	14
*	+23+45	45

The third main routine, called Split, accepts an expression and splits it into two operands. Let us refer to the two operands as First and Second. The behavior of Split is shown with some examples in the following table:

InString	First	Second
23	2	3
*234	*23	4
45	4	5
2+34	2	+34
+23+45	+23	+45

The Eval routine has two cases: Either it is dealing with a single number or it has an expression whose first character is an operator. The algorithm for Eval is as follows:

> if the expression is a number then
>   return the numeric value
> else
>   call Apply with the leading operator and the rest of the expression

So we see that Eval leaves the hard work for Apply.

The Apply routine must divide the expression into the two parts and then apply the operator to the two parts *after they are evaluated*. The algorithm for Apply is as follows:

> use the Split routine to divide the expression into the two parts, First
> and Second, depending on the operator:
> '+': return Eval(First) + Eval(Second)
> '*': return Eval(First) * Eval(Second)

We will see that the Split routine is not really very difficult, so that Apply leaves the hard work for Eval to do (it's only fair).

The Split routine must find the point at which the expression is to be divided into two operands. By studying a few examples, we see that the dividing point comes just after there is exactly one more number than operators as we view the expression from left to right. Review the previous table to see that this idea is correct. The algorithm for Split is as follows:

> set the variable Count to 0
> scan the expression from left to right, looking at single characters:
>   if the character is an operator then
>   set Count to Count − 1
>   if the character is a number then
>   set Count to Count + 1
>   when Count becomes equal to 1, divide the expression into two parts
>   just after the current character

Let us now trace these algorithms through an example. We begin with attempting to evaluate the expression +2*34. We explicitly trace only the Eval and Apply calls, assuming that Split works properly.

Level 1:	We invoke Eval with the parameter +2*34.
	Eval sees that the first character is the operation + and
Level 2:	invokes Apply with the parameters + and 2*34. Apply invokes Split with the parameter 2*34 and receives back the two parts 2 and *34.
	Apply
Level 3:	invokes Eval with the parameter 2.
	Eval sees the character '2' and returns the number 2.
Level 2:	Apply
Level 3:	invokes Eval with the parameter *34. Eval sees that the first character is the operation * and
Level 4:	invokes Apply with the parameters * and 34. Apply invokes Split with the parameter 34 and receives back the two parts 3 and 4.
	Apply
Level 5:	invokes Eval with the parameter 3. Eval sees the character '3' and returns the number 3.
Level 4:	Apply
Level 5:	invokes Eval with the parameter 4. Eval sees the character '4' and returns the number 4.
Level 4:	Apply applies the operation '*' to the numbers 3 and 4 and returns the number 12.
Level 3:	Eval receives the number 12 from Apply and returns the number 12.
Level 2:	Apply applies the operation '+' to the numbers 2 and 12 and returns the number 14.
Level 1:	Eval receives the number 14 from Apply and returns the number 14 to us.

The following diagram may help you follow the tracing. This diagram was constructed during the hand-tracing and represents the entire execution of the algorithm for the given input.

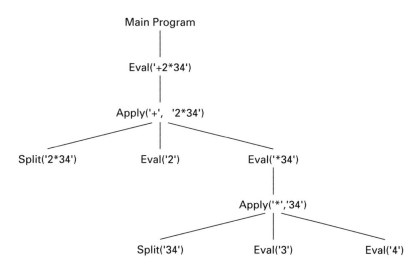

After tracing such a simple example and seeing the complexity of the behavior of the process, we may be mystified by the simplicity of the algorithms for Eval, Apply, and Split as compared to their synergistic behavior. The answer to the paradox of simplicity producing complexity is that the recursive process itself takes care of a substantial amount of bookkeeping, thus relieving the programmer of the easy but error-fraught steps of keeping track of who is invoking whom and who returns what to whom. We trust the example presented here dramatically illustrates the power of recursive thinking.

REVIEW

Terms and Concepts

algebraic methodology
analytic methodology
combinatorial coefficient
divide and conquer
empty set
geometric methodology
historical approach
infix
merge sort
mutually recursive

Pascal's Triangle
predicates
prefix
reasonig by analogy
recursion
selection sort
simulations
statistical methodology
subsequence
subset

EXERCISES

1. For each of the problem-solving strategies listed at the beginning of this section, find a problem that is best solved using the particular strategy.
2. Evaluate each of the following:
   (a) Factorial(8)
   (b) Factorial(0)

(c) C(5, 3)
   (d) C(1000, 0)

3. Write the eleventh row of Pascal's Triangle.
4. Hand-trace the execution of the algorithm for Reversed on the input string "fun".
5. Hand-trace the execution of the algorithm for merge sort on the array 3, 5, 7, 2, 1, 8, 6, 5.
6. Which of the following are subsequences of the string "abcdefg"?
   (a) abcdefg
   (b) gfedcba
   (c) a
   (d) (empty)
   (e) aa
   (f) beg
   (g) ach
7. Which of the following are substrings of the string "abcdefg"?
   (a) abcdefg
   (b) a
   (c) (empty)
   (d) aa
   (e) beg
   (f) def
8. (a) For the string InString, write an expression for Right(InString, 3) in terms of the built-in function Copy.
   (b) Write an expression for Right(InString, N).
9. (a) For the string InString, write an expression for Left(InString, 3) in terms of the built-in function Copy.
   (b) Write an expression for Left(InString, N).
10. Write all strings of length 2 using the three-letter alphabet {a, b, c}.
11. Write all of the divisors of 72.
12. Use the algorithm for counting divisors to calculate the number of divisors of 72.
13. Write all of the ways to represent the number 7 as a sum of positive integers.
14. Hand-trace the function Addends(7).
15. Write all of the subsets of {a, b, c, d}.
16. Hand-trace the function NSubs(3).
17. Translate the following infix expressions into prefix form:
    (a) 4 + 5 + 6
    (b) 4 * 3 + 2
    (c) (3 + 3) * (2 + 1)
    (d) 1 +2*3+4
    (e) 1 + ((2 + 3) + 4)
18. Evaluate the following prefix expressions:
    (a) ++123
    (b) +*123
    (c) *+123
    (d) **123

(e) +1*23
(f) *1+23
(g) +*1+2*3+456

19. Hand-trace the Eval–Apply–Split algorithms on the expressions +1*23 and +*1+2*3+456.

20. Enhance the set of valid prefix expressions by including the unary operator $, which means to square the biggest prefix subexpression that lies to the right. Some examples:

$+23 is equal to 25
+$23 is equal to 7
+2$3 is equal to 11
*2$+12 is equal to 18

21. Write a recursive algorithm to count the number of ways to divide a string of length N into pieces. For example, the divisions for the string "aaa" are

aaa
a aa
a a a
aa a

22. Write a recursive algorithm to generate r-digit binary sequences (strings of 0's and 1's) with no adjacent 0's. For example, the sequences for r = 4 are

1111
1110
1101
1011
0111
1010
0101
0110

23. Think of ways to represent some of the data objects that we have discussed in this section:
   (a) Sets of letters a, b, c, ...
   (b) Collections of sets of letters a, b, c, ...
   (c) Prefix expressions
   (d) N-by-N chessboards
   (e) N-by-N chessboards containing at most one queen per column
   (f) Collections of N-by-N chessboards

24. There are three basic ingredients to a *backtracking* algorithm:

   • a way to order the possible actions at each stage, so you do not keep trying the same one
   • a way to record the actions taken, and to "back up" the action after the recursive call returns
   • a way to know when a successful solution is reached

   A classic group of problems amenable to solution by backtracking involves *graph traversal*. For example, suppose you want to list all the paths from node 1 to node 5 in the following diagram, where the arrows indicate one-way streets. You do not want to revisit any node on the way. (One possible path is 1 → 4 → 5.)

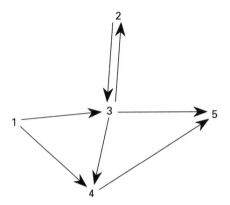

(a) Describe ways to handle the three basic ingredients mentioned before for a backtracking solution.
(b) Carry out a backtracking solution by hand.
(c) Repeat part (b) for this graph. You want to get from node 1 to node 7.

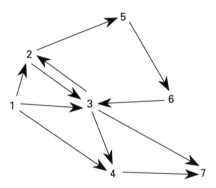

(d) Describe a general algorithm for solving the problem of traversing from node I to node J in a graph using backtracking.

10-2 RECURSIVE PROGRAMMING

We move in this section from the theory of recursive program design to the practice of using recursion in our programs. We find that it takes more than algorithms for effective recursive programming; we have concerns about data types and scope of variables and we discuss some data representation ideas. We present Pascal code for several examples discussed in the previous section. Only the most important ideas in the code are explicitly discussed; in many cases, the code stands on its own.

Factorial

We expect the code for the Factorial function to be short and simple, and it is; we present it in Figure 10-1. You may be surprised at the type that we have chosen for the Factorial function. The reason for the choice of *real* as the type is that even 8 factorial is larger than maxint. By using the real type, we extend our range to 20 factorial before we begin to experience round-off error. We have a suggestion in the exercises of a way to extend the range further.

The combinatorial coefficients can be calculated by the integer function Combinatorial, as is shown in Figure 10-2. Note that here, as in the case of the Factorial function, the use of var parameters is not only inappropriate, but illegal, because we use expressions in the recursive calls. It is legal to have both recursive calls to Combinatorial appear in the same expression.

```
function Factorial(N: integer): real;

{Written by: XXXXXXXXX XX/XX/XX}
{Purpose:    To calculate N factorial}
{Parameters: N - input, number for computation}

begin {Factorial}
  if N = 0 then
     Factorial := 1
  else
     Factorial := N * Factorial(N - 1)
end; {Factorial}
```

Figure 10-1 Recursive Factorial function.

```
function Combinatorial(N, M: integer): integer;

{Written by: XXXXXXXXX XX/XX/XX}
{Purpose:    To calculate a combinatorial coefficient, recursively}
{Parameters: N - input, row of Pascal's Triangle}
{            M - input, term in the row}

begin {Combinatorial}

{*** See if we're done}

if  (N = M) or (M = O) then
    Combinatorial := 1

{*** If not done, get lower-level values}

    else
      Combinatorial := Combinatorial(N-1, M) + Combinatorial(N-1, M-1)
    end; {Combinatorial}
```

Figure 10-2 Recursive Combinatorial function.

```
function Right (InString: string; Position: integer): string;

    {Written by:    XXXXXXXXX XX/XX/XX}
    {Purpose:       To return a cofinal substring of InString}
    {Parameters:    InString - input, string for substring extraction}
    {               Position - input, position to begin substring}
    {Functions used: Copy - (built-in) to extract a substring}
    {                Length - (built-in) to find the length of a string}

begin {Right}
  if Position < 1 then
    Right := InString
  else if Position > Length(InString) then
    Right := ''
  else
    Right := Copy(InString, Position, Length(InString) - Position + 1)
end; {Right}

function Reversed (InString: string): string;

    {Written by:    XXXXXXXXX XX/XX/XX}
    {Purpose:       To reverse a string}
    {Parameters:    InString - input string to reverse}
    {Functions used: Right - to extract a cofinal substring}

const
  Null = '';      {Empty string}

begin {Reversed}
  if InString = Null then
    Reversed := InString
  else
    Reversed := Concat(Reversed(Right(InString, 2)), InString[1])
end; {Reversed}
```

Figure 10-3 Recursive string reversing function.

Reversing a String

The function Reversed uses the function Right, which extracts a **cofinal** substring of a string. That is, Right returns a substring that starts in some specified position and extends all the way to the end of the string. See Figure 10-3.

Recursive Sorting

In this section, we present two versions of the procedure Sort. For both, we rely on the following set of global declarations:

```
const
  MaxSize = 1000; {Highest subscript}
```

```
type
   BaseType = integer;
   ArrayType = array[1..MaxSize] of BaseType;
```

By using this set of declarations, we can utilize the Sort procedures to sort different types of data by adjusting the definition of BaseType. We can also modify the maximum size of the array to be sorted by adjusting the value of the constant MaxSize.

We show the recursive selection sort in Figure 10-4. Note that the array X is a var parameter and that the procedure does not work otherwise. Another feature worthy of note is that the procedure as presented is not **stable.** A sorting technique is stable if two elements of equal value maintain their order relative to each other. For example, if we were to use our sort of Figure 10-4 on a hypothetical array consisting of a blue 2 followed by a red 2, then the resulting array would consist of the red 2 followed by the blue 2. To remedy this situation, we could change the comparison X[I] > Large to X[I] >= Large. Alternatively, we could change the *for* loop to the form:

```
for I := Last downto First do
```

For the second alternative, we would also want to initialize Large to X[Last] and Place to Last.

We show the recursive merge sort in Figure 10-5. Note that the merge sort procedure is stable because our merge algorithm is stable.

Subsequences and Substrings of a String

Recall that a subsequence of a string consists of zero or more characters of the string in the same order as they appear in the string. It is not required that the characters be consecutive in the string. A substring of a string is a subsequence consisting of consecutive characters of the string. In Figure 10-6, we present code for the Boolean function SubSeq, which determines if one string is a subsequence of another.

In Figure 10-7, we present code for the Boolean function SubString, which determines if one string is a substring of another. In addition to the function Right discussed before, we also use the function Left for extracting a **coinitial** substring of a string. That is, Left returns a substring that starts at the beginning of the string and extends to some specified position.

Strings of Length N Using M Letters

We continue to discuss programs dealing with strings. We show how to count the number of possible three-letter words in the English language (including lots of nonwords). We also illustrate how you might print all of those words, but we do not suggest that you try it. (Think about how many there are.) In Figure 10-8, we show the code for the function StringsNM(P, Q), which counts the number of strings of length P using Q letters. Because these values tend to be large, we use the type *real* for the function.

In the spirit of considering some interesting programming techniques, suppose that we do not just want to count all of the strings, but that we want to print a list of the strings. One way to accomplish this is to use a technique of building the recursive answers from the top

```
procedure Sort(var X: IntArray; First, Last: integer);

{Written by:  XXXXXXXXX XX/XX/XX}
{Purpose:     To sort an array with a recursive selection sort}
{Parameters:  X - update, array to sort}
{             First - input, left limit of portion of array}
{             Last  - input, right limit of portion of array}

    var
       I: integer;         {Loop index}
       Large: ArrayType;   {Largest element}
       Place: integer;     {Place largest element found}

begin {Sort}

{*** Check to see if done}

    if First < Last then
       begin

{*** Find largest element}

          Large := X[First];
          Place := First;

          for I := First + 1 to Last do
             if X[I] > Large then
                begin
                   Large := X[I];
                   Place := I
                end; {if}

{*** Exchange largest value with X[Last]}

          X[Place] := X[Last];
          X[Last]  := Large;

{*** Call upon Sort to do the rest}

          Sort(X, First, Last - 1)
       end {if}

end; {Sort}
```

Figure 10-4 Recursive selection sort.

to the bottom, rather than from the bottom to the top (as we do in building factorials, for example). For simplicity, suppose that we restrict the alphabet of letters to *a*, *b*, and *c*. We design a procedure PrintStrings to print all of the strings of length N using the letters *a*, *b*, and *c* by specifying the parameters:

```
procedure Sort(var X: IntArray; First, Last: integer);}
{Written by: XXXXXXXXX XX/XX/XX}
{Purpose:    To sort an array with a recursive merge sort}
{Parameters: X - update, array to sort}
{            First - input, left limit or portion}
{            Last - input, right limit or portion}

  var
    I: integer;           {Loop index}
    Large: ArrayType;     {Largest element}
    Place: integer;       {Place largest element found}
    Middle: integer;      {Midpoint of First and Last}
    LPlace: integer;      {Place on left half of array}
    RPlace: integer;      {Place on right half of array}
    XPlace: integer;      {Place in X array}
    Start: integer;       {Marks the rest of the . . . }
    Finish: integer;      { . . . array X to copy to Temp}
    Temp: ArrayType;      {Where array parts are merged}

begin {Sort}

{*** Check to see if done}

  if First < Last then
     begin

{*** Sort the bottom and top halves, if necessary}

        Middle := (First + Last) div 2;
        if First < Middle then
           Sort(X, First, Middle);
        if Middle + 1 < Last then
           Sort(X, Middle + 1, Last);

{*** Merge the two halves}

  LPlace := First;
  RPlace := Middle + 1;
  I := First;

  while (LPlace <= Middle) and (RPlace <= Last) do
     begin
        if X[LPlace] <= X[RPlace] then
           begin
              Temp[I] := X[LPlace];
              LPlace := LPlace + 1
           end
        else
           begin
              Temp[I] := X[RPlace];
              RPlace := RPlace + 1
           end; {if}
        I := I + 1
     end; {while}
```

Figure 10-5 Recursive merge sort (continues next page).

```
        if LPlace > Middle then
           begin
              Start   := RPlace;
              Finish  := Last
           end
        else
           begin
              Start   := LPlace;
              Finish  := Middle
           end; {if}

        for XPlace := Start to Finish do
           begin
              Temp[I] := X[XPlace];
              I := I + 1
           end; {for}

        for I := First to Last do
           X[I] := Temp[I]

     end {if}

  end; {Sort}
```

Figure 10-5 (continued)

StringSoFar — one of the strings still being formed

MoreToAdd — number of letters to be added to StringSoFar

We invoke the procedure to print all of the strings of length N by the call

```
PrintStrings('', N)
```

The algorithm is as follows:

    if MoreToAdd is equal to 0 then
      print StringSoFar
    else
      PrintStrings('a' + StringSoFar, MoreToAdd – 1)
      PrintStrings('b' + StringSoFar, MoreToAdd – 1)
      PrintStrings('c' + StringSoFar, MoreToAdd – 1)

We can see that the algorithm causes the strings to grow as they are passed downward by the recursive calls until there are no more characters to add to the string.

We show the code for the PrintStrings procedure in Figure 10-9.

Number of Divisors of an Integer

In order to implement the algorithm presented in the previous section, we need some help from a few small subprograms. First, we need an integer function Power for raising one integer to the power of the other. This function was discussed earlier in the book and is simply shown as part of Figure 10-10. For example, Power(2, 3) is 8.

```
function SubSeq(InSeq, InString: string): Boolean;

{Written by: XXXXXXXXX XX/XX/XX}
{Purpose:    To determine if InSeq is a {subsequence of InString}
{Parameters: InSeq - input, candidate for subsequence}
{            InString - input, string to check for subsequence}
{Functions used: Right - to extract a cofinal substring}
{                Pos   - (built-in) to find a substring of a string}

  const
    Null = '';                      {Empty string}

  var
    Place: integer;                 {Position of character}

  begin {SubSeq}

  {*** First, take care of empty sequence or string}

    if InSeq = Null then
      SubSeq := true
    else if InString = Null then
      SubSeq := false

  {*** Take care of non-empty sequence and string}

    else
      begin
        Place := Pos(InSeq[1], InString);
        if Place = 0 then
          SubSeq := false
        else
          SubSeq := SubSeq(Right(InSeq, 2), Right(InString, Place+1))
      end {if}

  end; {SubSeq}
```

Figure 10-6 Subsequence of a string.

Second, we need an integer function SmallDivisor that finds the smallest divisor (greater than 1) of a number. This function was discussed in Chapter 4 and is also located within Figure 10-10. For example, SmallDivisor(15) is 3.

Third, we use the integer function Degree that tells us the highest power of a factor that divides into a number. This function can also be found within Figure 10-10. For example, Degree(2, 24) is 3.

Finally, we also present our recursive function in Figure 10-10.

Obtaining a Number as a Sum

In this example, shown coded in Figure 10-11, we use an auxiliary function to provide a more straightforward interface to the calling program. We are ultimately interested in the number of ways that we can sum to a specified number. So at the top level, we want to simply call the integer function Addends, perhaps in a write statement such as

```
function Left(InString: string; Position: integer): string;

{Written by: XXXXXXXXX XX/XX/XX}
{Purpose:    To return a coinitial substring of InString}
{Parameters: InString - input, string for extraction of substring}
{            Position - input, last position for substring}
{Functions used: Copy - (built-in) to extract a substring}
{Length - (built-in) to find the length of a string}

begin {Left}
  if Position < 1 then
     Left := ''
  else if Position > Length(InString) then
     Left := InString
  else
     Left := Copy(InString, 1, Position)
end; {Left}

function SubString(InSub, InString: string): Boolean;

{Written by: XXXXXXXXX XX/XX/XX}
{Purpose:    To determine if SubString is a substring of InString}
{Parameters: InSub - input, candidate for substring}
{            InString - input, string to check for substring}
{Functions used: Length - (built-in) to find length of a string}
{            Left   - to extract a coinitial substring of a string}
{            Right  - to extract a cofinal substring of a sting}

  const
    Null = '';   {Empty string}

begin {SubString}
  if InSub = Null then
     SubString := true
  else if Length(InString) < Length(InSub) then
     SubString := false
  else if InSub = Left(InString, Length(InSub)) then
     SubString := true
  else
     SubString := SubString(InSub, Right(InString, 2))
end; {SubString}
```

Figure 10-7 Substring of a string.

```
Writeln('The number of ways to add to ', N, ' is :', Addends(N))
```

Once inside of Addends, we set up the loop of calls to the Auxiliary function AddendsAux.

The Power Set of a Set

The data structures involved in programming the algorithm as presented in the previous section are beyond the scope of this book. However, in this section, we present a procedure that performs a similar activity. The procedure, WriteSeq, prints all subsequences of a string

```
function StringsNM(N, M: integer): real;

{Written by: XXXXXXXXX XX/XX/XX}
{Purpose:    To count the number of strings of length N}
{            using M letters}
{Parameters: N - input, length of strings}
{            M - input, number of letters in alphabet}

begin {StringsNM}
  if N = 1 then
     StringsNM := M
  else
     StringsNM := M * StringsNM(N - 1, M)
end; {StringsNM}
```

Figure 10-8 Number of strings of a given length.

```
procedure PrintStrings(StringSoFar: string; MoreToAdd: integer);

{Written by: XXXXXXXXX XX/XX/XX}
{Purpose:    To print strings from the alphabet: a, b, c}
{Parameters: StringSoFar - input, string building up}
{            MoreToAdd   - input, number of characters left to add}

begin {PrintStrings}
  if MoreToAdd = 0 then
     Writeln(StringSoFar)
  else
     begin
        PrintStrings('a' + StringSoFar, MoreToAdd - 1);
        PrintStrings('b' + StringSoFar, MoreToAdd - 1);
        PrintStrings('c' + StringSoFar, MoreToAdd - 1)
     end {if}
end; {PrintStrings}
```

SAMPLE INPUT AND OUTPUT

```
<dialogue that supplies the value of MoreToAdd = 2>

aa
ba
ca
ab
bb
cb
ac
bc
cc
```

Figure 10-9 Printing substrings.

10-2 RECURSIVE PROGRAMMING

```
function Power (N, K: integer): integer;

begin
  if K = 0 then
    Power := 1
  else
    Power := Round(Exp(K * Ln(N)))
end; {Power}

function SmallDivisor (N: integer): integer;

  {Written by:    XXXXXXXXX XX/XX/XX}
  {Purpose:       To find the smallest divisor of N > 1}
  {Parameters:    N - input, number for smallest divisor}

  var
    Test: integer;          {Used to check for divisor}

begin {SmallDivisor}
  Test := 2;
  while (N mod Test) <> 0 do
    Test := Test + 1;
  SmallDivisor := Test
end; {SmallDivisor}

function Degree (Factor, Number: integer): integer;

  {Written by:    XXXXXXXXX XX/XX/XX}
  {Purpose:       To find the highest power of Factor that divides Number}
  {Parameters:    Factor - input}
  {               Number - input}

  var
    Total: integer;

begin {Degree}

  Total := 0;
  while Number mod Factor = 0 do
    begin
      Total := Total + 1;
      Number := Number div Factor
    end; {while}

  Degree := Total

end; {Degree}
```

Figure 10-10 Number of divisors of an integer (continues next page).

```
function NumDivisors (N: integer): integer;

   {Written by:     XXXXXXXXX XX/XX/XX}
   {Purpose:        To count the number of divisors of N, recursively}
   {Parameters:     N - input}
   {Functions used: SmallDivisor - to get the smallest divisor of N}
   {                Degree - to get the highest power of a factor}
   {                Power  - to raise an integer to an integer power}

   var
         Factor: integer;               {Smallest divisor of N}
         Multiplicity: integer;

begin {NumDivisors}

{*** See if we're done}

   if N = 1 then
     NumDivisors := 1
   else
     begin

{*** Get smallest divisor of N}

       Factor := SmallDivisor(N);

{*** Use it for recursive call}

       Multiplicity := Degree(Factor, N);
       NumDivisors := (Multiplicity + 1) * NumDivisors(N div
                      Power(Factor, Multiplicity))
     end {if}

end; {NumDivisors}
```

Figure 10-10 (continued)

and is shown in Figure 10-12. If we begin with the string 'abc', then the list of subsequences of the string is

> (empty)
> c
> b
> bc
> a
> ac
> ab
> abc

```
function AddendsAux(N, M: integer): integer;

{Written by: XXXXXXXXX XX/XX/XX}
{Purpose:    To provide the recursive calculation for Addends:}
{            number of ways to add to N using M as the lowest factor}
{Parameters: N - input, number to sum to}
{            M - input, lowest factor in sum}

  var
    I: integer;
    Total: integer;

begin {AddendsAux}
  if M = N then
    AddendsAux := 1
  else if M > N div 2 then
    AddendsAux := 0
  else
    begin
      Total := 0;
      for I := M to N - M do
        Total := Total + AddendsAux(N - M, I);
      AddendsAux := Total
    end {if}
end; {AddendsAux}


function Addends(N: integer): integer;

{Written by: XXXXXXXXX XX/XX/XX}
{Purpose:    To calculate the number of ways to sum to N}
{Parameters: N - input, number to sum to}
{Functions used: AddendsAux - to find sums with lowest factor}

  var
    I: integer;
    Total: integer;

begin {Addends}
  Total := 0;
  for I := 1 to N do
    Total := Total + AddendsAux(N, I);
  Addends := Total
end; {Addends}
```

Figure 10-11 Obtaining sums to a number.

Compare this list of subsequences to the list of subsets of the set {a, b, c} that we discussed in the previous section. We use the basic idea of the algorithm for power sets, but we use the top–down method that we used earlier in this section for printing strings.

The procedure WriteSeq has two parameters:

Prefix: a subsequence in formation

Rest: the remainder of the original string that can be used for further building of subsequences

If our original string is called InString, then at the top level we invoke WriteSeq with the command

```
WriteSeq('', InString)
```

to indicate that no work on subsequences has been done yet, and all of the original string is left to process. At the bottom level, Rest is the null string; at this point, the subsequence that is contained in Prefix can be printed. To see how WriteSeq works "in the middle," suppose that it has been invoked by

```
WriteSeq('ac', 'efg')
```

somewhere in the process of trying to print all the subsequences of the string 'abcdefg'. The recursion consists of making the two recursive calls:

```
WriteSeq('ac', 'fg')
WriteSeq('ace','fg')
```

The first call is for subsequences that do not involve 'e', and the second call is for subsequences that do involve 'e'. In both cases, the length of the parameter Rest is reduced by 1.

```
procedure WriteSeq(Prefix , Rest : string);

{Written by: XXXXXXXXX XX/XX/XX}
{Purpose:    To print subsequences of a string}
{Parameters: Prefix - input, building string}
{            Rest - input, rest of string}
{Functions used: Right - extracts cofinal substring}

  const
    Null = '';              {Empty string}

begin {WriteSeq}
  if Rest = Null then
    if Prefix = Null then
      Writeln('(empty)')
    else
      Writeln(Prefix)
  else
    begin
      WriteSeq(Prefix, Right(Rest, 2));
      WriteSeq(Prefix + Rest[1], Right(Rest,2))
    end {if}
end; {WriteSeq}
```

Figure 10-12 All subsequences of a string.

Mutual Recursion

The main issue of this section is how to reconcile the two conflicting ideas of defining procedures before using them and mutual recursion. From what we have discussed so far, it seems as though we are stuck with one of the two procedures calling the other before the other has been defined, and we know how the compiler deals with that situation—it gives a compile time error message. The solution to the quandary is provided by a mode of declaration known as **forward reference**. The idea is that we let the compiler know about the heading of the subprogram in advance, and present the body of the subprogram later on. For our situation, the order in which we present Apply and Eval to the compiler is

> Declare Apply as a forward reference.
> Define Eval (which uses Apply).
> Define the body of Apply (which uses Eval).

Thus, forward referencing allows us to achieve mutual recursion.

A complete program for the evaluation of prefix expressions is shown in Figure 10-13. We note two points about the syntax of the forward reference:

1. After the normal heading line of any subprogram that is declared as a forward reference, use the suffix "; forward".
2. When the body of the subprogram is defined, we must use an abbreviated form of the heading; we do not list parameters nor specify the type of a function.

We introduce the Code function to help the procedure Split to divide an expression into two pieces. The Code function provides the means for generalizing the program along the lines explored in the exercises.

DPT

1. Recursive algorithms have a good chance of "going off to never-never land" during the early stages of development and testing. Good design heads off most problems, but to be safe, you should save a version of any recursive program before running any test of it.

2. Be careful when using var parameters and global variables from within recursive subprograms. Quite often, you will find the lower levels of the recursion are having undesirable side effects on the upper levels. For example, if you change the loop indices I of Addends and AddendsAux of Figure 10-11 to a single global variable I, you find the program still runs, but produces erroneous results.

Testing

1. We must always test each of the base cases in a recursive solution. Because these cases are the building blocks for all the other cases, it is essential they function correctly.

2. The next level above the base case should be tested to be sure that the reduction to smaller cases is functioning correctly.

```
program PreFix;
{Written by:    XXXXXXXXX XX/XX/XX}
{Purpose:       To evaluate prefix expressions}
{Functions used: Eval - evaluates the expression}
  const
    EndOfData = '';           {Terminating value}
  var
    Expression: string;       {Input expression}
function Code (InChar: char): integer;
  {Written by:    XXXXXXXXX XX/XX/XX}
  {Purpose:       To return a code depending on the character}
  {Parameters:    InChar - input, character to encode}
begin {Code}
  if InChar in ['1'..'9'] then
    Code := 1
  else if InChar in ['+', '*'] then
    Code := -1
  else
    Code := 0
end; {Code}
procedure Split (InString: string; var Left, Right: string);
  {Written by:    XXXXXXXXX XX/XX/XX}
  {Purpose:       To split a string into two parts}
  {Parameters:    InString - input, string to split up}
  {               Left  - output, left part of split string}
  {               Right - output, right part of split string}
  {Functions used: Code   - to get code for character}
  {                Length - (built-in) gets length of string}
  {                Copy   - (built-in) extracts substring}
  const
    Null = '';                   {Empty string}
  var
    Count: integer;              {For operators and numbers}
    I: integer;                  {Loop index}
begin {Split}
  Count := 0;
  I := 0;
  while (Count <> 1) and (I < Length(InString)) do
    begin
      I := I + 1;
      Count := Count + Code(InString[I])
    end; {while}
```

Figure 10-13 Mutual recursion and forward reference (continues next page).

```
      if Count = 1 then
        begin
          Left := Copy(InString, 1, I);
          Right := Copy(InString, I + 1, Length(InString) - I + 1)
        end
      else
        begin
          Left := Null;
          Right := Null
        end {if}
end; {Split}

function Apply (Op: char; InString: string): integer;
forward;

function Eval (InString: string): integer;
  {Written by:    XXXXXXXX XX/XX/XX}
  {Purpose:       To evaluate a prefix expression}
  {Parameters:    InString - input, expression to evaluate}
  {Functions Used:  Apply   - to apply an operator}
  {                 Length  - (built-in) gets length of string}
  {                 Ord     - (built-in) position of character in set}
  {                 Copy    - (built-in) extracts substring}

  const
    Null = '';                          {Empty string}

  var
    FirstChar: char;                    {First character of InString}

begin {Eval}
  if InString = Null then
    begin
      Writeln('*** error in expression ');
      Eval := 0
    end
  else
    begin
      FirstChar := InString[1];
      if FirstChar in ['0'..'9'] then
        if Length(InString) = 1 then
          Eval := Ord(FirstChar) - Ord('0')
        else
          begin
            Writeln('*** error in expression');
            Eval := 0
          end
      else
        Eval := Apply(FirstChar, Copy(InString, 2, Length(InString) - 1))
    end {if}
end; {Eval}
```

Figure 10-13 (continues next page)

```
function Apply;

  {Written by:      XXXXXXXX XX/XX/XX}
  {Purpose:         To apply an operator to two operands}
  {Parameters:      Op - input, operator to apply}
  {                 InString - input, contains operands for operator}
  {Procedures Used: Split - to split InString into operands}
  {Functions Used:  Eval - to evaluate operands}

  var
    First: string;
    Second: string;

begin {Apply}
  Split(InString, First, Second);
  case Op of
    '+':
      Apply := Eval(First) + Eval(Second);
    '*':
      Apply := Eval(First) * Eval(Second);
    otherwise
      Writeln('*** Invalid operator')
  end {case}
end; {Apply}

begin {PreFix}

{*** Get user input until EndofData}

  repeat
    Write('Enter the expression (RETURN to exit): ');
    Readln(Expression);
    if Expression <> EndofData then
      Writeln('The answer is: ', Eval(Expression))
  until Expression = EndofData;

{*** Terminate}

end.
```

Figure 10-13 (continued)

3. When the reduction to smaller cases is different from the simple moving from N to N − 1, we should perform some **error-guessing** tests to see if we can cause the algorithm to skip over the bottom-level cases and plunge into an inescapable abyss.

4. Recursive programs are particularly vulnerable to **stress testing**. It is a good idea to attack a recursive routine with many tests involving maximum-size data.

REVIEW

Terms and Concepts

cofinal
coinitial
error guessing

forward reference
stable
stress testing

Pascal Syntax

Forward Reference

```
header line for subprogram A; forward;
other declarations
abbreviated header line for subprogram A
body of subprogram A
```

DPT

1. Save work before testing.
2. Be careful of var parameters and global variables.

Testing

1. Test each bottom-level case.
2. Test the next level up from the bottom.
3. Practice error guessing.
4. Perform stress testing.

EXERCISES

1. Write a Pascal program that discovers the lowest-numbered factorial that is calculated incorrectly by the function of Figure 10-1.
2. We can extend the range of the factorial function by defining a data structure for representing large integer values. One possibility is to declare the record structure:

```
const
  MaxSize = 1000;

type
  BigInteger = record
    Positive: Boolean;
    NumDigits: integer;
    Digits : array[1..MaxSize] of integer
  end;
```

The array Digits is intended to contain the decimal digits of a number. For example, the number 1024 would be represented in the data structure as

Positive: true

NumDigits: 4

Digits : . . . , 1, 0, 2, 4   (digits are right-justified in the array)

In order to use this new data type to assist in calculating factorials, we need three subprograms:

(1) **procedure** `Init(var BigInt: BigInteger; Value: integer);`

The task for Init is to assign an initial value to a large integer.

(2) **procedure** `Mult(Int: integer; BigInt: BigInteger;`
              `var Product: BigInteger);`

The task for Mult is to allow us to multiply an integer by a large integer in order to perform the step:

(k factorial) = k times (k – 1 factorial)

(3) **procedure** `PrintBig(BigInt: BigInteger);`

The task for PrintBig is to display a large integer on the screen.

Use these ideas just sketched to write a factorial procedure that allows the calculation of large factorials.

3. Suppose that we had a data structure defined as

```
Student = array [1..1000] of record
  Name: string[50];
  Major: string[15]
  end;
```

If we wanted a list of students grouped within their majors and alphabetically by name within each major, then we might sort the Student array first by Name and then by Major.

(a) Discuss the desirability of having a stable sorting algorithm for accomplishing the job.
(b) Write a Pascal program to read in the students and print them out in the order suggested.

4. Use an unstable sort for the program of Exercise 3(b) to observe the effects.
5. Enhance the PrintStrings procedure of Figure 10-9 by adding the letter "d" to the alphabet.
6. Enhance the PrintStrings procedure of Figure 10-9 by allowing the user to input the alphabet into an array.
7. Modify the code of Figure 10-11 so that each of the sums is printed as in this example:

$$1 + 1 + 1$$
$$1 + 2$$
$$3$$

8. Remove error checking from the function Right and cause it to have a run-time error.
9. Remove error checking from the function Left and cause it to have a run-time error.
10. Change the WriteSeq procedure so it maintains a global variable Count that can be printed after all subsequences have been printed.

EXERCISES

11. Generalize the program of Figure 10-13 as suggested in Exercise 21 of Section 10-1.
12. Write a program to print 10 rows of Pascal's Triangle.
13. Write a program to perform the algorithm of Exercise 22 of Section 10-1.
14. Write a program to perform the algorithm of Exercise 23 of Section 10-1.
15. Write a program to perform the algorithm of Exercise 25 of Section 10-1.

10-3 RECURSION, ITERATION, OR . . . ?

In this section, we consider questions of efficiency in the design and coding of our programs. We present tools for measuring the space and time our programs use and consider alternative methods for the solution of several of the examples we discussed in the previous two sections. We close the section with a list of points to summarize our discussion of recursion.

Program Measurements

When we are comparing alternative ways to solve a problem with a computer, we should consider the following categories:

1. Use of processing time
2. Use of memory space
3. Time to develop the program
4. Time to debug the program
5. Time to maintain the program

As a general rule, recursive solutions tend to do well in categories 3, 4, and 5. Because recursive solutions tend to be simple and small, the time needed to develop the programs, remove their bugs, and to modify the programs later usually is less than the time needed for nonrecursive solutions of the same problems.

However, recursive solutions do not tend to do very well in their use of computer processing time and the amount of computer memory space that they require (although there are exceptions). When we are writing and running programs on our own computer, we often do not care about the time that a program takes to run as long as it gets finished in "a reasonable amount of time." We usually do not care about memory utilization if the program does not require more than the amount of memory that we have in the computer. However, when we are programming for an environment that allows several programs to execute concurrently (**multitasking**) or that also allows several users to work concurrently (**multi-user**), we should be conservative in our use of shared processor time and computer memory resources.

There is no simple formula for obtaining the answer to the question of which one of several solutions for a problem is the best. Even if we have accurate statistics for each of the previous categories, it is not obvious how to compare the sets of numbers. Factors such as the predicted life span of the program, frequency of usage, relative importance of the program, and costs of programming and processing must enter into the decision procedure. The field of **software engineering** attempts to address categories 3, 4, and 5. The field of

algorithm analysis attempts to address the theoretical aspects of categories 1 and 2. We attempt to address some practical aspects of categories 1 and 2 in this section.

Measuring Time and Space

We use a tool that we call "StatPack" to aid in the measurement our programs' use of time and space. The StatPack package consists of a few subprograms that can be merged into a Pascal program.

Three Areas of Memory. Knowing how much static space a routine requires is helpful when determining how big a problem it can solve, or what other activities can be placed in a program with it and not exceed THINK's static space limit. Unfortunately, THINK Pascal has no easy way to measure how much static space is in use. You can estimate how much static space is used by adding up how much memory each static structure takes.

Another area of memory on the Mac is the *run-time stack*. Its major purpose is keeping track of the "state of the program" when a subroutine is called. All the information THINK needs to "pick up where it left off" once the subprogram completes is placed onto the stack. If we are deep into procedure calls (such as when processing recursively), we can run out of room on this stack, causing a run-time error. There is a function in the OSIntf unit called StackSpace, which returns the amount of free stack space. By subtracting the minimum amount of stack space free during the program's run from the amount that was free at the program's start, we can calculate the maximum amount of stack memory used.

StatPack uses the predefined function MemAvail to tell us, at any point during a program's execution, how much space is left in the *heap*, the place from which dynamic storage is allocated. By subtracting the minimum amount free during the program's run from what was free at the start, we can determine the largest amount of dynamic memory used. Since we use arrays in the examples that follow, there is no dynamic memory employed; StatPack returns zero as the amount used. We include dynamic memory measurement in StatPack for completeness; we can use StatPack to obtain information about heap space usage when we run programs that do use dynamic memory.

Timing a Routine. StatPack also employs TickCount, a long integer function defined in the ToolIntf unit. TickCount returns the number of *ticks* that have occurred since you turned on the machine; a tick is $1/60^{th}$ of a second. When TickCount reaches the largest long integer it can hold, it goes back to zero and keeps counting. TickCount only counts ticks when it is active — it can be suspended for a small amount of time during some Macintosh operations; TickCount can be "jumpy" in its behavior. Even so, since TickCount has almost the highest priority of execution of routines the Macintosh uses, our measurement will not be off by more than a tick or two. By subtracting the number of ticks at the end of a task from the number that had elapsed before its start, we obtain the time the task required.

In the interest of clarity and brevity, we only test each of the routines that follow for one or a few test cases. Such limited testing doers not prove that one approach is speedier than another in all cases. To test thoroughly for a routine's behavior requires a test plan similar to that used for testing program correctness: several cases are required, especially those that represent boundary conditions.

The code for StatPack is shown in Figure 10-15.

Notes

1. We do not need a *uses* clause to give StatPack access to the units in which MemAvail, StackFree, and TickCount are found. THINK Pascal has the access to those units built in.
2. THINK has a profiler that can measure, among other things, the amount of time each routine in a program takes. So we could have used it to time our routines. But the profiler does not measure space usage, so we would have needed to write code for that purpose anyway. We decided to incorporate in StatPack the code to do timings so we would not increase our program's complexity by including both StatPack and the interfaces to the profiler's routines to obtain the space and time measurements we seek.

```
var
   BeginTime: longint;
   HeapMostFree: longint;
   HeapLeastFree: longint;
   StackMostFree: longint;
   StackLeastFree: longint;

procedure InitStat;

   {Written by:    XXXXXXXXX XX/XX/XX}
   {Purpose:       To initialize the run-time statistics}
   {Functions used: MemAvail  - to get available heap memory}
   {                StackFree - to get free stack memory}
   {                TickCount - to get the system time in ticks (1/60}
   {                sec)}
begin {InitStat}

{*** Get the available memory}

   HeapMostFree   := MemAvail;
   HeapLeastFree  := HeapMostFree;
   StackMostFree  := StackSpace;
   StackLeastFree := StackMostFree;

{*** Get the time 1/60ths of a second}

   BeginTime := TickCount

end; {InitStat}
```

Figure 10-15 The StatPack package (continues next page).

```
procedure DisplayStat;

  {Written by:  XXXXXXXXX XX/XX/XX}
  {Purpose:     To display elapsed time and space used}

  var
    EndTime: longint;               {time at end of task in ticks}
    ElapsedTime: longint;           {elapsed time in ticks}

begin {DisplayStat}

{*** Display elapsed time}

  EndTime := TickCount;
  if EndTime >= BeginTime then
    ElapsedTime := EndTime - BeginTime
  else
    ElapsedTIme := (EndTime - BeginTime) + maxlongint;
  Writeln('The elapsed time is: ', ElapsedTime / 60.0 : 1 : 3,
          ' seconds.');

{*** Display maximum space used}

  Writeln('The maximum amount of dynamic memory used was: ',
        HeapMostFree - HeapLeastFree : 1);
  Writeln('The maximum amount of stack memory used was: ',
        StackMostFree - StackLeastFree : 1)
end; {DisplayStat}

procedure CheckSpace;

  {Written by:  XXXXXXXXX XX/XX/XX}
  {Purpose:     To check space utilization}

  var
    HeapFree: longint;
    StackFree: longint;

begin {CheckSpace}
  HeapFree := MemAvail;
  if HeapFree < HeapLeastFree then
    HeapLeastFree := HeapFree;
  StackFree := StackSpace;
  if StackFree < StackLeastFree then
    StackLeastFree := StackFree
end; {CheckSpace}

{*** StatPack ends here}
```

Figure 10-15 (continued)

To use this tool in your own programs, insert the code for StatPack just before the declarations of your subprograms. Be sure that your program does not have any name conflicts with the global variables and subprograms of StatPack. In particular, avoid the use of the following names:

Global variables: BeginTime
HeapLeastFree
HeapMostFree
StackLeastFree
StackMostFree

Subprograms: InitStat
DisplayStat
CheckSpace

In order to use the StatPack, do the following:

1. Place the following statement at the beginning of the executable part of each subprogram whose space usage you wish to measure:

```
CheckSpace
```

(You need not include this call if you only wish to measure time.)

2. After any user input to the program, place the following statement in the main program:

```
InitStat
```

3. Place the following statement in the main program immediately after the tasks you want to measure:

```
DisplayStat
```

It is important for you to note that the time and space statistics that StatPack reports are to be used for comparisons only, since the use of StatPack in a program increases the program's time and space requirements. (This is sometimes known as the **observer effect**.) When using this technique to compare your programs, be sure the numbers compared have been generated by the same computer model; memory configuration and processor speed vary from one model of computer to another.

A First Comparison

One technique for removing recursion from a program is to attempt to replace the recursion with **iteration** (the use of loops). It often occurs that a recursive solution is the easiest to produce, yet it might be an inefficient one, and an iterative approach runs much faster or uses less memory.

Subprograms that contain only one recursive call at the end of the code (called **tail recursion**) are the easiest to transform into iterative alternatives. To illustrate, consider the recursive algorithm for computing a factorial:

```
if N = 0 then
    Factorial := 1
else
    Factorial := n * Factorial(n - 1)
```

We can easily change this algorithm into one that uses a loop:

```
Total := 1;
loop for I going from 1 to N
    Total := Total * I
Factorial := Total;
```

Note that this nonrecursive algorithm still works for N = 0, but it is not as obvious an observation as it is with the recursive version of the algorithm. When we gather the time and space statistics for factorial functions employing these two algorithms (run on a Macintosh Plus with 1 Megabyte of memory), we obtain the following results:

ALGORITHM	MAXIMUM STACK SPACE	TIME
Recursive Factorial (N = 16)	756	0.050
Iterative Factorial (N = 16)	56	0.017

Since TickCount might be off by a few ticks (at worst about 0.33 seconds), these figures are not conclusive evidence that one approach is better than the other. We can obtain much better evidence by obtaining the factorial several times and comparing results. For N = 16, calculating factorial of N 1000 times in a loop produces a time of 28.617 for the recursive approach and a time of 21.083 seconds for the iterative one. Because the iterative solution is so much faster, and uses a smaller amount of stack space, we prefer it over the recursive one.

This result is far from universal. For instance, the same algorithms run using a different version of Pascal on the same Macintosh resulted in the recursive approach being about one-and-a-half times faster than the iterative one! The reasons one approach is faster than another has to do with how well the programming language converts recursive calls into assembly language for machine execution. The only way to be absolutely sure eliminating recursion will improve program performance is to try both the recursive and nonrecursive algorithms and compare the results.

The Fibonacci Numbers

The Fibonacci sequence introduced in the exercises of Section 4-2 provides an excellent example for comparison of solution techniques. In Figure 10-16, we show a recursive function that generates the Nth Fibonacci number.

The recursion the Fibonacci number function uses is not tail recursion, but a simple example of **tree recursion**. The transformation of the recursive algorithm into an iterative one is a bit more difficult in this case. Figure 10-17 shows an iterative version of the function.

The iterative function has a more complicated algorithm and uses more variables than the recursive function. The time to develop and debug the iterative solution is certainly greater than for the recursive one.

```
function Fibo(N: integer): real;

{Written by: XXXXXXXX   XX/XX/XX}
{Purpose:    To generate the Nth Fibonacci number}
{Parameters: N - input, which number to calculate}

begin {Fibo}
  if N < 3 then
    Fibo := 1
  else
    Fibo := Fibo(N - 1) + Fibo(N - 2)
end; {Fibo}
```

Figure 10-16 Fibonacci numbers: by recursion.

```
function Fibo(N: integer): real;

{Written by: XXXXXXXX   XX/XX/XX)
{Purpose:    To generate the Nth Fibonacci number)
{Parameters: N - input, which number to calculate}

  var
    First: real;
    Second: real;
    Temp: real;
    I: integer;

begin {Fibo}
  First := 1;
  Second := 1;

  for I := 1 to N - 2 do
    begin
      Temp := First;
      First := First + Second;
      Second := Temp
    end; {for}

  Fibo := First
end; {Fibo}
```

Figure 10-17 Fibonacci numbers: by iteration

In this case, there is another approach: a formula. It happens that we can calculate the Nth Fibonacci number directly by the formula:

$$\frac{(1 + \sqrt{5})^N}{\sqrt{5}}$$

The number $1 + \sqrt{5}$ is related to a venerable problem in geometry called the **golden section**, so we choose to call this constant by the name Golden in our third version of the

```
function Power(X: real; N: integer): real;

{Written by: XXXXXXXXX XX/XX/XX}
{Purpose:    To calculate X to the N}
{Parameters: X - input, base for the calculation}
{            N - input, exponent for the calculation}
{Functions used: Exp - (built-in) exponential}
{                Ln  - (built-in) natural logarithm}

begin {Power}
  Power := Exp(N * Ln(X))
end; {Power}

function Fibo(N: integer): real;

{Written by: XXXXXXXXX XX/XX/XX}
{Purpose:    To generate the Nth Fibonacci number}
{Parameters: N - input, which number to calculate}
{Functions used: Power - exponentiation}

  const
    Golden = 1.6180339887;
    Root5  = 2.2360679775;

begin {Fibo}
  Fibo := Power(Golden, N) / Root5
end; {Fibo}
```

Figure 10-18 Fibonacci number: by formula.

Fibo function, as shown in Figure 10-18. Also included in Figure 10-18 is a version of the Power function that is needed in the calculation.

We show the time and space results for the calculation of Fibo(20) in the table:

ALGORITHM	MAXIMUM STACK SPACE	TIME
Recursive Fibo(20)	924	34.983
Iterative Fibo(20)	64	0.017
Formula Fibo(20)	56	0.033

We see a dramatic example of the potential inefficiency of a recursive function. We would certainly not choose the recursive function as the best way to produce Fibonacci numbers even though it has the easiest formulation. How do we choose between the other two possible solutions? The fact that the iterative version only uses the addition of numbers with no fractional part means that the results are exact up to the degree of precision of the representation of real numbers. Because the formula uses the exponential and logarithm functions, we do not have the same level of confidence in the accuracy of the values. On this basis, we choose the iterative approach for the computation of Fibonacci numbers as the best in this case.

```
function Combinatorial(N, M: integer): integer;

{Written by: XXXXXXXXX XX/XX/XX}
{Purpose:    To calculate a combinatorial coefficient, iteratively}
{Parameters: N - input, the row of Pascal's Triangle}
             M - input, the entry in the row}
var
  Triangle: array [1..21, 0..22] of integer;
  Row: integer;
  Column: integer;

begin {Combinatorial}
  if (M = 0) or (M = N) then
    Combinatorial := 1
  else
    begin
      Triangle[1,0] := 1;
      Triangle[1,1] := 1;

      for Row := 2 to N - 1 do
        begin
          Triangle[Row, 0] := 1;
          Triangle[Row, Row] := 1;

          for Column := 1 to Row - 1 do
            Triangle[Row, Column] :=
                Triangle[Row - 1, Column - 1] +
                Triangle[Row - 1, Column]
        end; {for}

      Combinatorial := Triangle[N - 1, M - 1] + Triangle[N - 1, M]
    end
end; {Combinatorial}
```

Figure 10-19 Combinatorial coefficients: by iteration

Combinatorial Coefficients

One way to calculate the combinatorial coefficients iteratively is to use an array to hold the rows of Pascal's Triangle. We choose to use a rectangular array with rows ranging from 1 to 21 and columns ranging from 0 to 21. (See Section 7-1 for any desired details on the syntax for dealing with these types of array.) Our strategy for calculating Combinatorial(N, M) is to fill in the triangle for rows 1, 2, ..., N – 1, and then to use the recursive formula (once) to get our result.

We have already shown the recursive version of Combinatorial as Figure 10-2 in Section 10-2. We show the iterative version of the function as Figure 10-19.

Another approach is to use the mathematical formula for the combinatorial coefficient Combinatorial(N, M) given by

$$\frac{N!}{M!(N-M)!}$$

```
function Combinatorial(N, M: integer): integer;

{Written by: XXXXXXXX   XX/XX/XX}
{Purpose:    To calculate a combinatorial coefficient, by formula}
{Parameters: N - input, row of Pascal's Triangle}
{            M - input, entry in the row}

  var
    Num: integer;
    Denom: integer;
    Prod: real;

begin {Combinatorial}
  if N - M < M then
    M := N - M;
  Prod := 1;
  Denom := M;

  for Num := N downto N - M + 1 do
    begin
      Prod := Prod * (Num / Denom);
      Denom := Denom - 1
    end; {for}

  Combinatorial := Round(Prod)
end; {Combinatorial}
```

Figure 10-20 Combinatorial coefficients: by formula

(where N! is the factorial of N). This formula is best used in an equivalent form, obtained after some algebraic transformations of the formula. Assuming M is not greater than N − M, then this formula is equivalent to the previous one:

$$\frac{N}{M} \frac{N-1}{M-1} \frac{N-2}{M-2} \frac{N-3}{M-3} \cdots \frac{N-M+1}{1}$$

The fact that Combinatorial(N, M) = Combinatorial(N, N − M) means that we can use the above formula in every case by changing M to N − M, if necessary.

We show the code for the formula version of the Combinatorial function in Figure 10-20.

The results of running the three different solutions for the combinatorial coefficient for the case of Combinatorial(17, 8) are as follows:

ALGORITHM	MAXIMUM STACK SPACE	TIME
Recursive	564	242.883
Iterative	1012	0.017
Formula	58	0.017

```
function Reversed(InString: string): string;

{Written by: XXXXXXXXX XX/XX/XX}
{Purpose:    To reverse a string iteratively}
{Parameters: InString - input, string to reverse}
{Functions used: Length - (built-in) gets length of a string}

   var
     I: integer;
     WorkString: string;

begin {Reversed}
   WorkString := '';
   for I := 1 to Length(InString) do
      WorkString := InString[I] + WorkString;
   Reversed := WorkString
end; {Reversed}
```

Figure 10-21 Reversing a string: by iteration.

In this case, we can't be sure of the time comparison of the iterative and formula approaches (because of the "graininess" of TickCount's results) so we run each 1000 times. The result is 17.817 seconds for the iterative approach and 22.433 seconds for the formula approach, so the former is our preferred choice. (A thousand units of stack memory is still well within reason.)

Reversing a String

The recursive form of the Reversed function was shown in Figure 10-3 of Section 10-2. This provides another example of tail recursion that can be easily transformed into iterative form. We show the iterative form in Figure 10-21.

For the purposes of the comparison we use the string

$$abcdefghijklmnopqrstuvwxyz$$

The time and space statistics are as follows:

ALGORITHM	MAXIMUM STACK SPACE	TIME
Recursive	28678	0.083
Iterative	814	0.017

The timings are not informative; within the accuracy of TickCount, the numbers are virtually equal. So, we run each algorithm 1000 times in a loop. The recursive approach takes 92.000 seconds, and the iterative approach takes 10.333 seconds. Since it takes much less time, and significantly less stack space as well, we prefer the iterative approach.

There is another iterative algorithm that may have occurred to you as you considered the reversal problem. The alternative solution is to do a character by character replacement and avoid the concatenation. The alternative function is presented in Figure 10-22.

```
function Reversed(InString: string): string;

{Written by XXXXXXXXX XX/XX/XX}
{Purpose:    To reverse a string iteratively}
{Parameters: InString - input, string to reverse}
{Functions used: Length - (built-in) gets length of a string}
   var
     N : integer;
     I : integer;

begin {Reversed}
   Reversed := InString;
   N := Length(InString);
   for I := 1 to N do
      Reversed[I] := InString[N - I + 1]

end; {Reversed}
```

Figure 10-22 Reversing a string: character replacement

When the alternative iterative algorithm is run on the test string, its stack space is 302 and its time is 0.17 seconds. Because we cannot tell which of the iterative algorithms is better, we run both with the test strings 1000 times. The algorithm that uses concatenation had a time of 10.333 seconds and the algorithm that uses character replacement has a reported time of 4.167 seconds.

We conclude that the best way to reverse a string is to use the character replacement form shown in Figure 10-22.

Sorting

We compare quicksort and iterative selection sort from Section 6-3 with the merge sort and recursive selection sort from Section 10-2.

We have run timings of each sort with different sets of data. The results are shown in the following series of tables. (We leave stack space measurements for the exercises.)

Test Set 1: Array of 1000 randomly generated integers in the range from 1 to 10000.

ALGORITHM	TIME
Quicksort	3.767
Iterative selection sort	53.150
Recursive selection sort	31.833
Merge sort	3.700

In the context of random data, quicksort and merge sort show their superiority. Note that recursive selection sort is significantly faster than iterative seleciton sort.

Test Set 2: Array of 500 randomly generated integers in the range from 1 to 10000.

ALGORITHM	TIME
Quicksort	1.717
Iterative selection sort	13.467
Recursive selection sort	8.233
Merge sort	1.717

The tables for Test Sets 1 and 2 make it seem likely that the two selection sorts are $O(n^2)$, and quicksort and the merge sort are both $O(n \log n)$. (The "O" notation was introduced in Section 6-3.)

Test Set 3: Array of 1000 distinct integers in the range from 1 to 1000 in ascending order.

ALGORITHM	TIME
Quicksort	40.317
Iterative selection sort	52.950
Recursive selection sort	74.883
Merge sort	3.333

In this context, quicksort is at its worst. If the data are already sorted, or nearly so, then quicksort is not the sorting method of choice; merge sort seems best.

Test Set 4: Array of 1000 randomly generated integers in the range from 1 to 10.

ALGORITHM	TIME
Quicksort	3.900
Iterative selection sort	53.067
Recursive selection sort	31.583
Merge sort	3.700

Once again, we see that random data (even in a small range of values) are the context in which quicksort and merge sort show their superiority.

Test Set 5: Array of 1000 integers in the range from 1 to 10 in ascending order.

ALGORITHM	TIME
Quicksort	5.317
Iterative selection sort	59.950
Recursive selection sort	31.700
Merge sort	3.333

We see that quicksort is not slowed as much by sorted data in a small numeric range.

Test Set 6: Array of 1000 integers all with the same value.

ALGORITHM	TIME
Quicksort	4.417
Iterative selection sort	53.017
Recursive selection sort	31.350
Merge sort	3.400

The context wherein all data have the same value is one of the boundary conditions of sorting. Quicksort and merge sort do well in this context.

Test Set 7: Array of 1000 distinct integers in descending order.

ALGORITHM	TIME
Quicksort	43.150
Iterative selection sort	58.483
Recursive selection sort	53.233
Merge sort	3.300

Quicksort also does not do well when its data are sorted in reverse order.

Our conclusions are as follows: If you are sure that you have nearly random data, or if the range of values of the data is small, then use either merge sort or quicksort. If you think that the data are almost sorted, then use merge sort. Do not use either selection sort.

Prefix Expressions

We do not attempt to transform our algorithms into iterative form in this case. It is certainly possible to accomplish the task, but the development and debugging time do not warrant the effort. We analyze the performance of the program shown in Figure 10-14 of Section 10-2. The basis for our comparisons are differing prefix expressions. The following is a table of some examples:

EXPRESSION	MAXIMUM STACK SPACE	TIME
++++++++++++++++1111111111111111	20728	0.367
+1+1+1+1+1+1+1+1+1+1+1+1+1+1+1+11	20756	0.200
++++11+11++11+11+++11+11++11+11	5950	0.217

Since this prefix-evaluation expression has a number of recursive calls active at once, its stack-space requirements can vary significantly, depending upon the level of recursion that is attained while the program runs. To show the depth of calls, let us modify the Eval and Apply functions so that they add 1 to a global count when invoked and subtract 1 from the global count when they end. In addition, we have both Eval and Apply check if the global count is larger than a global variable that represents the largest count so far. If we begin the process by setting the largest value and the count both to 0, then we have a strategy for checking levels of recursion. The following table shows the results of the level checking on the expressions shown previously (all of which evaluate to 16):

EXPRESSION	HIGHEST LEVEL OF RECURSION
+++++++++++++++++1111111111111111	31
+1+1+1+1+1+1+1+1+1+1+1+1+1+1+1+11	31
++++11+11++11+11+++11+11++11+11	9

Notice how closely stack usage parallels the highest recursion level.

Another influence on the space requirements is that we used 255 as the maximum size for all strings in the program. By changing the maximum size from 255 to 80, we free up static space and use less stack memory when the Eval and Apply procedures are called. The maximum size chosen for all strings in a program can have a significant influence on that program's memory requirements.

Some Final Thoughts on Recursion

The discussion and examples of this chapter have pointed toward some conclusions that can be usefully applied to our programming efforts.

1. A recursive algorithm is often the first solution that we discover.
2. A recursive algorithm can be transformable to a nonrecursive, usually iterative, form.
3. Trying more than one solution to a problem is an advantage when we want to find the best (fastest, easiest to understand, least using of memory, etc.) solution.
4. Recursive solutions may have the smallest development, debugging, and maintenance times, but they may use more computer time and memory resources than nonrecursive solutions.
5. It is more likely that a recursive solution is best if the problem is complex (sorting, prefix notation).
6. There are techniques for analyzing the behavior of programs that can be used for judging program efficiency.
7. Recursion is indispensable as one of a programmer's tools.

REVIEW

Terms and Concepts

algorithm analysis
golden section
iteration
multitasking
multiuser

observer effect
software engineering
tail recursion
tree recursion

EXERCISES

1. (a) Modify the Factorial function so that it works by means of a "lookup table" embodied in a case structure. Put in the factorials from 0 to 16. Measure the performance against the iterative factorial. Which method of factorials do you recommend as best?

(b) Modify the Combinatorial function so that it references a global array containing the factorials from 0 to 16. Build the array iteratively in the main program before invoking Combinatorial. Measure the performance against the other Combinatorial functions. (Be sure to include the time to build the factorial array.)

(c) Repeat part (b) for 1000 calls to the combinatorial function. Only build the factorial array once. What conclusions can you draw?

2. If you wrote the extended range Factorial procedure as suggested in the exercises of Section 10-2, do the following:
   (a) Write an iterative version.
   (b) Measure the performance of the two forms.

3. Show that Fibo(50) is accurately calculated by the iterative approach, but not accurately calculated by the formula approach. What is the smallest number N for which the iterative approach fails? The formula approach?

4. Use a calculator to compute Fibo(N) for N = 2, 3, and 4 using the formula approach.

5. Draw a picture of the recursive levels of the calculation of Fibo(5) in the following manner:

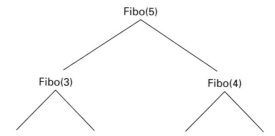

Turn it upside down. Now you see why this kind of recursion is called tree recursion.

6. (a) Modify the Power function that is used for the calculation of Fibonacci numbers so that it calculates by iteration instead of using the exponential and logarithm functions. Measure the performance of this method of calculation for Fibo(25).
   (b) Repeat part (a), but use the recursive Power function presented in Section 4-2.

7. By hand, calculate Combinatorial(5, 3) by the first formula given.

8. Repeat the picture drawing activities of Exercise 5 for the recursive calculation of Combinatorial(5, 3).

9. Find what size of string, if any, exhausts the run-time stack memory available by default when the recursive form of the Reversed function is used.

10. Write a nonrecursive merge sort for the special case when the number of elements in the array is a power of 2. Hint: Start at the bottom level with subarrays of size 1 and work upward to size 2, 4, ..., merging the two subarrays on the level below. Test the performance of this sort against the recursive merge sort for 512 randomly generated numbers in the range from 1 to 10,000.

11. How might you remove the restriction to arrays of the size of a power of 2 in Exercise 10?

12. Write an iterative version of the SubSeq function in Figure 10-6 of Section 10-2. Measure the performance against the recursive form.

13. Write an iterative version of the SubString function in Figure 10-7 of Section 10-2. Measure the performance against the recursive form.

14. Write a simple looping version of the NumDivisors function in Figure 10-10 of Section 10-2. Is it a good approach to solve this problem? Why or why not?

15. Write an iterative version of the Addends function in Figure 10-11 of Section 10-2. Measure the performance against the recursive form.
16. Write an iterative version of the WriteSeq function in Figure 10-13 of Section 10-2.
17. What would be some necessary ingredients of a nonrecursive solution of the PreFix program in Figure 10-14 of Section 10-2? Formulate a rough algorithm.
18. Write a Pascal program for a nonrecursive solution of the PreFix program in Figure 10-14 of Section 10-2. Measure the performance against the recursive version.
19. Find the maximum levels of recursion for the sorting procedures discussed in this section for all the test sets listed, and use StatPack to determine the run-time stack usage. What conclusions can you draw from these figures?

11   File I/O

OBJECTIVES

In this chapter, we explore **files** in some depth. Files were introduced in Chapter 5, and you have probably written some programs that used files. By the end of this chapter, you should be able to:

- use control break logic to use file data to produce reports
- merge two sequential files together
- update sequential files
- manipulate and update random-access files

11-1 INTRODUCTION

In this chapter, we pull together and review information about files with which you are already familiar. We then build on that knowledge by showing applications based on **control break logic** and sequential file **merging** and **update** strategies. In addition, we give a brief introduction to the concept of **random-access** files.

The presentation is not intended to be a complete discussion of file-processing techniques. Indeed, whole textbooks have been written on that subject. Nor do we give an exhaustive description of the Pascal file-processing commands. Our purpose is to indicate some methods for working with files using the Pascal language, expanding on what we learned in Chapter 5.

We begin with a brief review.

File Terminology

A file consists of a number of **records.** (Pascal has borrowed and generalized on the concept of record.) A record contains one or more values, frequently relating to one given entity. For example, we might have a record that contains the following **fields:**

Name
Social security number
Date of birth
Marital status
(and so on)

In this case, the record refers to a particular individual. Files can appear in many forms. For many years, punched cards were an important medium for input files. Data are encoded on a punched card by a pattern of holes that can be interpreted as character data by a card reader. In such a file, each data card might be a single record of the file. Another example of a file is a printed report. In this case, each line printed is considered to be one record of the file.

It is frequently desirable to store and maintain data in a more convenient form. For example, we might want to have one program put some information on a file and later use that information as input to some other program. A printed report is not appropriate in this application. We could have the first program create a set of punched cards to be read by the second program. However, this would require maintaining the deck of cards (which could be sizable) over an extended period of time.

Fortunately, today there are more convenient (and still economical) storage media for files. Two of the most commonly used are **magnetic tape** and **magnetic disk.** (In addition, **optical disk** systems are now on the market, and will probably be increasingly common as time goes on.)

The magnetic tape used by the computer to store a data file is analogous to the tape used for sound recording. Indeed, some (older) microcomputers use ordinary audio cassettes as a storage medium. The records of the file are placed on the tape, one after another, from first to last, as shown in Figure 11-1. In reading a file that has been written on tape, the computer has to read the records in order (sequentially). As a result, a magnetic tape is referred to as a **sequential-access** storage medium. A file stored on tape is accessed sequentially.

Likewise, a magnetic disk is analogous to the compact disk (CD) used to store sound. One form of magnetic disk you are familiar with is the diskette, or floppy disk, commonly used by microcomputers. In addition, you may be familiar with microcomputer hard disk devices, or perhaps with the disk devices used by minicomputers or mainframe computers. These devices all have the fundamental strategy for storing data in common, as shown in Figure 11-2. The data are stored on a series of concentric rings, rather than on one continuous spiral, as is true for a phonograph record. The disk is rotated at a high rate of speed by a device called a **disk drive.** The disk drive mechanism includes a **read/write head** on an arm that can be moved to any of the concentric rings, or **tracks**, of the disk. Again, this is somewhat analogous to the audio record player arm, which can be moved to any groove on the record.

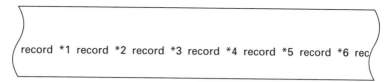

Figure 11-1 Tape file.

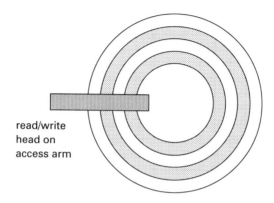

Figure 11-2 Disk file.

A magnetic disk is called a **direct-access** storage medium. In order to access a particular record (perhaps record 735), it is not necessary to read all the records up to the record. The read/write head can be moved directly to the track (concentric ring) on which the desired record is located. Since the disk is rotated by the disk drive, the desired record passes under the read/write head soon after the head is in place. This direct-access capability of the magnetic disk and disk drive does not, however, mean that the records of the file cannot be processed in order. If a file is stored on a disk, then it can be accessed either sequentially or directly.

Pascal Files

Pascal supports two types of sequential-access type files (and one type of direct-access file). The sequential types were introduced in Chapter 5; we discuss the direct-access type in Section 11-4.

The first sequential type we discussed was a **text file**, declared as type *text* in the *var* section of the program. A text file is a file of characters organized into lines. Although it is possible to read such a file one character at a time, we have preferred to read one line at a time. We have done so by making extensive use of THINK Pascal's string data types.

Text files in which a line contains several data items can be more difficult to use when not all the data are numeric. As a simple example, suppose that two programs each contain these declarations:

```
var
   LastName: string[25];
   FirstName: string[20];
```

Suppose program1 writes the data to a text file:

```
Writeln(FriendFile, LastName, FirstName);
```

and that later program2 reads the data:

```
Readln(FriendFile, LastName, FirstName);
```

Will this work properly? Probably not, unless the last name that was written was 25 characters long. For example, suppose that we have assigned

```
LastName := 'Frederickson'
FirstName := 'Arthur'
```

When the record is written, it contains the characters

```
FredericksonArthur
```

Now when the next program reads the data, there is nothing to tell it where LastName ends, so it reads the first 25 characters because LastName is string[25]. As a result, LastName becomes 'FredericksonArthur   ' and First Name contains the null string.

We could avoid this problem by padding the output of the last name with blanks to achieve a length of 25. However, the name we read in would then have the extra blanks at the end.

As another example, consider

```
Readln(Age, Sex)
```

where Age is integer and Sex is char. To enter the values 25 and 'F', what should the input line be? If we use

```
25 F
```

then Age would be 25 and Sex would be a blank. If we try

```
25F
```

THINK Pascal gives us an I/O error because THINK insists that numeric data be terminated by a blank or a return.

Again, we could get around this, perhaps, by issuing a Readln as

```
Readln(Age, Sex, Sex)
```

and using an input line

```
25 F
```

This would read 25 for Age, the blank for Sex, and then the F for Sex. However, this is not very satisfactory.

Because of these subtleties, we have tended to read one data item per record when reading from a text file or from the keyboard. This is a matter of defensive programming: avoid known pitfall areas.

The second type of file is the **binary file.** These are declared using a declaration similar to

```
type
   PersonFile = file of PersonRecord;

var
   FriendFile: PersonFile;
```

This illustrates the most common use. However, we can declare types such as

```
file of integer
```

In this case, the file's "records" are not Pascal records, but rather a single integer.

Binary files can be treated as sequential files (the way we have been using them) or as random-access files (which we consider in Section 3).

There are trade-offs to be considered in choosing between text files and binary files:

1. A text file can be processed in a text editor. Therefore, text files are frequently used as original input to a program or set of programs.
2. A text file is readable by humans. Files meant to be printed as reports are definitely text files.
3. As we have mentioned, there are certain subtleties to be avoided in reading text files. It may be desirable to arrange the input file with one value per line.
4. I/O is faster on binary files. The data are stored on the file in precisely the form in which they are stored in the computer. No conversion routines are needed to translate back and forth to text form.
5. One disadvantage of binary files is that they can require special protocols when transmitted over phone lines to remote computers. Typically, transmitting text files is easier.

Before we discuss new material, let us remind you very briefly of the file-handling features we have studied. For more information, review Chapter 5.

1. Type can be "text" or "file of *component type*"
2. Reset (*Pascal name, disk file name*)

   Rewrite (*Pascal name, disk file name*): removes any previous data
3. Read (*Pascal name, . . .*)

   Write (*Pascal name, . . .*)
4. Readln (*Pascal name, . . .*): these are for text files only

   Writeln (*Pascal name, . . .*)
5. Eof (*Pascal name*): becomes true as the last record is read
6. Close (*Pascal name*)

11-1 INTRODUCTION

7. Error trapping. We have used this to trap the error that occurs when a file does not exist. It can, however, be used to trap an error in any I/O statement, as shown here. (See also Exercise 1.)

```
IOCheck(false);                       {Turn off error messages}
some I/O statement                    {Reset, Read, etc}
IOCheck(true);                        {Turn on error messages}
ErrorOccurred := (IOResult <> 0)      {Check for error}
```

REVIEW

Terms and Concepts

binary file
control break logic
direct access
disk drive
file
field
magnetic disk
magnetic tape
merging

optical disk
random access
read/write head
record
sequential access
text file
track
update

EXERCISES

1. To demonstrate the use of error trapping in other than a file context, write a procedure GetScore as described here. This procedure obtains a valid test score between 0 and 100. There should be three possible error messages: "too low", "too high", and "not valid integer input". Use IOCheck and IOResult to trap this third error type.

   Exercises 2 to 5 refer to a binary file that contains inventory figures for a chain of drugstores. Each record of the file contains these fields:

DESCRIPTION	TYPE	NUMBER OF CHARACTERS/DIGITS
Item number	Numeric	5
Item name	Character	Maximum 20
Department code	Character	3
Inventory at each of nine locations	Numeric array	4 digits each

   The file is in ascending order by item number.

2. Write a program to create this file. In order to create the file, you read a set of input records. Each has exactly the information that will be put on the file and an additional field that contains the total inventory for the entire chain (numeric, five digits). The input file is a text file that is created by the user with a text editor. It is up to you to describe the exact layout of the input file.

   Your program is to perform the following correctness checks:

- The item name field must begin with a nonblank character.
- The department code must be one of the following eight codes: COS, DRU, TOY, CRD, PRE, HHG, CLO, or BKS.
- The sum of the individual inventory amounts must equal the total inventory (this helps catch data-entry errors).
- The item numbers must be in order.

In addition, perform the following "reasonableness" check:

- Each inventory amount must be between 0 and 3000, inclusive. Records with no errors are placed in the file; records with errors are not. All errors are listed on a text file, as illustrated:

```
12345 BLANK ITEM NAME
12345 BAD DEPT CODE
12345 BAD INVENTORY AMT (STORE 2)
12345 BAD INVENTORY AMT (STORE 9)
12345 INCORRECT TOTAL

*****************************************************
12479 BAD INVENTORY AMT (STORE 6)

*****************************************************
13780 OUT OF ORDER (PREVIOUS ITEM = 13792)

*****************************************************
```

3. This exercise is exactly the same as Exercise 2 except for the error-report form. In this case, it should be listed on a printed exception report, as illustrated:

```
                    EXCEPTION REPORT                PAGE 1
                    ----------------

ITEM NUMBER                 TYPE OF ERROR
-----------                 -------------

   12345                    BLANK ITEM NAME
                            BAD DEPT CODE
                            BAD INVENTORY AMT (STORE 2)
                            BAD INVENTORY AMT (STORE 9)
                            INCORRECT TOTAL
   12479                    BAD INVENTORY AMT (STORE 6)
   13780                    OUT OF ORDER (PREVIOUS ITEM = 13792)
```

Notice that you should continue checking for further errors even after finding one error. Also, notice that the output is "group indicated" by item number. If the list for a single item spans two pages, print the item number in a form such as "19345(cont.)" on the new page.

4. Write programs to create partial files containing the following:
   (a) All TOY items.
   (b) All items whose item number is between 10,000 and 30,000, inclusive.
   (c) All items where any single inventory amount is less than 30. The output record should contain only the item number, name, and department.

EXERCISES

5. Write a program to create a file where each record contains an item number and the total inventory for the entire chain.

11-2 SEQUENTIAL FILES: CONTROL BREAKS

In the next two sections, we examine two classical categories of algorithms for working with sequential files. Either can be used with text files or with binary files (used sequentially). In fact, for the programs of this section, we could even obtain input from the terminal. The only differences occur in the details of reading the fields of the input record. For simplicity, we assume that the input is a binary file.

The first algorithm category we consider is that of **control breaks.** Although we cannot claim that this is the most exciting class of algorithm to learn, it can certainly be argued that it is one of the most widely used. In any case, it should be in every professional's "toolbox," along with other problem-solving methods.

There are many instances, especially in business applications of the computer, where the data to be processed occur in groups. If there are special tasks to be performed when one group ends and another begins, we have the structure frequently referred to as a control-break structure. In this type of application, information contained within the data items themselves is generally used to determine when to move from one group to another.

An important consideration for this type of problem is that the records being processed must be prearranged into the groups involved.

An Example

Each data record contains a department number (integer), a salesperson number (integer), and an expense amount (real). The records are arranged with the salespersons for each department grouped together in the file. Write a program to create a summary listing, as illustrated in Figure 11-3.

We start with the realization that a loop is needed to process the data. We need at least the following variables:

Input:	Department	Integer	Employee department
	IDNumber	Integer	Employee number
	Expense	Real	Employee expense
Output:	DeptTotal	Real	Total for department
	GrandTotal	Real	Total for entire file

Many file-processing problems follow this general pattern:

```
initialization
while not Eof(file-designator) do
   begin
      read a record
      process the record
      print information
   end
```

```
                        EXPENSE TOTALS
                        --------------

          Department           Salesperson        Expenses
          ----------           -----------        --------

              100                 5000            1000.00
              100                 5001            1000.00
                              Department Total:   2000.00

              200                 8907             500.00
              200                 3798            1603.45
              200                 4359            1000.75
                              Department Total:   3104.20

              300                 2987             984.50
                              Department Total:    984.50

             1800                 3871            1500.00
             1800                 8340             390.25
             1800                 8469              50.75
             1800                 8307             500.00
                              Department Total:   2441.00

             2050                 3498              35.50
                              Department Total:     35.50

                                  Grand Total:    8565.20
```

Figure 11-3 Control break: desired output format.

However, the control-break logic requires a somewhat more complex algorithm because there are special tasks to be performed when we finish one group and start another. Somewhere after the read step, we insert a step that is something like this:

>   if this is a new department then
>   perform 'change of department' steps

The "change of department" steps include, among other things, printing the total for the previous department. In general, we must perform some "cleanup" steps for the old department and some "setup" steps to get ready for the new department. These general categories can overlap somewhat.

Note. In many programs, the test to check whether we have a new group comes immediately after the read step. However, there are instances when some preliminary processing must be done prior to determining whether a new group has occurred.

11-2 SEQUENTIAL FILES: CONTROL BREAKS

If we ask, "How can we tell if this is a new department?" the answer might be to compare the department number just read with the previous department number; we might, therefore, make an addition to our variable list:

Other: OldDept   Integer   Previous department number

With a little more thought, we might conclude that the first data record should be treated separately because there is no "old department number" with which to compare the first department number. We might be led to read and process that first record before we enter the loop because it will be treated differently from the rest. If so, we would come up with an algorithm something like this:

```
print headings
set GrandTotal to 0
read the first record
do 'setup' steps for the first department
print the first record
add the first record's expense to DeptTotal
as long as there is any data left
    read a record
    if Department is different from OldDept then
        perform 'change of department' steps ('cleanup' and 'setup' )
    print the record
    add the record's expense to DeptTotal
perform 'cleanup' for the last department
print GrandTotal
```

We perform the setup for the first department prior to the loop. This is sometimes referred to as **priming**. In addition, we must perform the cleanup for the last department after the loop, when we have run out of data.

To complete the algorithm, we must determine what is involved in setting up for a new department and cleaning up after an old department. To do so, we should review the required output. If we concentrate on the "department change," we should be able to determine most of what is required. Each step is labeled as "cleanup" or "setup".

This step should be obvious:

1. Print DeptTotal (cleanup).

Some others are not quite as obvious:

2. Add DeptTotal to GrandTotal. GrandTotal represents the sum of the individual department totals (cleanup).

3. Set DeptTotal back to 0 to prepare to accumulate a new total for the new department (setup).

4. Give OldDept the value of this record's department (setup).

Note.   As "cleanup" for the last department, we must perform steps 1 and 2. The "setup" for the first department consists of steps 3 and 4.

Adding these refinements to our algorithm, we obtain the program in Figure 11-4. This program reads its data from a text file. It also sends its report to a text file. The text file can then be printed (as often as needed) using the Print command. As we mentioned in Chapter 5, this is a handy method both for obtaining multiple copies of the report and for the situation where several microcomputers are sharing the same printer. (Another important reason is that it reduces the development time because output to a disk file is faster than output to a printer.) We use the OpenRead and OpenWrite procedures discussed in Chapter 5.

Control Breaks: General

The preceding example illustrates the control-break concept. There are some general comments we can make about planning this type of algorithm, which usually involves a loop that terminates at end of file. We discuss in some detail what types of steps generally appear before, in the body of, and after this loop.

Keep in mind that the underlying feature of the control-break structure is that the data are arranged in groups based on some field of the individual records. In addition to the usual analysis of the steps to be performed for each individual data record, we must determine the steps required because of the grouping. As a general rule, these steps fall into two categories:

1. Those steps used in starting a new group, such as initializing (or reinitializing) counters or accumulators or printing special lines of information.
2. Those steps used in finishing up an old group, such as printing summary information.

Whenever we encounter a new group, we must perform all these steps. The principal features of the algorithm are as follows:

1. Before the loop:
   (a) Initialize for the entire file (for example, GrandTotal := 0).
   (b) Read the first record.
   (c) Set up for the first group.
   (d) Process the first record.

2. In the loop:
   (a) Read the new record.
   (b) If a new group, finish the previous group and set up for the new group.
   (c) Process the record.

3. After the loop:
   (a) Finish the last group.
   (b) Print summary information for the entire file.

Most control-break problems fit fairly well into this general outline. For some applications, steps 2(b) and 2(c) must be modified slightly because the first record of each new group is processed slightly differently from the subsequent records in that group. However,

```
program ControlBreak;

{Written by:   XXXXXXXXX XX/XX/XX}
{Purpose:      To print a report for input data grouped by department}
{Procedures used: Header - to print headings}

  var
  DeptFile: text;                {input file}
  ListFile: text;                {report file}
  Department: integer;           {department #}
  IDNumber: integer;             {employee #}
  Expense: real;                 {employee expense}

  DeptTotal: real;               {total expense for dept.}
  GrandTotal: real;              {total expense for company}

  OldDept: integer;              {previous employee's dept. #}

{function Exists as shown in Appendix C is inserted here}

{procedure OpenRead as shown in Appendix C is inserted here}

{procedure OpenWrite as shown in Appendix C is inserted here}

  procedure Header;

  {Written by:   XXXXXXXXX XX/XX/XX}
  {Purpose:      To print headings}

    begin {Header}
      Writeln(ListFile, ' ' : 20, 'EXPENSE TOTALS');
      Writeln(ListFile, ' ' : 20, '--------------');
      Writeln(ListFile);
      Writeln(ListFile, ' ' : 14, 'Department', ' ' : 9, 'Salesperson',
              ' ' : 14, 'Expenses');
      Writeln(ListFile, ' ' : 14, '----------', ' ' : 9, '-----------',
              ' ' : 14, '--------');
      Writeln(ListFile)
    end; {Header}

begin {ControlBreak}

{*** Preliminary setup and initialization}

  OpenWrite(ListFile);
  Header;
  GrandTotal := 0;
```

Figure 11-4 Control breaks (continues next page)

```
{*** Handle first employee}

  Readln(DeptFile, Department, IDNumber, Expense);
  DeptTotal := 0;
  OldDept := Department;
     Writeln(ListFile, Department : 10, ' ' : 14,
             IDNumber : 5, ' ' : 15, Expense : 10 : 2);
  DeptTotal := DeptTotal + Expense;

{*** Handle other employees in loop}

  while not Eof(DeptFile) do
    begin
      Readln(DeptFile, Department, IDNumber, Expense);
      if OldDept <> Department then
        begin
          Writeln(ListFile);
          Writeln(ListFile, ' ' : 21, 'Department Total:',
                  DeptTotal : 16 : 2);
          Writeln(ListFile);
          Writeln(ListFile);
          Writeln(ListFile);
          GrandTotal := GrandTotal + DeptTotal;
          DeptTotal := 0;
          OldDept := Department
        end; {if}

      Writeln(ListFile, Department : 10, ' ' : 14,
              IDNumber : 5, ' ' : 15, Expense : 10 : 2);
      DeptTotal := DeptTotal + Expense;
    end; {while}

{*** Finish last department and print grand total}

  Writeln(ListFile);
  Writeln(ListFile, ' ' : 21, 'Department Total:', DeptTotal : 16 : 2);
  Writeln(ListFile);
  Writeln(ListFile);
  Writeln(ListFile);
  GrandTotal := GrandTotal + DeptTotal;
  Writeln(ListFile, ' ' : 26, 'Grand Total:', GrandTotal : 16 : 2);

{*** Close files and print terminating message}

  Close(DeptFile);
  Close(ListFile);
  Writeln('Report complete; it is in the file ExpenseReport')
end.
```

Figure 11-4 (continued)

this outline should help us obtain a good algorithm for any control-break problem we may encounter.

Using Subprograms with Control Breaks

In the preceding discussion, we have not indicated how subprograms fit into the control-break program logic. We have at least these four possibilities:

1. We can use a procedure for reading the data. This might be especially useful in two instances. First, we could use it to validate the input. Second, if the input file is a text file containing data for one record spread over several lines of text, it could be used to hide the details of reading the data. In either case, it would enable us always to translate the algorithm step "read a record" into a single line of Pascal code.
2. We can use a procedure for printing detail lines. In this way, we can proceed to a new page of output when we reach the bottom of each page. It is frequently helpful to pass, as an input parameter for this procedure, a Boolean flag indicating whether or not this is the first record in a new group. We might use a variable NewGroup for this purpose. (The first record in each group is frequently handled differently in the detail line printing routine.)
3. The processing of the record can very well involve complicated logic that warrants one or more subprograms.
4. The setup and cleanup steps themselves can be placed in subprograms. We discuss this possibility in what follows.

There are several possible reasons for placing the setup and the cleanup steps in subprograms. First of all, each one is generally used twice. For example, the setup steps are performed before the loop for the first record and in the loop whenever a new group is encountered. In addition, these steps could be fairly complex. The more complex they become, the more likely it becomes that we choose to place them in subprograms. Finally, using subprograms emphasizes the similar structure of the various control-break programs we write.

We reexamine our sample control-break algorithm to illustrate these ideas. For example, the algorithm for a SetUp subprogram is

set DeptTotal to 0
set OldDept equal to this record's department

This requires a procedure; the parameters are the department total (output), the current record's department (input), and the old department number (output).

For a CleanUp subprogram, we have

print DeptTotal line and three blank lines
add department total to grand total

The department total is an input parameter and the grand total is an update parameter for this procedure.

For the detail line routine, we have input parameters for the record to print together with the Boolean variable NewGroup discussed earlier. We write

```
if this is a new group
    add 5 to LineCount
    if LineCount > 45
        print headings
        set LineCount to 6
print the record
add 1 to LineCount
```

Note. This procedure is somewhat different from some earlier ones in its handling of the LineCount variable. This is to adjust to the fact that this program prints lines other than detail lines. If we simply count detail lines, we are unable to judge when we are near the bottom of the page. Rather than merely counting detail lines, we count all lines of output.

As a result, LineCount is set to 6 after printing headings. In addition, for a new group, we add 5 to LineCount. This counts the department total line we have printed and the one blank line before and three blank lines after that line.

Using these ideas, we develop the main program as shown in Figure 11-5.

Note. With the use of the NewGroup parameter for the detail line procedure, it is a simple matter to **group indicate** the output. For example, this output is not group indicated:

100	5.43
100	6.17
150	0.41
150	1.23
150	0.61

The same output group indicated would be

100		5.43
		6.17
	150	0.41
		1.23
		0.61

REVIEW

Terms and Concepts

control break
group indicate
priming

```
program ControlBreak;

{Written by:   XXXXXXXXX XX/XX/XX}
{Purpose:      To print a report for input data grouped by department}
{Procedures used: Header   - to print headings}
{                 Setup    - to initialize a new department}
{                 Cleanup  - to perform final actions for a department}
{                 GetData  - to obtain data}
{                 DetailLine - to print detail lines, with headings}

  const
    MaxLines = 45;              {maximum lines per page}

  var
    DeptFile: text;             {input file}
    ListFile: text;             {report file}
    Department: integer;        {department #}
    IDNumber: integer;          {employee #}
    Expense: real;              {employee expense}

    DeptTotal: real;            {total expense for dept}
    GrandTotal: real;           {total expense for company}

    OldDept: integer;           {previous employee's dept. #}

    LineCount: integer;         {counts report lines on page}
    NewGroup: boolean;          {for use by detail line printer}

{function Exists, as shown in Appendix C, is inserted here}

{procedure OpenRead, as shown in Appendix C, is inserted here}

{procedure OpenWrite, as shown in Appendix C, is inserted here}

  procedure Header;

    {Written by:   XXXXXXXXX XX/XX/XX}
    {Purpose:      To print headings}

  begin {Header}
    Writeln(ListFile, ' ' : 20, 'EXPENSE TOTALS');
    Writeln(ListFile, ' ' : 20, '--------------');
    Writeln(ListFile);
    Writeln(ListFile, ' ' : 2, 'Department', ' ' : 9, 'Salesperson',
            ' ' : 14, 'Expenses');
    Writeln(ListFile, ' ' : 2, '----------', ' ' : 9, '-----------',
            ' ' : 14, '--------');
    Writeln(ListFile)
  end; {Header}
```

Figure 11-5 Control breaks with procedures (continues next page).

```
procedure Setup (var DeptTotal: real; Department: integer;
                 var OldDept: integer);

  {Written by:   XXXXXXXXX XX/XX/XX}
  {Purpose:      To initialize a new group}
  {Parameters:   DeptTotal - output, set to 0}
  {              Department - input, current record's department}
  {              OldDept - output, set equal to Department}

begin {Setup}
  DeptTotal := 0;
  OldDept := Department
end; {Setup}

procedure Cleanup (DeptTotal: real; var Grand: real);

  {Written by:   XXXXXXXXX XX/XX/XX}
  {Purpose:      To perform final actions for a department that is}
  {              finished}
  {Parameters:   DeptTotal - input, total for the department}
  {              Grand - update, total for the company}
  {Globals used: ListFile - the Pascal name for the report file}

begin {Cleanup}
  Writeln(ListFile);
  Writeln(ListFile, ' ' : 21, 'Department Total:', DeptTotal : 16 : 2);
  Writeln(ListFile);
  Writeln(ListFile);
  Writeln(ListFile);

  Grand := Grand + DeptTotal
end; {Cleanup}

procedure GetData (var Department, ID: integer; var Expense: real);

  {Written by:   XXXXXXXXX XX/XX/XX}
  {Purpose:      To read one person's data}
  {Parameters:   Department - output, the department}
  {              ID - output, the employee number}
  {              Expense - output, the expense amount}
  {Globals used: DeptFile - the handle for the input file}

begin {GetData}
  Readln(DeptFile, Department, IDNumber, Expense)
end; {GetData}
```

Figure 11-5 (continues next page).

```
  procedure DetailLine (Department, ID: integer; Expense: real;
                        NewGroup: boolean);

    {Written by:    XXXXXXXXX XX/XX/XX}
    {Purpose:       To print a line of data, with headings when needed}
    {Parameters:    Department - input, the department}
    {               ID - input, the employee number}
    {               Expense  - input, the expense amount}
    {               NewGroup - input, is this a new department?}
    {Globals used: ListFile - the handle for the report file}
    {Globals modified: LineCount - the detail line counter}
    {Procedures used:  Header, to print headings}

  begin {DetailLine}
    if NewGroup then
      LineCount := LineCount + 5;
    if LineCount >= MaxLines then
      begin
        Header;
        LineCount := 6
      end; {if}
    Writeln(ListFile, Department : 10, ' ' : 14,
            IDNumber : 5, ' ' : 15, Expense : 10 : 2);
    LineCount := LineCount + 1
  end; {DetailLine}

begin {ControlBreak}

{*** Preliminary setup and initialization}

  OpenRead(DeptFile);
  OpenWrite(ListFile);
  Header;
  LineCount := 6;
  GrandTotal := 0;

{*** Handle first employee}

  GetData(Department, IDNumber, Expense);
  Setup(DeptTotal, Department, OldDept);
  DetailLine(Department, IDNumber, Expense, true);
  DeptTotal := DeptTotal + Expense;

{*** Handle other employees in loop}

  while not Eof(DeptFile) do
    begin
      GetData(Department, IDNumber, Expense);
      NewGroup := false;
      if OldDept <> Department then
```

Figure 11-5   (continues next page)

```
      begin
        NewGroup := true;
        Cleanup(DeptTotal, GrandTotal);
        Setup(DeptTotal, Department, OldDept)
      end; {if}
    DetailLine(Department, IDNumber, Expense, NewGroup);
    DeptTotal := DeptTotal + Expense;
  end; {while}

{*** Finish last department and print grand total}

  Cleanup(DeptTotal, GrandTotal);
  Writeln(ListFile, ' ' : 26, 'Grand Total:', GrandTotal : 16 : 2);

{*** Close files and print terminating message}

  Close(DeptFile);
  Close(ListFile);
  Writeln('Report complete; it is in the file ExpenseReport')
end.
```

Figure 11-5 (continued)

Program Logic: Control Break

1. Before the loop:
   (a) Initialize for the entire file (for example, GrandTotal := 0).
   (b) Read the first record.
   (c) Set up for the first group.
   (d) Process the first record.

2. In the loop:
   (a) Read the new record.
   (b) If a new group, finish the prior group and set up for the new group.
   (c) Process the record.

3. After the loop:
   (a) Finish the last group.
   (b) Print summary information for the entire file.

EXERCISES

1. There are several possible revisions to the output indicated in Figure 11-3. In general, it should be possible to make these revisions by modifying only the detail line routine, provided the totals are still printed in the same manner. Make the necessary changes for each of the following:

```
                        EXPENSE TOTALS
                        --------------

                        Salesperson         Expenses
Department Number  100     5000             1000.00
                           5001             1000.00

                        Department Total: 2000.00

                        Salesperson         Expenses
Department Number  200     8907              500.00
                           3798             1603.45
                           4359             1000.75

                        Department Total: 3104.20

                        Salesperson         Expenses
Department Number  300     2987              984.50

                        Department Total:   984.50

                        Salesperson         Expenses
Department Number 1800     3871             1500.00
                           8340              390.25
                           8469               50.75
                           8307              500.00

                        Department Total: 2441.00

                        Salesperson         Expenses
Department Number 2050     3498               35.50

                        Department Total:    35.50

                           Grand Total:     8565.20
```

Figure 11-6 Report format for Exercise 1.

    (a) Group indicate the data by department.
    (b) Group indicate by department; when a page break occurs in the middle of a department, the first line on the next page should look something like this:

```
4157 (CONTINUED)      16141          945.30
```

    (c) Obtain output in the format illustrated in Figure 11-6.

2. Write algorithms and variable lists for each of the following:
    (a) Each data record has a name, course number, and letter grade. Records are grouped by name. Output should be group indicated by name. For each person, print the number of courses taken and the number of courses failed.
    (b) Each data record has a department (six characters), name, rank (four characters), and salary. Records are grouped by department. Output should be similar to that in Figure 11-3.

```
        Grade              Name                Course
        -----              ----                ------

          F          XXXXXXXXXXXXXXXXXXXXXXXXX    XXX
                     XXXXXXXXXXXXXXXXXXXXXXXXX    XXX
                                .
                                .
                                .
                     XXXXXXXXXXXXXXXXXXXXXXXXX    XXX

          D          XXXXXXXXXXXXXXXXXXXXXXXXX    XXX
                     XXXXXXXXXXXXXXXXXXXXXXXXX    XXX
                                .
                                .
                                .
                     XXXXXXXXXXXXXXXXXXXXXXXXX    XXX

               (and so on through C, B, and A)
```

Figure 11-7 Report format for Exercise 4.

For each department, print the number of full professors (rank = 'PROF') and the average salary. Also count the departments.

(c) Modify the algorithm of part (b) to also find the department with the highest average salary.

(d) Each record contains a state abbreviation (two characters), a city name (20 characters), and a population figure to the nearest 1000. For example, 253 would denote 253,000. Records are grouped by state. Output should be similar to that of Figure 11-6. For each state, print the total population of the cities given and count the cities with population over 500,000.

(e) Modify the algorithm of part (d) to also find the total number of cities listed with population over 500,000 and the average population of all the cities listed (for the entire file).

(f) Each data record has a department number, employee number, and hourly wage. Use output similar to that in Figure 11-3. For each department, print the number of the person with the lowest hourly wage; also print the number of the employee in the entire company with the lowest hourly wage.

3. Write Pascal programs for each of the algorithms of Exercise 2.

4. Each record contains a numerical grade, course number, and name. The records are in ascending order based on the numerical grade. The letter grade is calculated by the rule: 0 to 59.99, F; 60 to 69.99, D; 70 to 79.99, C; 80 to 89.99, B; and 90 to 100, A. Write an algorithm to generate the report illustrated in Figure 11-7. Hint: Some preliminary processing of the data may be needed prior to determining if you have a new group.

5. Write the program for the algorithm of Exercise 4.

6. Each data record contains an ID number for a sample steel rod and the measured length of that particular sample. The records are arranged in ascending order based on the length of the samples. The report format of Figure 11-8 groups the samples; for example, the heading "1–2 inches" means "between 1 and 2, but not including 2 inches." Give an algorithm to generate this report. See the hint of Exercise 4. Notice that there can be "gaps" in the groups. After "16–17 inches" might come "23–24 inches."

7. Write the program for the algorithm of Exercise 6.

EXERCISES

```
         Group                  Sample #               Length
         -----                  --------               ------
      1-2 inches                  xxxx                xxx.xxx
                                  xxxx                xxx.xxx
                                    .
                                    .

                      xxx Samples In This Group

      2-3 inches                  xxxx                xxx.xxx
                                  xxxx                xxx.xxx
                                    .
                                    .

                      xxx Samples In This Group

                            (and so on)
```

Figure 11-8   Report format for Exercise 6.

```
         Division               Department              Employee
         --------               ----------              --------
           xxxx                    xxxx                  xxxxx
                                                         xxxxx
                                                         xxxxx
                                                         xxxxx
                                  xxxxx Employees In Dept xxxx
                                   xxxx                  xxxxx
                                                         xxxxx
                                                         xxxxx
                                                         xxxxx
                                  xxxxx Employees In Dept xxxx

         xxxxx Employees in xxx Departments in Division xxxx
           xxxx                    xxxx                  xxxxx
                                                         xxxxx
                                                         xxxxx
                                                         xxxxx
                                  xxxxx Employees In Dept xxxx
                                   xxxx                  xxxxx
                                                         xxxxx
(and so on)
```

Figure 11-9   Report format for Exercise 8.

8. Each data record contains a division number, department number, and employee number. The records are grouped by division and by department within each division. Give an algorithm to generate the report illustrated in Figure 11-9. This is an example of a *multiple-level control break*. Hint: Each new record could be the start of a new division; also, it could be the first record of a new department within the same division.

9. Each of these exercises refers to Exercise 2. State what assumptions you make on the order of the data.

   (a) Modify Exercise 2(b) to print a report group indicated by department and by rank within departments.
   (b) For Exercise 2(d), create a report group indicated by state, which lists cities group indicated by size, as shown here

   ```
   xx       0- 49        xxxxx...xxx
            50-100       xxxxx...xxx
   ```

   (and so on in steps of 50,000)

11-3 SEQUENTIAL FILES - MERGE AND UPDATE

Sequential files are most useful for applications that require all, or most of, the file's records. For applications that require only a small portion of the file, a direct file might be more useful. However, sequential files are frequently more efficient, both in terms of the actual space occupied on the storage medium and in the time required to process the entire file.

The Merge Algorithm

Because of these savings, sequential files are widely used. As a result, a number of techniques have been developed for efficient modification and utilization of this type of file. The **merge** algorithm discussed here is one example. Others are indicated in the next section and in the exercises.

Suppose we have two non-empty binary files, each of which contains records where the first field is an indentification number, and the remaining fields contain other information. Assume each of these files is known to be in ascending (low to high) order based on the ID number, and, moreover, that neither file contains any duplicates.

Our goal is to create a combined file with these same properties: in order by ID number and with no duplicates. The technique we use is called "merging" the files and is similar to the action when two lanes of traffic merge into one.

The basic idea is to compare IDs from the two files repeatedly, always placing the lower one into the output file. Here is a very rough algorithm. (Record 1 and ID1 refer to the data from the first file. Record 2 and ID2 refer to the second file.)

```
read a record from each file (to get started)
repeat
   take action based on comparing ID1 to ID2:
      a. (ID1 < ID2) put record ID1 into the output file
         read another record from file 1
      b. (ID1 > ID2) put record 2 into the output file
         read another record from file 2
      c. (ID1 = ID2) process a "duplicate" error
         read another record from file 1
         read another record from file 2
perform ???
```

Because we have not discussed how to terminate the loop, it is not yet clear what steps might follow it.

There are a number of options for processing a duplicate record. For this example, we choose to place the record from the first file on the output file and print an error message. Because both records have then been processed, we read a new record from each of the two files.

There are several ways to handle loop termination. For example, we might use a *while* loop with the condition

while (not Eof(File1) and (not Eof(File2)) do

When the loop terminates, then Eof(File1) is true, or Eof(File2) is true, or possibly both. We could write a decision structure based on these conditions.

This method is complicated because in Pascal, the end-of-file condition becomes true as the last record is read. Thus, for example, the code for the case where Eof(File1) is true but Eof(File2) is not has to do two things: process the remaining record from file 1 and then copy the rest of file 2 (if any) to the output file. To simplify matters, we might use Boolean variables File1Done and File2Done. File1Done signifies that we have attempted a read when no more records are in file 1, and similarly for File2Done. The step "read record from file 1" in the algorithm could be written similar to this:

```
if Eof(File1) then         {Previous read got last record}
   File1Done := true
else
   Read(File1, Record1)
```

A third possibility uses **sentinel records** on the input files. These are records whose ID number field is $+\infty$. By $+\infty$, we mean a value larger than any ID existing on either input file. For example, maxint would probably be appropriate for our integer IDs, because it is probably larger than any legal ID number.

Note. If we use this "plus infinity" technique, then the **sentinel value** "$+\infty$" must be chosen carefully. It must not be possible to use this value for actual data.

How does the sentinel record help us? Suppose that we reach the end of file 1 first. Then ID1 is maxint and the condition (ID1 > ID2) is true for each record of the second file until it also reaches its sentinel record. This causes the remaining records of file 2 to be copied to the output file. We terminate the loop when both sentinel records are reached.

In Figure 11-10, we present a procedure to accomplish the merge using this technique. The main program is to handle the file open and close operations. The types DataRecord and DataFile are defined in the main program. For the purpose of our procedure, we need only know that the data record contains an ID field. Likewise, we use a constant "Infinity" defined in the main program. Thus, this procedure could be used in a variety of contexts.

An important question for this procedure is: How did the sentinel record get into the input files? The answer is: Because these are binary files, a program created them. If they were text files created by a user, then that person would have had to put them there.

```
procedure MergeFiles (var File1, File2, MergedFile: DataFile);

{Written by:   xxxxxxxx, xx/xx/xx}
{Purpose:      To merge files}
{Globals used: Infinity - a constant larger than any ID}
{Parameters:   File1 - the first file to merge}
{              File2 - the second file to merge}
{              MergedFile - the resulting merged file}

  var
    Record1: DataRecord;      {first file record}
    Record2: DataRecord;      {second file record}

begin {MergeFiles}

{*** Prime the loop by reading from both files}

  Read(File1, Record1);
  Read(File2, Record2);

{*** Repeatedly put the smaller on the output}

  while (Record1.ID <> Infinity) or (Record2.ID <> Infinity) do
    begin
      if Record1.ID < Record2.ID then
        begin
          Write(MergedFile, Record1);
          Read(File1, Record1)
        end
      else if Record1.ID > Record2.ID then
        begin
          Write(MergedFile, Record2);
          Read(File2, Record2)
        end
      else
        begin
          Writeln('Duplicate ID: ', Record1.ID);
          Writeln('Tap <RETURN> to continue ');
          Readln;
          Write(MergedFile, Record1);
          Read(File1, Record1);
          Read(File2, Record2)
        end {if}
    end; {while}

{*** Put a sentinel record on the output file}

  Write(MergedFile, Record1)

end; {MergeFiles}
```

Figure 11-10 Merging sequential files.

Observe that the procedure puts a sentinel record at the end of the output file. Thus, the output file is suitable as input to the merge at some later date.

This raises an important point. If this technique is to be used for merging, then all the sequential files maintained by the organization must have a sentinel record. This affects every program that accesses those files. Perhaps a better approach is not to use an actual sentinel record, but to write the program to simulate the existence of a sentinel record. For example, rather than Read(File1, Record1), we could use

```
if Eof(File1) then       {last record has been read}
   Record1.ID := Infinity
else
   Read(File1, Record1)
```

Efficiency Note. Suppose that one of the files reaches the end long before the other. For example, suppose file 2 reaches the end of file with approximately 1000 records remaining in file 1. Then this procedure compares Record1.ID to "infinity" 1000 times in order to copy the rest of file 1. Isn't this inefficient? Couldn't we simply terminate the loop when either file is done and copy the rest of the other file?

The answer is partially yes and partially no. It is inefficient, and we could terminate the loop as suggested. (This would make the procedure slightly more complicated.) However, in a file merge, the inefficiency is very minor. The time it takes to do the 1000 comparisons is miniscule in comparison to the 2000 accesses to the disk (or to tape) used to copy the records. (In an array merge, on the other hand, the inefficiency is more significant.)

This basic merge algorithm is one of the most important in computer science. In addition to being the basis for various file-update algorithms, it appears in many contexts. For example, it is the basis for merge sort, discussed in Chapter 10. It finds application in some forms of data structure used to represent polynomials. And it appears in handling "sparse matrices," matrices most of whose entries are 0.

Sequential-File Update

In this subsection, we give some indication of how the merge algorithm can be used to build procedures for **sequential file update.** The exercises develop the theme further.

First, consider this situation. A **master file** contains a list of employees and their year-to-date earnings. A **transaction file** contains a list of transactions to be processed against the master file. In this case, the transaction file represents a weekly payroll. The transactions records contain employee number and this week's pay. Provided both files are in increasing order, we can write an algorithm similar to our first merge algorithm:

> read the first record from each file (to get started)
> repeat
>   take action based on comparing master ID (MID) to transaction ID (TID):
>   (a) (MID < TID). This means that this employee had no check this week. Write the master record to the output file, and read a new master record.
>   (b) (MID > TID). This is an error situation—a check was issued for an employee number not on the master file. Report the error, and read another transaction record.

(c) (MID = TID). Add the week's pay to the year-to-date figure. Write the modified master record to the output file, and read a new record from both files.

after the loop, perform any necessary final steps

As for the merge algorithm itself, there are a variety of ways to accomplish the loop control. Depending on the method used, there may have to be some action taken after the loop terminates.

In this example, the resulting output file becomes the input master file when the program is run the following week. Exactly how this is handled is up to the organization. Here are two possibilities at opposite extremes:

1. Start with a master MasterIn with all figures 0. Run this with a file Week1, creating MasterOut. Use a file copy to copy this to MasterOut for the second week, and so on.
2. Start as before, but call the output Master1. Use this as input for the second week, creating Master2. By the end of the year, you would have 52 files containing a complete record of the year.

For our final example, suppose that the transaction file contains a list of items to be deleted from the master file. A deletion is accomplished by simply not writing the record to the output. Thus, in the decision structure of the basic merge algorithm, we have

(a) (ID1 < ID2) same as merge
(b) (ID1 > ID2) error; read transaction file
(c) (ID1 = ID2) just read both files

REVIEW

Terms and Concepts

infinity (+∞)
master file
merge
sentinel record

sentinel value
sequential-file value
transaction file

Algorithms

Basic Method

read a record from each file to get started
repeat these take action based on comparing ID1 to ID2:
  (a) (ID1 < ID2) put record 1 on output file
      read another record from file 1
  (b) (ID1 > ID2) put record 2 on output file
      read another record from file 2
  (c) (ID1 = ID2) process a duplicate error
    read another record from file 1
    read another record from file 2
after the loop, perform ???

Loops

1. Terminate when Eof is *true* for either file.
2. Terminate when an attempt is made to read past the end of file for either file.
3. Use initial records and terminate when both values are +∞.
4. Same as item 3, but terminate when either is +∞.
5. Simulate the sentinel record.

Sequential-File Updates. Sequential-file updates can be based on the fundamental merge algorithm; differences occur in what is done for each of the three branches in the decision structure.

EXERCISES

1. Write a procedure similar to the one in Figure 11-10, but not using sentinel records. The loop should be terminated as soon as Eof is *true* for either file. Be careful to write the portion following the loop correctly.
2. Repeat Exercise 1 using Boolean variables File1Done and File2Done as suggested in this section. Terminate the loop when either is *true*.
3. Repeat Exercise 1, "simulating" the sentinel record as suggested in this section. Terminate when both ID values are infinity.
4. Repeat Exercise 3, terminating when either ID value is infinity.
5. Comment on the pros and cons of the approaches in Figure 11-10 and in Exercises 1 to 4.
6. Two files containing names and other data are to be merged based on the names. What is an appropriate value for "plus infinity" in this case?
7. Suppose files that are in order from high to low are to be merged. How would this affect the algorithm? What type of sentinel value is appropriate?
8. Write a procedure that, for a master file, accepts from the terminal a list of numbers to be deleted, as shown in Figure 11-10. It should warn the user if the number entered is lower than the previous entry.
9. (a) Write a procedure to merge three files rather than two.
   (b) Write a procedure to expand this to merge 10 files. Can you suggest a way to merge 10 files without writing a new program?
10. Sometimes students try to write the decision structure of the merge algorithm using three *if* statements:

    ```
    if Record1.ID < Record2.ID then
      {code for < as in Figure 11-10};
    if Record1.ID > Record2.ID then
      {code for > as in Figure 11-10};
    if Record1.ID = Record2.ID then
      {code for = as in Figure 11-10};
    ```

    Criticize this by finding a pair of files for which it would not work properly.
11. Suppose we modify the third branch of the merge algorithm (ID1 = ID2) to the following: print the error message, and read a new record from file 2. Does this work? Justify your answer.
12. Write procedures similar to Figure 11-10 for the following:

(a) A master file has records consisting of an item number, department, and quantity. A transaction file has records containing only an item number. Each record in the transaction file represents a record to be removed from the master file. Both files are in order by item number and have no duplicates.

Create an output file consisting of the records in the master file with the indicated records removed. Print an error message for any faulty transaction item numbers.

(b) The master file is the same as for part (a). The transaction file contains a list of changes to be made. Each transaction record contains an item number and a new quantity for that item. Both files are in order by item number and have no duplicates.

Create an output file consisting of the records in the master file with the new quantity for each of the indicated items. Print an error message for any faulty transaction item numbers.

13. Combine the merge (which adds records) with the delete and change procedures of Exercise 12. The master file is the same as for Exercise 12. Each transaction record contains:

Transaction code (A = add, D = delete, C = change)
Item number
Department (blank for codes D or C)
Quantity (blank for code D)

Both files are in order by item number and have no duplicates. Write a procedure to create an output file consisting of the records in the master file with the indicated additions, deletions, and changes.

14. Write a program to update the drugstore inventory file created in Exercise 2, Section 11-1.

You have a transaction file containing this information: an item number, an item name, a department code, an inventory for each of nine locations (an array), and a transaction code. Except for the transaction code, the information is precisely the same as that on the master file. The transaction code has the same meaning as in Exercise 13. The transaction record can leave blank (or 0) any of the fields not actually being used in that type of transaction. You can assume that the information on the transaction record has been edited.

The following are to be done for a change transaction:

- If the item name on the transaction record is not blank, then change the item name.
- If the department code on the transaction record is not blank, then change the department code.
- Add each element in the inventory array to the corresponding element in the master record.

Instead of printing errors on the terminal, create an exception file. This file has records containing all the fields of the transaction record and a code for the type of error:

- Trying to add a record already there.
- Trying to delete a record not there.
- Trying to change a record not there.
- A resulting inventory amount that is less than 0 or more than 5000. (For this error, leave the master record with the faulty inventories; assume the error will be corrected later.)

15. Update algorithms based on the file-merge algorithm have one serious drawback. They do not handle multiple transactions for a single master record. Computer scientists have devised an algorithm, known as the *balance line algorithm*, which does handle multiple transactions.

EXERCISES

The basic idea is this: Rather than putting master records directly to the output file, put them in a new master record. Apply the transactions to this new master record. After all transactions have been applied, write the record to the output. In rough form, the algorithm can be described as follows:

read a record from each file (to get started)
repeat these four steps :
   1. ActiveKey := lower of MasterKey, TransactionKey
   2. if the MasterKey is equal to the ActiveKey
      copy the master record to new master record
      read another master record
   else
      set the new master record empty
   3. as long as the TransactionKey equals the ActiveKey
      apply 0 or more transactions to the new master record
   4. if the new master record is not empty, write it to the output file

after the outer loop, do any necessary final steps

(a) By tracing the algorithm for some sample files, determine what the phrase "apply a transaction" means for the six possible combinations:

TYPE OF TRANSACTION	NEW MASTER RECORD
Add	Empty
Add	Not empty
Delete	Empty
Delete	Not empty
Change	Empty
Change	Not empty

(b) Refine the algorithm to write a procedure to update a master file, as outlined in Exercise 13.

(c) Refine the algorithm to write a procedure to update a checking account master file. Each master record has an account number and balance. Each transaction record has an account number, type (check or deposit), and amount. The output file has an account number and the resulting balance. Record all error situations in an error file.

11-4 RANDOM-ACCESS-FILE TECHNIQUES

Files are convenient for the long-term storage of data. As long as a file is updated fairly infrequently, sequential access can be adequate. For example, a mailing list for an organization might be treated as a **sequential file**. Generally, this information is used in its entirety to generate a set of mailing labels. Updating might occur only once a month or even less frequently.

Even when a file is updated frequently, sequential access can be appropriate. For example, the "hours worked" and other fields on a file used to generate payroll checks might change every week. However, in this case, most records in the file are modified. An algorithm that goes through the file sequentially making the changes is fairly efficient.

Sequential files become inadequate in situations where frequent changes occur to records scattered throughout the file. As we discussed in Section 11-3, each batch of changes to a sequential file requires going completely through the file. In addition, if we are using the file to look up records that are scattered throughout the file, we want a **random-access file**, a file in which records can be accessed directly in a random order. Even in applications where a sequential file is adequate, a random-access file may be more convenient. For example, consider an interactive payroll system. Using a sequential file, a payroll clerk could enter the hours for each person on the file. However, the clerk would have to do so in the same order as the records were listed on the file. With a random-access file, the values could be entered in any desired order, perhaps by several payroll clerks, one per department.

As a result of these and similar considerations, random-access files have become more and more important in computing. As a result, THINK Pascal has included facilities for using this type of file, although some versions of Pascal do not.

Note. These files go under a variety of names. The term **direct file** signifies the ability to access the desired record directly, without having had to access all the preceding records. The term random-access file, similarly, signifies the ability to access the records in "random" order. The term **relative file** signifies the fact that, in order to access a record, the program supplies the relative record number (or just record number). We generally refer to the files as random-access files, but we are free to use the terms interchangeably.

Random-Access-File Commands

We already know quite a bit about THINK Pascal random-access files. For THINK Pascal, a random-access file is any type of file, but opened differently than a sequential file. There are also a few additional procedural functions that allow us to use these files in a random fashion.

First, two useful concepts. Each record in a binary file has a **record number**. The records are numbered starting at 0. As a simple example, suppose we have a file containing five records (fields of name and major):

Sue	CPS
Sam	MAT
Joe	MGT
Mary	ENG
Eileen	HIS

We will soon learn how to read record 3. If we do so, we obtain the record (Mary, ENG) because the record numbers start at 0.

The file-management system maintains a **file pointer**, which is initialized to 0 when the file is opened. After any read or write, the file pointer points to (contains the record number of) the next record. For example, after we read record 3, the file pointer's value is 4. At this point, unless we do something to modify the file pointer, another Read reads record 4 (and a Write replaces the current value of record 4).

With these concepts in mind, let us describe various capabilities THINK Pascal provides. The first five are procedures and the last two are functions.

1. Open(*file designator, file name*). Connects the program's name for the file (the file designator variable) and the file's name on the disk (the disk file name string), then opens the file for random access and sets the file pointer to 0 (that is, the first record of the file). Unlike a file opened with Reset or Rewrite, a file opened with Open can be both read from and written to.

2. Read(*file designator, variable*). Reads the record indicated by the file pointer, and advances the file pointer to the next record (adds 1 to the file pointer). In a text file, a "record" is taken to be 1 character, so a Read of a random text file works the same as a Read of a sequential text file — the next character is read, and the file pointer moves to the next character. (Readln can also be used on random text files, and works the same as when used on sequential text files.)

3. Write(*file designator, variable*). Writes the record indicated by the file pointer, and adds 1 to the file pointer. This replaces the previous data (if any) stored in that record. Write and Writeln of random text files works the same as when used on sequential text files.

4. Seek(*file designator, N*). Sets the file pointer to the Nth record, where N is a longint expression. The value of N should lie between 0 and the file size.

5. Close(*file designator*). Closes the file. This is necessary to make sure that all changes are reflected in the file on the disk. Your program should close all the files it opens.

6. Eof(*file designator*). This Boolean function's value is *true* if the file pointer is positioned beyond the end of file, otherwise *false*.

7. FilePos(*file designator*). This longint function supplies the current value of the file pointer (0 for the first record, and so on).

To illustrate these ideas, we show some segments of Pascal code. In each, we assume that the files are opened and closed by other portions of the program. We work with the direct file described previously; each record has a name and an age. We assume these declarations for the files and records involved.

```
type
    StudentRecord = record
        Name: String50;
        Major: String3
    end;
    StudentFile = file of StudentRecord;

var
    Person: StudentRecord;
    ClassFile: StudentFile;
```

We assume that a procedure GetData(Person) prompts the user for a person's name and major.

The first segment writes 25 records to the file, numbered 0 to 24. (The file was opened using Rewrite.)

```
for I := 1 to 25 do
  begin
     GetData(Person);
     Write(ClassFile, Person)
  end {for}
```

The second segment illustrates how we can add a record to the end of an existing file:

```
GetData(Person);
NewPosition := FileSize(ClassFile);
Seek(ClassFile, NewPosition);
Write(ClassFile, Person)
```

Suppose, for example, that the file size is 23. Then there are currently 23 records numbered 0 to 22. The Seek sets the file pointer to record 23, so that the Write puts the new record right after record 22.

Our third segment reads a series of record numbers from the user and prints the corresponding data from the file. For record numbers equal to the file size or larger, an error message is printed.

```
repeat
  Write('Enter a record number (negative to quit): ');
  Readln(RecNum);
     if RecNum >= FileSize(ClassFile) then
        Writeln('Too High')
     else
        if RecNum >= 0 then
           begin
              Seek(ClassFile, RecNum);
              Read(ClassFile, Person);
              with Person do
                 Writeln('Name: ', Name, ' Major: ', Major)
           end {if}
until RecNum < 0
```

Finally, we present a segment that changes all 'CPS' majors to 'CSC'. (The file has just been Reset.)

```
while not Eof(ClassFile) do
  begin
     Read(ClassFile, Person);
     if Person.Major = 'CPS' then
        begin
           Person.Major := 'CSC';
           Seek(ClassFile, FilePos(ClassFile) - 1));
           Write(ClassFile, Person)
        end {if}
  end {while}
```

Notice that, if we did not use a Seek to "back up one," we would have overwritten the wrong record.

Random-Access-File Algorithms

The examples that follow illustrate some basic techniques for working with random-access files. The major difficulty with these files is that the program must know the proper record number. If this number is read from some other file or from the user, as in the previous example, then the user must know the record numbers of the records to be processed. There are a number of techniques that have been devised for this purpose. Studying them in detail typically occupies a major portion of a course in file processing. We just touch on some of the issues.

Here is an example that illustrates a simple technique for determining record number:

A small liberal arts college maintains a student data file. Among other things, the file contains a four-digit student number, the total number of credits attempted to date, and the number of grade points earned to date. When the file was originally created, it was decided to use the student number itself as the record number. A file was created containing records 0 to 9999, where each record contained a flag telling whether that student number was active.

The student number can be viewed as a **key** to the record; given the student number, we know which student's record we wish to see. In this case, we have the record number equal to the key.

The procedure in Figure 11-11 updates this file. To do so, it reads a sequential file containing a series of student numbers, credit hours attempted during one semester, and grade points earned during that semester. Using the given student number, it retrieves the student's record, updates the record, and writes it back onto the file.

Notes

1. It would not be necessary to include the student number on the record because this number is the same as the record number.
2. A field of the record indicates whether that record number is active. Requests to update an inactive record are logged on an error file. (The record number is, however, assumed to be valid, that is, between 0 and (file size − 1).
3. We assume that the main program handles opening and closing the file.

Using the record number as the key can be a problem. When the record number is the key, then we must know the key to obtain the record. Moreover, this key must be numeric, and the number of digits allowed in the key is limited. There are many applications where it is more convenient to use an alphabetic key. For example, when students come in to check their records, they may not remember their student numbers. Their names might be a more convenient key.

As a similar example, consider a file that lists the local tax rate for the cities, towns, and so forth in a given state. For such a file, a convenient key would be the locality name or perhaps an abbreviation of its name. If the file is set up with this alphabetical key, then some means must be provided in the program to determine the desired record number, given the locality name.

```
procedure UpdateQP (var StudentFile: MasterFile; var UpdateList:
    TransactionFile; var ErrorLog: text);

{Written by:   XXXXXXXXX XX/XX/XX}
{Purpose:      To read a sequential transaction file, and add data to}
{              the records of a master student file}
{Parameters:   StudentFile - the file of student records}
{              UpdateList  - the file of transactions}
{              ErrorLog    - a text file for error messages}

  var
    Semester: UpdateRecord;              {figures for this semester}
    Student: StudentRecord;              {master record}
    RecNum: integer;                     {record number}

begin

  while not Eof(UpdateList) do
    begin
      Read(UpdateList, Semester);
      RecNum := Semester.StudentNumber;
      Seek(StudentFile, RecNum);
      Read(StudentFile, Student);
      with Student do
        begin
          if not Active then
            Writeln(ErrorLog, 'Inactive record: ', RecNum)
          else
            begin
              Hours := Hours + Semester.Hours;
              QP := QP + Semester.QP;
              Seek(StudentFile, RecNum);                {back up}
              Write(StudentFile, Student)
            end {if}
        end {with}
    end {while}
end; {UpdateQP}
```

Figure 11-11 Updating a random access file.

A number of techniques have been devised to handle these and other considerations when working with random-access files. These techniques are beyond the scope of this text (although we do indicate some possibilities in the exercises). However, keep in mind that once the record number is calculated, the Seek, Read, or Write is identical in form to those presented in our examples.

Inactive Records

The example in Figure 11-11 illustrates one important aspect of working with random-access files. It is possible that there can be "gaps" in the file. In THINK Pascal files, those gaps are *logical* rather than *physical* gaps. That is, if a file contains record 200, it also contains records 0 through 199. However, some of those records may not contain meaningful information.

One way to deal with this is indicated in Figure 11-11. A Boolean field of the record can indicate that the record is inactive. Another possibility is to set some field of the record to a specific "dummy" value. For example, a name field that is null might signify an inactive record.

Whatever technique is used, all programs that access the file will have to apply the technique consistently. We would, perhaps, have a program to create the original file containing nothing but inactive records. Later, other programs would change some records to active status. We might also have a procedure to delete a record. For the file used in Figure 11-11, it could do so by setting

```
Student.Active := false
```

and then writing the record. Notice that a "deleted record," as used here, is one that is logically deleted, not physically deleted. The record is still there; it has just been marked inactive.

REVIEW

Terms and Concepts

direct file
file pointer
key
random-access number

record number
relative file
relative record number
sequential file

File Operations

1. Read, Readln, Write, Writeln, Close, Eof: Same as for sequential files.
2. Open: Opens a file for random access.
3. Seek(*file designator*, N): sets the file pointer to the Nth record (generally, N is in the range $0 \leq N \leq$ file size).
4. Function FilePos(*file designator*): shows the current value of the file pointer (record number).

Random-Access File Algorithms

1. Need to know desired record number.
2. Can mark records as inactive (deleted) in a variety of ways.

EXERCISES

1. Rewrite Case Study No. 9 (Section 6-4) to use random-access files rather than arrays. Use the items number as the key to the item file and the customer number as the key to the customer file.

2. A direct file contains a list of persons and companies to whom a church typically writes checks. Write the following set of routines for the church treasurer.

   Note: Each record contains the account name (25 characters) as it is to appear on the checks. If the name is '*', the account has been deleted.

   (a) *Lookup.* Given an account number (record number), display the account name.
   (b) *Addition.* Given a new account name, add it to the end of file. (Make sure it isn't a duplicate.)
   (c) *Printout.* Print a list of the current contents of the file: record number and account name. Ignore deleted records.
   (d) *Deletion.* Given a record number, mark it as deleted. (First display the name on the screen and verify that this is the one the user wanted to delete.)
   (e) *Compression.* Remove all deleted records by copying the valid records to a temporary file, reopening the account file, and then recopying the valid records.

3. A direct file keeps a list of checks written by a church. A control file contains one record with three fields: the first check number in the file, the last check number in the file, and the last check number printed and sent. For the other records, the check number is the record number, and the records contain these fields:

DESCRIPTION	TYPE
Date (yymmdd): 870407 is April 7, 1987	String
Payee (three-digit code)	Integer
Budget category (two-digit code)	Integer
Amount (dollars, cents): 1013,45 is $1,013.45	Record with two integer fields

   The "payee" code refers to the file of Exercise 2. The "budget category" code refers to a similar file that lists budget category items.

   Give subprograms for the following. Assume the main program has opened the files.

   (a) *New Check.* Given a date, "paid to" code, "category" code, and amount, add a check to the end of the file. First, however, make sure that the given date is after the date of the last check written and that both codes are valid. Set a Boolean parameter OK to indicate success or failure.
   (b) *Check List.* Create a printed list of the checks on the file with these columns: date, number, paid to (name, not code), budget category (name), and amount. As an optional extra, group indicate by date; that is, print the date only when it changes. Print the dates in the form mm/dd/yy.
   (c) *Partial List.* Modify part (b) to print only those checks whose dates lie between two given dates, inclusive.
   (d) *Check Print.* Print all checks that have not yet been printed. Devise a reasonable check layout. Print the date in the form "January 16, 1988". Print the amount preceded by asterisks, as in "***35.49". Also print the amount in the form "EXACTLY 35 DOLLARS AND 49 CENTS".
   (e) *Budget Summary.* Create a printed report showing how much was spent in each budget category between two given dates. You can assume that the budget category file records contain a field for use as an accumulator.

4. How would you modify the program of Exercise 3 so that the first check written in the year would be record 0, the next record 1, and so on? (For a church whose first check was 1927, this would save almost 2000 empty records.)

EXERCISES

5. An employee file contains records 0 to 999. Among the fields is a LastName field set to '*' for unused records. For several applications, we wish to access the records in alphabetical order by last name. Write the following collection of program segments to accomplish this (see also Exercise 6).
   (a) Write code to set up an array of records with fields RecNum and Name. For record I in the array, RecNum is the record number and Name is the name of the Ith active record on the file. (Skip unused records.)
   (b) Sort the array into alphabetical order by name.
   (c) Create a sequential file that contains the record number field from the sorted array, one number per file record.

6. See Exercise 5. If we are given a list of record numbers to be processed, we can easily process a direct file in that order. Use the file created in Exercise 5(c) to display a printed list of the name, hourly rate, department, clock number, marital status, and number of dependents in alphabetical order by last name. Make reasonable assumptions about the structure of the master file.

7. See Exercise 5. Rather than creating a separate file to get an alphabetical listing, we could have each record in the master file show which record is next in alphabetical order. Each record might contain these fields:

DESCRIPTION	TYPE
Name	String
"Next": a three-digit number showing which record number comes next in alphabetical order	Integer
Other data	Miscellaneous

Suppose that a control file contains only a single number ("First") that tells which record is first in alphabetical order. Also, suppose that the "Next" field for the person who is last contains the number −1.

   (a) Write a program to print the file as in Exercise 6, using the control file to get started and using the "Next" field to move through the file.
   (b) Write algorithms for inserting a new employee and for deleting an employee. Each involves changing some of the "Next" fields in the file (and, perhaps, the "First" field in the control file).

8. In this exercise, we explore simple *hashing* and *collision-handling* strategies for determining where a record should be placed in a direct-access file.
   (a) Suppose we want to place some records in a file that we have set up to have 10 empty records, numbered from 0 to 9. The records have keys that are four digit numbers. Let us follow the rule: Try to place the record in the location (that is, record number) indicated by the last digit of the key. (This rule is an example of a simple *hashing function*.) What record would that rule have us use for the following keys: 1403, 1695, 1138, 5689, 4122, and 8904?
   (b) These records ran well. There were no *collisions*, that is, no two records yielded the same output from the hashing function. (We might put it as "no two records hashed to the same location.") In the more general case, we must use some collision-handling strategy. One approach has a number of names, including the very descriptive "consecutive spill." For example, "if the record hashes to location 4 and that is full, put it in 5; if that is full, put it in 6; and so on." Using this strategy to handle collisions and the same empty file and hashing function as in part (a), show where these records would go: 1403, 1795, 1138,

2014, 1183, 8998, and 3114. (Notice that locations can be full because of collisions or due to records that have already spilled out of their hash location.)

(c) What should you do with a record that "spills" past location 9, which is the last location in the file? The usual method is to treat the file as if it were circular, so that location 0 follows location 9. Continuing with the file in part (b), add these records: 9000, 8615, and 4029.

(d) A *probe* is the act of examining a location to see whether it is empty. For example, putting in 1403 required one probe because location 3 was empty. How many probes did each of the other records require?

(e) Write a program to create a file containing 10 empty records, numbered 0 to 9. Each record contains a key and a name. Read data from the user to be placed into the file. By using the hashing function (hint: use the mod function) and the collision-handling method described previously, the program should insert the records. At the end, it should print the file in order by record number to verify that it worked correctly. Note: The loop that examines locations to see if they are empty should have three ways to terminate: an empty location is found, a duplicate key is found, or all 10 locations have been examined and none is empty (file is full).

(f) Modify part (e) to handle more keys by setting up a file of size 100. Modify your hashing function appropriately.

(g) If you placed 75 records into a file of size 100 using the program of part (f), about how many total probes would you expect it to take? (See part (d).) To answer the question, write a program that does the steps described in what follows in a loop and reports the statistics. The steps are initialize the file to contain 100 empty records; generate random keys and place them into the file, counting the probes for nonduplicate keys; and terminate the loop when 75 different keys have been inserted.

EXERCISES

Appendix A

Additional THINK Pascal Features

In this appendix, we describe a few features of THINK Pascal that were not covered in the body of the text. These topics are "extra" in the sense that it is possible to get by quite adequately without them. (We have done so in all the program examples in the text.) However, there are instances in which some of these additional capabilities prove useful in designing and writing (especially larger) THINK Pascal programs; we discuss those here.

THINK Pascal also has several other advanced features, which include those that allow us to take full advantage of the Mac's built-in windowing, graphics, and sound generating capabilities. Since these are advanced features, we leave them for programming courses that follow the first, introductory one for which this book is intended.

A-1 TRANSFER STATEMENTS (LABELS, GOTO, EXIT)

Pascal permits us to define a **label** and use a **goto** statement. In THINK Pascal, labels are strings of digits between 0 and 9999, and must be declared in a label declaration of the form

```
label 10, 100, 200;
```

for example. The label declaration precedes the constant declaration in a program or procedure. A label is attached to a statement by writing the label, a colon, and then the statement, such as

```
10: if X = Y then
        A := B + C;
100: Y := X + Z;
200: for i := 1 to 10 do ...
900 ;
```

Notice in the last example that the label is attached to a null statement. The statement

```
goto 900
```

causes the program to start executing statements at (transfers control to) the statement labeled 900.

Generally, a *goto* can be used to transfer into, within, or out of the body of a loop, the true or false part of an *if-then-else*, the body of a *with* block, or even into or out of a procedure or function.

For example, the following code is valid:

```
.  .  .
label 10;
.  .  .

begin
   .  .  .
   while ... do
      begin
         .  .  .
         if ... then goto 10;
         .  .  .
      end;
   .  .  .
   10: ;
   .  .  .
end.
```

Transferring into the middle of a statement from outside of it (such as jumping to one of the statements within the *begin* and *end* of a *for* loop) is legal, but definitely not recommended—the effects of such a jump are often unpredictable. For example:

```
label 10;
.  .  .
begin
   .  .  .
   if  ... then goto 10;
   .  .  .
   for I := 1 to 100 do
      begin
         .  .  .
         10: ;
         .  .  .
      end;
   .  .  .
```

If the jump to statement 10 is made, we have no idea how many times the *for* loop executes, nor that the value I has during each pass through the loop. Writing a program with unpredictable behavior is not a good idea.

The *goto* statement is very controversial. Historically, it has been used in ways that have made programs extremely difficult to understand. As a result, some individuals (and some companies) completely forbid its use. Others use it only in a few well-defined situations. For example, some might use the *goto* to leave a nested loop when an error is discovered.

A-1 TRANSFER STATEMENTS (LABELS, GOTO, EXIT)

> **Note.** THINK Pascal does place some restrictions on how a *goto* can be used. For example, it is illegal to branch out of the *then* part of an *if* statement into the *else* part of the same statement, or out of a procedure into a statement that is nested within another procedure. The exact rules are somewhat cumbersome to remember; perhaps it is best just to remember to use a *goto* only in a situation where it will always have predictable behavior.

As an example of the controlled use of the *goto*, consider the procedure XXXX (which follows) that does some unspecified process. During the course of this process, two error conditions could be detected. The procedure is to quit processing upon discovering an error. Here are two solutions:

```
procedure XXXX( . . . );
label 900
begin
   . . .
   if error #1 exists then
      begin
         Error := 1;
         goto 900
      end;
      . . .
   if error #2 exists then
      begin
         Error := 2;
         goto 900
      end;
      . . ..
900: end;

procedure XXXX( . . . );
begin
   . . .
   if error #1 exists then
      Error := 1
   else
      begin
         . . .
         if error #2 exists then
            Error := 2
         else
            begin
               . . .
            end
      end;
```

The use of the *goto* avoids nesting decisions. You might want to ponder the form of the two solutions if there were, say, five possible errors instead of only two.

Many programmers use the *goto* statement to terminate the execution of a procedure. However, because of the tendency to abuse the *goto*, those who use it in this fashion may feel uncomfortable doing so. THINK Pascal provides an alternative that achieves the same result but without opening the Pandora's box of the unrestricted use of the *goto*. This alternative is the **Exit** procedure. Exit (*ProcName*) means "leave the procedure (or function) called *ProcName*." It is equivalent to a *goto* that branches to the end of the given procedure. In the previous example, the statement Exit (XXXX) could replace each "goto 900" statement. We would not declare or use the label 900 in this case.

Notes

1. Even the use of the *Exit* is somewhat controversial. If you are programming for someone else, find out if it is allowed.
2. The *Exit* procedure is not available in standard Pascal.

A-2 VARIANT RECORDS

Records were first introduced in Chapter 5 and used extensively in the following chapters. The Pascal record structure is useful both as a way to organize our data in a program and as an implementation of the record concept for files.

The Pascal record data type includes a capability not discussed in the body of the text: the ability to contain what is called a **variant part**. (The records we have used previously contained only a **fixed part**.) As an example of a record structure with a variant part, suppose we want to store data on various people associated with a college. These people are in three categories, with the following associated data to be stored:

Faculty:
  Name
  Permanent address
  Position (faculty)
  Highest earned degree
  University awarding this degree

Student:
  Name
  Permanent address
  Position (student)
  High school graduated
  Combined SAT score

Staff:
  Name
  Permanent address
  Position (staff)
  Job description

One approach would be to define data types as follows:

```
type
   PositionType = (Faculty, Staff, Student);
   PersonalData = record
       Name: string[50];
       PermAddress: string[150];
       Position: PositionType;
       Degree: string[8];
       University: string[25];
       HighSchool: string[20];
       SAT: integer;
       Job: string[15]
     end;
```

For each person, the data that did not apply would be left as null, or zero. But it would waste storage, as inapplicable fields would still be present in each instance of the record.

The alternative is to define a record with both a fixed part and a variant part:

```
type
   PositionType = (Faculty, Staff, Student);
   PersonalData = record
       Name: string[50];
       PermAddress: string[150];
       case Position: PositionType of
          Faculty: (Degree: string[8];
                    University: string[25]);
          Student: (HighSchool: string[20];
                    SAT: integer);
          Staff: (Job: string[15])
     end;
```

Notes

1. The fields Name and PermAddress form the fixed part of the record. Every record of this type contains these fields.
2. The Position field is called the **tag field**. It determines whether the remainder of the record consists of a degree and university, or a high school and SAT score, or a job description.
3. The remainder of the record is the variant part. It consists of a list of fields for each value of the tag field. This list is enclosed in parentheses. It can be empty, but the parentheses are required in any case.
4. The variant part of a record must follow its fixed part.

With a variable Person of type PersonalData, we can write code similar to these examples:

```
Person.Name := 'Joe Smith'
Person.Position := Staff
Readln(Person.SAT)
```

```
with Person do Job := 'President'
if Person.SAT > 1000 then . . .
```

Note. It is up to the programmer to maintain consistency. For example, the assignment

```
Person.SAT := 1215
```

is allowed even if Person.Position were Faculty. The results are unpredictable.

As an example of how the variant record concept might be used, consider the program of Figure 6-10. In that program, we used two files, a control file and a data file. The control file contained a single record that gave the number of students, tests, and programs represented in the data file. An alternate approach is to place this count as the first record in the data file. To do so, we would redefine the StudentRecord type as

```
type
    RecordType = (ControlRec, StudentRec);
    StudentRecord = record
        case Indicator: RecordType of
            Control: (NStudents: integer;
                      NTests: integer;
                      NPrograms: integer);

            Student: (Name: String20;
                      TestList: TestArray;
                      Exam: integer;
                      ProgList: ProgramArray;
                      Average: real;
                      Letter: char)
    end;
```

We would do away with the control file, with the variable Control declared to be of type StudentRecord. (Control.Indicator would have the value ControlRec.)

What are the advantages and disadvantages of using variant records? They allow us to store data when the records share some information but have some information that is different. In doing so, they save space. In the PersonalData example, each record using the original form is about 95 bytes, but only about 56 with the variant record form. (Space is allotted for the fixed part and the longest of the alternatives in the variant part.)

Another advantage is that they can remove the need for control files. On the other hand, the syntax is more difficult and can lead to confusion on the part of the programmer or the reader of the program.

As a final comment, we note that the tag field variable can be omitted. This is an advanced topic that we do not pursue in this text.

A-3 NESTED PROCEDURES

You have seen many examples of procedures and functions in this book. For the rest of this section, we use the word procedure, but what we discuss here applies equally to functions.

We have declared user-defined procedures within a program unit after the variables have been declared and before the program's executable statements. Variables referenced within these procedures have been one of the following:

1. arguments of the procedure
2. local variables, accessible only within the procedure
3. global variables, accessible everywhere within the program (unless the name was as in 1 or 2)

In Pascal, we can define a procedure within another procedure (and in turn define a procedure within that procedure, to as many levels of nesting as we like). Such procedures are called **nested procedures**. The effects are to limit access to the procedures nested within another, and to create variables whose scopes lie between local variables and the global variables discussed previously.

Consider, for example, the program in Figure A-1.

```
program Nested;
var
   I, J, K: integer;
   procedure P1(X1, X2: integer);
      var
         L, M, N: integer;
      procedure P2(Y1, Y2: integer);
         var
            O, P, Q: integer;
      begin {P2}
         .
         .
         .
      end; {P2}
      procedure P3(Z1, Z2: integer);
      var
         R, S, T: integer;
      begin {P3}
         .
         .
         .
      end; {P3}
   begin {P1}
      .
      .
      .
   end; {P1}
begin {Nested}
   .
   .
   .
end.
```

Figure A-1   Nested procedures.

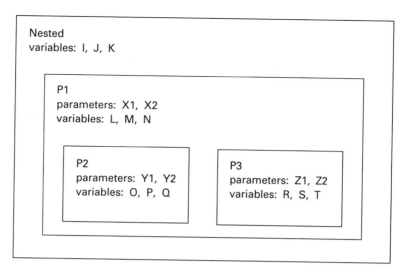

Figure A-2.

In this example, procedures P2 and P3 are defined within procedure P1. They are said to be nested within P1. This has implications concerning the scope of the program's variables. For the discussion that follows, it may be helpful to refer to Figure A-2, which shows P2 and P3 defined within P1, and P1 defined within the main program Nested.

The variables I, J, and K are global, as before. They can be referenced in any of the procedures P1, P2, and P3, or in the main program. The variables O, P, and Q and the parameters Y1 and Y2 are local to P2 and can only be referenced there. Likewise, R, S, T, Z1, and Z2 can be used only within the body of P3. The variables L, M, and N and the parameters X1 and X2 can be referenced within the body of P1. Moreover, they can also be referenced within the bodies of P2 and P3 because P2 and P3 are declared within P1. Visualize the boxes in Figure A-2 as one-way mirrors that allow us to look out from (but not into) a procedure, and imagine being inside the body of a procedure. The variables you can see as you look out are those variables this procedure can reference.

The portion of a program in which a variable can be referenced is called that variable's **scope**. Thus, the scope of the variable L in the example consists of the bodies of procedures P1, P2, and P3. In general, the scope of a variable is the procedure in which it is declared and any procedure nested within that procedure. However, declaring a variable within a procedure "masks" or "hides" variables of the same name that were declared outside of that procedure. For example, suppose that procedure P3 declared a variable L. Then the scope of the variable L defined in P1 would no longer include P3; any reference to L within P3 would refer to the L declared in P3.

What are the disadvantages and advantages of nested-procedure definitions? The primary disadvantage is obvious: They considerably complicate determining a variable's scope. They also make it less likely that the compiler will detect the failure to declare a variable. As a result, nested procedures should be used with some care.

There are, however, at least two important advantages. One is found with a package of programs a developer might supply. The person writing the package may want to place

A-3 NESTED PROCEDURES

subprograms within the modules that use them. These modules are not visible to the user of the package, so he or she do not have to avoid the module names in choosing identifiers.

A second advantage is illustrated by the QuickSort procedure of Figure A-3. This procedure is a modification of Figure 6-14 (page 490); the changes are in italics.

```pascal
procedure QuickSort (var A: IntegerArray; N: integer);

   {Written by:   XXXXXXXXXX XX/XX/XX}
   {Purpose:      To sort an array, using the quicksort technique}
   {Parameters:   A - update, the array to sort}
   {              N - input, the upper bound of the portion of the array}
   {                  to sort}
   {Procedures used:  QSort, to perform the actual sort}

      procedure Partition (Low, High: integer; var PivotLocation: integer);

         {Written by:   XXXXXXXXXX XX/XX/XX}
         { Purpose:     To partition an array into three parts:}
         {              1. values less or equal to the pivotal element}
         {              2. the pivotal element}
         {              3. values greater than or equal to the pivotal element}
         {Parameters: Low, High - input, the portion of the array to partition}
         {            PivotLocation - output, the location for the pivot}
         {                            element}
         {Procedures used:  Swap, to swap two elements of the array}
         {Globals modified: A (from QuickSort), the array being partitioned}

            var
              I: integer;              {used to locate large values}
              J: integer;              {used to locate small values}
              Pivot: integer;          {the pivotal element}

            procedure Swap (var I, J: integer);

              {Written by:   XXXXXXXX  XX/XX/XX}
              {Purpose:      To swap two integers}
              {Parameters:   I, J - update, the integers to switch}

                 var
                   Temp: integer;      {holding variable}

              begin
                 Temp := I;
                 I := J;
                 J := Temp
              end;

         begin {Partition}
            I := Low;
            J := High + 1;
            Pivot := A[Low];

            repeat
```

```
            {*** Move I to right looking for a value >= the pivot}

                repeat
                    I := I + 1
                until (I = High) or (A[I] >= Pivot);

            {*** Move J to left looking for a <= the pivot}

                repeat
                    J := J - 1
                until A[J] <= Pivot;

            {*** Swap if the values are out of order}

                if I < J then
                    Swap(A[I], A[J])

            until I >= J;

        {*** Put the pivotal element in the proper place, and return the value}
        {    of its subscript to the calling module}

            Swap(A[Low], A[J]);
            PivotLocation := J

        end; {Partition}

        procedure QSort (Low, High: integer);

            {Written by:    XXXXXXXXXX XX/XX/XX}
            {Purpose:       To sort an array, using the quicksort technique}
            {Parameters:    Low, High - input, the portion of the array to sort}
            {Procedures used: Partition, to partition the array into two}
            {                 subarrays QSort, called recursively to sort the two}
            {                 subarrays}
            {Globals modified: A (from QuickSort), the array being sorted}

            var
                PivotSub: integer;          {Location of pivotal element}

        begin {QSort}
            if Low < High then
                begin
                    Partition(Low, High, PivotSub);
                    QSort(Low, PivotSub - 1);
                    QSort(PivotSub + 1, High)
                end {if}
        end; {QSort}

    begin {QuickSort}
        QSort(1, N)
    end; {QuickSort}
```

Figure A-3   (continued)

The advantages to this arrangement are as follows:

1. The main program can invoke QuickSort using

   `QuickSort(TestArray, TestSize)`

   rather than

   `QuickSort(TestArray, 1, TestSize)`

   Having to supply the parameter 1 seems unnatural.
2. The recursive calls do not have to pass the parameter A; Partition and QSort are defined within QuickSort, so the scope of its parameter A includes those procedures. This speeds up the program only slightly, as A was a var parameter. If the array A had been a value parameter, the improvement would be quite significant. (For example, try writing a recursive binary search using the two approaches. If the array to be searched is passed as a value parameter, as one would do to avoid inadvertently changing the array's values, the difference in speed is significant.)
3. The procedure Partition is a specialized procedure that only seems useful within the context of the quicksort algorithm. Defining it within QuickSort thus seems reasonable.
4. The procedure Swap could be defined inside of any one of several places: Partition, QuickSort, QSort, or the main program. It has been placed inside Partition because that is where it is used. However, it is a utility procedure, so we might reasonably have chosen to define it in the main program. In this way, a main program that needed to do some swapping could reference the procedure.

A-4 UNITS

Introduction

We have used predefined units throughout the text to take advantage of built-in Macintosh features. For example, rather than spending time writing our own random-number generator, we used the Random function in the QuickDraw unit (which THINK automatically accesses for us).

THINK allows us to define our own units. Units have several advantages:

1. They are self-contained blocks of Pascal that can be compiled separately from the main program (or other units) that employ them. This feature allows us to write, test, and then use these modules in any program. Developing large programs is also faster: if we make a change to a unit, we only need to recompile its several lines — not all 20,000 or 50,000 lines of the program.
2. They help promote information hiding. The structure of units is such that the user of the unit is only allowed to use the constants, types, variables, functions, and procedures the writer of the unit explicitly makes available. These items are often called **public**. All the lower-level details of how these items are defined are hidden from the program using the unit; these details are **private**. If the private part of a unit needs to be changed, the program employing the unit does not require modification; only the unit itself is affected.

3. They promote software reuse. You have seen how easy it is to employ a unit in a program; this ease makes units an attractive alternative to rewriting code.

4. Units speed the development of large program projects involving several programmers. Once the public objects of the units are defined, a programmer can write the unit with minimal communication with colleagues. The private details of the unit are hidden from all users of that unit; the programmer need not worry that how she implements the unit will have side effects when used in a program. Since communication among programs is one of the most time-intensive activities during a large project, reducing the need for programmers to communicate speeds program development.

Defining a Unit

A unit has three parts: a *header* that names the unit; an *interface* part, which declares the public objects; and an *implementation* part, which declares the private objects and contains the details of the procedures and functions in the interface part. The header, interface part, and implementation part appear in the unit in that order; the unit's definition ends with an *end* followed by a period.

The header has the form

```
unit unit name;
```

where the *unit name* is a name we give to the unit (such as SortRoutines).

The interface part begins with the word *interface* and can contain constant, type, and variable declarations, written the same way as we did for a THINK program. It also contains the heading lines of procedures and functions we wish to make public.

The implementation part begins with the word *implementation* and can contain constant, type, variable, procedure, and function declarations. These objects and routines cannot be employed by a program using the function. Their usual purpose is to serve as aids to the public procedures and functions. The implementation part also contains the full declarations of the public procedures and functions, except that their header lines do not need to list parameters or the function result type; only the word *procedure* or *function* need appear, followed by the routine's name and a semicolon.

An Example

Suppose we placed several sorts into one unit called SortRoutines. We could include quicksort, selection sort, merge sort, and so on; the user then could call the sorting procedure that worked best with the data at hand. In Figure A-3, we present the beginnings of defining SortRoutines by including the QuickSort procedure from the previous section. To include this procedure in a unit, we do the following:

1. Define type IntegerArray and the QuickSort procedure in the interface part of the unit to make them available to the program using the unit.

2. Place the procedure Swap into the implementation part of the unit, since we only want our sort routines to have access to it; although potentially useful to a user, it is not the purpose of this unit to swap variables.

The resulting unit definition is shown in Figure A-4.

```
unit SortRoutines;

interface

  type
    IntegerArray = array[1..1000] of integer;

  procedure Quicksort (var A: IntegerArray; N: integer);

implementation

  procedure Swap (var I, J: integer);

    {Written by:    XXXXXXXX    XX/XX/XX}
    {Purpose:       To swap two integers}
    {Parameters:    I, J - update, the integers to switch}

    var
      Temp: integer;      {holding variable}

  begin
    Temp := I;
    I := J;
    J := Temp
  end;

  procedure Quicksort;              {(var A: IntegerArray; N: integer)}

  {Written by:    XXXXXXXXXX XX/XX/XX}
  {Purpose:       To sort an array, using the Quicksort technique}
  {Parameters:    A - update, the array to sort}
  {               N - input, the upper bound of the portion of the}
  {               array to sort}
  {Procedures used:   QSort, to perform the actual sort}

    procedure Partition (Low, High: integer; var PivotLocation:
                         integer);

    {Written by:    XXXXXXXXXX XX/XX/XX}
    {Purpose:       To partition an array into three parts:}
    {               1. values less or equal to the pivotal element}
    {               2. the pivotal element}
    {               3. values greater than or equal to the pivotal element}
    {Parameters:    Low, High - input, the portion of the array to}
    {               partition}
    {               PivotLocation - output, the location for the pivot}
    {               element}
    {Procedures used:   Swap, to swap two elements of the array}
    {Globals modified: A (from Quicksort), the array being partitioned}

      var
        I: integer;             {used to locate large values}
        J: integer;             {used to locate small values}
        Pivot: integer;         {the pivotal element}
```

Figure A-4   Quicksort defined in a unit (continues next page).

```
   begin {Partition}
     I := Low;
     J := High + 1;
     Pivot := A[Low];

     repeat

{*** Move I to right looking for a value >= the pivot}

         repeat
           I := I + 1
         until (I = High) or (A[I] >= Pivot);

{*** Move J to left looking for a value <= the pivot}

         repeat
           J := J - 1
         until A[J] <= Pivot;

{*** Swap if the values are out of order}

         if I < J then
           Swap(A[I], A[J])

     until I >= J;

{*** Put the pivotal element in the proper place, and return the}
{    value of its subscript to the calling module}

     Swap(A[Low], A[J]);
     PivotLocation := J

end; {Partition}

procedure QSort (Low, High: integer);

{Written by:     XXXXXXXXXX XX/XX/XX}
{Purpose:        To sort an array, using the quick sort technique}
{Parameters:     Low, High - input, the portion of the array to sort}
{Procedures used: Partition, to partition the array into two}
{                              subarrays}
{                 QSort, called recursively to sort the two subarrays}

   var
     PivotSub: integer;      {Location of pivotal element}

begin {QSort}
  if Low < High then
    begin
      Partition(Low, High, PivotSub);
      QSort(Low, PivotSub - 1);
      QSort(PivotSub + 1, High)
    end {if}
  end; {QSort}
```

Figure A-4   (continues next page)

```
    begin {Quicksort}
         QSort(1, N)
    end; {Quicksort}

end. {unit SortRoutines}
```

Figure A-4   (continued)

Notes

1. IntegerArray must be defined in this unit (or in another unit that appears before this one in the *uses* list). Since unit definitions are the first declarations of a program, defining IntegerArray in the program using the unit results in its declaration appearing after its use, something THINK does not permit.
2. The array A is still global to Partition and QSort, since they are defined within the QuickSort procedure. We have left Partition and QSort nested inside QuickSort because they are procedures unlikely to be needed by any other sorting method we might add to the unit. The user of the unit cannot call Partition and QSort because they are "hidden" within QuickSort. We could have hidden the routines by placing them in SortRoutine's implementation part, but, since they would no longer nested, we would need to pass A as a parameter.
3. THINK allows us to restate the parameter list in the implementation of the QuickSort procedure, but only if it is exactly as it appears in the interface part of the future. We relist it but also commented it out. This approach allows us to remind ourselves of the parameter definitions without referring back to the header line in the interface section, and also prevents us from inadvertently changing them.

Compiling and Using a Unit

For a unit to be ready for use, it must be added to the project using it. To compile a unit, use the Compile to Disk selection under the Compile menu. THINK will know you are compiling a unit because of the word *unit* (instead of *program*) in the header. THINK will flag any compilation errors it discovers. Once your unit is compiled error-free, it is not recompiled when you compile and run the program that uses it.

To use a unit, we need only include its name in the *uses* clause after the program header and add the name of the disk file in which it is stored to the project.

As an example, suppose we wanted to use the SortRoutines unit. The start of the program would look something like this:

```
program SortAList;
uses
   SortRoutines;
```

If the disk file in which SortRoutines is located is called SortUnit, we would add this file to the project (using the "Add File . . ." command from the Project menu.)

Once the SortRoutines file is located and the unit "used," we can now use any of the public constants, types, variables, procedures, or functions SortRoutines contains as if they

```
program SortAList;

{Written by:   XXXXXXXX    XX/XX/XX}
{Purpose:      To demonstrate the use of the programmer-defined unit}
{Units used:   SortRoutines, to use QuickSort}

   uses
     SortRoutines;

   const
     NumItems = 500;                  {number of items to be sorted}

   var
     I, J: integer;                   {index into array A}
     A: IntegerArray;                 {array to be sorted}

begin {SortAList}
   GetDateTime(RandSeed);             {Seed the random number generator}
   for I := 1 to NumItems do          {Generate the numbers}
     A[I] := Random;
   QuickSort(A, NumItems);            {Sort them}
   for I := 1 to NumItems div 10 do   {Print them}
     begin
       for J := 1 to 10 do
         Write(A[10 * (I - 1) + J], ' ');
       Writeln
     end
end. {SortAList}
```

Figure A-5   Using a unit to sort a list.

were defined directly within our program. We close this section with Figure A-5, which shows a simple program that uses the SortRoutines unit to quicksort a list of 500 random integers.

Appendix

B Syntax Diagrams

In this appendix, we use syntax diagrams to describe the syntax of the THINK Pascal language components we have discussed. This provides a handy visual way to determine what form each construct of the language must follow in order to be syntactically correct. In reading the diagrams, take verbatim those items in ovals or circles. Items in rectangles are to be filled in by specific instances of the concept described. For example, the diagram

indicates "any identifier," followed by the := operator, followed by "any constant," followed by a semicolon. Valid instances of this diagram might be

```
A := 3;
CutOffPoint := 155.27;
```

(For items enclosed in rectangles, you will find the concepts further explained in other diagrams or in the notes.)

Along with some of the diagrams, we include some semantic notes (comments about the meaning of the construct). These notes should be considered as general guidelines, rather than as an exhaustive reference. For additional information, you can refer to the index entry for the item being described.

B-1 BASIC PROGRAM LAYOUT

Program

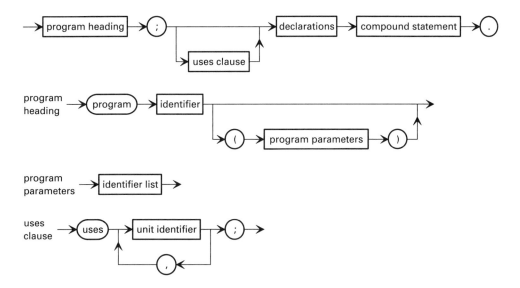

1. The *identifier* is the program name.
2. The *program parameters* can be only *input* and *output*, are optional, and are ignored by the compiler.
3. The *compound statement* is called the *body* of the program.
4. The *uses clause* is a list of all units to be incorporated in this program.

Comment

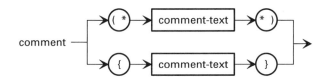

1. The *comment-text* can be any text not containing the character "}" [if the comment started with a "{"] or a "*)" [if it started with "(*"].
2. Comments can be placed in the program at any spot where a blank space is allowed (although THINK will move comments embedded in a line of code to the end of that line).
3. Comments do not affect the program's meaning.

Declarations

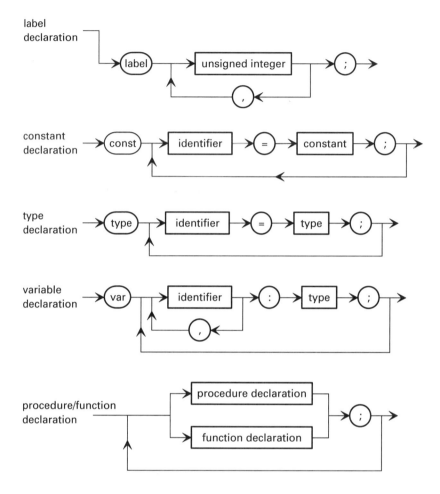

1. In standard Pascal, this order must be followed; THINK relaxes the rule.
2. *Const* defines named constants that the program cannot modify.
3. *Type* gives names to user-defined types. This is frequently useful; it is mandatory if variables of that type are to be passed as parameters.
4. *Var* declares variables whose scope is the module in which this declaration occurs.
5. Function and procedure declarations can be mixed. The general rule is that a sub-module must be declared before it is used.

Function Declaration

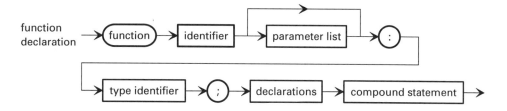

1. The *identifier* is the function name.
2. The *parameter list* is optional.
3. The *type identifier* is the type of the function's returned value. It must be a named type: a built-in type (*real, integer, char, boolean, string*), a named pointer type, a named scalar or subrange type or a named string type. It cannot be a record, array, file, or set type.
4. The *compound statement* is the body of the function. It should include at least one statement assigning a value to the identifier that is the function name. (This causes the answer to be sent back to the module using the function.)

Procedure Declaration

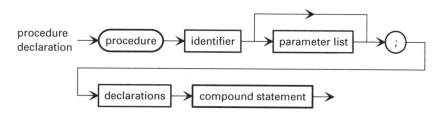

1. The *identifier* is the procedure name.
2. The *parameter list* is optional.
3. The *compound statement* is the body of the procedure. It should *not* attempt to assign a value to the procedure name identifier.

Parameter List

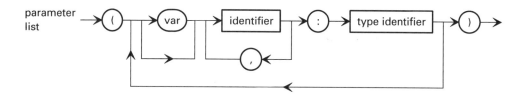

1. The parameters in the list are called formal parameters.
2. The effect of the var is to make the identifier(s) that immediately follow it variable parameters. Its effect ends at the end of that list (at the colon).
3. If the var is omitted, the identifiers in the list (up to the colon) are value parameters.
4. For a variable parameter, the corresponding actual parameter must be a variable. Any reference to the formal parameter is directed to the corresponding actual parameter.
5. For a value parameter, the corresponding actual parameter can be any expression. Its value is passed in when the module is invoked; no value is ever passed back with a value parameter.
6. The parameters must be named types (built-in or user-defined).

Forward Declarations

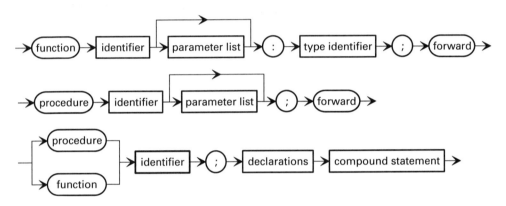

1. Forward declarations allow the body of a procedure or function to be separated from its declaration. This is useful in cases of mutual recursion or in a large program where submodules are alphabetized.
2. The module is first declared using the directive *forward* to notify the compiler that the body is found later. This declaration includes all the usual parameter and function-type information.
3. Later, the declarations and body of the module are supplied. That module is identified by an abbreviated declaration of the module: just the word *procedure* or *function* followed by the module name (no parameter or function type information need be supplied here).

B-2 PROGRAM STRUCTURES

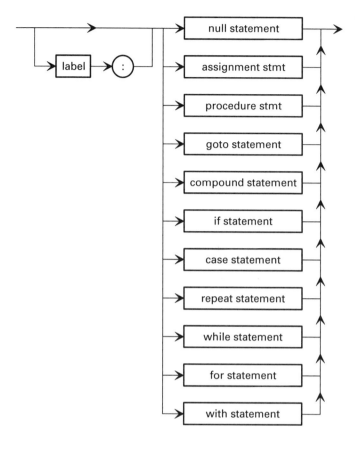

1. The *label* is the statement label. It must have been defined in the label part of the declarations of the module in which it appears.
2. Statement labels are needed only when a *goto* statement is used. Use of the *goto* statement is discouraged.
3. The *null statement* consists of nothing. For example, the compound statement

   ```
   begin
     T := 5;
     X := 3;
   end
   ```

   contains two assignment statements followed by a null statement.

Assignment Statement

1. The *identifier* is either a function or variable name.
2. A function name is assigned a value inside the function body to pass back the answer to the calling module.
3. The specific variable referred to by *identifier* is determined by using the scope rules. Look first for any local definition of the identifier. If there is none, look in the successive surrounding modules, going back to the main program.
4. The types of the identifier and of the expression must be the same, with some exceptions. For example:

    (a) Integer values can be assigned to real variables.

    (b) Any two string types are considered compatible (truncation might occur).

    (c) Subtypes (of the same base types) are considered compatible.

5. Expressions are described in detail in what follows.

Procedure Statement (Call)

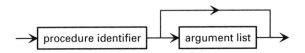

1. The *argument list* is optional.
2. The named procedure is invoked. When it terminates, execution continues at the next statement following the call.

Argument List

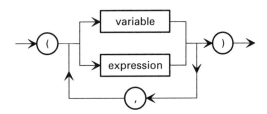

1. Arguments are also called actual parameters.
2. The argument list must match the parameter list for the module being invoked:

    (a) Correct number of arguments.

    (b) Correct types for each argument.

    (c) Must be a variable for a "var" parameter.

3. For var parameters, the subprogram works directly with the variable in the argument list.
4. For value parameters, the value of the expression in the argument list is calculated and sent to the matching parameter in the subprogram; no value is ever returned.

Goto Statement

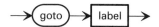

Compound Statement

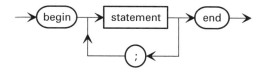

1. This is Pascal's way of allowing multiple statements where the syntax calls for one (for example, as the body of a *while* loop).
2. The statements are executed in order from first to last.

If Statement

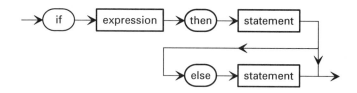

1. The *expression* must be of type boolean.
2. If the value of the expression is *true*, the statement following the *then* is executed.
3. If the value of the expression is *false*, the statement following the *else* is executed. (If there is no else, nothing is done.)
4. In either case, execution continues with the statement following.
5. In case of ambiguity, as in

   ```
   if X > 5 then if Y > 10 then T := 5 else T := 10;
   ```

   the "dangling else" goes with the closest unmatched *if*. The meaning of this example is "if X > 5 then perform the if-then-else statement 'if Y > 10 then T := 5 else T := 10'."

Case Statement

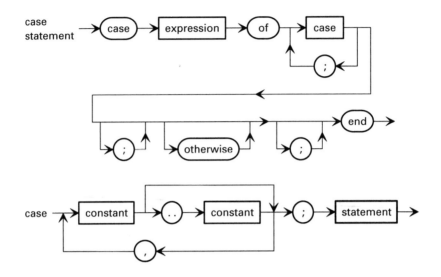

1. The semicolons just before the *otherwise* and just before the *end* are optional.
2. The type of the *expression* and those of the constants must be the same; they must be *integer*, *char*, *boolean*, or a user-defined scalar.
3. The values indicated by the constants and by the ranges *constant..constant* must be unique. For example, having 3 and also 1..4 is illegal.
4. The *expression* is evaluated and its value compared to the lists of constants and ranges. If a match is found, the corresponding statement is executed.
5. If no match is found, the statement following *otherwise* is executed. (If there is no *otherwise*, it is an error.)

Repeat Statement

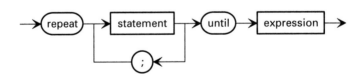

1. The *expression* is of type *boolean* (i.e., a condition).
2. The list of statements is called the *body* of the *repeat* loop.
3. The body is executed, and then the *expression* is evaluated. If the condition is *false*, the process is repeated.
4. When the condition is *true*, execution proceeds to the next statement of the program.

While Statement

1. The *expression* should be of type *boolean* (i.e., a condition).
2. The *statement* is called the *body* of the *while* loop.
3. The *expression* is evaluated; if it is *true*, the body is executed. This process is repeated as long as the condition remains *true*.
4. When the *expression* is *false*, execution proceeds to the next statement of the program.

For Statement

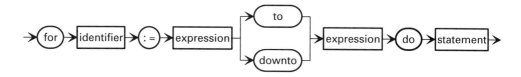

1. The *statement* is called the *body* of the *for* loop.
2. The *identifier* must be a variable of type *integer*, *char*, *boolean*, or a user-defined scalar. Its type must match that of the expressions.
3. The *identifier* is called the *loop-control variable*.
4. If the form *expression1 to expression2* is used, the loop-control variable successively takes on the values in the range expression1..expression2. For each value, the loop body is executed. (If the range is empty, the body is not executed.)
5. If the form expression1 *downto* expression2 is used, the control variable takes on the value in the range expression2..expression1, in decreasing order. (If the range is empty, the body is not executed.)
6. The loop-control variable can be used but not modified within the loop body.
7. After the body has been executed the indicated number of times, execution proceeds to the next statement in the program. At this point, the loop-control variable's value is undefined.

With Statement

1. The *variable* must be of a record type.
2. Within the statement following *do*, references to fields of the indicated variable can be made without the prefix variable. For example,

    with Student **do** Readln(Name)

in place of

```
Readln(Student.Name)
```

B-3 UNIT STRUCTURE

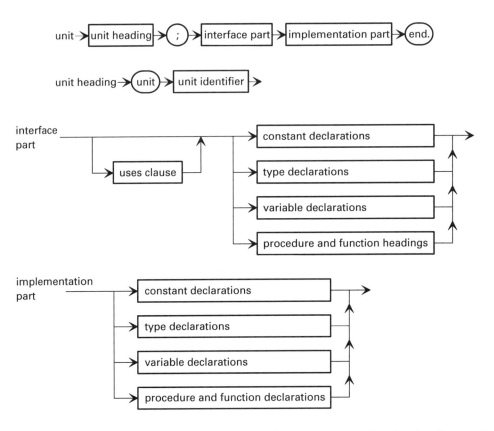

1. The order of constants, types, variables, and procedure and function headings and declarations can be intermixed, provided all items are defined prior to their use.

B-4 DATA STRUCTURES

Type

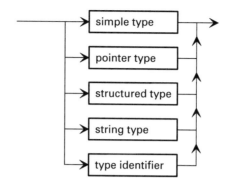

1. *Type identifier* refers to a type that has been defined in the type portion of the declarations.

Simple Type

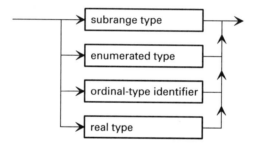

1. *Ordinal-type identifier* is the identifier naming a user-defined ordinal type.
2. Ordinal types include the subrange and enumerated types, and user-defined versions of these types; they do *not* include type *real*.

Subrange Type

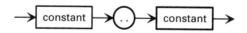

1. The constants must be of the same type. That type must be *integer, boolean, char,* or a user-defined scalar.
2. The Ord value of the first constant must be less than or equal to that of the second constant.
3. The legal values for entities of this type are values lying between and including the two constants.

Enumerated (Scalar) Type

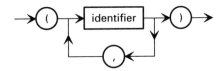

1. The identifiers form a list of legal values for the type.
2. The order in which they are listed is significant. (It is used by the Ord, Pred, and Succ functions, and for determining the meaning of *for* loops. The first item in the list is number 0.)
3. The identifiers must be unique.

Pointer Type

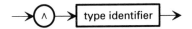

1. The *type identifier* can be defined after it is used to define the pointer type.
2. There is a predefined constant *nil* that is a possible value for any variable of any pointer type.

Structured Type

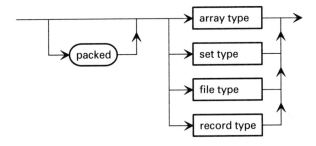

1. The word *packed* relates to how the data are stored in the computer memory; packed items are compressed, allowing them to occupy less memory, but often at the cost of slowing down access to them (perhaps making a program run more slowly).
2. The components of packed data types cannot be used as actual var parameters.

String Type

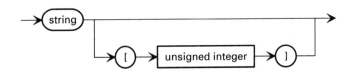

1. The *unsigned integer* must be an integer in the range 1 to 255. It indicates the maximum length of the string. If no length is given, a length of 255 is assumed.
2. The type *string* (without a specified size) is considered to be a named type.
3. As the program is running, the current actual length of the string is automatically maintained.

Array Type

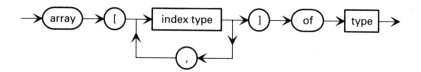

1. The *index type* must be an ordinal type, that is, a subrange type or enumerated type, either predefined or user-defined.
2. The notation using several *index types* is a shorthand notation. For example,

    `array[1..3, 5..17] of integer`

    is shorthand for

    `array[1..3] of array [5..17] of integer`

3. Array elements are referenced by indicating indexes (subscripts) in the given range. For example,

    `A[2,10]` or `A[2][10]`

Set Type

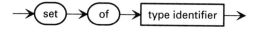

1. The *type identifier* must indicate a *boolean*, *char*, *string*, or user-defined enumerated or subrange type.
2. Sets size defaults to at most 256 items; the Ord values of the set elements must lie from 0 to 255. (So a set of the subrange 100..200 is illegal.) In THINK, set can contain up to 65536 items by changing the setting in the "compile options" menu selection.
3. Every set type includes the value [ ], the empty set.

File Type

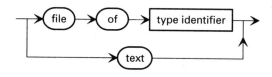

1. The predefined type identifier *text* denotes "packed file of char." Moreover, for this type of file, the procedures Readln and Writeln can be used.
2. For all other file types, only Read and Write can be used.
3. A common use involves having the type be a record type.
4. In addition to the standard I/O operations, THINK Pascal provides facilities that allow random access to the values in the file.

Record Type

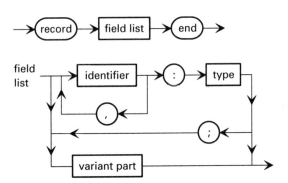

1. The *identifier* denotes a field of the record.
2. Field values within a variable of record type are denoted by indicating the variable name, a period, and the field name. For example,

   ```
   Student.Name
   ```

   (But also see the *with* statement diagram.)
3. The fields of the record, in turn, can be structured types, including arrays and records.

Variant Part

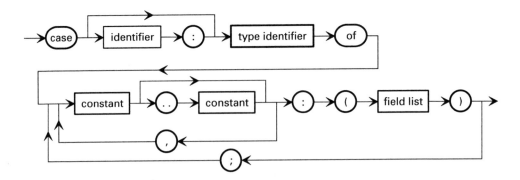

1. This feature allows the list of fields within the record to depend upon the value of a field within the record.

2. It is the programmer's responsibility to ensure consistency.

3. The identifier determining which list of fields is to occur can be omitted.

B-5 EXPRESSIONS

It is possible to give syntax diagrams for expressions. However, they are probably more useful to a compiler writer than to a person who is writing programs in Pascal. Instead, we summarize some of the important points concerning expressions.

1. Expressions can contain combinations of

constants
variables
fields of records
array elements
pointer references
function invocations (syntax is the same as procedure invocation)
sets
strings

(Any use of a function name in an expression is interpreted as an invocation of that function.)

2. Subject to rules involving compatibility, these can be combined using the following operations to form *simple expressions*:

parentheses for grouping
+, –, *, /, div, mod
not, and, or

There cannot be two operators in a row. For example, A * – B is illegal; use A * (–B) or –A * B.

3. Simple expressions can be combined, using

<, =, >, <=, >=, <>, in

The result will be Boolean.

4. The precedence is

not
*, /, div, mod, and
+, –, or
<, =, >, <=, >=, <>, in

Within each list, the order is "left to right." (Parentheses can be used for grouping.)

5. The operators +, –, *, and / can be applied to integers or reals. The result is real, except that the sum, difference, or product of two integers is integer.
6. The operators *div* and *mod* can only apply to integers. The results are truncated division and remainder, respectively.
7. The operators *not*, *and*, and *or* apply only to Boolean values. The result is Boolean.
8. The comparisons <, <=, >, >=, =, and <> apply to any *real, integer, string, char, boolean*, or user-defined scalar type. For *char, boolean*, and user-defined scalars, the result is based on the Ord value of the operand. String comparisons generally yield alphabetical comparisons.
10. The operators +, –, and * when applied to sets are set union, difference, and intersection, respectively. The operators <, >, <=, >=, =, and <> denote set inclusion and set equality tests. The operator *in* determines if a value is an element of a set.
11. Among the functions available are

Sqr	Round	Ord	Odd
Sqrt	Trunc	Chr	Eof
Abs	Cos	Succ	Random
Exp	Sin	Pred	
Ln	Arctan		
Copy	Tan		
Pos	Concat		
Length			

12. Constants can be signed or unsigned numbers, or constant identifiers and strings, or the predefined constants *nil* or *maxint*.
13. Identifiers begin with a letter, followed by zero or more letters, digits, or underscores (in any order). Identifiers can be as long as 255 characters.
14. Sets can be denoted by a list of expressions enclosed in square brackets. The expressions can be ranges (for example, ['A'..'Z', 'a'..'z']) and they can be variables (for example, [0, 1, Sum]).
15. Fields of records are denoted by the record name, a period, and the field name (for example, Student.Age).
16. Array elements are denoted by the array name and a list of subscripts enclosed in square brackets (for example, A[5], B[7,2], and B[7][2]).
17. Pointer references consist of the pointer variable name followed by "^" (for example ListHead^). Very frequently, pointers point to records, whose fields can be indicated using the usual field notation (for example, ListHead^.Name).
18. Integer constants consist of sequences of digits (the value must lie between –*maxint* and *maxint*).
19. Real constants contain either a decimal point, an exponent part, or both. The syntax diagram is

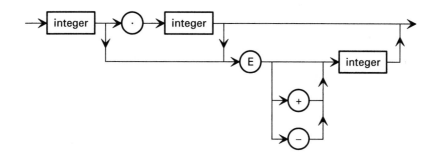

The exponent part indicates a power of 10. For example, 1.2E3 means 1.2 times 10^3.

20. String constants consist of any string enclosed in single quotes (i.e., apostrophes). The character for apostrophe is represented by two consecutive apostrophes, as in

```
'don''t'
```

Character constants have the same form as string constants of length 1.

Appendix

C File Utilities

In this appendix, we present some utility subprograms that are useful in dealing with files.

C-1 EXISTS

Here is a Boolean function that can be used to determine the existence of a file.

```
function Exists (FileName: string): boolean;

{*** Comments}

   var
      DummyFile: text;                  {used to check file name}

begin {Exists}
   IOCheck(false);                      {turn off error messages}
   Reset(DummyFile, FileName);          {try to open for input}
   IOCheck(true);                       {turn them back on}
   Exists := IOResult = 0;              {return true if ok, false otherwise}
   Close(DummyFile)                     {don't leave files lying around open}
end; {Exists}
```

C-2 OPENREAD

The following is a general-purpose procedure for obtaining the name of an existing file from the user and opening the file for reading. Note that the type of the file is specified by the global type FileType, so that the procedure can be used in different contexts.

```
procedure OpenRead (var InputFile: FileType);

{*** Comments}

  var
    FileName: string;         {file name on disk}
    ValidName: boolean;       {entered name exists?}

begin {OpenRead}
  repeat
    Write('Enter the name of the input file: ');
    Readln(FileName);
    ValidName := Exists(FileName);
    if not ValidName then
      Writeln('***File does not exist.')
  until ValidName;

  Reset(InputFile, FileName)    {open the file for input}
end; {OpenRead}
```

C-3 OPENWRITE

Here is a procedure for obtaining the name of a file and opening the file for writing. There are two issues to deal with: "Does the file already exist?" and "Is the filename valid?"

```
procedure OpenWrite (var FileVar: FileType);

{*** Comments}

  var
    FileName: string;         {Name of the file}
    ValidName: boolean;       {Indicator for file name}
    Answer: char;             {User response}

begin {OpenWrite}

{*** Ask the user for the filename}

  ValidName := false;

  while not ValidName do
    begin
      Write('Enter the filename: ');
      Readln(FileName);
      if Exists(FileName) then
        begin
          Write('File already exists. Delete (Y, N)? ');
          Readln(Answer);
          if Answer in ['Y', 'y'] then
```

```
          begin
            ValidName := true;
            Rewrite(FileVar, FileName)
          end {if}
        end
      else
        begin
          IOCheck(false);
          Rewrite(FileVar, FileName);
          IOCheck(true);
          if IOResult = 0 then
            ValidName := true
          else
            Writeln('Invalid filename. Re-enter.')
        end {if}
      end {while}
  end; {OpenWrite}
```

C-4 FILEBUILD

When writing a program to deal with files of records, it is convenient to have an easy method of building samples for testing. The following is a utility that can be easily customized for any such file. To customize FileBuild, you must modify the declaration of RecordType and the fields used in the ReadRecord procedure. (These portions are in italics.)

```
program FileBuild;

{*** Comments}

  type
    RecordType = record
      {Fill in the field definitions}
      end;
    FileType = file of RecordType;

  var
    FileVar: FileType;        {File designator}
    RecordVar: RecordType;    {Record variable}
    Quit: boolean;            {User wants to quit?}

  {function Exists is inserted here}

  {procedure OpenWrite is inserted here}

  procedure ReadRecord (var RecordOut: RecordType; var Quit: Boolean);
  {*** Comments}
    const
      EndOfData = ???;   {Give appropriate terminating value}
```

```
    begin {ReadRecord}
      with RecordOut do
        begin
          Writeln;
          Writeln('Enter fields of record: ');
          Write(' ???: ');
          Readln(???);
          Quit := ??? = EndOfData
        end {with}
    end; {ReadRecord}

begin {FileBuild}

{*** Open the file}

 OpenWrite(FileVar);

{*** Process the file}

 repeat
    ReadRecord(RecordVar, Quit);
    if not Quit then
       Write(FileVar, Recordvar)
 until Quit;

{*** Close the file}

 Close(FileVar);

{ *** Print message and terminate}

 Writeln(message)
end.
```

C-5 FILELIST

Our last file utility is a program to display the contents of a file of records. FileList asks for a Return after each record of the file is displayed. Once again, you can easily customize this utility by modifying the declaration of RecordType and the fields used in the WriteRecord procedure. (The portions to customize are in italics.)

```
program FileList;

{*** Comments}

type
   RecordType = record
     {Fill in the field definitions}
     end;
   FileType = file of RecordType;
```

```
var
  FileVar: FileType;        {File designator}
  RecordVar: RecordType;    {Record variable}

procedure Pause;

{*** Comments}

begin {Pause}
  Writeln;
  Writeln(' ' : 23, '<Tap Return to continue>');
  Readln;
  Page
end; {Pause}

{function Exists is inserted here}

{procedure OpenRead is inserted here}

procedure WriteRecord (RecordIn: RecordType);

{*** Comments}

begin {WriteRecord}
  with RecordIn do
    begin
      Writeln;
      Writeln('Fields of record: ');
      Write(' ???: ');
      Writeln (? ? ?);
    end; {with}
  Pause
end; {WriteRecord}

begin {FileList}

{*** Open the file}

 OpenRead(FileVar);

{*** Process the file}

  while not Eof(FileVar) do
    begin
      Read(FileVar, RecordVar);
      WriteRecord(RecordVar)
    end; {while}

{*** Close the file}

 Close(FileVar);

{*** Print message and terminate}

 Writeln;
 Writeln('End of file reached.')
end.
```

Appendix

D The ASCII Characters

In a few places in the text, we have used features specific to ASCII, the underlying code set that represents character data in the Macintosh. ASCII is an acronym for the longer phrase "American Standard Code for Information Interchange." The code is ancient history compared with the short time line of the computer field and thus contains some codes that have lost or changed their original meanings. When the ASCII code appeared (circa 1963), the teletype terminal was a predominant input/output device; thus, some of the codes specifically relate to that artifact.

There are code sets other than ASCII that are used with computers. The major alternative is the EBCDIC code set found on mainframe computers manufactured by the IBM Corporation. The name EBCDIC is an acronym for "Extended Binary-Coded Decimal Interchange Code."

The purpose of having standard code sets is to ease communications among various computers and devices so that, for example, an 'A' tapped on a keyboard, processed by a computer, communicated to another computer via a modem, processed by the second computer, and printed by a printer still appears as an 'A'.

There are two main ways in which the particular code set can affect Pascal programs. The first way has to do with the particular values of various "control characters" that produce effects such as beeping, backspace, top of form, and so on. The second, more subtle way, is the inherent order of characters enforced by the particular code set used. This collating sequence has a direct effect on programs that sort string or character data. For example, the order of the three strings:

```
Elephant
e. e. cummings
E4
```

would be in ASCII:

```
E4
Elephant
e. e. cummings
```

and in EBCDIC:

```
e. e. cummings
Elephant
E4
```

The behavior of an individual character code varies not only with the code set the computer uses but may also depend on a particular brand of printer, plotter, or modem that is being used. Not all printers advance to the top of a new page when an ASCII form feed character is sent (most do, however). And on the Macintosh, different character fonts have different symbols that correspond to an ASCII code. For instance, ASCII 65 [chr(65)] is normally the character 'A'. But in Macintosh fonts that do not use standard characters sets, ASCII 65 can be quite different:

FONT	ASCII 65
Monaco	A
Times	A
Symbol	A
Cairo	♩
Mobile	🌲

To be in complete control of the environment, the programmer may need to study manuals for the computer, printer, modem, etc., being used. The possible combinations are almost endless, but there is common adherence to standards (official or de facto) for several classes of devices; for example, ASCII or EBCDIC code sets for computers, Hayes-compatible codes for modems, and PostScript-compatible codes for laser printers.

The following is the standard ASCII code set, giving the decimal codes, the standard mnemonic abbreviation, and the Monaco characters (THINK's default character font for program output). Remember, these often change for a particular font (but for most character, rather than graphic, fonts, the characters adhere quite closely).

Ord	Standard	Monaco Font Character	Comments
0	NUL		The null character
1	SOH		
2	STX		
3	ETX		End of text
4	EOT		End of transmission
5	ENQ		
6	ACK	\	Acknowledgment
7	BEL		Beep (or bell)
8	BS		Backspace
9	HT		Tab
10	LF		Linefeed
11	VT		Vertical tab
12	FF		Form feed (top of form)
13	CR		Carriage return (Return key)
14	SO		
15	SI		
16	DLE		
17	DCI		
18	DC2		
19	DC3		
20	DC4		
21	NAK		Negative acknowledgment
22	SYN		Communications synchronization
23	ETB		
24	CAN		Cancel
25	EM		
26	SUB		End of file
27	ESC		Escape (Option key)
28	FS		
29	GS		
30	RS		
31	US		Unit separator
32	SPC		Blank space (space bar)
33	!	!	Exclamation point
34	"	"	(double quote)

Ord	Standard	Monaco Font Character	Comments
35	#	#	(pound sign)
36	$	$	Dollar sign
37	%	%	Percent sign
38	&	&	Ampersand
39	'	'	Single quote (apostrophe)
40	(	(	(left parenthesis)
41	)	)	(right parenthesis)
42	*	*	(asterisk)
43	+	+	Plus sign
44	,	,	Comma
45	-	-	Hyphen (minus sign)
46	.	.	Period (decimal point)
47	/	/	Slash (division sign)
48	0	0	Zero
49	1	1	One
50	2	2	Two
51	3	3	Three
52	4	4	Four
53	5	5	Five
54	6	6	Six
55	7	7	Seven
56	8	8	Eight
57	9	9	Nine
58	:	:	(colon)
59	;	;	(semicolon)
60	<	<	(less than)
61	=	=	Equal sign
62	>	>	Greater than
63	?	?	(question mark)
64	@	@	("at" sign)
65	A	A	First uppercase letter
66	B	B	
67	C	C	
68	D	D	
69	E	E	

Ord	Standard	Monaco Font Character	Comments
70	F	F	
71	G	G	
72	H	H	
73	I	I	
74	J	J	
75	K	K	
76	L	L	
77	M	M	
78	N	N	
79	O	O	
80	P	P	
81	Q	Q	
82	R	R	
83	S	S	
84	T	T	
85	U	U	
86	V	V	
87	W	W	
88	X	X	
89	Y	Y	
90	Z	Z	Last uppercase letter
91	[	[	Left bracket
92	\	\	(back slash)
93	]	]	(right bracket)
94	^	^	Caret
95	_	_	Underscore
96	`	`	Back quote
97	a	a	First lowercase letter
98	b	b	
99	c	c	
100	d	d	
101	e	e	
102	f	f	
103	g	g	
104	h	h	

Ord	Standard	Monaco Font Character	Comments
105	i	i	
106	j	j	
107	k	k	
108	l	l	
109	m	m	
110	n	n	
111	o	o	
112	p	p	
113	q	q	
114	r	r	
115	s	s	
116	t	t	
117	u	u	
118	v	v	
119	w	w	
120	x	x	
121	y	y	
122	z	z	Last lowercase letter
123	{	{	{ (left brace)
124	|	|	| (vertical bar)
125	}	}	Right brace
126	~	~	Tilde
127	DEL		Delete (rubout)
128		Ä	
129		Å	
130		Ç	
131		É	
132		Ñ	
133		Ö	
134		Ü	
135		á	
136		à	
137		â	
138		ä	
139		ã	

Ord	Standard	Monaco Font Character	Comments
140		å	
141		ç	
142		é	
143		è	
144		ê	
145		ë	
146		í	
147		ì	
148		î	
149		ï	
150		ñ	
151		ó	
152		ò	
153		ô	
154		ö	
155		õ	
156		ú	
157		ù	
158		û	
159		ü	
160		†	
161		°	
162		¢	
163		£	
164		§	
165		•	
166		¶	
167		ß	
168		®	
169		∂	
170		™	
171		´	
172		¨	
173		≠	
174		Æ	

Ord	Standard	Monaco Font Character	Comments
175		0	
176		∞	
177		±	
178		≤	
179		≥	
180		¥	
181		µ	
182		∂	
183		Σ	
184		∏	
185		π	
186		∫	
187		ª	
188		º	
189		Ω	
190		æ	
191		ø	
192		¿	
193		¡	
194		¬	
195		√	
196		ƒ	
197		≈	
198		∆	
199		«	
200		»	
201		…	
202			
203		À	
204		Ã	
205		Õ	
206		Œ	
207		œ	
208		–	
209		—	

Ord	Standard	Monaco Font Character	Comments
210		"	
211		"	
212		'	
213		'	
214		÷	
215		◊	
216		ÿ	
217		ƒ	
218			
219			
220			
221			
222			
223			
224			
225			
226			
227			
228			
229			
230			
231			
232			
233			
234			
235			
236			
237			
238			
239			
240			
241			
242			
243			
244			

Ord	Standard	Monaco Font Character	Comments
245			
246			
247			
248			
249			
250			
251			
252			
253			
254			
255			

127 to 255 are not official ASCII codes; these are used for various characters, depending upon the font. As you can see, Monaco does not use some of these ASCII values.

References

The following are sources where you can obtain additional details about the Macintosh computer and the THINK Pascal for the Macintosh programming environment.

Chernicoff, Stephen. *Macintosh Revealed Volume One: Unlocking the ToolBox*, second edition. Hayden Books, 1985.

Rose, Caroline, et. al. *Inside Macintosh: Volumes I, II, and III, IV, and V.* Addison-Wesley Publishing Company, Inc., 1985, 1986, 1988. © Apple Computer, Inc., 1985, 1986, 1988.

Symantek Corporation. *THINK Pascal User Manual.* © Symantek Corporation, 1988, 1990, 1991.

Index

A

Accumulator. *See* Loops.
Actual parameters. *See* Parameters.
Algorithm, 2
Algorithm analysis, 667
Aliasing. *See* Pointers.
and (operator), 106–08
Antibugging, 258–61
Arguments. *See* Parameters.
Arrays:
    algorithms:
        condition-controlled, 440–43
        count-controlled, 436–40
    copying portions, 444–45
    declaring, 203–04, 434–35
    indexing, 456–57
    initializing, 443–44
    introduction to, 200–03, 206–07
    limits for storage of, 449
    out-of-bounds conditions, 204, 243
    parallel, 458–59
    of pointers, 616–25
    processing elements of, 445–47
    of records, 48, 378–79, 460–62
    referencing, 435–36
    searching, 441–43
    shifting elements of, 445
    syntax diagram, 751
    testing algorithms using, 447–48, 467, 470
    three or more dimensions, 544
    two dimensional:
        computing with, 537–38
        file I/O with, 536–37
        interactive I/O with, 534–36
        introduction to, 531–34
        used for matrices, 538–44
    when to use, 432–34
ASCII character set, 395, 761–70
Assertion, 240
Assignment statement:
    general, 37–38
    numeric, 38–45
    string, 45–47
    syntax diagram, 743–44

B

Backus-Naur form (BNF), 67
Balance line algorithm, 711–12
Base case. *See* Recursion
Base type. *See* Sets
Big oh of N. *See* Order N notation
Big strings. *See* Strings
Binary file. *See* Files
Binary search. *See* Searching

Boolean expressions. *See* Expressions
Boolean operators. *See* Logical Operators
Boolean variables, 125–27
Bottom-up testing. *See* Testing
Boundary conditions, 29, 263
Boundary testing, 79
Bubble sort. *See* Sorting
Bugs, 27, 258

C

Calling program, 147
Caret (^ operator), 595
Case structure, 112–14, 127–29
   syntax diagram, 746
Case study:
   no. 1, 30–33
   no. 1 continued, 76–79
   no. 2, 129–34
   no. 3, 151–60
   no. 3 continued, 176–80
   no. 4, 313–23
   no. 5, 324–26
   no. 6, 326–40
   no. 7, 413–19
   no. 8, 419–28
   no. 9, 499–14
   no. 10, 514–25
Character conversions (in strings). *See* Strings
Character strings. *See* Strings
Character variables, 10, 11, 45
Chr. *See* Functions
Class testing. *See* Testing
Close. *See* Procedures
Cofinal substring. *See* Strings
Coinitial substring. *See* Strings
Collisions (when hashing). *See* Hashing
Combinatorial coefficients, 630–31, 674–76
Comments, 10
Compile-time errors. *See* Errors
Compiler, 4
Compiler directive, 44
Compound statement, 67
Concatenation. *See* Functions, 46
Conditions. *See* Expressions
Constants, 8
Control breaks (of a report), 690–97
   example using, 690–95
   multiple level, 704

programming with, 693, 696
using subprograms with, 696–01

D

Dangling else pitfall, 124–25
Dangling pointer. *See* Pointers
Data structures, 457. *See also* Arrays, Files, Records, Sets, Types
Debugging, 258–61
Debugging aids, 30
Decision structures, 66–76, 124–29
Declarations, 8, 10–12
   syntax diagrams, 740–72
Defaults, 23
DeMorgan's Laws, 108
Design (of a program), 18, 63–64
   modular, 150–51
   top-down, 154, 271
Diagnostic prints. *See* Trace prints.
Direct access storage medium, 685
Direct file. *See* Files
Disk name (of a file), 348
Disk:
   disk drive, 684
   magnetic, 684–85
   optical, 684
Dispose. *See* Functions
div (integer division), 91–92
Division by zero pitfall, 119
Documentation, 3, 156, 428, 524–25
Driver program, 151
Dummy value. *See* Terminating value
Dynamic memory. *See* Memory

E

EBCDIC, 761–62
Editing input. *See* Input.
Editor, 3
Empty string. *See* Null string.
Enumerated type, syntax diagram, 750
Enumerated types. *See* Types.
Errors:
   compile time, 28
   logic, 28
   run-time, 28
Executable file, 4
exit (statement), 725

Expressions:
    conditional, 69–70
    logical, 105–08
    relational, 69–70
    rules for forming, 753–55

F

Factorial, 629–30, 647–48, 671
Fibonacci sequence, 671–73
Field (of a record), 372, 386
File pointer, 713
Files:
    binary, 373–76, 687
    error trapping with, 402–04
    I/O with, 683–21
    master, 708–09
    random-access (direct access, relative), 713–18
        examples using, 714–17
    searching, 407–09
    sequential, 712
        merging, 705–08
        updating, 708–09
    syntax diagram, 751–52
    text, 347–66, 685–86
        adding lines to, 354–56
        basic operations, 348–49
        closing, 348–49
        displaying, 350–53
        interactive processing of, 356–58
        modifying, 360–63
        opening, 348–49
        printing, 350–53
        reading, 348–49
    searching in, 358–60, 365–66
    used as standard I/O, 363–64
    writing, 348–49
    trade-offs between binary and text, 687
    transaction, 708–09
    utilities. *See* Functions, Procedures
Flag, 244
Formal parameters. *See* Parameters
Functions
    calling (invoking), 91
    file utilities
        Exists (check if file present), 756
        FileBuild (build a test file), 758–59
        FileList (print a file's contents), 759–60
        OpenRead (open file for input), 756–57
        OpenWrite (open file for output), 757–58
    from the OSIntf unit:
        GetDateTime (time in seconds), 191
        MemAvail (heap space available), 667
        StackSpace (stack space available), 667
    from the SANE unit:
        Str2Num (string to number), 564–65
        Str2Num example, 566–69
    from the ToolIntf unit:
        TickCount, 667
    standard:
        Abs (absolute value), 88, 90, 100
        ArcTan (arctangent), 100
        Chr (character), 45
        Concat (concatenate), 46, 554
        Copy (substring), 554
        Cos (cosine), 100
        Dispose (release memory being pointed to), 598–99
        Eof (end of file?), 714
        Exp (e^x), 100
        FilePos (current position in a file), 714
        Include (add substring into string), 555
        Int (integer part of real), 100
        Length (of a string), 553–54
        Ln (natural logarithm), 100
        New (obtain storage for item pointed to), 597–98
        Odd (is number odd?), 164
        Omit (string with a substring removed), 555
        Pos (substring's position in a string), 554–55
        Round (round), 95, 100
        Sin (sine), 100
        Sqr (square root), 88–89, 100
        Sqrt (square root), 100
        Trunc (truncate), 94–95, 100
    string example, 556–59
    user defined, 139–46
        example, 139–42
        form, 143–45
        parameters with, 143–44
        steps in writing, 144–46
    when to use, 289–91

G

Global variables, 277–81
Golden section, 672–73
goto (statement), 722–25
Graph traversal, 645–46
Group indicate (in a report), 697

H

Hand-tracing (a program), 28, 259
Hashing, 720–21
Heap. *See* Memory.
Hierarchy chart, 152–53
High-level language, 2

I

I/O. *See* Input/Output. *See also* Files
Identifiers, 8
If -then, if-then-else structure, 22, 67, 70–73
   syntax diagram, 745
Implementation, 20
In (set operator). *See* Sets
Inactive records (of a random-access file), 717–18
Incremental testing. *See* Testing
Indentation (of program statements), 68
Index (of an array), 434
Infix expressions, 640
Information hiding, 585
Input device, 2
Input parameter. *See* Parameter
Input, validation of, 244–48
Input/Output, 13
Insertion sort, 497
Instant window, 30
Integer expressions, 42–44
Integer overflow. *See* Numeric overflow.
Integer-to-real conversion, 95–96
Integers, 8–9
   number of divisors, 635–36, 652–53, 656–57
   ways to represent as sum, 636–38, 653–54, 658
Interpreter, 4
IOCheck function, 402–03
IOResult, 402
Iteration, 670

L

label (statement), 722
Laptop computer, 2
Library, 4
Life, Conway's Game of, 549–50
LIFO (last in, first out), 603
Linear search. *See* Searching.
Linked lists, 601–02, 612–16
Linker, 4
Literal, 45
Local variables, 277–81
Logic errors. *See* Errors
Logical expression. *See* Expressions
Logical file name, 348
Logical operators, 106–08
longint, 12
Loops:
   accumulating, 164, 167–71
   controlling, 19
   counting, 164, 166
   finding largest, 164, 171–75
   finding smallest, 164, 175–76
   for-do, 188–89, 191–92, 194, 197–99
      syntax diagram, 747
   initialization of, 164
   inner, 235
   multiple termination conditions, 237–44
   nested, 234–37
      examples, 238–40
   off by 1/2 errors, 241–43
   off by one errors, 241–43
   outer, 235
   planning, 213–17
      examples, 220–27
   repeat-until, 185–86, 188, 194–99, 217–20
      syntax diagram, 747
   termination of, 164
   testing, 178–82
   used when searching. *See* Searching
   while-do, 186–88, 197–99, 217–20
      syntax diagram, 747

M

Machine language, 2
Mainframe computer, 2
Master file. *See* Files
Matrices. *See* Arrays

maxint (predefined identifier), 92–93
Measuring program performance, 666–82
MemAvail. *See* Functions
Memory:
    dynamic, 602
    heap, 667
    run-time stack, 667
    static, 602, 667
Merge sort. *See* Sorting
Merging files. *See* Files
Microcomputer, 2
Minicomputer, 2
Mixed-mode computation, 93
mod (remainder of integer division), 91–92
Modular design. *See* Design
Modules. *See* Functions, Procedures
Multiple-way branches, 66, 108–12
Multitasking, 666
Multiuser, 666
Mutual recursion. *See* Recursion

N

Named type, 275
Nested decision structures, 114–17
    testing, 117–18
Nested procedures. *See* Procedures
New. *See* Functions
nil (pointer constant), 598–99
Node (of a list), 602
not (operator), 106–08
Null string. *See* Strings
Numeric operators, 38–40
Numeric overflow, 44

O

Object file, 4
Observe window, 30
Operating system, 3
Operator precedence, numeric, 39–42
or (operator), 106–08
Ord. *See* Functions
Order N notation, 480
Ordinal types. *See* Types
Output device, 2
Output parameter. *See* Parameter
Output position, 83

Output:
    formatting, 82–88
    of integers, 83–85
    of reals, 84–85
    to the printer, 86–87
Overflow (numeric). *See* Numeric overflow

P

Page. *See* Procedures
Parallel arrays. *See* Arrays
Parameters:
    actual, 270
    formal, 270
    input, 276–77
    introduction, 91
    matching types, 273–76
    output, 276–77
    reference, 277
    update, 276–77
    value, 246, 271–73
    var, 246–47, 271–73
Pascal's triangle, 630
Pascal, Blaise, 4
Pascal, versions of, 5
Path name, 351
Path testing. *See* Testing.
Physical file name, 348
Pointers:
    advantages of, 605–06
    aliasing, 607
    assigning value to, 596–97
    dangling, 598
    declaring, 595–96
    disadvantages of, 606
    example of use, 599–05
    introduction, 594–627
    obtaining data for, 597–99
    saving time and space with, 616–25
    syntax diagram, 750
    using appropriately, 606–07
Portability (of programs), 93
Power set. *See* Sets
Pred. *See* Functions
Predicates. *See* Strings
Prefix expressions, 640, 679–80
Probe. *See* Hashing
Problem-solving approaches, 628–29

Procedures:
    advantages of, 59–60
    introduction, 54–63
    nested, 727–32
    from SANE unit:
        example of, 566–69
        Num2Str (number to string), 563–64
    standard, 57, 59
        Close (close a file), 348, 714
        Delete (delete substring), 559–60
        Insert (insert substring), 560–61
        Open (open a random-access file), 714
        Page (go to top of new page), 87
        Read (read an item), 714
        Readln (read a line), 13, 59
        Reset (prepare to read a file), 348
        Rewrite (prepare to write a file), 348
        Seek (go to a record of a random-access file), 714
        Write (write an item), 12, 714
        Writeln (write a line), 12, 57, 84–85
    syntax diagram, 744
    user defined, 54–65
    value parameters with, 192–93
    when to use, 289–91
Processing unit, 2
Profiler, 668
Program, 2
    syntax diagrams, 739
Program flow structures, 18–19
Program performance. *See* Measuring program performance
Programming environment, 4, 6
Programming language, 2
Programming style, 23
Prompt, 12

Q

Quicksort. *See* Sorting

R

R option (in Project menu), 204
Random numbers, 190–92
Random-access files. *See* Files
Range Checking, 204, 401–02
Read/Write head (of a disk), 684–85
Readln. *See* Procedures
Real (type), 8–9
    fractional part of, 96
    inaccuracy of, 90, 93
    integer part of, 96
Real expressions, 42–44
Real-to-integer conversion, 93–95
Real-to-real conversion, 96
Record number (of a random-access file), 713
Records, 165, 372–79
    arrays of, 378–79
    assignment with, 376
    containing arrays, 462–65
    files of, 373–76
    files with, 404–09
    ordinal types with, 404–09
    as parameters, 377–78
    processing, 376–77
    structure, 372–73
    syntax diagrams, 752–53
    tag field, 726–27
    variant, 725–27
Recursion, 287, 302–05, 628–82
    mutual recursion, 640–43, 660–63
    problems involving, 629–43
    programming, 646–66
    tail recursion, 670–71
    tree recursion, 671
Reference parameter. *See* Parameter
References, 771
Refinement (of program design), 18
Relational operators, 105
Relative file. *See* Files
Repeat-until loop. *See* Loops, 20
Reset. *See* Procedures
Retyping. *See* Types
Rewrite. *See* Procedures
Right justification, 83
Run-time errors. *See* Errors
Run-time stack. *See* Memory
Running a program, 4

S

SANE. *See* Units, Functions, Procedures
Scope (of variables), 277–81, 729
Searching, 244. *See also* Arrays
    binary search, 481–83
    linear search, 478–80
    loops used with, 244
Selection sort. *See* Sorting
Semantics, 110

Semicolon, use of, 23, 73
Sentinel. *See* Terminating value
Sequential access storage medium, 684
Sets, 107, 379–83
    assignment with, 380
    base type, 379
    declaring, 379–80, 382
    difference of, 380
    empty, 379
    example, 383–85
    I/O of, 381–82
    inclusion (subsets), 381
    intersection of, 380
    membership (in), 379
    power set, 638–39, 654, 657–59
    syntax diagram, 751
    union of, 380
    used as parameters, 382–83
Sieve of Eratosthenes, 529
Software engineering, 666
Sorting:
    bubble sort, 497
    comparing various methods, 677–79
    merge sort, 632–33, 649, 651–52, 677–79
    quicksort, 487–92, 677–79
        defined in a unit, 733–36
        used from a unit, 736–37
        using nested procedures, 730–32
    selection sort, 484–87, 648–50, 677–79
    stable, 649
Specification, 17
Stack, 475–76, 602–03
StackSpace. *See* Functions
Statements, 8
Static use of memory. *See* Memory
StatPack (program performance package), 667–70
Step into/Step over, 30
Storage, 2
Strings, 10–11, 45–46, 551–93. *See* also Functions, Procedures
    accessing individual characters, 552
    big strings (greater than 255 characters), 583–88
        testing, 588, 590
    cofinal substring, 648
    coinitial substring, 649
    comparison of, 552–53
    null, 46
    number of length N from M letters, 635, 649, 653–54
    reversing, 631–33, 649, 676–77
    routines:
        BigConcat (concatenate two big strings), 587–88
        BigCopy (get substring of big string), 585–88
        BigLength (obtain length of big string), 585–86
        BigReadln (read in big string), 585–86
        BigWriteln (write out big string), 584–85
        LowCase (convert characters to lower case), 582–84
        LowtoUp (convert characters to upper case), 581–83
        Pad (pad string with spaces to given size), 578–79
        Replace (replace substring with another), 579–81
        RunOf (make string of repeated character), 577–78
        Trim (remove trailing spaces), 576–77
    subsequences and substrings of (predicates), 633–35, 649, 653–54
    syntax diagram, 750
Stub (for subprogram), 151
Subprograms. *See* also Functions, Procedures
    nested invocation, 287–89
    planning, 291–92
        examples, 292–302
    reasons to use, 270–71
Subrange. *See* Types
Subscript (of an array), 434
Succ. *See* Functions
Supercomputer, 2
Syntax diagrams, 67, 738–55
Syntax rules, 18

T

Tag field. *See* Record
Tail recursion. *See* Recursion
Tape (magnetic), 684
Terminating value, 19, 706
Testing, 28–30, 261–67
    bottom-up, 151, 266–67
    class, 262
    error-guessing, 663
    incremental, 150–51
    path, 264
    stress testing, 663

Testing (*continued*)
  top-down, 151, 266–67
  unit, 155
Text files. *See* Files
Text window, 26, 60, 63
THINK Pascal, running THINK programs, 5
TickCount. *See* Functions
Top of form, 83
Top-down design. *See* Design
Top-down testing. *See* Testing
Trace prints, 259–61
Tracks (of a disk), 684–85
Trailer value. *See* Terminating value
Transaction file. *See* Files
Translator, 4
Tree recursion. *See* Recursion
Truncation of strings. *See* Strings
Two dimensional arrays. *See* Arrays
Type checking, 400–02
Types:
  ordinal, 107
  retyping, 397
  scalar, 393–98
    Chr function with, 394
    Ord function with, 393–97
    Pred function with, 394–95, 397
    Succ function with, 394–97
  subrange, 399–400
  syntax diagrams, 749–53
  user-defined, 393–410
  user-defined ordinal, 396–99
    as indices of arrays, 398–99
    as indices of for loops, 398
    assignment with, 396
    comparisons with, 396–97
    I/O of, 397–98

U

Unit testing. *See* Testing
Units, 561, 563, 733–37
  OSIntf, 667
  SANE, 561, 563

syntax diagrams, 748
ToolIntf, 667
user-defined, 732–37
  compiling, 736–37
  header, 733
  implementation part, 733
  interface part, 733
  private part, 732–33
  public part, 732–33
  using, 736–37
Update parameter. *See* Parameter
Utility, 4

V

V option (of Project menu). *See* Numeric
    overflow
Validating input. *See* Input
Value parameter. *See* Parameters
Var parameter. *See* Parameters
Variable list, 19
Variables, 8
Variant records. *See* Records

W

While-do loop. *See* Loops
Wirth, Niklaus, 4
With statement, syntax diagram, 747–48
Write. *See* Procedures
Writeln. *See* Procedures
{$R+}, {$R-}. *See* Range checking
{$V+}, {$V-}. *See* Numeric overflow

^ *See* Caret
* (multiplication), 39–41
+ (addition), 39–41
- (subtraction), 39–41
- (unary minus), 39–41
/ (real division), 39–43
@ (pointer operator), 597